Principles and Practice of Business Continuity

Tools and Techniques
2nd Edition

Jim Burtles KLJ, MMLJ, Hon FBCI

Kristen Noakes-Fry ABCI, Editor

ROTHSTEIN PUBLISHING

a division of Rothstein Associates Inc.
Brookfield, Connecticut USA
www.rothsteinpublishing.com

ISBN: 978-1-931332-94-1 (Perfect Bound)
ISBN: 978-1-931332-95-8 (Epub)
ISBN: 978-1-931332-96-5 (PDF)

Upon registration, paid purchasers of this book are entitled to a free download of the **Business Continuity Toolkit**, extensive supplemental licensed material. See instructions on back page.

ISBN: 978-1-931332-94-1 (Perfect Bound)
ISBN: 978-1-931332-95-8 (Epub)
ISBN: 978-1-931332-96-5 (PDF)
Library of Congress
Control Number: 2015948289

a division of Rothstein Associates Inc.
Philip Jan Rothstein FBCI, Publisher
4 Arapaho Road
Brookfield, Connecticut 06804-3104 USA
203.740.7400 • 203.740.7401 fax
info@rothstein.com
www.rothsteinpublishing.com
www.rothstein.com

Upon registration, paid purchasers of this book are entitled to a free download of the **Business Continuity Toolkit**, extensive supplemental licensed material. See instructions on back page.

Keep informed of the latest crisis communication, crisis management, and business continuity news.
Sign up for Business Survival™ Weblog: Business Continuity for Key Decision-Makers from Rothstein Associates at www.rothstein.com/blog

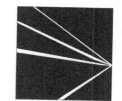

Dedication

This book, along with its contents and the ideas which it might inspire, is dedicated to those hopeful professionals who aspire to protect and preserve the many organizations upon which we all rely and depend. I firmly believe that the practice of business continuity is an essential element of ongoing operational success and its principles should be applied without restraint or dogmatism to safeguard the infrastructure of modern society.

This dedication applies to all those who have the wisdom and foresight to think ahead, plan and prepare for the worst, and adopt a positive attitude toward the future, but who are ready to welcome opportunity whenever it presents itself.

Acknowledgments

- Throughout my career I have received continuous support, encouragement, and tolerance from my wonderful wife. Without her moral and intellectual backing I would have tripped and fallen many times on my way towards achievement and recognition within my chosen field.

- During the revision, expansion, and improvement of this second edition, my esteemed editor, Kristen Noakes-Fry, has gently but determinedly guided me through the maze of differing viewpoints and alternative ways of expressing the underlying concepts. She has been instrumental in the development and delivery of a piece of work that we can both be proud of. We are also grateful to Melvyn Musson for reviewing the manuscript when it was in progress and making a number of valuable suggestions.

- I want to thank Lyndon Bird for his input to the SMARTRisk process and subsequent permission to make it available to our readership.

- I am also particularly grateful to Deborah Higgins for the inspiration behind, and the permission to use, the DICE model decision-making process.

- Thanks to Bob Arnold and *Disaster Recovery Journal* (DRJ) for granting generous permission to use their glossary within this book and to include other DRJ materials in the downloadable **Business Continuity Toolkit**.

- Many of my ideas were sparked or refined by intelligent conversation with friends and colleagues, including the late Steve Bisbey, David Green, Alan Heath, Jason Jarret, Peter Merrick, Mike Mikkelsen, John Robinson, Phil Rothstein, Allen Smith, Jim Stephens, and Steve Yates, as well as all of my students and customers over the years.

Author's Introduction to the Second Edition

The aim of this second edition of *Principles and Practice of Business Continuity: Tools and Techniques* is to provide a balanced, student-friendly textbook to help you establish yourself as a competent practitioner of business continuity (BC). While philosophy and the principles remain the same, the book has been restructured and updated in five parts to represent the five main phases of learning and development. Each part consists of three or four chapters devoted to specific areas of knowledge or competence. Techniques are subtly refined to represent current practice with additional information included. To assist you in your learning, you will find discussion questions and useful examples at the ends of chapters, supported by a wealth of downloadable practical material (accessible once you've registered your book). Pausing for reflection at regular intervals like this will reinforce the learning process, as well as enable you to evaluate and appreciate your progress.

New material in this edition includes:

- Expanded glossary of terms currently in use in the industry.
- Suggestions for additional reading at the end of each chapter.
- A comprehensive index.
- A new section on governance, exploring how resilience can fit into the larger picture of the organization.
- Information about professional certification options.
- Multiple choice questions at the end of each chapter inviting you to check your understanding.
- A "Food for Thought" section in each chapter letting you apply what you have just read to your experiences at work and in the community.

You will follow my lead in exploring the subject of BC management as I explain the basic principles and describe what my experience has shown to be good practice. By the end of this book, you should be prepared to engage in all of the activities associated with the development, delivery, and maintenance of a sound BC program.

Part I: Preparation and Startup

- At the start of the book, you will look at how and why BC came into existence. This glimpse at history leads naturally into some thoughts about the science behind the basic principles. The practical aspect opens up with ideas about launching a program and getting to grips with the operational risks and threats – and understanding the concept of resilience.

Part II: Building a Foundation

- Risk management is a well-established discipline, and much of our BC work is often predicated upon the work done by others in this area. The BC discipline works towards a practical understanding of the impacts and consequences of risk, which leads to designing an appropriate continuity strategy to meet the precise needs of your organization.

- Business impact analysis (BIA) is an especially valuable contribution to the development of continuity and resilience in any enterprise.

- You will explore the basic continuity strategies and how to select the most appropriate one to meet your organization's needs and the budget.

Part III: Responding and Recovering

- Important in this context is the emergency response aspect, preparing to deal with a business interruption. Understanding the management and control of the effects and consequence of such an event leads you naturally towards the need for restoration and recovery of facilities, resources, and equipment.

- Next, you will look at disaster recovery, the various methods technical people use to rebuild or recover the support services and functions. This is an area in which you, as a BC specialist, may need to rely upon the skills and experience of other professionals.

Part IV: Planning and Implementing

- Armed with a rounded knowledge of the prerequisites, you are ready to develop and construct the actual BC plans based on the types and levels of plans that cover the various aspects of a disruptive event. You will work with a model that has five distinct types of plans, which you can adapt to fit the needs and structure of your organization.

- Having covered the build-up towards – and the actual development and delivery of – the BC plans, you will move on to consider the longer term aspects of the management program, including the process of developing and applying the requisite support and delivery skills, looking after the resources, and keeping the plans up-to-date.

Part V: Long-Term Continuity

- This second edition concludes with a new section on the function of resilience in corporate governance. You will consider the review or audit program as a means of ensuring the ongoing suitability of the system and its components as well as its strategy, plans, and resources. Finally, you will learn what to expect in your future career in BC, your role in the company, and what professional certifications are available to you.

Imagine that you are about to embark on an educational cruise though the world of BC. I am the experienced traveler who has planned your itinerary, this book is your curriculum, and our phase model is an outline map of the lands you will be visiting. If you are working with a tutor or mentor, you should look to that person as your tour guide to ensure that you get to appreciate the landscape and learn about the people, places, and culture you encounter along the way. By the end of the journey, you should be familiar with all aspects of BC, ready to advise and guide others.

Jim Burtles

London, United Kingdom

February, 2016

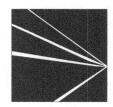

Foreword

The time that has passed since the first edition of Burtles' *Principles and Practice of Business Continuity: Tools and Techniques* was released (2007) has witnessed countless changes in organizational governance, business structure, and corporate goals.

Working as a shift leader on Honeywell Level 64 mainframes in the late 1970s, I was involved in a few emergency nightshifts of my own, when the room-filling beast of a computer would power itself down for many unknown reasons. I remember that my first action to get the machine up and running again was to open and slam the doors on the shed-sized processor cupboards and open and close the drawer under the operators' teletype in a tried and tested sequence!

It is difficult at times to believe the changes in working practice and technology that have taken place since then. Each successive update to the technology within an organization has required the business model to drive, or in some companies to follow, that change. As each change to the operational and processing methods employed has taken place, so the business continuity model has been required to mature alongside. Changes have been both internal, as mergers and acquisitions have occurred or business models and methods have changed, and external, as litigation and regulation have shaped commerce. The globalized world in which companies now operate requires an advanced capability of business continuity.

While occasionally tipping its hat to the idea of significant relationships with the other practitioner schools of organizational resilience, this second edition of *Principles and Practice of Business Continuity: Tools and Techniques* concentrates on the key capability of continuing to deliver products or services at acceptable redefined levels following disruptive incidents – business continuity in a nutshell. Burtles has created an easy-to-follow five-part structure within the book which permits the reader to follow his widely experienced knowledge of the definition, delivery, and maintenance of a business continuity program within an organization.

Burtles offers a brief look at the history of business continuity, which provides an insight into the necessities of establishing business continuity. In addition, he looks at operational risks, identifying the threats and potential impacts if the risk profile becomes active in any way, and introducing the contemporary concept of organizational resilience. In the first few chapters, he establishes the purpose of business continuity, clarifies the association between risk and appropriate continuity strategies, and explains the application of a business impact analysis cycle. Burtles then deals successively with the concepts of emergency response and the design required for restoration and recovery of services and products required by the organization; examples of the plan types that the business practitioner may wish to create against the structure of the organization; and a final chapter that details the means of governance of the business continuity program, both within the organization and in the support of the levels of resilience that management might expect in a modern business. Whether you regard Burtles, himself, as a guide or as a mentor, the results of this book should familiarize you with the various facets and requirements of business continuity creation to a level of excellence.

Chapter by chapter, the book builds knowledge of business continuity management techniques, much in the sequence of the professional practices established by the Business Continuity Institute's *Good Practice Guidelines*. Each chapter of the book is complemented by a set of questions and/or exercises to check your understanding – a task that requires organized business continuity thought processes to complete – and suggestions for further reading in the specific subject matter of the chapter. This level of enforcement will ensure understanding and promote best practices in line with Burtles' ideas and advice.

As a past designer of business continuity management systems, service continuity methods, and operational control systems, I have now moved into the world of lecturing others to do the same. You can rest assured that, by my estimation, this new edition by Burtles can contribute greatly to the systems capability that the business continuity practitioners, both new to the field and currently operating, are expected to design. The Business Continuity Institute's *Good Practice Guidelines* provides the current body of knowledge for the profession in terms of how to practice the discipline. In addition, a book such as *Principles and Practice of Business Continuity: Tools and Techniques* puts the skin on the bones of business continuity and provides wider knowledge of the activities associated with design, development, delivery, and management of business continuity for all sizes and types of organizations.

A part of business continuity is the scanning of the horizon to ensure that the business that you write the continuity management systems for is covered for almost every eventuality. Back when I loaded disk packs and tabulation paper in the back of a Ford Cortina to ensure overnight processing could take place at a reserve site, little did I think that this process would grow into a professional discipline called "business continuity." I could not have anticipated that business continuity would encounter so many developing challenges of the modern world, not only to meet the needs of the practitioners' own organizations, but also to permit their companies to remain competitive within the global marketplace at the times of highest stress.

Owen Gregory MBCI MBCS
Senior Lecturer
Buckinghamshire New University
High Wycombe, Buckinghamshire, UK

Foreword

We've all heard the saying "It's not what you know but who you know." This saying is true in my case, as it specifically applies to knowing Jim Burtles. As I began my career in emergency management, I first became aware of Jim as a respected author and expert in the field. I must admit that I was a little star-struck when I first met him as my instructor years later in a Business Continuity Institute (BCI) Good Practice Guidelines training course. At the time, I was working in a large public sector organization in the UK. As business continuity (BC) practitioners so often do, I felt a little isolated and despondent and was considering a change in direction.

It was Jim's enthusiastic teaching and passion for the subject that reignited my own passion for the subject. I realized that I could revive and learn to harness my enthusiasm and, combined with increasing my knowledge and skills, I could demonstrate the value of good BC management and make a difference. Thanks to Jim's expertise, advice, and positive attitude, I went on to become a certified practitioner and joined the BCI as a member. I would like to thank Jim for unintentionally persuading me to stick with BC as a profession and for introducing me to the BCI, where I am one of the many people Jim has brought into the field.

In this second edition of *Principles and Practice of Business Continuity: Tools and Techniques*, Jim describes himself as the experienced traveler, but I see him as the experienced guide with some great stories to tell with great lessons built in. Jim takes us on a journey, from the origins of BC to how it is practiced today. Because he is a founder of the discipline and continuing contributor to the growing body of knowledge in BC, with Jim we are in steady hands.

Jim's friendly narrative and ability to read the minds of the readers provides us with answers to many of the questions we often ask ourselves, such as, "So, what does this mean in practice?" He uses examples to illustrate his recommended approach to the subject along with suggestions for where to go for further information.

A common issue for practitioners is how to get the attention of the top management. For that, Jim's advice about being a good communicator and the importance of being patient and persistent is invaluable. Another frequent challenge for practitioners is to be able to demonstrate the value of BC and illustrate some return on investment. Jim suggests methods to calculate potential loss, which can be applied in your workplace to help answer those difficult questions.

This new edition builds on and expands on the original by posing questions at the end of each chapter inviting us to check what we have just read, making this book ideal for self-study for practitioners. Jim has written many exam questions as part of the BCI exam development group and knows how to test the reader's knowledge. I really like the thought-provoking "Food for Thought" sections that encourage readers to think about how they might apply this knowledge. Among other excellent resources, the downloadable **Business Continuity Toolkit** contains good examples of what can be used in the workplace to help practitioners develop their own documents.

Jim is a founding member of the BCI and key player in the BC profession, and I am lucky enough to now hold a senior position in the BCI myself and to work alongside Jim in many capacities. We have collaborated on developing teaching materials and models, co-presented our work to a global audience, and worked together to develop examination questions for the globally recognized certificate of the BCI (CBCI) credential. I am thrilled to be writing this foreword and happy to be able to give something back to Jim for all the many years he has contributed to the discipline and to my own career.

I would encourage anyone working in the field of BC and resilience to read this newly revised book. It tackles the emerging subject of organizational resilience as a governance issue and states the importance of collaboration between disciplines with which I wholeheartedly agree. Building a network of people and collaborating with others is a consistent message throughout this book and one to which I have listened and continue to follow.

As Head of Learning and Development at the Business Continuity Institute, I have been involved in a number of key industry developments – the *Good Practice Guidelines 2013*, the *British Standard on Crisis Management* (*BS 11200*), and *Organizational Resilience* (*BS 65000*) – and most recently as a member of the working group developing the International Standard for organizational resilience. I am proud to represent and to meet many BC professionals all over the world, and I know that this second edition of *Principles and Practice of Business Continuity: Tools and Techniques* will make an excellent addition to our resources, and should form an essential part of every practitioner's learning and development.

Deborah Higgins MBCI
Head of Learning and Development
The Business Continuity Institute

bci Business Continuity Institute

Table of Contents

Copyright ii

Dedication...iii

Acknowledgments..iv

Author's Introduction to the Second Edition..v

Foreword by Owen Gregory vii

Foreword by Deborah Higgins ix

Part I: Preparation and Startup 1

Chapter 1: What, Why, and How 3

1.1	A Brief History of the Business Continuity Profession	4
1.1.1	The Early Years	4
1.1.2	Organizations, Standards, and Laws	4
1.1.3	Business Continuity Today	5
1.2	The Business Continuity Professional	6
1.2.1	The Stages of Professional Competence	6
1.2.2	Understanding the Challenges of the BC Profession	6
1.2.3	The Business Continuity Professional as Communicator	7
1.3	Guidelines for Practical Business Continuity	7
1.3.1	A Practical Application of PAS 56	8
1.4	Six Disruptive Scenarios (What Can Go Wrong)	9
1.4.1	The Six Essential Elements	9
1.4.2	Physical Disruption	10
1.4.3	Technical Disruption	11
1.4.4	A Recovery Hypothesis	12
1.5	The Backlog Trap	12
1.5.1	How a Backlog Develops	12

1.5.2   Reducing the Backlog 13
1.5.3   Backlog Persistence 13
1.5.4   Efforts to Improve Efficiency 14
1.6   The Decision Point and Business Tolerance 14
1.6.1   Factors for Determining the Decision Point 15

Chapter 2: Roles and Responsibilities 21

2.1   The Key Players 22
2.1.1   Roles in the BC Management Structure 22
2.1.2   Selecting the Sponsor 23
2.2   Key Considerations 24
2.2.1   The Right Level of Support 25
2.2.2   The Role of the Sponsor 25
2.3   The Other Team Players 26
2.3.1   BC Manager 26
2.3.2   Senior Managers 26
2.4   The Teams 27
2.4.1   Crisis Management 28
2.4.2   Emergency Response 28
2.4.3   Facilities Recovery 28
2.4.4   Systems Recovery 29
2.4.5   Function Restoration 29
2.4.6   Non-Participants 29
2.5   A Collaborative Network 30
2.6   Your Business Continuity Infrastructure 32
2.6.1   UK Gold, Silver, and Bronze Management Levels 32
2.6.2   US National Incident Management Structure and Incident Command System...33
2.6.3   Applying the Gold, Silver, Bronze Structure to Your Own Game Plan 34
2.7   As You Embark on This Journey 35

Chapter 3: Getting Started 39

3.1   A Viable Game Plan 40
3.1.1   Kick-Off Meeting 40
3.1.2   Action Plan 40
3.1.3   Lead Them Step-by-Step 41
3.2   Deliverables and Other Outcomes 41
3.2.1   Initial Project 42
3.2.2   Permanent Process 42
3.3   A Launch Argument Formula: Seven Principles 42
3.3.1   In-House Ownership 42
3.3.2   Five Examples 43
3.3.3   Observance 44
3.3.4   Cognitive Marketing 44
3.3.5   Reach and Withdraw 45
3.3.6   Remain Realistic 46
3.3.7   One Step at a Time 47
3.4   Board-Level Motivators 47
3.4.1   External Influences 47
3.4.2   Internal Factors 48

3.4.3   Practical Considerations 49
3.4.4   Suitable Timing 50
3.5   Scaling to Fit 51
3.6   Standards and Their Interpretation..51
3.6.1   Compliance Issues 53
3.7   Hidden Benefits...53
3.8   The Auditor's Role 54

Part II: Building a Foundation..59
Chapter 4: Understanding Your Risks 61

4.1   Risk from a Business Continuity Perspective 62
4.1.1   Risk and the Six Disruptive Scenarios 62
4.1.2   The Regular Risk Management Review 62
4.1.3   Individual Interviews 63
4.1.4   Group Interviews 63
4.2   Risk Assessment Methods 63
4.2.1   Quantitative and Qualitative Methods 63
4.2.2   A Simple Quantitative Approach 64
4.3   Six Stages of Grid Impact Analysis 64
4.4   Risk Acceptance 66
4.4.1   Three Categories of Non-Transferable Risk 66
4.5   The Cost of Loss 67
4.5.1   Loss of Profit 67
4.5.2   Invisible Costs...68
4.6   Investment Wisdom 69
4.7   Defensive Measures..69
4.7.1   Causes of Business Interruption...70
4.7.2   Effects, Symptoms, and Consequences 71
4.8   QwikRisk...71
4.8.1   The Four Risk Groups..71
4.8.2   The Four Strategies...72
4.8.3   Matching the Risk with the Strategy 73
4.9   SMARTRisk 73
4.9.1   Key Features of SMARTRisk...74
4.9.2   Output of the SMARTRisk Process...74
4.10   Risk Reporting...75

Chapter 5: Impacts and Consequences......................................79

5.1   From Risk to Impact 80
5.1.1   Disruption Scenarios 80
5.1.2   Team Involvement..81
5.2   Business Impact Analysis Project..81
5.2.1   Organizing the Project...82
5.2.2   Collection of Impact Data – Choice of Method 82
5.2.3   Data Collection via Questionnaires 83
5.2.4   Data Collection via Interviews 83
5.2.5   Business Impact Analysis Workshops..84
5.2.6   Combining Questionnaire, Workshop, and Interview Methods 85
5.3   Business Impact Analysis Report...85

5.3.1	Assessing the Effects of Disruption and Business Impact	86
5.3.2	Determining Loss Exposure	87
5.4	Facilitated Business Impact Analysis	87
5.4.1	Interactive Impact Modeling	87
5.4.2	Results of the Exercise	89
5.4.3	Applying the Modeling Exercise to the BC Plan	89
5.5	Dependency Modeling	90
5.5.1	Creating the Dependency Model	90
5.5.2	Identifying Criticalities	91
5.6	Five Step Functional Analysis	91
5.6.1	Define the Critical Function	92
5.6.2	Agree on the Functional Drivers	93
5.6.3	Agree on the Main Business Functions	93
5.6.4	Identify the Functional Relationships	94
5.6.5	Criticality	95

Chapter 6: Continuity Strategies and Options 99

6.1	Selecting Practical Strategies	100
6.1.1	Disaster Response Considerations	100
6.2	Disaster Recovery Options	100
6.2.1	Dual Systems	100
6.2.2	Harmonic Recovery	101
6.2.3	Hot Site	101
6.2.4	Mobile Recovery Services	101
6.2.5	Cold Site	102
6.2.6	Portable Cold Site	102
6.2.7	Reciprocal Agreement	102
6.2.8	Second Site	103
6.3	Business Continuity Options	103
6.3.1	Alternate Sourcing	103
6.3.2	Emergency or Standby Stock	104
6.3.3	Buffer Stock	104
6.3.4	Redeployment or Relocation	104
6.3.4.1	Working from Home	105
6.3.5	Reduction of Operations	105
6.3.6	Termination or Change	106
6.3.7	Bypass Arrangements	106
6.3.8	Outsourcing	106
6.4	Strategy Selection	107
6.4.1	Initial Research	107
6.5	Backup and Restore Procedures	109
6.5.1	Locating and Cataloging Corporate Information	109
6.5.2	Identifying Critical Information	109
6.5.3	Information Protection and Replication	110
6.5.4	Storage Considerations	110
6.5.5	Types of Records for Backup and Retention	112
6.6	Information Recovery	113
6.7	Integrating and Coordinating Disaster Recovery with Business Continuity	114
6.7.1	Difficulties in Bringing the Fields Together	114
6.7.2	Finding the Common Ground	114
6.7.3	Working Together Smoothly	115

Part III   Responding and Recovering 119

Chapter 7: Emergency Response 121

7.1	Factors to Consider in an Emergency Response Team 122
7.1.1	Performance Concerns 122
7.2	Assembling the Right Emergency Response Team 124
7.2.1	Selection 124
7.2.2	Thorough Training, Education, and Exercising 125
7.2.3	Appropriate Tools for the Job 126
7.3	Command and Control 127
7.3.1	Command and Control Post Logical Structure 128
7.3.1.1	Emergency Communications 129
7.3.2	Command and Control Post: Physical Structure 129
7.3.2.1	Essential Features 130
7.3.2.2	Desirable Features 131
7.3.2.3	Ideal Characteristics 132
7.4	Phased Incident Management 133
7.5	Communications 134
7.5.1	Lack of Certainty 134
7.5.2	Withholding Information 135
7.5.3	Conflicting Information 135
7.5.4	Lack of a Firm Decision 135
7.5.5	Fear of Starting a Panic 136
7.5.6	No Means of Communication 136

Chapter 8: Emergency Preparedness 141

8.1	Identifying and Maintaining Emergency Resources 142
8.1.1	Access Control 142
8.1.2	Inventory Control 142
8.1.2.1	Establishing the Inventory 143
8.1.3	Financial Control 143
8.1.4	Service and Repair 144
8.1.5	Updates and Changes 144
8.1.6	Asset Retention 144
8.1.7	Feedback 144
8.2	Disaster Actions and Modes 145
8.2.1	Tools and Supplies 145
8.2.2	Skills 146
8.2.3	Resources 146
8.2.4	Arriving at a List of Requirements 147
8.3	Battle Boxes 148
8.3.1	Strategy 148
8.3.2	Characteristics 148
8.3.3	Contents 149
8.3.3.1	Inspection and Assessment 149
8.3.3.2	Rescue and Recovery 150
8.3.3.3	Office Support 150
8.3.3.4	Security and Isolation 151
8.3.3.5	Emergency Response 152
8.3.3.6	Crisis Management and Public Relations 152

8.3.3.7   Command Post Support 153
8.3.4   Maintenance and Update 153
8.3.4.1   Appoint a Responsible Person 153
8.3.4.2   Shelf Life of Contents 153
8.3.4.3   Photograph the Contents 153
8.3.4.4   Schedule Checks 154
8.3.4.5   Create a Battle Box Checklist 154
8.4   Recovery Facilities 155
8.4.1   Functional Resources 155
8.4.2   Functional Facilities 155
8.5   Liaising with Other Groups 156
8.5.1   Regulators 156
8.5.2   The Community 156
8.5.3   Insurers 156
8.5.4   Competitors 156
8.5.5   Neighbors 157
8.6   Liaising with Police and Emergency Services 157
8.6.1   Local Authorities 157
8.6.2   Emergency Services: Police 158
8.6.3   Emergency Services: Fire and Rescue 158
8.6.3.1   Importance of Portable Fire Extinguishers 159
8.6.3.2   Fire Training 159
8.6.3.3   Assisting the Fire Service 159
8.6.4   Emergency Services: Floods 159
8.7   Disaster Recovery 160
8.7.1   Salvage and Restoration 160
8.8   Contact Lists 160
8.8.1   Emergency Services 160
8.8.2   Internal Contacts 161
8.8.3   External Contacts 162

Chapter 9: Salvage and Restoration 167

9.1   Scrap or Salvage? 168
9.1.1   Insurance Issues 168
9.1.2   Professional Help 169
9.2   Denial of Access Issues 170
9.2.1   Causes of Denial of Access 170
9.2.2   Denial of Access for Public Security 171
9.2.3   Denial of Access by Health and Safety Officials 172
9.2.3.1   Death or Serious Injury 172
9.2.3.2   Structural Damage 172
9.2.3.3   Contamination 172
9.2.3.4   High Rise Buildings 173
9.2.3.5   Main Street and Industrial Locations 173
9.3   Site and Structures 173
9.3.1   Deterioration of Materials 173
9.3.2   Other Problems 174
9.4   Precautions after an Event 175
9.4.1   Precautions after Fire 175

9.4.2   Precautions after Flood (Including Firefighting Water) 175
9.4.3   Precautions after Contamination 175
9.4.4   Precautions after Blast 175
9.4.5   Unsafe Structures 176
9.5   Equipment and Technology 176
9.5.1   Problems of Running Applications on Different Equipment....................177
9.5.2   Issues after the Event...177
9.5.3   Damaged Media 178
9.6   Documents and Records Retrieval 178
9.6.1   Four Categories of Documents 179
9.6.2   Other Types of Documents...179
9.6.3   Emergency Response and Recovery Issuees for Documents 180
9.7   Electronic Equipment 180
9.8   Process Equipment 181
9.8.1   After Fire 182
9.8.2   After Flood 183
9.8.3   After Contamination 183
9.8.4   After a Blast..184
9.9   Regulating Access to the Site 184

Chapter 10: Disaster Recovery

Chapter10: Disaster Recovery 189
10.1   What is Disaster Recovery?..190
10.1.1   Characteristics of Disaster Recovery Plans 190
10.1.2   Aspects of Disaster Recovery...190
10.2   Technology and Support Services 191
10.2.1   Range of Services 191
10.2.1.1   Technical Services 191
10.2.1.2   Facilities 191
10.2.2   Rules to Maximize Resilience 192
10.2.3   Alternate Routing...192
10.3   Systems Recovery 193
10.3.1   Technical Expertise 193
10.3.2   Up-to-Date Recovery Strategies 193
10.3.3   Documented and Tested Procedures 194
10.4   Disaster Recovery Sites..194
10.5   Backup and Restore 194
10.5.1   What is Backup?..194
10.5.2   Backup and Restore Procedures 194
10.6   Backup Regimes 195
10.7   Business Records 196
10.7.1   Business Value 196
10.7.2   Source Information 196
10.8   Critical Records 197
10.8.1   Guidelines for the Selection of Critical Records.......................................197
10.8.2   Types of Critical Records 197
10.8.2.1   Software...197
10.8.2.2   Central Records 198
10.8.2.3   Operational Records 198
10.8.3   Storage of Critical Records...199

10.8.3.1   Backup Media..199
10.8.3.2   Data Storage Conditions...200
10.8.4   Backup Life Cycles..200
10.8.4.1   Creating a Backup Schedule for Record Types...............................201
10.8.4.2   A Typical Backup Schedule...202
10.9   The Data Recovery Process...202
10.9.1   Recovering the Data..203
10.9.2   Assembling the Data..204
10.9.3   Synchronizing the Data...204
10.10   Recovery Requirements...205
10.10.1   Golden Rules of Recovery...205
10.10.2   Rotation or Re-Use of Media..205
10.10.3   Management and Control..206
10.10.4   Backup Hints and Tips..206

Part IV: Planning and Implementing 211
Chapter 11: Plans and Planning 213

11.1   Hierarchy of Plans..214
11.1.1   Areas of Responsibility..214
11.1.2   Plan Types and Responsibilities..216
11.2   The Plan Development Process..216
11.2.1   Design and Structure..217
11.2.1.1   Relation of Plan Type to Area of Responsibility.............................218
11.2.1.2   Purposes of the Plan Types...219
11.3   Content of a Basic Plan: Business Recovery Plan............................220
11.3.1   Document Control Information...220
11.3.2   Contents..221
11.3.3   Layout...221
11.3.4   Organization Charts..222
11.3.5   Definitions..222
11.3.6   Scenarios...222
11.3.7   Roles and Responsibilities...223
11.3.8   Activation Process...223
11.3.9   Decision Criteria...223
11.3.10   Escalation Procedure...224
11.3.11   Action Lists...225
11.3.12   Reference Information...225
11.4   Emergency Response Plans..225
11.5   Crisis Management Plans...226
11.6   Function Restoration Plans...226
11.7   Disaster Recovery (DR) Plans...227
11.7.1   Disaster Recovery Modules...227
11.8   The Use of Commercial Planning Tools..228
11.8.1   Evaluation Considerations...229
11.9   Scaling to Fit...230
11.10   Preparation and Delivery of a Draft Plan.......................................230
11.10.1   Points to Look for in Template or Format......................................230
11.10.2   Preparing the Final Draft...231

Chapter 12: Exercise Preparation 235

12.1	Getting Started with BC Exercises	236
12.1.1	Capability and Confidence: Educating Personnel	236
12.2	The Five-Stage Growth Path	237
12.2.1	Desktop Exercise	237
12.2.2	Walkthrough	238
12.2.3	Active Testing	238
12.2.4	Command Post Exercise	239
12.2.5	Full-Scale Exercise	240
12.2.6	Frequency of Testing	241
12.3	Testing Plans and Procedures	241
12.3.1	Disaster Recovery Testing	241
12.3.2	Systems Recovery Checklist	242
12.4	Elements of Exercise Development	243
12.5	Background: Objectives and Purpose	245
12.5.1	Stating the Purpose	245
12.6	Buildup	246
12.7	Developing the Script for the Exercise	247
12.7.1	The Script Process Deliverables	247
12.7.1.1	Script Content	249
12.7.1.2	Interrupts	250
12.8	Quality	250
12.8.1	Realism	250
12.8.1.1	Methods for Achieving Realism	251
12.8.2	Scope	252

Chapter 13: Crisis Management and Communications 257

13.1	Understanding the Dimensions of a Crisis	258
13.1.1	Surprise	258
13.1.2	Uncertainty	259
13.1.3	Exposure	259
13.1.4	Urgency	259
13.2	Communicating with Internal and External Groups	259
13.2.1	The Corporate Statement	260
13.2.2	Internal Groups and Staff	260
13.2.3	External Groups and the Media	261
13.2.3.1	Media Policy	261
13.2.3.2	Ground Rules for Dealing with the Media	261
13.3	Crisis Communications Team	262
13.3.1	Creating the Team	262
13.3.2	Responsibilities	263
13.4	Managing the Media During a Crisis	264
13.4.1	Controlled Media Response	265
13.4.1.1	Holding Statements	265
13.4.2	Handling Media Telephone Calls	265
13.4.2.1	Preparation for Media Calls	266
13.4.2.2	Response Protocol	266
13.4.2.3	Social Media	267
13.4.3	Press Releases	267

13.4.3.1   Preparation and Content..268
13.4.3.2   Layout and Style..268
13.4.3.3   Points to Avoid 269
13.4.4   Interviews..269
13.4.4.1   Press Conferences 270
13.4.4.2   Guidelines for Spokespersons..270
13.4.4.3   Make Use of the Internet...271
13.4.4.4   Prepare Fast Facts for Background 272
13.4.4.5   Avoid Door-Stepping Journalists 272

Chapter 14: Exercise Management and Delivery 277

14.1   Exercise Delivery..278
14.1.1   Exercise Coordination and Control..278
14.1.2   Potential Problems 281
14.1.3   Preparation and Practice 281
14.2   Safety: Isolation and Security..282
14.2.1   Creating Isolation...283
14.2.2   Setting Up Security 283
14.3   The Ideal Scene 283
14.4   Lessons: The Feedback Stage...284
14.4.1   Exercise Debrief 284
14.4.2   The Exercise Report 285
14.4.3   The Exercise Review...286
14.4.4   Full Sequence of Feedback 286
14.5   Tracking the History 286
14.5.1   Records and Reports...286
14.5.1.1   Records 287
14.5.1.2   Reports 287
14.5.2   Recording 288
14.6   Kick-Off...288
14.6.1   Announcement and Notice...288
14.6.2   Cautions 289
14.6.3   Rules of Engagement 289
14.6.4   Keeping It Going 290
14.7   Advanced Techniques..290
14.7.1   The Command and Control Exercise Scale..291
14.7.2   Cabaret Exercising 292
14.7.3   The Bang and Echo Program 293

Part V: Long-Term Continuity..297

Chapter 15: Auditing and Maintaining Your Plans..................................299

15.1   Terms of Reference for Review 300
15.2   Steps in Review Process..300
15.2.1   Facilities 301
15.2.1.1   Facilities Testing 301
15.2.2   Resources 302
15.2.2.1   Resources Testing 303
15.2.2.2   Reviewing Dynamic and Stable Plan Content 303
15.2.3   Output Phase 304
15.2.3.1   Status Reports and Activity Reports 304

15.2.4	After the Reports	305
15.3	Auditing	305
15.3.1	The Audit Process	308
15.3.2	Rules of Audit	308
15.3.3	Policy	309
15.3.4	Compliance	309
15.3.5	Finance	309
15.3.6	Investment	310
15.3.7	Expenditure	310
15.3.8	Prudence	310
15.3.9	Purposes	310
15.3.10	Achievement	311
15.3.11	Claims	311
15.3.12	Concerns	311
15.4	Completing the Audit	311
15.4.1	Audit Checklists	311
15.4.2	Checklist Construction	312
15.4.3	Audit Reports	313

Chapter 16: Governance in the Resilient Organization 317

16.1	Horizon Scanning	318
16.1.1	Future Potential Moments of Vulnerability	318
16.1.2	Geographic and Economic Horizons	318
16.1.2.1	Geographic Horizon: Locations and Marketplaces	318
16.1.2.2	Economic Horizon: Supply Chains and Value Chains	318
16.2	Disruption from Relocation or Expansion	319
16.2.1	Reorganization or Restructuring	319
16.2.2	Survival of BC in Times of Economic Downturn	320
16.3	Tiers of Governance	320
16.3.1	Corporate Governance	322
16.3.2	Strategic Direction	322
16.3.3	Operational Management	322
16.3.4	Routine Supervision	323
16.4	Creating the Integrated Infrastructure	324
16.5	Relationship Between Governance and Business Continuity Standards	325
16.5.1	ISO 22301	326

Chapter 17: Your Future in Business Continuity 331

17.1	The Long-Term Management of Your BC Plans	332
17.2	Challenges	332
17.2.1	Lack of Understanding and Appreciation	333
17.2.2	Change of Ownership or Leadership	333
17.2.3	Lack of Priority	333
17.3	Opportunities	333
17.4	Professional Certification	334
17.4.1	The Business Continuity Institute (BCI)	334
17.4.2	Disaster Recovery Institute International (DRII)	335
17.4.3	International Consortium for Organizational Resilience (ICOR)	336
17.4.4	Other Professional Certifications Available	336
17.5	What's Next for Business Continuity	336
17.6	A Parting Word	337

Appendix A: Making Decisions Under Pressure 341

A.1	Decision-Making Protocols	341
A.2	Fight or Flee	342
A.3	Black Swan	342
A.4	Routine Mission	343
A.5	The Dark Serpent	343
A.5.1	Attack	343
A.5.2	Retreat	344
A.5.3	Evade	344
A.5.4	Ignore	345
A.5.5	Succumb	345
A.5.6	Taking Advantage of the Dark Serpent	345
A.6	Carousel Solution	346
A.7	Foxy Thinking	347
A.7.1	Foxy Scenario Planning	348
A.8	The DICE Model	349
A.8.1	The Six Key Elements	350
A.8.2	Application	350
A.8.3	Values	351
A.8.4	Information – Gather Information and Intelligence	351
A.8.5	Strategy	351
A.8.6	Authority – Powers and Policy	352
A.8.7	Tactics – Options	352
A.8.8	Actions and Review	353
A.8.8.1	Actions	353
A.8.8.2	Review: Recording What Was Done and Why	353
A.9	Learning from Hindsight	355

Appendix B: Case Study: Organic Resilience at Rushmore Enterprises 357

B.1	Organic Resilience Approach	357
B.2	The Basic Processes in Functional Relationships	358
B.2.1	Emergency Supplies	360
B.2.2	Emergency Production or Acquisition	360
B.2.3	Emergency Stores or Inventory	361
B.2.4	Emergency Communications	362
B.2.4.1	Receiving Information	362
B.2.4.2	Sending Information	363
B.2.5	Protective Strategies	364
B.2.5.1	Defense as a Strategy	365
B.2.5.2	Recovery as a Strategy	365
B.2.5.3	Copycat or Simulation Strategy	366
B.2.5.4	Supplementing as a Strategy	367

Appendix C: Working with People 369

C.1	Health, Safety, and Welfare	370
C.2	Emergency Working	371
C.2.1	Fatigue and Isolation	371
C.2.2	Rotating Tasks	371
C.3	Rewards and Acknowledgment	372

C.3.1   Benefits of Debriefing 372
C.4   Emotional Reactions to a Crisis 372
C.4.1   The Five Discoveries of Stress 373
C.4.1.1   Discovery of Fear 373
C.4.1.2   Discovery of Excitement 374
C.4.1.3   Discovery of Capability 374
C.4.1.4   Discovery of Chaos 374
C.4.1.5   Discovery of the Numbness of the Unknown 375
C.4.2   Post-Crisis Exit Effect 376
C.4.2.1   Delayed Exit Phenomena 376
C.5   Specific Forms of Counseling 377
C.5.1   Restabilization 377
C.5.2   Traumatic Incident Reduction (TIR) 378
C.5.3   Debriefing Sessions 378
C.5.4   Self Help 379
C.6   A Family Contact Team 380

Appendix D: Emergency Evacuation and Back to Normal 383

D.1   Emergency Evacuation: The Starting Point..383
D.1.1   Site Review 384
D.1.2   Emergency Evacuation Process and Timing..385
D.1.3   Test and Rehearsal Regime...386
D.2   Back to Normal: Reverse Recovery or "Revacuation"..........................387
D.2.1   The Timing..387
D.2.2   Migration and Commitment Points 387
D.2.3   Stumbling Blocks to the Return to Normal...388
D.2.3.1   Overconfidence 388
D.2.3.2   Apprehension 388
D.2.3.3   Bravado 388
D.2.3.4   Insufficient Recuperation 388
D.2.3.5   Catching Up and Forward Loading 389
D.2.4   Reverse Criticality 390
D.2.5   Troubleshooting 390
D.3   Back to Normal 390
D.3.1   Exit Housekeeping 390
D.3.2   The Debriefing Process 391
D.3.3   Inventory Check 391
D.3.4   Prevent a Recurrence 391
D.3.5   Opportunity 392
D.3.6   Public Relations 392

Glossary 393

Index 411

About the Author 431

Credits 432

Registration 436

Figures

Figure 1-1.   How Business Continuity Functions as an Umbrella......................................5
Figure 1-2.   The Six Types of Planning to Recover Business Operation 8
Figure 1-3.   BCM Process Model with a Choice of Entry Points and Optional Work Patterns 9
Figure 1-4.   Six Disruptive Scenarios Can Cause Loss of Essential Business Elements............11
Figure 1-5.   How a Backlog Trap Develops and Persists.......................................13
Figure 1-6.   How Backlog Relates to Recovery 15
Figure 1-7.   Decision Point for Declaring a Disaster 16
Figure 2-1.   Relationship of Roles in BC Management Structure..............................22
Figure 2-2.   Five Functional Teams for Organizing Response and Recovery 27
Figure 2-3.   The Gold, Silver, Bronze Command and Control Structure 32
Figure 4-1.   Risk Matrix Output Example Using QwikRisk......................................72
Figure 5-1.   Determining Dependencies and Connections to Core Business Processes 90
Figure 5-2.   Determining Critical Functions 92
Figure 5-3.   Functional Map of Core Functions 94
Figure 7-1.   Gold, Silver, Bronze 128
Figure 7-2.   Command Flows 129
Figure 7-3.   Points of Contact for Inbound and Outbound Communications Traffic...........130
Figure 7-4.   The Three Phases of Incident Management 133
Figure 8-1.   Disaster Actions and Modes 145
Figure 9-1.   Reporting Structure 184
Figure 9-2.   Controlling Access to the Area..185
Figure 10-1.   Effective Disaster Recovery Process..195
Figure 10-2.   Accuracy of Records Deteriorates Over Time....................................201
Figure 10-3.   The Logic of Data Recovery 203
Figure 11-1.   Roles in the Typical Organizational Structure................................215
Figure 11-2.   Key Tasks to Be Performed in an Emergency 215
Figure 11-3.   Hierarchy of Plans Related to Tasks and Functions 216
Figure 11-4.   Three Key Modules in Disaster Recovery Plan..................................227
Figure 12-1.   Gradient Learning: The Five-Stage Growth Path 237
Figure 12-2.   Exercise Elements 243
Figure 12-3.   Purpose in Action 246
Figure 12-4.   The Deliverables 248
Figure 12-5.   Blast Cones 251
Figure 13-1.   Dimensions of Crisis..258
Figure 14-1.   Exercise Elements 278
Figure 14-2.   Exercise Teams 279
Figure 15-1.   Three Areas of Interest in the Review Process 300
Figure 15-2.   Major Audit Activities 308
Figure 15-3.   Typical Types of Questions 312
Figure 16-1.   Tiers of Governance 321
Figure 16-2.   Core Characteristics 321
Figure 16-3.   An Integrated Robust Business Infrastructure 325
Figure 16-4.   Business Continuity and Strategic Alignment 326
Figure A-1.   The Dark Serpent 344
Figure A-2.   Scenario Planning 348
Figure A-3.   The DICE Model 351
Figure B-1.   The Basic Organic Structure 357
Figure B-2.   Request/Response Relationship...358

Figure B-3.   An Organic Enterprise 358
Figure B-4.   Basic Functional Relationships..359
Figure B-5.   Emergency Supplies..360
Figure B-6.   Emergency Production or Acquisition 361
Figure B-7.   Outsourcing or Emergency Stock 361
Figure B-8.   Emergency Communication Strategies 362
Figure B-9.   Defend the Function..365
Figure B-10.   Recover the Function...365
Figure B-11.   Copycat (or Simulated) Function..366
Figure B-12.   Supplement the Function 367

Tables

Table 5-1.   Assessing Effect of Disruption 86
Table 5-2.   Areas of Concern in Loss Exposure 87
Table 5-3.   Sample Worksheet for Impact Modeling..88
Table 8-1.   Sample Battle Box Checklist 154
Table 8-2.   Sample Contact List for Emergency Services...161
Table 8-3.   Sample Contact List for Internal Resources..161
Table 8-4.   Sample Contact List for External Contacts 163
Table 11-1.   Strengths and Weaknesses of Commercial BC Software 229
Table 12-1.   Summary of the Five Stages and Their Characteristics................................240
Table 14-1.   Five Levels of Command and Control...291

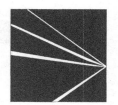

Part

I

Preparation and Startup

Part I: Preparation and Startup
Part II: Building a Foundation
Part III: Responding and Recovering
Part IV: Planning and Implementing
Part V: Long-Term Continuity

Preparation and Startup, covered in our first three chapters, explains what the subject is, explores the reasons behind it, and prepares you with the practical information about what can be achieved, what should be achieved, and how to go about it. You will be able to apply this information whether you are looking forward to a possible business continuity (BC) career, about to create a BC program, or already on the job in BC.

Chapter 1 – What, Why, and How

- Introduces you to the subject and those who engage in it.

Chapter 2 – Roles and Responsibilities

- Explains what you can expect and what might be expected of you and how to set up a BC management structure.

Chapter 3 – Getting Started

- Tells you how to get management buy-in and launch an effective BC program.

1

What, Why, and How

In this chapter we will be looking at the reasons why your organization should engage in business continuity (BC) since you need to be able to convince colleagues and decision-makers of the advantages and benefits of committing to a fully developed BCM program. Armed with the basics of BCM, an understanding of the tools, and familiarity with the techniques, you will be in a position to approach a BCM program in a professional and competent manner.

This chapter will help you to:

- ☑ Define BC in practical terms.

- ☑ Trace the history of the BC discipline as it evolved into the present day.

- ☑ See what it takes to be a BC professional.

- ☑ Understand the six disruptive scenarios that can cause business interruptions.

- ☑ Relate the backlog trap to the process of efficient decision-making in the face of disruption.

1.1   A Brief History of the Business Continuity Profession

Before we set out on this adventure together, it might be useful for you to have some background information about our relatively young profession and its origins. Bear in mind that in many ways the development of the profession has been a reflection of the businesses it seeks to protect; therefore, it is still evolving in sympathy with the dynamics of modern commerce in our changing world. In other words, nothing is set in concrete; the basic concepts will always remain true, but the tactical and technical details may well change over time.

1.1.1   The Early Years

In 1974, Norm Harris, then Director of Data Processing at the First National Bank of Ohio, put together what has been recognized as the first *disaster recovery plan*. This plan was aimed at recovering the information technology (IT) capability in an era when mainframes were the only available form of computing. These machines were massive, costly, and relatively fragile, which meant availability was a constant source of concern to the IT managers of the time. Although the idea of a planned recovery caught on fast among a number of forward-thinking managers and directors, the majority of decision-makers were quite happy to keep their heads firmly buried in the sand.

> **...business managers and executives began to realize that the only valid form of protection was full protection.**

A few years later, in the early 1980s, midrange systems began to appear, and real-time processing increased the need for high availability. Computer users were becoming dependent on having immediate access to their business applications. As a result, a new style of plan emerged which embraced the users' needs rather than simply serving the IT department. These rather more comprehensive plans were known as *contingency plans* and broadened the horizons for our emerging profession. The users spoke common or garden-variety business language rather than IT jargon, which meant that company decision-makers finally began to understand some of the arguments and appreciate the benefits of this planning idea.

Gradually, business managers and executives began to realize that the only valid form of protection was full protection. This thinking meant that plans of a broader scope were required. A book about continuity planning by the late Ronald D. Ginn, an advocate of Norm Harris's principles, soon led to the adoption of the term business continuity around the world (Ginn, 1989). Soon, business continuity plans covered the full spectrum of the business enterprise.

1.1.2   Organizations, Standards, and Laws

The UK-based Business Continuity Institute (BCI, www.theBCI.org) was founded in 1994 and published the first set of standards, which were developed in collaboration with the Disaster Recovery Institute (DRI), which later changed its name to Disaster Recovery Institute International (DRII, www.DRII.org). These standards of competence defined the skills and formed the basis for evaluating the capability of a BC practitioner. Shortly after that, the phrase *business continuity management* (BCM) emerged as the term to describe this discipline in the framework of modern governance.

By the turn of the century, BCM was becoming recognized as a core discipline within many sectors of both government and commerce. BCM techniques were used to prepare for the possible appearance of the millennium bug and for the resulting chaos which many of the gloom-and-doom merchants were predicting. One school of thought is that we were very lucky and the millennium continuity was entirely the result of very thorough preparation. On the other hand, some responded that the whole thing was exaggerated and that a lot of time, money, and effort had been wasted. As a result, it took BCM a couple of years to recover its image and return to center stage as the bastion against disasters, emergencies, crises, contingencies, and hiccups.

Over the decades during which contingency planning gradually emerged from disaster recovery and matured into the BC of today, a number of membership organizations sprang up to meet the needs of a growing community of pioneers and their fellow travelers. At the same time, many of the regulatory bodies around the world began to recognize the need for continuity of services and operations. Today, most of them expect, require, or advise the realistic implementation of business continuity measures within their industry.

> **One of the key characteristics of the early pioneer was a passion and enthusiasm for the subject...**

In recent years, more and more government bodies have issued standards or recommendations relating to BCM, and several countries now have legislation promoting the adoption of BC measures in both the private and public sectors. The most obvious and inclusive of these efforts has been the UK's Civil Contingencies Act 2004, which even requires local government to promote BC throughout the business community.

One of the key characteristics of the early pioneers was a passion and enthusiasm for the subject coupled with good communication skills. This is not surprising because it was, and still is, a fascinating field with many variations and opportunities for fresh thinking and constructive activity. It was their enthusiasm that attracted others to join them or support them. Nowadays, the majority of practitioners in the field still display a keen interest or fascination for what is, after all, such a beneficial subject. This sincerity is essential to arouse the vital spark of interest in our target audience, who are the managers of today and the leaders of tomorrow. Thus, the key to success for any BC manager is an ability to communicate (which includes both talking and listening), coupled with enthusiasm for the subject.

1.1.3 Business Continuity Today

Figure 1-1 correlates the disciplines, products, and processes that may be considered to relate to, impinge upon, or contribute to, the practice of BCM. In your role as a BC manager, you will need to have a basic understanding of, and a relationship with, each of these areas of responsibility and action. Understanding these relationships is important because the protection and resilience of the overall enterprise stems from the ongoing collaboration of a number of disciplines.

Both the security policy and BCM must span the whole of the enterprise. Testing,

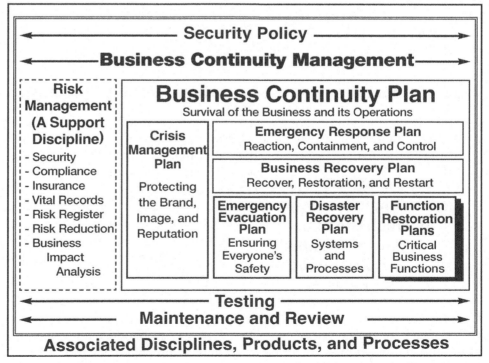

Figure 1-1. How Business Continuity Functions as an Umbrella

maintenance, and review processes must span the whole BCM program, which also requires the support of risk management.

BC plans, which are the tangible products of BCM, include modules or components to address the various aspects of response, recovery, and continuity. Crisis and emergency response are also shown as separate plans or modules. All of these plans, or elements, comprise the overall BC plan which is, in effect, a set, or a suite, of plans.

1.2   The Business Continuity Professional

1.2.1   The Stages of Professional Competence

Wherever you are in your BC career – student, beginner, or practitioner – you will be at one of the three stages of professional competence in the BC profession.

- First, you have to learn the language and understand the concepts. This is like being at school getting ready to face the world.
- Then, in the second stage, you have to learn how to apply that knowledge and act the part. This is a form of training where you will be looking to others to guide and advise you as you move forward and learn the ropes. After a while you will be in a position where you have acquired, or absorbed, enough expertise to approach the work on your own without someone standing by, ready to hold your hand.
- Eventually, at the third stage, you will become an expert, ready to show others, and play a leading role, with the ability to adapt the tools and techniques to suit the occasion and the environment.

If you are a student or beginner, you will be in some phase of completing your basic schooling, largely comprised of reading through this book and practicing with the materials in the downloadable **Business Continuity Toolkit** included with this book. You will be working with a tutor or mentor, ready to embark on a practical training program, possibly some form of apprenticeship in which you will learn the ropes, sheltering under the wing of an established professional. If you already have some experience as a practitioner, you will be using the advice in this book to enhance your current skills and to lead others as they pursue a challenging career in BC.

1.2.2   Understanding the Challenges of the BC Profession

However, if you are at the beginning stages of the BC profession, you are probably still wondering what sort of person takes on this kind of work and what might be expected of you if you decide to follow in the footsteps of the professionals we have described. BC, as its name implies, is all about protecting the whole of the organization and ensuring that all of its essential component parts are able to function. Ideally, this continuity should be achieved without any noticeable interruption, but a realistic aim is minimal interruption. Absolute continuity is rarely achievable and usually prohibitively expensive. We are looking at adequate protection rather than absolute prevention; rapid recovery rather than instantaneous revival. Within the domain of BC we have to remain pragmatic with our aims and expectations.

> **...BC gives a person a very thorough grounding in the way in which the many departments and activities work together...**

Over the years, I have had the pleasure of helping a number of young graduates who were attached to the BC teams of large organizations in, and around, the city of London. It was part of my job to teach them the basics of BC and help them integrate into the world of commerce. They were at the start of their career path and still exploring the possibilities of where that might lead. A common theme was the way in which they learned much more about the way the organization worked than any of their fellow graduates who were placed in other departments.

I have come to the conclusion that working in BC gives a person a very thorough grounding in the way in which the many departments and activities work together as an integrated whole. Although it might not lead you to a deep grasp of all the minutiae, it does allow you to see and understand the whole picture. The only other people who typically learn as much about what is really happening right across the spectrum are the auditors, who also get to visit and interview people from all departments as a natural part of their work. By starting their careers in BC, these young people had the advantage of being able to work out which part of the organization best suited their talents.

1.2.3   The Business Continuity Professional as Communicator

In my experience, the person who is most comfortable and successful as a BC practitioner is a good communicator who is patient and persistent. If you develop those skills, you will find it a rewarding occupation because what you are doing is extremely valuable and appreciated, especially when something goes wrong and BC comes to the rescue.

A BC professional needs to be a good communicator in the fullest sense of the word. In this context, a good communicator is one who can get other people to understand what he or she is talking about. It is equally important that you are a careful listener, able to understand what other people are trying to explain to you; this is where the patience and persistence comes in. Many times you will find yourself dealing with people who are engaged in quite complex and unfamiliar activities. On the one hand, you will need to gain a basic understanding of what they do and what they need; on the other hand, you will have to persuade them to apply your principles to their activities so that, working together, you can work out sensible solutions to problems which may never have occurred to either of you separately. You have to remain sincere, and maintain your credibility, throughout the whole process. In addition, you need to be able to make effective presentations to small gatherings of important people, engage in deep and meaningful conversations with people at all levels, prepare professional looking reports and plans, and demonstrate enthusiasm for what you do.

1.3   Guidelines for Practical Business Continuity

In 2003, the British Standards Institution (BSI) released a publicly available specification (Marsh & McLennan Companies, 2004). PAS 56 provided a "generic management framework for incident anticipation and response, as well as describing evaluation techniques and criteria." At the time of publication in 2003, the BSI stated PAS 56 would be withdrawn upon "publication of its content in, or as, a British Standard." Please note that PAS 56 was replaced by BS 25999 in 2006. In 2012, ISO 22301 was introduced, and both PAS 56 and BS 25999 were withdrawn. (For more detail on ISO 22301, see Chapter 3 of this book.) In the UK, the Civil Contingencies Secretariat adopted PAS 56 as its paradigm of good practice, and many groups followed suit. Since then, other standards have emerged but the underlying principles and concepts have evolved rather than changed. Although some of the models that I describe here were not carried forward into the new standards, I still like to use them as explanations of the practical side of BC. However, for certification purposes, you will need to consult the details of current standards.

Full protection of the whole business can come only from the completion of all three phases at all four levels...

You will return to the subject of published standards in Chapter 3 of this book, when you will be looking at the standards and guidelines you may turn to as references.

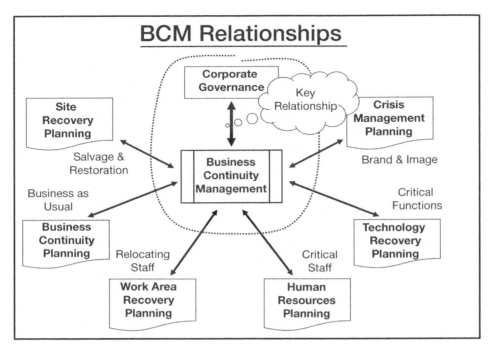

Figure 1-2. The Six Types of Planning to Recover Business Operation

PAS 56 linked the discipline of BCM with corporate governance, which was also emerging as a subject of considerable interest to managers and executives, although the subject of corporate governance had not been formally standardized. As shown in Figure 1-2, this prototype standard called for six different types of planning to protect and recover various aspects of the business operation.

It went on to suggest that there should be four basic strategies and three different levels of strategic planning. The overall BCM program was comprised of six stages, each with its own defined objectives and outcomes. Although the actual model has not been carried forward, the underlying concepts have been retained in subsequent standards.

1.3.1   A Practical Application of PAS 56

For the first edition of this book, we developed a practical interpretation of what we understood to be the aims and concepts of PAS 56. As shown in Figure 1-3, it is a BCM process model which offers you a choice of entry points and a number of optional work patterns. This model enables you, as the BC manager, to select the degree of protection which is required at each of the various levels. Then, you can build towards those particular goals with a series of projects over a timeframe of your own choosing. Of course, this will all be carried out in collaboration with your colleagues, managers, and executives.

In our business protection model there are three consecutive or sequential phases for each of the four levels of protection:

 ▸ Phase One, **Establishment** identifies the basic needs.
 ▸ Phase Two, **Basic Protection** implements the protective measures.
 ▸ Phase Three, **Consolidation** develops the skills and proves the capability.

The four levels of protection represent the main areas of coverage:

 ▸ Level One, **Crisis Response** is about protecting the brand and image.
 ▸ Level Two, **Emergency Response** is about dealing with the incident.
 ▸ Level Three, **Restoration and Recovery** is about business processes.
 ▸ Level Four, **Backup** is about protecting vital information.

Full protection of the whole business can come only from the completion of all three phases at all four levels, but the advantage of offering a degree of choice will make it much easier for you to obtain buy-in. Furthermore, each of the tasks can be seen to deliver a distinct degree of protection or resilience. You can demonstrate that progress is being made with a series of visible deliverables, revealed at regular intervals. This approach is generally more attractive than one where everybody has to wait a long time before they see any substantial result.

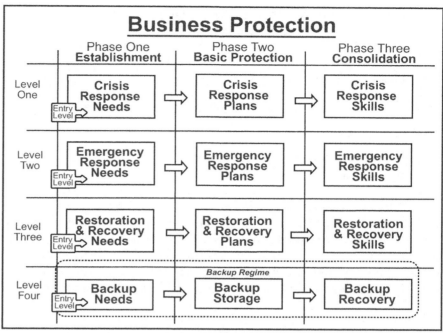

Figure 1-3. BCM Process Model with a Choice of Entry Points and Optional Work Patterns

In many ways, BCM is an almost endless learning curve because throughout the entire program you will be gaining insights, learning lessons, and applying them. It is a continuous series of improvements derived from analyzing what is known, understanding what is possible, and preparing for what is likely.

1.4 Six Disruptive Scenarios (What Can Go Wrong)

BC works on the assumption that certain effects can and will happen, irrespective of the actual cause. It is based on considerations about a range of possibilities which may be completely unpredictable but do need to be treated pragmatically. You should also bear in mind that BC is principally concerned with protecting, and sustaining, what should be happening at a tactical or operational level rather than the rather more philosophic and intangible aspects of policies, strategies, and values.

The focus is on the noticeable effects rather than the obscure causes of an incident...

In order to prepare for almost any eventuality it helps if you can categorize those eventualities. Then you can address the categories rather than prepare to deal with each and every one of the many and varied abnormalities which might intrude upon the business operation. From a BC perspective, I assert that there are only six disruptive scenarios which you need to plan for. Once the incident has occurred, the precise cause is irrelevant, but you must have a strategy which covers the ensuing effects.

1.4.1 The Six Essential Elements

Six essential business elements combine to enable the cash flow, or income stream, which drives and sustains the typical enterprise. Most of the things that can, and do, go wrong, and all business disasters, crises, or interruptions, are variants of those six scenarios, which we will discuss in detail later in this chapter. *If you and your organization are prepared to deal with these six generic circumstances, you will be able to recover from any business disaster.*

Three *physical* disruptive scenarios you need to prepare for are:

1. Loss of access.
2. Loss of people.
3. Loss of supplies.

Three *technical* disruptive scenarios you need to prepare for are:

1. Loss of communication.
2. Loss of function.
3. Loss of data.

Like many of my colleagues, I had accepted without question some of the traditional beliefs about the causes of disasters, their effects, and the subsequent consequences. However, after reviewing some of the materials I had used over the years, I saw the possibilities of a new model. This model, presented here for the first time in Figure 1-4 below, provides a clear, practical foundation for your preparation and planning. The focus is on the noticeable effects rather than the obscure causes of an incident. As the BC manager, you will be responsible for working out how to contain the effects and thus reduce the consequences.

All businesses depend upon some form of cash flow for their continued existence. Most commercial enterprises will be engaged in activities which result in a positive cash flow in return for the delivery of its goods or services. Governmental and charitable bodies may be expected to dispense goods and services in a form of outbound or negative cash flow. In either case an interruption to the delivery results in a loss or a drain on the cash reserves. If this situation is not addressed in time, then the business is at risk of losing its income and without funds it will soon be forced to close its operation. By focusing on effects, rather than causes, you will be adopting a similar viewpoint to that of a doctor who prescribes a course of action, or medication, to deal with the symptoms and reduce any long term consequences. The actual cause is mainly of academic interest. The patient is not particularly interested in whether it was a virus, a bacterium, or a toxin that caused the swelling and the pain – she wants to be able to relax and get to sleep at night.

In essence, these six disruptive scenarios are those situations that are liable to cause the unexpected and detrimental loss of your essential business elements. We can regard them in two groups: three physical types of disruption and three technical types of disruption which need to be addressed. Any effective BCM program needs to cover each of these disruptive scenarios. Also, bear in mind that you could lose more than one of these elements at the same time. This could be a direct result of the initial cause or it could be a domino effect in which the outcome of one difficult situation leads to another problem.

1.4.2   Physical Disruption

Loss of access is the category which covers all those circumstances where personnel are denied access to premises or facilities. This might include anything from an earthquake which has destroyed the premises to a storm which has damaged the property or a broken key that won't open the door. The BC plan has to provide a solution which is likely to involve access to alternative facilities or, in some instances, an instant repair capability.

Loss of people means that personnel are unable or unwilling to carry out their normal tasks. This might be due to absence caused by sickness or injury or they may have withdrawn their labor for some reason or cause which they subscribe to. Other possible problems include extreme weather conditions, lack of transport, changes of circumstance, violence on the streets, or a blockade. BC plans need to cover this eventuality through the use of alternative or temporary people who may require specific training or qualifications. Detailed working instructions and scripts might also be required to support such plans.

Loss of supplies means a shortage of ingredients or materials to support the production and delivery of normal goods and services. This may be caused by damage to existing stocks or the storage area where they are held. Such problems can be due to extreme weather conditions, power failure leading to loss of heat or cold, flooding, or fire. Loss of supplies may also be

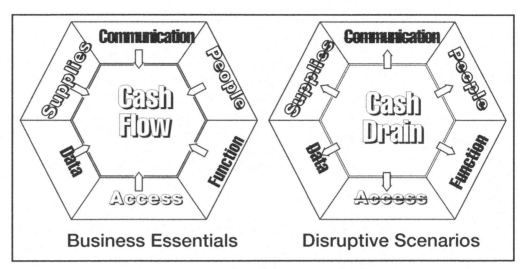

Figure 1-4. Six Disruptive Scenarios Can Cause
Loss of Essential Business Elements

due to a failure within the supply chain causing stock to be delayed or not delivered. BC plans need to ensure the timely supply of all such materials under emergency conditions. This may entail pre-arranged purchase orders, alternate suppliers, or comprehensive shopping lists. The details of the arrangements will vary according to the urgency, volumes, and uniqueness of the supplies involved.

1.4.3   Technical Disruption

Loss of communication describes the situation in which some or all of the important communication systems become ineffective or corrupted for whatever reason. This may be caused by storm damage, power outage, flooding, or problems with service providers. It is also possible that authorities may wish to limit or shut down the services in a particular area. This especially applies to mobile phone networks. Satellite and landline communications are rather more difficult to control.

Loss of function occurs whenever an important item of equipment is out of service for some reason. This might be due to poor maintenance, unscheduled maintenance, power failure, accidental damage, vandalism, or the equipment may simply be unavailable or unusable for some reason. Perhaps the lease has run out or the certificate of assurance has expired. BC plans should cover this situation, typically by providing, or enabling access to, alternative equipment. Another solution might be to outsource the related activity while the original equipment is restored.

Loss of data is any situation where one or more functions of the business are unable to access important information. This might be due to some form of technical or system failure which renders the data inaccessible. It could also be caused by corruption somewhere within a database which renders the data unusable or unreliable. Critical information which the business depends on for current activities may be missing, incomplete, or inaccessible. BC plans must address these possibilities and establish means to recapture, retrieve, or replace the missing information.

While there may be literally thousands of causes for a disaster and hundreds of possible consequences, your BC plan has to deal effectively with only these six disruptive scenarios: loss of access, people, supplies, communication, function, and data. Furthermore, the plan needs to offer guidelines only, rather than detailed directions, except where particular procedures require specific instructions. Remember that a BC plan should be interpreted according to the circumstances, and those circumstances can't be accurately predicted – they have to be assessed and translated at the time.

> ## Underpinning the need for BC…is the unexpected accumulation of an unmanageable work load.

Obviously, expertise which comes from practical experience will prove to be a tremendous asset whenever the BC plan is invoked. The benefit of competence and confidence developed through regularly exercising your BC plan is an essential ingredient of any reliable performance. You will find this to be especially true under trying circumstances, such as in the wake of a disaster.

1.4.4 A Recovery Hypothesis

I contend that any BC plan which covers each of the six disruptive scenarios – loss (or impairment) of access, people, supplies, communication, function, or data – provides the basis for recovery from any physical disaster. I have come to this conclusion after 35 years of practical experience in the disaster recovery services industry and the BC profession.

1.5 The Backlog Trap

Underpinning the need for BC and a planned response to any serious business disruption is the unexpected accumulation of an unmanageable work load. This is an almost invisible danger that is often overlooked or ignored because people simply do not understand it or appreciate its implications. I first described and published my thoughts on this phenomenon in 1993 in a paper entitled "The Backlog Trap" (Burtles, 1993). In the full paper (available in the downloadable **Business Continuity Toolkit**), the theory is underpinned with a mathematical formula which enables you to calculate the precise nature and scale of the impact on your business, taking account of its style of operation.

1.5.1 How a Backlog Develops

The concept of the backlog trap was originally discovered within an IT setting, but its implications apply to any business system, process, or operation which may be subject to fluctuations in performance or availability. Fluctuations in this context could be due to such factors as mechanical failures, technical problems, routine maintenance, lack of supplies, or misunderstandings. Whether these fluctuations were expected and planned for or came as a complete and total surprise isn't really important. The catching up still needs to be done.

Returning to "normal" from a "system down" situation generally takes at least five times the duration of the downtime and it could take considerably longer. This figure of five times is based on the assumption that you are able to increase the effective work rate by 25% in order to clear the backlog.

A backlog starts to grow immediately once the system fails or falters because the business need continues unabated. Most businesses have little or no capacity for dealing with the backlog; so it tends to dwell as an unrecognized but denigrating burden. In other words, the business becomes slower in the delivery of its goods and services to the customer. This level of service can have a negative effect on staff morale and relationships that will affect the way in which customers perceive the business. From the perspective of customers, what was once a reliable resource has now become a doubtful source of supply, and they begin to look elsewhere, where they are likely to be made to feel most welcome.

1.5.2   Reducing the Backlog

There are two ways of reducing the backlog: 1) you can have more people working or 2) the same number of people working longer hours. Without additional trained staff available, you would have to extend the working period to clear the backlog. Typically, this means increasing the working day from 8 hours to 10 hours for the duration of the emergency. Alternatively, you might try extending from a five-day week to one of six or even seven working days. Theoretically, an extended work period may appear to be a workable solution, but it can be difficult to organize and is often fraught with operational problems caused by fatigue and other considerations such as staff willingness or availability of supplies or other resources.

Because of the tendency to return to usual working methods *before* the whole of the backlog has been tackled, the backlog tends to persist. The persistent backlog becomes self-perpetuating and thus becomes accepted as the "new normal."

Figure 1-5 shows the backlog trap in a graphic form. This may be easier to recognize and understand than a complex argument or a set of mathematical symbols. The purpose here is to show you the relationships, together with the potential scale and timeframes, of the factors involved in the build-up and the persistence of an outstanding body of work which builds up whenever our systems let us down unexpectedly.

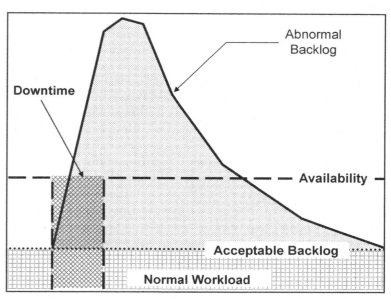

Figure 1-5. How a Backlog Trap Develops and Persists

1.5.3   Backlog Persistence

In one common example of backlog persistence, invoices are sent out late, subsequent queries are raised on them simply because they are late, and more work is then required to handle the queries which makes it even more difficult to get the invoices out on time. Also, these delays affect things such as cash flow.

The backlog will probably also include, or impose, additional work, such as changes to procurement and delivery procedures. Often, the outage will have created circumstances which require different reports and forecasts to be made in order to establish the new status and manage the business accordingly.

We tend to think that as soon as the engineer has given us back our system or component, all of our troubles are over and we can attack the backlog. In actual fact, of course, we still have to recover and restart the system, extending the effective downtime. Although what is usually recorded and plotted as downtime is the system outage as perceived by the operator(s), it is the overall duration of abnormal working or the effect on the end-users and hence the customers which impacts the business.

A further hazard is that overloaded workers, and systems, are more prone to errors and failures, which compound the effects of an outage. For example, a couple of weeks ago, my local dry cleaners had some technical difficulties which prevented them from doing any dry cleaning for three or four days. The boss decided they should work longer hours to catch up, which meant that some of the staff became very tired and slightly careless. Somehow, some of the shirts and trousers which customers brought in did not have their labels firmly attached. The labels came off during the cleaning process, and for the next couple of weeks, there was chaos in the shop while infuriated customers had to help the staff search for their items of clothing. Understandably, this poor service led to some upsets and arguments between staff and customers. The company lost customers (and income) as a result of the mix-ups and responded by raising their prices; it remains to be seen whether the changes in pricing will lead to more profit or less business.

1.5.4   Efforts to Improve Efficiency

Earlier we gave the example of a business improving its effective work rate by 25% in order to reduce the backlog within five times the duration of the downtime. This optimistic figure is based upon two assumptions:

- ◗ This particular business normally runs at 70% efficiency.
- ◗ In an emergency, the business can increase its efficiency to 95%.

If management does not declare a disaster at or before this decision point...you are endangering the continued success of the business.

100% efficiency is an unrealistic possibility even for the most advanced and well managed operation. On the other hand, 70% efficiency is rather sluggish. An already efficient business is likely to find it difficult to improve its efficiency. The implication here is that the well managed enterprise is more exposed than its fumbling counterpart and, consequently, it is more in need of continuity plans and procedures. If the work rate is increased by only 20%, the ratio of business exposure to downtime becomes 6:1 and at 10%, it drops down to 11:1. A 5% increase gives a backlog exposure ratio of 21:1. (**Note:** A 20% increase assumes a business running at 70% can achieve 90% in recovery mode; a 10% increase assumes a business running at 80% can achieve 90% in recovery mode; and a 5% increase assumes a business running at 90% can achieve 95% in recovery mode.)

Key Messages

1. Until the backlog is reduced to an acceptable level, the business is still at risk.
2. The business exposure is at least five times the duration of the downtime. This figure assumes the operation in question is currently running at less than 80% efficiency and yet it is able to approach 100% efficiency in the aftermath of an emergency.

1.6   The Decision Point and Business Tolerance

The real danger of backlogs for complex operations, such as IT, is the very short period of time in which a problem can escalate to a potential disaster. If you ask the end-users how long they can manage without the system (period of tolerance), you will get an answer based on what they perceive as the "acceptable backlog" condition. Therefore, as shown in Figure 1-6, you must take the backlog trap into account and divide their period of tolerance by a suitable factor in order to determine the true *business critical point* – which is the latest moment, or longest time, end-users can afford to be without a working system. From that figure, you must then deduct the time taken to recover, restore, and restart the system; this calculation gives the "decision point" at which a disaster has to be declared. If management does not declare a disaster at or before this decision point – or fails to invoke your emergency measures in time – then you are endangering the continued success of the business.

Up until the decision point you are within the "problem phase" which is followed by the "disaster phase." During the initial problem phase someone should be able to detect, investigate, and repair the fault. *Failure to*

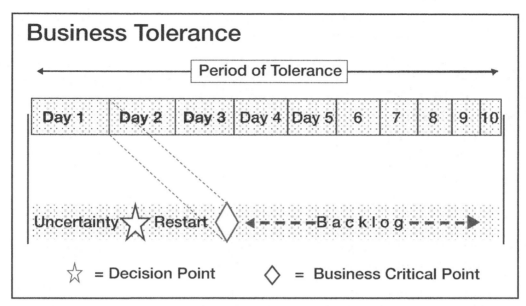

Figure 1-6. How Backlog Relates to Recovery

resolve the problem before reaching the decision point opens up the disaster phase. If a conscious decision is not made by this point in time, the whole enterprise is in a state of disaster without realizing it. This is literally a worst case scenario.

1.6.1 Factors for Determining the Decision Point

As shown in Figure 1-7, the timeframe in which you have to make a decision about declaring a disaster may be very much shorter than anyone realizes. There are a number of factors to be taken into account when determining the decision point. As I mentioned earlier, these concepts were originally developed within an IT context, but the principles apply to any business process or activity.

Sample Set of Decision-Making Criteria

A disaster should be declared, and the emergency response team alerted, whenever any of the following conditions apply:

- ✦ Access to the premises has been denied for more than 60 minutes, irrespective of the cause.
- ✦ Telecommunications have been unavailable to more than 50% of the staff for more than 30 minutes.
- ✦ Power has been unavailable to more than 50% of the site for more than 90 minutes.
- ✦ The main computer system has been unavailable to more than 50% of the accounts staff for more than 2 hours.

If any of these conditions is likely to be met within the next 30 minutes, the BC director (or manager designated in the BC plan) should be advised of the situation without delay.

The above example is meant to be an illustration of the language and style rather than a model set of disaster criteria. You will need to develop and agree upon your own set of criteria in collaboration with your colleagues.

▸ **System Recovery:** The procedures for rebuilding a computer system to the condition where it is ready to accept data and applications. System recovery depends on having access to suitable hardware.

> Because of the enormous leverage the backlog can have…problems which used to be mere inconveniences now become quite serious.

▸ **System Restore:** The procedures required to get a system into an operable condition where it is possible to run the application software against the available data. System restore depends on having a live system available.

▸ **Application Restart:** The procedure or procedures that return the applications and data to a known start point and get the users restarted. Application restart is dependent upon having an operable system.

Because of the enormous leverage the backlog can have on the business and the reduced tolerance due to market pressures, problems which used to be mere inconveniences now become quite serious. Indirect or environmental causes, such as loss of power, air-conditioning faults, cabling problems, and so on, can lead to a significant loss if we do not adhere strictly to our pre-determined decision point.

In order to ensure the timeliness of an adequate recovery, you will need the decision-making process to be formalized and adhered to with a clear set of criteria which are objective rather than subjective. These criteria must be supported by empowerment to enable whoever is available to invoke the disaster recovery procedure to act without hesitation for fear of reprisal. In other words, it is the situation which should determine the outcome rather than someone's judgment or opinion; the decision should be event-driven rather than emotionally motivated.

Your decision-making criteria should refer to measurable dimensions or factors, such as elapsed time or extent of the failure. It is not helpful to depend upon estimates of what might happen or how the situation may evolve over time. A far more reliable approach is to inspect the actual circumstances rather than attempt to predict any of the likely outcomes.

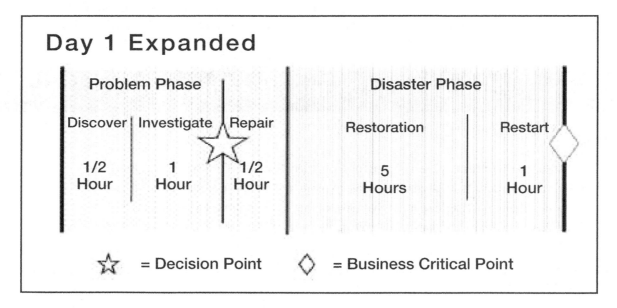

Figure 1-7. Decision Point for Declaring a Disaster

Self-Examination Questions

1. The business continuity profession is
   A. a long-established profession with concepts and procedures that have stood the test of time.
   B. a relatively young profession based in well-established concepts but still-evolving procedures.
   C. a brand-new profession in which concepts and procedures are changing with the times.

2. Back in the 1970s, the first type of plan designed to help businesses deal with incidents impacting their ability to function was called a
   A. disaster recovery plan.
   B. contingency plan.
   C. business continuity plan.

3. In 1994, the first set of business continuity standards was published by the
   A. Business Continuity Institute (BCI).
   B. Disaster Recovery Institute International (DRII).
   C. Occupational Safety and Health Administration (OSHA).

4. The overall aim of business continuity management (BCM) is to achieve which of the following after a disaster or other incident that threatens the operations of the business?
   A. Absolute continuity, since anything less puts the company at a competitive disadvantage.
   B. Minimal interruption, since absolute continuity is prohibitively expensive.
   C. Whatever amount of interruption is considered acceptable under published standards.

5. In their correct order, what are the three essential phases of a BCM process model that will protect the whole business?
   A. Basic Protection, Consolidation, Establishment.
   B. Establishment, Consolidation, Basic Protection.
   C. Establishment, Basic Protection, Consolidation.

6. Which of the following are the six business-disruption scenarios that a BC plan must prepare for?
   A. Loss of access, loss of people, loss of supplies, loss of communication, loss of function, and loss of data.
   B. Loss of access, loss of people, loss of cash flow, loss of communication, loss of function, and loss of data.
   C. Loss of access, loss of people, loss of supplies, loss of communication, loss of function, and loss of market share.

7. After a business experiences a stoppage in operations due to a crisis incident, how long does it take to eliminate the backlog and have the business return to normal?
   A. Four times the duration of the downtime.
   B. Five times the duration of the downtime.
   C. Six times the duration of the downtime.

8. Once the system goes down and a backlog begins to accumulate, there is a point in time by which management must put the crisis response plan into action to avert a disaster. This point in time is called the
   A. business critical point.
   B. business tolerance point.
   C. decision point.

Food for Thought

Just to make sure that you have a clear idea of what BC is, where it came from, and how you might engage with it, I suggest that you reflect on what you have learned so far. This leads naturally on to the question of your role within the profession.

To help you develop your own picture of what this is all about, it would be useful for you to challenge some of the basic concepts and ideas which we have covered in this first chapter. Here are some questions for you to discuss, debate, or simply think about. Obviously, the more you engage in the process, the more you are likely to gain from it.

Exercises

1. We have suggested that cash flow is the lifeblood of any business operation.
    > What are the key business drivers for your organization besides cash flow?
        ⌃ Consider various types of organization and how they might vary in this regard.

2. We have described the six essential elements of a business operation.
    > Explore the practical possibilities of each of these elements and how their loss might affect an organization.
        ⌃ Give a couple of examples for each of them.

3. Describe a few real life examples of disruptions that you are aware of.
    > Would some pre-planning have helped, or do you think that was how they managed to do so well?

4. Can you think of any other realistic possibilities which you might need to consider when developing your own plans?
    > Take account of the type, and style, of your business and its location from an environmental and political perspective.

5. Translate our definitions of *system recovery*, *system restore*, and *application restart* to apply to a manufacturing process instead of a computer.
    > Try to get a precise wording that is a true definition rather than a vague impression which is subject to interpretation.

Looking Forward

Now that you have an idea of what is involved and why you should be doing it, in the next chapter we will be looking at whom you should be working with and how to approach them for their support. Much of what you have learned so far will help you to explain the purpose and importance of BC to them and explore how the work might be tackled within your organization.

Downloadable Business Continuity Toolkit

You can download a fuller description of the backlog trap together with other useful supplementary materials from the **Business Continuity Toolkit.**

References

Burtles, J. (Spring 1993). The backlog trap. *Survive! The Business Continuity Magazine.*

Ginn, R. D. (1989). *Continuity planning: preventing, surviving, and recovering from disaster.* Elsevier Science Publishing Company (out of print).

Marsh & McLennan Companies (July 2004). *PAS 56 guide to business continuity management.* Retrieved from http://agsc.org.uk/uploads/docs/PAS56guidetoBCM.pdf

For Additional Reading

Business Continuity Institute (2013). *Good practice guidelines.* Available from http://www.thebci.org/index.php/resources/the-good-practice-guidelines (May be downloaded free by BCI members, or purchased by non-members.)

Hiles, A. (Ed.). (2011). *The definitive handbook of business continuity management* (3rd ed.). Chichester, West Sussex, UK: John Wiley & Sons.

2

Roles and Responsibilities

Now that you have a broad understanding of what business continuity (BC) is, where it came from, and why we need it, you can begin to think about the people you will be working with. At the same time, you will need to know why, and how, they are going to be involved in the subject. That involvement may well depend upon how you approach them, what you tell them, and what you think you can offer them. How and where BC should sit within the corporate structure is something you will need to figure out for yourself. It will also be necessary for you to work out a simple infrastructure, or hierarchy, for those who will be engaged in supporting the development and delivery of the BC program.

This chapter will help you to:

- ☑ Understand and define the roles of key players involved directly in BC management.

- ☑ Make a compelling case for BC plans, procedures, and resources to top level decision-makers.

- ☑ Identify people and groups throughout the organization who can support the BC effort.

- ☑ Organize response and recovery teams.

- ☑ Create a continuity infrastructure using the Gold, Silver, Bronze model.

2.1   The Key Players

In any organization, no matter what the size, all disciplines have a hierarchy, and the BC management structure is no exception. Although you, as the BC manager, will play a leading role in the development and delivery of the BC program, you will need to engage with several others who will contribute to its success. In this section we will look at the possibilities and the implications of their involvement. There has to be someone who:

   ▶ Spearheads the work. In BC, it is the *sponsor*.

   ▶ Leads the work across various departments, divisions, or zones. In BC, it is the *program manager*, who acts as subject matter expert.

   ▶ Supervises and administers the work at a local level. In BC, it is the *departmental deputies*, or subject interpreters.

   ▶ Supports the work from a technical perspective. In BC, it is the *technical specialists*.

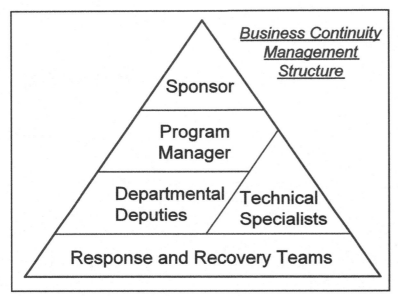

Figure 2-1. Relationship of Roles in BC Management Structure

This *command and control structure* is similar to that of a military establishment, the classic role model for any effective organization. (See Section 2.7 below for how command and control can work in your BC infrastructure.) The comparison is particularly relevant for those of us who practice BC because the military is set up, trained, and equipped to deal with unwelcome and unexpected events. When called to action, members have to be able to think and work under difficult and stressful conditions.

Figure 2-1 shows how these various roles relate to each other. Company policy, orders, authority, and funding are fed downwards through the layers from the top of the pyramid to the people at the bottom; reporting works upwards from layer to layer so that no one is bypassed in either direction and we are all kept in the picture.

2.1.1   Roles in the BC Management Structure

Sponsor: Your sponsor will be someone who has the ear of top management and access to those who can allocate budget. Typically, this would be a member of the board of directors. In the military model, this post would be held by a senior officer.

Program Manager: Strategy, instructions, techniques, and tactics are generated and organized within the second layer. This is where the program manager enters the picture, someone who is able to interpret corporate policy into practical and affordable measures that people can work with and believe in. Typically, this would be your BC manager who brings the knowledge, skills, and tools of the profession with him or her. The military equivalent might be a junior officer.

Departmental Deputies: The application, adaption, and implementation of BC measures and plans are carried out at the third level. You will need someone to act as your representative and active participant in each of the key business areas. Usually this will be a part-time commitment by someone who is involved in the management, administration, or supervision within that department or division. They will be looking to the BC manager to provide them with the skills, tools, and techniques which may be necessary to fulfill their role. These are the sergeants and corporals in our BC battalion.

Technical Specialists: Throughout the organization there will be a need for the co-option and cooperation of those with specialist knowledge of the techniques, tools, and facilities which are in regular use within that part of the business operation. These are the technical specialists whom you may need to call upon from time to time. Their military equivalent would be the engineers, artillery, or cavalry who support the main operation.

> **...the compliance officer may be the one who brings the matter to the board's attention.**

Response and Recovery Teams: Finally, you will need various response and recovery teams to put the plans into action under battle conditions. Members of these teams are selected from those who work within the various departments on a routine basis, but they will have been prepared to respond to a business interruption, working on the protection and recovery of the key business operations. Their military equivalents are the soldiers on the ground. Those who are not involved in your BC program can be likened to the civilian population which the army is trying to protect.

2.1.2   Selecting the Sponsor

In practice, the sponsor is often a fairly obvious choice. It is usually someone at board level, or the equivalent. This is the person who has been able to convince the rest of the board that they do need to at least consider some form of BC. Once upper management begins to accept the idea – usually reinforced by reference to statistics, regulations, and standards that apply – they will begin to look to this person as their potential savior and place the burden firmly upon his or her shoulders. Soon after considering the idea as a possibility, they will probably come to realize that this is an investment they can't afford to miss. Reports and feedback from the initial analyses will reveal to them that the required outlay is relatively small and the returns could be literally lifesaving.

In a regulated industry, the compliance officer may be the one who brings the matter to the board's attention. The compliance officer is charged with making sure that the organization complies with all the relevant rules and regulations, which commonly include a need for BC. Often the compliance officer will not want to take on the role of sponsor because it might be seen as a conflict of interest. In this instance, the responsibility will be given to whoever shows the most enthusiasm for the subject. Whichever of these routes has led to the appointment, the result is someone who has volunteered rather than someone who has been coerced. This considerate approach helps to ensure the success of the program.

On the other hand, in cases where the sponsor is not an enthusiastic volunteer, but has been selected arbitrarily, there may be little or no passion for the subject. Thus, the BC program often stalls after a year or so. Plans and procedures are developed and delivered as promised at the outset, but after that the program sits on the shelf gathering dust. During this period of inactivity, lack of practice and lack of confidence inevitably compromise the organization's capability to recover.

Another difficult situation is one where the person who has been given responsibility for launching and driving the BC program lacks the necessary authority, or respect, to address the issues or access the requisite resources. This can lead to a partial solution in which some areas of the business achieve a degree of resilience while other key departments remain exposed. (See Chapter 3 for a detailed discussion of how to launch the program.)

Hopefully, you will bring enthusiasm for the subject with you, and your sponsor will inspire a positive attitude which will affect and infect the people with whom you engage.

2.2   Key Considerations

For purposes of this section of the book, I am going to assume that you have completed your education, served your apprenticeship, and you are now thinking about setting up your own BC management system from scratch. You may not yet be at that stage in your career. You may be a student, or a new member of an established BC team. However, to be prepared for the future, you do need to understand and appreciate what happens at this crucial stage of the game in which the foundations are laid.

The secret of long-term success is to embed the components of success into the launch...

Before you embark on this adventurous voyage, it is best if you prepare yourself with a map of where you expect to go, how you might get there, and what to expect when you arrive. You will also want to know how to recognize and confirm your destination. Here are some key considerations which you need to take into account:

▶ A sound *game plan* forms the wisest starting point, which means knowing what should be developed and delivered and how to convince others of the need (touched on in Section 2.7.2 below and covered in detail in Chapter 3).

▶ Board-level *motivation* is the key to success, taking external as well as internal factors into account. Added value is an obvious benefit to them (will be covered in Chapter 3).

▶ A *modular approach* is best, suiting those modules to the size and structure of the organization (will be covered in Chapter 3).

▶ An increasing number of *standards* is in existence today, and these standards may need to be interpreted to suit the nature of your organization (will be covered in Chapter 3).

▶ Support from the *auditor* or audit department is a distinct advantage, but be aware that the auditors may require education before they are ready to lend that support (will be covered in Chapter 3).

As we have already suggested, every project or program requires someone to take the lead and make it happen. All too often, good ideas gain token support for a brief while, and then they are abandoned in favor of some other more meaningful, more ambitious, more achievable, or politically appropriate prospect. *The secret of long-term BC success is to embed the components of success into the launch of this important program.*

I have identified six components of success. The first three will be covered in this chapter:

1. The right *level of support* behind the concept.
2. An enthusiastic, and popular, *sponsor* to lead the project.
3. A well-structured *team of key players*.

The remainder will be covered in detail in Chapter 3 and subsequent chapters. They include:

4. A viable *game plan* with regular milestones.
5. A clear *vision of the deliverables* and other outcomes.
6 One or more *motivators* that carry weight at board level.

There may well be other factors that can generate energy, funding, and enthusiasm for the tasks ahead. If you cannot generate real enthusiasm at the outset, you must at least gain acceptance for the work; over time, your enthusiasm – coupled with the obvious progress and success – will engender a much more positive attitude among your colleagues. Familiarity with the culture and the personalities involved may help you to judge the right ingredients. In any case, it is wisest to wait until you have prepared the ground before you launch yourself into the unknown.

2.2.1   The Right Level of Support

In order to start your BC program and get it up off the ground and flying, you are going to need support from the highest levels in your organization. For any attempt at BC to be successful, it needs to be approached as a permanent fixture rather than a temporary attachment. The support for it needs to be stable and wide-ranging, which means getting the attention and the backing of one or more of those who can command respect and support throughout the entire enterprise. Of course, this is an ambitious starting point, but it is the only effective way of ensuring the long-term cooperation of your colleagues, an allocation of funds, and protection of the resources against hijacking.

… run a short exercise, making sure that all members of the executive team either take part or get to know the results.

In a typical commercial organization, we are looking to gain the support of the chief executive or the managing director, i.e., someone who is in a position of unquestionable authority. Without his or her support it will be difficult to launch the program, much less sustain its momentum beyond the first few stages. The ideal would be a commitment to support the BCM program from the entire senior management team. However, it is unrealistic to expect to generate such wholehearted support without some outside influence, such as a regulatory body imposing the need or a catastrophe causing these individuals to feel exposed.

One effective way to attract attention to the existing exposures and the advantages of pre-planning is to run a short exercise, making sure that all members of the executive team either take part or get to know the results. It does not need to be a large-scale or complex exercise. Something short, sharp, and to the point is the best approach. The point you want to make is that they are ill-prepared to deal with a serious incident which could occur at any time. The evidence for their exposure will come out of the exercise, and a little research will soon provide you with plenty of evidence to suggest how things can, and do, go wrong even in the best-run firms.

Try to get a few minutes of their time during one of their regular meetings or bring them together for a special exercise. Ask them, for example, to imagine their building has just been damaged by fire which, after all, is a common occurrence. Ask them how they would cope with such a situation. Be realistic and press them for full details:

- What would they want to do and what would they use?
- When would it actually be done?
- Where would it be done and who would do it?
- How would they manage and control the situation?

Hold a dummy staff briefing and a dummy press briefing at which they have to explain their actions to others. Finally, you should finish with a debriefing or a debate about the issues and concerns which have been raised. If no issues or concerns appear, then it is probably time to think about moving on. You can lead a horse to water but you can't make him drink.

2.2.2   The Role of the Sponsor

As we have said, an important matter like this requires a sponsor who can engender support and act as a focal point for the project. This role does not require him or her to be actively engaged in the actual development and delivery processes. You only require this person's visible support. It helps if you can educate your sponsor to the level where he or she can understand and appreciate the purpose and perceive the benefits of the project. The sponsor does not need to know all of the details, but he or she should certainly have a clear grasp of the grand design.

Again, an exercise is likely to help to get the key messages across. Not only should your report highlight the weaknesses in the current situation, but it should also form the basis of discussions regarding what should be done. During this discussion, your potential sponsor will hopefully emerge. All you have to do is watch, listen carefully, and ask that person to act as your sponsor and ally while you do all the support work. Because the sponsor's name will appear from time to time as the executive with responsibility for what is, after all, a key project spanning the whole enterprise, there should be plenty of kudos in it for the sponsor. This of course presumes the program is ultimately successful.

Once you have gained your sponsor, be sure to work closely with the person and make him or her feel part of the team which is going to deliver some very valuable benefits. While you will be focusing on protecting the business and making it resilient, other benefits may well emerge from taking a careful look at the infrastructure and the way it works.

2.3   The Other Team Players

Apart from the sponsor, there are several others whom you need to be able to identify and empathize with, as shown in Figure 2-1. Although you may be the only one with direct responsibility for BC, you will not be working entirely on your own. Throughout the program you will need to be working with others; although the relationships may be intermittent, they will be of a lasting nature because you are engaged in an iterative process and will return time and again to the same areas, gradually improving and enhancing as you learn about the subtleties of the operation. Also, bear in mind that the operation itself moves on to reflect the ongoing changes and improvements in technology, regulations, and the marketplace.

In the early stages, there may well be some changes in your portfolio of players and the business areas they represent. It will take some time before your tentative working model of the business operations comes to match reality.

2.3.1   BC Manager

The second in command will be the BC manager whose responsibility spans the whole enterprise. In this role, you will be expected to bring all the BC skills and knowledge to the table. You will also be expected to disseminate that information and distribute the associated tools and techniques to those who will be working with you in the development and delivery of the requisite plans and processes.

You will need to work closely with senior managers to develop the high-level response plans which they will require to deal with an emergency or a crisis. An *emergency* in this context is something going badly wrong and a *crisis* is a situation where there is a potential for bad news. In either case, these people will need plans and procedures to guide them through the event and its consequences, together with training to prepare them for a successful performance under stressful conditions. The kinds of people we have in mind are the heads of department and C-level executives; they are the ones who will be expected to lead the company, especially when the going gets tough. Here, we are looking at building the command and control team (or teams) who will be in overall charge of the response and subsequent recovery.

2.3.2   Senior Managers

Immediately below these people you will need to work with senior managers from each of the core business operations. They will be expected to lead the activity recovery teams which you will be helping them to set up. The members of these recovery teams will be hands-on middle managers and supervisors who are familiar with the intricacies of the business at a local level. Those are the people who will be able to provide you with the knowledge and practical information that will form the basis of your detailed continuity plans. Once they have helped you to develop the plans, they will need to exercise those plans in order to prove that they can be made to work.

Because BC plans require ongoing maintenance to ensure their currency and relevance it is helpful to have someone appointed as a local administrator with the responsibility for the upkeep and distribution of the plans. Preferably, these will be people who are already engaged in routine administrative tasks within their department. This will ensure that they understand the local language, jargon, and personalities as well as being familiar with the way things work at grass roots level. They may also assist in making sure that the requisite resources and facilities are also kept in good order. Because they will be acting as your local representative, these people will require some basic training in the plan development process. They will also need to understand what you are trying to achieve and how it should be done. It is a good idea to involve them in the early stages of your research when you are talking with their colleagues to establish where the problems might lie and how to deal with them.

> **Match the BC framework to the shape, size, and culture of the organization...**

2.4   The Teams

When something goes wrong and you have to invoke your BC plans, teams of people will have to carry out a number of tasks to restore order and enable the organization to continue, or resume, its business operations. These are the response and recovery teams which are set up to reflect the structure and work flows of the organization as a whole. This book gave you an overview of the disciplines, plans, and processes which are involved in Chapter 1, where it showed you the relationship between the various types of plans. Each of these plans is basically a set of guidelines and objectives for a team with specific responsibilities. Bear in mind that you are not able to provide them with precise or detailed instructions, nor would you want to. It isn't possible to know the exact circumstances in which these plans will be put into practice; so the teams must be allowed to interpret and adjust their actions to fit the situation. (**Note:** As you select the key players on your team, you will also need to make sure to have a trained *backup* person for each position on the team. This will be discussed further in later chapters.)

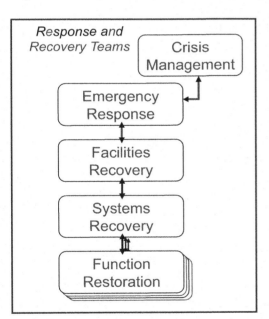

Figure 2-2. Five Functional Teams for Organizing Response and Recovery

Just as this book is unable to define the circumstances which might cause you to summon these teams into action, it can't be specific about the number and sizes of the teams which you might require. Match the BC framework to the shape, size, and culture of the organization you are trying to protect. At the higher level, you can be pretty sure that you will want only one team to take care of crisis management and another one to take charge of the emergency response.

The layout and number of the teams and people who are involved in facilities recovery, systems recovery, and the restoration of critical functions will need to reflect the way in which the business works. This is where your knowledge of the organization and its internal structure will come to the fore. If you are still new to the company then you will need to work with your sponsor to gain a basic understanding.

2.4.1   Crisis Management

Because *crisis management* is about defending and preserving the brand, image, and reputation of the whole enterprise and its products or services, we have to look to the very highest level for the members of this special team. Typically we would expect the CEO to lead this team which would be comprised of a few select people, such as the company secretary, together with the director of sales and marketing, head of public relations, financial controller, and an administrator. Normally, I would expect the sponsor to suggest who should be in the crisis management team. He or she would also be the best person to approach them and get them to agree or nominate others who would be better suited to the role. There is often a certain amount of personal politics involved here; so this task is best left to someone of a fairly senior rank who knows the people well enough to understand and handle the nuances of operating at that level.

2.4.2   Emergency Response

The *emergency response* team will be on duty in the *command and control center* and overseeing the response to any emergency situation that might arise. Consequently, you are looking to find someone with enough authority to take on such a responsibility and act as the team leader. Apart from the question of authority, you are also expecting this person to be able to remain calm under pressure, liaise with the crisis manager, and inspire those around him or her to work together under difficult circumstances. (**Note:** More about the command and control center will be explained in Chapter 7 when this book explores emergency response in more detail.) In many cases, the sponsor has turned out to be the one who was best placed to assume this role, but that may not always be the case.

The rest of the emergency response team has to be made up of people with sufficient knowledge and rank to be able to handle the various tasks and responsibilities. These are the three basic roles, which would be supported by a relatively small group of people, each of whom would handle a particular aspect of the response and recovery operation. Typically, these roles are:

- ▸ Communicating with the other teams.
- ▸ Coordinating the emergency responders.
- ▸ Handling technical aspects of the recovery operations.

Because these teams may be summoned at any time and the work can be quite demanding, have at least two deputies lined up for each of the roles. These deputies will be able to provide cover for absences and they could also be available for shift work as is often necessary.

2.4.3   Facilities Recovery

For *facilities recovery*, most organizations of any significant size have someone who is responsible for facilities management. An alternative title would be estates management. This group looks after the premises, making sure that you have a fully functioning and safe working environment. These are very practical people with experience in dealing with problems and fixing things, so they are ideally suited to our purpose. They are also going to be very useful because they know exactly what does, and can, go wrong. What is more, they probably know how to fix it or whom to turn to for help. Obviously, the head of the facilities management team is the ideal person to head up the facilities recovery program. The size and content of the facilities management support group will depend upon the scale, complexity, and layout of the premises for which they are responsible.

2.4.4   Systems Recovery

Systems recovery for technology is also known as *disaster recovery*. The systems recovery team is usually almost self-defining. Whoever is responsibility for running the systems on a daily basis should be your natural team leader and his or her support group will be the technicians who work with that person. In many instances, where systems support is outsourced, you may have to depend upon your supplier for the requisite skills and this may require a certain amount of negotiation with regard to the contract and its implications. Clearly, your company will want, and expect, an adequate level of support in this regard.

> **Build yourself a network of collaborators…as a source of inspiration, reference, or assistance.**

Systems recovery plans need to be fairly specific about what has to be achieved and provided because of the technical implications. Systems, programs, applications, and workstations all have to be compatible and properly connected. The other important responsibility for this team will be the recovery of the databases which support the systems. You will need to work closely with these technical people in order to ensure that all of the systems recovery plans are fit for purpose and kept up-to-date with all the changes, features, and patches which are applied from time to time.

2.4.5   Function Restoration

Function restoration is the basement level of your BC planning, the point at which you plan for the restoration of the many critical or important functions of the business. In the initial stages, you may not be in a position to know, or even guess, which teams will be required. This type of information will emerge only as you begin to develop a deeper understanding of the organization during the assessment and analysis stage of your BC program.

As you gain a better understanding of how the organization works, you will be able to assess just which functions will require restoration and the type of people who will be able to support that work. For the time being, you should assume that there will be a restoration plan and team for each of the key operations. Over the years, I have usually ended up with between five and seven plans and teams at this level. Here, I am excluding customers who operate from multiple sites. On one occasion, a client required us to develop plans for up to eight teams, although they never envisaged invoking all of these plans at the same time. I mention this to give you some idea of scale.

Your relationship with each of these functional recovery teams and their plans should be through the local administrator who will be responsible for supporting the development and maintenance of these plans. However you will both need to work closely with the manager or supervisor of that function in order to develop a proper understanding of what is needed, wanted, and practical.

2.4.6   Non-Participants

Quite a large proportion of the staff will have no direct involvement with BC. However, you should not ignore them. Throughout the BC program you must make a point of keeping them informed about what you are doing and planning. You will be depending on them and their loyalty should things go wrong. Without their tacit support, you will never be able to reduce the inevitable backlog and return the business operation back to normal.

Because of their daily exposure to difficulties, problems, subtle differences, and alterations, they are also a valuable source of ideas and information which could prove useful. Draw on their experience to develop and improve the way in which you try to avoid and solve problems. Build yourself a network of collaborators to whom you can look as a source of inspiration, reference, or assistance.

2.5   A Collaborative Network

What really distinguishes a subject matter expert from the rest of us is the peripheral network of potential collaborators which have been acquired over the years. If I approach my doctor, who is a general practitioner, I know he will be able to refer me to all sorts of specialists who offer additional, peripheral, or complementary forms of therapy or investigation. He is my source of holistic medicine, even though many of the services are actually delivered by his circle of professional acquaintances. In addition, he is often able to pass on some of their advice which he has absorbed over the years.

In a similar way I can rely on my local garage to redirect me or advise me on various aspects of looking after my car. They will know what to do, or where to go, if I have a dent, or a scratch, a worn tire, a noisy exhaust, or torn upholstery. As a BC practitioner I have also built up a series of useful relationships. Indeed, when I first set up my own private practice, I set up something we called "The Phoenix Society," a group of individuals who promised to help each other deal with any problems which arose in any of our small startup businesses. One of our key assets was our joint promissory fund. We all shared a promise to help any of our fellow members with an interest-free loan if they got into financial difficulty. Obviously, there was a lot of trust and some strict rules attached, but it provided us all with a degree of comfort as we set out to become self-supporting.

As an aspiring young BC practitioner, you will also need to develop a network of associates who can extend your knowledge and skill base as well as provide supporting services. Areas where you should be looking for help in this connection include people who practice disciplines which can support, enhance, or extend your BC program. Below are some of the fields in which they operate and how they can prove useful. This list is not meant to be exhaustive, but it should give you an idea of where to start. As you build your professional network, your list will probably evolve into something bigger and broader than you might imagine at the start.

Complementary Disciplines

Facilities Management: You will find that facilities managers are very practical people who are regularly doing things which contribute to the continuity of the overall business operation. They are the ones who deal with such diverse problems as broken floor boards and leaking roofs, blocked drains and blown fuses, air-conditioning failures and people stuck in an elevator. Solving problems and making things run smoothly are routine for them; so you will find they are level headed and resourceful when the lights go out or the alarm goes off – ideal companions in a BC situation.

Human Resources or Personnel Management: You will need to develop a good working relationship with those who are responsible for the recruitment and the welfare of the contingent of people who form the most important and valuable asset of any business enterprise. Whenever things go wrong, it is the HR or personnel department which has to deal with the personal implications at both the group and the individual level. They will be able to help you make your plans user friendly and they will be able to provide you with up-to-date information about the numbers and types of people you need to take account of in your plans.

Emergency Planning: In your local authority there will be an emergency planning officer who is responsible for dealing with emergencies which occur on a community scale. In turn he or she will report to, or be a part of, a higher level team which is responsible for dealing with large-scale events within a command and control structure which goes right up to, and beyond, a national level. These people will be aware of the large-scale risks and how the community plans to deal with such events. You need to be aware of these plans so as to ensure that they do not conflict with, or compromise, your plans for such issues as disaster recovery.

For international approaches to handling business disruption, you may wish to become acquainted with the International Association of Emergency Managers (IAEM), (http://www.iaem.com), an international nonprofit organization of emergency management professionals with more than 9,000 members worldwide. IAEM publishes *Principles of Emergency Management* and holds conferences covering best practices in handling emergency management challenges to protect property, lives, and the environment during emergencies and disasters.

In the US, the National Emergency Management Association (NEMA), (http://www.nemaweb.org), "provides national leadership and expertise in comprehensive emergency management; serves as a vital emergency management information and assistance resource; and advances continuous improvement in emergency management through strategic partnerships, innovative programs, and collaborative policy positions."

In the US, the Federal Emergency Management Agency (FEMA), (http://www.fema.gov), has a mission to "support our citizens and first responders to ensure that as a nation we work together to build, sustain, and improve our capability to prepare for, protect against, respond to, recover from, and mitigate all hazards."

The primary purpose of FEMA is to coordinate the response to a disaster in the US that overwhelms the resources of local and state authorities. Once the governor of the state in which the disaster occurs declares a state of emergency and formally requests assistance from FEMA, the federal government will respond to the disaster. The only exception to this requirement is if the emergency or disaster takes place on federal property or to a federal asset. In addition, during the recovery, FEMA provides experts to assist state and local governments, and funding for rebuilding efforts, including low interest loans in cooperation with the US Small Business Administration. FEMA also funds training of response personnel throughout the US and its territories.

In the UK there is the Environment Agency which maintains publicly available live flood warning maps (http://maps.environment-agency.gov.uk). Large-scale threats to the community are managed by a series of local resilience forums (LRFs) in the UK, where "…multi-agency partnerships are made up of representatives from local public services, including the emergency services, local authorities, the NHS, the Environment Agency and others. These agencies are known as Category 1 Responders, as defined by the Civil Contingencies Act" (https://www.gov.uk/local-resilience-forums-contact-details).

Technicians: A number of technical people will be responsible for the delivery, upkeep, and maintenance of the technical resources which support your business operations. Typically these will be the people who look after your computers, but there are many other areas where you might find there is a regular need for specialist skills. You will find that they are experienced in solving technical problems and can highlight potential problem areas and recommend sensible solutions, especially at the operational and recovery level of continuity planning.

Internal Audit: Most organizations have an internal audit function, responsible for ensuring that everybody keeps to the rules, and that the organization, its risks, and operations are effective and reflect sound practice. You will find that the auditors have a sound overview of how the business operates as a whole. They have a unique perspective because they engage in regular in-depth conversations with all departments throughout the company. In time, they will also want to check how well you have implemented and are managing your BC program.

Compliance Officers: In a regulated industry such as the finance sector there may be a requirement for a compliance officer who is responsible for ensuring that the company adheres to the rules and regulations. This role requires him or her to be familiar with all the standards and regulations which apply. You might find that the regulations include specific instructions or guidelines in regard to BC. Therefore, you should seek them out and find out what they would like to see in place before you get too deeply involved in setting out your BC area of responsibility.

Risk Management: Risk management aims to prevent or mitigate any foreseeable risks. Since all risks cannot be eliminated, this function also involves dealing with the after-effects of incidents and events. This means that these people try to deal with the basic causes of interruptions and failures. Therefore, their actions are often a precursor to BC, which seeks to deal with the effects of interruptions and failures. You will need to work closely with risk management because there is likely to be a great deal of overlap between what they are trying to do and what you are trying to do. In fact, many organizations place risk management and BC within the same department. In some organizations, risk management and insurance are a combined department or function.

Insurance: Insurance deals with the final link in the cause, effect, and consequence chain. Your insurer may be asked to cover the long-term costs of the consequences of an incident, although not all companies take out insurance for every eventuality and many types of incident are not normally covered. You will find it useful to find out who is responsible for insurance in your organization and what they believe is covered. Your principal concern is to establish what is *not* covered.

2.6   Your Business Continuity Infrastructure

By now you should have a reasonable idea of whom you should be working with and for. You also need to understand how they should be organized, what you can expect from them, and what they should be expecting

> **Gold, Silver, and Bronze ...symbolize the strategic, tactical, and operational levels...**

from you. For your BC organization to be effective you will need to arrange these people and their roles into a hierarchy with a reporting structure and a broad outline of their duties and relationships.

Once you have a sound BC infrastructure in mind and your work progresses, you will be able to place the people and work out the types of plans and other materials which they will require. At first some of your

choices will be tentative and subject to review, but as you move forward you will be able to develop a clear idea of how all the plans and people fit together into the various groups and teams. The hierarchy will also suggest what they will require in the way of information from above and support from below.

2.6.1   UK Gold, Silver, and Bronze Management Levels

At this early stage you are looking to identify the players who will fit into the BC infrastructure. You might not know their names yet, but you should be able to recognize them as potential candidates whenever you are introduced to them. In recent years, many practitioners have come to refer to the three levels of command and control as Gold, Silver, and Bronze (College of Policing, 2013). These metallic colors are used to symbolize the strategic, tactical, and operational levels of authority and their responsibilities. The accompanying diagram shows how these groups work in conjunction with each other.

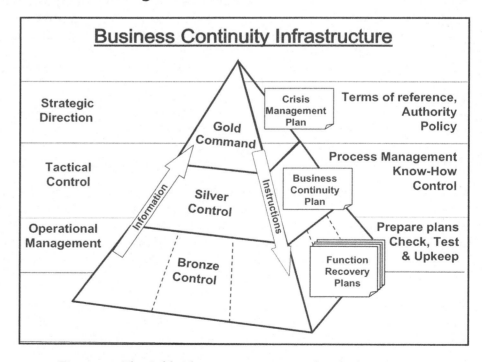

Figure 2-3. The Gold, Silver, Bronze Command and Control Structure

This Gold, Silver, Bronze command and control model was developed in 1985 by the UK Metropolitan Police Service and has since been adopted by many who expect to be dealing with emergencies and the emergency services. It provides a reporting and decision-making structure which is independent of rank and can reflect the scale and complexity of the situation as it unfolds.

The title of "Gold, Silver, Bronze" for this command and control structure was invented by Chief Superintendent David Stevens, of Scotland Yard. One of his colleagues, Inspector Peter Power, was responsible for developing the idea into a systematic approach to emergency management and he became its principal advocate. In 1993, Peter retired from the police force and in 1995 set up his own consultancy specializing in crisis management and BC. In 2012, the Gold, Silver, Bronze model was adapted for ensuring the security of the Olympic and Paralympic Games when they were held in London (HM Government, 2013). Due to the scale, duration, and complexity of this operation, a number of subsidiary roles were developed, but the basic principles of responsibilities, reporting, and decision-making remained the same. A parallel command and control structure was developed for the BC aspect of the operation with liaison at each level between all those who might be involved in the event of an incident. This involved the Olympic Delivery Authority, which was responsible for BC alongside a number of other organizations that provided various support services such as security, communications, transport, catering, first aid, and medical facilities. Up to 200,000 people were engaged in this project, which ran smoothly without any major incidents, thanks to the good planning and preparation (HM Government, 2013).

Although the Gold (strategic), Silver (tactical), Bronze (operational) model was developed in the UK and is a standard for emergency response there, this highly workable operational structure can be applied in countries throughout the world.

2.6.2   US National Incident Management Structure and Incident Command System

In the US, the National Incident Management Structure (NIMS) – administered by the Federal Emergency Management Agency (FEMA), an agency of the US Department of Homeland Security – provides a structure for responding to local and regional disasters by means of multi-agency deployment. The Incident Command System (ICS), developed by the US Department of Homeland Security in 2004, is a subcomponent of NIMS. An ICS is based upon a changeable, scalable response organization providing a common hierarchy within which people can work together effectively. These people may be drawn from multiple agencies that do not routinely work together, and ICS is designed to give standard response and operation procedures to reduce the problems and potential for miscommunication. ICS has been summarized as a "first-on-scene" structure, where the first responder of a scene has charge of the scene until the incident has been declared resolved, a more qualified responder arrives on scene and receives command, or the Incident Commander appoints another individual Incident Commander.

ICS is usually organized around five major functional areas: command, operations, planning, logistics, and finance and administration. A sixth functional area, intelligence, may be established if deemed necessary by the Incident Commander, depending on the requirements of the situation at hand.

Some of the more important "transitional steps" that are necessary to apply ICS in a field incident environment include the following:

▶ Recognizing and anticipating the requirement that organizational elements will be activated and taking the necessary steps to delegate authority as appropriate.

▶ Setting up strategically located incident facilities, as needed, to support field operations.

▶ Establishing the use of common terminology for organizational functional elements, position titles, facilities, and resources.

▶ Evolving rapidly from providing oral direction to developing a written Incident Action Plan.

2.6.3   Applying the Gold, Silver, Bronze Structure to Your Own Game Plan

The principal advantage of the Gold, Silver, Bronze labeling system is its intrinsic simplicity in creating a clear chain of command. It gives you an immediate impression of how the structure works, which is especially useful to the outsider or newcomer. While terms such as strategic, tactical, and operational might be more specific, they can also be rather confusing to those who are not familiar with the language or this particular type of jargon. Of course, the relationships, responsibilities, and the duties become quite clear once the definitions have been given and understood, but this may not happen in the confusion of an emergency situation where this response structure is likely to be convened.

> **... put together a game plan outlining what you want to achieve and how you intend to go about it.**

Before you can start gathering the information which will form the basis of your BC plans and accompanying arrangements, you will need to put together a game plan outlining what you want to achieve and how you intend to go about it. As you move forward you will doubtlessly encounter a few surprises and experience a few frustrations; so you will have to be flexible in your approach, although the final objectives should remain the same.

The principal objective here is for you to be able to develop and deliver a suite of BC plans which have been properly exercised and proved to work. These plans will need to be complemented by reliable access to adequate resources to implement them in time of need. To achieve this aim you will require the support of a sponsor, together with a high-level executive policy statement which outlines the company's intentions and requirements in this connection.

Use the BC infrastructure model (Figure 2-3) as a reference, but you will need to develop the Bronze level configuration to align with the infrastructure of your own organization. It is unlikely that you will need to alter the Gold and Silver levels. These upper levels are a reflection of corporate governance which remains more or less the same throughout all commercial and non-commercial enterprises. Further down, at the Bronze level of operational management, you will often come across significant, and sometimes subtle, differences which echo the culture, industry, and style of operation. This is where you need to gain a thorough understanding of how the business works in practice, and that information can only come from those who are actually engaged in the work. High-level intentions are passed down to management as orders, issued as instructions by supervisors, and then translated into actions on the shop floor.

At this point, it might be useful to gain a deeper understanding of the infrastructure and its implications. Here is a brief summary of the responsibilities, relationships, and workflows of this model in action. Remember that it is designed for an effective response to an emergency situation in which there is little room for error, no time for formalities, and a lot of pressure on all concerned. This means that some of the interactions may differ from what people are used to under normal conditions (whatever that might mean).

- **Gold Command** is the top-level team that provides the strategic direction. Prior to the event the team members, or their peers, will have developed or endorsed the terms of reference for the whole of the BC program. When, and if, the occasion arises they will use the crisis management plan as their guide, although they will be at liberty to alter it or even abandon it if that is what the circumstances dictate. They will also have been responsible for the BC policy and are the authority behind that policy.

  Their principal concern will be to address all of the issues relating to the brand, image, and reputation of the organization, leaving the actual work of response and recovery to those who report to them. Where necessary they will issue orders or instructions but only if circumstances warrant their involvement in management or operational issues. Each level within this command and control structure has to be empowered to make decisions and take action without continuous reference to a higher authority; otherwise the system becomes totally ineffective, embedded in protocol, procedures, and politics.

▸ **Silver Control** is the high-level management team that provides the tactical control. These team members are responsible for managing the response to an emergency or any situation which looks as though it may develop into an emergency. It is at this level that the situation is brought under control. Because these people know how the business normally works, their experience as managers will enable them to deal with problems and difficulties as they arise. Apart from their knowledge and experience they will have the BC plan to guide them. Again, deviation is possible, but should only be considered where circumstances dictate and with Gold level approval.

Their main concern will be the safety of all the people who may be affected by the incident. After that they will be trying to arrange for the protection and restoration of the facilities, information, and communications. They will depend on the skills of the various Bronze level teams to help them meet these objectives, together with the resources which are available to them. In an ideal world those resources will have been prepared in advance as part of the planning process, but in reality the response will have to be based upon what is actually available rather than what should be there.

▸ **Bronze Control** is the operational management level which will include a number of teams that can be called upon to protect, recover, restore, or replace the core critical business functions. These teams will report upwards to Silver control and will be working with *function recovery plans*, sometimes known as *activity recovery plans* or *department recovery plans*. At this level some of

> **...key players...can help you along the way with their knowledge, assistance, or authority.**

the plans will need to contain quite specific instructions about how certain tasks are to be tackled. Nevertheless, they still remain guidelines which need to be interpreted because you cannot be certain of the circumstances, or the problems, which these teams will encounter.

The arrangement of plans and teams at this level will need to reflect the way in which the business normally operates. Within each of the supported departments, someone will be expected to assist in the development and delivery of the plans for their area. These teams will also be largely responsible for checking and testing their plans to make sure that they are fit for purpose. The local BC administrator will be expected to keep the plans up-to-date under the guidance of the BC manager who will also plan and coordinate the test and exercise program.

The Gold, Silver, Bronze model is a relatively simple concept which can easily be adapted to suit the typical business disruption scenario. On the other hand, NIMS ICS is a rather more complex framework designed to cope with emergencies which impact a whole community. A basic understanding of the ICS structure may prove to be very beneficial if your organization is caught up in a large-scale incident, in which case you would know what to expect and whom to turn to.

2.7   As You Embark on This Journey

At the outset of your campaign to implement BC – or to play a meaningful part in its development, delivery, or maintenance – your game plan needs to take account of what you know so far about the subject and the environment in which you will be working. For many who are new to the subject and the environment, there may be some hazy areas; so you shouldn't be looking to put too much detail into the plan at this stage. Over the course of the next few weeks, months, and years, that plan will probably need to be reviewed and refined, but without it you are likely to get lost or led astray.

▸ Start off with a clear statement of what you want to achieve, taking account of what you know so far. In the early stages, this work program is a project; so it is best to define the current situation as your start point.

▸ Then, define what you see as the target situation, and work out the steps which might get you to that destination.

▸ Add some milestones which you can associate with specific deliverables, and then work out an approximate timeframe. This is your draft itinerary, but you might need to be prepared to make a few adjustments along the way once you get to see some of the sights, explore some of the side roads, bump into one or two obstacles, and work out what to do about the "No Entry" signs.

▸ You will also need to identify who the key players might be: people who can help you along the way with their knowledge, assistance, or authority. At this stage you might not know them by name, but you should be able to figure out what sort of positions they hold and how they could help.

Self-Examination Questions

1. In a business continuity command-and-control structure, the key player who leads the work across various departments, divisions, or zones is called the

    A. departmental deputy.

    B. program manager.

    C. sponsor.

2. Which of the following is an important consideration when selecting a sponsor for the business continuity (BC) program?

    A. The sponsor should be able to put the BC plan into action under crisis conditions, having prepared to respond in a way that recovers key business operations.

    B. The sponsor should be able to interpret corporate policy into practical and affordable measures that people can work with and believe in.

    C. The sponsor should have the ear of top management and have the communications skills and level of respect necessary to convince them to approve the BC program.

3. Key components of success for any BC program include

    A. the right level of support for the program, an enthusiastic sponsor, and a good team of key players.

    B. a BC command-and-control structure that puts the response-and-recovery teams at the top.

    C. a compliance officer acting in the role of sponsor.

4. One effective way to begin building support for a BC plan among top management is to

    A. run a short exercise designed to demonstrate how the organization is not prepared to deal with a crisis.

    B. offer a top manager a highly visible role on your BC project team.

    C. lobby government officials to issue regulations requiring all companies to have BC plans.

5. For which of the following response-and-recovery teams would the CEO be the best leader?

    A. Crisis management team.

    B. Emergency response team.

    C. Facilities recovery team.

6. One person who needs to be in the collaborative BC planning network is

    A. the head of the legal department.

    B. the local facilities manager.

    C. the head of sales and marketing.

7. In the BC infrastructure developed by Inspector Peter Power of Scotland Yard, the Gold, Silver, and Bronze levels refer to

    A. the different levels of financial losses that will likely be caused by different types of disasters.

    B. quality rankings awarded to various response-and-recovery teams, based on their performance.

    C. the strategic, tactical, and operational levels of authority and responsibility.

8. In the Gold, Silver, and Bronze command-and-control structure, the management of the response to an emergency (to protect the safety of people and protect and restore physical and other assets) is handled by team members at which level?

    A. Gold.

    B. Silver.

    C. Bronze.

Food for Thought

It would be useful at this stage if you were to go through the mental exercise of applying what you have learned so far to an imaginary scenario in which you are looking to initiate a BC management program. Look at a small, a medium, and a large example to see how the size and complexity of the organization may affect your approach and offer different challenges. If you are already on the job, engaged in BC or a related discipline, then you might also go through the same process using real life as your background. However, I would suggest going through the imaginary scenarios first as a kind of dry run to get used to the process.

Exercises

If you were about to embark on a BC program, who are the kinds of people you would target as your potential allies, supporters, and interested parties? At this stage, you will have only a rough idea of their positions and what they actually do, so don't waste too much time trying to be precise. You are trying to see how the principles might work based on what you know so far.

1. Run through this exercise for a familiar successful retail establishment.
    - Who do you see as the people you will need to engage with for the various roles in your BC program?
    - What are you hoping to get from each of these people?
    - How are you going to approach them and convince them that they should support your BC program?

2. Do the same exercise for a shopping mall that you know.
    - Does the larger scale make much difference?

3. Go through the same thought process for a large supermarket chain which has many stores and a warehouse.
    - Presumably there are more unknowns in this more complex scenario but hopefully the principles still apply.

You might also consider how you would approach this task for a local primary school, a larger secondary school, and a university campus.

Looking Forward

Having looked at who might and should be involved, this book moves on in the next chapter to consider how you go about developing a more detailed, viable game plan. This means you will need to explore what the expected deliverables and outcomes might be and think about what should and could motivate these people to offer you their support and active participation when and where it is required.

Downloadable Business Continuity Toolkit

You can download materials from the **Business Continuity Toolkit** that will assist you in explaining the points made in this chapter to management and colleagues.

References

College of Policing (2013). *Command structures.* Retrieved from http://www.app.college.police.uk/app-content/operations/command-and-control/command-structures

HM Government (2013). *Inspired by 2012: The legacy from the London 2012 Olympic and Paralympic Games.* Retrieved from https://www.gov.uk/government/uploads/system/uploads/attachment_data/file/224148/2901179_OlympicLegacy_acc.pdf

US Department of Homeland Security (2008). *National incident management system.* Retrieved from http://www.fema.gov/pdf/emergency/nims/NIMS_core.pdf

For Additional Reading

Business Continuity Institute (2013). *Good practice guidelines.* Available from http://www.thebci.org/index.php/resources/the-good-practice-guidelines (May be downloaded free by BCI members, or purchased by non-members.)

Hiles, A. (2014). *Business continuity management: Global best practices* (4th ed.). Brookfield, CT: Rothstein Publishing, chapter 2.

3

Getting Started

The first two chapters of this book have given you a broad overview of the subject so that you can begin to understand what business continuity (BC) is all about. You have looked at who you will be working with and how they might fit into an overall program. Now you need to know something about why and how you should approach the development and delivery of a BC program that suits the needs and culture of your organization. You will also need to think about how that program should relate to the relevant rules, regulations, and standards that might apply.

This chapter will help you to:

- ☑ Understand why your organization needs a BC program.

- ☑ Design and develop a suitable program.

- ☑ Create a launch argument in support of BC to present to decision-makers.

- ☑ Adapt the BC process to fit your organization.

- ☑ Appreciate the standards and guidelines which might apply to your work.

- ☑ Explain the benefits which can accrue from an effective BC program.

- ☑ Engage in a helpful dialog with your auditors as you move forward.

Of course, I am assuming that you are going to be starting from scratch and are, therefore, covering the whole process from the very beginning. However, it is quite possible that you may be joining an existing program in which much of this initial work has already been done. In that case, I am giving you some background information which will enable you to appreciate what has happened so far and correct any misunderstandings which might have arisen in the audience. Here the term *audience* is used to cover all those who are likely to be the beneficiaries of your BC program. You will be coming along with a fresh pair of eyes and may spot oversights or gaps which others have not yet covered.

> **As soon as you get management to understand that there is a definite need... follow it up with a viable solution....**

3.1   A Viable Game Plan

Until you are ready to make your first bid for support and responsibility, it is wise to keep your own counsel. You might not get a second chance; so it makes sense to know exactly what needs to be done before you attract the wrong kind of attention. It's a bit like an election campaign: you only get one day at the polls, but you may have to spend weeks preparing. If you succeed in gaining sufficient votes, you will be able to keep your promises – otherwise, you will soon be forgotten.

As soon as you get management to understand that there is a definite need, you must be able to follow it up with a viable solution, a clear route map of what needs to be achieved and how it can be done.

3.1.1   Kick-Off Meeting

Your game plan needs to include some form of introductory event – a kick-off meeting – to launch the program. The purpose is to establish the need firmly in the minds of senior managers and to ensure you get their buy-in. For best results you need to have some facts and figures to illustrate and support your argument. Obviously, these examples need to be credible and relevant; so you need to carry out some research about what has gone wrong recently in their neck of the woods. You will be looking for examples in which there was an opportunity for loss of business or reputational damage, particularly ones to which they can relate. Also, there may be some relevant legislation, regulations, or standards that apply to their industry or area of operations.

Because these kick-off meetings are so vital to the successful launch and subsequent progress of the BC program, I developed a *launch argument* formula which I have used quite successfully over the past 30 years (described in detail in Section 3.3 of this book).

3.1.2   Action Plan

At the meeting, or very shortly afterwards, you'll want them to agree to an *action plan* with defined outcomes and responsibilities. Initially your action plan (at least the public version) may include only the early stages of the project, which include identifying the potential risks, the impacts, and some possible strategies. If there are no risks and the impacts are negligible, then there is no need to proceed any further. On the other hand, if the early stages of the project reveal a need for action, then the impetus will come from those early results, such as your risk report or the impact analysis.

While it is extremely unlikely that you will discover a risk-free environment or one in which the impacts are negligible, this is a good line of reasoning at the beginning because it does not commit them to a full program of work. That level of commitment will only come if, and when, you can present them with incontrovertible evidence that something has to be done because the existing precautions are inadequate or insufficient. It is not going to help your case if you suggest that their measures are nonexistent or totally useless. They could regard such a negative judgment as aggressive and are likely to respond accordingly. At this stage, it is important to remember that you are trying to find allies rather than develop enemies.

Over the years I have carried out literally hundreds of such investigations, and in every case I have found at least four or five reasons why we (they and I) should proceed to develop and test a full set of BC plans. However, you must regard it as a series of tasks, each moving on from its predecessor. At the end of each stage, you should give them the impression that:

> **The ideal message would be: "The worst is over but there is still a bit to do..."**

- ▪ Something positive has been achieved.
- ▪ There is still some work to be done.

The ideal message would be: "The worst is over but there is still a bit to do if you want to reap the full benefit of all the good work that we have done so far."

3.1.3 Lead Them Step-by-Step

If you start off trying to sell a full-scale BC program to top management, you may meet resistance because they may not want to over commit themselves and the company, especially to something which they don't yet fully understand or appreciate. You will find that it is far more effective to lead them step-by-step towards their own solution. Try to let them get the impression that most of this was their idea. Later on, as the program develops, they will begin to appreciate your external view, extensive knowledge, and sincere capability – but that level of trust is going to take time to develop and mature.

In a large organization, with its many divisions and business units spread across several locations, your game plan will need to take account of the diverse nature, scale, and layout of the enterprise. Clearly, you cannot make it all happen at once. You might need to build recovery plans for one business unit or process at a time before developing emergency response plans for each location. Once a particular location has been addressed, you can then move on to the next one. After all the regional offices and branches have been covered, you are in a position to tackle the head office. When you have completed all recovery and emergency response plans, you can start on the crisis response plan for the whole enterprise. Of course, you may choose a different sequence, but the overall game plan remains the same: a series of deliverables with a logical sequence. Note that NFPA 1600 defines a crisis management or response plan as "the ability of an entity to manage incidents that have the potential to cause significant security, financial or reputational impacts" (National Fire Protection Association, 2013).

3.2 Deliverables and Other Outcomes

Each phase, or stage, of your BC program will have one or more deliverables and outcomes. To ensure you gain, and retain, the support or buy-in of management, it is best to provide them with a regular supply of achievements. Set yourself a few milestones, at reasonably frequent intervals, each with an outcome and a deliverable. If the outcome does not, of itself, provide a deliverable then you have to write a report which fulfills the need. Without regular evidence of your existence and progress, it is all too easy to be ignored or forgotten by senior management.

The program should start off as an implementation project designed to establish BC and its supporting elements. Once the basics are in place and the challenges have been met, the second phase, which is an administrative process rather than a project, begins. Perhaps the project team may move on after handing over to a group focused on routine maintenance and updating. Both groups have a key role to play, but they are different roles and may call for different types of people.

3.2.1   Initial Project

During the initial project phase the emphasis is on exploring the possibilities and developing the procedures. In many large-scale organizations the startup team forms a center of excellence which provides ongoing support for a number of local administrators. The startup team visits each department, division, or location and carries out the project part of the program before moving on to their next target area. In this way, the core group builds up knowledge and skill without getting bogged down with too much of the detail. For the central core group, BC is a unique and interesting vocation with a worthwhile outcome, while the local administrators are more likely to see it as an important job that needs to be done properly with due care and attention to detail.

3.2.2   Permanent Process

> **…bring the BC discipline to management's attention, provide the tools, and help along the way.**

BC management is a permanent, iterative process which it is usually best to approach as the second phase following on from an initial project. A different attitude and mindset are required for the ongoing maintenance process. This is when things are more or less stable and attention to detail and accuracy come to the fore. Administrative teams are given a set of tools and procedures to enable them to carry out regular reviews, revise the procedures where necessary, and keep the records up-to-date.

3.3   A Launch Argument Formula: Seven Principles

My arguments for a BC launch are normally based upon seven principles. Occasionally, circumstances might dictate that I follow some in-house rules, in which case I apply as many of my principles as I can without straying too far from the given requirement.

- ▸ Ensure in-house ownership.
- ▸ Provide five relevant examples.
- ▸ Display observance.
- ▸ Allow cognitive marketing.
- ▸ Reach and withdraw.
- ▸ Remain realistic.
- ▸ One step at a time.

3.3.1   In-House Ownership

From the very outset you need to make it perfectly clear that company leaders are the owners of the whole program, which is going to be for the benefit of their business, their customers, and their staff. As a consultant, or a facilitator, you will be bringing the skills, tools, and techniques to the party but, in the long term, they will need to do the bulk of the work themselves because they are the only ones who really understand all the nuances and subtleties of how the business actually operates on a day-to-day basis. As outsiders, you and I can only set them up and point them in the right direction.

Now, I can hear some of you saying that you are not consultants or that you do not consider yourselves as outsiders. However, from a practical perspective, *all* BC practitioners are external to the business activities which they seek to protect. Your task as a BC professional is to bring the BC discipline to management's attention, provide the tools, and help along the way. Throughout this process, you will be transferring skills to managers at various levels, after which you will stand back and let them get on with it. As the center of competence, you will remain available as a reference source and support center.

It is vitally important that the business operators own their BC plans and procedures. These documents and their implications must never be seen or regarded as items on the shelf which have been brought in from outside. They need to be seen as the living, breathing components of survival in the event of something going wrong – as it inevitably must.

It is important for you to make it clear that your involvement should be not seen as an eternal commitment. Too often, I have seen consultants who seem unable to "let go." They come in and set up a permanent program which requires them to return time and time again, to review and update the plans and procedures ad infinitum. Often their excuse is that the subtleties and complexities of the methodology require specialist knowledge or training. Of course, they have not passed on that vital knowledge or training to their customers, leaving them in the dark and dependent. BC customers should not be regarded as a captive audience to be enslaved but as independent and fully capable free spirits who can, and should, take responsibility for their own success and survival.

3.3.2   Five Examples

Having assured the top management team that you do not see them as a soft touch and that you are going to make their people responsible for, and capable of, continuity, you need to convince them that it is necessary. The best way to get this message across is to use some real-life examples of things going wrong. You can quote statistics, such as the number of fires that have occurred or the frequency of power outages, but numbers don't create vivid pictures in the listeners' minds, and it is colorful images that carry weight in an intellectual argument. Carry out some research about unexpected and disruptive events which have recently occurred.

…develop a body of knowledge which will give you the confidence to put forward a good argument….

I always try to offer five instances of significant events. Anything less than five leaves room for explanations or excuses. Here I am thinking of responses like: "Oh that couldn't happen to us, we've got security guards." "Our local authority has flood plans." "The fire service has that under control." On the other hand, more than five makes you sound like a merchant of doom trying to predict the very worst, and the worst has never happened to us – yet.

The rule here is *recent, relevant, and remarkable.*

- *Recent* makes it more interesting because they may not know the full details. The 1896 earthquake in San Francisco or the destruction of Pompeii is unlikely to persuade a business person of the need to pay attention to what comes next.
- *Relevant* makes it even more interesting because it is closer to home and, therefore, more meaningful. Relevance means something which happened locally, something which happened to someone your listeners know, or something which happened in a place like theirs.
- *Remarkable* tends to ring alarm bells and make people wonder whether they have got that base covered. Wondering leads them towards worrying, and worry can spark action. Here we are looking for the unexpected which could be a question of something unusual, a matter of scale, or surprise that it was allowed to happen.

Five different types of events will add variety and help your audience to see things from alternate perspectives. Almost always, there will be a recent fire which made the news. Another common disruptive scenario is bad weather, which could take the form of hurricanes, tornadoes, floods, freezing conditions, or dust storms. Power outages are also commonplace in most parts of the world. Tsunamis and earthquakes can occur in many regions. Transport problems are yet another common cause of disruption. Pollution may also be a contender in some areas and some industries.

Of course, in some industry sectors there may be a regulatory requirement for BC, but that could result in a tick-in-the-box solution which may prove to be quite ineffective in a real emergency. Something which simply appeases regulators or satisfies auditors is not necessarily going to generate enough support and enthusiasm to thoroughly prepare for the worst case scenario.

Before confronting your audience with these scenarios, think about how you would respond to any challenges which they might throw back at you. Make sure you have your facts and figures at your fingertips, and it might help if you have a couple of additional similar examples up your sleeve to reinforce the message you are trying to get across. In other words, try to develop a body of knowledge which will give you the confidence to put forward a good argument based on facts delivered with a convincing degree of certainty.

3.3.3   Observance

I find that it improves my image if I demonstrate my powers for observation. It shows that I am on the ball in the sense that I know what I am doing and also in the sense that I am alert and taking their case seriously. You may work for the company and are not coming in as a consultant, but, as I said earlier, from a practical perspective *all* BC practitioners are external to the business activities which they seek to protect. When you look at your company from a BC perspective, you are looking at it with new eyes.

Before I cross the threshold of a new customer for the first time, I take a few minutes driving through the surrounding area looking for clues about running a business in that part of the world. I am looking to see if there are any potential problems in the immediate neighborhood. Is there ease of access? Are there any factors which might affect staff or visitors should they have to evacuate the premises? The sort of things I am looking for are signs of parking restrictions, busy roads, catering facilities, and somewhere where they can take shelter or gather together in comfort and safety. Perhaps there is a company parking lot which could be used as an assembly area, or there might be a park nearby.

As I enter the premises and pass through reception, I make a point of checking the emergency evacuation signs and any instructions about fire alarms or other emergencies. Sometimes the receptionist or the security desk will point out whether the company plans to have a fire drill or test the alarm. In a really well organized, or a particularly hazardous, location there will be safety or evacuation instructions available for visitors. Often these instructions are incorporated into the visitor's pass.

In any case, I usually find enough little snippets to be able to make a few casual remarks about the environment in which the company appears to operate. Even if I am wrong about my interpretation of what I've seen, at least I was paying attention, and the experience has had a chance to teach me something useful.

3.3.4   Cognitive Marketing

Cognitive marketing is a conversational concept which I have constructed for myself as a psychological tool for use in a teaching or a marketing situation. It is a relatively simple concept, but it only works if you are careful and patient when applying it.

If you want someone to believe something, then you should allow them to discover it for themselves. When you stumble across a useful piece of information or clear understanding, you are much more likely to accept it and trust it because it is yours, it is your discovery. This moment of cognition or realization embeds that piece of data into the private and personal area of your mind and memory. From then on, it becomes a part of you. On the other hand, if someone were to simply tell you that same fact, you will remember it or grant it significance only if it aligns with what you already know.

Example

In 1993 an enterprising young businessman by the name of Richard Pursey was thinking about launching a disaster recovery service. His intention was to provide customers with rapid access to an emergency supply of PCs. The reasoning behind this was simple: in the event of a disaster, companies need people, premises, and computers in order to be able to do business. People and premises, at that time, were in plentiful supply, but it was not easy to obtain large supplies of PCs at short notice.

Richard met the recently knighted Andrew Lloyd Webber at a dinner party (they both lived in the same neighborhood). Andrew spoke enthusiastically about a new musical (*Sunset Boulevard*) he was working on and after a while he turned to Richard and said, "Tell me what's going on in your head these days?" Richard explained how important it was for commercial organizations to have access to computers, especially if they had just lost their premises due to a fire or some other kind of emergency. Andrew interrupted with a big smile on his face. "There is a business opportunity here! I'd like to invest in it if you think you could make it work." Rather than argue or elaborate, Richard was sensible enough to smile and offer his hand.

Richard went home with a check for £150,000 in his pocket. Andrew went home thinking he had just invented what we now call "business continuity." A new disaster recovery service named *Neverfail* was launched shortly afterwards. To this day, Andrew Lloyd Webber still believes that he created a new industry when he discovered that his friend had a problem at the back of his mind.

3.3.5   Reach and Withdraw

Another subtle way of persuading people to want what you might be able to offer is a technique that I call *reach and withdraw*. It is a subtle form of teasing in which you reach out towards them with a tentative offer of something enticing. Then, when you have gained their attention and interest, you withdraw or walk away. Their natural instinct is to follow you because you have caused them to want something at a subconscious level. For the moment they are like putty in your hands – until someone or something else catches their attention.

In a BC launch context, I use this technique to show them that some desirable objects can emerge from the BC process. The most appealing benefits at this early stage are those which are tangible rather than virtual. Something tangible which they can touch and feel is going to be more meaningful than the promise of some virtual service that they don't yet fully understand. If it can be seen to exist physically, then there is no doubt that it is real, whereas a promise, a description, or a fancy title carries very little weight in a hypothetical argument.

The way it works is like this. I arrive with a bag of hidden goodies. The bag is obvious because I put it on the desk and make sure it is always close to hand. There is a subtle unspoken message here: I value what's in that bag, it's precious. When we get around to discussing the business of the day, which is "when things go wrong," I reach into the bag and produce a newspaper clipping or a photo of a recent disaster. This is an illustration to reinforce what I am saying, food for thought but not something to dwell on. So I put the picture down and move on to talk about what might be useful if ever something like that happened to them.

I mention that one possibility would be to send someone on a training course, at the end of which he or she would come back with a binder full of ideas and solutions. I reach into my bag and produce a course manual which I put on the desk. Shortly afterwards, I add a few other goodies which the student might acquire: some sample documents, a few templates, and a mounted certificate.

I suggest that if they were to sign up with a disaster recovery service, for example, then they would get an instruction manual and some invocation instructions, together with a map showing how to get there. More stuff out of the bag. By now, I have amassed quite a pile of useful items.

> **Whenever possible, support your ideas with powerful visual aids...**

Then I suggest that, as an alternative, they may prefer to rely on their own resources and appoint one of their staff to prepare some BC plans. This leads me to describe the outcomes of such a program and, one by one, a series of reports and plans emerges from the bag.

In closing, I say, "Armed with all these sources of information, I would feel quite confident about dealing with whatever might happen, but you might see things differently." At this point, I gather up all my goodies and put them back in the bag ready to walk away.

Usually my withdrawal leads to someone wanting to explore this whole subject in a bit more detail. "Don't run away, we were just getting interested in what you were saying."

3.3.6   Remain Realistic

Throughout this argument, which is, after all, a sales campaign, you have to remain realistic and try not to exaggerate. Two methods of creating realism are:

▪ Use *relevant references*, stay real, and avoid flights of fancy.
▪ Use *images* to convey solid messages.

Relevance will be achieved if you stick with local, or at least familiar, reference points. Stick with reality, don't exaggerate, and avoid flights of fancy. Try to bear in mind your customers' areas of interest and their background. Keep your examples within the experience of the listeners. There is no point in talking about a plague of red frogs that has only ever occurred once on a remote island in the Pacific, unless, of course, you happen to be in that part of the world.

Imagine you were a football or soccer player getting ready for an important match. Would you be interested in hearing about how my uncle prepares the village green for a cricket match? You might prefer to know what David Beckham says about being mentally prepared. I can't tell you because I don't know, but we could discuss it and share our views.

Images are our most powerful communication tools. The whole purpose of any dialog is to create pictures in the mind of the receiver; otherwise, nothing meaningful occurs.

Whenever possible, support your ideas with powerful visual aids. Throughout the argument, remember that words and sounds don't always have the same impact as visible physical objects. They do say that "a picture paints a thousand words." I would add that 3D is better than 2D. In other words, a realistic model is even more powerful as a means of conveying a message than a painting or photograph. The addition of mass into the mental equation literally adds weight to your argument. Even something as simple as the "goody bag" in the section above offers an impactful visual message not possible in a thousand words.

In my pocket I always carry a Swiss penknife and often use it as an example of planning ahead, preparing for the unknown, and excellent workmanship. Whenever I talk about it, I show it to people and then let them handle it so they can get the feel of it. If they open it up they can see how it works and imagine themselves using it. From then on it symbolizes to them just how practical I am, especially if I embroider the conversation with a few tales about making use of the scissors, screwdriver, tweezers, and sharp blades. It does more for my credibility than asking them to read a two-page CV.

3.3.7   One Step at a Time

Although you and I know that BC is a continuous program with a number of stages, many of which are reiterative, it is best to allow management to focus on one task at a time rather than try to get them to commit to supporting a long, complex, and probably expensive campaign. It is better to approach it as a step-by-step process in which each step will lead inevitably towards the next. You should also allow for each of these steps to deliver a final outcome, at least in the minds of your sponsors.

For example, the first step in the BC process would be to carry out some form of investigation regarding the potential threats and the defense measures which are already in place. It is reasonable to suppose that the report at the end of this process will contain recommendations about dealing with the threats. However, you should also allow for the possibility that there may appear to be no need for further action. Although, in fact, this is a rather remote possibility it should not be ruled out. Otherwise, you will be seen to be instigating a self-fulfilling prophecy, a short-term project with a hidden long-term agenda.

Another school of thought maintains that it is best to gain board-level commitment to BCM in entirety at the outset. If you can achieve that, then you have gained support for the whole of the program. It is a bold approach which brings dividends if you can pull it off; however, you may prefer the more tentative incremental style.

3.4   Board-Level Motivators

The launch presentation which we have just explored is a means of creating interest in the subject and possibly promoting some debate. Hopefully it will help you to gain the support of a board-level champion. However, it is unlikely to generate more than a token commitment from a financial perspective, and without any funds your program is not going to last very long. Beyond the initial launch, you may need to build a proper business case in order to justify the anticipated investment involved in setting up a permanent BC process. You will be asked to submit a proper proposal with some numbers attached.

This book will explore four particular aspects of the *business case* for investing in a BC program. A solid case can be built within these principal dimensions:

- External influences, i.e., understanding the drivers.
- Internal factors, i.e., estimating the impacts (backlog trap).
- Practical considerations, i.e., adopting the techniques.
- Suitable timing, i.e., developing the opportunities.

These ideas can also be grouped according to *why*, *how*, and *when*.

The ideas presented here are based on generalities rather than local knowledge, and you will need to adapt them to fit your own particular circumstances.

3.4.1   External Influences

In almost any industry or sector there will be a number of external influences which affect the manner in which the company is managed and operated. These are often referred to as *business drivers* because they do steer the business in what others see as the right direction.

Government Guidelines, Regulations, and Standards

Your local or national government may issue guidelines or regulations which suggest or require some form of BC planning or preparation. In some parts of the world, local governments actively promote BC. In the UK this is a direct result of the *Civil Contingencies Act 2004* which requires local government to offer support in this area. The Monetary Authority of Singapore issues *Business Continuity Management Guidelines* to its financial institutions and expects auditors to check for compliance against these guidelines.

> If a business collapses unexpectedly or if someone gets hurt...it can result in an investigation that could lead to a court case.

In South Africa, all listed companies are required to follow the governance principles which are outlined in the *King Report III 2009*. The report includes references to what it calls "business rescue and integrated sustainability" which can be achieved through BC.

Those industries which are regulated are normally required to comply with a detailed code of conduct or guide to good practice. Almost all of them have some reference to the need for BC planning. (For more about standards, see Section 3.6 below.)

Risk of Liability or Negligence

Another important external factor is often overlooked. In the event of something going wrong, somebody is going to be liable. If a business collapses unexpectedly or if someone gets hurt as a result of negligence, it can result in an investigation that could lead to a court case. At the inquiry or in the courtroom, the prosecuting counsel is probably going to ask for evidence of proper planning and training to deal with such an event. Even if the lawyer fails to impress the judge, there is no doubt that the media will have a field day.

The likely charges are criminal negligence or corporate manslaughter, and the penalties can be quite harsh. In the UK, for example, *The Corporate Manslaughter and Homicide Act 2007* facilitates the prosecution of corporate entities where a death is caused by a breach of a duty of care, and senior management failings are a substantial element of such a breach. The suggested starting point for a fine following a corporate manslaughter conviction is £500,000 according to the sentencing guidelines.

Although there have been relatively few prosecutions to date, organizations should not be lured into a false sense of security. Recent figures suggest that the UK Crown Prosecution Service investigated 40% more corporate manslaughter cases in 2012 than it did the previous year.

From a public relations perspective it is good corporate citizenship to be fully prepared to meet the needs and expectations of the staff and customers. Meeting these needs includes offering staff a sustainable and safe working environment while offering customers a continuous supply of goods and services. Therefore a weak or missing BC program must be seen as a sure sign of poor corporate citizenship and inadequate governance.

3.4.2   Internal Factors

Failure to Exercise Plans

In an ideal world any organization of any substance would already have a policy in place which supports the requirement for regular exercising of their BC arrangements. Of course, there are many enterprises which are somewhat less emphatic about the need to prepare for the inevitable. There are three likely reasons for a lackadaisical approach to risks and threats: either they don't know, they can't see, or they simply don't care. In the latter case it might be easier to walk away than bang your head against a brick wall. Where there is lack of knowledge or vision, then you can offer to open their eyes or provide them with some facts.

Failure to Review Physical Risks

Offer to conduct a review of the physical threats with a view to identifying whether there is a need for some BC measures. This only needs to be a simple overview which can be carried out fairly quickly without much effort. An hour spent with the facilities manager, or an equivalent staff member, will soon reveal whether further action should be considered.

Unfortunately, spare capacity is probably rather limited, and the team spirit may not survive the incident.

Backlog Trap

Perhaps the most important factor which allows top management to underestimate the need for some effective response and recovery procedures is the backlog trap which this book covered in the first chapter. It is easy and natural to assume that the return to business as usual is just a matter of engendering a bit of team spirit, calling for a concerted effort, and making full use of the spare capacity. Unfortunately, spare capacity is probably rather limited, and the team spirit may not survive the incident.

3.4.3 Practical Considerations

Before top executives agree to authorize you to embark on something relatively new to them, they will want some reassurance that you know what you are doing and how you are going to go about it. Some basic decisions need to be made here before you can put forward a proper business case.

Reassuring Management About Sources of Techniques

Executives will want answers to questions like: "Where do you get your ideas from?" "Whose methodology or techniques will you be using?" "How will you adapt it to fit our organization?" "Will it fit into our culture?" "Can we really afford it?"

You should reassure them that any of the standards or guidelines which you use as your reference will allow sufficient flexibility to enable you to adapt the concepts behind their recommendations to fit their needs and requirements. Explain that all of these models will have been developed by people with some degree of expertise, and because no two organizations are alike at the detail level, experts will have drawn up their guidelines to be relatively flexible and user-friendly rather than pedantically precise or restrictive. However, you should be prepared to give them a clear picture of how you propose to approach the work. (See Section 3.6 below.)

Deciding Whether to Select a Consultant

Whether you want to call for any outside help will depend upon your own confidence and capability as well as the corporate culture. Some companies regard consultants or other external experts as unwelcome and unnecessary, whereas others see them as helpful and unavoidable. Where specialists are frowned upon, you will need to work out how you are going to acquire the skills and techniques to do the job yourself, perhaps in collaboration with others. If you think that you might be allowed to bring in outside help, then you should do some research into who might be able to help and how the person you are considering would like to approach the job.

Explore a range of choices: If you are looking to refer to consultants, then you need to be fairly selective and explore a range of choices. Consultancy practices come in all sizes and varying degrees of specialization; bigger is not necessarily better. What matters most is the background, skill, and experience of the individual with whom you will be working. Make sure that you get to meet this person and understand his or her approach before you commit to using this consultancy and its methodology. In particular, you need to ensure that there will be some skills transfer included in the project so that you do not have to rely on the consultant permanently.

Ideally, your consultant should be able to provide you with references which show familiarity with your industry sector and your part of the world. You also need to establish that the consultant will follow good practice and can deliver a complete package which will suit your needs.

Review qualifications: Make sure that companies being considered are properly qualified and experienced, especially if you are looking for them to take the lead throughout the work. In any case, it is well worth checking their references, looking for evidence that they have experience that is relevant to your industry sector and your part of the world; otherwise, the expertise is irrelevant. If the consultant has a certificate, that qualification will prove that he or she has at least had some formal education in the subject. Ideally, that certificate should be aligned to a recognized standard or a code of practice, such as ISO 22301 or *Good Practice Guidelines 2013*.

> **…the whole organization should be dealt with gradually…rather than one single massive effort.**

A more robust and meaningful qualification would be membership of the Business Continuity Institute (BCI) because this shows that the consultant has proved his or her knowledge in an examination and has some practical experience in the subject. Statutory membership of the BCI entitles the consultant to have letters after his or her name and also means that the consultants follow an ethical code of professional practice and are competent in following the discipline of BC. Statutory or official grades include Associate Member (AMBCI), Member (MBCI), Associate Fellow (AFBCI), and Fellow (FBCI).

In addition, BCI offers a certificate (CBCI) or a diploma (DBCI) to recognize those who have demonstrated their knowledge of the subject in a formal examination. CBCI is awarded to those candidates who passed the CBCI examination but have not achieved full statutory membership. DBCI is awarded to those who have an academic qualification by taking a distance learning program in partnership with Buckinghamshire New University.

Evaluate methodology and software: Ask whether your consultant, or external adviser, will recommend, endorse, or insist upon using a particular methodology or software at any stage of the game. If he or she expects you to use a proprietary software tool, there will no doubt be an associated cost of which you should be aware. Another issue could be the question of where that software and associated information is expected to be located. It may or may not be wise to entrust the intimate details of your business operation to what is, in effect, a third party. You also need to seek assurance that their approach will be compatible with any standards with which you may want to align or comply.

3.4.4   Suitable Timing

Because the risks and threats, whatever they may be, are eternally present, it makes sense to implement your protection and recovery program as soon as realistically possible. However, there are often many more pressing and apparently important tasks to be considered, especially when viewed from a high-level corporate perspective. On the other hand, there are often quieter periods when top management can afford the time and energy to consider some of the secondary issues which they tend to hold in abeyance most of the time.

You need to choose the right moment to make your bid for their attention. This means you need to be aware of what I call the "corporate chronology." There will be regular busy times of the year and month, occasional frantic periods, and a few periods of relative calm and stability. Obviously, you have to time your bid for their attention so that other more pressing matters don't conflict.

In addition, there may be seasonal concerns. For example, one of my clients who was in the jewelry trade reckoned to do 90% of his turnover in the six-week period before Christmas and about 8% in the four weeks before St. Valentine's Day. Thus, for 42 weeks of the year, his shop was there simply to establish his presence in the market in readiness for the few weeks when he expected to make a profit. Needless to say, there were times of the year I didn't get to visit him.

3.5 Scaling to Fit

Your overall game plan should take account of the number of business divisions, units, and locations. This means that the whole organization should be dealt with gradually as a series of relatively small projects rather than one single massive effort.

Thus, you may end up with a large number of plans with several relating to each location. In order to manage and maintain these plans it is desirable for them all to follow a similar layout and form part of a well-organized structure. The easiest way to do this is for you to emulate the structure of the organization itself. Regard it as a series of separate entities, each of which is a relatively independent business unit or function. Harmony is achieved by means of a management hierarchy which you can represent through an overarching emergency response plan for each location. At an even higher level, you can prepare a crisis response plan to cater for the protection of the brand and image of the whole enterprise.

By adopting an approach which is based on a separate plan for each business entity, you can use the same tools and techniques no matter how large or diverse the enterprise is. Of course, you can combine the plans for all of the entities at one location to form a local master plan, which consists of a number of similar modules. However, each entity will only need to have and to use the particular module which covers its recovery procedures. Further details of this modular approach to BC will be revealed in Part III of this book, which addresses the shape and contents of the various types and levels of plans.

3.6 Standards and Their Interpretation

Your top management is likely to want assurance that whatever you do in pursuit of your desire to deliver BC will align with the recognized standards. They may not know what those standards are, but they will be pretty sure that something exists and will expect you to be in a position to reassure them.

As you can imagine, a number of existing and planned standards cover BC and related subject matter, many of which are of local or limited scope and applicability. However, four key regions can be identified, in which BC is a well-established and recognized discipline: the international scene, UK, US, and Australia.

International

In 2012, the International Organization for Standardization (ISO) published *ISO 22301:2012, Societal security – Business continuity management systems – Requirements*, which specifies a system for managing an organization's business continuity arrangements. This document is rather formal in style in order to facilitate auditing for compliance and certification. It is supported by *ISO 22313:2012, Societal security – Business continuity management systems – Guidance*, which offers more practical advice about implementing and running a BC management system. There is also *ISO/IEC 27031:2011, Information security – Security techniques – Guidelines for information and communication technology* [ICT] *readiness for business continuity*, which offers guidance on the ICT aspects of BC management. This latter aspect of the BC discipline is also commonly known as disaster recovery.

According to Andrew Hiles, ISO 22301, because of its emphasis on preparedness rather than recovery, "will become the most applied standard world-wide," possibly winning "long-term commitment to BC from the C-suite." Compared to previous standards, Hiles notes that the compliance requirements of ISO 22301 "will cause more maintenance effort, but should result in more consistent and continually improved efforts within BCM" (Hiles, 2014).

United Kingdom

Prior to the release of ISO 22301, BC standards progressed through two iterations in the UK. In 2003, the British Standards Institution (BSI) offered Publicly Available Specification *PAS 56* for review and comment. In 2006, BSI introduced British Standard *BS 25999*, a two-part BC management standard. *Part 1 – A Code of Practice* offered pragmatic implementation guidance, and *Part 2 – A Specification* formally specified a set of requirements for a BC management system. In 2012, both PAS 56 and BS 25999 were withdrawn and replaced by ISO 22301.

The Business Continuity Institute (BCI) published *Good Practice Guidelines* (GPG) *2013* as an independent body of knowledge for good practice in BC around the world. The terminology and concepts used in these guidelines are in line with those used in ISO 22301.

United States

Published by the National Fire Protection Association, *NFPA 1600: Standard on Disaster/Emergency Management and Business Continuity Programs* has been described by many experts as a clear and unambiguous outline of what to do and how to do it in a sensible progressive manner. Originally published in 1995 as a set of recommendations for good practice, it was upgraded to the status of a standard in 2000.

The 2013 edition of NFPA 1600 includes:

- ▸ A section covering training and education.
- ▸ A comparison between the standard and *Professional Practices* published by the Disaster Recovery Institute International (DRII). (**Note:** *Professional Practices* is intended as a guide for practitioners and a tool for auditors. The body of knowledge covers the 10 core disciplines of BC management.)
- ▸ An annex or appendix about using NFPA 1600 as a Management System Standard.

NFPA 1600 is deemed critical for emergency management officials in the private, public, and not-for-profit sectors, and for professionals charged with BC.

Australia

Two guides published by Standards Australia, *HB 292-2006: A practitioner's guide to business continuity management* and *HB 293-2006: Executive guide to business continuity management*, offer an overview of what they describe as "generally accepted practices" and emerging new practices, particularly in Australasia, the US, and the UK. The practitioner's guide also points out that what works well in one organization may not suit a different one, advising that caution be exercised when deciding exactly how BC should be implemented. The executive guide explains why a business enterprise should invest time, money, and effort into protecting the interests of all its stakeholders.

For a truly comprehensive overview of all the relevant standards and regulations that apply in different regions around the world, you should consult *BCM Legislations, Regulations, Standards and Good Practice*, published by the BCI. The 84-page document summarizes the current legislation, regulations, and standards that exist both nationally and internationally for BC management (Business Continuity Institute, 2014).

3.6.1 Compliance Issues

Many of our major industries and sectors are governed or regulated by sets of rules, regulations, or guidelines and, as time goes by, more and more of our business operations will be in a position where they have to take compliance issues into account as a regular part of their organizational governance. Inevitably, BC is being included as a key component of such compliance.

With regulations, standards, and statutes increasingly adding to the administrative burden, many executives are beginning to wonder whether it is even possible to comply with all of these rules. Surely, some of these independently formulated models are going to be at odds with each other which must mean compliance with one directive or guideline is almost bound to lead to non-compliance in another area.

...there will be many opportunities to spot better, and safer, ways of doing thing.

This leaves decision-makers with the question of which to choose in order to be the least exposed – or is it better to ignore them all and take a chance? The regulators, watchdogs, and other authorities will gradually persuade us that opting out is neither in their best interest nor ours. Eventually, the authorities will take measures to ensure we do comply with their guidelines or standards.

When it comes to BC, we are in the fortunate position that the various standards which have sprung up around the world do tend to align with commonly accepted good practice. As a profession, we have been careful to make sure our expert opinion was taken into account during the development of almost all of these sets of formal documentation. The concepts behind these outlines are really very similar, although the detail may differ according to local ways of doing things – and then there is the inevitable jargon which creeps in to confuse the issue.

After all, BC is mostly structured common sense; so it should always be recognizably similar in its approach, even if some of the specifics are variable. Compliance, then, is largely a matter of interpreting the concepts behind the standard and applying those concepts to your particular situation and circumstance. Any reasonably competent reviewer, auditor, or inspector should understand that this is the only way to make BC fulfill its intention rather than use it as a means of obtaining a tick in an obscure box.

3.7 Hidden Benefits

Whereas most people know and accept that BC provides both resilience and protection for the core business operations, many fail to appreciate the hidden benefits which can spring from such a program. There are several areas where BC can deliver bonuses, and there are other areas where BC principles, processes, or procedures can be used to advantage.

Some of the areas where BC management can help will include:

- *Mergers of businesses, operations, or functions.* By viewing the project as a planned emergency, the benefits will include risk identification and reduction as well as the means for prompt recognition and response to any out-of-line situations which may develop during the merger.

- *Relocations or the establishment of a new operation.* In the same way, the transfer of existing operations or the establishment of new operations should be approached as a potential emergency. In addition, the event can be viewed, and used, as a real-life emergency response exercise with a number of lessons to be captured for future occasions.

- *Functional and procedural improvements.* During the assessment and analysis stages of BC, there will be many opportunities to spot better, and safer, ways of doing things. As a result, you could end up with a robust business operation which is not only stronger but also more effective.

- *Sales and marketing strategies.* By looking at the marketplace from the perspective of BC, using scenario planning techniques, you can help decision-makers to gain a fresh perspective on long-term sales and marketing strategies.

- *Sales and marketing opportunities.* In the event of changes in the market, those who are best prepared to spot the changes and respond rapidly and effectively are likely to gain market share in both the short term and the long term. BC plans should take such matters into account and develop techniques and strategies which are designed to maximize such opportunities.

- *Flexibility in operating procedures.* While preparing for a possible emergency, the continuity planning process will naturally identify alternate ways of serving the corporate mission or meeting customers' needs. Most, if not all, of these ideas can be employed to provide flexibility, if required.

- *Improving the utilization of key resources.* The early stages of BC require a fairly thorough analysis of the functioning of the organization and the way it employs and manages its key resources. Because this work is carried out from a relatively unbiased viewpoint, the output can be seen as a relatively honest appraisal of resource utilization. There is an obvious opportunity here to review and improve the current way of doing things. However, if any significant changes are made, the analysis will need to be revisited.

3.8   The Auditor's Role

Wherever there is an internal audit function, you have an immediate ally who can help to set the scene for the successful launch of a BC program. There is a strong chance your internal auditor or audit department will already be aware of the benefits of BC. On the other hand, if your auditors are not up to speed on the subject, then a short period of education should soon bring them around to recognizing that a BC program would be a distinct advantage.

…without a proper BC plan, you could be in breach of data protection legislation…

BC is also an essential part of protecting the data which is held by an organization. The implication here is that without a proper BC plan, you could be in breach of data protection legislation which is common to most countries in one form or another. The only exception might be a claim that your records do not contain the names and addresses of any individuals and therefore you can claim exemption. However, there are very few organizations where this applies in practice.

In the longer term, your auditors can help to keep the program rolling by asking to see evidence of progress, such as reports of tests and exercises. They might even wish to cast their eye over the actual plans themselves. Although auditors may not have the expertise to make meaningful comment, they can express interest or concern in their annual reports, which will be seen and read at the highest level.

Self-Examination Questions

1. The kick-off meeting for the business continuity (BC) program must be designed to
   A. verify that all response-and-recovery teams are ready to go into action.
   B. confirm with the legal department that the BC program is in compliance with regulations.
   C. establish the need for a BC plan in the minds of senior managers and ensure their buy-in.

2. When developing the action plan for the BC program, it is important to
   A. achieve a series of deliverables with a logical sequence.
   B. encompass all the organization's needs in one initial step.
   C. impress management with your expertise so they let you implement the program the way you see fit.

3. Which of the following is NOT one of the seven principles used as the basis for a BC program launch?
   A. Provide five relevant examples.
   B. Reach and withdraw.
   C. Use scare tactics.

4. Cognitive marketing can be described as
   A. appealing to the audience's intellect rather than to their emotions.
   B. persuading someone of an idea by allowing them to discover it for themselves.
   C. carefully observing the environment of an organization for details that may be useful.

5. Which of the following would be an example of an external influence to include in the business case for BC?
   A. Failure to exercise BC plans.
   B. Industry guide to good practice.
   C. Assurance that BC practices will be adapted to the organization.

6. Of the following standards, which is likely to become the most applied internationally because of its emphasis on preparedness?
   A. ISO 22301.
   B. NFPA 1600.
   C. BS 25999.

7. Relocating the firm's operations or initiating new operations
   A. is not related to BC, and such business activities should never be confounded with disaster preparation and recovery.
   B. intersects with BC only in that the new premises or operations will need to be incorporated into the scope of the BC program.
   C. can be approached as a potential emergency, with lessons learned captured from the exercise.

8. The BC manager should view the organization's auditors as
   A. natural allies, as they have an interest in data recovery and a penchant for reviewing tests of the organization's systems.
   B. probably uninterested, as their expertise lies in the organization's financials and BC has a holistic focus.
   C. possible opponents, since the costs of BC can be difficult to incorporate into the cost-accounting structure.

Food for Thought

In this chapter we have begun to look at how to get your BC program off the ground in what we have called a *launch argument*. Here we are using the term *argument* to suggest a meaningful debate in which you aim to persuade others to accept your point of view.

Now try to imagine how you might apply those principles to your own organization. You could also consider how you would approach the task in relation to a college or a nearby shopping mall with which you are familiar. Another possibility would be to use the example of a company where a family member or friend works.

Exercises

1. How and when might you be able to arrange the opportunity to deliver a launch argument?
   › Who will form the audience for this argument?
   › Will it be a specially arranged meeting or a regular scheduled meeting?
   › How will you ensure that you get the chance to air your views?

2. Develop a draft launch argument.
   › What recent and relevant events could be used to illustrate your argument?
   › Which five of these recent events will you use in your presentation?

3. Define exactly what you expect to gain from this meeting.
   › Make a list of the possible outcomes and rank them in order of probability and preference.
   › How do you propose to ensure that you get the best of the possible outcomes?

4. What additional advantages or side benefits would support your argument?
   › Rank them in order of their value or attractiveness to the organization.
   › Develop the top three into a meaningful message, i.e., get the wording and sequence right.

5. Who might be able and willing to support or add weight to your argument?
   › Will you be referring to regulators, standard makers, or legislators?
   › How will you go about enlisting the aid of auditors?
   › What about suppliers, customers, or the local community?

Downloadable Business Continuity Toolkit

You can download information and tools from the **Business Continuity Toolkit** that will help you make the case for BC to management.

References

Business Continuity Institute (2014, January). *BCM legislations, regulations, standards and good practice.* Retrieved from www.bcifiles.com/BCMLegislationsandRegulationsJan2014.pdf

Hiles, A. (2014). *Business continuity management: Global best practices* (4th ed.). Brookfield, CT: Rothstein Publishing, chapter 2.

National Fire Protection Association (2013). *NFPA 1600 standard on disaster/emergency management and business continuity programs.* Retrieved from http://www.nfpa.org/assets/files/AboutTheCodes/1600/1600-13-PDF.pdf, p. 1600-5.

For Additional Reading

Business Continuity Institute (2013). *Good practice guidelines.* Available from http://www.thebci.org/index.php/resources/the-good-practice-guidelines (May be downloaded free by BCI members, or purchased by non-members.)

Part

II

Building a Foundation

| Part I: Preparation and Startup |
| Part II: Building a Foundation |
| Part III: Responding and Recovering |
| Part IV: Planning and Implementing |
| Part V: Long-Term Continuity |

Understanding impacts and consequences is essential to your business continuity (BC) preparation. At the base of all of your efforts will be how effectively you identify possible threats, deal with the symptoms of that threat, and prevent the consequences of a threat in the event that it materializes.

In Part I, you explored the practical aspects of getting started in BC. Now, in Part II, **Building a Foundation**, you will do the basic research and information gathering that will allow you to identify threats and critical functions and make the choices that will protect the survival of the business.

Chapter 4 – Understanding Your Risks

> Describes how to assess the risks and explain them to others.

Chapter 5 – Impacts and Consequences

> Covers analyzing the risks and understanding their consequences.

Chapter 6 – Continuity Strategies and Options

> Presents alternative approaches to implementing practical BC.

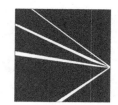

4

Understanding Your Risks

By now you should have an appreciation of business continuity (BC) and why it is important. Once you have successfully launched a BC program, as covered in Chapter 3, the next important stage is to understand the specific reasons why your organization actually needs to have plans in place. So far, your people have been asked to consider only generalities and concepts which need not necessarily apply to their environment.

You will need to explore precisely why, and where, the business enterprise might be exposed to specific threats and risks. Once you are able to explain how such an event might impact the business operation, your explanation will lead to the development of plans and procedures to deal with an interruption.

This chapter will help you to:

- ☑ Approach the need for risk assessment from a BC perspective.

- ☑ See the difference between qualitative and quantitative risk assessment.

- ☑ Discover, evaluate, and report risks.

- ☑ Focus on the possibility rather than the probability of an occurrence.

- ☑ Apply several risk analysis methodologies, such as Grid Impact Analysis, QwikRisk, and SMARTRisk.

- ☑ Present your findings in a simple but effective manner.

4.1   Risk from a Business Continuity Perspective

For background, you need to be aware of the key definitions within the world of risk management. As the concept of resiliency is added to traditional BC, one of your tasks will be to integrate these concepts in how planning and decision-making are conducted at all levels in your organization. Your goal is to balance the two main areas of risk management:

> **Enterprise risk** – This is the area in which you work to mitigate events that may impact the organization in terms of people, facilities, information technology (IT), and assets.

> **Operational risk** – This is the area in which you work to mitigate vulnerabilities in business operations, including the effectiveness of processes, analysis of downtime, governance, and reporting – making processes work better.

4.1.1   Risk and the Six Disruptive Scenarios

The regular scope of risk management is rather wide and concerns itself with many aspects of risk which are not pertinent to the purpose of BC and, thus, are well outside your remit or specific task.

In considering risk as it applies to BC, you need to be concerned only with those threats which are likely to result in one of the *six disruptive scenarios* that were introduced earlier in Chapter 1:

> Loss of access.

> Loss of people.

> Loss of supplies.

> Loss of communication.

> Loss of function.

> Loss of data.

Any of these situations would be made worse if you were either unaware of the loss or unable to assess the situation through lack of information about the circumstances. Therefore, your risk assessment needs to be based on those risks which can lead to these potential outcomes.

Theoretically, you could develop a set of plans to cope with almost any situation; however, it seems reasonable to identify the most significant threats and then to plan accordingly. Your information about these threats ensures support for the program because you will be able to demonstrate a definite need together with a sound solution to a known set of problems.

4.1.2   The Regular Risk Management Review

In most organizations, some form of risk management protocol will already be in place. The identification, assessment, and mitigation of risk are integral elements of any conscientious management system and a basic requirement of good governance. For example:

The UK Corporate Governance Code (September 2012) C.2 states that: "The board is responsible for determining the nature and extent of the significant risks it is willing to take in achieving its strategic objectives. The board should maintain sound risk management and internal control systems" (Financial Reporting Council, 2012). It goes on to say: "The board should, at least annually, conduct a review of the effectiveness of the company's risk management and internal control systems.... The review should cover all material controls, including financial, operational and compliance controls." Similar codes, regulations, or guidelines are in place around the world.

4.1.3   Individual Interviews

One way of being prepared would be to speak with managers and supervisors and ask for their opinions about these types of risk. From their input, you can compile a risk report which gives a broad indication of the existing threats. In addition, these managers will probably be able to suggest ways of dealing with these threats. Thus, you will begin to form the basis for your basic BC plans.

> **No executive is going to release funds and resources based on…hearsay and subjective impressions.**

Of course, this is a rather informal approach and depends to a large degree on the skill and knowledge of both the interviewer and the interviewees. Most of us would prefer to use a more structured approach because that is more likely to produce a consistent and credible result. No executive is going to release funds and resources based on what might be perceived as nothing more than hearsay and subjective impressions. They will expect to see some degree of rigor in your approach before they are willing to commit to supporting any further work based on those results.

When carrying out this type of investigation allow enough time to go through all of the questions but try not to outstay your welcome. To get a clear and accurate perspective and to eliminate bias it is best to interview at least three people for each area of the business. If you speak to two people and they give very different answers, it is very difficult to judge what the truth might actually be. If you have two other opinions, it is much easier to establish whether people are biased in their opinion or judgment. Their bias may be based on any number of factors including not wanting to admit their ignorance, lack of time, lack of interest, an earlier misfortune, temporary dissatisfaction, innate pessimism, lack of confidence, or an optimistic nature.

If you should be unlucky enough to get three very different views, then there is either something wrong with your approach or you have identified some serious concerns about the way that particular area of the business is being run. If there are fewer than three people available for interview, you will have to judge whether the differences are significant and how their views differ from other parts of the same organization.

4.1.4   Group Interviews

One way of obtaining an initial overall view is through a facilitated discussion with a representative group of managers. This will also help to develop their buy-in because you are openly drawing them into the process. You are also demonstrating that you value their opinion and are basing your approach upon their input rather than seeking to impose an externally influenced solution of your own invention.

> **The most useful number you can calculate is the "cost of absence," or the "cost of loss."**

However, in most organizations you will be expected to adopt a methodical approach to risk assessment, and I am going to offer you a choice of methods. You need to select which of these is appropriate to your needs and expectations.

4.2   Risk Assessment Methods

4.2.1   Quantitative and Qualitative Methods

There are two distinct approaches to risk assessment: one seeks to identify the risks and *quantify* them; the other approach tries to gain a general impression about the risks and *qualify* them.

  ▸ The *quantitative methods*, which seek to put a numeric value against the risk, usually depend on having reliable statistics from which to extrapolate the future. In practice, these figures are not readily available and, in any event, the past may no longer reflect the future. Yesterday's problems will have been superseded as we improve our technology and skills.

 ▸ I recommend, and propose to examine, the *qualitative approach*. A typical qualitative method is to use a checklist of questions which people are asked to rate individually. Although you are making use of numbers in this approach, the result is qualitative in the sense that the numbers are comparative estimates rather than accurate numerical reflections of probability based on statistical analysis.

4.2.2   A Simple Quantitative Approach

Although I recommend a qualitative approach, I will include a few words about a relatively simple quantitative approach. The most useful number you can calculate is the "cost of absence," or the "cost of loss." This is a straightforward calculation of the costs associated with not running an operation or process, less any savings which might occur during the outage.

To calculate "cost of loss," you need to account for all the components of cost, such as:

 ▸ Labor or staffing costs.
 ▸ Costs of raw materials and supplies.
 ▸ Final finished product value.
 ▸ The overhead costs of accommodation, etc.
 ▸ Costs associated with starting or commissioning systems and processes.
 ▸ Run-down costs associated with closing down any key systems or processes in a safe manner.
 ▸ Costs of borrowing.
 ▸ Penalty costs, etc.

Then you can establish the true cost of an outage and judge what you should, or could, afford to spend on protecting the operation or process. That is proper risk management – reducing the cost of risk, both potential and actual.

One method of assessing the quality and extent of risk is to look at *all* the areas concerned, evaluate them individually, and develop an impression of the *total risk*, a relative value which can be used as a progress indicator.

You can download a risk assessment tool from the **Business Continuity Toolkit**.

4.3   Six Stages of Grid Impact Analysis

Grid impact analysis is a formal method of analyzing complete systems to identify their critical components. It looks at everything that might be concerned with the flow of information through the business. Grid impact analysis can, and should, be extended to look at all flows through the business, such as cash, materials, people, resources, etc.

There are six stages in this exercise:

1. Data collection.
2. Data mapping.
3. Grid analysis.
4. Issues and needs.
5. Reporting.
6. Implementation.

Stage 1: In the data collection stage, the analyzing team needs to be familiar with the applications, operating procedures, configuration, personnel, and environment, and team members should be armed with lists of applications, libraries, and configurations.

Stage 2: In the mapping phase, each activity, function, or process is mapped against its essential resources or needs.

Stage 3: Then each intersection is considered in terms of its likelihood of failure and the options for alternate mechanisms. Wherever there is an alternative available, the risk is considered minimal but where there is no alternative, the risk has to be seen as critical. Where a resource is essential to a number of activities, functions, or processes, then it has to be perceived as super critical or very high risk.

The natural consequence of the reporting stage will be a request...to develop and deliver a solution to the problems...

Stage 4: The final product of this exercise will be a list of issues and needs in priority sequence, together with cost and/or resource estimates.

Stage 5: Once you have collated and organized all the data, you need to report your findings. The manner in which you present your conclusions and recommendations to top management will depend on corporate culture. It is normal to deliver a verbal summary in a face-to-face meeting with an opportunity for questions. This should be followed up by a written report. The natural consequence of the reporting stage will be a request, order, or instruction for someone, such as yourself, to develop and deliver a solution to the problems which you have highlighted.

Stage 6: The final, and ongoing, stage is the implementation of the appropriate strategies which top management will have selected, or devised, as a result of your analysis and reporting. This is where your skill and knowledge will be put to the test.

The essential characteristic of this method is the data mapping and the subsequent grid analysis.

For example, here is the initial mapping carried out to show which parts of the business use various resources.

Table 4-1. Initial Mapping

→Resource Operation↓	Switch-board	Water Supply	Lighting	Computer	Laser Printer
Tele Sales	*Critical*	Not used	Needed	*Critical*	Needed
Help Desk	*Critical*	Not used	Needed	*Critical*	Useful
Reception	Useful	Not used	Useful	Useful	Not used
Marketing	Useful	Not used	Useful	Useful	Useful
Accounts	Not used	Not used	Useful	*Critical*	*Critical*
Manufacturing	Not used	*Critical*	Useful	Useful	Not used

When the information is analyzed, we get this picture:

Table 4-2. Analysis of Information

→Resource Operation↓	Switch-board	Water Supply	Lighting	Computer	Laser Printer
Tele Sales	✓✓✓	X	✓✓	✓✓✓	✓✓
Help Desk	✓✓✓	X	✓✓	✓✓✓	✓
Reception	✓	X	✓	✓	X
Marketing	✓	X	✓	✓	✓
Accounts	X	X	✓	✓✓✓	✓✓✓
Manufacturing	X	✓✓✓	✓	✓	X

From this initial analysis, it is clear that the water supply is critical to the manufacturing operation; accounts say the laser printer is critical; the switchboard is very critical because it is critical to two key functions; and the computer is supercritical because it is seen as critical by at least three key business functions.

> **Once the implications are fully understood, a sensible strategy can then be proposed or selected.**

Further analysis might reveal that an additional printer should be provided, mainly to support accounts. While the water supply is critical to manufacturing, the risk of losing it may be considered low, and therefore no action needs be taken.

The final action would be to investigate the options and costs for recovery of the switchboard and the computer. Once the implications are fully understood, a sensible strategy can then be proposed or selected.

4.4   Risk Acceptance

Over the years I have explained my theory about risk acceptance to boards of directors and management teams because I think it is important that they should understand how others might view their *appetite for risk*. Such an understanding helps decision-makers to appreciate the need for BC.

4.4.1   Three Categories of Non-Transferable Risk

Based on the assumption that customers are concerned about receiving a reliable service, my contention is this: Smart customers will expect to deal with smart suppliers, who recognize three categories of *non-transferable risk*:

1. Constant, line of business risk   or   *common hazards*

2. Regular, judgmental risks   or   *regular chances*

3. Irregular, arbitrary risks   or   *random perils*

Smart customers:

▶ Accept that a smart supplier allows for the *common hazards* when setting a realistic price. Higher risks mean higher margins.

▶ Expect smart suppliers to cover their *regular chances* by ensuring their staff are properly trained and qualified to make sound judgments.

▶ Do not wish to share the *random perils* experienced by a supplier that chooses to let them down through lack of foresight.

You can apply the same line of thinking to your own suppliers and their management style, evaluating the degree to which they meet the definition of "smart suppliers." In fact, you might consider preparing a draft risk acceptance report about your key suppliers as a case study for your top management team to ponder over. Such a report could lead to some interesting questions.

> **The actual cost of loss can be calculated as the loss per hour…less any potential savings which might accrue…**

4.5 The Cost of Loss

The actual cost of loss can be calculated as the loss per hour (or any other appropriate unit of time) less any potential savings which might accrue as the result of not carrying out some operations. For instance, if you are unable to make deliveries you might save on fuel and labor. The end result is the *effective loss per unit of time.*

Once you know what it would cost you to lose a significant part of a major business unit, you can begin to assess the true value of suitable protective measures.

Aggregate Loss   less   Any Savings   =   Effective Loss

4.5.1 Loss of Profit

Loss of profit is the bottom line figure that will interest senior executives, once they understand the implications and likelihood of something going wrong.

Let us look at some figures for a small business that loses its ability to function for some time because of a disruption:

Turnover	=	$10 M per year
Desired Profit	=	12%
	=	$5,000 per day (approx.)
Cost of disruption	=	$5,000 per day x 5
		(Allowing for the Backlog Effect)
Loss of Profit	=	$25,000 for one day's outage

For such a medium-sized company this amount of money should easily cover the cost of protection for their core systems. From the cost of a day's outage we can estimate the potential annual loss due to system downtime by taking into account the total time lost in a typical installation. This might easily amount to 3 days per annum.

A) Annual Loss of Profit

Annual Outage	=	3 days per year
Each Outage	=	$25,000
Potential Annual Loss	=	$75,000 per year

If you can prevent the consequences of one outage, the preventative measures are paid for. If you can prevent two, you can show a profit!

The *invisible costs*... are, perhaps, the most expensive of all.

Another way of looking at the costs of a disruption is to take into account the wasted worker hours because your people are unable to work effectively during the disruption and the subsequent return to normal. If we assume the cost of employment of an average member of staff to be $20,000 a year, including benefits, overhead, etc., and that each staff member works 8 hours a day for 200 days a year, we can work out the cost of a disruption in terms of wasted time and effort of the user population. For this size of company, we can assume there will be about 40 users.

B) Cost of Disruption

$\dfrac{\text{Staff x Salary}}{\text{Days x Hours}}$	=	Cost per hour		
$\dfrac{40 \times 20,000}{200 \times 8}$	=	$500/hour		
Potential Annual Loss	=	$75,000 per year		
1 hour of disruption + Backlog Effect	=	6 x $500	=	$3,000
1 day of disruption + Backlog Effect	=	48 x $500	=	$24,000
Therefore, 3 days of disruption per year	=	$72,000 a year		

This second calculation seems like confirmation at first glance, but we should realize that:

The total financial impact is actually   A+ B + ???

The first calculation was about *income* and the second one was about *overhead*. Under normal business conditions, the income covers the overhead with a small margin which is the profit. The positive covers the negative. During a disruption, the income is lost but the overhead continues unabated. This is a double whammy situation – a negative income combined with negative overhead amounts to a large financial impact.

These simple calculations are the obvious, easy to identify items which form the visible "tip of the iceberg." However, other deeper parts are even more significant. The additional areas to be considered will probably be specific to your particular business and marketplace.

What else might affect the profitability or soundness of your company? Consider the potential consequential losses. If they are not easily measured, they are unlikely to be covered by insurance. If they are not easy to anticipate, they are probably outside the scope of your insurance.

4.5.2 Invisible Costs

The *invisible costs*, which are notoriously difficult to evaluate are, perhaps, the most expensive of all. By their very nature, they are unrecoverable and they affect the business in an insidious manner which renders them virtually unrecognizable.

The *invisible assets*, which are subject to these invisible losses, are those intangibles which add to the value of the business but do not appear on the balance sheet, such as:

▸ **Cost of opportunity.** The costs associated with the opportunity to do business are rarely taken into account in our contingency plans, although they are commonly quite significant.

▸ **Goodwill.** Goodwill is generally a value assigned to the reputation of an organization in the marketplace, above and beyond the value of physical assets. It becomes a consideration in mergers and acquisitions.

▸ **Corporate image.** Similar to goodwill, relating to brand and perception – the corporate identity as perceived by the public.

> **Awareness precedes action, but it is understanding that precipitates action.**

These "invisibles" can take a long time before they evidence themselves as costs or losses, which may place them outside of the finite indemnity period of your insurance coverage. However, even if they were within the time period they are probably outside the scope of coverage due to their elusive nature which makes them virtually impossible to describe, to measure, and to predict. Such "black swans" are more or less uninsurable.

A famous example of such an "invisible cost" was when Gerald Ratner wiped £500 million from the value of his jewelry company, Ratners Group, with a remark he made on 23 April 1991. In a speech at the Institute of Directors, he described one of his cheap products as "total crap." He resigned in 1992, and the name of the company was changed to Signet Group in 1993 (Doing a Ratner, 2007). Yet his company had the most advanced BC and DR plans in place. They even arranged to have two separate data systems running in parallel during the run up to Christmas when they were at their busiest.

4.6   Investment Wisdom

Investment wisdom is the term I use to describe the rationale behind any capital expenditure. Top managers are cautious about spending capital unless they can perceive a worthwhile return on that investment. In contingency planning, as in many other fields of endeavor, a 90% rule is in operation. For almost any area of risk, it is possible to achieve 90% protection at a reasonable cost, using standard basic measures. To achieve a higher degree of assurance, one has to resort to a higher level of protection, which can involve an unreasonable cost. For example, one can make the computer room secure by making it "invisible" at a very low cost, simply by specifying no windows and no identifying signage. Sensible locks and restricted access will also enhance security up to the 90% level. However, to go beyond the 90% protection level, one has to either go for sophisticated access control systems or begin to address security for the whole building or site.

A simple principle applies to any BC program: Awareness precedes action, but it is understanding that precipitates action.

The first step has to be some form of risk identification, or assessment, followed up with a formal report which is circulated among the senior executives or, at least, comes to their attention.

4.7   Defensive Measures

It is necessary for you to establish exactly what the risks are, identify appropriate defensive measures, and prioritize those measures. Some costs and additional effort will be involved, although the full implications may be the subject of a further review which looks at those specific measures your executives decide to consider as the most likely solution to the problems you have highlighted.

There are three types of defense to consider:

- Protective measures.
- Recovery services.
- Contingency plans.

The sequence in which these measures are implemented depends to a large extent upon the results of the investigation into the current risks – once an Achilles' heel has been revealed, it becomes easier to identify the most realistic and effective strategy for defensive action. As these three types of defense are interdependent, it is obvious that attention must be paid to all of them before true business resilience can be expected.

There are as many causes as there are disasters, as each one is a unique combination of events and circumstances. However, it is possible to categorize them into broad groups which may help to make them more comprehensible.

Nevertheless it must be recognized that contingency measures must be designed to cope with the effects, irrespective of the causes.

4.7.1   Causes of Business Interruption

The major groupings of causes are:

Natural hazards – those in which no one can be blamed or bear responsibility.

Man-made hazards – those in which someone could be held responsible for contributing to the event, or events, which caused the disaster, whether by intent, neglect, or accident.

Deliberate man-made hazards – those in which someone is to be blamed for intentionally allowing or causing events to happen which contribute to the disaster.

Accidental man-made hazards – those where it is reasonable to suppose that ignorance or incompetence, rather than an evil intention, was behind the action, actions, or lack of action, which led to the disaster.

Natural Hazards

- Storm damage
- Flood
- Subsidence
- Lightning
- Snow bound
- Frost damage

Man-Made Hazards (Accidental)

- Operator error
- Explosion
- Fire
- Fire extinguisher discharge
- Water leaks

Man-Made Hazards (Deliberate)

- Break-in
- Fraud
- Arson
- Strike
- Riot
- Vandalism
- Bomb damage
- Bomb hoax

Man-Made Hazards (Indirect)

- Power failure
- Telecommunications failure
- Smoke damage
- Floods from fire fighting

4.7.2 Effects, Symptoms, and Consequences

Basic Effects

To review an important point made earlier, there are six basic effects which can have disastrous consequences:

1. Loss of Access.
2. Loss of People.
3. Loss of Supplies.
4. Loss of Communication.
5. Loss of Function.
6. Loss of Data.

Symptoms

The perceived symptoms might be such signs as loss or lack of:

- Access.
- Environment.
- Personnel (temporary loss).
- Control.
- System function.
- Communication.
- Data.
- Data integrity.

Consequences

Secondary effects or consequences would include:

- Interrupted cash flow.
- Loss of image.
- Brand damage.
- Loss of market share.
- Lower morale.
- Loss of staff.
- Costs of repair.
- Costs of recovery.
- Penalty charges.

These lists are not necessarily exhaustive, but they do give a fair indication of what you might need to consider.

4.8 QwikRisk

QwikRisk is a simple and quick tool for you to analyze risks and bring them to the attention of your top management to gain their support. It is carried out as a group activity in which you will be acting as the facilitator. (For background on QwikRisk, see the note at the end of this chapter.)

This exercise can lead the group to identify a suitable handling strategy based on… each type of risk.

4.8.1 The Four Risk Groups

The facilitator starts the facilitation by explaining to the executive group that risk has two principal dimensions – probability (P) or likelihood, and impact (I) or cost. You can illustrate these two dimensions and their relationships by drawing a couple of lines, or arrows, on a flipchart or a whiteboard. You can go on to explain, "If we plot our perceived risks against probability and impact, we can determine the severity." This exercise can lead the group to identify a suitable handling strategy based on the intrinsic characteristics of each type of risk.

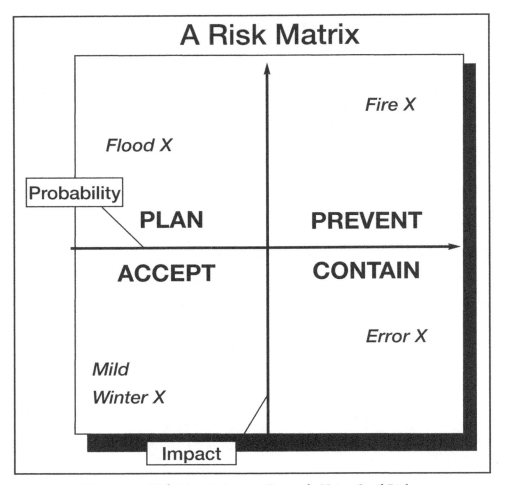

Figure 4-1. Risk Matrix Output Example Using QwikRisk

Figure 4-1 is an example of the output generated by this approach. There will be four groups of risk emerging from this process:

1. High Probability/High Impact
2. High Probability/Low Impact
3. Low Probability/High Impact
4. Low Probability/Low Impact

4.8.2   The Four Strategies

So the four strategies are:

1. Prevent
2. Accept
3. Contain
4. Plan (for)

4.8.3 Matching the Risk with the Strategy

▶ Risks which are deemed to be *high probability and high impact* should be *prevented*. This means you should implement preventative measures. The cost of this approach is justified because this type of risk is likely to happen and it would be very costly if it did occur.

▶ Risks which are *low probability and low impact* can be *accepted* because they are unlikely to happen and even if they did they would not seriously affect the business.

▶ Risks with a *high probability but low impact* can be expected to occur on a reasonably frequent basis, but they do not have major impact on the business. Because of their frequency we must address them, but there is no need to go so far as to prevent them. The solution is to arrange for *containment* measures which can help us to recognize them and stop them from getting out of hand.

▶ Finally, we have a number of risks that are *low probability but high impact*. Because of their low frequency, it is not worth implementing expensive preventative or complex containment measures, yet we do need to be prepared to deal with them as they could prove to be very costly. Therefore, these are the kind of events for which we should be developing *continuity and recovery plans*.

You can capture the output from this exercise and include it as a diagram in the body of your report. Alternatively, you could just refer to the four groupings and list the concerns under the appropriate activity headings with a short comment on how the four groupings are derived and how the results were developed.

4.9 SMARTRisk

As a regular member of what used to be the Risk and Audit Committee of the Business Continuity Institute (BCI), I was involved in the development of *SMARTRisk* (the Small to Medium Assessment of Real Threats risk assessment and reporting method), a simple means of recognizing and reporting operational risks within an organization. We were looking for a method which could easily convey its essential messages to the directorate. The method also needed to be suitable for use in a small- to medium-sized company where governance and risk management is usually practiced by those who are reliant upon a sound, sensible technique to achieve their aims in this regard. Being a global membership organization, we also needed to have an approach which was transparent and easy to translate.

Subsequently the Risk and Audit Committee has been superseded by the Risk and Governance Committee, but it has retained the SMARTRisk method as the basis of its ongoing risk audit and review procedure. The method has also been adopted by a number of BCI members for use in their own professional practice. The feedback has been very positive: people around the world have found the system easy to understand, simple to use, and effective as a means of communication.

Some users have also introduced various degrees of automation into the process, but this book focuses on the original manual method. Personally, I believe that unsophisticated pen and pencil methods add an extra degree of involvement and understanding compared to automated methods, where the calculations tend to be invisible. I think visibility of the number crunching adds weight to the result in the mind of the researcher which communicates itself in the presentation.

Automation comes in various forms which range from using a spreadsheet to capture the basic information up to specialized software which transfers the entered data straight into a visual display revealing past, current, and possible future results.

4.9.1   Key Features of SMARTRisk

The main features of the SMARTRisk methodology are:

» The risk calculation process allows the results to be displayed on a graph which separates degrees of concern using straight lines.

» Risks are classified according to a scheme which is derived from the Australian Standard AS 4360, Risk Management.

» It uses red, amber, and green coloring to indicate the level of concern. This is commonly referred to as the RAG coding system.

» It uses a limited range of whole numbers which makes it easy to follow.

Risk assessment is generally accepted to be a combination of three factors:

1. Level of threat or probability.
2. Level of harm or impact.
3. Degree or extent of mitigation measures which are in place to avoid the risk or manage its consequences.

> **...we multiply the mitigation factor by itself to produce a... balanced view of risk.**

It is normal practice to multiply the factors for probability and impact in order to determine the risk potential or the level of perceived danger. Mitigation, however, is one-dimensional, which results in a much smaller range of numbers. In the SMARTRisk system, we multiply the mitigation factor by itself to produce a number which is in the same range as the risk potential. This gives us a balanced view of risk.

By dividing the risk potential by the mitigation factor we end up with a final risk score. Where the mitigation exceeds the potential, the final score will be a number less than one, and that is our aim with all risks. If the final score is higher than one, we classify that as a danger which requires special attention. A score of less than one is classified as acceptable, which calls for regular management. If the score is below 0.5, we classify that as a risk which is under control and warrants occasional monitoring.

When investigating and evaluating the risk factors, we stick to whole numbers in the range from 1.0 to 5.0. This results in a range of results running from a minimum of zero up to a maximum of 25, which can be represented easily on a small graph. It also ensures that we end up with a simple target of keeping the final scores below 1.0.

For the purpose of good governance, the SMARTRisk method covers the full range of normal business operations by reference to the 12 areas of business risk as defined in the Risk Management Standard ISO 31000.

4.9.2   Output of the SMARTRisk Process

The output takes two forms:

» Risk register.
» Risk map.

The *risk register* gives full details of the threats as they are perceived by the owners of the various operations. It is a record which reflects the views of the owner when interviewed by the investigators. The owner describes the risk in his or her own terms, and then evaluates the probability and likely impact on a scale of 1 to 5. After that, the owner describes the mitigation measures which are in place before coming up with a mitigation score. The investigator multiplies the figures to produce a risk score which is then compared with previous results to gauge progress. The *risk map* is a simple graphic display of the risks in a format which indicates the current situation and highlights areas of concern.

Having two people conduct the interview gives a more rounded view, and it is also a valuable means of ensuring that all the team members are up to speed with the technique.

Soon after the introduction of SMARTRisk, the BCI board of directors called for the resulting risk map to be updated and presented at every board meeting to provide a "heads up" on the current situation. This means each meeting can begin with a quick snapshot of where the organization stands and explain the situation to any new directors or visitors.

Although the SMARTRisk methodology was developed with a small company in mind, it has been employed effectively in a number of large international corporations. In particular, the resultant SMARTRisk map has been welcomed as a useful tool which can provide top management with a snapshot view of the current status and progress in regard to major risks.

> **Your report needs to break through these barriers of complacency and generate a positive response...**

A full description of SMARTRisk, complete with templates for the risk register and the risk map, can be found in the **Business Continuity Toolkit**.

4.10   Risk Reporting

No matter how you go about investigating the risks and threats to your business, it is almost certain that you will uncover some potential problems which should be addressed. In the past, these gremlins may have simply been ignored or people have assumed their luck was invincible. Another possibility is a general consensus regarding the inevitability or a sustained belief that there are no affordable solutions to these rather unlikely problems. The most common form of ostrich thinking is based on the idea of it being someone else's responsibility. Perhaps they feel it is the government's duty to help them out or maybe it is "some other department" that should be worrying about such imponderable issues.

Your report needs to break through these barriers of complacency and generate a positive response; so don't pull your punches, but don't stray from the truth or make any statements which you cannot substantiate. Include some potential solutions to the problems you have highlighted, preferably with a range of choices so that decision-makers can select what they perceive to be the best choice. If you offer only one option, it might simply be accepted or rejected, but if you offer three or four, then the odds are in favor of readers discussing them before making a rational selection, and it is unlikely they will choose the wrong one, providing you give them enough data.

For best results, your report needs to explain the merits and drawbacks of each tentative solution, including those which you don't really expect, or want, them to choose. You may need to be patient as you await the budget to support their choice, but then Rome was not built in a single day.

Self-Examination Questions

1. In considering risk as it applies to business continuity (BC), which of the following threats do you need to be concerned with?
   A. Only those threats that are specific to your department, location, or region, as defined by your job description as a BC manager.
   B. Only those threats that are likely to result in one of the six disruptive scenarios described in Chapter 1 (loss of access, people, supplies, communication, function, or data).
   C. All possible threats to your company, as identified in your corporate risk-assessment report.

2. What is one of the main problems with quantitative risk assessment?
   A. Reliable statistics are difficult to gather and may not be accurate predictors of future problems.
   B. Rating "cost of absence" or "cost of loss" is not a useful quantitative method.
   C. Making comparative estimates produces qualitative rather than quantitative data.

3. What is the purpose of grid impact analysis in a BC context?
   A. To analyze the flow of information through the business for the purpose of identifying where information bottlenecks may occur
   B. To map how money flows through the organization for the purposes of understanding how different levels of financial support affect the organization's different components
   C. To analyze all flows (e.g., of information, cash, people) through a business for the purposes of identifying the critical components of the business

4. Common hazards, regular chances, and random perils are three categories of
   A. appetite for risk.
   B. enterprise risk.
   C. nontransferable risk.

5. If one of a business's key systems (e.g., information technology, production facilities, product delivery) becomes disrupted, the effective cost of that disruption equals
   A. the cost of the disruption per unit of time.
   B. the cost of the disruption per unit of time minus any savings from not operating the disrupted system per unit of time.
   C. the cost of the disruption per unit of time plus the cost of repairing the disruption.

6. Which of the following costs are unrecoverable and perhaps the most expensive of all?
   A. Costs of absence
   B. Invisible costs
   C. Penalty costs

7. For which of the following risk groups is a containment strategy appropriate?
   A. High probability/low impact
   B. Low probability/high impact
   C. Low probability/low impact

8. When you submit a risk report to top management, what is the most effective way of breaking through complacency about risk and persuading leaders to address identified risks?
   A. Keep it simple: identify one major risk and offer one clear, incontrovertible solution to the problem.
   B. Give them a wake-up call: identify as many risks as possible and state in the strongest possible terms why each risk must be addressed immediately.
   C. Give them choices: identify the risks you have detected and offer options for addressing each risk, explaining the merits and drawbacks of each potential solution.

Food for Thought

This chapter has taken you on a short guided tour of the ways in which you might approach a risk assessment project as part of the build-up towards establishing a BC program. It is also possible that you may be asked to carry out this type of work in connection with an existing program, in which case you may be expected only to review and update the current risk register. In either case, you need to make sure that you feel comfortable with this important aspect of the work.

As in previous episodes of Food for Thought, I should like you to apply your mind to a real or imaginary situation in which you are the BC manager and you are contemplating the establishment of a BC program. Assume that you have a free hand, and think about how you would set about assessing the risks within the various departments of your organization.

It is also worth considering that many organizations will already have a risk manager or a risk management department in place. Most managers will already be familiar with monitoring and managing risks. Your communication skills will come into play leading the company to the best risk solution without stepping on too many toes.

Exercises

1. Choose which risk assessment tools or techniques you would want to employ.
   - ❯ What is the reasoning behind that choice?
   - ❯ Would you want to employ more than one?
     - ⌄ When and why would you use different methods?

2. Develop an outline schedule for conducting a full BC risk assessment.
   - ❯ What are the steps involved and how long do you think it might take?
   - ❯ Who will need to be involved?
   - ❯ How much of their time will you occupy?
   - ❯ How will you ensure their cooperation?

3. Decide how the results will be reported or published.
   - ❯ What is the scope of the audience?
   - ❯ What restrictions would you, or should you, impose?

4. Consider the longer term in regard to risks and BC.
   - ❯ How often should the results be reviewed?
   - ❯ How will you go about these reviews?
   - ❯ How do you ensure the program doesn't falter?

5. Address opposing or differing views.
   - ❯ Do you propose to liaise with the risk manager or is this something separate?
   - ❯ How will you deal with those who resist or wish to avoid your risk assessment?

Looking Forward

You should now be in a position to find out whether there really is a need for BC within your organization. You should also be ready to begin sharing that result with your colleagues and enlist their support.

Think about what should and could motivate these people to offer you their support and active participation.

Armed with a basic knowledge of the potential threats to your organization, you can move on in the next chapter to develop a deeper understanding of what is needed and wanted to ensure continuity within your business.

Downloadable Business Continuity Toolkit

From the **Business Continuity Toolkit**, you can download questionnaires to assist you in conducting an assessment, as well as more information about SMARTRisk, examples of its use, and templates you can adapt to present your findings.

References

"Doing a Ratner" and other famous gaffes (22 Dec. 2007). *The Telegraph*. Retrieved from
    http://www.telegraph.co.uk/news/uknews/1573380/Doing-a-Ratner-and-other-famous-gaffes.html

Financial Reporting Council (2012). *The UK corporate governance code*. London, UK: Financial Reporting Council.

For Additional Reading

Bernstein, P. (1998). *Against the gods: The remarkable story of risk*. New York, NY: John Wiley & Sons.

Burroughs, G. (Q2 2012). How thorough is your risk assessment. *Continuity: Magazine of the Business Continuity Institute*. Retrieved from http://www.bcifiles.com/Q22012.pdf, p. 38.

Committee of Sponsoring Organizations of the Treadway Commission (COSO), (2004). *Enterprise risk management – integrated summary: Executive summary*. Retrieved from
    http://www.coso.org/documents/COSO_ERM_ExecutiveSummary.pdf

Engemann, K. & Henderson, D. (2012). *Business continuity and risk management: Essentials of organizational resilience*. Brookfield, CT: Rothstein Publishing.

Graham, J. & Kaye, D. (2006). *A risk management approach to business continuity*. Brookfield, CT: Rothstein Publishing.

Hiles A. (Ed.). (2011). *The definitive handbook of business continuity management* (3rd ed.). Chichester, West Sussex, UK: John Wiley & Sons.

Praxiom Research Group Limited (2015). *ISO 31000 2009 translated into plain English*. Retrieved from
    http://www.praxiom.com/iso-31000.htm

Note: I developed *QwikRisk* as a way to develop outline risk strategies in the early 80s when I was working for IBM. The name is entirely original, although I derived the technique from a decision-making tool in common use at the time. When I joined SafetyNet, I developed and delivered its PlanStart customer training course, which included a session on QwikRisk. In 1995, I incorporated QwikRisk into the "A to Z of Business Continuity" training course I developed and delivered internationally. Since then, I have used the title and technique in my own consultancy work. About 3,500 students around the world can bear witness to my claim to be the originator of the method and the title. – Jim Burtles Hon FBCI

5

Impacts and Consequences

Business impact analysis (BIA) is a unique process which is at the very heart of business continuity (BC) management. Building on the risk analysis, BIA is all about evaluating the impact to the business of potential losses in meaningful, quantitative, and qualitative terms. The ability to conduct a proper BIA for an organization is considered by most professionals to be one of the most important aspects of BC practice. No other profession or trade carries out this type of work, which provides us with an in-depth understanding of the health and welfare of all the core activities that make up a business operation.

This chapter will help you to:

- ☑ Recognize how risk analysis relates to BIA.

- ☑ Understand the role of BIA in creating a BC program.

- ☑ Become familiar with a range of analytical techniques.

- ☑ Conduct a dependency modeling exercise to gain valuable insights.

- ☑ Use BIA results to help form BC strategies and plans.

During the risk assessment stage you will have gained an understanding of how the business functions and gained insight into its core functions. Now it is time to visit the people who work within those functions and discover what really makes the business operations tick, in a process that is generally known as BIA. Over the years, I have developed a number of subsidiary techniques or variations on the theme which I will be sharing with you in this chapter.

5.1   From Risk to Impact

So far in this book, we have looked at how and why you would initiate and launch a BC program. Now we are going to look at what many regard as the most important stage of the whole process, the stage that completes the first phase of your learning. It is time to consider the implications of the risks which you looked at in Chapter 4. An analysis of the impacts and their consequences will enable you to discover where BC is needed and what it should offer.

Continuity plans... reduce the extent of that exposure by enabling key business operations to be resumed in time...

As the focus changes, so does the language. What were *risks* or *threats* in the previous chapter now become *exposures to loss* and *dormant difficulties*. In the last chapter you looked at risk assessment, which was about identifying what might threaten your critical functions. In effect, this enabled you to locate potential troubles and demonstrate the need for BC. Now you need to understand the full business implications in order to develop suitable response strategies and put together practical recovery plans. Such analysis means you have to dig a bit deeper; much of what we would like to know from a BC perspective can be hidden, vague, or uncertain.

BIA takes a fairly thorough look at the business operation using techniques and processes which are unique to BC. Your aim is to work out what harm can be done if the unexpected should occur and what that will mean in the longer term. Armed with this sort of knowledge, you can then start to prepare effective plans which address the real issues.

5.1.1   Disruption Scenarios

Because of the innate complexity of this specialized area of investigation and the variability between the many diverse environments where BIA has been used, a number of differing approaches have been used. These techniques range from relatively simple to highly complex. To begin, this book will take you through the area on a gradient, starting with an explanation of what you are trying to do and why.

For example, regular fire drills, like risk assessments, are commonly used and understood. However, less commonly understood is fire exposure analysis (FEA), an advanced look at the same area which aims to prove much more useful. While you might describe a standard office fire drill as the foundation course, an FEA is the equivalent of an advanced graduate course. Although FEA has often been used in a BC context to raise awareness, it is more relevant to *emergency evacuation planning* (Burtles, 2014).

Basically, an FEA sets out to capture the cost to the business of a serious fire, which is the common cause of disruption. You can do this by estimating the commercial value of all the information and work in progress which would be lost. The method involves a spot check on the destruction, loss, or damage of current paperwork. When this process is carried out as part of a regular fire drill, a truly representative result can be obtained.

In preparation for the development of BC plans and procedures, you need to capture information about the character of the business operations, what they might require, and the timeframes to which they work. The term *impact* is used because you are trying to discover what immediate losses you might suffer and have to deal with. *Consequences* are those awful longer-term possibilities that BC seeks to prevent or at least contain.

Whenever one of the disruptive scenarios occurs, the business suffers a *loss exposure*, i.e., it is exposed to the possibility of a loss. That might be a loss of opportunity through being unavailable, or it may be a financial loss through incurred costs or impeded transactions. Continuity plans and measures seek to reduce the extent of that exposure by enabling key business operations to be resumed in time to contain the effects. So you need to establish which operations are critical, what their recovery timeframes are, and what is required within those timeframes.

5.1.2   Team Involvement

Another useful aspect of carrying out a BIA is the opportunity to engage with people throughout the business, expose what you are doing, solicit their support, and engage them in the process. It is a useful tool for embedding BC into the business culture although that is not its primary purpose.

Previous chapters looked at the type of people with whom you need to work and the roles they should play, and discussed the formation of a team structure for response and recovery. It is during this analysis stage that you will get to meet the people who work at the coalface or closest to the frontline. This is your opportunity to identify those individuals who are best placed and suited to populate your response and recovery teams.

5.2   Business Impact Analysis Project

One way of looking at this whole BC program is to compare it with the creation of a landscape painting. The aim, in both cases, is to create an image which, from the customer's viewpoint, looks like the real thing. An artist will prepare by looking at the scene from several points of view to gain a true perspective and in the process will make a few pencil sketches of the features he, or she, wants to capture. Your equivalent of the artist's sketching stage is the analysis of the impacts and consequences. This is where you prepare for the creation of your masterpiece. It's how you can get a clear idea of what it is that you are trying to replicate or protect. To begin, look at the types of sketch you may wish to draw before you put brush to canvas.

> **BIA is a process by which you will identify and quantify the costs to the enterprise of the effect of a disaster or an emergency...**

- ▸ **BIA:** This is the quintessential BC process that you can use to establish the key parameters and dimensions that your BC plans and preparations will be based upon.
- ▸ **Facilitated BIA:** This analysis is a variant on the regular BIA process, which you may choose to use either as an introduction to the subject in order to develop an overview, or as your preferred method. Personal preference, location, and culture will influence your choice.
- ▸ **Dependency Modeling:** This structured method is a means of establishing the inter-functional relationships to help you select which functions should be included in your BIA.
- ▸ **Functional Analysis:** This analysis is another way of looking at interdependencies within the business by determining which functions are critical. Critical functions are those which require the protection provided by your BC measures.

To begin, explore each of these techniques in turn, starting with the regular BIA process, which is the basis of standard practice. Once you understand what each of them offers, you can select which ones suit you best. You can mix and match them in accordance with your needs and circumstances. At the end of the day, you will need to make sure you can demonstrate that you have been thorough in your approach.

5.2.1   Organizing the Project

BIA is all about evaluating the impact to the business of potential losses in meaningful, quantitative, and qualitative terms. Essentially, BIA is a process by which you will identify and quantify the costs to the enterprise of the effect of a disaster or an emergency – with results expressed in financial or non-financial terms. Most professionals consider the ability to conduct a proper BIA to be one of the most important aspects of BC practice. Indeed, the Business Continuity Institute (BCI) rates BIA as a very valuable core competence. The process described in this chapter is derived from the original 10 professional competencies as defined and agreed upon by the BCI (Business Continuity Institute, 2013).

For best results, your first step is to identify and obtain a *project sponsor*. Then, with that person's backing, you can move on to defining the objectives and scope for the BIA project. There are a number of considerations to be taken into account when you are just beginning to organize your BIA project.

- **Methodology.** You need to choose an appropriate BIA project planning methodology or tool. The choice will, to some extent, depend on the corporate culture, the scale of the operation, and your personal preferences. However, as it is primarily a *data collection* exercise, most people prefer to work with the simplest of tools which can offer flexibility and ease of use.

- **Communication.** You need to identify whose input you require and then inform the participants about the BIA project and its purpose. The initial communication should also explain how you propose to engage them in the project and the degree of commitment you expect.

- **Training.** You need to establish whether there is any need for training for those involved in the BIA project. If so, you need to set up a training schedule and ensure the training schedule is completed satisfactorily before moving on to the next stage.

- **Project leader.** It is also essential that the project leader has a sound understanding of the purposes and culture of the organization. Otherwise, you may need to reconsider the choice of project leader or engage him or her in some form of induction training.

- **Agreement.** You will need to obtain agreement with the project sponsor about the time scales and deliverables before embarking on the full data collection and reporting project.

5.2.2   Collection of Impact Data – Choice of Method

A number of methods can be used to gather the input for a BIA, but whatever method is used, senior management support is essential to guarantee the success of the process. The BIA process requires locating a great deal of information, much of which is not easily available because no one has looked at things in this way before. Thus, you may find that there are no convenient records for people to turn to and provide you with a fast response.

The most appropriate choice will again be dependent on those corporate factors of scale and culture, taking into account your own personal preference.

- You need to decide how you are going to collect your impact data from those who are involved in the running or management of the various business units or functions. Options include the use of questionnaires, interviews, workshops, or a combination.

- Whichever the collection method, you will need to agree how the potential impacts are going to be quantified. Because many of the operations or functions cannot really be gauged in purely monetary terms, bear in mind that *non-financial* measurements must be considered for this purpose.

- You will need to agree on what type of non-quantifiable impact information you are looking for and how you will evaluate it. This is where a good understanding of the business culture and its aims becomes a distinct asset. How do you judge a malfunction in meaningful terms?

- If you decide to make use of a questionnaire, then you will need to compile a list of questions and a set of completion instructions. Before you circulate the questionnaire, check it for style and content to ensure that the recipient, or user, has a clear idea of what you are looking for. It is well worth getting several opinions regarding ease of use and clarity of purpose.

- You will also need to settle on the analytical methods you intend to use. This could be a purely manual process, or you may elect to use some form of computer-based method to carry out the actual analysis. Some people make good use of spreadsheet tools such as Excel for this stage of the work.

You have the option of choosing from various ways of gathering the information you need as the input to your BIA. Each approach has its inherent advantages and disadvantages.

5.2.3   Data Collection via Questionnaires

At first sight, a standard questionnaire may seem to be the easiest way to gather the information, and it does have certain merits. However, the devil is in the details of how the process of distributing and collecting these questionnaires is handled. If you plan simply to send out a large form for everybody to fill in, you may be very disappointed with the result, since you are unlikely to get a 100% rate of return. Almost everybody will have better, or more urgent, things to do. There needs to be some sort of incentive to drive their cooperation. This might take the form of pressure from above, an understanding of the need coupled with an appreciation of the long-term benefits, or some kind of reward or acknowledgment system.

Considerations for the use of questionnaires include:

- Plan the design and contents of the questionnaires. The level of detail required will affect the style of questioning and the size of the document. If you fail to ask for enough detail, you will be working on assumptions or false premises. On the other hand, if you ask too many questions, or make them too complex, the results will be unreliable because people will tend to guess rather than spend time and effort researching the facts to provide precise answers.

- As you prepare to distribute and collect the questionnaires, provide a clear explanation of the purpose and your requirements to the participants, such as departmental managers. One way of handling this is to set up a series of local project kick-off meetings to distribute and explain the questionnaire. People will have the chance to ask questions and get a feel for what is expected of them, including the amount of work involved and the anticipated timeframes.

- Be ready to support respondents during their completion of questionnaires. Without this cooperation, they will either skip some of the difficult parts or provide the wrong answers due to their misunderstanding or ignorance.

- Review all of the completed questionnaires and identify those for which follow-up interviews will be required to obtain clarification or additional information. Then arrange for these follow-up discussions.

5.2.4   Data Collection via Interviews

A BIA interview will need to follow a standardized format for information collection; otherwise, you are not going to get a consistent picture. It is important that the interviewees are not rushed in verbalizing their answers. The core issue is to identify those critical functions which are truly vital to the business. It is on that basis that you are going to build your recovery strategy and tactics; so all the answers do need to be validated to some extent.

A good starting point is to interview those who are responsible for managing and maintaining the overall facilities and resources.

Interviewing individuals can be a very rigorous and time-consuming approach. However, it does inspire confidence in the final result because of its very thoroughness. In order to ensure an accurate impression, interview at least three people from each business unit or function. If you interview only one person, there is no way of knowing whether the result is skewed. If you get two very differing viewpoints, there is no way of knowing which is the more correct. When you bring in a third person, it is more likely that you will be able to judge where the truth lies.

> A structured interview is a very good way of gaining the necessary detailed information to complete the BIA.

> If the interviewees are not absolutely clear about the scope and purpose of the BIA interview, this could cause some potential reluctance to release the type of information you are looking for.

> Once you reassure all participants that the aim of the BIA is to protect business assets in the event of a business interruption, they will feel less threatened by the process and be more likely to give accurate information.

> Before you begin interviewing, pre-define the basic data to be collected and organize it into a logical sequence.

> Your initial interview notes will need to be reviewed and verified by the interviewee before they are incorporated into your analysis. This review ensures accuracy and clarity and provides an opportunity to spot any errors or misunderstandings.

> Allow time for some follow-up interviews if the initial analysis shows a need to clarify or add to the data already gathered.

Get the broad picture first and then focus on the more specific aspects of the individual business units or functions. A good starting point is to interview those who are responsible for managing and maintaining the overall facilities and resources. Because of their wide-ranging responsibilities, these initial interviews typically last a couple of hours. Once you have the broad picture, you can move on to look at the detail, setting it into context with the established background. Once again, the initial interview in each area of inquiry may cover a bit of contextual information before focusing on details. These primary interviews usually last around an hour, and the other cross-checking interviews should only take about 45 minutes. In between interviews, allow plenty of time to cross-check your notes and record the key messages and facts.

5.2.5   Business Impact Analysis Workshops

Bringing people together into a workshop environment is another way of collecting the information required for a BIA. The main advantage of this technique is that you can generate an immediate consensus of opinion through discussion. Furthermore, the debate – and subsequent cross-flow of ideas and opinions – tends to inspire a deeper perception of the more obscure aspects and implications of the business operation.

One disadvantage of the workshop approach is the challenge of getting all the key players together for several hours. In a large organization, it may not be possible to get everybody together at one time, which might mean running a whole series of such events.

Before embarking on a BIA workshop, or series of workshops, get a clear idea of what needs to be done and how you are going to make sure you get the result you are looking for.

> Develop a workshop agenda with timings and a clear set of objectives. If you don't know what you are trying to achieve – and stick to it – the workshop might get hijacked.

> Identify the appropriate level of management participation and get their agreement to take part. Without their willingness, you will not get very far.

> Someone, presumably you, will have to act as the facilitator and leader during the discussions. This does require the ability to manage an audience and steer them towards a conclusion. Ideally, you are looking for a unanimous opinion but might need to settle for compromise here and there. Consensus is often rather difficult where you have strong characters pulling in opposite directions, simply because of their different standpoints and conflicting responsibilities.

> Before closing and thanking everyone for their cooperation, make sure that the objectives of the workshop have been met.

> Outstanding issues should be identified and the responsibility for their resolution agreed, together with target dates.

With a few notable exceptions, the average response to any sort of questionnaire without any follow-up is likely to be low…

5.2.6   Combining Questionnaire, Workshop, and Interview Methods

You have seen that the various possibilities for data collection range from sending out a questionnaire, through running a workshop, to conducting a series of interviews. However, these are not mutually exclusive approaches. Each has its advantages and disadvantages, and perhaps a sensible blend can eliminate most of the drawbacks and profit from the combined benefits.

The most obvious improvement is to use the questionnaire as a tool to support your interview process. With a few notable exceptions, the average response to any sort of questionnaire without any follow-up is likely to be low, especially when some of the questions are not easy. A great deal of chasing and reminding is required to make a significant difference to the return rate. But the underlying principle of getting the answers to a standard set of specific questions is sound; so use the questionnaire as the basis for an interview which is, in effect, the follow-up. Send out the questionnaires in advance; book a date and time for the interview; go through the questions together.

The workshop can be used as a way of introducing the subject and the concepts to prepare the way for a more productive response at the interview stage. Such a kick-off event might simply be a platform for introducing the need for BC covering corporate policy, anticipated timeframes, and the expected benefits and outcomes. On the other hand, you may wish to engage attendees in exploring the subject together by carrying out a high-level facilitated BIA exercise as described in Section 5.4 in this chapter. The number and size of these kick-off events will need to be tailored to suit the scale and spread of the enterprise. Usually, you can get much better interaction with relatively small audiences.

5.3   Business Impact Analysis Report

Once the data has been collected and analyzed, it is time to prepare a BIA report detailing the initial impact findings and any issues which have been raised. Prominence should be given to the principal conclusions which should include:

- A list of the mission-critical activities (MCAs).
- Recovery point objectives (RPOs).
- Recovery time objectives (RTOs).
- Minimum acceptable level of business continuity (LBC).

Often, these findings are expressed collectively in terms of the tolerance threshold, stating the percentage of recovery or response that is required within a particular timeframe, e.g., "25% availability of resources and 100% of the data base is required within 12 hours with an 80% certainty."

- Initially, this report should be issued as a draft to all participating managers, requesting their feedback and corrections.
- Following this, review the management feedback and, where appropriate, revise findings accordingly or add to the outstanding issues.
- Where necessary, set up a workshop or meeting with the participating managers to discuss the initial findings.
- Ensure that the original findings are updated to reflect changes arising from these meetings.
- Prepare the final BIA report in accordance with the organization or house standards.
- Prepare and deliver a formal presentation of your BIA findings to peers and executive bodies, as appropriate.
- When you present your findings to senior management or executives, you have an obvious opportunity to enhance the profile of your project and demonstrate clearly the value of the work you have been doing.

5.3.1   Assessing the Effects of Disruption and Business Impact

Table 5-1 below shows the areas of consideration during a BIA investigation. It can be used as an *aide memoir* when conducting interviews or running workshops.

Table 5-1. Assessing Effect of Disruption

Effects Of Disruption	
Loss of assets: physical assets, information assets, intangible assets	
Disruption to the continuity of service and operations	
Violation of law/regulation	
Public perception	
Impact of Disruptions On Business	
Financial	Environmental
Customers & suppliers	Operational
Public relations/credibility	Personnel
Legal	Other resources
Regulatory requirements/considerations	

5.3.2   Determining Loss Exposure

Table 5-2 below covers the areas of concern in regard to loss exposure in the event of a malfunction or interruption of the normal business operations.

Table 5-2. Areas of Concern in Loss Exposure

Quantitative	Qualitative
Property loss	Human resources
Revenue loss	- Morale
Fines	- Confidence
Accounts receivable	- Loyalty
Accounts payable	- Social responsibility
Legal liability	Brand
Overtime	Image
Additional expenditure	Reputation

In the downloadable **Business Continuity Toolkit** you will find a generic questionnaire that you can use as the basis for your BIA interviews.

5.4   Facilitated Business Impact Analysis

The traditional BIA process is to interview the key players individually and then analyze their answers. An alternate approach can be useful to truly engage the participants in a rather more transparent process. Your choice of method is bound to be influenced, or determined, by the type and scale of the enterprise coupled with personal preferences.

Since managers are highly motivated to prevent such impacts, they…have a common interest in developing … the basis of a solution.

Impacts can occur in many ways and over various time scales. Some of the potential losses discussed in this chapter and previous chapters are difficult to quantify, while others are difficult to spot. All of these dangers are the concern of the regular management team. Since managers are highly motivated to prevent such impacts, they will have thought about these matters and have a common interest in developing a better understanding together with the basis of a solution.

5.4.1   Interactive Impact Modeling

An interactive impact modeling session is perhaps the most effective way of raising BC awareness together with the BIA process of identifying the business exposure to loss. It is a form of workshop involving the leaders of the core business processes.

Impact modeling is a three-stage process, which is orchestrated by you as the facilitator. As facilitator, you will need to arrange a suitable venue and a convenient date as well as persuade the right people to attend.

Stage 1

For each business process you ask the team members to consider and list what they perceive as the *dormant difficulties* – problems which could have a direct, or indirect, impact on the business. A checklist of generic problems may stimulate their Stage 1 thinking. You can use materials from the downloadable **Business Continuity Toolkit** to assist you in going through the stages.

Stage 2

Taking each dormant difficulty in turn, the team should then consider the tangible costs for various time scales. The concept of a business cycle may help them to qualify the appropriate time scales. A typical business cycle may be measured in days, hours, or even minutes, depending on the nature of the business and its trading environment. A short time scale would be one business cycle or less, a medium time scale would be several business cycles, and a long time scale would be many business cycles. The tangible costs would be such things as loss of profits, additional costs, accumulating overheads, backlogs, and extended credit.

At this point in your analysis, it is necessary to highlight only the areas and scales of these tangible costs. Your aim is to develop an overall picture rather than gather precise details.

Stage 3

Once your team has worked through the tangible costs, the team moves on to Stage 3, in which you ask them to consider the intangible costs for each dormant difficulty. Many of these intangibles may be difficult or impossible to quantify, and they may occur only over a long term. However, they do provide a valuable insight into the need to be prepared for all sorts of unknown problems.

You can record and present the output of all three stages in the form of a table. It is probably easier to manage if you use a separate sheet for each of the key business processes or operations. Personally, I print out a handful of worksheets and mount them on a clipboard at the start of the day's interviewing. The worksheet will look something like Table 5-3.

Table 5-3. Sample Worksheet for Impact Modeling

Process: Owner:		
Dormant Difficulties	**Tangible Costs**	**Intangible Costs**

5.4.2   Results of the Exercise

The output of the impact modeling presents a clear picture of the actual impacts on the business, both in terms of the potential problems and the probable costs. Ideally, the results of this exercise should be documented properly in a report which you distribute to all of the participants.

However, from a BC planner's perspective, you need to extend the investigation to determine:

- ‣ Which areas require protection.
- ‣ Degree of business tolerance.
- ‣ Minimum service levels acceptable to the business.

This type of information is elicited as you move forward in your planning by using the output from impact modeling as a starting point and pursuing the inquiry further to obtain consensus about the BC objectives and requirements.

5.4.3   Applying the Modeling Exercise to the BC Plan

A well-constructed BC plan requires a definition of what are known as the *mission-critical activities*, together with the *recovery point* and *recovery time objectives*. You also need agreement about the required *level of BC*. Naturally, you will need to make sure that these specialist terms are properly explained to the participants before they can realistically consider their dimensions. These parameters are particularly important in the development of disaster recovery plans, which address the recovery of systems and databases. Terms used to describe this process include:

> **When assessing the potential impact of a threat...all of these dependencies must be taken into account.**

Mission-critical activity (MCA): A critical operational or business support service, or product related activity which enables an organization to achieve its business objectives, taking into account seasonal trends and timing issues (Business Continuity Institute, 2013).

Recovery point objective (RPO): The point in time to which work should be restored following a BC incident which interrupts or disrupts an organization.

Recovery time objective (RTO): The timescale in which mission-critical activities must be recovered.

Level of business continuity (LBC): The minimum level of continued output of products or services acceptable to an organization in achieving its business objectives.

Once you ensure that these terms have been explained and understood, the facilitator can get the participants to express their opinions on these issues. As soon as they have voiced their initial opinions and explained why they have reached their particular conclusions, it should not be too difficult to come to an agreement about each of these parameters.

Another approach to applying the model to the BC plan would be to engage the same team in a *functional analysis* during which they are asked to build a model of the functional relationships from which you can then determine the type of information you need to develop your BC strategies and plans. The functional analysis method is described later in this chapter in section 5.6.

5.5   Dependency Modeling

The aim of a BIA is to identify the critical business functions and understand their relationships in order that appropriate measures or controls can be devised and put into place to ensure these functions can remain operational. By doing this, an organization can prevent any business interruption from impacting upon services to its clients.

When assessing the potential impact of a threat to an organization, it is vital that all of its *dependencies* and connections have been plotted and agreed upon. In order to understand the impact profile of the organization, all of these dependencies must be taken into account.

In the downloadable **Business Continuity Toolkit**, you will find details of *dependency modeling* analysis. In this useful extension to the overall BIA process, you work with your interviewees to develop a picture of how their operation depends upon others, and vice versa. Basically, it is a way of looking at the business connections, their relationships, and dependencies. In a large or complex organization, this extra level of detail can prove to be helpful when you start to look at developing practical plans and solutions. Additional research on the interdependencies between departments, systems, and processes is worth the effort, since it will not only help your BC plan but will also give management valuable data for improved decision-making (Asnar, Y. & Giorgini, P., 2008).

5.5.1   Creating the Dependency Model

By using the type of dependency model shown in Figure 5-1 below, all the connections of an organization can be established, and the criticality of its business functions established.

The dependency analysis process requires an interactive discussion between the analyst and those responsible for managing or overseeing the core functions of the business. During that discussion, each of the suggested areas should be investigated. You should be aware of, and remain alert for, the possibility that some functions may have dependencies and connections which are not shown here.

When analyzing dependencies, it is vital that sufficient depths of detail are obtained and all dependencies taken into account. In order to achieve this, the dependency model can be adapted to a variety of levels. It can be used for an overview of the organization as a whole, or to provide detail at a business function or process level.

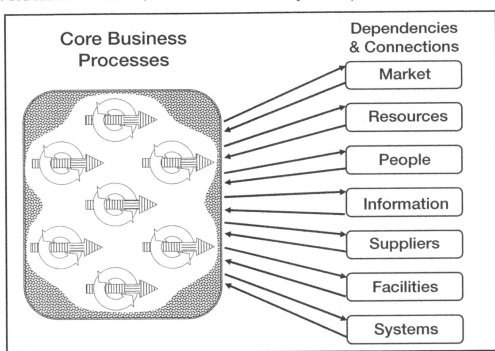

Figure 5-1. Determining Dependencies and Connections to Core Business Processes

5.5.2   Identifying Criticalities

A detailed analysis may reveal that certain processes within a function are less critical than others with different recovery profiles based on their criticality. Therefore, simply because a business function is critical, it does not necessarily follow that all of the processes within that function will be critical, too.

In order to measure the criticality of a business process, figures relating to financial loss are typically used. However, there are many areas of loss, both tangible and intangible. Every organization's culture and its approach to risk management will differ based on its rating of critical business functions. For example, some organizations place reputation as their most important asset and will not tolerate any damage to it.

In this context, a *tangible impact* means something which might cause one of the three *physical* disruptions which we mentioned in Chapter 1 (see 1.4.1 The Six Essential Elements). For example, any threats to the health and safety of people would lead to their withdrawal from service. You may also lose their services due to travel difficulties, a strike, or civil disturbances in the area.

Other tangible impacts include the loss of supplies due to fire, flood, or theft. Earthquakes, storms, explosions, or riots could have a similar effect. You could also lose the ability to either receive or deliver goods and services. Of course, damage to the building or its facilities is another factor which you need to take into account.

Intangible impacts refer to the effects of so called *technical* disruptions such as the loss, or perhaps the corruption, of functioning equipment, communication services, or important data which are often caused by, or associated with, a *physical* disruption.

The secondary or unintended effects will include possible breaches of standards, regulations, or legislation especially within well-regulated industries. In some cases, this could lead to the loss of license to trade, although this might be an extreme. Other secondary effects include threats or damage to the brand, image, and reputation of the organization. All of these disruptive scenarios are liable to lead to some form of financial damage unless the situation is handled properly. The financial effect is most commonly and easily recognized because finances can be measured and compared in accurate and meaningful terms.

You can expand on this definition to provide a more refined model to allow for varying degrees of criticality.

When reporting the results, it usually helps to include a graphic image of the relationships in your report or presentation, enabling the reader to actually see what you mean. Otherwise, your readers might find themselves struggling with unfamiliar words and phrases, or familiar words in an unfamiliar context.

5.6   Five Step Functional Analysis

A functional analysis exercise is a relatively straightforward way of getting common agreement among the executive staff of what is critical and why it is critical. The process is run as a workshop activity among the executives, with representatives from all of the main business functions.

There are five steps to the process:

1. Agree upon the definition of a critical function.
2. Agree upon the functional drivers.
3. Develop and agree upon the main functions.
4. Develop and agree upon relationships for each of the functional drivers.
5. Agree upon their criticality according to the definition from step 1.

Your aim is to reach agreement at the end of each step before moving on to the next part of the process. This approach ensures progress without the need for continuous reiteration and argument.

The definition of a critical function can be agreed upon by proposing a self-evident definition and ensuring that everyone understands and accepts the definition. During these discussions, the wording may need to be revised to suit the circumstances, preconceived notions, and the culture of the organization. You might consider including your initial draft definition in, or with, the invitation to participate in the analysis.

5.6.1   Define the Critical Function

Your initial definition could be something like: *A critical function is one which performs an essential service in satisfying the core needs of the business, i.e., its output or service is required on a frequent or permanent basis, and delays are not acceptable.*

You can expand on this definition to provide a more refined model to allow for varying degrees of criticality. You might, for example, identify two or three levels of criticality, each with its own set of priorities and considerations based on its relationship with other functions.

All of the critical functions would meet the basic definition as above, but further analysis might reveal them to be highly critical or even super critical in some cases. The distinction between these different categories would be the way in which they serve or interrelate with some (or all) of the other critical functions.

A *super critical* function would be one whose services are essential to the long-term success of the business. We are talking here about the absolute showstopper. For example, the absence of such a super critical function might incur a loss of the license to operate, impose a serious health risk, or cause an infringement of the law. Another way of defining a super critical function would be because it serves several critical functions.

Any function upon which a super critical function depends has to be regarded as highly critical because of its relationship with the super critical function.

Highly critical functions would in turn have their own dependencies. Functions providing essential services to a highly critical function must at least be critical. If they serve a number of highly critical functions then they should also be regarded as highly critical.

Here we are only concerned with the essential service contributions to the dependent function. We are not concerned with subsidiary or minor contributions.

By the end of this first step you should have reached a consensus about the definition(s) of critical functions in the context of your organization.

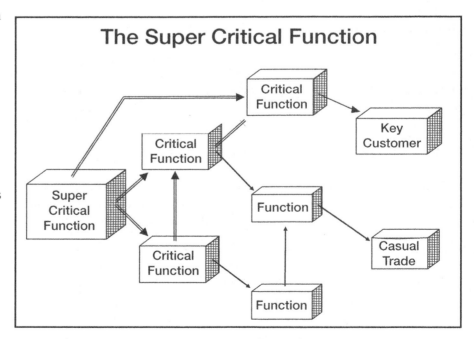

Figure 5-2. Determining Critical Functions

5.6.2   Agree on the Functional Drivers

The *functional drivers* are those forces which contribute to the fulfilment of the core purpose or mission of the business. They are unique to each organization, and so it is essential that they be defined and agreed upon as part of this process.

However, you can suggest a typical set of such drivers as the basis of your discussion. A few suggestions will give the participants a better idea of what you are looking for. Then they can modify and improve on somebody else's ideas rather than have to develop their own from scratch. Modification and adaptation are so much easier than original invention.

> **...functional drivers – the invisible forces driving the business towards its destination.**

These basic drivers can be summarized as:

1. *Cash-flow* – contributing to the income or profitability of the company.
2. *Service* – the ability to meet the expectations of customers.
3. *Operations* – the capability to sustain normal operations.
4. *Image* – the public perception or image of the function, the company, and its products or services within the marketplace.
5. *Compliance* – complying with the rules and regulations which are imposed by regulators, legislation, or corporate policy.

Naturally these typical functional drivers may need to be modified or refined to suit the nature of your particular business and style of operation. Almost certainly, there will be concerns about cash-flow and prudent controls in any emergency situation.

After some discussion, you should reach agreement about these functional drivers – the invisible forces driving the business towards its destination.

5.6.3   Agree on the Main Business Functions

Once you have agreed on the four or five main functional drivers, it is time to consider the main functions and plot them on a whiteboard or a flip chart. From the key function selection list in the downloadable **Business Continuity Toolkit**, highlight all of those functions which correspond roughly to the identifiable key departments or business units in your enterprise.

Don't be too keen to eliminate the less important ones at this stage, because their true importance is due to their interactions with other functions. That importance will become apparent when you see how the business drivers work through the organization.

Bear in mind that this is largely a visual process; you are trying to build a picture of how the critical parts of the business function in relation to each other. You are principally concerned with the relationships and interdependencies rather than the inner workings of the functions themselves.

▸ It is a kind of logic map; it doesn't need to be geographically correct.

▸ Distances are irrelevant and relationships come later – so the components can go anywhere for the time being.

▸ Although there may be a dozen or more main functions, it is likely that you will identify only about half a dozen really critical functions.

▸ Plotting the way in which the functional drivers act between these core functions will help to identify which of them are truly critical.

The important thing at this stage is for all the participants to be happy that all of the main functions have been included in this preliminary picture.

5.6.4   Identify the Functional Relationships

The next stage of this analysis is to plot the way in which the functional drivers act between the various functions.

Take each functional driver in turn and get the group to tell you how those drivers act between the various functions. Where do they come from and where do they go to? Draw an arrow on the map to represent the flow of each relationship as it is called out.

When you have all of the arrows in place for all of the business drivers you can establish a weighting for each of the relationships. This can be indicated on the map by the width of the arrow. A thick arrow shows a major influence or high volume of traffic between the two entities.

The use of color also helps to distinguish between the different functional drivers, but a fairly accurate picture can be built in simple black and white.

Once you have agreement that the map or picture is fairly complete and reasonably accurate, you can move on to get agreement as to which of these functions are the main functions.

Then you can remove the subsidiaries or perhaps redraw the map. Redrawing the map provides an opportunity to remove the superfluous elements and obtain a more open layout, which will make it easier to read and understand. It also allows everybody to check the validity of the resultant model.

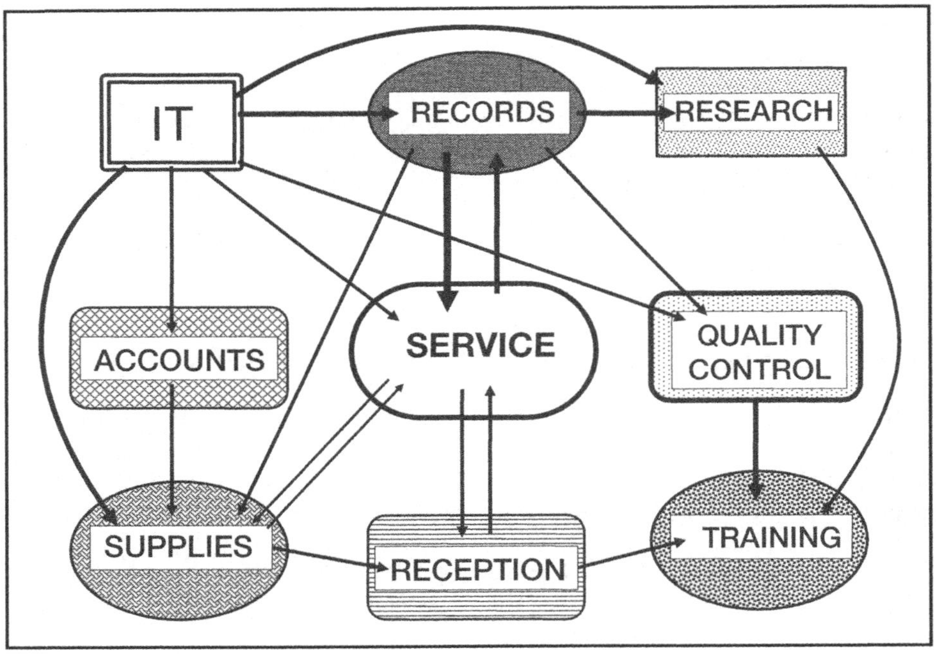

Figure 5-3. Functional Map of Core Functions

The result is a functional map of all the core functions showing their logical relationships within the business. You can also see how they work together, providing goods or services to the customers, maintaining a regular cash flow, meeting the mission statement, and satisfying the aims of the directors while protecting the brand and image and demonstrating accountability. It is a clear picture of the complete business cycle.

Now you have a graphical representation of the main functional processes. The dynamic relationships between the key functions will become apparent, providing a visual demonstration of the relative criticality of those functions.

5.6.5   Criticality

From Figure 5-3, it becomes obvious which of the key functions are super critical. In this example, Service and IT (information technology) are super critical because most of the business is relying on their services.

On the other hand, you can see that Accounts and Training are noncritical. They absorb rather than generate the flow of their functional drivers. It is therefore likely that the overall business enterprise could manage without these two functions – at least in the short term.

The fact that a function is shown to be noncritical does not mean it is superfluous. It simply means it is a non-urgent function and therefore its resources can be redirected or redeployed in the event of an emergency. It can be a useful source of people and resources.

The majority of the functions in our example must be regarded as highly critical because they are major contributors to the super critical function of Service.

Interestingly enough, IT is a super critical function but has no internal dependencies. It is a provider rather than a consumer of services. However, it clearly has external dependencies such as power and communications, but they do not figure on this particular version of a functional analysis.

Finally, we can see that Research and Supplies should be regarded as critical. Neither is providing major inputs to any highly critical or super critical functions but they are of themselves essential to the functioning of the business operation as a whole.

Once you have reached agreement about the critical rankings in this manner, you will have a prioritized list of the business functions which should be featured in the emergency management section of your BC plan or plans.

Self-Examination Questions

1. Which of the following statements about business impact analysis (BIA) is true?

   A. BIA is a brand-new process that's still not that well understood by business continuity (BC) professionals.

   B. BIA is a common practice that has long been adopted by professionals in many fields.

   C. BIA is a unique process that is only carried out by business continuity management (BCM) professionals.

2. What is the difference between impacts and consequences?

   A. Impacts are the immediate losses caused by a disruption, while consequences are the long-term problems that are caused by disruptions and their impacts.

   B. Impacts can easily be measured in dollar terms, while consequences are more nebulous and thus require a BIA to determine.

   C. Impacts pose a severe danger to the business, while consequences are more easily managed.

3. What is the primary purpose of a BIA?

   A. To analyze all flows (e.g., of information, cash, people) through a business for the purpose of identifying the critical components of the business

   B. To identify and quantify the costs to the enterprise of the effects of a disaster or an emergency

   C To clearly differentiate impacts from consequences

4. What is the most effective way to combine the various methods of data collection during the BIA process?

   A. Distribute questionnaires, conduct follow-up interviews, and then hold a workshop.

   B. Begin with interviews, hold a workshop, and then distribute questionnaires.

   C. Start with a workshop, distribute questionnaires, and then follow up with interviews.

5. What are the three stages of the interactive impact-modeling process?

   A. 1) List dormant difficulties, 2) consider tangible costs, 3) consider intangible costs

   B. 1) List mission-critical activities, 2) consider dormant difficulties, 3) consider intangible costs

   C. 1) List dormant difficulties, 2) determine loss exposure, 3) consider tangible costs

6. The point in time by which work should be restored following a BC incident is known as the

   A. mission-critical activity (MCA).

   B. recovery point objective (RPO).

   C. recovery time objective (RTO).

7. When assessing the potential impact of a threat to an organization, it is vital to plot and agree upon all of the threat's _____ and consequences.

   A. causes

   B. dependencies

   C. exposures

8. On a map of all the core functions in an organization, with arrows showing the dynamic relationships between the functions, what indicates that certain functions on the map are supercritical?

   A. Many arrows point outward from the functions, indicating that the functions generate rather than absorb the functional drivers of the organization.

   B. Arrows only point toward the functions, meaning the functions are the key receivers of the functional drivers of the organization.

   C. An equal number of arrows point toward and away from the functions, meaning the functions are well integrated into the organization.

Food for Thought

This chapter explored the implications and possibilities in connection with developing a thorough understanding of the risk and impacts which might apply to your organization. You have learned about a number of different approaches, and now it is time to think about which you will choose to use. As you tackle the exercises below, you will find it helpful to consult the downloadable **Business Continuity Toolkit**.

Here are some questions for you to reflect upon. Use one, or more, of the case study situations from any of the previous chapters. By now, you should know which scenarios are best suited to your viewpoint and background. The more variety and depth you add to these exercises, the more benefit you will reap in the long run.

Exercises

1. Before you can do any sort of impact analysis, you need to sell the idea to top management, telling them why and how it should be done.
    > Whom do you think you should be talking to?
    > What will you say to them?
      ⌃ How do you think they might respond?

2. Think about how you would conduct a functional BIA (FBIA).
    > Whom will you turn to for help in organizing the FBIA?
    > Who would you want to invite?
      ⌃ Consider roles or job titles rather than specific nominees.

3. Prepare your opening presentation for an FBIA.
    > Would you want or expect to use slides?
      ⌃ Practice the opening with a flipchart.

4. Develop a work plan for a full BIA.
    > What documentation will you need?
    > How long do you think it will take?
      ⌃ Consider the number of sessions and their duration, match appointment schedules, and write up the results.

5. Conduct a five step functional analysis as instructed in Section 5.6 of this chapter for your case study organization.
    > How many critical and super critical functions?
    > Are there any business lessons to be learned from this?

Looking Forward

At this point, you are familiar with the process of identifying threats. Next you will make the choices of how to be prepared.

Downloadable Business Continuity Toolkit

There are several key documents which complement the material in this chapter, including checklists and questionnaires, in the downloadable **Business Continuity Toolkit**.

References

Asnar, Y. & Giorgini, P. (2008). *Analyzing business continuity through a multi-layers model*. Retrieved from
   http://disi.unitn.it/~pgiorgio/papers/bpm08.pdf

Business Continuity Institute (2013). *Good practice guidelines 2013*. Retrieved from
   www.thebci.org/index.php/resources/the-good-practice-guidelines (May be downloaded free by BCI
   members, or purchased by non-members.)

Burtles, J. (2014). *Emergency evacuation planning for your workplace: From chaos to life-saving solutions*.
   Brookfield, CT: Rothstein Publishing, pp. 211-225.

For Additional Reading

"Professional Practices" is published by DRI International (DRII) and can be found at
   www.drii.org/certification/professionalprac.php

"Continuity of Practice Requirements" is published by the Association of Chartered Certified Accountants
   (ACCA) and can be found at www.accaglobal.com/content/dam/acca/global/PDF-members/practisinginfo
   /PI%20handbook%202015.pdf It is a document about the legal requirement of continuity which applies to
   this specific profession.

6

Continuity Strategies and Options

Now that you have identified risks and their consequences, it is time to consider developing a disaster response strategy. At this point, you begin to flesh out the requirements and contents of your business continuity (BC) plans and procedures. Now that you understand the problem, you can begin to design suitable solutions and make practical choices which will be the basis of those plans.

This chapter will help you to:

- ☑ Begin the implementation of BC by selecting, or developing, a strategy.

- ☑ Develop processes and procedures to suit the strategy.

- ☑ Revise strategies to align with budgets and other considerations.

- ☑ Address the need for the recovery and restoration of data.

- ☑ Initiate a sound backup regime to ensure reliable data recovery.

6.1 Selecting Practical Strategies

So far, a lot of discussion and research has revealed some interesting facts, suggested some parameters, and perhaps even caused some concerns. This next stage, however, will lead directly to key activities requiring expenditure and capital investment. Before presenting management with a tentative strategy, you must establish some ballpark figures and viable alternatives. In other words, you need to build a sound business case in order to move forward.

During this key stage of strategic thinking and serious decision-making, you will require the involvement and support of your BC sponsor. His or her full engagement will help to ensure you get firm commitment to the strategies which will form the basis of any further progress.

As the BC manager, you will be responsible for determining and guiding the selection of practical BC strategies. These operating strategies have to take full account of the recovery time and recovery point objectives, protecting and maintaining the organization's critical functions.

6.1.1 Disaster Response Considerations

There are two principal aspects to this subject area:

- Disaster Recovery.
- Business Continuity.

Disaster recovery is all about recovering the technology and information systems that support the business. Over the years, a number of approaches have been developed to address the many issues arising from hardware or software failures. Many of these techniques have been refined and have been incorporated as features on some modern systems to provide built-in resilience. Nevertheless, it is still useful to understand the principles in order to make sure you know just what kind of resilience you can expect.

Business continuity, on the other hand, is more about the basic resources and processes which enable the normal business operations. It is concerned with people, workspace, and emergency procedures and processes.

To begin, let's take a look at the various approaches together with their drawbacks and advantages. The descriptions here provide a conceptual overview. The specifics will vary in accordance with the actual products and services concerned. My purpose here is to familiarize you with what is possible so that you can appreciate the similarities and differences among the possible alternatives. Obviously, you will encounter many areas in which you might benefit from the advice of someone with technical knowledge and an understanding of your organization's particular needs.

The question of selecting a suitable disaster recovery site and arranging storage is revisited in Chapter 10, which looks at disaster recovery in depth.

6.2 Disaster Recovery Options

Several basic approaches to disaster recovery (plus a number of combinations or variations) can be taken.

6.2.1 Dual Systems

In *dual systems*, the principle is to have two sets of equipment with the workload divided across them, thus providing a means of obtaining complete independence from the impact of hardware and software failures. At its extreme, only one system is used at any one time. Whenever there is a failure in the primary or working system, the workload is transferred to the secondary or idle system (fallback). An enhanced variant is the full mirror-image concept, in which the database of the secondary system constantly shadows the one on the primary system to enable a rapid recovery by avoiding the need to restore the database. The second system may be physically at a distant location to avoid loss or failure of both systems at one time.

A side benefit of the basic dual systems approach is that by careful installation and management, one can improve, or enhance, performance or productivity by allocating differing user types to different processors. In an emergency, some of the workload is put on standby until the failure has been remedied.

6.2.2   Harmonic Recovery

Harmonic recovery is the term I use to describe the next stage in the evolution of automated fault tolerant computing systems. Secondary parallel processors, or "catchers," shadow the primary operational processors ready to step in and catch the work in hand if any of the primary processors should fail. While harmonic recovery requires a considerable investment in technology and technique, it does provide for virtually instantaneous system recovery under all circumstances.

When it is properly implemented, this harmonic recovery concept can be extended to provide several levels of recovery to protect against multiple failures of facilities, systems, and services. Recovery times can be measured in minutes and seconds rather than days or hours. Indeed, the response is so fast there is often a need to delay the system from going into recovery mode immediately each time a user fails to respond quickly enough to an error message or hesitates while inputting data.

6.2.3   Hot Site

A *hot site* service is one in which the vendor provides a standby site fully equipped and configured, ready, and available at short notice for the organization to transfer and continue essential operations and processes. A guarantee of the number of hours it will take for your recovery site to be set up and ready for use is typically part of the vendor contract. With a dedicated hot site, some travel may be required since a regional disaster may mean that the closest available hot site is in another region, possibly several hours away.

Since these are accessible systems with the emphasis on ample disk capacity and communications capability, it is possible to relocate key personnel to the hot site, where they can continue business as usual. This is a potentially expensive option since access is strictly limited to those who subscribe to the service and thus share the cost of ownership along with the running costs. Technical support staff, specialists in restoration techniques, are on hand to assist the subscriber's personnel in the event of a disaster or a test. Onsite testing is encouraged to ensure that all subscribers are able to make best use of the services available. After all, the disaster recovery center has no other purpose than to support customers in their hour of need. Bear in mind that most hot site contracts set a limit to the number of days the hot site can be used before you must move out.

6.2.4   Mobile Recovery Services

In the mid-range arena, *mobile recovery* makes it possible for you or a vendor of this service to mount your whole system and its peripherals in a 40-foot articulated trailer. Space is limited, but it can be a viable solution, providing you still have somewhere to park after the disaster. It would be worth touring one of these trailers as part of your research since the workstations and other areas in the newer mobile units are often set up very efficiently and attractively.

Minimal technical support from the vendor should be expected. Some pre-disaster investment will be necessary to provide a facilities panel with electrical and communication connectivity close to a suitable parking site. You will need to obtain appropriate zoning approval and parking permits in advance. You should allow 48 to 72 hours before the system function is returned to the end-users. While it might be possible to improve on this sort of timing, there is no guarantee everything will run smoothly under emergency conditions. It is not an ideal short-term strategy; it is more suited to the medium term.

Mobile recovery is often available as an option from the hot site service providers and can prove quite beneficial in an incident which is not a total disaster or where the incident and its implications can be predicted and prepared for in advance. For example, you might make use of mobile recovery services during a refit of the computer suite or a major upgrade to the core systems, where the mobile site can be parked somewhere convenient to the staff members who will be using it (in contrast to a hot site, which may be located in another part of the country and require travel).

6.2.5   Cold Site

This *cold site* option means keeping, or renting access to, an empty room with power, air conditioning, and a raised floor. Whenever such a facility is set aside as a potential cold site it often gets commandeered for another purpose. Unfortunately, it is not a recovery strategy which can be tested regularly because it depends upon going out to the marketplace and acquiring a complete set of equipment, commissioning it, and testing it before putting into service. (If you are working with a commercial vendor, you will have some testing options available rather than making all the arrangements yourself. Also, you can make arrangements with equipment leasing companies to provide a basic configuration of equipment within a specified timeframe in the event of an emergency.)

While it is a relatively inexpensive option, the cold site cannot be relied on as a first line of defense, but may make sense as a medium- or long-term recovery strategy for use while the home site is being rebuilt. Some hot site vendors often have cold site space available as an option in their locations. Often, the vendor will configure the site for you, but it will require more time, since the site will be set up to order. Because use of a hot site is often limited to a certain number of days or weeks, the vendor often includes the option of assisting you in moving to one of the vendor's cold sites if your stay at the facility is going to be extensive.

6.2.6   Portable Cold Site

This *portable cold site* strategy is based on a type of small temporary prefabricated modular building (developed in the US in 1955 as PortaKamp and in 1961 in the UK as Portakabin) which can be delivered and erected onsite, typically within 48 to 72 hours. Like the static cold site, this approach presupposes a suitable system available to be located and installed within an acceptable timeframe. It also depends on having a suitable piece of firm, level ground where it can be erected, with zoning and building permits arranged in advance.

The temporary modular building has the same advantages and disadvantages as any cold site with the additional caveat of having somewhere suitable to erect it. Where the home site has a large unoccupied parking area for vehicles, a parade ground, or other hard surface area available for use, then this might be another option for the medium- or long-term strategy.

6.2.7   Reciprocal Agreement

The *reciprocal agreement*, a mutual aid agreement in which another organization can bring its disaster to your doorstep – or you can bring your disaster to their doorstep – is not really a feasible solution, although it is often proposed. Reciprocal agreements are a sure-fire recipe for enmity, frustration, and bitter disappointment. Without a profit, or return, or a real guarantee for either party, there is no real motivation for this approach to work in the harsh reality of a major incident. And, in the event of a situation causing regional business interruption, neither of you will be available to the other. Its only advantage is the rather attractive price tag, and its principal disadvantage is the propensity to fail when it is most needed.

6.2.8   Second Site

This *second site* option means owning and running a standby site of your own which doesn't have a full-time workload. Generally, only very large-scale operations can absorb the full cost of setting up a separate, dormant data processing facility. The major drawback is the lack of real-life recovery skills which can be developed only through experience.

However, some large organizations do have multiple data centers which provide a high degree of resilience and may enable them to absorb much of the workload when one site experiences some difficulties. With three or more sites in the network, there is an even higher degree of resilience. On the downside, all of the sites do need to remain compatible at all times, which may entail simultaneous upgrades across multiple sites. Careful planning and some serious investment are required to avoid major exposures.

Once a threat is recognized and confronted as a realistic problem, the resolution is often self-evident.

Often the organizations which invest in multiple sites as a BC measure have outgrown the capacity of the disaster recovery service providers. Due to sheer size, or their degree of specialization, they are obliged to become self-sufficient at all times.

If there is an Achilles' heel in this strategy it would be the organization's vulnerability to a planned and sustained attack on their systems. For some organizations this can be dismissed as an extremely unlikely scenario.

6.3   Business Continuity Options

Certain emergency procedures should be developed to cope with the implications of situations such as denial of access, infrastructure failure, and loss of personnel or other key resources. Many of the possible solutions will emerge through the risk and impact analysis. Once a threat is recognized and confronted as a realistic problem, the resolution is often self-evident. People who are exposed to risks are generally aware of them and should have already considered how they might either avoid the consequences altogether or be better prepared to deal with them.

You may wish to take a look at some other continuity solutions before making your recommendations to the owners of the business operations. They are additional choices to the disaster recovery strategies outlined above; they are not replacements.

It might be necessary, or at least advisable, to carry out a simulation of some sort to prove the validity of a method before committing to it as a strategy. Such pre-testing may be limited to market research or, if it is a well-known and proven method, you might assume it is going to work for you and will be subject to a test in due course as one of the regular BC elements.

6.3.1   Alternate Sourcing

In order to obtain better control over such matters as quality, price, and delivery, the supplies of materials, goods, and services are often taken from a limited (or even a single) source. There is a danger here of the restricted supply line becoming a *single point of failure*. Such dependencies can easily lead to shortages in an emergency situation. An alternate sourcing capability is the natural bypass to this type of problem; while it might incur some additional costs, it does improve continuity of service to the customer. There are often considerable advantages to using a limited range of suppliers, but these incentives do have to be offset against the higher level of risk associated with such a dependency.

> **Staff mobility and willingness to relocate temporarily is another factor which needs to be checked out.**

Alternate sourcing as an emergency measure does mean you need to set up a reliable short-term, rapid response capability which can provide adequate supplies on demand. Obviously, the details of how this is to be achieved will be unique to every situation, but the basic strategy is simple enough for almost anyone to adopt fairly easily, once you have the help of those who are familiar with the market for those goods or services. Once the principle and its implications have been accepted, the solution should not be difficult to develop and implement. Any additional costs associated with this approach can be accounted for as an integral part of the price of resilience.

6.3.2   Emergency or Standby Stock

In some circumstances, it may be possible to set up an emergency stock which is set aside specifically to bridge any gaps in the normal supply chain. Such stocks may need to be updated or refreshed from time to time. There will be a number of implications to be considered, especially those which are inherent in the nature of the goods or supplies concerned. Shelf space and shelf life are the most obvious factors which can affect the regular stock management procedures. Other aspects to be taken into account include storage conditions, seasonality, batch tracking or source identification, and any other special characteristics of holding long-term stock.

The most obvious disadvantage is the additional cost involved in establishing the storage space together with the additional overhead of extra stock. On the positive side you are likely to be more resilient as well as immune to minor problems with transport and deliveries.

6.3.3   Buffer Stock

By increasing the quantities of stock in hand it may be possible for the business to continue working while alternate sources are being sought, commissioned, or delivered. The technique of buffering the stock assumes there is a system or procedure in place to make sure the contents of the store are used on a first-in, first-out (FIFO) basis so the supplies are always relatively fresh. Of course, this technique may not be suitable for materials or goods which have a short shelf life or require special storage conditions.

Exactly the same arguments apply to this strategy as to the previous one. The main difference is in the way the stock gets managed and used. The investment requirements are similar in both cases. The shelf life and cost are the key factors in choosing between these two concepts.

6.3.4   Redeployment or Relocation

Sometimes it is possible to transfer the operation or the people to another site or location in an emergency. Some careful planning and research needs to be done to ensure that sufficient capacities of supplies and resources are going to be available in an emergency.

This approach is particularly attractive where there is already some spare capacity which can easily be made available for use in an emergency. Staff mobility and willingness to relocate temporarily is another factor which needs to be checked out. It is wrong to assume that people would be happy to change their travel or working patterns at a moment's notice. They must be consulted and given the opportunity to comment before such plans are finalized.

The main challenge with this approach is the dynamics of the business which may alter so as to inhibit or prevent you from making use of this capability. It is something which will need to be monitored if this type of response is adopted as a basic strategy.

6.3.4.1 Working from Home

Modern technology and communications offer the flexibility of working from home – either full-time or a few days a month – a common strategy for many organizations, allowing them to attract the best possible staff while removing the constraints of travel and family issues. In fact, some companies, which contain many "knowledge workers," recruit experts from all over the world, giving them the advantage of working full-time from their home offices and communicating electronically with the corporate office and each other. It is a useful option but it does require a certain amount of advance planning and investment if it is to work well. The benefits of recruiting a good staff have to be carefully weighed against the potential problems. The maturity and reliability of the staff members are important considerations. Of course, the option of working from home doesn't suit some types of business operation, especially those where specialized machinery or industrial processes are involved. However, it is particularly well suited to tasks which require only access to a desk with a computer and broadband communications.

If the option of working from home is approached properly, it can be a very effective and affordable solution to a number of problems. One approach is to allow working from home for a few days per week or month. One small company (25 full-time staff), as part of its BC plan, has introduced the idea of regular monthly "work from home" days for most of its staff. As a result, all staff members are familiar with the process and everything is in place and ready to cope with the closure of company premises. To ensure that someone is always in attendance from each department, staff members share a common diary for scheduling their days at home. They all have access to a teleconferencing facility which is in regular use for staff meetings.

Some of the concerns for this company included ensuring that each of the participants had access to a suitable, private office space. Information security meant extending the existing policy and practices to include remote working. Other considerations were access to good communications, ownership of the facilities, and liaison between workers and managers to ensure continuity of service to their clients. All of this was discussed and settled before they launched the first trial, which was successful because of the careful planning.

6.3.5   Reduction of Operations

In some circumstances, it may be possible to reduce the scale of operation during the emergency period. This can perhaps be augmented by buffering the output, e.g., warehousing a supply of finished goods prior to dispatch to the client base. Here, you are looking at a variant of the buffered stock principle with the buffering in the outbound rather than the inbound stream. When calculating the quantities to be held, one must take account of the time that will be taken to re-establish operations and rebuild the stock levels. A second emergency which led to a supply chain failure, despite your precautions, could be very embarrassing.

One potential advantage is the extra time available for the stock to mature before dispatch, although some types of goods may tend to deteriorate in storage. The extent and impact of these changes might depend to a large degree on the storage conditions as well as the intrinsic nature of the products. Buffering might also allow variations in the production rate to accommodate busy periods, staff holidays, or downtime for maintenance, etc. Of course, the real advantage, from the customer perspective, is continuity of supply.

Drawbacks include the potential for deterioration or even contamination while goods are held in extended storage. The costs associated with holding additional stocks are another consideration but they can easily be worked out and balanced against the risk, and consequential loss, of non-delivery.

6.3.6   Termination or Change

Changing or ending the service, product, function, or process should also be considered as a strategic option. Although it may seem drastic at first sight, it is worthy of consideration. This course of action is most appropriate where a product or service has a limited life span and is approaching obsolescence or replacement. There are, of course, marketing and many other issues which will affect such a strategy and the associated decision or invocation criteria. These questions need to be resolved at a fairly high level before adopting this strategy. While it seems like a contradiction of terms to think of termination as a continuity strategy, you must bear in mind that you are mainly concerned with ensuring continuity of the business as a whole rather than the survival of every component part.

The advantages and disadvantages of this approach are dependent upon such unique factors as the line of business, the type of product, season of the year, ease of change, customer demand, customer preferences, and many others. It has to be a matter for investigation on behalf of, and in agreement with, the owners of the operation.

6.3.7   Bypass Arrangements

Under some circumstances, it may be expedient to bypass some of the normal processes or procedures in order to speed up the overall operation or to satisfy customer demands. Where applicable, such emergency arrangements do need to be thought through and properly authorized, subject to certain very specific conditions. There will also need to be some safeguards in place to ensure standards are maintained to at least the minimum acceptable level.

The major disadvantage of this approach is the danger to the brand and reputation once the story gets out that there has been some corner cutting. Almost inevitably, the public will get to know about your emergency arrangements; the manner in which they are told and the information they are given is vital to the success or failure of this strategy. If there is any doubt about the wisdom of this approach, don't do it.

One large organization bypassed its billing procedure for 24 hours due to a system failure. None of its customers complained and its competitors saw it as a smart publicity stunt. The cost of this "surprise campaign" was put down as a marketing expense. Very few people knew this was all part of an agreed upon BC strategy. The alternative strategy would have been a complete replication of its data center, but the organization chose to take the more customer-friendly approach.

6.3.8   Outsourcing

When production ceases entirely, due to an emergency, it might be prudent to satisfy the customers by supplying them directly from an alternative source, even in some cases a competitor. While this may be rather more costly than supplying them from your own production line, it will at least help to retain the customer's loyalty. After all, it is usually far more cost-effective to retain existing customers than it is to obtain new ones. Obviously, the way in which the story is managed can have an enormous influence on the success of such a strategy.

One rather useful version of outsourcing is the *emergency call center* which can replicate an organization's regular call center operations. The key elements in this type of scheme are the ability to redirect the telephone traffic and the provision of suitable scripts for the call agents. Several companies now offer this type of specialist support.

The key advantage of outsourcing is customer retention, at a known additional cost. The main disadvantage is there may not be a practical solution if your product has unique features or characteristics. Another problem is the risk of the customer who may prefer the alternative product, especially if the price is attractive enough. On the one hand, it may not be practical because there is no realistic alternative to your product or it may be too risky because the alternative is too close for comfort. Sometimes there is a very fine line between the different types of risk which are inherent in the alternative strategies. Once again, it is the owners of the operation who have to make the final decision.

> **…your task is to pave the way for the decision-makers and then to implement their decisions.**

6.4   Strategy Selection

Decisions about the recovery and continuity strategies discussed earlier in this section should be made at the highest level. Even if the assessments and judgments are delegated to a lower level, the implications warrant the final decisions to be understood and endorsed from the very top. These strategies represent the direct application of corporate policy.

The selection process needs to be:

- Based on contributions and opinions from all relevant levels and perspectives.
- Based on a full understanding of the options available.
- Based on a full understanding of the implications.
- Rigorous and transparent, i.e., well-researched and openly discussed with those who are responsible for running the relevant functions.

The outcome needs to be:

- Endorsed and funded at executive level.
- Understood and supported at management level.
- Implemented and tested at operational level.

Someone has to take on the key task of masterminding the accumulation and collation of the technical, operational, and financial information about each of the various options. This knowledge base will form the foundation for the debate and decision-making which is at the heart of the strategy selection process. Building and maintaining this accumulation of facts, opinions, ideas, caveats, and reservations would normally be your responsibility. As BC manager, you may not need to be deeply involved or make the actual decisions; your task is to pave the way for the decision-makers and then to implement their decisions.

6.4.1   Initial Research

At the initial research stage, it is often useful to call in a few specialist service providers and consultants to get their views on the subject. If you invite them in to simply talk about an outline strategy you may pick up some sound advice and get a few ideas of what is practical as well as a few examples of what has already been done by other people. There is no need to get too deeply involved with them at this early juncture although you may feel their support and assistance could be of benefit. While expert opinion can be seen as expensive, it is often cheaper, faster, and more effective than the alternative of learning from your own mistakes.

The complete strategy selection process will include some or all of these steps or deliverables:

- A list of feasible options.
- Estimates of size, suitability, and costs.
- Operational considerations.
- Operational preferences.
- Management considerations.
- Business case.
- Executive input.
- Deliberations and decisions.

The business impact analysis (BIA) will already have uncovered a few suggestions based on the practical experience of your operational people; so you will have some useful clues as to what are regarded as realistic possibilities. Make a list of these and compare them to the various outline strategies described earlier. You should then be able to eliminate some of the more obvious non-starters. This should leave you with a short list of feasible options.

Armed with a list of feasible options, gather as much information as you can about each one of them. The decision-makers will want to know about the costs, terms, and conditions, etc., while the operational people will want to know about compatibility, suitability, and procedures. Management will be interested in such matters as the availability, size, and scope of each option. Gradually, you will be able to pull together a catalog with estimates of the size, suitability, and costs of the feasible options.

The business case with facts and figures...can then be developed and put before the executives.

You will then be ready to meet with the operational people and discuss the advantages and disadvantages of the various options. You may want to do this in a workshop format, in a series of small meetings for each unit or division, or perhaps on a one-to-one basis with the operational managers and their supervisors. The detail of this stage of the process will be governed by the nature and culture of the organization concerned. What you are trying to capture is an understanding of the operational considerations for each of the alternatives so that you can determine their preferences from an operational perspective.

You might find it useful to pull these preferences and the reasoning behind them into a report so the management can review, and ponder over, the pros and cons of each strategy. They will want to add their own considerations before you begin to build a proper business case with recommendations to the executive group. Your sponsor should be involved at this stage because you will benefit from his or her support as you move towards dealing with the executives and obtaining their commitment to a set of recovery and continuity strategies.

The business case with facts and figures, supported by some practical considerations, together with recommendations from the business units and their management can then be developed and put before the executives. The executive group may, in their wisdom, want to see some further detail, alterations, or additions before coming to a final conclusion. On the other hand, if you have done your homework correctly, they may move straight on to the decision-making. If they do not reach an immediate conclusion, then your role will be to support them during their journey through their deliberations towards the final decision-making process.

Armed with their decision about recovery and continuity strategies, you can move on to start developing the actual plans themselves.

6.5 Backup and Restore Procedures

Any successful recovery and restart of modern information-based business systems and processes will depend heavily upon the existence of adequate backup and recovery procedures. This means that the development of procedures to ensure the availability of critical data, information, programs, and documents under all circumstances is a crucial aspect of business continuity.

Without adequate backup, a full recovery may be impossible.

Due to the technical complexity of some aspects of backup and restoration, it is an area where you will require the assistance of your technical support team. You should also be aware that such a technical topic is subject to continuous changes and improvements, and so the optimum solutions are likely to change over time.

The essential outcome of this stage of BC planning is a robust backup regime which can be relied upon to preserve and deliver the critical information required by the core business operations under any and all circumstances. In most organizations there will already be some form of backup strategy in place. You have to ensure that the existing procedures do meet the corporate needs from a business or operational perspective rather than from the somewhat limited view of the information technology (IT) department or systems administrators. Reviewing the current arrangements and moving towards good practice should be seen as a joint venture between the BC and the technical teams. The backup review and assurance process, as discussed in the following sections, comprises four stages:

- ◗ Develop a catalog of all the corporate information.
- ◗ Identify which information is critical to the business.
- ◗ Review and refine information protection and replication strategies and procedures.
- ◗ Review and test the information recovery procedures.

6.5.1 Locating and Cataloging Corporate Information

This step involves determining the content, location, and relevance of the different categories of information and documentation that is normally held within the organization. Much of the intelligence about the many kinds of records will have been established during your BIA investigations. You are not concerned with individual records and documents, just the *types* that exist, and where and how they are held.

Then you need to confirm, or establish, some clear guidelines for the classification of information and documentation. It has to be the responsibility of the owners or custodians of these materials to do the actual classification in accordance with the guidelines. Obviously, the guidelines need to be approved and signed off at executive level.

The classification process should categorize all of the information according to the medium on which it is held and its value to the business. Thus, you might have several categories of electronic data, such as permanent records of high value, temporary records of high value, temporary records of medium value, transient records of low value, and personal records of low value but confidential.

6.5.2 Identifying Critical Information

Once you have compiled an information catalog, the organization can identify what is critical. While you may be able to set up the procedures and carry out the tasks, it is the business owners who must make the judgments about what is critical and what is peripheral or noncritical. They need to identify and confirm which information and documentation are critical to the key business needs of the organization. The easiest way to approach this is on a unit-by-unit basis, starting with those parts of the business where you might expect large volumes of records. Usually, the actual critical volume is far less than the total volume.

6.5.3   Information Protection and Replication

Once you have established which records are deemed critical, you need to select and recommend the most appropriate methods of backup. This will be a consultation exercise, carried out with those who are normally responsible for the storage and management of those records. For example, the IT department will probably be responsible for looking after millions of electronic records, many of which will be deemed critical. They should also be able to say which parts of the database are particularly volatile and which parts are fairly static. This may be an indication of criticality and value but it must be confirmed by the actual users of those records.

> **...duplication of information is to be preferred to replication because it is quicker and more reliable.**

Working with the owners, you need to determine which types and groups of information should be backed up. Essentially, this means having a usable spare copy available in case something goes wrong. The technical people will need to establish which methods are available for the duplication or replication of all classes or categories of critical information. In this context, you need to distinguish between the duplication of records and the replication of records.

- **Duplication.** I use the term *duplication* to mean the simultaneous creation of more than one copy at the source, i.e., as the original information is created, recorded, or captured. Thus, there is always an alternate version which could be retrieved. In practice, this may be achieved through the use of a data processing operation which automatically creates duplicate original records when certain types of transaction are completed.

- **Replication.** On the other hand, I use *replication* to mean the copying of existing records, subsequent to their creation. For example, you might be in the habit of taking a scan or photocopy of original documents before working with them. Copying of electronic data onto backup tapes is another example of replication.

Wherever it is practical, duplication of information is to be preferred to replication because it is quicker and more reliable. A one-step action with an immediate result is better than a multi-step delayed process. There is less chance of failure and a higher degree of accuracy.

Technicians will need to set up regular schedules for the replication or backing up of all critical records. They will also need to think about how and where they are going to store the volumes of information needed for backup purposes. This means they have to work out how much storage space they will need and identify suitable storage facilities.

6.5.4   Storage Considerations

A suitable storage facility needs to be safe and secure; therefore, it has to be outside the potential emergency zone of the home site. It also has to offer secure but convenient access for the deposit and retrieval of records. Another key requirement is a controlled environment – dust-free, temperature-controlled, and protected from sunlight. You will find it worthwhile to visit a number of sites which offer data storage facilities to get an idea of what is required and what is actually available. Your technical people will probably know who offers such services in your area.

Together with the technical team, you will need to make sure regular schedules are established for the safe transfer of your backup records to suitable storage facilities. Here I am referring to traditional media such as paper and tape which require physical handling. The same principles apply to offsite storage facilities which use an electronic data feed. Some hot site vendors include offsite storage as a convenient support service – very useful when you need to make use of their recovery facilities.

Once the records are placed safely in storage you need to concern yourself with understanding the required retention periods. If you simply keep adding to your backup you will soon run out of space. Not only that, but you will have more records than you need which means your recovery could gradually become more complex and time consuming.

Therefore, you need to be able to purge your storage from time to time and remove those records which are no longer useful or valuable. If you keep your backup on reusable media then the media can be recycled. Otherwise, out-of-date materials need to be treated as confidential waste when they are removed from storage.

When things go badly wrong…you need…real backup to load onto real systems in order to bring about a real recovery.

The required retention period for business related information will depend upon the regulations for your industry and legislation in regard to corporate governance. You should turn to your company secretary or your compliance officer for advice in this connection. There may be penalties imposed if such records are lost or destroyed. On the other hand, confidential or potentially embarrassing records could introduce an additional risk of exposure in the event of an official investigation. Such an investigation might be connected with the discovery process in connection with litigation, or a government action.

Media which can be recycled is usually managed on what is known as a grandfather, father, and son cycle in which several sets of media are used in rotation. The sequencing and scheduling of backup will depend on how dynamic, and critical, the database is rated by those who are responsible for managing the backup regime. If their evaluation is at odds with the business needs then the business owners should be alerted and the procedures updated accordingly.

RAID (**R**andom **A**rray of **I**ndependent **D**isks) technology is a data storage system that uses multiple disk drives to improve performance or reliability. There are several variations, but the basic principle is to distribute the data across several disks using error protection or recovery techniques to enhance the availability of information. Your technical team can advise you about its use and suitability.

Data deduplication, or intelligent compression as it is sometimes known, is a means of reducing the volume of data or backup by ensuring that regular patterns of data are not endlessly repeated. This is achieved by including references to a single example of a particular block of data, such as an attachment to an email. Although this is not a backup strategy per se it can substantially reduce the volumes involved. Data compression is a simpler version which seeks to avoid long sequences of similar characters, such as strings of zeroes.

In the early days of computing, we managed with relatively small amounts of data which were held on large and cumbersome storage devices which commonly failed. To illustrate how data storage has changed, I recall that, in 1984, I attended a computer users' conference in Granada where an IBM research engineer held up a small device no larger than a cigarette packet. He predicted, "Within 12 months, a device like this could hold up to 20 megabytes of data." After a pause for effect, he went on, "That is more information than anyone will generate in a lifetime." I laugh when I remember this, since I now produce that much information every time I use my camera!

Modern technology has transformed the ways in which data can be stored and backup can be managed. These changes have been driven by market needs and enabled by the availability of more sophisticated techniques for information transfer and data recording.

The demand was created by the exponential growth of contemporary databases fed by the Internet and the explosion of graphics and other storage-hungry applications. Meanwhile, advances in recording techniques have made in-flight data copying virtually transparent to the user. The other factor that has enabled dramatic advances is the increased bandwidth of modern telecommunications through the use of fiber optics and other smart technologies.

Consequently, backup can now be available online permanently, and data recovery can be achieved almost instantaneously – if everything goes according to plan! However, there is still a need for traditional offsite backup as a worst-case-scenario recovery measure.

When things go badly wrong, as they inevitably must – then you need to have access to real backup to load onto real systems in order to bring about a real recovery. Thus, it is worthwhile to consider how you manage and handle backup that is recorded on portable media.

6.5.5   Types of Records for Backup and Retention

Basically you need to consider four types of records as separate categories or classes for backup and retention purposes: *primary*, or long-term, records; *stable*, or medium-term, records; *dynamic*, or short-term, records; and *archive*, or permanent, records.

Primary records are those which are unlikely to change on a regular basis such as operating systems, applications, and procedures. Such records will only need to be backed up when there is a major change to the systems, procedures, or the software. These copies may be held in storage for many months, if not years, and therefore need to be handled as long-term copies.

Stable records are those which are only likely to change gradually as occasional alterations are made to their content, such as customer records, project plans, and management information. These copies will need to be backed up and replaced reasonably frequently, perhaps once a month or once a week depending on the nature of the business. As their shelf life is relatively short they will not require any special attention during storage, although they must obviously be kept in suitable conditions.

Dynamic records are those where the details are likely to change frequently; therefore their contents are of a rather temporary nature, although the structure might be quite stable. Because of their transient nature, these records will need to be backed up incrementally or continuously. Incremental backup is where the copies of records are automatically updated at regular intervals. Continuous or real-time backup reflects all changes to the database as and when they occur. This improves the recovery capability but it does require additional processing resource. There are many subtle variations available so this is an area where you should seek specialist advice before getting too deeply involved.

Recovery point objective (RPO) is another important concept in relation to backup and recovery. This is a rather elusive concept which is referenced in most modern standards or guidelines. The RPO identifies the last safe point within the business operation and thus describes the required restart position. It is an important parameter in determining your backup and recovery strategy. You should start by defining it from the users' point of view, and then your technicians can work out how to meet those requirements.

Archive records are those which are more or less permanent and of long-term value, such as company records and legal documentation. Storage times may be dictated by legal or regulatory requirements as well as the perceived needs of the business. These records will only need to be backed up when there are changes in the records themselves, improvements to the system, or modifications to the procedures. Consequently, you can expect them to be held in storage for many years, and it is important to take deterioration into account.

▸ *Deterioration* in this context refers to the media itself as well as the reading and writing equipment which provides access to the information itself. Most electronic media are made of plastic and plastic does eventually become brittle, a process which can be accelerated by exposure to heat or ultraviolet light, which is why the media should be kept under stable, cool conditions and shielded from daylight. In addition, there is a tendency for tapes to stretch and sag under their own weight and so they should be rewound to re-tension them every six months or so.

> **...confer with the technical team members...that their procedures meet with your needs, which are the needs of the business.**

▸ Another major concern with long-term storage is *compatibility* of the equipment. Over the years technological changes could provide a challenge when it comes to reading records recorded with an earlier technology. In fact, different pieces of equipment from what appears to be the same stable with similar features cannot always be relied upon to read what was written on another device. Compatibility checks are an essential precaution when considering data recovery, especially with something as precious as your backup.

▸ Another potential problem is poor *labeling*, which can cause chaos because nobody is sure which is which. Bad handwriting, faded ink, and labels falling off are typical causes of frustration.

▸ Validating the content of archive recordings (as well as other types of backups) is also essential. Without regular testing, there is always a possibility that the backup media are unreadable, contain wrong or incomplete data, or empty.

6.6   Information Recovery

The final phase of your review and assurance of the backup and recovery regime is to look at the information recovery process, together with the supporting procedures. This is all about making sure all of the critical information can be properly restored, with certainty and timeliness, in the event of a disaster. In the case of all the electronic records, you will need to confer with the technical team members to get confirmation that their procedures meet with your needs, which are the needs of the business.

Some of the questions you need to discuss with them include:

▸ Have they considered the most suitable *sequence* of records and files for an efficient recovery of the complete system? If so, have they organized the layout of the backup so as to improve the restoration time? For example, if the longest records are at the beginning of a tape then it will take longer to reach the short records at the rear of the tape; as there are probably more short records than long records this is not a very efficient way of transferring the data. Remember, the index is written at the start of the tape and the search for the next record may begin with going back to read the index to locate it. The ideal recovery arrangement is for the smallest records to be at the beginning of the tape and the biggest at the end of the tape.

▸ Have they thought about the *compatibility* of the reading equipment at the recovery site and the writing equipment at the home site? If so, have they tested it? How can they be sure the two sets of equipment will remain compatible at all times, taking the life of our long-term records into account?

▸ Do they have *robust procedures* for preparing, transporting, storing, and retrieving the backups? Do they subject the retrieval and recovery procedures to regular, thorough tests at the recovery site? Do they include archived records in any such tests?

Of course, you will need to extend your review and assurance of the backup and restore procedures to include all of those critical records which are not held in electronic form. These may include drawings, microfiche, books, and paper records. Storage conditions are an important consideration because paper and film can deteriorate quite rapidly if they are kept under warm, moist conditions. There is also the question of fire and the damage which might result from the protection or firefighting measures. (Water and foam are not good companions for paper and film.) A good record management system is also important, as individual records can be difficult to trace without reliable index and location aids.

6.7   Integrating and Coordinating Disaster Recovery with Business Continuity

Working from the information gained during the risk assessment and the BIA, you need to develop suitable recovery and continuity strategies and recommend them for implementation. In order to achieve this, you have to understand the options and compare them with the needs and demands of the business operation.

- *Disaster recovery* is the technical aspect which will require the support and skills of the technicians.
- *Business continuity* is more concerned with ensuring the availability of facilities and resources.

Disaster recovery (DR) is primarily a technical field, whereas BC is a very broad, pragmatic field.

- DR has to be quite precise in the sense that all the components need to be compatible and arranged in the right order.
- BC, on the other hand, has to be adaptable to meet the needs of the day.
- Historically BC originates from DR, but over the years they have tended to drift apart.

For this BC and DR coordination…you need to have links and references between the two sets of plans and procedures.

Both of these aspects may require considerable amounts of expenditure and investment; as the BC manager, you will need to prepare your case carefully and thoroughly. As the work progresses, you will also need to monitor and manage the program to make sure that the outcome is in line with expectations and fit for purpose. This result can be achieved only through an ongoing interactive dialogue with all the key players. Tell people what is going on, solicit their support, and seek their opinion throughout the whole process. You don't always have to do what they ask, but it is wise to welcome and acknowledge their input.

6.7.1   Difficulties in Bringing the Fields Together

Disaster recovery focusses on restoring computer systems together with their software and databases. There is an implicit need for specialist knowledge which almost invariably involves technical language. Practitioners have also evolved a unique jargon for the specialized procedures and techniques associated with BC. Because of the language barrier each discipline has created and the different concerns and interests, you might find it difficult to combine the two groups into one harmonious whole. However, if you don't manage to bring them together, it is unlikely that anyone else will.

6.7.2   Finding the Common Ground

There is a good deal of common ground in the way the two disciplines approach the planning process.

- Both are trying to avoid disruptions and cope with them if they cannot be avoided. This involves developing an understanding of how the business operates, figuring where the problems might lie, and developing practical solutions.

▸ Both should see eye to eye on the need for regular exercising or testing to check the plans and prepare the people.

It is also important to realize that these plans are interdependent and may need to be put into practice more or less simultaneously.

6.7.3 Working Together Smoothly

For this BC and DR coordination to work smoothly under difficult or stressful conditions, you need to have links and references between the two sets of plans and procedures.

▸ There should be similarities in style and layout to make it easier for the users to understand.

▸ Consistency in language is another helpful factor, and they should both be derived from the same corporate policy.

▸ It may be necessary to amend or amalgamate the existing documentation if separate policies are in current use.

It is in the interest of both parties to ensure that things run smoothly when something goes wrong. So you should enlist the support of your BC sponsor to make sure that you have access to the right people in the technical team who can work with you to align and coordinate the two approaches. Ideally, they should be integrated, but that may take some time to achieve.

Self-Examination Questions

1. The two principal aspects of any disaster response strategy are
   A. disaster recovery and business continuity.
   B. harmonic recovery and business continuity.
   C. disaster recovery and mobile recovery.

2. In the context of disaster recovery options, a standby site that is fully equipped, ready, and available at short notice for the organization to transfer its essential operations and processes to is called a _____.
   A. cold site
   B. dual system
   C. hot site

3. To avoid shortages when a supply chain becomes a single point of failure, one should consider using _____ to set up reliable rapid-response capability that can provide adequate supplies on demand.
   A. alternate sourcing
   B. buffer stock
   C. emergency or standby stock

4. The decision about which disaster recovery and business continuity strategies to adopt should be made
   A. by the frontline supervisors, who will be responsible for implementing those strategies.
   B. by the middle-level managers, who will be responsible for coordinating the response and recovery.
   C. at the highest level of company management.

5. Any successful recovery and restart of modern information-based business systems and processes depends heavily upon the existence of adequate _____.
   A. alternate sourcing
   B. backup and recovery procedure
   C. mobile recovery services

6. Which of the following is the best means of backing up critical information?
   A. Duplication
   B. Replication
   C. Restoration

7. For purposes of backup and recovery, which type of records are unlikely to change on a regular basis; will only need to be backed up when there is a major change to systems, procedures, or software; and will need to be held in storage for the long term?
   A. Archive records
   B. Primary records
   C. Stable records

8. Deterioration, compatibility of equipment, and poor labeling are all issues that may adversely affect _____ records.
   A. archive
   B. primary
   C. stable

Food for Thought

Chapter 6 has taken you forward into the second phase of the BC development model to determining your response strategies. This is where you gain an understanding of what is needed, what is possible, and what is practical. Once again, you will find yourself in communication with the rest of the organization, asking questions, analyzing the responses, and offering realistic solutions.

This chapter has covered the broad outline of the various continuity strategies and options which are available. You need to reassure yourself that these choices make sense to you because they form the basis of what comes next.

Exercises

It is worth reflecting on what you have learned so far and how it applies to the job in hand. Here are a few areas for deliberation.

Let us assume that you are about to present to top management in a bid to gain support for what you consider to be a sound BC and DR strategy.

1. Consider the choices to cover a loss of access.
   - What are the choices?
     - Which are likely to be available and affordable?
     - Which are likely to be reliable and suitable?

2. We looked at a number of BC strategies.
   - How would you describe the range of BC strategies?
   - Which would you propose for your organization?
     - How would you defend that choice?

3. Think about the selection of a BC strategy.
   - How do you suggest that selection should be made?
   - Who would be involved?
   - What part would you play in this process?

4. Prepare a strategy selection bid.
   - How, when, and where would you make that bid?
   - How would you put your argument together?

5. Consider the development and delivery of a backup and restore regime.
   - What would you recommend?
   - Who should take responsibility for managing and monitoring this?
   - What would you do or say if others opposed your views or interference?

Looking Forward

Now you should be well on your way towards putting together a set of BC plans. You have learned how to initiate the BC program, worked out what is needed, and begun to understand what can be done. In Part III, you will be looking at what is involved in emergency response and how you should prepare to organize and manage that response.

Downloadable Business Continuity Toolkit

You can download useful documents and guidelines from the **Business Continuity Toolkit**, which will help you assess commercial services available in your part of the world and plot your progress and look ahead to the next steps.

For Additional Reading

Georgetown University (2014). *Systems and operations continuity: Disaster recovery*. Retrieved from http://continuity.georgetown.edu/dr

Kirvan, P. (2011). How to write a disaster recovery plan. *Computer Weekly*. Retrieved from www.computerweekly.com/feature/How-to-write-a-disaster-recovery-plan-and-define-disaster-recovery-strategies

The Disaster Recovery Guide (2014). *Disaster recovery planning from A-Z*. Retrieved from www.disaster-recovery-guide.com

Part

III

Responding and Recovering

Part I: Preparation and Startup
Part II: Building a Foundation
Part III: Responding and Recovering
Part IV: Planning and Implementing
Part V: Long-Term Continuity

At this point in the process, you are ready to consider the implications of your disaster response and the subsequent recovery actions. This analysis will bring you closer to being able to develop your continuity plans and procedures. You will also start to collate and organize the resources, people, and facilities which may be required to support the protection, recovery, and restoration of your critical business activities. Once you have determined the risks and understood the impacts, you will begin to form strategies to ensure continuity of the business operations and survival of the enterprise, which will be addressed later in the book.

Chapter 7 - Emergency Response

▸ Recognize and react to an emergency situation.

Chapter 8 - Emergency Preparedness

▸ Get ready to deal with the unexpected.

Chapter 9 - Salvage and Restoration

▸ Understand what can be done to repair and restore your damaged facilities.

Chapter 10 - Disaster Recovery

▸ Restore your data processing capability.

7

Emergency Response

Now you have begun to develop a practical business continuity (BC) strategy, building on the knowledge gained during the exploratory procedures of risk assessment and business impact analysis (BIA). That information should provide you with the basis of an initial outline or a skeleton plan. Now you have to work up that sketch into something more meaningful and practical by adding some detail about who does what, when, and how in the event of a disruption, such as a disaster or emergency. It is time for you to put some flesh on the bones of your skeleton plan and develop some robust response procedures.

This chapter will help you to:

- ☑ Understand how people are likely to react in an emergency situation.

- ☑ Select and train the emergency response team (ERT) to take charge during an emergency.

- ☑ Set up and equip a command and control center.

- ☑ Organize phased incident management.

- ☑ Ensure the safety and welfare of your people, especially in an emergency evacuation.

- ☑ Prepare to communicate effectively in times of emergency.

7.1   Factors to Consider in an Emergency Response Team

Perhaps the single most important factor in determining the long-term success of an enterprise during a crisis such as a disaster or other major disruption is the performance of the emergency response team (ERT). It is the team members' performance on the day which counts rather than any procedures, plans, or resources. These are the people who either recover the situation or break the company by the way in which they conduct themselves during those first few precarious moments. They are also the ones who can create their own catastrophe in a careless, unguarded moment, causing a great deal of damage.

7.1.1   Performance Concerns

What factors are likely to impinge upon their performance in the wake of a disaster? We are all familiar with the effects of stress, which can seriously hamper one's ability to cope with a traumatic or stressful situation. On the other hand, most of us are not quite so familiar with the effects of *eustress* which is a positive reaction to the effects of stress that often occurs. Eustress allows some individuals to excel under difficult conditions. The main point to be made here is that the range of individual coping strategies is much wider than is commonly realized.

Building an effective team all comes down to how people respond to a dramatic incident. Some people are overwhelmed by the situation. Their mental self-defense mechanism calls for some kind of armor or somewhere to hide. Because there is nothing ready to hand, they mock up a crude suit of mental armor in which they can hide and feel protected. A bit like King Arthur hurriedly dressed for a surprise battle in Sir Lancelot's spare suit of armor.

Dr. Vali Hawkins Mitchell notes the huge responsibility that a manager has for the emotional health of workers in the wake of a disaster, explaining that "if the manager is clueless and unprepared for a disaster, or has no concept about the effects of disaster on human emotions, chaos can increase and escalate the emotional consequences." She adds, "Managing a disaster is not about controlling the disaster; it is about managing the emotions of the moment" (Hawkins Mitchell, 2013, pp. 236-237).

Following are some of the responses you can expect to encounter, based on what I have observed over my years of handling these difficult situations.

Some Typical Emotional Responses and Defense Mechanisms

▸ **Take Refuge in What Worked Before.** When the incident is, or appears to be, a repeat of an earlier similar occasion, some people will adopt the previous suit of ill-fitting armor. But for them it is better than nothing. It worked before – so why shouldn't it work now? As soon as the incident is over, they could afford to shed the armor but may not be capable of recognizing the endpoint of the event. Therefore, they tend to remain within their protective shell, just in case. Eventually they forget it is there and the massive, clanking suit of armor becomes a permanent protection, distorting their view of the world and restricting their activity. Struggling to walk in an iron suit with a constricted view through the visor becomes their safe approach to life and its problems. After a while, the original impromptu solution becomes the permanent defense against everything. Although it was hastily developed in response to an unwelcome and unexpected danger, it does seem to work. Its apparent effectiveness reinforces the unconscious belief in its value; thus, its drawbacks get to be accepted as the long-term price of safety and survival. "So what if people laugh at my umbrella? Someone has to keep the god of thunder at bay."

These people, who appear to have withdrawn into their shell, can be recognized by their reluctance to take any positive action. They will want to stand back while other people deal with the situation; you might think of them as shy. For everybody's sake they need to be made to realize that the danger is over and they can prove themselves to be useful. The trick is to get them involved doing something useful; this will allow them to escape from their trap and move on. You can activate them by asking them to perform a simple task like "Could you check whether the bins have all been emptied?" or "Can you make sure all the clocks show the correct time?" Soon, they will become absorbed in the task before them and return to the real world.

▸ **Escape into the Past.** Another escape route is to move away from the incident through the dimension of time. Because of the person's uncertainty about the end point, the safest refuge appears to be at a point in time long before this incident started. This means of escape leads to the person's estrangement from present time activities with his or her attention fixed firmly on a safe moment from the past. The person is unwilling to look to the future because of the attendant risk of meeting those dangers from which he or she desperately wants to escape. The challenge for these people is to recognize their temporary defense mechanism, recognize its limited long-term value, and develop the courage to discard it. Any repetition re-stimulates or refreshes the hidden or subconscious memory and the response mechanism. Repetition has the chronic effect of reinforcing the coping strategy into an automatic response to almost any stimulation. Counseling can help them with this process. However, people have to actually deal with it themselves. The counselor cannot do it for them, nor can he or she apply it to them or for them. What counseling can do is to provide the questions and offer support and guidance while the subject searches for his or her own answers.

In an emergency situation, these "escapees" will give the impression that they don't realize anything has happened, and they will try to carry on as usual. This will probably lead to a certain amount of confusion because some of the usual tools and places will be unavailable. The solution for these people is to ask them to do something different; they need a change. Asking them to do a menial but different task can release them from their moment of the past and allow them to enter present time. Something like: "Can you go round and make sure all the cupboards are shut, empty, or open?" might help them to face up to reality. Avoid giving them too much responsibility like putting them in charge of something; that could make their situation worse rather than better.

▸ **Accept and Take Action.** Of course, there are those clear-sighted individuals who see the incident for what it is and figure out a way to cope with the situation in the moment. They may employ a coping strategy they have used before; in that case, they know it works and can approach the problem with some confidence. For example, people who have learned to swim would have no difficulty when confronted by a dog stranded by a flood. They know that if the water happens to be rather deep, they could swim to safety, and so they would confidently try to rescue the stranded pet. Others may succeed by acting on the spur of the moment; they may not even consider the depth of the water because they are much too concerned about the plight of the poor dog. Either way, those people who are able to confront and deal with the situation manage to see the incident right through to an end point. Thus, they can recognize when it's all over and feel free to move forward unhindered, boosted by their own sense of competence.

These are the competent ones, who are ready to grit their teeth and get on with it. You can easily recognize them because they look alert and are prepared to listen. They will probably step forward to offer their assistance. You will have been able to spot these people during the BC exercises and workshops; they are the sort of people you want to have on your response teams. If they are not already involved in the response or recovery process, then you might recruit them for some spontaneous minor management roles. Invite their support by asking something like: "We are looking for volunteers to organize the sandbags." Or, "Can someone organize the teas and coffees?" Make use of their willingness and capability, and they will feel better about themselves with the added bonus that they are being helpful.

▶ **Become an Overwhelmed Misfit.** In the wake of any exciting or dramatic incident there may be a number of people around who are "surplus to requirements," an odd assortment of misfits, orphans, lost souls, trespassers, opportunists, and incompetents wandering around in various states of confusion and helplessness. Many of them will want to help, more for their own benefit than to serve any truly useful purpose. They are driven by the need to participate because they feel overwhelmed by the situation, and a contribution of some sort will make them feel less threatened. Unfortunately, they are probably out of their depth and unable to cope, more of a liability than an asset.

...the ERT is the group of *executives* who manage and control an emergency situation...

These spare bodies must be made "useful" or removed from the scene, without upset or offense. Such people are quite vulnerable at this time and need to be handled sensitively. It is far better for you to find something innocuous for them to do than refuse their help. Perhaps they can be useful in a relatively simple task at a safe distance. Maybe they can make a few phone calls to reassure other members of staff that everything is under control, or you might send them home to get some rest in case you need them to relieve others at a later stage. They could prove quite useful acting as temporary chauffeurs or security guards.

As we have seen, different people will have differing reactions, but giving them something to do will help them and the community to deal with the situation. The important thing is to communicate with them and invite their support. Find something for them to do rather than ignore them or leave them with nothing to occupy their hands and minds.

7.2   Assembling the Right Emergency Response Team

It is very difficult to predict exactly how any one individual is going to react in any particular situation. Indeed a person's behavior will depend upon a wide variety of factors which include state of health, state of mind, training, experience, beliefs, and responsibilities. How many of these diverse influences can we anticipate in advance of the specific event? This is especially difficult to judge, as many of these motivators are extremely variable on a daily or even hourly basis. All kinds of reaction must therefore be expected, recognized, and allowed for. More importantly, how can we create a team that is prepared to cope with both the event and themselves?

Disaster Recovery Institute International defines the ERT as "qualified and authorized personnel who have been trained to provide immediate assistance" (Disaster Recovery Institute International, 2015). In this book, I will extend that concept of "personnel" to mean that the ERT is the group of *executives* who manage and control an emergency situation on behalf of the enterprise. In other words, these people are in charge of the destiny of the total enterprise, with all the attendant responsibility. It is crucial that they perform well, both as individuals and as a well-matched team. To create a successful ERT, I recommend that you adopt a combination of:

▶ Careful selection.
▶ Thorough training.
▶ Appropriate tools for the job.

7.2.1   Selection

The selection process should start with a clear definition of the roles and responsibilities that are to be allocated. (More detail about who exactly should be on your various teams is covered in Chapter 11.) Then, it is a matter of choosing the most appropriate of those who are likely to be available. This choice will be influenced by a number of factors such as their regular position and their drive to succeed, often disguised as ambition. You also need to consider the potential mixture of different personalities, personal attributes, relevant experience, communication skills, and a willingness to serve in this capacity. One volunteer is worth a dozen conscripted men or women.

7.2.2   Thorough Training, Education, and Exercising

Having selected the team, you must then prepare them for the task.

Your ERT members will need to have the right set of abilities, skills, and knowledge. Therefore, your training or development program should seek to assess and monitor their abilities, enhance their skills, and provide them with the knowledge they might require. Realistic, risk-free, practical exercises are the obvious approach. However, to gain the full benefit, team members must be observed carefully and the program adapted to fit their needs as they evolve. At the same time you need to ensure the right mix of skills, abilities, and personalities. Nobody should be exempt from such a review process.

Much of the expertise in evaluation and decision-making will be an extension of their normal role as senior executives. Because of their overall familiarity with the business, the damage limitation or control aspect of the job should also come quite naturally.

Abilities: Ability can be assessed by observation or examination. The ability you seek is the latent capability to perform well under difficult conditions. While ability may be enhanced by intensive training and practice, it is unlikely that you can afford the time and effort to make a significant difference. It is far easier to choose those who already possess the capability to cope with an emergency situation.

> **The skill required will be practical expertise to deal with abnormal or out-of-line situations.**

Skills: Skills, however, can be cultivated through a reasonable amount of practice or exercise. The skill required will be practical expertise to deal with abnormal or out-of-line situations. In order to sustain a high degree of skill there is a need for regular ongoing practice or training. Fire and rescue workers who are continually exposed to critical circumstances can be expected to retain the highest level of coping skills simply because of their regular involvement. The military maintains soldiering skills by constant drilling and training. In the commercial world, you cannot expect to attain and retain such finely tuned skills. You need to have sufficient practice to be able to recognize the limits of your skills and have the wisdom to call for help from professionals before things get worse.

Knowledge: Knowledge can be acquired by study or experience; however there is little need for your team to know all there is to know. Knowledge is the possession of, or access to, relevant information. You can provide the team members with most of the information they require in the form of checklists, contact lists, and other reference materials. Even if they were to memorize all of the available data, it is unlikely they would be able to recall it in the excitement of the moment. Traumatic situations cause dispersed attention and short-term memory loss. Indeed, these are the key symptoms of trauma.

The Task Set for the Team: There are 4 groups of tasks the ERT is primarily responsible for.

1. Evaluation.
   - ❑ Resources available.
   - ❑ Skills available.
   - ❑ Shortfalls.

2. Strategic decisions.

3. Tactical decisions.

4. Damage limitation.

7.2.3   Appropriate Tools for the Job

Management and Control Model

The gold, silver, bronze control model is commonly used by the police and other emergency authorities, particularly in the UK, and it can easily be adapted to meet your purpose (College of Policing, 2013). It provides empowerment and control in a manner which everyone can understand and respect.

Bronze: In the typical crisis situation, bronze control would take charge of the actual incident area. Bronze control would be a single point of contact, in charge of liaison, access, and communications within that inner zone. Access to this region would normally be restricted to the recovery and salvage teams, together with the emergency services.

Silver: The immediate surroundings, perhaps the whole building, or even the complete site would come under the supervision of silver control. This would be another single point of contact, perhaps with a higher level of authority, in charge of liaison, access, and communications within the outer zone of the incident. Typically, this team would be responsible for organizing and controlling the essential border activities (such as parking arrangements and dealing with members of staff and the public in and around the site) and coordinating deliveries and supplies into and out of the site area.

Gold: Meanwhile, gold control would be more concerned with dealing with external interests, such as customers, the media, and the authorities. This would be the highest level of corporate authority, representing the company's interests and taking full responsibility for the ongoing management of the incident.

> **...working members of the ERT will be far less prone to traumatization.**

Regular communication between these three control teams ensures everyone sings from the same hymn sheet and the recovery efforts are neither restricted by lack of support nor compromised by interruptions and distractions.

Capabilities Required

The principal tool for the team members is their capability to think clearly and make important decisions under pressure, supported by a set of simple guidelines, together with some basic information such as contact lists and team structures. Underpinning their direction and decision-making, there has to be a complete set of plans (as covered in Chapter 11), enabling the ERT to call for a coordinated, structured approach to the recovery of all the essential business functions.

Empowerment: In an emergency situation there is no time, or space, for a large hierarchical command chain. Authority must be delegated to those who are in the best position to be effective. They should, therefore, possess the skills to handle the recovery. To make sure this happens, you need to train all those who might be called upon to serve on the ERT. (Training of the team is covered later in this chapter.)

Dealing with Trauma: In the wake of an emergency, it is normal for people to be traumatized and feel uncomfortable in what used to be their safe workspace. If they are not given appropriate support and counseling, many of them may eventually leave as a result. Although you should recognize the need for such services, this type of work is not the responsibility of the ERT. However, a good debriefing, during which everybody has the chance to air views and vent feelings, can be a very constructive way of providing first line support for all those who were involved or affected. Generally, because they will be actively involved, the working members of the ERT will be far less prone to traumatization. The opportunity to be causative rather than the victim of circumstance is a powerful remedy for those who are in the front line. They will undoubtedly feel bad if it all goes horribly wrong, but that will not necessarily happen. After all, you are going to choose them carefully, train them properly, and support them effectively.

Communication: Your ERT will need to communicate with a wide range of interested parties, each with his or her own viewpoint and needs. The members of this broad and varied audience will need clear, relevant, comforting messages, which are both understandable and useful to them. In order to achieve this clarity, you must avoid jargon, waffling, and "official speak." There should be an open dialog with absolute honesty. You cannot hide the truth; it will emerge with, or without, your help. If the truth is released, you have little to fear; if it escapes, it will seek revenge. An authoritative speaker, who is fully prepared to deal with any skeletons in the closet, should make all communications with sympathy and compassion. All messages need to be composed carefully, based on a core of factual statements. The content of the messages should also be consistent even if the language has to be tailored for different groups of readers or listeners. It will do no harm to remind everyone of the "good news" to give a positive balance. Dealing with the outside world via the media, or through your own communication lines, does require a delicate touch and sound delivery technique which can only be acquired through careful preparation and proper training. According to James E. Lukaszewski, "Most bad news initially comes from negative phrases habitually and carelessly used by the spokesperson.... Eradicate the use of these and the vast, vast majority of your bad news will be controllable" (Lukaszewski, 2013, p. 193).

> **...command and control can be achieved only by creating a definite point of control.**

Decision-Making: Decision-making under pressure and strange circumstances is not always easy but it can be learned and practiced. All the major decisions, such as whether to invoke the plan, should be based on facts and criteria. The criteria can be agreed in advance, while the facts can be established at the time of the incident. All decisions should be recorded and adhered to, without fear of countermand or retribution. This can only be achieved by making sure the team is fully empowered to make strategic and tactical decisions, whatever the implications, and that the members work within a set of approved guidelines. If these guidelines are meaningful and familiar to them, the members of the ERT are going to feel comfortable about making sound judgments without debate or delay.

7.3   Command and Control

A single point of control is the only effective way to manage a loose collection of people who are suddenly plunged into a dynamic project. Any other approach will lead to loss of control as different groups divert from the original intention. Such diversions can be the result of differing interpretations or they may be due to changes of circumstance as the situation evolves.

An emergency situation is an extreme case of the dynamic project. The whole purpose is to change the circumstances. The original intention may be modified many times before normality is re-established. Even normality itself may change radically. Under such erratic conditions, command and control can be achieved only by creating a definite point of control. The command and control post symbolizes the need for an effective chain of command and a common source of information and instructions. It should also facilitate these essential elements of emergency management.

Therefore the command and control post should not only be practical, it should also look the part. Appearance and feel play psychological roles in demonstrating that all is well and everything is under control or is coming under control.

Needs of Emergency Management

Over the course of many years, I have observed the activities of ERTs from a wide range of backgrounds and expertise. This has led me to draw a number of conclusions about the basic nature of emergency management.

You need to distinguish between the various types and scales of organization which might require a command post. At one end of the scale there is the military need to command a whole army, engaged in complex operations. Very large-scale enterprises may have to deal with issues spanning several continents. On the other hand, many businesses operate from quite limited accommodation and minimal resources.

> **The ERT derives great benefit from delegating routine functions and specialist tasks to a *management support group.***

Environmental and transport agencies are often faced with major disasters which are the focus of world attention. Telecommunications, electricity, and water companies have to keep track of vast networks. The majority of organizations have relatively simple, and infrequent, emergency command and control needs, but they can certainly learn from the experiences of the minority. You can assist in this connection by distilling the experience of the minority down into some basic concepts which might apply to the general case of the majority.

Returning to the three-level command and control model (HM Government, 2013), it is apparent that bronze control is responsible for the operational aspects surrounding the incident. This is a very practical hands-on type of role. Bronze control will need to coordinate their activities with the emergency services on the ground.

Silver control is responsible for the tactical approach to the incident and managing communication within the control structure. The role is a combination of control and command duties and there has to be a high level of awareness of the implications. Silver control will be able to liaise with the emergency services' headquarters or through a liaison officer if one is appointed.

Gold command assumes overall control with responsibility for the overall strategy, high level decision-making and external communications. Gold command deals with the press and other interested parties. All external requests for information, or access, must be referred to gold command. Neither bronze nor silver control is in a position to deal with such matters, and they must resist any temptation to make comments or pass information to outsiders.

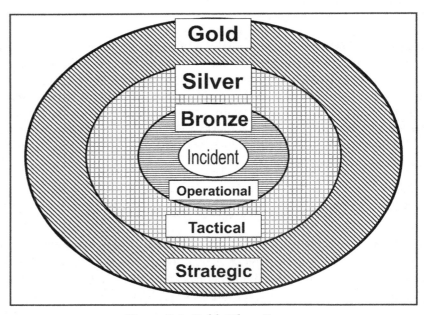

Figure 7-1. Gold, Silver, Bronze

7.3.1   Command and Control Post Logical Structure

A sound logical structure provides the basis of an effective command and control post. There are four essential functions that need to work together in close harmony during what can be a very demanding and stressful period.

Communications – Receipt and dispatch of information and instructions.

Administration – Recording and management of information and instructions.

Intelligence – Analysis and interpretation of information and verification of instructions.

Control – Decision-making based on the information and instructions available.

In Figure 7-2, you can see how the ERT fulfils the central role of silver control with the crisis management team acting as gold command. The diagram also shows the key activities for each unit and section.

The ERT derives great benefit from delegating routine functions and specialist tasks to a *management support group*. The support group comprises three sections, each concerned with a particular aspect.

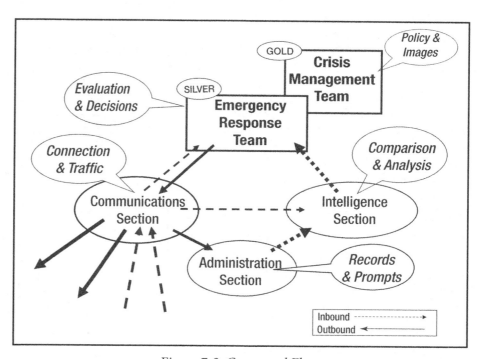

Figure 7-2. Command Flows

- The *communications section* is essentially the switchboard/reception function. These section members establish contact on behalf of the ERT, receive and route all incoming calls, and pass on messages. Visitors would also be greeted by this section.

- An *administration section* would be responsible for keeping a history log, typing up interim reports, and reminding the ERT of any deadlines, appointments, or checkpoints. These section members would also be responsible for ensuring that visitors are checked in and out.

- The *intelligence section* would be concerned with analyzing what is happening and filtering out the essential key facts on behalf of the ERT. These section members would also be expected to spot trends and provide statistics where appropriate. The intelligence section would also be in a position to brief visitors or to brief relieving personnel before they join the main group.

7.3.1.1 Emergency Communications

In Figure 7-3, you can trace the paths for the lines of communication between the teams and their audiences. There are single points of control for all inbound and outbound traffic.

7.3.2   Command and Control Post: Physical Structure

Clearly, the physical layout of the command and control post will depend largely on what is available.

Some essential features may limit the options to be considered. In addition, some desirable features will affect the final choice, while some ideal characteristics are potential enhancements. The perfect command and control post would combine all of these features and characteristics.

7.3.2.1 Essential Features

Secure, safe accommodation: The command and control post needs to be secure to ensure that everything is there and ready for use after lying idle for some time. It also needs to be a safe place in the event of an emergency. This means it should be robust and protected against any fires or floods which may strike the business premises. A mobile command and control center can serve a number of sites and be set up somewhere safe yet convenient, near to the actual disaster site. Independent communications and power do need to be provided.

Guaranteed, easy access: The command and control post must be accessible at all times under all circumstances including worst-case scenarios.

Weatherproof: The command and control post is likely to be put into service as a result of, or during, the very worst weather conditions. So it does need to be a safe haven, providing shelter from the storm, as well as being a secure working environment.

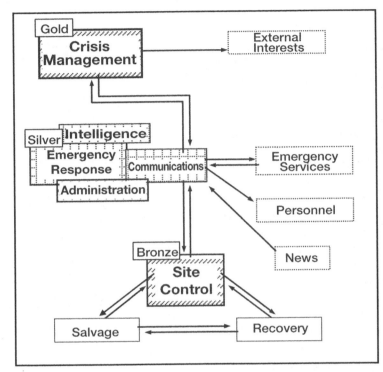

Figure 7-3. Points of Contact for Inbound and Outbound Communications Traffic

Table and chairs: At least one table and sufficient chairs for those who will be working in the command and control post.

Adequate lighting: As the emergency situation may last well into the night, it is essential to have enough lighting available for the ERT.

Communication facilities: There should be full communication facilities available in the command and control post. It may be necessary to remain in contact with the emergency services, the recovery teams, the rescue teams, the public, the news services, head office, other locations, regulatory bodies, and other interested parties.

> ‣ Phone lines for incoming and outgoing calls.
> ‣ A fax machine on a separate line.
> ‣ Cell phone charging stations.
> ‣ Backup power.
> ‣ Satellite phones.

Whiteboard or flip chart: The team will need some means of recording and displaying the key action points, outstanding actions, milestones, targets, and timeframes as well as a summary history log. You will also need to ensure there is a fresh supply of pens and paper.

Always ready: The command and control post should be kept in a constant state of readiness so as to eliminate delays in responding to an emergency.

Contact lists: Up-to-date contact details for all emergency suppliers and services should always be held in the command and control post, preferably in hardcopy format.

Draft statements: It may save time if there are some pre-prepared draft statements. Details of the situation are unknown but some basic facts and advice can be provided for the team to draw up their first draft statements for the staff and others. Support and goodwill depend upon getting some positive messages out as early as possible.

Event history logs: Full details of what happened and when; what actions were taken, when and why should be recorded at the time. This record may contain valuable lessons for the future and could even be required as evidence in due course.

7.3.2.2 Desirable Features

Separation of duties and facilities: Confusion is reduced if the various duties and functions are kept separate. Labelling will also help to remove doubt and confusion, provided it is clear, up-to-date, and reliable.

> ...seek the advice of corporate communications, who are the experts in this field.

▸ Separate inbound from outbound traffic.
▸ Separate support from control functions.

News channels: It could be helpful to know what is going on, or being said in the rest of the world.

▸ Radio, TV, and Internet.

Wall clock: Serves to remind everybody of the time and is a common reference for logging purposes.

Photocopier: Copies of various documents may be needed for distribution or for record purposes. The ideal is to have a multi-purpose printer which can also function as a fax machine, a scanner, or a photocopier.

Laptop or desktop PC: This will allow the teams to send and receive emails as well as text messages. It will also provide them with access to the Internet so they can track what is happening in the rest of the world.

Standby power: It is possible that mains power will be unavailable for much of the time during an emergency. A standby generator would be a useful asset.

Dedicated purpose: Ideally the accommodation for the command and control post should be dedicated to the purpose and equipped for emergency use. A commandeered resource can only be regarded as a compromise.

Loudhailer or megaphone: A device to amplify the voice can be useful when directing traffic, controlling crowds, or addressing staff after they have gathered at the emergency assembly area.

Battle boxes: A permanent command and control post might be the ideal place to store emergency supplies such as hard hats and reflective jackets.

Social media: Your corporate communications group should have rules in place to restrict, limit, or control the use or abuse of social media. There are some companies which use these facilities on a regular basis as a means of communicating with their staff or customers. Those rules should cover what is likely to happen in an emergency situation although the temptation to post a comment or a picture may be difficult for some people to resist.

Your BC plans should draw everybody's attention to these rules, emphasizing the importance and the implications of controlling what the world sees and hears when the organization is under stress. Obviously, this is an area where you should seek the advice of corporate communications, who are the experts in this field. According to James E. Lukaszewski, "To effectively control social media usage by both the enterprise and employees, a documented strategy…should be developed with the involvement of all relevant stakeholders…. This holistic approach to integrating emerging technologies into the enterprise helps to ensure that risks are being considered in the context of broader business goals and objectives" (Lukaszewski, 2013, p. 235).

7.3.2.3 Ideal Characteristics

The perfect command and control post would have all of the above features which are necessary to support the basic functions of the ERT. It would also have some, or all, of the following characteristics.

Briefing area: A separate briefing area can be used in a number of ways. It can be used to:

> • Brief visitors without disturbing or interrupting the core activities.
> • Brief incoming team members before they relieve their colleagues.
> • Debrief outgoing team members after they have handed over to their colleagues.
> • Receive briefings from authorities or emergency services.
> • Rehearse before press briefing and as an emergency press briefing room.

Breakout area: A breakout area can be used to allow members of the operational team to relax during the quieter moments, if they occur. It might also be used to debate the finer points of an argument away from the core activities.

Controlled parking: Members of the ERT, and their authorized visitors, should be able to park close to the command and control post and all other vehicles should be kept well away from the area.

Refreshments: There should be facilities in the command and control post, or nearby, for drinks and light refreshments. In an extended operation hot meals might be required.

Sleeping area: Key players may prefer to remain on the premises between shifts rather than travel, especially if they are on call during these times. Sleeping bags would be useful here. A bed might also prove to be useful in the case of dealing with injuries or illness.

Shower or washing facilities: People will want freshening up or a thorough cleaning, particularly if they should have to work under dirty or hazardous conditions.

Soundproofing: Protection from the noise of the outside world can help people to focus on what they are doing. This could be a distinct advantage during the commotion which often surrounds an emergency.

Good ventilation: Fresh air is essential.

Alternative exits/entrances: There should be more than one way into and out of the command and control post. People arriving or leaving may wish to remain anonymous or unseen, or they may simply wish to avoid others. Safe egress is another consideration.

> • One doorway can be set aside exclusively for emergency use, while another one is for general use.
> • In an emergency, any particular doorway may not be available for use. Without an alternative access, the command and control center could be compromised.

7.4   Phased Incident Management

From a management perspective, you should regard the management of any form of incident as a phased activity. In the anticipation phase, everyone is half expecting something to happen but hoping it won't. As the moment approaches, the anticipation and excitement build to a crescendo. At least, this is true where there is some forewarning of a change of circumstances. In the case of the truly unexpected, there is a sudden explosion of excitement rather than a gradual surge. This phase is characterized by a steady buildup of risk and it is terminated when the risk manifests itself as an actual event.

Once the incident has occurred and the new circumstances emerge, there is an immediate need to confront and deal with the situation. You need to bring things under control. It is time to contain the effects of the imposed changes and address the immediate issues. This is a time of intense and often chaotic activity, which is characterized by the significant reduction of risk.

When the immediate problems have been addressed and the situation has been brought under control, or at least stabilized, it is time to be concerned with the longer term. There is an obvious need to recover from the trauma and excitement and begin to reconstruct the future.

The recovery phase is the one which tends to dwell.

At each of these stages or phases, the team characteristics must change to meet the anticipated activity set. On the other hand, it is not wise to replace the whole team when there is so much happening and everybody is engrossed in what they are trying to do. Also bear in mind that fatigue will take its inevitable toll if these people are allowed to remain on duty for too long. Intense concentration can be very tiring.

One solution is to have extended casual handovers in which each team member hands over to his or her replacement independently of the rest of the team. The casual aspect means that the team membership gradually changes over time rather than a sudden and complete transformation. This ensures a degree of strategic continuity rather than a series of step changes.

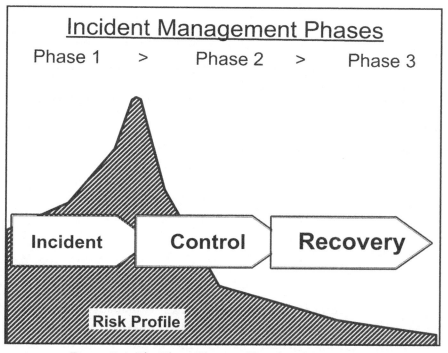

Figure 7-4. The Three Phases of Incident Management

The extended aspect means the incoming team member is briefed before joining his or her outgoing partner. Then they can sit and watch for a while, until they feel they understand what is going on and what is likely to be expected of them. Before leaving, the outgoing person will stay and watch his or her partner for a while, just in case of a question or need for further guidance. If necessary, the outgoing team member may remain on standby for a while. This could be because his or her particular skill or knowledge is likely to be called into play at some stage or perhaps there are some doubts about the status of the incoming team member who may have limited experience or knowledge in some areas.

Figure 7-4 shows a risk profile of incident management. During the initial first phase, the buildup to the incident might be a slow and gradual increase of risk or there could be a sudden and abrupt rise as the incident occurs. Once the incident has occurred, the risks are usually brought under control fairly quickly because of the perceived urgency of the situation. The recovery phase is the one which tends to dwell. This is where you deal with the backlog and try to get back to normal; somehow there is less urgency, and complacency begins to set in.

Phase 1 is about preparation, monitoring, and activation; it is an integral part of business as usual.

- Preparation is deliberate.
- Monitoring is passive.
- Activation is dynamic.

Phase 2 is about deliberate activity in a dynamic situation; it establishes control and initiates the response.

- Establishing control.
- Containing the incident.
- Activation of the recovery procedures.
- Initiating the crisis response.

Phase 3 is about the ongoing management of a key project; it aims to resume normalcy and avoid a recurrence.

- Restoring business processes and activities.
- Recovering the infrastructure.
- Returning the business to normal.
- Preventing a recurrence.
- Learning the lessons.
- Applying the lessons.

7.5   Communications

In an emergency there is an urgent need to inform everybody about what has happened, what is being done, and what they should do. There will be several reasons why this will be difficult, if not impossible. (More about communications in a crisis or disaster will be covered in Chapter 13.) These difficulties might include:

- Lack of certainty about what actually happened.
- Information being withheld for security or other reasons.
- Conflicting information from different sources.
- Lack of a firm decision.
- Fear of starting a panic.
- No means of communication.

7.5.1   Lack of Certainty

In the very early stages of an incident there will be a desperate clamoring for a clear explanation. However, there is also likely to be a great deal of confusion and uncertainty, which tends to cloud the real issues and provide several conflicting versions of the apparent truth. There is a natural tendency for people to jump to conclusions based on their assumptions, fears, and imagination. The opportunity for rumor and conjecture tends to breed a sense of insecurity which leads to all sorts of fears and wild explanations. Before long, many versions of the story are being passed around by word of mouth. Sometimes this leads to debate or even argument about what really happened, or is happening. On other occasions, one particular story begins to emerge as the most plausible explanation, and before long it is accepted by all and sundry as being the authorized version of events.

Once this "self-authorized" account is established in the minds of the people it might be rather difficult to convince them otherwise. Any facts or reports you provide which run counter to this commonly held belief will be suspect on the grounds that you are trying to deceive by withholding the truth. This leads to speculation about why you are not being honest and so the media tends to move on to the conspiracy theory phase, with the story becoming further embroidered with a plethora of legends, myths, memories, and bad dreams. At this stage, anybody coming up with the true facts will be branded as an evil spirit who is trying to mislead everybody for some nefarious reason.

> **...any delay in relaying the truth...makes it very difficult to correct the usual rumors...**

Therefore, any delay in relaying the truth to those affected or interested makes it very difficult to correct the usual rumors and tales that will abound. Tell them what you know as soon as you can, even if it is only part of the truth. Obviously, you should promise to let them have more details as they come to light, preferably with an estimate of when you will get back to them.

7.5.2   Withholding Information

Sometimes, information is withheld out of security considerations. Or it may be withheld because no one feels authorized to release the information, or simply because no one has thought about telling the information to anyone else. Whatever the reason, withholding information about what happened is a poor idea because it fails to instill a sense of trust. While it makes sense that you should avoid naming names or making accusations, it is essential that you do provide some basic data about what happened before the rumor mill starts to generate the counter truths which may prove difficult to dispel.

7.5.3   Conflicting Information

If there are differing versions of the story emanating from the source, i.e., the actual scene of the incident, then it may pay to try to verify which version is the nearest to the truth. However, if it is not yet possible to reach certainty, it is probably wisest to issue both versions, with the caveat that you are getting conflicting reports. A delay in telling your version can only lead to the rampant spread of disinformation which is, at the very least, counterproductive.

7.5.4   Lack of a Firm Decision

There is no excuse for poor, or slow, decision-making. You need to have plans which provide clear guidance on how to reach a decision about what to do. This decision-making process will be based on matching the known facts with certain criteria. In the event of uncertainty the plan should indicate a default option. The plan should also provide empowerment for the right person to make such decisions.

If you do not have plans which cover this point, nobody will have any sympathy and the world at large will regard you and those around you as incompetent. This book covers what goes into such plans, and how to create them.

7.5.5   Fear of Starting a Panic

This is usually an unfounded fear. People would much rather face up to the truth, no matter how awful, than be kept in the dark. Panic is not a natural reaction for the majority of people. The natural tendency is to try to behave rationally, based on knowledge of the circumstances and the associated threats. It is only when they are denied knowledge of the circumstances or the threats that they are likely to behave irrationally. The normal reaction to any situation is based on the instinct for survival which generally provokes rational behavior rather than mass panic. You must distinguish between people hurrying and people panicking. Panic only occurs when rational behavior, which might include hurrying, doesn't seem to be working as a survival strategy.

7.5.6   No Means of Communication

Again, while there is no excuse for being unprepared, your pre-planning should include alternative means of communication for use in an emergency. Telephone lines may or may not be working; if they are working, you may not have access to a handset or the people you want to speak to may not be at the normal place of work.

Under normal circumstances, mobile phones offer a pretty reliable means of communication which is independent of either party's current whereabouts. However, in an emergency there is a good chance the local network will be overwhelmed. The phone company's response to this phenomenon is to impose "call gapping" which restricts the number of calls getting through at any one time. By re-dialing once or twice, you can usually overcome this artificial limitation. Once a call is connected, the actual service is normal.

Under certain circumstances, however, the authorities may impose controlled access to mobile networks in the vicinity of an incident. This means you will not be able to use your mobile phone, unless you move away from the area.

Your plans should take account of these factors when considering how to relay messages to your people during an emergency. Notices, or posters, are a reliable low tech form of communicating with anyone who is passing by. There is also the initial opportunity to speak directly to those who are gathered at the assembly point. This will probably be a one-time possibility which is likely to include the advice to go home or retire to some other location. It is unlikely they will remain gathered at the assembly area for any length of time without good reason.

In addition to the question of communicating with people who have been evacuated, there is the prior need to inform them of the need to evacuate, where to go, and how to get there. This preliminary contact will depend on whatever communication systems are available. In the absence of some form of public announcement system, you may have to depend on your fire marshals to relay the message to all the people in their area. In the event of a minor emergency which doesn't require the attention of the ERT, any messages in connection with evacuation would probably be delivered by the security people. However, the mechanism should be the same for both instances.

Self-Examination Questions

1. What is likely to be the single most important factor in determining the success of an enterprise during a crisis or disaster?

    A. The validity and effectiveness of the business continuity (BC) plan

    B. The performance of the emergency response team (ERT)

    C. The extent to which the organization follows published standards and regulations

2. Because different people respond to a high-stress crisis situation in different ways – some more functionally than others – managing a disaster is first and foremost about

    A. managing the emotions of the moment.

    B. implementing the emergency response plan.

    C. making sure everyone is actively engaged in disaster response.

3. The emergency response team (ERT) is the group of _____ who manage and control an emergency situation on behalf of the enterprise.

    A. executives

    B. professional specialists

    C. frontline workers

4. The four essential functions that the command and control post must perform to effectively manage a crisis are as follows:

    A. 1) command, 2) control, 3) communications, and 4) intelligence

    B. 1) communications, 2) administration, 3) intelligence, and 4) control

    C. 1) communications, 2) empowerment, 3) intelligence, and 4) decision-making

5. In the three-level command and control structure, the ERT fulfills the core function of the _____ level.

    A. gold

    B. silver

    C. bronze

6. What are the three phases of incident management?

    A. 1) Crisis Management, 2) Emergency Response, and 3) Site Control

    B. 1) Prevention, 2) De-escalation, and 3) Resolution

    C. 1) Preparation, 2) Control, and 3) Recovery

7. In the aftermath of a crisis incident, when should the ERT release information about what has happened, what is being done, and what people should do?

    A. As soon as possible – tell people what you know as soon as you can, even if it is only part of the truth.

    B. Once all the data are complete and verified – tell people what you know only when you know it's the whole truth.

    C. Once the crisis is under control – there's no point in releasing information when an active crisis could change that information at any time.

8. In a crisis, the ERT withholds some important information about the crisis because the team believes that releasing the information could cause a panic. Is this likely to be a wise decision?

    A. Yes, starting a panic is the worst-case scenario in a crisis and should be avoided by any means necessary.

    B. Maybe, if releasing the information could cause other problems for the company even if it does not set off a panic.

    C. No, the fear of panic is usually unfounded, and people always want to know the truth, no matter how bad the situation is.

Food for Thought

In this chapter we have looked at how people are likely to respond to an emergency and how you might manage the situation as it unfolds. The implications are that you need to plan and prepare for such a situation in order to ensure the health and safety of those who visit, work, or reside in your premises. Emergency response and evacuation is a core basic element of business continuity. One could claim that it is the most important element of BC because people's lives could depend on how well you approach this piece of work.

Exercises

To align what you have just learned with the reality of the world in which you live and work, consider the place where you normally work or study as your reference, and consider the following questions. You could also use a shopping mall or a college campus as an alternative venue or to get a comparison. Going through the exercise more than once will help to reinforce the learning and give you a clearer idea of the various possibilities and implications. (For detailed information about evacuation procedures, see Appendix D of this book.)

1. Where would you expect to go in the event of an evacuation?
   > Is this a guess or do you know?

2. Which route, or routes, would you expect to take?
   > How would you know which one to use?

3. What do you expect to happen when you get there?

4. How would you seek to improve any aspect of the evacuation plans or procedures?

5. Who should be on the emergency response team (ERT)?
   > How would this team be invoked or called together?

6. How and where do you envisage the team setting up a command and control center?
   > Bear in mind what exists, and would be available, on site.

Looking Forward

Now that you understand the basics of emergency response and evacuation, you should be in a position to apply what you already know and get ready to deal with the inevitable. This next chapter will build on your basic knowledge to help prepare your organization to deal with such a situation when, and if, it arises.

Downloadable Business Continuity Toolkit

The **Business Continuity Toolkit** contains material on emergency management team selection and training. You will also find instructions for handling an emergency and tools to illustrate your talks on the subject.

References

College of Policing (2013). *Command structures.* Retrieved from http://www.app.college.police.uk/app-content/operations/command-and-control/command-structures

Disaster Recovery Institute International (2015). *International Glossary for Resilience.* Retrieved from https://www.drii.org/glossary.php

Hawkins Mitchell, V. (2013). *The cost of emotions in the workplace: The bottom line value of emotional continuity management.* Brookfield, CT: Rothstein Publishing.

HM Government (2013). *Inspired by 2012: The legacy from the London 2012 Olympic and Paralympic Games.* Retrieved from https://www.gov.uk/government/uploads/system/uploads/attachment_data/file/224148/2901179_OlympicLegacy_acc.pdf

Lukaszewski, J.E. (2013). *Lukaszewski on crisis communication: What your CEO needs to know about reputation risk and crisis management.* Brookfield, CT: Rothstein Publishing.

For Additional Reading

For help in preparing emergency plans in the US, see
https://www.osha.gov/SLTC/etools/evacuation/expertsystem/default.htm

For information about emergency response and recovery planning in the UK, see
https://www.gov.uk/emergency-response-and-recovery

8

Emergency Preparedness

So far this book has looked at the reasons why you would need to have some form of business continuity (BC) arrangements and who should be prepared to respond when things go wrong. By now, you should have a clear idea of how to develop a suitable strategy and select the right people. The next step – which will be explored in this chapter – is to provide those people with the tools to do the job.

This chapter will help you to:

- ☑ Understand what tools, supplies, and resources may be required in an emergency situation.

- ☑ Create a "battle box" to ensure that emergency supplies are available and usable when the occasion demands.

- ☑ Arrange, manage, and store those items safely and securely.

8.1   Identifying and Maintaining Emergency Resources

Resources and facilities are the physical assets of BC.

▸ *Resources* are those basic goods, supplies, or devices which you rely on to work effectively whenever you are operating in a BC mode. People and information are key resources in any business environment.

▸ *Facilities* include the equipment or accommodation which enables us to work with those resources. Buildings and computers are key facilities in the business world.

Essential goods and supplies allocated for recovery purposes need to be secured, preferably at the recovery site, where they are easy for the recovery team to locate. You need to have the right kind of supplies in place, and the right amounts in stock, to support the business recovery activities. Also, you need a procedure in place to replenish those supplies when the business begins to move into full functional mode after the initial recovery. Resources would include such goods and supplies as essential raw materials and components for production processes, stationery for the office, and food and drink for the people. It would also include the emergency support items kept in *battle boxes*, special kits for emergency use (covered in 8.3 below).

> **The regular feedback keeps you on track... managing the right things, in the right way.**

Maintenance is an essential long-term aspect of BC, because those resources and facilities will need to be permanently ready for an incident, ensuring that they will be there for use in an emergency situation, whenever it may occur.

Maintenance of BC resources and facilities is mostly about control and management. Feedback from rehearsals, tests, audits, and reviews will indicate where particular attention is required. The regular feedback keeps you on track, ensuring that you are controlling and managing the right things, in the right way. The control side of your maintenance program for these facilities and resources is about:

▸ *Access control* to prevent unauthorized use of your property.

▸ *Inventory control* to ensure you have what you need.

▸ *Financial control* to ensure you are cost-effective.

▸ *Service and repair* to ensure everything is in working order.

▸ *Updates and changes* to ensure everything is compatible.

▸ *Asset retention* to make sure you do not lose your property.

8.1.1   Access Control

Access control is about preventing the wrong people from using your resources and facilities, but allowing the right people to make use of them at the right time. If you do not control access, resources and facilities may be misused and fall into disrepair. You run the risk of missing items, untidiness, wear and tear, damage, etc. Reduce this possibility by limiting opportunities.

8.1.2   Inventory Control

Inventory control is a means of ensuring everything is in the right place and in good order when you need it. If you do not control your inventory, it will soon disappear and someone will want to know who is responsible.

Basically, an inventory is a list of your assets, and you need to keep track of them to exercise control. At all times you should know what you've got and where it is. For each type of item you should also keep track of:

▸ Quantities and where they are held.

▸ Serial numbers and features, where appropriate.

▸ Utilization: who used it, when, and why.

▸ Service records or notes on condition or shelf life.

At all times, the BC inventory should reflect the actual current business need. Again, you are reliant upon feedback from the owners of the operation.

For example, my car is a capital item, but the fuel is a running cost I have to budget for.

8.1.2.1 Establishing the Inventory

Before you can control or manage an inventory, you have to create it. You may have inherited a well-catalogued list of assets, but let us assume you are starting from scratch. The first step is to go around the business and establish exactly what is there for BC purposes. You must also establish what is actually required. There will be some clues in the business impact analysis (BIA), but now you need to refine those broad requirements down to more specific detail. The only certain way to accomplish this is to visit each of the critical functions and ask questions. The result of this exercise will be an initial inventory and a shopping list or a wish list.

You have to keep track of the status of all of the items on your inventory, adding to it as necessary. Occasionally, some of the items can be released when they are no longer regarded as essential. Meanwhile, you need a process to convert the shopping list into emergency reserve property, in order to extend your inventory. If you encounter any doubts about whether an item should be listed as an actual, or potential, BC asset, then it is best to assume it is one. To help you keep track of your inventory you can use a card index, a paper-based system, simple computerized documents, or a sophisticated database, but the principle would still be the same.

8.1.3 Financial Control

Financial control is all about making sure you are cost effective, and being able to show it. There are two broad categories of finance you need to deal with: the *short-term running costs* and the *long-term capital cost*.

▸ An organization manages and funds the short-term, day-to-day running costs by budgeting, and you will be expected to stay within your budget. A budget sets a total limit but is not normally specific about the detailed expenditure. While a budget gives you the flexibility to spend money according to your needs, as they occur, you may find yourself in a desperate situation in which the budget does not allow for something crucial, which means you will have to resort to applying for some capital expenditure.

▸ Capital expenditure permits you to acquire those major items outside of your budget, normally by means of a purchase order process in which you request the funds for a specific item. Often, this will include the need for a business case to support the application, especially where the sum of money is fairly large.

For example, my car is a capital item, but the fuel is a running cost I have to budget for. My printer is a capital item, but paper and cartridges are casual or budgetary items.

8.1.4   Service and Repair

Some of your BC resources and facilities will need to be serviced from time to time – as a regular requirement or simply performed as needed, usually after a specified number of hours of use. As the responsible person, you need to know who is able to carry out regular repairs of routine items, preferably at a reasonable cost and without undue delays or arguments about payment, delivery, workmanship, or availability. You will also have to make the arrangements for this repair work to be carried out as and when necessary, preferably at a time when the risks are relatively low and the business is fairly quiet.

Without resources and facilities your program is doomed to failure…

Other items may need to be repaired occasionally. Your inventory control should make you aware of any items which get damaged, start to malfunction, or show signs of wear. You may need to engage in regular tours of inspection to check for damaged, or missing, items. These visits are also a chance to make everyone aware of why you need these things, reinforcing the BC message about preparedness.

8.1.5   Updates and Changes

Over time, most business systems are upgraded to include more features or capability, or to cure or prevent problems. Any systems which are to be used for BC purposes need to be kept up-to-date in order to remain compatible with all those improvements. Otherwise, they can become a liability in an emergency situation. The BC manager has to monitor these changing needs and respond to them. Indeed, BC should be involved in major changes or upgrades to any of the core systems.

From time to time the business may change its operations or the equipment and systems it employs. These changes can be due to:

- Expansion or contraction plans.
- Acquisitions or mergers.
- Changes of method.
- New technology.
- New products and services.

Whatever the reason behind the change, BC needs to be there to support the change – and then protect the new way of doing things, once all of the changes have been implemented successfully. Of course, that includes updating BC plans and procedures accordingly.

8.1.6   Asset Retention

Any resource or facility which is reserved for BC purposes can seem to be standing idle for long periods. Casual observers may assume it is spare capacity which they could usefully employ for their own purpose. At first, they may want to have only temporary use, but over time they will attempt to establish permanent rights to your assets.

It is important that this danger is recognized at the highest level and your ownership is fully recognized. Any BC program depends entirely on the immediate availability of its resources and facilities. Without resources and facilities, your program is doomed to failure, and failure of BC opens the way to failure of the whole business.

8.1.7   Feedback

Feedback from the business and the BC program is a means of keeping everything on the right track. You need it to make sure you are controlling and managing the right things in the right way. Tests, exercises, and rehearsals are all designed to explore the limitations of your preparations through practice. So, they are a valuable source of feedback from a practical point of view.

Reviews and audits of the plans and procedures are designed to reveal weaknesses and areas for improvement. Most of these flaws will come from the many relatively minor changes which are made over time. This means the feedback from reviews and audits is helpful to make sure your arrangements are kept up-to-date.

8.2   Disaster Actions and Modes

During the period of time spanning an emergency and the response, there are several distinct modes. Each of these modes has its own characteristics, and timeframe, and you should bear this in mind when allocating resources and personnel. Not everybody is suited to every situation. As shown in Figure 8-1, with BC firmly in place, you are in **ready mode**, prepared for any eventuality. This is a semi-permanent mode which persists until something untoward happens.

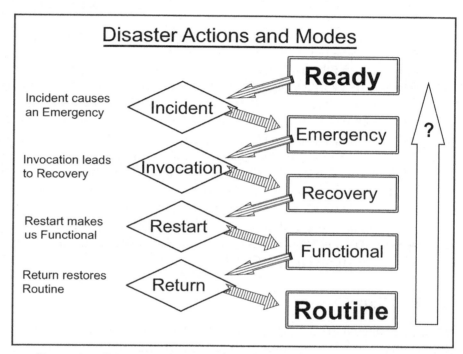

Figure 8-1. Disaster Actions and Modes

▸ **Emergency mode.** Immediately after an incident you must have instant access to all of your emergency resources and facilities to support prompt action. Ease of access is the key factor in emergency mode.

▸ **Recovery mode.** With the incident more or less under control you need secure access to your critical resources and facilities to support the initial recovery procedures. Secure but guaranteed access is the key factor in recovery mode.

▸ **Functional mode.** Once the recovery is complete, you need regular access to the full set of resources and facilities to support the core functions of the business. Regular but secure access is the key factor in functional mode.

Finally, you are able to return and settle back into **routine mode**. You are back to normal and everything needs to be made ready again.

8.2.1   Tools and Supplies

A bewildering variety of jobs needs to be done during the recovery from an emergency. Tools and supplies for dealing with various aspects of the emergency, recovery, or restoration might be considered to be the responsibility of the *emergency manager*. The core business operations may also require certain tools and supplies in order to provide a minimum level of service in the first phase of their recovery. Those items are the responsibility of the *business units*.

Business-specific skills cannot be bought off the shelf.

However, without you prompting them, those business unit managers may not think about such preparations. You should draw the matter to their attention and perhaps offer your help, but there are limits to what you can do on your own. Give some careful thought to come up with a realistic list of what items each department is likely to need. This sort of thinking requires an intimate knowledge of the operation and its implications.

1. The first task is to decide what might be needed. The result will be a sort of shopping list. Then the list will need to be refined to pare it down to the real essentials. It is perfectly normal for people to put more items on the list than are really necessary. You should also ask them to reflect on the possibility of selecting items which might have alternate uses. For example, my Swiss penknife can serve as a sharp blade, a screwdriver, a pair of scissors, or even a light hammer if necessary. I often use this image as an illustration of flexible thinking when discussing emergency requirements with a business unit.

2. The second task is to decide what quantities might be needed during the first phase of the recovered operation. This is going to depend on the minimum level of service they expect to be providing as well as the rate at which these things get used. The other consideration is how soon these items can be obtained from suppliers rather than from an emergency stock. You will have established the timeframes and levels of service during the earlier BIA work which we covered in Chapter 5.

3. The third and final task is to set up an emergency stock, or to make arrangements for an emergency supply, which is likely to meet the immediate needs of the business. Later in this chapter, you will find instructions for creating a *battle box*.

8.2.2   Skills

Working with your emergency guidelines and action lists, you can establish what skills are likely to be needed. Much of the work is simply an extension of the normal routine activities for some of your people. In this case, it is a relatively simple matter of identifying and listing the skills you might need during the rescue, recovery, and restoration and then seeking out those who possess such skills.

Imported skills. Some of the skills can be imported as, and when, required. For example, loss adjusters, salvage engineers, and builders would come into this category. The solution to this type of shortage is for you to develop a list of useful contacts.

Business-specific skills. Business-specific skills cannot be bought off the shelf. These have to be discovered, or developed, from within, sometimes from people who have recently retired or moved on. In an emergency they might be prepared to help out.

Special command and management skills. Command and management skills which are likely to be required only in an emergency need to be developed through practice in exercises and tests. Without regular on-the-job training, it is unlikely that anyone will be able to cope successfully with the demands and stresses of emergency response and management.

8.2.3   Resources

Denial of the use, or failure, of your normal resources is a common emergency situation. Your contingency plans have to take this into account. While it is true that the additional resources may never be used in a crisis, they should certainly come into regular use for practice or training. The cost of the additional resources has to be set against the perspective of what it might cost the enterprise if it is not equipped properly to meet the demands of an emergency. Complete failure to rise to the needs of the moment is, by comparison, very expensive.

To determine the minimum resources which should be held in anticipation of a disaster, you will need to go back to the owners of – or those responsible for – the super-critical and highly critical functions that you identified earlier. They should be able to tell you what they will require to sustain their end of the main business driver relationships with other entities.

> ▸ First of all, the owners need to agree on the *minimum level of service* they can afford to provide. Here we are using the word "afford" to reflect customer expectations rather than costs to the supplier. For example, for the subscriber network of a mobile phone company, that minimum may be 50% (or even higher), whereas for the accounts department, it may only be 10%. Minimum service level is usually expressed as a percentage of normal capacity, although it can be expressed as turnaround or delivery time. You need to take account of the nature and style of business as well as the way in which service is perceived and managed within that particular department.

…you will probably need to get the budget sanctioned by your BC sponsor.

> ▸ The other dimension the owners must agree upon is the *tolerance threshold* or how long the business can afford to be without the use of its critical functions or processes. In the case of our phone company, this would be a matter of hours and minutes for the network, but it could be several days for the accounts department. Everybody will expect instant service, but few will worry if their bill is a week late.

You should then be able to determine the *minimum recovery capability*, which is a combination of the *tolerance threshold* and the *minimum service level*. For its subscriber network, our phone company might want to be able to recover at least 50% of the full capacity within two hours. Accounts, on the other hand, may want to reach only 10% by the end of the week.

8.2.4   Arriving at a List of Requirements

With this combination of time and quantity in mind, it is possible for you, with the help of departments or business units, to estimate what is needed to support that level of recovery capability. Each group can map out its short-term emergency requirements in the sense of what they need. After you have run a couple of these workshop-type investigations, you should get to be quite skilled at it and be able to embed the concept of BC into the culture at a local level. The resulting list of requirements is the basis of a *resource contingency plan*.

> ▸ Some of these items can probably be obtained at relatively short notice, i.e., within the period of tolerance. These can go onto a shopping list so they can be identified and acquired with minimum delay. However, bear in mind that in the event of a significant event, others may also be chasing after the same items. You may need to consider some sort of contractual arrangement or even going further afield to alternate suppliers – if that is possible!

> ▸ Other items will require either some form of contract for rapid deployment or they will have to be held in reserve. At this stage, you may need to look at the sums of money involved before committing to a solution. Capital outlay and expenditure need to be taken into account here, and you will probably need to get the budget sanctioned by your BC sponsor. Probably you will have to develop a business case and make a formal bid for approval in line with corporate policy. This reflects the business aspect of BC.

8.3   Battle Boxes

Many of the required resources, tools, and supplies can be held in readiness in *battle boxes.*

8.3.1   Strategy

The first step in developing a battle box strategy is to figure out the intended purpose. What do you expect to deal with and how will the box support you or those who will need to use it? For example, there may be a potential need to carry out a damage assessment after a fire or an explosion. Or you might think the box ought to contain essential business items to support the unit at an offsite location. You may need a number of different boxes to cope with the various scenarios you envisage.

Their shelf life and workload will vary according to a number of factors. For example, a salvage engineer may carry a battle box in the car and use it every day, whereas a bank may place several battle boxes in key locations and never need to use them.

With such a wide range of needs and considerations, any practical advice about contents, size, number, and location must be of a general nature. All of these aspects need to be taken into account when preparing a battle box. While most battle boxes can be kept relatively small because they are intended for only a known quantity of items, it is probably wise to have enough room to allow the items to be found easily and for other items to be added over time.

8.3.2   Characteristics

Type of container: The actual container needs to be rugged enough for its planned duty and secure enough to prevent pilfering or borrowing. It is worth thinking about alternative uses, such as a seat or a platform. Possibly the marshals might be able to stand on it at the designated assembly area so they can act as a rallying point and to give instructions to the people.

Portability: Consider the circumstances in which the battle box may be deployed and whether it will need to be moved or should it be regarded as a fixture. If it is to remain static, then it should be permanently mounted. Otherwise it needs to be fully portable. A portable battle box should either be light enough and small enough to be carried in one hand, or it should have wheels. Remember that the person who is moving it may have to negotiate his or her way through a damaged building, climb stairs or ladders, and get through doorways. The person may very well be carrying a flashlight while keeping one hand free for support or balance. A safety light mounted on a hard hat or a belt will be an advantage in these circumstances because it leaves the wearer free to use both hands. For portability, large toolboxes with wheels are available from hardware stores and make ideal battle boxes.

Color coding and labeling: Consider the use of color to increase visibility and to give an external indication of purpose, location, responsibility, or ownership. Any coloring or labeling must be permanent and waterproof; so sticky labels are not suitable. Color codes should be bold in order to ensure easy identification in poor light or by those with weak color vision. Bold patterns such as stripes, circles, or squares make recognition easier. In the same way, any labeling should be written in large bold characters. If you use symbols, remember that they do not replace the need for words. Also avoid acronyms, since they are likely to cause confusion in an emergency situation.

Accessibility and security: A battle box is useful only if people can get at it; so its location needs to be considered carefully. It must be kept somewhere where it is likely to be accessible under all circumstances. If it has to be kept under lock and key, you have to make sure that everyone who might need urgent access to the box will have all of the keys and passes to gain access. If the box is not kept under lock and key, then you have to make sure it is under secure supervision at all times. Perhaps you can leave it with your security guards. An alternative to locking is to use breakable seals, but this is not a very secure or reliable form of protection. Thieves and trespassers show little respect for such fragile devices. Another approach to security would be to lock the items into place within the battle box so that the user has to break a seal or undo a lock to gain access to any of the valuable items. A common way of securing the contents is to have a lock (or locks) on the box itself. Combination locks save the need for issuing sets of keys, but one has to ask: "Will they be able to remember the combination in an emergency situation?"

> **If someone should borrow your flashlight ... that person is compromising your recovery capability....**

Security in this context covers three distinct areas of concern:

- **Unwarranted access to sensitive data.** Any plans, contact lists, or other records stored in your battle box must be regarded as sensitive data and access to this type of information should be controlled on a "need to know" basis. You should bear this in mind when deciding what to include and where to locate your box.

- **Protection of valuable items against theft.** Much of the essential material in a battle box will be easily replaceable in terms of intrinsic value but the reason for its presence in the box is its instant availability rather than long-term economy. However, your plan may also call for the inclusion of relatively valuable equipment which could be a temptation for would-be thieves. Therefore, you must make sure such items are hidden from view and properly secured. This may mean placing all of your emergency resources in a locked room or cabinet.

- **Casual or unauthorized use of the contents.** It is often very tempting for people to borrow something which doesn't seem to be in regular use. That borrowing soon develops into a permanent loan. Whatever you put in the box will have an emergency value out of all proportion to its intrinsic or real value. A cheap battery could be a lifesaving resource in an emergency, whereas an expensive camera may have a limited practical value. If someone should borrow your flashlight with every intention of putting it back, that person is compromising your recovery capability in exactly the same way as if he or she were a hardened criminal seeking to get rich at your expense.

8.3.3   Contents

The actual contents of your battle box will be determined largely by its intended purpose, or purposes, and the needs and preparedness of its users. For example, they may expect to have their own protective or high visibility clothing, or on the other hand, may expect to find it in the battle box. This will partly depend on the nature of the business and its culture. It will also depend upon what you see as the most practical solution. There are several categories of use that can affect what is held in a battle box.

8.3.3.1 Inspection and Assessment

If your battle box is to be used to support site inspection and damage assessment, you should consider including some or all of the following items. The actual quantities of these items will depend on the number of people you expect to deploy for these tasks.

- Hammer, for testing, access, and sampling.
- Probes (long sticks used to check and test).
- Hard hats.
- Plastic bags for samples.
- Boots.
- Strong knife to take samples.
- Site plans.
- Tape recorder.
- Rope.
- Binoculars.
- Safety glasses.
- Work gloves.
- Camera (with flash).

- Mobile phone or walkie-talkie.
- First aid kit.
- Whistles to summon help.
- Floor plans.
- Reflective jackets.
- Overalls.
- Flashlights or torches.
- Chalk.
- Spare batteries.
- Face masks.
- Clipboard & pen.
- ID or security pass.
- Checklist of critical items.

This list, like the others that follow, is neither exhaustive nor exclusive. You should consider all of the items in all of the lists before making a final choice to suit your particular purpose and environment.

8.3.3.2   Rescue and Recovery

If your battle box is expected to be used for the rescue and recovery of resources, equipment, and records, then you have to consider dealing with flooding and fire damage. You must also assume that the rescue and recovery work will need to be done without power and in darkness.

Consider this list in conjunction with the items suggested above:

- Rescue plan (indicating what is to be rescued and where from).
- Colored labels (to indicate point of origin). These should be self-adhesive and can be pre-printed with a reference code that matches the coding in a prepared logbook or record sheet.
- Action plan (update and pass to security for safety of rescuers).
- Cart for transport of wet documents, etc.
- Access code, key, or pass to data backup.
- A supply of plastic bags.
- Waterproof clothing.
- Washing kit.

- Staple gun.
- Overshoes.
- Buckets.
- Stirrup pump.
- Plastic sheeting.
- Cleaning rags.
- Cling film.
- Screwdrivers.
- Carryall bags or totes.
- Hose pipe.
- Bolt cutters.
- Folding crates.
- Crowbar.

8.3.3.3   Office Support

You may require support for the normal office functions during an emergency. In the case of a power outage you may need to think about light and warmth for the staff or even an alternative source of power. This could range from a couple of battery lamps to a portable diesel generator.

You should also consider what might be required in the case of relocation to another site, or area, which may not have everything in place to support the normal business needs. Redeployment is a variation on the same theme but is usually taken to mean that the original unit or team is split across a number of spare places.

...a complete change... can easily lead to a feeling of discomfort...

The main problem with redeployment is having the right management skills and communication procedures to retain both the team spirit and departmental effectiveness, since people are now operating in strange and unfamiliar surroundings. The combination of a complete change of environment, unfamiliar faces, and missing the members of their normal group can easily lead to a feeling of discomfort, which must be managed sympathetically.

Before considering the transfer of processes and procedures to an alternate location it will be necessary to ensure that there is technical compatibility. A compatibility plan will document the differences you may encounter and indicate how to resolve any problems which those differences may pose.

The items to be included for supporting office functions are more concerned with the detailed running of a business unit and would normally be developed, held, and used at a departmental or unit level.

Consider the inclusion of some or all of the following items:

- Emergency stationery.
- Company seal.
- Kettle.
- Postage stamps.
- Check books.
- Clock.
- Desktop items, e.g., calculators.
- Receipt book.
- Cups and spoons.
- Radio.
- Credit cards.
- Staff contact list.

- Reference materials.
- Petty cash.
- Tea, coffee, sugar.
- Departmental recovery plan.
- Credit listings.
- Internal directory.
- Thumbtacks, push pins.
- Key client contact list.
- Carrier bags.
- Compatibility plans and data.
- Any tools or devices that may help to achieve compatibility.

8.3.3.4 Security and Isolation

A common requirement is for a battle box to support those responsible for implementing security and isolating different parts or areas of the site. These people will need to have the tools and accessories to mark out and highlight specific areas and to inform people about the temporary arrangements for access, etc. Communication may take the form of signs, sounds, or vocal signals. The items for this type of battle box might include some or all of the following items:

- Plastic cards and marker pens for temporary signage.
- Spray paint for marking unsafe areas or areas of high priority.
- Loudhailers or megaphones for voice messages.
- Tape for cordoning off areas.
- Cones for marking off areas.

- Portable horn.
- Security vests to identify security personnel.
- Access register (list of key holders and their access limits).
- Swipe cards and master keys.
- Security passes.

8.3.3.5 Emergency Response

Emergency response or emergency management is all about controlling the situation while the recovery and restoration teams attempt to re-establish the business operation. You need to coordinate the activities of your own teams with those of the emergency services to ensure that any losses are minimized and the situation is contained. Essential attributes are the skills and attitudes, which can come only from experience and training.

To make emergency response easier, your battle box might support several aspects of emergency management and control. The three main areas would be those of:

- Communication and control.
- Health and safety.
- Identification of property or inventory control.

For communication and control, consider holding any or all of the following:

- Clip-on ID badges (for issue to all non-uniformed personnel).
- Emergency response plan.
- Site plan.
- Visitors' log.
- Emergency services contact list.
- Activity and handover log.
- Team roster.
- Company credit card.
- Emergency purchase orders.

For health and safety, consider holding any or all of the following:

- Hazard list, listing key concerns. (Potential health and safety issues due to materials or equipment.)
- Details of hazardous or toxic materials kept on site or nearby, together with relevant handling advice.
- Protective clothing for any known hazards.
- Emergency lighting for passage ways and work areas.
- First aid kit.
- "Keep out" signs.
- List of nearby doctors, with phone numbers.
- List of nearby hospitals with emergency wards.

For identification of property before removal, consider holding any or all of the following:

- Prioritized unit recovery plan indicating the most critical areas.
- Site plan indicating location of services, hazards, and critical areas.
- Release forms (authority for removal of property and equipment).
- Removal log (who took what, when, and where).
- Location identification scheme to track what came from where.
- Preprinted sticky labels for each building, floor, or unit.
- Spray paint and stencils.

8.3.3.6 Crisis Management and Public Relations

In the event of an emergency, you may need to handle the crisis aspects of the event. This means that your people will have to be able to receive reports and collate information as well as prepare statements about the situation to be delivered externally. Some organizations may have a fully functioning public relations department or even a press briefing room, whereas others may have no experience in this area at all.

Crisis management for the average organization will depend largely on finding somewhere to operate from, such as a nearby hotel room. Ideally this would be arranged in advance. The alternative is to rely on ad hoc availability, an arrangement which is a contradiction in terms. To support a crisis management team, your battle box may contain some or all of the following:

- Mobile phones and chargers (separate phones for incoming and outgoing calls).
- Prepared draft statements that address typical issues.
- Laptop and printer (to prepare statements and faxes).

- Company logo suitable for use as a backdrop.
- List of critical contacts (stakeholders, regulators, trade press, key clients, etc.).
- Business cards with emergency contact details.

8.3.3.7 Command Post Support

In a large organization there may be a requirement to set up a command post to direct the complex recovery and restoration operations. This sort of set up will require some additional resources to aid the management and control of the emergency activities. Consider holding any, or all, of the following:

- Laptop loaded with some event management software and the business continuity plans.
- Details of insurers and insurance policies.
- Contact list of emergency support organizations.
- Emergency lighting equipment.
- Maps of the area.

- A mobile office (a caravan or a vehicle).
- Contacts for maintainers of key plant and equipment.
- Details of loss adjusters or loss assessors.
- Flip charts (and pens) to record and track activities and display information.

8.3.4 Maintenance and Update

8.3.4.1 Appoint a Responsible Person

Appoint a person to be responsible for checking the contents of all battle boxes at regular intervals, someone who has the authority, or the budget, for replacing or replenishing as necessary. Base the assessment on a simple checklist to ensure everything is covered.

Set up a schedule with the dates of required checks…and submission of reports to the corporate risk manager.

8.3.4.2 Shelf Life of Contents

Keep track of any items which have a limited shelf life compared to their expected storage life. Short life items will need to be replaced on a regular basis, well before their expiry date, which makes better sense than waiting until they are beyond their useful life. Items which are removed may be used on an as-required basis; they should still be in working order.

8.3.4.3 Photograph the Contents

It is useful to include photographs of the contents of each box laid out for inspection. The contents can then be laid out and compared with the photo for a quick visual check of contents and condition.

8.3.4.4 Schedule Checks

Set up a schedule with the dates of required checks (for example, January 31 and July 31) and submission of reports to the corporate risk manager. If your battle box is deployed in a test, an exercise, or an emergency situation, the checks in Table 8-1 should be carried out at the end of the test or emergency. These checks should be an integral part of the training in order that the users become familiar with the box and its contents during the process.

8.3.4.5 Create a Battle Box Checklist

Table 8-1 gives you a sample battle box checklist. A typical battle box inspection would require some or all of those checks to be carried out at regular intervals, as discussed above. However, the actual interval between checkups will depend to a large extent upon the shelf life of its more vulnerable contents. The emergency response manager or the BC manager is expected to supervise checks on all battle boxes within his or her area of responsibility.

Table 8-1. Sample Battle Box Checklist

Action	Check
Remove contents and lay them out for inspection. (Compare contents with reference photo stored in battle box).	
Check that all batteries are in good condition. (Check them for leakage and charge).	
Check for damage or deterioration of box and its contents.	
Check for signs of dampness, desiccation, or decay (e.g., sticky tape may no longer be sticky).	
Check documents for legibility and accuracy. (Lists, maps, and plans may be out of date.)	
Check that all pens still work. (Replace wherever there is doubt.)	
Check for evaporation or leakage of liquids.	
Check the actual contents against the contents list.	
Check labeling and color coding.	
Review adequacy of contents. (Has anything changed so as to affect the use or purpose of the box and its contents?)	
Make a note of the dates of inspection and replenishment.	
Remove and replace any pens which are over 12 months old.	

8.4   Recovery Facilities

Recovery facilities need to be kept in permanent readiness, which means you have to maintain them as if they were in constant use. To meet this state of readiness you need to consider several aspects:

- Cleaning and routine maintenance.
- Opening up procedures.
  - ❑ How does the recovery team gain entry to the secure premises?
- Provision and maintenance of building services.
  - ❑ Heating.
  - ❑ Lighting.
  - ❑ Air conditioning.

If the recovery site is not dedicated to your exclusive use, take steps to ensure you have guaranteed access in an emergency. If you have no guaranteed access, then you need to know (with some degree of certainty) how to resolve any contentions which might arise. Once the facilities are being used in recovery or functional mode, establish regular security arrangements. These security arrangements must be appropriate for fully operational business premises, bearing in mind the local environment and the factors which led to the invocation.

While time is of the essence, the supply chain doesn't move at the speed of your thoughts or needs.

8.4.1   Functional Resources

Once the core business functions are fully restored, these functions will be requiring regular supplies of their normal quantities of goods, products, and services, such as raw materials, stationery, mail, and power. Most of these resources can be diverted from the normal place of delivery to the recovery site. But some planning and forethought is needed to make sure the changeover is successful and there are no logistical, or other, problems to put further strains on the business. The emergency and the recovery were stressful periods, and now people want to get down to dealing with their backlog.

Diversion of resources: The successful diversion of resources depends on having the proper arrangements in place long before the event. Suppliers will want to have notice of your intentions and how you will let them know about the alternate arrangements. It would be rather awkward if someone diverted your supply chain by accidentally triggering the emergency arrangements. You need to have some kind of check-back or verification system in place to call someone back to confirm the emergency status before altering the logistics.

Extra supplies: You may need extra supplies to replace those lost in the incident. Once again, consult with the owners of the various business functions to establish the requirements. Obviously, they will give you an indication of their expected requirements during the initial planning stages, but it is equally important to review these requirements immediately after the emergency has been declared and the recovery plans have been activated. While time is of the essence, the supply chain doesn't move at the speed of your thoughts or needs. It runs at a steady and deliberate pace, which is why it is so stable and reliable.

8.4.2   Functional Facilities

As the business moves from recovery to functional mode, there will inevitably be a demand for more facilities. In effect, the business will be expanding rapidly at this time. You need to be prepared to meet the demand and allow for expansion or extension of the facilities. This requires detailed planning regarding the quantities involved and the timing of the expansion in order to meet the service-level needs of the business.

Once the facilities are fully occupied, you should assume they will remain occupied for some while. Long-term use means considering the regular maintenance and repair of the facilities. You will also have to organize routine tasks such as waste collection, office cleaning, window cleaning, internal and external security, compliance with health and safety regulations, fire drills, and evacuation plans.

8.5   Liaising with Other Groups

8.5.1   Regulators

Many industries have regulators or monitoring bodies which will also be involved in, or at least concerned with, emergency response planning. You need to establish contact with your own compliance officer or whoever is responsible for dealing with the regulators for your industry.

8.5.2   The Community

> **...there may well be benefits of scale when a large cooperative seeks to invest in solutions to common problems.**

Any business enterprise, whatever its purpose, has a responsibility towards the local community. After all, it draws its staff and possibly customers from the neighborhood, all of whom can influence its success or failure in the long run. Apart from that, there is a moral, and perhaps a legal, obligation to act as a good corporate citizen. For many successful companies, good citizenship is regarded as a cornerstone of their relationship with the world at large.

Many areas have BC or community resilience initiatives in which BC, emergency planning, and related disciplines are discussed and community schemes are developed. These may be sponsored or promoted by the local authorities or chambers of commerce or they may simply be self-sufficient groups of likeminded people. There is a considerable advantage in sharing knowledge about each other's activities and any associated risks. In addition, there may well be benefits of scale when a large cooperative seeks to invest in solutions to common problems.

If you are in an area where such a group doesn't yet exist, then I would strongly advise you to get together with other leading members of the community to develop one. This approach is especially appropriate where several companies occupy a business park or share a building.

8.5.3   Insurers

As a BC manager, you should be familiar with the terms of the various insurance policies which may be relevant when dealing with an emergency and its aftermath. It is worthwhile getting to know the people you might be dealing with in the event of a claim and discussing how they might view things under various circumstances. Emergency decisions are easier and more prudent if they are based on a proper understanding of the implications.

8.5.4   Competitors

Others who are in the same line of business may see your disaster as a welcome opportunity – that is, until they think about it. Then they might realize there could also be dangers to the industry as a whole, and thus to themselves, if one of their number is seen to be foolhardy, grasping, or unreliable. These are common outcomes once the media begins to report on any unfortunate incident. While crisis management is generally regarded as protecting the brand and reputation of one company, wisdom suggests that protection of the brand and image of the whole industry is a logical progression from that more familiar, self-centered view.

Now that BC is becoming a recognized subject for discussion, a trend among trade associations is to look at common risks and tentative solutions, sharing ideas and exploring the possibilities of cooperative endeavors. Associations are also a useful source of relevant case studies. One can learn a great deal from the experience of others, especially if their operations are in any way similar to your own.

If there is no BC working group within your trade association, then you should be asking why. On the other hand, if one already exists, you should be getting involved.

8.5.5   Neighbors

From a BC perspective, one of the key questions has to be "What do our neighbors do and how do they do it?" Over the years, I have often been astonished at the surprising way in which sound businesses have been brought to their knees by events occurring on nearby premises. The astonishment was usually caused by the innocence of the victims. They rarely knew they were sharing a major risk, and most of those who were aware of the risks were content to accept them or forget about them.

It is absolutely essential that your emergency response plans take account of the threats which may be posed by your neighbors. Take the necessary steps to identify your neighborhood risks. Find out what other people are doing in the areas around you and carry out a full risk assessment on each of them. Most importantly, take steps to deal with the issues raised. Of course, this has to be a two-way dialogue; they should be made aware of any risks and threats coming from within your operation.

8.6   Liaising with Police and Emergency Services

The BC manager should take responsibility for recommending policies and establishing procedures for the coordination of emergency management, crisis management, business recovery, and service restoration activities with the relevant external agencies (such as local, state, and national authorities, emergency responders, civil defense, and Coast Guard) while ensuring compliance with any applicable laws, codes, or regulations.

In practice, this will mean identifying and establishing proper liaison procedures for emergency management and coordinating the company's response activities with the various agencies that may be involved in dealing with the emergency or its implications. There is also a need to be familiar with the various laws and regulations concerning emergency management in the context of your own organization and its activities in relation to the local environment.

Ideally, you should also become involved in running emergency management exercises in conjunction with these external agencies wherever possible. Most of the "blue light" responders will be conducting regular exercises which you should at least be aware of and, preferably, participate in. Exercises which include the full span of the community are more realistic and thus more effective than those which are held in isolation. Of course, this level of cooperation may not be easy or practical in some parts of the world.

8.6.1   Local Authorities

You should be able to establish contact with an emergency planning officer through your local city hall or county hall. Presumably, there will be an equivalent post in most parts of the world. In the US, for example, there are local representatives of the National Emergency Management Agency (NEMA). In the UK every city or county will have one or more emergency planning officers who are charged with the responsibility for dealing with any emergencies which might affect their community. These people will already be in close contact with all of those official, voluntary, and commercial organizations that might be engaged in preparing for, or dealing with the aftermath of, a major incident. Their expertise and knowledge can prove to be very helpful, but they are unlikely to share it with you unless you ask.

A number of emergency services may be involved in responding to and dealing with the results of an emergency. Principal among them will be the police and the fire service, perhaps supported by the ambulance service or paramedics.

8.6.2   Emergency Services: Police

If the incident is considered to be the result of criminal activities, then the affected area will be treated as a crime scene. It will be cordoned off while the police and perhaps the fire service carry out their forensic investigations, and some items may be held as material evidence with the implication that you will be denied access to them. The evidence might include such items as computers, backup tapes, and documentation which could seriously hamper your recovery – another valid reason for having multiple copies of critical data.

Throughout the emergency, security of the premises and their contents must be seen as a major issue. You need to make sure your security people are able to raise the level of security during such times. Whenever property is damaged, unoccupied, or in darkness for any length of time, you face the risk of theft, trespass, or vandalism.

In many communities, local security personnel are encouraged to work closely with the police whenever there is a major incident. A large part of this work involves sharing information about current risks and threats, as well as sharing the need for manpower in such routine activities as manning cordons or patrolling exposed areas. One of the fringe benefits of this arrangement is the additional intelligence which becomes available to those businesses whose security personnel are involved in such cooperative arrangements.

8.6.3   Emergency Services: Fire and Rescue

The fire and rescue service provides absolutely essential assistance in any serious emergency. Apart from its main role of protecting property in using fire fighters, it also bears the humanitarian burden of rescuing people and saving lives.

Clearly, these tasks are made easier if emergency personnel are familiar with your premises, layout, contents, activities, and the kind of people who are likely to be found there, including staff, visitors, and passersby. Also, tell them about any especially valuable or delicate items which might require particular or urgent attention in the event of a fire or other emergency.

Many small fires are put out by occupants of the building using the firefighting equipment at hand.

Under normal conditions, the fire service responds to an alert within a few minutes, dispatching tenders and ladders according to the category of your premises. Once its personnel are onsite they can radio for additional support as needed. They will be aware of any major fire hazards in the area and will act accordingly. Their training will enable them to spot specific hazardous substances and take the appropriate measures.

While the site is a "fire ground," these experts are in charge of access to the site and they are directing the operation. After a fire, they will remain on the scene until the site is properly damped down and there is no further danger of anything reigniting, or until everybody is safe and there is no further threat to life and limb.

8.6.3.1 Importance of Portable Fire Extinguishers

Your primary line of defense against fire is the range of portable fire extinguishers you are required to have on your premises. Obviously, they are unsuitable for a big blaze, but most fires start out as something fairly small. According to the fire engineers who study these matters, the average fire takes about 90 seconds to establish itself as a serious fire and about 4 minutes to get out of control, i.e., requiring expert attention. Many small fires are put out by occupants of the building using the firefighting equipment at hand.

8.6.3.2 Fire Training

In order for your own people to deal with fires using normal firefighting equipment, you must provide them with some training. People need to know how to use the equipment and be confident of its effectiveness in their hands. People must understand what they are dealing with. Confidence comes only from practice. Research has shown that most people fail to recognize the true danger of the situation in the event of a fire, especially when they know the building or are accustomed to the smell of smoke.

8.6.3.3 Assisting the Fire Service

You can help the fire service by reducing the chances of a fire breaking out. It is important to realize that fires can be started and sustained only if the three components of combustion are present. Fire depends on the simultaneous availability of:

1. Fuel or combustible material.
2. A source of heat or ignition to start or sustain the fire.
3. Oxygen (or fresh air) to support the combustion process.

If any one of these elements is removed, the fire is extinguished. Until the actual cause of ignition is eliminated, there is the ongoing danger of something reigniting. This is why firefighters damp everything down to deal with any remaining hot spots long after the initial blaze appears to have been brought under control.

Smoke detectors become less effective over time, as their sensing mechanisms become obscured by accumulated dirt. Their effective life, without cleaning or replacement, depends upon the working conditions and where they are placed. Have them checked regularly.

Sprinkler systems are usually reliable and effective, unless someone has turned them off for some reason such as maintenance or to cure a leak. Therefore, it would be wise to check regularly that any sprinkler systems on your premises are in full working order.

Prove that your fire detection and alarm system works from end to end. Have it checked by the fire engineers who are responsible for its regular maintenance.

8.6.4 Emergency Services: Floods

Often the fire department is called in to deal with flooded premises, pump out basements, etc. If there is a realistic chance of your premises becoming flooded, then you should identify where you can acquire suitable pumping equipment. If your site is vulnerable to flooding, someone in your organization should be responsible for monitoring the long-range weather forecast and raising an alert if heavy rains are predicted. This should give you a day or two in which to implement and finalize your flood precautions.

If you are unsure whether your premises are vulnerable to flood you should contact your county (or city) emergency planning officer. In the US you can review flooding information from the US Geological Survey at https://water.usgs.gov/floods, and from the US Federal Emergency Administration (FEMA) at https://msc.fema.gov. It is also worth asking emergency planning officers what steps they will be taking during periods of restricted emergency services.

In the UK, the Environment Agency is responsible for the management of inland waters and health and safety in connection with them. In the US, the US Army Corps of Engineers (USACE) is responsible for maintaining 12,000 miles of inland waterways, the US Coast Guard is responsible for safety, and federal laws and regulations cover environmental health and safety.

8.7 Disaster Recovery

Because of the complexity and sequential nature of this type of activity, disaster recovery plans usually contain detailed instructions and procedures. In addition, there may be a need to recover the working environment. The additional items to support your disaster recovery team (or teams) might include some or all of the following:

- Disaster recovery plans.
- CD or thumb drive copies of key applications.
- Capital plant inventory.
- Emergency backup procedures.
- Dimensions of large glass windows.
- Duct tape and scissors.

- Systems manuals.
- Backup and retrieval procedures.
- Capital plant recovery strategy.
- Emergency security procedures.
- Details of recovery service contract and procedures.

8.7.1 Salvage and Restoration

It is often necessary to clean up the site to deal with the after-effects of fire, flood, chemical spillage, explosion, storm damage, or vandalism. (Salvage and restoration are covered in detail in Chapter 9.)

8.8 Contact Lists

Certain of the accompanying instructions and comments are specific to the UK but the principles are universal. You should be able to adapt them easily to your own company and local area.

8.8.1 Emergency Services

Obtain the published contact numbers from the local telephone directory or an Internet search. Determine which hospitals have an accident and emergency department.

Table 8-2. Sample Contact List for Emergency Services

Agency	Phone Number
Fire and Rescue Service	
Police	
Ambulance Service	
Hospital (Accident & Emergency Dept.)	
Hospital (Accident & Emergency Dept.)	
Hospital (Accident & Emergency Dept.)	

8.8.2   Internal Contacts

Identify all those who may prove to be useful in the event of an emergency situation. Make a special note of those with long service and local or specialist knowledge whose background could prove to be invaluable in an emergency.

Fire marshals and trained first aid people should be identified for each floor or section. Where applicable, find out who would represent the parent company in the event of an emergency. Heads of departments and their deputies should be identified within the plan. They may be required to assist in roll calls and in identifying, locating, and communicating with their staff.

Table 8-3. Sample Contact List for Internal Resources

Role	Name	Phone/Alternate
Fire Marshals		
First Aiders		
Parent Company Representative		
Deputy Facilities Manager		
Facilities Manager		
Departmental Contacts		
Other Internal Contacts		

8.8.3   External Contacts

‣ **Alternative premises.** Identify those real estate agents who specialize in commercial properties in your area. Also identify potential premises which could be adapted to your needs. Consider inquiring through the parent company about such premises.

‣ **Associates.** Try to identify all those who may be useful sources of resources, information, and/or skills, which could be put into service to satisfy urgent needs.

‣ **Computer hardware and peripherals.** Identify sources of replacement and repair for the key items of equipment in each location.

‣ **Computer software and applications.** Identify sources of replacement and technical support for the key computer applications, i.e., those which are essential to the business. In particular you should establish whether there are specific dependencies such as "dongles" or special license conditions which might affect recovery or restoration onto another machine.

> Identify convenient potential storage facilities…for regular storage of emergency supplies…

‣ **Counseling services.** The British Association for Counseling and Psychotherapy keeps a register of recognized counselors, some of whom may specialize in this type of work. For more information, see http://www.bacp.co.uk/

‣ **The Traumatic Incident Reduction Association (TIRA).** Based in the US, this is an international membership body whose members specialize in traumatic incident reduction. For more information, see http://www.tir.org/index.html

‣ **Critical customers.** Each division or business unit should indicate their most critical customers, i.e., those who warrant special consideration in the event of an emergency which might delay completion or delivery of goods, information, or services.

‣ **Document salvage.** This is a specialized field. However, you may only need to recover the information, in which case photocopying may serve your needs. If the original physical documents need to be saved, then you can freeze them to preserve them until a document salvage service has been identified.

‣ **Insurance broker.** Your accounts department or risk manager will be able to identify your insurance broker.

‣ **Loss adjuster.** The insurer normally calls in the loss adjuster. It should be possible to pre-appoint a specific loss adjuster. The loss adjuster will know whom to call in to provide the various salvage and recovery services.

‣ **Networks and communications.** Identify who provides and services your communications links, who supplies and maintains your private exchanges and handsets, and who supplies and maintains your modems and cabling systems to your computers. Also consider cellular carriers and the possibility their services may be interrupted.

‣ **Office supplies.** Identify suppliers for all of your basic business needs, preferably more than one.

‣ **Offsite storage locations.** Identify convenient potential storage facilities which might be used for regular storage of emergency supplies or backup. Also, identify potential storage facilities which might be used for short-term or temporary storage in the event of an emergency.

‣ **Press and media contacts.** Identify those trade journal and other media contacts that have been established over the years. This information may be useful to the emergency response team (ERT).

‣ **Public services.** Identify those departments and services which may be useful during the reconstruction or restoration of the business, such as surveyor, gas, electricity, environmental health, parking permits, sewage, waste disposal, and water.

▸ **Salvage engineers.** Salvage engineers are often called in by the loss adjuster but it is better to have them pre-appointed so they can become familiar with your specific needs and priorities. Your insurers, or their loss adjusters, should be able to help you identify a suitable firm of salvage engineers.

▸ **Security companies.** In the wake of an emergency there may be a need to implement extra security if the normal access controls are damaged or compromised.

▸ **Spare capacity.** Identify where there may be spare capacity within the organization (or its closest allies) to conduct business operations or services. Spare capacity should be identified for all of the major needs of the organization such as office accommodation, specialized computing and process equipment, warehousing, and bulk storage.

▸ **Transport services.** Consider the need for removal specialists who can assist with a complete relocation in an emergency. Also allow for the regular movement of equipment and people between shared locations where an operation has to be split across more than one site. It may be necessary, or advisable, to run a shuttle transport service rather than depend on people making their own way back and forth.

Table 8-4. Sample Contact List for External Contacts

Agency	Contact Name & Company	Phone
Alternative Premises		
Associates		
Computer Hardware & Peripherals		
Computer Software & Applications		
Counseling Service		
Critical Customers		
Document Salvage		
Insurance Broker		
Loss Adjuster		
Networks and Communications		
Office Supplies		
Offsite Storage Locations		
Press and Media Contacts		
Public Services		
Salvage Engineers		
Security Companies		
Spare Capacity		
Transport Services		
Water Company		

Self-Examination Questions

1. The basic goods, supplies, or devices that the recovery team relies on to work effectively when the organization is in BC mode are called _____.
   A. battle boxes
   B. facilities
   C. resources

2. _____ is an essential long-term aspect of BC because the organization's resources and facilities need to be permanently ready for an incident, whenever it may occur.
   A. Innovation
   B. Maintenance
   C. Process improvement

3. With BC firmly in place, the organization is in _____ mode, prepared for any eventuality. This is a semipermanent mode that persists until a crisis occurs.
   A. functional
   B. ready
   C. routine

4. Where can many of the resources, tools, and supplies that the organization will need in a crisis be held in readiness?
   A. Battle boxes
   B. Hot sites
   C. Recovery facilities

5. The contents of the organization's battle boxes will largely be determined by
   A. how large a budget the company is able to allocate to them.
   B. state and local safety regulations.
   C. their intended purposes and the needs of their users.

6. Various categories of skills are likely to be needed during emergency response. In this context, the skills of loss adjusters, salvage engineers, and builders would fall under which category?
   A. Business-specific skills
   B. Imported skills
   C. Special command and management skills

7. During disaster recovery, the minimum level of service that key business functions can afford to provide is
   A. the most basic level of service that will still meet customer expectations.
   B. the best level of service they can provide while keeping costs to a minimum.
   C. the best level of service they can provide given their reduced budgets during a crisis.

8. To make emergency response easier, the battle box should support these three aspects of emergency management and control:
   A. Access Control, Inventory Control, Service and Repair
   B. Emergency Mode, Recovery Mode, and Functional Mode
   C. Communication and Control, Health and Safety, and Identification of Property or Inventory Control

Food for Thought

In this and the previous chapter, you have had an overview of how people respond to an emergency and how you might prepare to help them deal with the situation. That process has entailed trying to envisage the likely scenarios, the practical response options, and what would be needed to support those responses. To help you understand the implications and adapt these ideas to your own situation, go through the following exercises.

Exercises

Using a work or study environment think about what might happen, and what would be required, or expected, in some typical emergency situations. Imagine that, apart from the emergency services, you are the first on scene in each of the following scenarios.

1. There has been a massive fire that has now been extinguished; the fire and rescue service are about to retire from the scene.
   > What would you try to do?
   > What would you expect and want to find?
   > What would you need to help you?

2. There has been a violent impact; either an explosion or an earthquake. Fire and rescue services are dealing with another related incident.
   > What would you try to do?
   > What would you expect and want to find?
   > What would you need to help you?

3. There has been a severe storm causing widespread loss of services and extensive damage. The emergency services are overwhelmed for the time being.
   > What would you try to do?
   > What would you expect and want to find?
   > What would you need to help you?

4. Based on the results of the above exercises, design an emergency kit that you would like to have available for yourself in readiness for such an event.
   > What would it look like (size and type)?
   > What would it contain?
   > Where would you keep it?

Looking Forward

This chapter and the previous one have looked at short-term measures concerned with responding to, and dealing with, the unexpected. Now you need to look at the medium-term implications and what can be done to restore some semblance of normality. The next chapter deals with salvage and restoration or returning your property to a useable condition.

Downloadable Business Continuity Toolkit

You may download model emergency response plans, manager's notes, and checklists in the **Business Continuity Toolkit**.

For Additional Reading

Cabinet Office (2011). *Emergency preparednesss. Chapter 5: Emergency planning.* Available by selecting Chapter 5 at https://www.gov.uk/government/publications/emergency-preparedness

Federal Emergency Management Agency (2013). *Emergency preparedness resources for businesses.* Available from https://www.fema.gov/media-library/resources-documents/collections/357

9

Salvage and Restoration

In the wake of a disaster, your policies and plans will need to address issues of recovering, restoring, and refurbishing your facilities and equipment. In this chapter, you will be exploring who can help you, how they might approach the work, and what you can do to assist them. This information and guidance are based upon the opinions and knowledge of salvage and recovery engineering specialists.

This chapter will help you to:

- ☑ Make your site safe and the buildings habitable.

- ☑ Understand what is involved in recovering, repairing, or replacing your technology.

- ☑ Protect and recover documents and records – know what to do and what not to do.

- ☑ Know the special requirements of electronic equipment.

- ☑ Take steps to protect and restore specialized processing equipment.

Note: The information in this chapter is intended to give you some general guidelines and points to consider in your planning, based on the author's experiences. Your organization may be covered by any number of specific local, state, and federal standards and regulations. Your insurance company may have rules and regulations that vary from those in this chapter. Work with your facilities management team, your insurance company, and your legal department to ensure that all current applicable requirements are included in your planning and procedures.

9.1   Scrap or Salvage?

Wherever salvage is possible, it is usually much cheaper and often quicker than total replacement. From a business continuity (BC) perspective, salvage is to be preferred because you end up with familiar tools and avoid all sorts of installation and commissioning problems. Almost invariably, because of technological progress, the acquisition of any new equipment will entail an upgrade or a major change. Meeting the needs for such upgrades implies familiarization with all the new features, or even re-training in many cases. Clearly, these are the sort of issues which are best avoided in any recovery situation. Far better to stick with what you know when you are under pressure and in a hurry.

The final decision about salvage, repair, or replacement will have to balance these different factors…

It is important to realize that important issues need to be taken into account when considering the re-instatement of affected equipment. The choices include salvage, repair, or replacement of the items involved. There are several ways of looking at this and there may be conflicts between those points of view. From a practical perspective, each of these options can have an impact on the performance, reliability, and service life. Esthetically there may be differences in the appearance which could be important in some contexts.

You may encounter serious issues in relation to warranties, service contracts, and residual value, depending on the manner in which the work is carried out. Urgency could override sound judgment in this area, and a costly decision may have to be made in the face of expediency. Seek agreement from all interested parties before anyone is instructed to take any specific action. Ideally, these conversations should take place well in advance of the incident; ad hoc independent decisions could compromise the value or long-term usefulness of the items concerned.

You should seek advice and guidance from your insurer (via their loss adjuster), the maintainer or supplier, the owner, and the prospective salvage engineer. The principal question will be: "How will this affect the future value, reliability, and service life of the equipment?" The other dimension of this puzzle is the speed of recovery: "How long will it take, and how long have we got?" The final decision about salvage, repair, or replacement will have to balance these different factors, and the selection process should be recorded for future reference.

It is essential for you to make an *inventory* of all the equipment and materials that are disposed of; otherwise, you will lose track of everything, including what might be useful information or even evidence in the subsequent inquiry. Appoint someone to create and maintain an inventory of all the equipment which has been damaged or lost and of everything that is replaced or repaired. Set up a process to track employees and other people in attendance onsite throughout the salvage and restoration work. The most important issue is to keep track of everything removed from the site, making a note of who took what and where it was supposed to be going. Get a signature for everything of value which is removed for whatever reason.

9.1.1   Insurance Issues

Under the terms of your insurance, you have a duty to minimize or mitigate the loss as far as you can. Salvage and restoration play a major role in this and may help you to recover the business operation in a more effective and timely manner. Many organizations are either uninsured or self-insured and in those instances there is perhaps an even greater pressure to contain the costs.

One of the common misunderstandings with regard to insurance is the question of consequential loss and where it applies. In the UK, consequential or indirect loss is covered under the law. For the US and other countries, consult your insurance company and attorney to make sure you have insurance that covers loss as a result of being unable to use property or equipment.

There is also the issue of primary and secondary claims. If you do not have a primary claim, then you may not be eligible for consequential loss. For example, if you lose business as a result of a fire on someone else's premises, you may not be able to claim the loss on your insurance because that would be a secondary claim and you don't have a primary claim. Your only remedy may be to sue the other people, assuming they stay in business and are solvent after the fire. It is worth noting that even when a decision is made in favor of replacement, a temporary reinstatement of the original damaged equipment may keep you in business while you are going through the lengthy process of selection, installation, commissioning, and training for the new configuration. Once again, these are legal and insurance questions that need to be addressed well in advance of a salvage and restoration situation.

9.1.2   Professional Help

As discussed above, whether to scrap or salvage a particular piece of equipment, or item of furniture, is a matter of judgment. In this instance, you will be able to benefit from the advice of professionals. After all, you will seldom have met such a situation, whereas the professionals are dealing with them regularly. Professional help to cope with an incident is available from a number of directions.

Loss adjusters help to negotiate any insurance claim and will also advise on how best to minimize the overall damage to the business, while staying within the terms of the policy. The insurer is normally responsible for appointing a loss adjuster. Many insurers prefer the loss adjuster to be the first person onto the site, before any salvage work begins. In practice, the insurer will not complain if salvage work is started before the loss adjuster arrives, providing they can see that the salvage work is minimizing the loss. In a multiple tenancy situation there is a likelihood of multiple insurers (owner, lessee, and tenants) with overlapping, or conflicting, interests. It is part of the loss adjuster's job to sort out what each insurer is responsible for, and to guide you in making your claim.

Loss assessors are an optional extra, possibly helpful if you have not planned beforehand. The assessor works directly for the client on a commission basis (a percentage of the amount paid by the insurer) to help the client formulate a claim. The cost of employing the professionals will normally be covered by your insurance policy, because they will be minimizing the cost to the insurer as well as minimizing the impact on your business. One of the functions of the loss adjuster is to advise on this. Where you do not carry insurance coverage, you will need to engage the services of a loss assessor to provide advice on these issues.

Salvage engineers are able to make tests to establish the nature and severity of contamination, and will direct the cleanup operations. The client usually appoints the salvage engineer, on the advice of the loss adjuster. Salvage is often a very labor-intensive operation and the salvage engineer may be able to train and lead your own staff. Not only does this reduce the overall cost but it is a welcome opportunity for your staff to become usefully involved. Active participation will help them come to terms with the incident and the after effects. You should plan to summon the salvage engineers to your site as soon as possible after any incident which causes damage to the environment, the structure, or the contents of your property. Delays could allow the situation to deteriorate, causing irreparable damage.

Service engineers, from your equipment maintainers, can work with the salvage engineer and loss adjuster to identify which equipment can be salvaged. They can also make sure such equipment works after cleanup, and accept it back into regular maintenance. As mentioned earlier, you will need to address some important issues here, and you should not assume that the obvious solution is the best solution in the long run; dialog should always precede decisions in this area.

Other professionals, such as architects, surveyors, engineers, or even insurance brokers may be called on as necessary.

> **The professionals... will have access to the requisite knowledge, skill, clothing, and equipment...**

You should steer away from using unqualified people, e.g., your own staff, office cleaners, or existing contractors. The fact that they have no professional indemnity could be the least of your worries. Salvage can involve some very skilled and delicate tasks at one end of the scale and it can be downright hazardous at the other end. The professionals will be aware of the most current local, state, and federal standards and will have access to the requisite knowledge, skill, clothing, and equipment to enable them to carry out a wide range of tasks, under circumstances which are often difficult and dangerous.

9.2   Denial of Access Issues

After an emergency, you could be denied access to your building for days, or even weeks, for a number of reasons. Handling the issues involved will require patience. Eventually, when people are able to enter on your behalf, they will need to have very clear instructions in order to make proper use of the opportunity. They will also need to know precisely where to find whatever you have asked them to look for, such as backup tapes, key records, or other vital items.

In any case, the first people to enter the building must record what they find. Digital cameras are a useful means of compiling an accurate record of the extent and degree of the damage. They provide an instant image with the opportunity to retake the shots immediately if there is any doubt about the quality or content of the pictures. Some will even allow the user to record their thoughts and impressions as an on-the-spot voice message.

9.2.1   Causes of Denial of Access

The duration of the delay of access will depend largely on the scale and severity of the damage as well as the nature of the incident. Several issues might affect access to your premises and an estimate of the time scales involved.

Insurance: Your insurer could delay your access while it conducts an investigation. If there is a potential claim against another party (for example, a contractor did something which may have caused the fire) your insurer may insist upon its own forensic scientists examining the site. Any attempt to start clearing or restoration operations against the advice of your loss adjuster could prejudice your insurer's legal claim against this third party, which could be grounds to repudiate your insurance claim. Also, your business interruption insurance policy probably does not provide cover where you are in a cordoned off area but have not sustained damage. If you have any doubts or concerns about this, then you should check your policy.

Explosion: If there is an explosion, emergency services will be dealing not only with damage but also with a crime scene and the potential for further explosions. Their primary concern will be the health and safety of the public which obviously includes your people. Forensic investigations by the police and explosive experts may take many hours, and the area has to be declared safe before forensic teams can begin their search for clues and evidence. It is likely to be 48 hours or more before you are allowed an initial entry to the site under escort. You may need to deal with contamination, dust, and debris which could include shards of glass. There may be fire damage as well as flood damage caused by the sprinkler system or firefighting activities. It may be many months before the building can be made ready for occupation if it has sustained significant structural damage.

Fire: After a fire of any consequence the fire service and the police may carry out a forensic investigation to determine if arson or other crime is connected to the incident. Fires are often started by criminals as a diversionary tactic to occupy the emergency services while they commit their criminal acts. You should allow for denial of access of up to 24 hours before you are allowed to inspect the scene for yourself. If the building has been smoke-logged, it may be several weeks before it is fit for occupation. Apart from the smoke damage, there will also be significant amounts of water which can cause problems of corrosion and mildew. Subsequent dehumidification, decontamination, and deodorization are tasks for professionals and may take many weeks.

Injury: If there is an injury which could be considered to be an industrial injury, it could take a week or more for an official investigation to be carried out before the site can be touched. Further delays might be caused by essential preventative or safety measures before people are allowed back into that area.

Flood: The damage and the delay will depend on the nature of the event which led to the flood. If the flooding is serious, there is always the danger of contamination by chemicals and sewage, which can lead to a substantial amount of work to decontaminate the premises and contents. It will also take several days or weeks to dehumidify and deodorize the premises. Often, there is a need to redecorate or refurbish. In any case, flooding could lead to an interruption of several days or even weeks.

9.2.2   Denial of Access for Public Security

The police will always give top priority to public safety; therefore, if there is a danger, or an imminent danger, they may erect a security cordon and allow nobody to enter. If your site is inside this cordon, you will be denied access along with everybody else. Remember that your business interruption insurance policy probably does not cover situations in which you are in a cordoned-off area but have not sustained damage. If you have any doubts or concerns about this, then you should check your policy. Reasons for a security cordon include:

Bomb alert: Depending on the location and prevailing circumstances, the police are likely to deny any access to the area for up to 12 hours while they investigate the scene and the cause of the alert.

Suspicious package or bomb threat: A bomb threat, or a suspicious package, will involve immediate evacuation until the police have made a thorough search. If there is intelligence to support the view that the threat is real, the cordon will tend to be the same as for an actual explosion, i.e., 500 meters from the target area, and the investigation might last up to 24 hours.

Terrorist bomb: The security cordon will entail an exclusion zone of not less than 500 meters. Safety checks by the police and explosive experts could take up to 24 hours. It is worth taking a large-scale map of your area and drawing a 500-meter circle around your premises to get some idea of the extent of such a cordon. You could also draw a similar circle around any obvious iconic targets in your area to see whether that would affect access to your premises. Bear in mind that the cordon is likely to extend to convenient control points rather than a precisely measured 500 meters; they will tend to err on the side of caution.

Armed siege: Nobody will be allowed within range, which probably means line of sight. This type of event can take days while the police try to negotiate a peaceful settlement.

Fire in a nearby building: If there is a risk of toxic fumes, an explosion, or structural collapse, it could lead to immediate evacuation of the area. It could take anywhere from several hours to several days before you are allowed back into your building. If a fire occurs at night you will certainly be denied access until the following morning. You will always have to wait until the fire service declares the building safe. The fire service may insist on a thorough investigation before you get access, which could take a few days. Among other things, they are determining the cause of the fire to eliminate the possibility of another outbreak. They will also want to be absolutely sure the fire has been completely damped down and there is no chance of reigniting. There have been cases where flammable material has smoldered for days and then burst into flame when disturbed and exposed to the air. If the fire service suspects arson, they will inform the police, who may take several days to carry out their forensic examination before you are given access.

9.2.3   Denial of Access by Health and Safety Officials

9.2.3.1 Death or Serious Injury

It can take several days for registered asbestos removal contractors to carry out their work.

If a death or serious injury has occurred as a result of a breach of safe working regulations (for example, a blocked fire exit or unsafe storage of chemicals), your federal agency responsible for safety in the workplace may be involved: Health and Safety Executive or Factory Inspectorate in the UK, and Occupational Safety and Health Administration (OSHA), an agency of the US Department of Labor, for example. The federal agency has the power to prevent you touching the area of the accident until its investigation is complete. This can take several weeks.

9.2.3.2 Structural Damage

If a building appears to be dangerous, for whatever reason, the police may require emergency strengthening work to be carried out before allowing anyone to approach, or enter, the building. The only exception would be the contractors who are carrying out the work. They would be required to adopt the appropriate safety measures, such as protective clothing.

High winds can pull window panes and cladding from a damaged building. The wind speed is important, and the police may deny access to the area if the wind speed is rising, or is expected to rise. Everyone entering the area would need to wear proper safety clothing: gloves, boots, and a hard hat.

9.2.3.3 Contamination

Contamination of any sort must always be taken very seriously. Cutting corners when attempting to deal with contamination can be an expensive mistake.

Asbestos: Many buildings contain asbestos in the materials used for cladding, insulation, partitions, or roofing. Although these materials are safe enough if they are left undisturbed, they may be broken up and spread around by fire and the water used to extinguish the fire. If there is a suspicion of asbestos contamination, tests must be carried out before any further work is permitted. These tests are relatively simple: samples are removed and inspected under a microscope. The various types of asbestos can be recognized by the distinctive shapes of their fibers. If there is any trace of blue asbestos (crocidolite) or brown asbestos (amosite), all of the asbestos-bearing materials must be cleared before anyone enters. It can take several days for registered asbestos removal contractors to carry out their work. They have to tent the contaminated area to prevent the spread of contamination, then they have to remove the asbestos and dispose of it as well as having it independently analyzed.

PCBs: PCBs (polychlorinated biphenyls) were once extensively used as insulating coolants in electrical switchgear and transformers, so it may well be present in older equipment. If the equipment is damaged in a fire, the PCBs can be spread with the smoke. These substances are highly carcinogenic, which means decontamination is essential before anybody is allowed to enter. It may be very difficult to find someone who is willing and able to deal with PCB contamination and your building could become a ghostly testament to the foolishness of earlier generations.

Other chemicals: Tests will be needed to detect traces of any dangerous chemicals which are known (or suspected) to be onsite. Bear in mind that many ordinary chemicals can produce dangerous mixtures in a fire after accidental mixing due to the damage, breakage, or leakage of containers.

9.2.3.4 High Rise Buildings

Multiple occupancy: If your organization is not the only occupant of the premises, you may have to join a queue with the other tenants for a short time-slot in which to retrieve essential items. This means your retrieval and inspection team will need to be fully briefed about what they should be looking for and where they should expect to find it. They may need to have passwords, keys, access codes, or access cards to reach secure items or enter secure areas. You must also be aware that there may be no power which might affect the security systems within the building. Depending on the system and its features, the lack of power may make it easier, more difficult, or impossible to reach the secure areas.

Falling glass: This is a much bigger problem with high rise buildings. There is a higher risk of glass falling and it is much more difficult to replace glass before you can use the building again. Anti-shatter film can reduce the potential for damage and injury.

Power failure: Since there is often no power after a fire, you cannot depend on being able to use the elevators or escalators. Thus, if power is interrupted, you may anticipate the physical problems of walking up and down many flights of stairs, perhaps carrying heavy loads.

9.2.3.5 Main Street and Industrial Locations

Wherever there are members of the public around, you may expect an increased chance that the police will deny access in the interest of public safety. You would be well advised to check the building materials for asbestos, especially if the building was built or re-clad between 1965 and 1985, and have it analyzed for asbestos content. (See the discussion of asbestos above.) Asbestos cement sheeting is very common on factory roofs and cladding, and can become friable after being subjected to high temperatures in a fire. There may also be asbestos insulation and lagging on pipe-work, especially in the more inaccessible places. If asbestos is found, you need expert advice about how to deal with it. It may be considered to be safer to leave it rather than disturb it. In any case, you should notify the Health and Safety Executive or OSHA about any asbestos which is found.

9.3   Site and Structures

Be aware that any changes made to the property during restoration may need planning permission. If the zoning or building codes in the area have changed since the building was built or altered, planning permission could even be needed just to restore the building to its previous state.

9.3.1   Deterioration of Materials

The principal concern for your site is the deterioration of materials through chemicals or high humidity: the problem is that the deterioration may not be immediately visible. By the time it becomes noticeable, it could be too late to do very much about it. If the problem had been recognized at the time of the incident, most, if not all, of the damage could have been avoided or prevented.

Hydrochloric acid: Produced by burning plastics such as PVC, hydrochloric acid can penetrate concrete, causing corrosion of the reinforcing steel, which leads to the concrete bursting because the products of corrosion occupy more space than the steel itself.

> **Any attempt to renovate before the drying out is complete…will delay the restoration project even further.**

The gaseous products of combustion from one kilogram of plastic will crystallize on relatively cool surfaces and then proceed to absorb water from the atmosphere to produce 1.4 liters of neat hydrochloric acid. The acid then permeates its surroundings and continues its inevitable chemical progress towards a stable compound like rust.

Hydrochloric acid also corrodes other metal surfaces, including the many hidden surfaces. Removing the corrosion and the contamination should restore the item back to its full function, preventing further deterioration. Deterioration is prevented only if the work is carried out properly; irreparable damage can be caused by the enthusiastic amateur who may do more harm than good.

Humidity: Very wet buildings will take a long time to dry out. It takes approximately one month for every inch of wall thickness, if it is left to dry naturally. The building cannot be fully redecorated and refurnished until the process of drying it out is complete. Any attempt to renovate before the drying out is complete will quickly reveal signs of dampness, such as staining and peeling paint, which will delay the restoration project even further.

Fungal attack can be an issue (rot or mold) as a wet building slowly dries out. Corrective treatment with the appropriate fungicides should help to reduce the scale of the problem. Some cleaning to remove the mold or fungus may also be necessary before the building is fit for decoration and occupation.

9.3.2   Other Problems

Hazardous materials: In the past, particularly during the 60s, 70s and early 80s, an asbestos mixture was often sprayed onto pipe work and other structures as a fire-resistant insulating material.

If such materials have been used on your premises, you will need to have some of the sprayed asbestos removed by a professional in order to check the underlying structure. This asbestos contamination hazard will require specialist attention and may cause further delays while they carry out the investigation and remove the hazardous materials. (See the discussion of asbestos earlier in this chapter.)

Smoke: Smoke travels up any natural chimneys, such as service risers, elevator shafts, stairways, ventilation shafts, or air conditioning ducts and will contaminate them in the process, causing problems and delays during the recovery and reinstatement of your operations.

Smoke and fumes from other people's fires may affect your premises, especially if the fumes are deemed to be toxic and require evacuation measures. Explore this risk before something does go wrong and causes you a problem. Do you know what kinds of goods, materials, and chemicals are held nearby and what would happen if there were a fire in the area?

Air conditioning: Air conditioning intakes sited close to the top of chimneys or other outlets can draw fumes back into the building and circulate them to parts which were previously undamaged. When there is a danger of smoke or fumes, air conditioning systems should be shut off immediately and should not be used again until the danger is over and the contamination has been dealt with properly.

Corrosive and contaminating substances can travel and persist inside the air conditioning system and may also penetrate the ceiling and floor voids. Because much of the ducting is likely to be almost inaccessible, complete decontamination of an air conditioning system can be quite a major undertaking.

Foul water: The presence of foul or stagnant water presents a serious bacterial risk. Warm, dry weather conditions will make the situation worse, while a cold spell will reduce the risk. Rain could spread the risk.

9.4   Precautions after an Event

9.4.1   Precautions after Fire

Beware of the fire restarting; reigniting is always a major concern for fire fighters. Flammable materials can smolder for days and then burst into flame when there is a draft or movement which allows more oxygen on to the hot spot. Keep fire extinguishers handy whenever you are moving rubble after a fire; the fire could flare up again as you open doors and start to move stuff around.

9.4.2   Precautions after Flood (Including Firefighting Water)

There is always a serious health risk from foul water; therefore, the people working in the flooded environment must be adequately protected.

> **...it is wise to check for other contaminants as well as the original one.**

- If there is any chance the water was contaminated by sewage or dirt, workers must be protected against disease. The commonest diseases likely to be present in dirty water are hepatitis, leptospirosis or Weil's disease, and AIDS. Don't take any chances.

- If there is any chance the water was contaminated by chemicals, workers must be protected against poisons. At the very least, this means waterproof protective clothing.

- If the flooding was severe, or long-lasting, it is likely the water will have soaked into the fabric of the building, taking its contaminants with it. There may be a need for decontamination as well as drying out and deodorization.

- Mildew and rot may begin to appear as the building dries out which will require specialist treatment to treat the cause, prevent further spread, and deal with the staining.

9.4.3   Precautions after Contamination

Wherever contamination is known or thought to have taken place, it is wise to check for other contaminants as well as the original one. The principle concerns are asbestos which can cause asbestosis, any chemicals which might be irritants or toxic, and the spread of contagious diseases. All of these require laboratory testing to identify the type and extent of the contaminant. In the case of biological testing for disease, the cultures may take several days to mature before a definite conclusion can be reached. If you expect to be dealing with toxic waste, be sure that your methods are in compliance with all local, state, and federal laws and regulations.

- Protective clothing is needed by those who are taking samples and those who have to deal with the contamination.

- Lockable containers are required for the collection and disposal of any dangerous chemicals.

- The dismantling, decontamination, reassembly, and reconditioning of the air conditioning plant and the associated ductwork may be a significant concern.

9.4.4   Precautions after Blast

After an explosion the main concern, apart from structural damage, is often the presence of glass shards or fragments of glass which can be found almost everywhere. The result is a constant risk of injury when cleaning, including the inside of cupboards and filing cabinets. Anybody picking up and handling documents will need to use extra caution.

▸ Glass fragments will be imbedded in materials such as curtains and in furnishings such as chairs. Consider the immediate replacement of all soft furnishings and furniture after a serious blast.

▸ Glass fragments may also be impaled in the fabric of the building. Under the enormous forces of an explosion, shards of glass can penetrate several inches into the brick or concrete structure of a building and present a significant hazard to the unwary.

▸ Glass dust, which can be difficult to see in poor lighting conditions, gets everywhere and can easily cause injury.

9.4.5   Unsafe Structures

If there are unsafe structures as a result of the blast, all sorts of problems may need to be resolved in order to enable the resumption of normal operations. The best advice is to seek help from specialists. Your loss adjuster (or loss assessor) should be able to make suitable recommendations.

▸ It may be necessary to protect the unsafe structure from the wind to reduce the chance of collapse or further damage. There might also be a need to protect the exposed parts from the weather in order to protect people and equipment.

▸ If mechanical or electronic equipment has to be kept running after a fire or an explosion, you should change, or clean, air filters frequently in order to prevent blockage by the dust and soot which will abound in the atmosphere for several weeks after the event.

▸ Your salvage team will need to recover materials and dispose of waste, which will mean hiring containers. You may require permission from the local authority (and the landlord, where applicable) to site these containers. If you are going to be disposing of toxic waste, then you will need to use lockable containers.

9.5   Equipment and Technology

...unskilled attempts... can lead to a complete loss of some or all of the vital information.

Much valuable information is stored electronically on all sorts of media, both as working data and as backup. This may take the form of CDs, DVDs, diskettes, tapes, thumb drives, or hard disks. All of these carriers are sensitive to a number of environmental factors which may be present before, during, and after a disaster.

It is important to realize that unskilled recovery efforts could cause further damage. In the worst case, unskilled attempts to clean the media or recover the data can lead to a complete loss of some or all of the vital information. Once the media is damaged, the data may be irretrievable. On the other hand, skilled specialists can often recover information after what might appear to be severe damage.

You can also expect the ever-present problem of knowing precisely which items contain the data you need. All too often incorrect, unclear, misleading, or missing labels cause unacceptable delays while the required records are found and eventually restored.

Other typical post-disaster concerns include:

▸ Difficulties and delays physically retrieving backup media from a damaged building.

▸ Deliberate or accidental erasure, either as a direct result of the incident, an error amidst the confusion, or as another blow from the unseen enemy who caused the whole affair.

▸ Some, or all, of the offsite backup might be incomplete, out-of-date, or irretrievable.

▸ Malfunction, or incompatibility, of the equipment used to gain access to the data.

▸ Physical distortion of tapes or disks, for example, caused by heat or old age. Skilled data recovery technicians may be able to help, depending on the degree of distortion and the accompanying deterioration of the recorded signal.

▸ Contamination of recording surfaces by chemicals or dust. Again this can often be overcome by skilled technicians but there are serious risks associated with any do-it-yourself efforts.

9.5.1　Problems of Running Applications on Different Equipment

When you are forced to move to alternate premises or use borrowed equipment, you may encounter a number of problems to be overcome before you can run your applications on different hardware.

▸ Sometimes the software is keyed to your particular hardware and will not run on machines with unregistered or unauthorized serial numbers. This is a security measure often imposed by software developers to prevent pirating of their intellectual property. Often you can obtain an extension to the licenses for use in disaster recovery mode. It is an issue which can be resolved only through the software provider and will be highlighted by testing your disaster recovery plan.

▸ Another protection mechanism which can be used by the suppliers of proprietary software is the use of "dongles" or access control devices which have to be connected to the machine before you can access the application on that machine.

▸ If your application is normally run on an earlier, perhaps obsolescent, model of computer or operating system, or it depends on some special feature, this may require an update, an upgrade, or a special modification.

▸ Some, or all, of your data or software, may be stored on an obsolete media format, and you may have difficulty finding suitable equipment to read and transfer the information to a working alternate operating environment.

▸ The index track may be damaged in some way meaning that although the information is still recorded, the pointer to its actual location has been lost. Specialists might be able to recreate the index from the content of the data, but it is likely that any relationships between records will have been compromised. Synchronization of a relational database may not be possible in these circumstances.

▸ Where assistance or support is required from suppliers or their agents you may have a problem of proving entitlement. They may not want to help you unless you can prove that you do have a legal right to use that software on that equipment at that location.

9.5.2　Issues after the Event

Recovery from clean, undamaged media is usually straightforward, providing you have access to the appropriate reading equipment. On the other hand, recovery of the data from damaged media can be an expensive and slow process.

- Unskilled attempts to recover the data from dirty or damaged media will invariably cause more harm than good. Furthermore, they cause unnecessary delays.
- Data stored on magnetic or optical disks is often recoverable, even when the computer equipment is severely damaged.
- Data stored on magnetic tapes is almost always readable, providing the tape itself is intact.
- After a fire, smoke contamination of the moving parts of a hard disk will lead to immediate data loss if the disks are powered up.
- Media stored in a data safe are protected for a limited time, depending on the fire rating of the safe (typically 1-2 hours). This may not be long enough in a big fire.

After flood: Water will not penetrate tightly wound tapes, so contamination should be limited to the edges of the tape. The data should be retrievable once the tapes have been properly cleaned.

After contamination: Transfer the data to clean media, dispose of the old media, and arrange for the reading equipment to be serviced.

After blast: Dust and glass may contaminate tapes which are held in open racks or placed on shelves. The abrasive effect of dust, especially glass dust, can lead to serious damage of both the tapes and the reading equipment.

9.5.3   Damaged Media

Failure of hard disks often occurs after a fire, flood, or explosion. This is usually because the device is switched on in an attempt to recover the data. Soot, chlorides, and dust will affect the vulnerable surfaces and correct operation of the disk unit is unlikely.

If tapes have suffered contamination (smoke, dust, or chemicals), you may be able to restore the information by first cleaning the tapes, and then running them once through a tape drive to transfer the contents to a new tape. Then the contaminated tapes should be scrapped and the tape reader serviced to remove all traces of contaminant.

Get expert help to:

- Remove dust and smoke by running tapes through a tape cleaner. Discard the tapes once you have recovered the data.
- Remove water from tapes by rewinding the tape several times carefully without attempting to read the data until all the water has been removed. If beads of moisture get between the read head and the tape, the tape will be ruined and the head may be damaged.
- Transfer information to an undamaged reel of tape, using a clean tape drive.
- Check the information before live use.
- Discard all contaminated media. Do not take a chance on cleaning and re-using contaminated media.

9.6   Documents and Records Retrieval

The aim of commercial document recovery is to produce documents you can read, handle, and store.

Mold will begin to appear within 48 hours under moist conditions, if the temperature is above 6°C. Removal of the marks, or stains, left by mold is almost impossible.

- Wet paper is very heavy and is very easily damaged by handling. It is an unpleasant job, as the documents to be recovered are usually dirty, wet, and smelly.

> Loose papers which are left lying on desks will probably not be recoverable after a fire, flood, or explosion.

> Some ink-jet printer inks are extremely water-soluble, and will disappear at the first trace of moisture. Where possible, you should consider changing to a non-soluble ink.

> If the information on such documents is important, it is better to scan the document and store the contents electronically, or file a photocopy, rather than file the paper itself.

9.6.1 Four Categories of Documents

The salvage of paper documents can be broken down into four categories, depending on what must be retrieved, the type of document, and the paper quality. We will refer to information recorded on individual sheets of paper as *loose* format, i.e., easily separated into individual pages. On the other hand, books and magazines are in *bound* format, i.e., separation is either difficult or even unacceptable.

Record retrieval – loose documents: Record retrieval can be summarized as the relatively simple act of recovering the information without the need for the original document. In this instance, a photocopy, an electronic record, or perhaps even a photograph will meet the requirements of the users of the information.

Original document retrieval – loose documents: Original document retrieval involves retention and restoration of the original document as the valid record. This may be because of a legal or similar statutory requirement or the document itself might have an intrinsic value. Restoration of the original document is a more difficult task than the relatively straightforward retrieval of the recorded information; therefore it is likely to prove to be a rather more costly option. It certainly requires much more patience and expertise to restore an original document.

...difficulties of handling and treating such documents and their bindings can be labor intensive.

Book retrieval – bound documents: Retrieval for bound volumes – even when they have not been deeply penetrated by the smoke, fumes, and/or water – requires a great deal of time and effort with its attendant costs. On the one hand, there is a clear advantage that the pages will have been protected by being confined between covers, but the difficulties of handling and treating such documents and their bindings can be labor intensive. In many ways, the techniques are similar to those used in the restoration of paintings, except that the materials are very much more fragile.

Art paper retrieval – bound documents: Art paper, or coated paper, which has been finished to a high gloss or treated in some other special manner, does present a special set of problems. In effect, the finish is a smooth coating of glue. Once this type of paper gets damp and begins to dry out, the leaves will fuse together and become permanently bonded. This is the type of job that requires the ultimate in skill and patience for any chance of success, and success can rarely be guaranteed.

9.6.2 Other Types of Documents

Personal documents: Many individuals will have some documents in their offices which are critical to their personal effectiveness (for example, personal contact lists). In practice, it is very difficult to safeguard or recover such information, but you should be aware that the loss of such documents could impede recovery and the restoration of normal services.

Transient documents: Papers which are of temporary value such as invoices, delivery notes, and orders can be a problem. There may be thousands of such documents being processed at the time of an incident, representing a significant amount of cash and work effort, and it may be very hard to know what has been lost with any degree of certainty. It is worth structuring the normal workflow so as to capture the information in electronic form as soon as possible after it enters the company (and, of course, to backup the electronic data).

Microfiche and microfilm: These are susceptible to softening through contact with water. They can also suffer as a result of smoke or chemical attack as well as fire. The main hazard is mechanical damage suffered as a result of careless handling, especially after softening or sticking has occurred through water damage.

9.6.3 Emergency Response and Recovery Issues for Documents

Fire, water, and dust present special sets of problems. In many cases, recovery will have to deal with the effects of all three.

- Get critical documents out of the damaged building, as early as possible, so business can continue.
- For cataloging, you need to know the origin of every document removed from the building – preferably, which desk it came from, but certainly which room or section.
- Charred documents are particularly fragile and need very careful handling.
- Documents absorb moisture. Because water is usually used in firefighting, you will be dealing with water damage as well as fire damage.
- The chemicals which are likely to be present in, or near, a fire zone will attack both the paper and the ink. This may bleach the documents or even cause them to disintegrate.
- Smoke particles are likely to cause major problems if they are not removed fairly soon, because of the acids which tend to condense on the particles of soot.
- Sheets of paper must all be dried individually. Take care with this process, since it is easy to reassemble documents incorrectly.
- Water-soluble ink will become illegible and may stain other documents.
- Wet paper is heavy and easily damaged.

Sealing the documents: You can prevent uncontrolled drying or crumbling of documents by keeping them closed and wrapping them gently in cling-film. Store the sealed documents temporarily in archival-sized boxes to aid handling and identification.

Freezing the documents: Freezing documents will prevent mold growth and provide protection against damage while they are being handled. A commercial frozen food trailer can be used as an emergency freezer and it should be easy to hire. If you don't have a dedicated parking area and intend to park the trailer in the road, you will probably need permission from the local authority which may take several days to arrange.

Handling microfiche: Wrap microfiche trays, or film spools, in cling-film to contain and stabilize their environment until specialist help is available to deal with them. Move them as little as possible; they are very fragile while wet or moist. It is worth considering transferring the images to a digital format that can be backed up as an integral part of the corporate database or knowledge base and be subject to the same security regime.

9.7 Electronic Equipment

With electronic equipment there is always the danger of extra damage occurring after the main incident. The key concerns will be:

- Users switching equipment on to see if it works. This can cause both mechanical damage and electrical damage.
- Static discharge which can damage the circuitry.

- Physical damage while equipment is moved around during cleanup operations.
- Smoke contamination of circuit boards, leading to irreversible chemical corrosion.
- Smoke contamination of disk motors and other electromechanical components.
- Short circuits caused by the presence of water.
- Direct damage from heat to both casings and circuit boards.
- Blockage of filters by dust and smoke particles leading to overheating and subsequent failure.
- Equipment being accepted back onto a normal maintenance contract after it has been salvaged.

Corrosion: Damage increases rapidly with time if nothing is done. The speed with which corrosion damage occurs will depend on the conditions. In extreme conditions of heavy contamination in a hot, moist environment, it is vital that salvage begins no later than 24 hours after the incident has occurred. In warm, dry conditions, unpowered equipment will resist corrosion for a longer time. In either case, it should not be assumed that equipment is a total loss just because there has been a delay.

> **...in a hot, moist environment, it is vital that salvage begins no later than 24 hours after the incident...**

9.8   Process Equipment

In an emergency situation, once everybody is accounted for and the premises are made safe, the first priority will be to get back in operation.

To save time and effort in the critical period following an incident, arrange now with your insurance company (or broker) and your equipment supplier for a list of suitable specialist loss adjusters and salvage engineers, whom you can contact directly.

You should then appoint your experts and discuss your situation with them, so they will be prepared to act swiftly in an emergency.

Important points to discuss include:

- What does your insurance policy cover and what is excluded?
- Is your recovery strategy consistent with the insurance policy?
- When equipment is restored and returned to service there is a risk of early failure. How long after the original incident are you covered by your insurance for equipment failure caused by the effects of the incident?
- Will your equipment supplier, or specialist maintainer, accept restored equipment back onto a regular maintenance contract and are there any special conditions attached?

After the event: Get agreement from all interested parties before starting work on reinstatement. These will include such people as:

- Your insurer; this will be arranged through the loss adjuster.
- The maintainer and/or manufacturer of your key items of equipment and plant.
- The owners of the equipment and plant, which may be the subject of a lease or hire purchase agreement.
- Your salvage engineer, who may have been pre-appointed or called in by the loss adjuster.

In general:

- Turn off power.
- Vent smoke.
- Immediate actions: Call professional help immediately.
- Do not switch on any equipment which may be damaged, wet, or contaminated. If there is any doubt – assume the worst, don't hope for the best.
- Remove or disconnect all power supplies including any uninterruptible power supplies and on-board batteries. The tiniest amount of current can do untold damage.
- Do not move damaged, or contaminated, equipment unless absolutely necessary. If you do move it, handle it as if it were in full working order – do not assume it is destroyed.
- Preserve and protect equipment in the meantime to slow the rate at which damage occurs.
    - ❏ Remove excess water from around the equipment.
    - ❏ Cover items with plastic sheeting, and place dehumidifiers under the sheeting. If you don't own dehumidifiers you can rent them – your loss adjuster or salvage engineer will be able to help you identify where you can get them.
- Protect any areas which are still uncontaminated to avoid cross-contamination from affected areas.
- Ask a salvage engineer to carry out tests to confirm where there is contamination and which areas remain uncontaminated.
- Stabilize the environment (leave it alone as far as possible).

9.8.1   After Fire

Even small fires can cause contamination problems.

- Heat from a fire will cause direct damage, but electronic equipment can stand temperatures of up to 70°C if it is switched off (at least 55°C if it is operating). Casings, external knobs, and switches can be quite seriously melted without any thermal damage to the electronics because the casing provides some protection.

> **While Halon is being phased out, a number of other similar gaseous extinguishants are available...**

- Soot (carbon particles) will settle on circuits and components inside equipment. This will cause short-circuits if electrical power is applied. Soot will also absorb water and acids, creating a moist environment which stimulates corrosion.
- Water used for firefighting will flood the building at the level where the fire is burning and any floors below it, carrying dirt, acids, and other contaminants.

- When PVC is burned it produces gaseous hydrogen chloride, which combines with airborne water vapor to form hydrochloric acid. The acid will condense on cool surfaces throughout the building, including circuit boards inside equipment in areas that may not appear to be affected by smoke.
- Unpowered circuits are reasonably resistant to attack but any electrical activity may cause shorting and electrolytic corrosion. Exposed metal surfaces (steel, stainless steel, galvanized steel, aluminum, brass, and copper) will corrode rapidly. Water and humid air accelerates the process of corrosion.
- Halon-based fire suppression systems are no longer used in UK and Australia, and in the US such systems are banned from new production, although some reuse is possible. While you are unlikely to be using Halon fire extinguishers, you should be aware of the chemical's negative effects. When Halon is heated to above 400°C, hydrogen bromide gas is formed; this combines with moisture in the air to form hydrobromic acid. As the temperature drops, the acid condenses, causing rapid corrosion of metal surfaces and circuit boards. Very little hydrogen bromide would normally be released when

Halon is used to put out a fire. But, if the gas comes into contact with a source of residual heat such as a furnace, or a large mass which has been heated by the fire, a continuous stream of hydrogen bromide may be formed, causing serious ongoing corrosion.

▸ While Halon is being phased out, a number of other similar gaseous extinguishants are available, which work on the same principle. They remove the free oxygen from the immediate vicinity of the flame. In order to do this, they need to be chemically vigorous, usually based on compounds of bromine or fluorine. Whenever they strike a hot surface, they are liable to break down and produce some very corrosive chemical byproducts.

Key activity: Ventilate the whole building to dispel smoke as quickly as possible, along with any other airborne contaminants. Carpets, curtains, paper, and other damp materials should be removed from the area to reduce the moisture content of the air. This will speed up the overall drying out process.

9.8.2   After Flood

▸ Dirty water will have left sludge and possibly chemical contamination on, and inside, everything it reaches. This will cause damaging short circuits if the equipment is powered up, and the damp atmosphere will encourage corrosion.

▸ Water may have soaked into the fabric of the building. This will result in abnormally high levels of humidity long after the bulk water has been removed. Remember that humidity is the principal cause of corrosion and deterioration.

▸ Key activities: The main requirement is to minimize corrosion while waiting for the equipment to be cleaned by removing water and lowering the relative humidity of the air to below 45%.

  ❏ Remove or isolate all power, including battery backup supplies, to prevent shorting.

  ❏ Gently tilt equipment so any water will run off the circuit boards rather than remain on the boards and evaporate, leaving sediment which can lead to chemical and electrical problems.

  ❏ Remove water from around the equipment.

  ❏ Cover the equipment with plastic sheeting, or tarpaulins, to protect it from falling water.

  ❏ Place dehumidifiers (not heaters) under the sheeting. Heaters will only make the situation worse.

  ❏ Allow plenty of air to move through the affected area to remove moisture. Open all windows and doors to encourage a free flow of air through the whole area.

  ❏ Carpets, curtains, paper, and other damp materials should be removed from the area to reduce the moisture content of the air. This will speed up the overall drying out process.

9.8.3   After Contamination

If the dust contains metal particles or carbon, it may conduct electricity, causing short circuits. On the other hand, insulating dust can isolate electrical contacts, causing open circuits. You should also bear in mind that some dusts are dangerous to health (for example asbestos or glass fragments from an explosion).

▸ Key activities:

  ❏ Do not switch equipment on.

  ❏ Remove or isolate all power, including any battery backup or uninterruptible supplies.

  ❏ Eliminate the source of dust to prevent further contamination.

  ❏ Seek professional advice on the nature of the dust (toxicity, etc.). This may involve sending samples for chemical or biological analysis.

❑ Dry powder extinguishers are not recommended for use on electronic equipment, but it does happen. These dry powders can be quite corrosive and toxic. It is a specialist's job to clean off the dry powder – do not attempt to do this yourself.

9.8.4   After a Blast

Be wary of glass fragments and particles. Modern electronic equipment is normally shock resistant, but contamination being driven inside the casing can be a problem.

▶ Key activities: Apart from the obvious signs of physical damage after a blast, the main concerns and activities are the same as for contamination, which are described above.

9.9   Regulating Access to the Site

In the aftermath of a major incident, many people will require access. The insured, tenant, owner, or occupier may not be granted access until the emergency is over. Access may also be denied to loss adjusters, or assessors, who are viewed as their representatives. Access may be controlled by the police or the fire service. It is important to handle the relationships between the interested parties and control or restrict access as needed.

Figure 9-1 shows the reporting structure of those involved in the salvage operation, working on behalf of the beleaguered victim, known as "the insured."

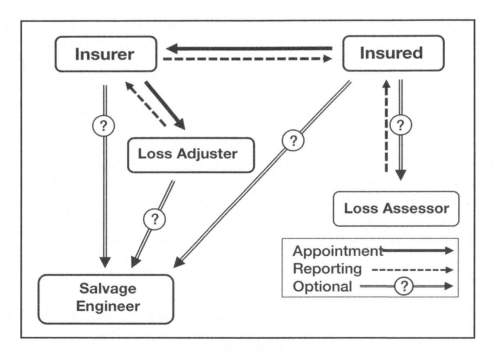

Figure 9-1. Reporting Structure

Figure 9-2 shows who is likely to be involved in controlling access to the disaster area and the premises within that area.

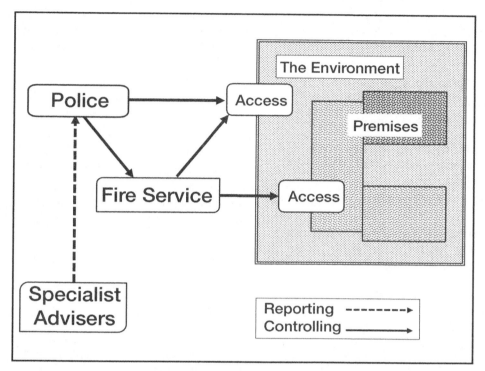

Figure 9-2. Controlling Access to the Area

Once the area is declared safe and investigations are complete, the area is subject to the normal security arrangements. However, those arrangements may no longer be suitable in the new situation.

Once you are allowed to return to the site, you may need to:

- Post additional security guards to control access to the site and prevent unauthorized removal of goods or materials.
- Put up perimeter fencing to provide an additional level of physical security and reduce the temptation to trespass. You could be held liable if someone enters the premises and harms themselves in the damaged structure.
- Board up any open doorways or windows for weather protection and access denial.
- Cover the roof for weather protection.
- Make arrangements for debris management and removal.

Self-Examination Questions

1. From a business continuity (BC) perspective, which of the following is the best approach to dealing with damaged equipment when attempting to recover from a disaster?

   A. Replace it with new equipment.

   B. Salvage it.

   C. Replace it if it's old; salvage it if it's new.

2. After a crisis incident involving one of the company's facilities, instruct the first people to enter the building

   A. to determine whether it is safe for others to enter.

   B. not to talk to law enforcement or firefighters about what they see there.

   C. to record what they find.

3. If a death or serious injury has occurred as a result of a breach of workplace safety regulations,

   A. a federal agency responsible for safety in the workplace may deny workers access to the facility for a long time.

   B. criminal charges are possible, and the company should hire a lawyer before anyone talks to the police.

   C. a lawsuit is almost certain, and the BC manager must turn over emergency management to the legal department.

4. When repairing and restoring a building, you must always first

   A. check building codes and obtain any needed permissions.

   B. determine whether it would be less expensive to build a brand-new structure instead.

   C. settle any lawsuits caused by the incident in case the building contains evidence.

5. When recovering equipment, technology, and data after a damaging incident, one of the gravest dangers is that

   A. insurance might not cover the losses if skilled specialists do not do the recovery work.

   B. proprietary information might fall into the hands of competitors disguised as workers.

   C. unskilled attempts to clean the media or recover the data could lead to the loss of some or all of the organization's vital information.

6. When salvaging paper documents, which of the following types of salvage is the quickest and simplest to perform?

   A. Book retrieval – bound documents

   B. Original document retrieval – loose documents

   C. Record retrieval – loose documents

7. In extreme conditions of heavy contamination in a hot, moist environment – like after a fire has been extinguished – it is vital that salvage of electronic equipment begin no later than _____ after the incident.

   A. 12 hours

   B. 24 hours

   C. 48 hours

8. After a disaster incident, which of the following is NOT likely to be involved in controlling access to the disaster area and the premises within that area?

   A. Fire department

   B. Legal department

   C. Police department

Food for Thought

In this chapter we have looked at the technical and logistic issues which you might need to take into account when recovering from physical damage to your equipment or premises. It is a rather specialized field in which you may not have any direct experience. To gain a more meaningful grasp of what might be involved, try these exercises.

Exercises

Try to imagine what resources or facilities should be regarded as essential and what you should or could do to facilitate their recovery and re-use.

1. What are the critical resources that you depend on in your working environment?
    > First, make a list of the items.
    > Then make a note of the protective measures you could or should take.
    > How would you retrieve and restore them after a major fire or storm?

2. What are the critical resources that you depend on in your living environment?
    > As before, make a full list of the items.
    > Then make a note of the protective measures you could or should take.
    > How would you retrieve and restore them after a major fire or storm?

3. What are the critical resources that your local community depends on?
    > As before, make a full list of the items.
    > Then make a note of the protective measures you could or should take.
    > How would your community retrieve and restore them after a major fire or storm?

4. What are the critical resources that your city, county, or state relies on?
    > As before, make a full list of the items.
    > Then make a note of the protective measures they could or should take.
    > How should they retrieve and restore them after a major fire or storm?

Looking Ahead

In this chapter, you looked at medium-term measures concerned with salvage and restoration or returning your property to a useable condition. In the next chapter, you will look at the complex technical issues associated with protecting and recovering your information technology which is at the heart of any modern business operation. That will lead on to developing the longer term plans, strategies, and procedures for the recovery and return of the overall business operation.

Downloadable Business Continuity Toolkit

You can download more information from the **Business Continuity Toolkit**.

For Additional Reading

British Damage Management Association (BDMA). See http://www.bdma.org.uk

National Fire Protection Association (2013). *NFPA 1600: Standard on disaster/emergency management and business continuity programs.* Available from http://www.nfpa.org/codes-and-standards/document-information-pages?mode=code&code=1600

Restoration Industry Association (RIA). See http://www.restorationindustry.org

Note: Much of the material in this chapter is based on research which I carried out on behalf of Survive, a UK-based membership organization devoted to BC. The organization ceased to trade in 2007.

10

Disaster Recovery

In previous chapters you have looked at how you would launch a business continuity (BC) program within your organization, understand the risks, and prepare to deal with an emergency. The next step is to discover what you need to do to ensure the recovery of your information technology (IT) systems and electronic data together with your communications technology.

This chapter will help you to:

- ☑ Identify the critical equipment and the services on which you depend.

- ☑ Prepare to be able to rebuild or restore your data systems.

- ☑ Determine what you need to have in place to accommodate your system users.

- ☑ Initiate a sound backup regime to ensure reliable data recovery.

- ☑ Ensure that you have adequate recoverable and accessible backup for all your essential data, information, and records.

10.1   What is Disaster Recovery?

Disaster recovery is that essential element of the BC management program which aims to restore the essential support services, thus enabling the core business functions to provide continuity of service to clients and client functions. Typically, disaster recovery plans cover the procedures to restore the technical services such as computing, Internet connectivity, and telecommunications, but the same principles can be applied to other types of equipment and services.

10.1.1   Characteristics of Disaster Recovery Plans

Disaster recovery plans tend to be technical, specific, and detailed, with little or no room for interpretation or deviation. Because they are concerned with technical and mechanical matters, things often have to be done in a particular sequence and approximation is not good enough. Such plans will include specific instructions, sequential task lists, and detailed procedures. There will be a tendency to avoid generalities and focus on the specifics.

...the main thrust is the resilience of the service and availability of the data to the users.

A disaster recovery plan takes an approach different from a BC plan. For example, a BC plan might suggest "access to office accommodation for 6 staff will be needed as a matter of some urgency." In contrast, a disaster recovery plan may state "6 desks in 360 square feet of ground floor office space with 120-volt single phase power should be available within 12 hours."

10.1.2   Aspects of Disaster Recovery

There are two distinct aspects of disaster recovery:

- Satisfying the ongoing need for business support systems through the recovery and restoration of essential facilities and resources.
- Preserving the integrity and availability of critical information through backup and recovery procedures.

These two aims are interdependent; there is no point in achieving one without the other. You need the systems and equipment in order to run the applications and provide the services, but they are ineffective without the data behind them. In addition to the regular issues of data security, confidentiality, access control, performance, and compatibility, the main thrust is the resilience of the service and availability of the data to the users.

As you saw in Chapter 6, a number of continuity strategies can provide resilience in various degrees. However, your actual choice of strategy will be influenced by a number of factors which will be covered in this chapter. Cost may or may not be a major factor, but you do need to get a clear perspective on financial implications. Factors to be considered include:

- The resilience, or the recovery, of technology and support services in general.
- Systems recovery, which includes the recovery or restoration of operating systems, software, and data.
- Network and Internet connectivity.
- Disaster recovery sites or services, the facilities and resources necessary to enable a recovery to take place.
- Work area recovery, providing suitable accommodation and resources for the general user population.
- In-house or third party options, the choice between having a contract with a specialist service provider and setting up your own independent solution.

Once you have explored the continuity options, return to the subject of establishing and maintaining the *backup regime*, which is the other essential ingredient of disaster recovery.

10.2   Technology and Support Services

One of the most important tools of modern business is communications systems. Without communications, there is no business activity. Communications technology, along with almost all of your other support services, is computer-based. Indeed, a modern telephone exchange is nothing more than a large computer with lots of remote users. Therefore, it makes sense to integrate the development and management of our telecommunications and data networks with your IT services. This integration makes life much easier than a set up in which two separate groups of technicians attempt to work in parallel or in competition with each other.

In most business operations, the majority of such services are provided and managed by an external organization. It is only the very large institutions, or those with specialized needs, that can justify developing their own dedicated services. Thus, it may be safe to assume you are able to rely on the support of your external service providers in a disaster recovery situation.

If you are seeking to provide total resilience within your own facilities, you will need to cover a number of services and utilities in some detail during your investigations and subsequent protection program. On the other hand, if you intend to make use of an alternative site or service provider, then you will be able to regard service failure as one of the effects with which your plans can cope, as long as your alternate site is not subject to the same interruption.

10.2.1   Range of Services

The range of services you may need to consider within your disaster recovery planning can be divided into two main groups. Technical services usually come under the control of an IT manager. All the other services are commonly called facilities, run by a facilities manager.

10.2.1.1 Technical Services

> Telephony, which includes the external service as well as the internal switchboard and communications network. If you have a call center, then you might regard this as an extension of the telephony system or perhaps as a separate function which requires its own dedicated disaster recovery plan.

> Internet, which includes the cabling and distribution network as well as the actual service from your service provider. This can be a very critical function in any organization which does a large proportion of its business over the Internet.

> Intranet, which is your own private version of the Internet which may be run by your own technical people or it might be outsourced to a specialist service provider.

> News and information services, which may be essential tools for some business units where trading and decision-making are dependent upon up-to-date information.

10.2.1.2 Facilities

> Electricity, which is essential to power all of your technology, heating, lighting, and electromechanical equipment together with conveniences such as elevators and escalators.

> Air conditioning, which may be used to maintain an effective working environment as well as protect equipment, such as servers, from overheating.

> Water supply, which may be required for drinking, hygiene, cooking or as a coolant or an ingredient in processing operations.

> Sewage, which is the removal of water after it has been used for any of the above purposes. If you can't get rid of the incoming water then you have a problem of the same magnitude as an interruption to the water supply.

10.2.2   Rules to Maximize Resilience

There are some rules which you can apply to these services and the companies that provide them in order to maximize your resilience or minimize the kinds of *exposure* that were discussed earlier in the chapters on risk and business impact analysis (BIA).

1. **Make sure you know exactly what you are dealing with.** Do not make assumptions about what you are entitled to, what is being delivered, and how it is being delivered. In some cases, it will take a lot of effort to uncover your hidden exposures. Often the service provider would prefer for these exposures to remain hidden or may not even be aware of the exposure or the implications. Over the years, I have acquired an assortment of devices, attachments, and features which make up my office system. Many of them are from the same source and others come from all over the place. When something goes wrong, do I turn to the supplier, the manufacturer, or someone on the Internet? If there is a question about compatibility, who takes responsibility? Luckily I have backup and two laptops. Alternatively, I could buy a totally new setup, complete with technical support.

> ...it is always possible to install a backup generator as an alternative power source.

2. **Carry out a thorough risk assessment of all the critical services.** Consider worst-case scenarios and examine evidence of the protective or resilient measures that the outside supplier claims are in place. Check out the whole of the service, not just your immediate interface. During recent large-scale flooding in the West of England, most power substations had thick walls to keep the water out. However, some villages lost power for weeks because their substations were not properly protected. They found out the hard way.

3. **Reduce your dependence on any one supply route or supplier for critical services.** Where alternate and separate supply routes are not viable or available, investigate alternate suppliers. If these options are not available, flag the exposure as a major threat to BC and investigate another recovery strategy. For example, there may only be one water main and no alternative supplier. The resolution might be to hold a stock of bottled drinking water and a small reservoir for other uses. The reservoir could be incorporated into the landscaping as a water feature, serving an aesthetic as well as a practical purpose.

10.2.3   Alternate Routing

The principles of alternate routing are derived from the third rule and apply to any service delivered through cabling, such as telephone lines, electricity supply, Internet access, computer links, signaling systems, or information services. You should always strive for:

> Multiple entry points into the building with physically separate supply lines to each entry point.

> Alternate or diverse routing of the supply lines to and from the central or local distribution point.

> Separate distribution points for each supply route.

Multiple entry points with diverse routing to separate distribution points ensure protection from the consequences of a failure somewhere along the supply route. All too often I have discovered that clients with supposedly separated power supplies or telephone lines have separation only as far as the nearest manhole. In fact, they require, and may even be paying for, separation right back to the source of supply, which is the local substation or telephone exchange.

Of course, with electrical power it is always possible to install a backup generator as an alternative power source. If you invest in this approach, make sure it will provide the required level of support during an emergency. A number of questions need to be resolved:

▸ Do you have sufficient capacity to supply all of your needs, both now and in the future? Allow for spare capacity as it is unlikely the plant will run at 100% efficiency.

> **Learning the language or jargon is quite an exercise in itself.**

▸ Do you have sufficient reserves of fuel to last throughout the emergency in the event of a shortage or delay in resupply? In fact, the emergency might be caused by a problem in the fuel supply chain.

▸ Has the generator been tested under full load and run for several hours to ensure it is capable of sustaining a full working load for an extended period? This is to ensure there are no unexpected problems with noise, vibration, exhaust systems, overheating, or degradation over time.

▸ Do you have either an uninterruptible power supply (UPS) system to handle the transition from utility to generator power, or a process to address short-term power outages until the generator kicks in?

With air conditioning, you may have a limited choice about alternative or backup, but it is quite possible that the staff can manage without it at certain times of the year. However, your computer room cannot function for very long without some form of air conditioning; racks of disk drives and servers generate a considerable amount of heat and would soon fail without its cooling effect. It is important that the air conditioning plant is serviced regularly.

10.3   Systems Recovery

Systems recovery, which is generally taken to mean the recovery of IT, Internet, and intranet services, is a complex and highly technical field. Many options and techniques are available to provide various degrees of continuity or resilience with a vast array of improvements, enhancements, and alternatives. The need for recovery and resilience measures, together with continual advances in technology, lead to fresh solutions appearing on the market. Some of them may simply be a revamp or re-branding of previous offerings and others may be significant breakthroughs. Simply staying abreast of what is currently available in this technical field is a specialized task. Learning the language or jargon is quite an exercise in itself.

10.3.1   Technical Expertise

If you are a technical person reading the latest literature on the subject, able to translate what you have read and heard into a meaningful strategy, then you should be able to come up with some suggestions about how to approach systems recovery within your own organization. On the other hand, if you are a BC manager who is trying to adopt a holistic approach, then you will need to get some technical advice in this area. Expertise about what is possible will come from suppliers of equipment and solutions and from other sources. Knowledge about what is required will come from your business unit managers, working with your technical people. Your role is to bring these groups together to thrash out a realistic systems recovery strategy for your organization.

10.3.2   Up-to-Date Recovery Strategies

Once you have a systems recovery strategy in place, revisit it on a regular basis. Both the possibilities and the requirements are almost certain to change over time. At a minimum, a biannual review should be held.

10.3.3 Documented and Tested Procedures

The key to systems recovery is a well-documented set of procedures which is regularly and rigorously tested and continually improved. Tested procedures allow you to establish a reasonable degree of certainty about the recoverability of the systems, while at the same time developing the skills required to support the recovery procedures. Another benefit is the opportunity to spot and apply improvements to those recovery procedures.

10.4 Disaster Recovery Sites

...such a technical topic is subject to continuous changes...with optimum solutions likely to change over time.

As discussed in Chapter 6, a standby or recovery site provides a solution to the majority of the problems posed by a disaster. An alternate site is a reliable means of dealing with denial of access, operational failures, and loss of data, providing you have the plans, procedures, and backup in place to support alternate site recovery. The ideal recovery site would be immune from all of the threats to the regular business operations at the normal business location.

10.5 Backup and Restore

10.5.1 What is Backup?

The term *backup* means a recoverable copy (or copies) of your vital records; this includes all of the data and documentation you need to hold for recovery purposes. Without proper backup, disaster recovery is virtually impossible. If you don't have the data, all the skills and resources in the world cannot put your business back together again. Any information which is held as backup must be regarded as both valuable and highly confidential and treated accordingly. Make sure recoverable copies of this vital information are always available:

- In the right format, for an easy recovery.
- In the right place, for a speedy recovery.
- Complete and current, for a total recovery.

You need to consider and understand several aspects of the process before you can create and run an effective set of procedures to produce the results you need with a fair degree of certainty at all times and under all circumstances.

10.5.2 Backup and Restore Procedures

The essential outcome of this stage of BC planning is a robust backup regime which can be relied upon to preserve and deliver the critical information required by the core business operations under any and all circumstances. While most organizations will already have some form of backup strategy in place, you have to ensure that the existing procedures meet corporate needs from a business or operational perspective rather than from the somewhat limited view of the IT department or systems administrators. Reviewing the current arrangements and moving towards good practice should be seen as a joint venture between the BC and the technical teams.

Due to the technical complexity of some aspects of backup and restoration, you will require the assistance of your technical support team. Be aware that such a technical topic is subject to continuous changes and improvements, with optimum solutions likely to change over time. The essence of effective disaster recovery is to able to ensure the constant *availability* of:

1. Records and information to provide input to the business functions.
2. Functional capability to provide a base for the business functions.
3. Plans and procedures to make effective use of the functional capability.
4. Skills and knowledge to interpret the plans and procedures effectively.

A key element of such a process is a robust backup regime to take care of the first of these four requirements, preserving and recovering vital records and information. This element will be covered in detail in this chapter. The other aspects of the process will be covered in other chapters.

As Philip Jan Rothstein notes, "Data backup technologies have come a long way since early mainframe days when open-reel tape was the only practical backup vehicle. Mass volumes of open-reel tapes have been supplemented by pocket-size media with orders of magnitude of more capacity and reliability.... Of course, the volume of data to backup has grown as well, constantly stretching the limits of backup media and speed" (Rothstein, 2003).

Another important consideration is that growing data communication bandwidth and connectivity have paved the way for backup independent of physical media or transport. Where offsite backup at one point was dependent on what was sometimes referred to as CTAM – "Chevy Truck Access Method" – contemporary backup schemes are as likely to be based on remote connectivity. Add to this technological advances such as cloud computing, and the whole issue of data backup can become challenging in some respects and simpler in others.

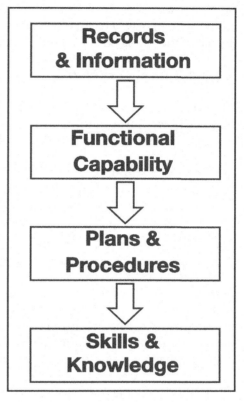

Figure 10-1. Effective Disaster Recovery Process

10.6   Backup Regimes

There are three main stages to the overall backup process to be controlled and managed. First, you have to create the records. Then, you must store those records. Finally, you have to be able to retrieve those records and recover the information from them. The control and management of this process is called a *regime*.

Although the technical details will vary from case to case, the model backup regime can be summed up as follows:

1. **Create:** Record all of the essential information, including:
   ▶ Any data which is critical to the business.
   ▶ Any original or source information.

2. **Store:** Store those records securely
   ▶ Until they are either replaced or out of date.

3. **Recover:** Then you can recover all of the information
   ▶ In an emergency or test situation.

...these business records represent the intellectual working capital of the whole business....

10.7   Business Records

Every business unit will generate records, require records, process records, or use records in some way. As a result, the average business enterprise acquires vast numbers of records.

Some of these records will be of an ephemeral nature, subject to change, replacement, or removal. Others will be unique pieces of history which may never alter but could easily be lost or forgotten. The majority will fit somewhere in between these two extremes. In total, these business records represent the intellectual working capital of the whole business, both now and in the future.

10.7.1   Business Value

The value is in the information which can be derived from the data rather than the record itself. Sometimes, the true business value is in the unique combination of records, from various sources, which are available to an organization. Business value includes:

▸ The cost of acquisition of the data or its purchase price.

▸ The full potential for profit over time or the long-term value.

▸ Replacement costs, if replacement is at all possible. Very often, it may be impossible to recapture original information once it has been lost, altered, or compromised.

▸ The value of the information to others or its commercial value.

▸ A rarity value to information which is unique, particularly rare, or difficult to obtain.

However, it is the owners of the business operations who should be asked to judge, or decide, what information is critical and which records need to be backed up – taking into account any legal or regulatory requirements which apply to the line of business or area of operation. In most regulated industries, an appointed compliance officer is tasked with ensuring that regulations are followed consistently, since there may be severe penalties for non-compliance.

10.7.2   Source Information

You must also consider the special value to the business of original or *source information*. In this context, original information is taken to mean any information which was developed or created by, or on behalf, of the organization. Source information is the basic concept, fundamental design or initial model from which functional, or working, versions of the idea can be derived or generated. For example, a computer program would be written by people in *source code*, but the computer would not be able to understand this first draft. The source code has to be converted into *machine language* for the benefit of the computer; the process is known as *compiling*; the result is a working application. If, at some later stage you want to modify the machine code, it is necessary to change the source code and re-compile the application.

Source information may take the form of:

▸ Original research material.

▸ Formulas or recipes.

▸ Software.

▸ Licensed material.

▸ Intellectual property.

▸ Patents.

▸ Copyright.

▸ Trademarks.

10.8   Critical Records

10.8.1   Guidelines for the Selection of Critical Records

As the BC manager, you cannot be expected to know about all these various types of records, the information they hold, and their relative value. Nor, for that matter, can the systems people be expected to know about such matters. Collection of this type of intelligence should be an intrinsic part of the BIA process, which is designed to capture input to the BC and disaster recovery plans for each department or business unit. Once again, it is the owners of these operations who have to decide and declare what is critical, what is desirable, and what is dispensable in an emergency.

You should regard a record as critical and include it within your backup regime if the information or the document is any of the following:

> **Difficult to replace:** Unnecessary costs and avoidable delays in rebuilding your database would occur if this record is not backed up.

> **In regular use:** There is a high degree of reliance or dependence on the information, simply because it is used in many ways or by many people.

> **Confidential:** You have to be able to demonstrate the information is used, held, and controlled in a secure manner. *Information security* requires the use of sound backup and recovery procedures.

> **Marketable:** It contains information of value to the client base or to another organization or individual.

> **Rare or unique:** It may be impossible to replace the record or the information it holds. Often the record itself may have an intrinsic historic or antique value as an artefact.

...critical records may be governed by a legal requirement to ensure that they are retained for specific periods of time....

> **About personnel:** It contains information about past, present, and future employees. Such records are subject to data protection legislation which calls for information security, implying the need for backup.

> **About customers:** It contains information about past, present, and future clients. Such records may also be subject to data protection legislation wherever the clients are identifiable as individuals.

> **About product or service records:** It contains information which is acquired for various reasons during the development, manufacture, shipping, and servicing of products.

10.8.2   Types of Critical Records

Certain types of records should be considered as critical by their very nature and therefore should always be included in any backup schedule or routine. These *mandatory backup records* include software, central records, and operational records.

10.8.2.1 Software

Keep backups of all the software which is in regular authorized use, such as:

> *Operating systems* complete with any special features and patches which may have been applied from time to time. If these modifications are missing, the users may experience the operating difficulties they

were supposed to cure, or incompatibilities which render systems unusable. The operating system is the basic background software which is needed to run the computer as a working system, hence the name.

▶ *Application software* complete with any features, patches, or other modifications which may have been applied. Applications are often supplied as an integral part of a package or suite of software, and the complete package should be considered as part of the backup.

▶ *Supporting documents* such as operating manuals should also be included with the backup. Otherwise, you may encounter difficulties establishing operating rights and solving technical problems. Specific license information may be essential to restore an application.

10.8.2.2 Central Records

A number of records are held centrally on behalf of the organization as a whole. Apart from their value as records, critical records may be governed by a legal requirement to ensure that they are retained for specific periods of time with the implication that they must be recoverable throughout that period. These central records might include:

▶ Company records which track and forecast cash flow, budgets, and financial data. Such information will have a limited distribution with access restricted to certain key personnel, such as the company secretary and the financial director. For security reasons, they may require special arrangements to be made for the capture, storage, and retrieval of this class of information.

▶ Accounts information such as billing information, orders received, and customer details which might include such sensitive information as special discounts, credit limits, and history. Just like the company records, accounts information may be governed by a requirement to be handled in a special manner.

10.8.2.3 Operational Records

Operational records serve to support or represent the needs and requirements of clients during ongoing day-to-day activities. These records will tend to be dynamic, with frequent changes and perhaps a short life cycle. However, they are essential to management and control of normal business operations. The operational group of records would include:

▶ Procedures and instructions, giving details of how various tasks and operations are to be carried out. Some of these jobs will be of a routine nature, or they may be customized to suit the requirements of a particular project or client. Generally, the procedures and instructions will have a broad application, and any variations will be described in a specific job sheet or project plan. Many of the basic procedures and instructions may depend upon or refer to the equipment supplier's manuals, which should be included as part of the backup.

▶ Work in progress information, such as job sheets, plans, and drawings. These may be unique to a specific job or project, and as work progresses they might be updated or modified to reflect changes or deviations. Such records cannot be replaced because they have become customized out of all recognition from the original draft; backup has to be current to be at all useful.

▶ Client information, such as details of contracts and specifications of a customer's particular requirements. Much of this information will be relatively static, although there could be important changes from time to time triggered by a new contract, a major review, or changes to regulations. Perhaps both the original and the revised or new versions will need to be held as backup, at least for a time.

▶ Project and process control records, which track or control the use of materials and ingredients. Very often there is a long-term need to maintain accurate records of the complete manufacturing, storage, and delivery cycle of goods, especially in the food and drugs sector. Backup must take account of these requirements.

10.8.3   Storage of Critical Records

At various times and dates throughout the year, you will put backup copies of all your critical records into storage where they will remain until they are retrieved or need to be replaced. While they are in storage, these records must be held secure and kept up-to-date. The repository where these records are held and maintained may be an actual physical location, or a virtual location which resides somewhere within your data processing network. In an emergency, you must be able to recover all of the data and information from those records without undue delay and with a high degree of certainty.

10.8.3.1 Backup Media

In recent years there has been a huge escalation in the volumes of data held on our systems. Advances in technology and an ever more demanding business environment mean that techniques and procedures from the past can't always be relied on as models for the future. However, the fundamentals of data handling and protection still apply. First you will explore the basic principles and then look at how you might approach your own backup and recovery program.

Wherever and however you retain your backup, the data has to be held on some sort of storage medium. Essentially there are four different types of media in current use. The choice is between magnetic tape, hard disk, optical storage, and solid state devices.

Consider that each of these media has a finite life, as a function of physical longevity, declining reliability over time, damage or environmental exposure, and technological obsolescence – consider how you would recover data from a 5.25-inch floppy diskette today!

Magnetic tape has been around for a very long time and has proved to be a very effective and reliable medium for storing large volumes of data over long periods. Its principal drawback is the fact that access is sequential. Every time you try to read something, you have to start from the beginning of the tape. Although the access to a specific record might be slow, the rate of reading or writing sequential data is quite fast. This means that for backup purposes all of the records need to be arranged in the right sequence to reduce the number of times the tape has to be restarted during the recovery process. Otherwise the recovery can be very slow. Because it is a relatively simple but highly refined technology, tape is a very cost-effective way of storing large volumes of data.

Hard disk enables rapid access to all records because the read head, or heads, can go directly to any particular sector of the rotating disk. The principal advantages of disks include low access times, high capacity and ease of use. However, because of their mechanical complexity, they tend to be more expensive and are relatively fragile, especially when being handled or transported.

Optical storage is a relatively slow, low capacity and low cost medium which includes DVDs, CDs and Blu-ray discs. For archive purposes they can be prepared in what is known as "Write Once – Read Many" (WORM) format which means the data cannot be changed once it has been written to the disc. This ensures that data integrity cannot be compromised by subsequent changes. The reading and writing of optical discs can be automated through the use of an auto-changer, a mechanical handling device which operates like a jukebox. This is particularly useful for backing up and restoring large capacity databases.

Solid state is the latest form of data storage. These devices are also known as flash drives, thumb drives, flash memory, or memory sticks. Because there are no moving parts in a solid state drive, access is very fast. Although they are expensive compared to traditional disk or tape drives, they do offer a convenient and reliable medium for backing up relatively small databases. It seems likely that their capacity will continue to increase and their cost will decrease over time.

10.8.3.2 Data Storage Conditions

Each particular type, or class, of record will have its own life cycle based upon its currency and completeness.

Your backup may be held online, near-line or offline. Online backup can also be physically located offsite in a separate storage location where it can be protected from any disruptions which occur at the host site. If it is held online and onsite then it will be subject to the same storage conditions as the rest of your system components. This section applies to those forms of backup which are subject to separate storage.

▶ Backup should always be kept in a secure offsite location where it is accessible at any time. In the case of physical media which must be retrieved, this offsite place should be fairly close to the recovery site, which is where the records will be needed in a hurry if there is ever an emergency, but sufficiently isolated to ensure it is not exposed to concurrent threats or vulnerabilities.

▶ At all times, access should be restricted to those who are responsible for backup or recovery as outlined in your BC plan. Everybody and everything else should be excluded from the backup facility and its contents. The facility should be dedicated to the one sole purpose. A shared space is not at all suitable for backup storage.

▶ Backups should be protected from unauthorized disclosure to at least the same degree as the primary data. At a minimum, encryption and password controls should be required for access.

▶ In order to prevent ageing and deterioration, backup copies must be kept in a stable, clean, and dry, controlled environment.

▶ The contents of the backup store should be physically and logically well organized and properly documented, just like a library. In fact, it is a library but a very private one rather than a public one.

    ❑ Everything must be clearly labelled so it is easy to locate at all times.

    ❑ Your labelling and cataloguing should include the date and time of recording, together with any version control data which applies. It may be a long time before some items are needed and people cannot be expected to remember, or work out, whether any particular record is the right level or version. It is far better to have an excess of information available than to have doubts about the value or validity of any of the contents of your backup store.

10.8.4   Backup Life Cycles

Here you will look primarily at the creation and organization of near-line or offline backup. However, you will also look at the implications of online backup which is a rather more advanced but not necessarily a foolproof recovery method.

Each particular type, or class, of record will have its own life cycle based upon its currency and completeness. You can divide your records into three categories from a backup perspective. They can be regarded as *dynamic*, *stable*, or *primary* records.

▶ **Dynamic records** are those which are subjected to many changes on a regular or random basis, e.g., customer or operational transactions, accounts, word processing, or email. Dynamic records, or at least their many changes, must be backed up frequently. You may need to rebuild the database from a full backup, together with a series of journals, or logs, which capture recent changes. Alternatively, your system might continuously update your backup as each transaction is completed, in readiness for a straightforward recovery at any time.

▶ **Stable records** are those which have relatively few changes due to their semipermanent nature, e.g., name and address files, parts catalogues, and lists of components. Stable records need to be backed up on a regular basis. It is best to back them up as a complete set rather than individual items. This saves recreating a whole series of files and folders from various sources.

▸ **Primary records** are those original or source materials which are only likely to be updated or replaced occasionally, e.g., operating systems, application programs, standards, and reference materials. Backup copies of primary records must be replaced occasionally and this is best scheduled on an as-required basis. This means you should take a backup copy of all the primary records immediately after any significant change to a major component of the system.

Over time, their value as backup will deteriorate because their accuracy will diminish as changes are made to the live records. Figure 10-2 shows how this deviation occurs and develops over time in the typical system environment.

Your backup schedule must take account of these differences and the requirements of the recovery process. Obviously, your backup schedule has to recognize the specific needs of the business, but you can work from some general guidelines.

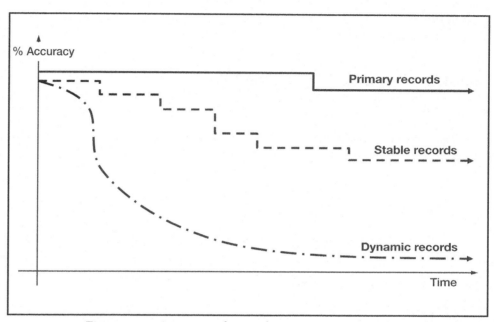

Figure 10-2. Accuracy of Records Deteriorates Over Time

10.8.4.1 Creating a Backup Schedule for Record Types

Dynamic Records: Copy the changes to dynamic records at least once a day, preferably on a more frequent basis, if it is practical. Complete copies should be taken at least once a week. Your technical team may be able to keep a continuous mirror, or shadow, image of all database changes. This is usually referred to as online backup and ensures speedy recovery. The principle behind this technique is to copy every change to the primary database as it is written to disk and apply the same change to the secondary database. The secondary database may sit on separate disks or dedicated partitions within the primary database. Alternatively it may be housed on a separate, parallel system.

Online backup may not provide an absolute solution but it does offer a first line of defense...

However it is a relatively costly approach because it does require additional processing power and double the amount of disk space to accommodate the secondary image. Because it is online it is also vulnerable to the same risks as the primary system; this would include accidental deletion or corruption as well as the possibility of being attacked by a virus, a hacker, or a malcontent. Online backup may not provide an absolute solution but it does offer a first line of defense for those situations where high availability is of paramount importance. Full protection would require the supplement of an alternative backup procedure.

Stable Records: Take a copy of all the stable records at least once a month, or immediately after any major changes to the system or the records.

Primary Records: Copy all primary records whenever some, or all, of them are replaced or updated for some reason. You should also make fresh copies whenever there are any significant changes to the recording system or media type. Increasingly, complex business environments tend to depend on multiple, interdependent databases, files, and systems, and there is no single point where a backup is practical – or even possible. For example, seemingly integrated systems may depend on multiple web servers managing the customer-facing interface, on back-end servers or mainframes handling processing and housing primary databases, and on external vendor systems providing input or processing. In this kind of environment, a static backup may be all but meaningless and a more sophisticated backup scheme will be necessary. This will need to be a design consideration for the core processing applications. As just one example, data snapshots for each transaction may be captured and stored with copies of the external data.

10.8.4.2 A Typical Backup Schedule

Full Backup

When a new system is installed or an old one is upgraded, take a copy of everything on the system. This to include:

> *Primary, stable,* and *dynamic* records.

Regular Backup

At frequent intervals – at least every month or so – take a copy of all the changeable records on the system. This to include:

> *Stable* and *dynamic* records.

Daily Backup

At the end of each day (or more frequently) take a copy of all the dynamic records on the system. This to include:

> All *dynamic* records.

Occasional Backup

Whenever any of the original or source material is changed or replaced, take a copy of all the primary records on the system. This to include:

> All *primary* records.

10.9   The Data Recovery Process

You will find it useful to review the logic of the data recovery process. The danger is highest when you are trying to solve an unexpected problem without knowing the cause or appreciating the implications of your corrective actions. Once you have retrieved the backup from your storage, it has to be subjected to a three-stage process.

Stage 1: **Read** the raw data from storage.

Stage 2: **Assemble** and consolidate the data.

Stage 3: **Check** and synchronize the data.

The logic of the data recovery, reassembly, and synchronization process is shown graphically in Figure 10-3.

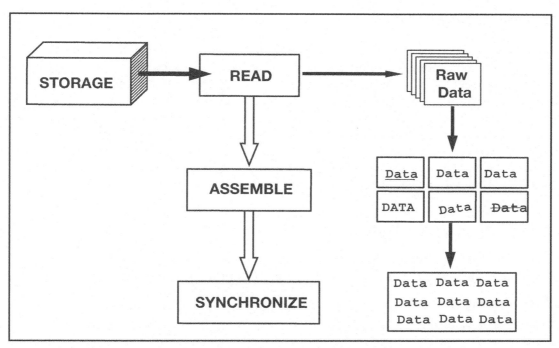

Figure 10-3. The Logic of Data Recovery

10.9.1   Recovering the Data

First you must be able to access all those records which are stored in your backup repository. There should be security protocols to be addressed to give you the authority to do so. If your backup is physically held offsite you may need to arrange for the media to be moved to the recovery site. Online or near-line backup should be readily available once you have addressed any security issues.

In order to recover your database you need to be able to read all of the data in its raw or stored format, which may not be the way it was laid out originally. For storage purposes, it may have been compressed, encrypted, enhanced, or fragmented in some way.

- Compression techniques are used to save space. For example, there is no point in recording long strings of the same character. It is easier to make a note of how many times the character is repeated and simply insert the required number of them at the right point during the rebuild.

- Encryption techniques would be used for security reasons and would usually cause the records to be longer and more complex than the original raw data.

- Enhancing techniques might be used to capture changes, updates, and alterations to the original records. This might consist of pointers and links to other static or dynamic records which are reserved for supplementary information.

- Fragmentation can occur when the system handles sections of large files in parallel rather than sequentially. This is a means of speeding up both the recording and the reading process.

When you do start to read the data your system will simply read the data in the sequence it is presented. This is a direct reflection of the way in which the data was gathered and arranged when recording the backup. The layout of the backup may not reflect the way the data was held in memory. For example, it may be stored on a linear device or a two-dimensional matrix device, perhaps holding information which is to be regarded as multi-dimensional. So the output from this initial read operation is a mixture of raw data which comes from many sources and is to be treated and presented in many different ways.

10.9.2   Assembling the Data

Then, the raw data has to be assembled into the appropriate format to act as the local input for the various operating systems and applications. These programs need access to the various types of records they expect to find so they can manipulate the data within the system's memory and present information to the user via external feeds or interfaces, screens, printers, or other output devices. Assembling and consolidating the data is normally carried out automatically by the data backup/recovery software. This takes time and effort; so it might to be a relatively slow process. The system will have to allocate space for each record and build a series of pointers so it knows where to find each record within a particular area or space such as a file or a folder. If the operating system differs in any way from that on the original processor where the records were created, then the assembly operation might be compromised.

10.9.3   Synchronizing the Data

Once the database has been rebuilt in this way, the operating system will need to check all of the records and synchronize them. This is to make sure the database fits together properly with no gaps or overlaps. It will also check to see that each record and file is complete. Whenever information is committed to the database, the system will automatically calculate and attach additional parity checks and other system security data. This extra information tells the system whether the data is in the right format, whether it is complete, whether it appears to contain any errors, and how it is related to any other data within the database. For instance, a *checksum* figure might indicate how many bits and how many bytes there should be within each record. Very often, if there is a minor error in the recording or reading of the media, the system will detect the error and be able to reconstruct the data using the inbuilt data checking mechanisms.

> **The final result of all this juggling with records, data, and checksums is a functional database...**

The database can be fully synchronized *only* by applying all of the changes and updates that have occurred since the last regular backup was taken. One common practice is to capture only the recent changes to dynamic records in a transaction log file or the interim or daily backup. During a recovery, all interim changes have to be applied to the database as it was captured in the last full backup. This process may entail one or more time-consuming update runs and adds to the complexity of the process with further opportunities for errors and mistakes.

In recovery mode, the data restore system goes through all this system information and attempts to repair any errors based on the mixture of parity and data checks attached to various records. Again, this should all take place automatically, but it can take up time and processing power. Obviously, if the system discovers an error which it can't fix for itself then it will raise an alert. Manual intervention by technically competent specialists may be required at this stage to identify the cause of the problem and respond to any error messages. It can require a considerable degree of expertise to deal with such an error without aggravating the situation. In the worst case, the only certain solution could involve going back to an earlier generation of backup.

The next step is validation. Even when the recovery software has done its job accurately and perfectly, you have no guarantee that the data restored is current, accurate, or even usable. A predefined acceptance testing process is essential. Such testing involves, for example, entering test transactions, running reports or data retrievals which can be matched against known results, retrieving specific transactions, and comparing data or functions against specific criteria. In a perfect world, this would all fall neatly into place. However, a better plan is to assume an imperfect world – and have procedures in place to address errors or inconsistencies.

The final result of all this juggling with records, data, and checksums is a functional database which is ready for the business users to return to work. The system can then present them with their data in the correct and familiar layout.

10.10 Recovery Requirements

10.10.1 Golden Rules of Recovery

There are a few essential requirements for any successful recovery, which is the only kind of recovery that is acceptable. These can be encapsulated into the **Golden Rules of Recovery**:

1. You must be able to retrieve and read all of your data.
2. There must be enough space to hold all of the data.
3. The connectors, adapters, and devices must be available at the recovery site.
4. They must be kept in good working order.
5. All of the media must be undamaged and easily identifiable.

The same principles apply to whichever media you are using. Photographic materials such as microfiche require suitable reading equipment to be available at the time and place of the recovery. They must also be kept free from dirt and moisture at all times. These recording methods are still in use where large-scale images need to be preserved such as architectural drawings or original works. However, you should ideally capture and use digital images, especially for backup purposes.

10.10.2 Rotation or Re-Use of Media

It is common practice to rotate reusable physical media in a grandfather, father, and son sequence to ensure that there are always at least three generations of backup available. Apart from the use of a previous generation as a measure of last resort when there are problems with the most recent one, the earlier versions might be needed to retrieve previous versions of particular records. Previous records might be needed for audit, error correction, or forensic work. While this is not the prime purpose of backup, it is occasionally an advantage to have these alternatives available.

While the three-generation concept arose from the inherent uncertainty of recovery from reusable media, it is perfectly valid to apply the same concept to single-use media. In fact, it makes even more sense to retain the most recent of the earlier generations if they cannot be recycled.

If you are backing up onto reusable media, then the labelling and tracking system has to take this into account. Your labelling should allow you to trace the history of each item of media. Any tape or disc which shows signs of wear or errors should be removed from the backup cycle. You may be able to redeploy the item somewhere else in a less critical or more tolerant environment.

Every time a reusable tape or disc is erased and written upon, the medium itself is slightly degraded. This is because, depending on the technology, it is not always possible to totally eradicate the previous signals and over time there may be a gradual buildup of background noise. At the same time the recorded signal may diminish slightly as the medium loses its sensitivity. Most of the time, and for most applications, the slight imperfections are perfectly acceptable and cause few real problems, but with backup you are looking to work with 100% certainty. Therefore, as a rule of thumb you should:

▸   Remove any suspicious media from the backup cycle and, in any event, remove all media from the backup cycle after an appropriate number of read or write operations.

▸   Use only the finest quality media for backup purposes – there is no point in saving a few pennies when dealing with records worth millions.

Any media which are discarded from the backup regime should be subjected to secure disposal, which means physically destroying the tapes or discs. It is not possible to erase all traces of your recordings from such materials. A "ghost signal" always remains, which can be detected and recovered by an unauthorized person with a little determination, a good reason, some patience, technical knowhow, and the right equipment.

10.10.3   Management and Control

Management and control of the backup is about balancing the needs against the restrictions, or the ideal versus the practical. You need to consider:

 ▶ Record life in relation to the need for data currency – dynamic records have a short shelf life.

 ▶ Record volumes in relation to the storage space. Available storage has to be sufficient to accommodate the volume of records being generated, both now and in the foreseeable future.

 ▶ Ease of access for retrieval purposes in relation to the security arrangements which are made to protect the records and the information they hold.

The primary objective is to be able to manage and control the backup in readiness for a test or an emergency recovery, which could occur at any time. In order to ensure meeting this objective certain parameters must be established. Although the BC manager may be able to offer advice and guidance in this area, it is the business owners who have to make the final judgments and decisions about their needs and requirements. Here are the main factors which need to be determined in the development of a set of effective long-term backup procedures:

 ▶ What procedures will be used to generate the backup and what volumes and frequencies can be expected?

 ▶ How long must you hold the various items and classes of backup in storage?

 ▶ When should you remove items from the store or purge them? Should this be done on a particular occasion, in a special sequence, or before or after a certain operation?

 ▶ How often should you be replacing individual devices within the backup store?

 ▶ How will media be stored and tracked so as to ensure the right set (or sets) of records can always be retrieved?

 ▶ How will you control access to the backup store?

 ▶ Who will have right of access and how will they gain access?

 ▶ How and when will the backup materials be moved to and from the backup store in a secure manner?

 ▶ How will the rotation of the actual media be managed?

Throughout the implementation of this regime you must bear in mind that any item of backup, whatever the medium, should always be retrievable at any time without delay or confusion.

10.10.4 Backup Hints and Tips

 ▶ Transfer archived data to new media every two years to avoid media ageing or format obsolescence. Format obsolescence can happen whenever there is a change of writing and reading equipment, software, or techniques.

 ▶ Position data safes in a place where they can always be reached easily, for example, on the ground floor against an outside wall, preferably with a lintel to provide a break out point allowing the safe to be dragged out through the wall. Of course, consider security as well as environmental implications such as theft or flooding.

Self-Examination Questions

1. Because they are concerned with technical and mechanical matters, disaster recovery plans tend to be

    A. loose and theoretical, leaving plenty of discretion to the IT managers who are most familiar with the technology at the site.

    B. focused on helping the recovery personnel decide what is salvageable and what must be replaced.

    C. technical, specific, and detailed, with little or no room for interpretation or deviation.

2. The essential ingredients of disaster recovery are

    A. satisfying the ongoing need for business support systems and preserving the integrity and availability of critical information.

    B. restoring physical facilities, restoring information technology, and recovering full operational capability.

    C. keeping the business functioning during a disaster, recovering full operational capability after the disaster, and demonstrating to customers that such disasters will be prevented in future.

3. The two main groups of services you need to take into account in your disaster recovery plan are

    A. information technology and finance.

    B. regulatory services and technical services.

    C. technical services and facilities.

4. Which of the following are the three main stages of a robust backup regime, without which disaster recovery is impossible?

    A. 1) creating records of all essential information, 2) storing those records securely, and 3) being able to recover those records in an emergency

    B. 1) establishing a disaster recovery site, 2) installing the same information technology there as at the main site, and 3) frequently backing up all data to a secure cloud

    C. 1) installing information security systems, 2) frequently updating them based on newly emerging threats, and 3) frequently backing up all data to a secure cloud

5. Regularly used software, central records, and operational records are all

    A. business support systems.

    B. mandatory backup records.

    C. supporting documents.

6. For backup purposes, there are three classes of records, each with its own life cycle:

    A. central records, operational records, and software

    B. critical records, supporting records, and backup records

    C. dynamic records, stable records, and primary records

7. The three stages of the data recovery process are

    A. 1) read the raw data from storage, 2) assemble and consolidate the data, and 3) check and synchronize the data.

    B. 1) restore physical facilities, 2) restore information technology, and 3) recover all data using that technology.

    C. 1) verify that the data is correct and complete, 2) reject any incorrect or corrupted data, and 3) assemble and consolidate the correct and complete data.

8. Which of the following is NOT one of the Golden Rules of Recovery?

    A. The organization must be able to retrieve and read all of its data.

    B. There must be enough space to hold all of the data.

    C. All of the media must be identifiable with research and repairable if damaged.

Food for Thought

Previously this book has discussed the need for BC and how you might examine the risks and impacts before developing suitable strategies to deal with disruptive scenarios or emergency situations. Then you looked at how the organization should respond to, and manage, such an emergency. Finally, you explored how you might prepare to recover your technology in a process known as disaster recovery. This is, perhaps, the most complicated aspect of BC because of its complexity and technical aspects. To ensure that you have a clear grasp of disaster recovery and its implications, try to apply what you have learned to circumstances you are familiar with or can imagine.

Exercises

If you consider your personal environment for work and study as a business operation you should think about applying the principles of BC to that situation which means developing and implementing your own disaster recovery strategy.

A large part of your personal environment will be based on access to technology such as a PC or laptop, telephone, Internet access, and community services.

1. Make a list of all the technical resources which you use regularly.
   > Identify which ones you consider to be essential or critical.

2. Make a list of all the reference material which you use regularly, e.g., contact lists, books, and websites.
   > Identify which ones you consider to be essential or critical.

3. Make a note of the recovery or replacement strategies which are available for your essential technical resources.
   > Select which of these strategies are practical and affordable.
   >> Shouldn't you be doing something about this or perhaps you have?

4. Make a note of the backup and recovery strategies which are available for your essential reference materials.
   > Select which of these strategies are practical and affordable.
   >> Shouldn't you be doing something about this or perhaps you have?

5. Apply this logic to a nearby business with which you are familiar.
   > Do you think that they have any of these procedures in place?

6. Consider the development and delivery of a backup and restore regime.
   > What would you recommend?
   > Who should take responsibility for managing and monitoring this?
   > What would you do or say if others opposed your views or interference?

Looking Forward

So far you have covered most of the basics of BC and now you should be in a position to look at the development and delivery of the plans which are the tangible manifestation of all your hard work. However, that will not be the end of the road. These plans are like a doctor's prescription: they show there has been a proper diagnosis, but they are not a cure in themselves. Treatment in this case involves developing the capability to use those plans to ward off disability or incapacity, a capability that comes from testing and exercising.

Downloadable Business Continuity Toolkit

You may download the checklists and other information to assist you in evaluating possible solutions from the **Business Continuity Toolkit**.

References

Rothstein, P. J. (2003). Can you really count on your backups? *Information Security Magazine*. Retrieved from https://www.rothstein.com/articles/backups.html

For Additional Reading

Disaster Resource Guide, a downloadable annual guide to disaster recovery goods and services is available at http://www.disaster-resource.com

Downloadable guidance on disaster recovery planning from the Ready Campaign of the Federal Emergency Management Agency (FEMA)/Department of Homeland Security (DHS) is available at http://www.ready.gov/business/implementation/IT

Part

IV

Planning and Implementing

Part I: Preparation and Startup
Part II: Building a Foundation
Part III: Responding and Recovering
Part IV: Planning and Implementing
Part V: Long-Term Continuity

You are now entering a most important part of this adventure through the intricacies of business continuity (BC) management: the process of preparing the plans which are at the heart of the BC program. At this point, you will begin to develop and document the procedures and processes of BC in a form that is suitable for use under emergency conditions, a major task with many implications. You will examine some of the guiding principles for the activities involved in developing such a plan or set of plans. In addition, you will be looking at how you manage and develop those plans, the resources, and the people in order to ensure that your BC capability can be retained and enhanced over time.

Chapter 11 – Plans and Planning

▸ Shows you how to create and deliver the various types of BC plans.

Chapter 12 – Exercise Preparation

▸ Prepares you for holding a meaningful BC exercise.

Chapter 13 – Crisis Management and Communications

▸ Explains how to protect the value of your enterprise through managing communications.

Chapter 14 – Exercise Management and Delivery

▸ Tells how to run a BC exercise that will give you the results you need.

11

Plans and Planning

Thus far, you have explored how and why you should develop a business continuity (BC) policy and discussed strategic and tactical issues. Much of this work has been about the discovery, collection, and collation of information about how the organization works and what it might need in the event of a disruption. Now it is time to think about applying that information to produce a set of BC plans or modules.

This chapter will help you to:

- ☑ Understand the range and types of plans which you might need.

- ☑ Work out how those plans fit together to support your organization.

- ☑ Develop the characteristics and contents of the various plans.

- ☑ Draft a beginning plan.

- ☑ Evaluate the use of software tools to support the planning and maintenance process.

11.1 Hierarchy of Plans

Perhaps the major influence on the type and number of plans will be the scale of the enterprise or the operation. For a large organization which is spread across a number of sites or locations, there will probably be some six or seven types of plans. Each of these plans will serve a different purpose and may be used in isolation under certain limited circumstances; whereas a major emergency may necessitate the use of most, or even all, of the plans.

The decision to follow the procedures outlined within one of your contingency plans is generally referred to as an *activation*. Part of the activation process should be concerned with considering the activation of other plans or the raising of alerts. An *alert* is the procedure for warning team leaders of circumstances which might lead to an activation. In a smaller organization, some of the plans may serve as *modules* that are combined to create a smaller number of plans, each with a broader scope.

Therefore, I shall describe the full range of plans as though they were separate entities, which they may be in many cases. However, they should all follow a similar structure. By using a consistent format, you can regard your plans as modules within a suite of plans. Each module is designed to help one of the teams fulfill a particular purpose in response to an emergency situation. Consistency allows you to move people, or even tasks, from one team to another, if the occasion should warrant. It also makes the maintenance and education process much easier for everybody concerned.

11.1.1 Areas of Responsibility

By looking at the main roles in the typical organizational structure, you can see how individual actions in these roles are likely to change when the organization, or its activities, is threatened or disturbed.

Directors: At the top of the organization, the directors are normally concerned with policies and strategies to ensure the long-term success of the enterprise.

Executives: Applying those strategies and running the overall business operation is the responsibility of the executives who are in regular dialogue with the directors.

Managers: The managers then run the individual business units or functions, each contributing to satisfying the needs of the clients and the expectations of the executives. Again there is regular dialogue with executives.

Operators and Technicians: The operators perform the tasks required by the business functions and report to the managers. The technical support people ensure that the systems and processes are properly developed and maintained in accordance with the business requirements. They report and provide advice to the managers and they also provide support and guidance to the operators.

This structure and the interfaces are shown in Figure 11-1.

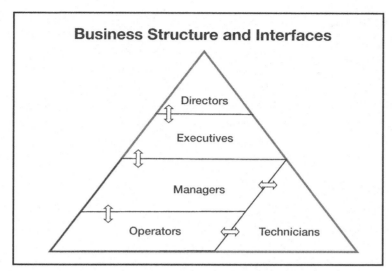

Figure 11-1. Roles in the Typical Organizational Structure

The key tasks these five key classes of personnel are likely to face in an emergency situation are shown in Figure 11-2.

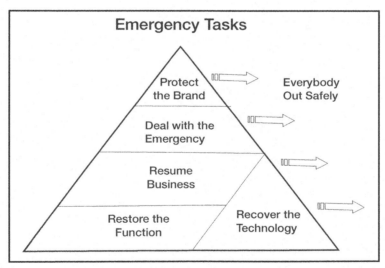

Figure 11-2. Key Tasks to Be Performed in an Emergency

In the case of a physical threat to the premises, the major task at all levels is to ensure everyone can get out safely under all circumstances – the number one priority for any enterprise no matter what the line, or style, of business might be. Therefore, the personal safety of everyone on the premises is a concern of all parties, although it might well be the direct responsibility of the security manager. However, many business disruptions will not require the emergency evacuation of personnel. In Chapter 1 you saw how business disruption involves both physical and technical scenarios. The need for evacuation is associated only with a physical disruption. Where relocation of personnel is required by technical or other issues, it is neither an emergency nor does it require an evacuation, and the appropriate response is covered by the other plans.

- The directors will need to protect the brand, image, and reputation of the enterprise. This represents the long-term value of the business. A blemish to the reputation can have disastrous consequences.

> ### They need to be written in plain language, conveying simple messages, and providing clear directions.

- Executives should focus their attention on dealing with the emergency by establishing control and setting out to contain the effects so as to reduce the damage and costs.

- Meanwhile the managers will be concentrating on resuming the business operation so as to sustain the customer interfaces.

- While the technicians recover the systems and services, the operators will be restoring the actual business functions behind the customer interface.

11.1.2   Plan Types and Responsibilities

Each of these tasks will be supported by a particular type of plan, as demonstrated in Figure 11-3.

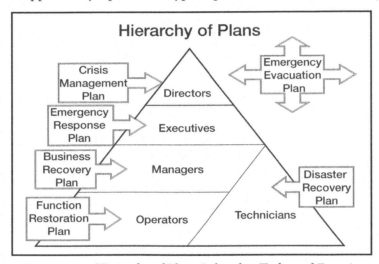

Figure 11-3. Hierarchy of Plans Related to Tasks and Functions

The preparation of *emergency evacuation plans* was covered in Chapter 7, Emergency Response. This leaves five main plan types still to be explored in detail.

- *Crisis management plan*
- *Emergency response plan*
- *Business recovery plan*
- *Function restoration plan*
- *Disaster recovery plan*

Later in this chapter, you will have the opportunity to explore the business recovery plan as a sample because it is very typical and has a broad application. Its structure and format can be adopted later as the basis for all of the other types of plans.

11.2   The Plan Development Process

Bear in mind that any BC plan is going to be used in times of stress or uncertainty. While these documents are designed for use in an emergency they are far more likely to be referred to during training exercises; but they must be suited to both. More importantly, they are definitely not intended to represent intellectual capital, to stimulate debate, or offer a persuasive argument. They need to be written in plain language, conveying simple messages, and providing clear directions.

Golden Rules for Writing a Plan

> Avoid jargon or unfamiliar words. Special or obscure meanings cause misunderstandings which can lead to mistakes.

> Avoid the use of acronyms. If you have to use them, include a clear explanation every time they appear.

> Remove the clutter. There is no need to include anything that is not directly related to the purpose of the plan.

> Make it easy to read. Use large clear typefaces; include simple diagrams. Leave wide margins or spaces for the users to make notes or corrections.

> Use color sparingly. It can be difficult to discern in poor light, especially for those who are color blind.

> Number every page and indicate the total number of pages. Doing that provides a useful means of checking for missing pages. There is often a suspicion that there should be another list at the back.

> Include version control information, such as the release level or issue date. Everyone should work with the same version.

> Treat contingency plans as the confidential documents they are. They contain information which could be very useful to anyone with bad intentions.

> Pay particular attention to the presentation and appearance of your plans. They are valuable documents which should be treated with respect. Scruffy collections of ill-assorted papers tend to devalue the contents in the eyes of the beholder.

Because BC is an ongoing reiterative process, i.e., regularly repeating the same steps in a continuous learning and improvement cycle, it is difficult to define an absolute start point. You can't really design the plans until you know something about what goes into them. (The main content has already been reviewed in previous chapters.) In sum, there are five basic stages to the development of any of the various plan types or modules:

1. Select and agree upon the overall design and structure of the plan. This chapter will focus on the design and structure of your plans before offering you some hints about the preparation and delivery of a draft plan.

The major benefits stem from the process of inspection, deliberation, and agreement...

2. Determine data requirements and gather the data. (Covered earlier in this book in Chapters 4 and 5.)

3. Determine strategy for the key phases of response and recovery. (Covered earlier in this book in Chapter 6.)

4. Allocate the emergency tasks and responsibilities. (Covered earlier in this book in Chapter 7.)

5. Prepare the draft plan. (Covered at the end of this chapter.)

11.2.1 Design and Structure

Preparing a plan or module starts with the selection or development of a suitable design and structure. Over the years, many people have designed and worked with thousands of BC plans with varying degrees of success. Therefore, it makes sense to tap into the wealth of knowledge and experience that must exist, rather than attempt to start from scratch with little or no guarantee of a successful outcome. This chapter will take you through the underlying concepts and then move on to looking at a range of templates. You can either adopt or adapt these templates for your own use, or you can continue your search for a suitable model elsewhere. Either way, it will help if you have a clear understanding of how these documents differ from other types of documents and from each other.

These documents are unique in the sense that they are intended to be used only under times of stress and difficulty. Even stranger, you probably cannot expect to ever use them under those particular circumstances. The major benefits stem from the process of inspection, deliberation, and agreement rather than the possession of the plans themselves. Further benefits are to be gained from the exercises and tests based on these plans. The plans should be seen as your emergency vehicles rather than your transport systems; they are useful tools but not complete solutions.

The typical structure or hierarchy of a business enterprise can be compared to a Greek temple. The foundation of this structure is the financial investment or capital which enables the enterprise to acquire supplies and resources. Supplies and resources are fed into the various business functions by their administration and each of these functions is subject to supervision. The management team runs the overall business in support of the corporate mission.

This working structure needs to be replicated in an emergency situation where the primary intention is to restore some degree of normality as quickly and effectively as possible.

Under these conditions the foundation investment, or capital, is in the form of reference information. This translates into the skills and knowledge which support the various business unit recovery plans. The supervision and management of these activities is outlined in the emergency response plan, which supports the immediate needs of the business as a whole.

While this temple model does provide us with a generalized overview of how BC management works in practice, it is rather simplistic and doesn't give a clear indication of the full range of plans that may be required. In order to get a more accurate and detailed view of the plan types, you need to look at the levels of responsibility and the types of tasks which the plans must support.

11.2.1.1 Relation of Plan Type to Area of Responsibility

In most organizations there are five key classes of personnel, each with particular levels of interest and types of concerns. Earlier in this chapter, Figure 11-3 showed the relationship between plan types and areas of responsibility. Many of these interests and concerns will be shared with others, but in practice the actions and responsibilities of individuals will reflect their position within the hierarchy. Almost separate to the main thrust of the business operation is the general concern for the health and safety of everyone in times of danger. This is usually the concern of the security people who watch over and protect the others without being integrated into the core business functions. Indeed, the very nature of their job precludes them from developing close links or relationships with any particular area or group. They have to retain a degree of independence.

Figure 11-1 illustrates the various levels and how they interface with each other under normal operating conditions. The directors set the corporate policy which the executives interpret as the strategy for their division. The managers decide on the tactics to meet those strategies while the operators carry out the routine functional tasks. The technicians devise the operational techniques and offer ongoing support to the operation. Meanwhile, the security team monitors everyone and the scenario in which they operate.

At the higher levels, the general dialogue is vertical but at the lower level it is more likely that the technicians, operators, and managers will work together to develop and maintain systems, procedures, processes, and techniques that serve the business well. Team spirit or esprit de corps tends to flourish at this level in any really successful enterprise.

This model is realistic and useful because it enables you to derive a working structure for your contingency plans based on who will be using them and their intentions. If you can match their intentions with the purposes and strategies which you build into the plans then you should be able to develop a set of plans which represent a working model of good practice. As a result, your deliverables should be fit for purpose because they are actually derived from the true purpose.

All of these key role types should be reflected within the BC plans, setting the parameters, defining the roles, and outlining the responsibilities at each level. Ideally, there should be a separate plan, or set of plans, covering each level. These "horizontal" plans should also take account of the "vertical" interfaces to the levels immediately above and below. Thus, one plan might cover management activities with links into the operational and technical recovery plans, as well as liaison with the executive team.

Personnel at each of these levels will have a particular concern in an emergency situation. At the same time, they will all share the common primary concern which is to get everybody out to safety. Once this has been achieved they will want to focus on their area of responsibility. In your planning you need to make sure that all of the key responsibilities are covered and there are no gaps.

> **Perhaps the wisest approach is to…keep the modules separate until you have finished the first draft…**

- The *directors* will need to focus on protecting the brand, image, and reputation of the enterprise. This activity is called crisis management, and any emergency is likely to give rise to concerns which need to be dealt with in this manner. On the other hand, a crisis might develop without any physical basis that could be seen as an emergency. Crises are all about perception whereas emergencies are actual real events where something happens, or fails to happen. As a crisis is likely to span the whole business, there would normally be one central corporate group which acts on behalf of the enterprise.

- While the directors look after the brand, members of the *executive team* will have to deal with the implication of the emergency, containing the incident and directing the responses. They need to establish and maintain command and control of the situation allowing others to deal with restoring the business and its dependencies. Emergencies tend to span a particular site or location, so you would expect to find an emergency response capability at each location, perhaps with a central point of command and control.

- *Managers* will want to organize the resumption of essential business activities to support the customer interface and to meet customer demand or expectations. These business resumption activities will be directed and coordinated by the central executive team but the managers will be fully engaged in the effort to enable the return to business as usual.

- Managers will depend on the support of the *technical team* which will be concentrating on recovering the technology and the associated services. While the managers and technicians are reconstructing the working environment, the *operational people* will be trying to restore the various critical business functions. At this level there may be a need for a number of separate plans to address the many differing needs. On the other hand you may prefer to use a modular approach in which these various activities are dealt with as separate, but integrated, chapters or modules within a single plan that spans a particular operation or location.

Perhaps the wisest approach is to assume a modular plan structure but keep the modules separate until you have finished the first draft of your plans. At that stage, it should relatively easy to merge them into a single document, providing you have been consistent in the construction of the modules.

11.2.1.2 Purposes of the Plan Types

Altogether there are six different plan types (as in Figure 11-3), each serving a distinct purpose, but covering all of your emergency needs among them. We covered the emergency evacuation plan in previous chapters. You will need a separate evacuation plan for each building, site, or location. The remaining plans are summarized here.

▶ **Business recovery plans** are required by the managers of each of the various business units to give them the means to resume the core business operations which they manage. All of these plans should allow for close cooperation with the emergency response team as well as the technical and operational teams. (This is the prototype plan in Section 11.3).

▶ **Emergency response plans** support the short-term initial reaction to an emergency situation. The longer term recovery may be supported by an *emergency management plan* to cover a rather more proactive long-term approach once the situation has been brought under control.

▶ **Crisis management plans** are needed to support the directors in getting the right message across, at the right time. An emergency response plan will help the executives to establish command and control. The crisis management and the emergency response plans should allow for regular dialogue between these two high-level teams that need to work in harmony to ensure that they are seen to be working to the same agenda.

▶ **Function restoration plans**, which might be regarded as a subset of the business recovery plans, will support the operational teams that will be responsible for restoring the critical business functions. These people will be working to the instructions of the managers who will be interpreting the business recovery plans in accordance with the implications of the scenario and subsequent developments.

▶ **Disaster recovery plans** will enable the technicians to recover or rebuild the key systems, services, and applications which support the critical business functions.

11.3   Content of a Basic Plan: Business Recovery Plan

Start with a detailed look at the *business recovery plan*, which serves as a basic BC plan which covers the core activities. Once you understand this central tool, you can move out towards the other parts of the downloadable **Business Continuity Toolkit**, which are all linked to the procedures set out in this fundamental document. The BC plan will also be the receptacle for the essential reference information you will be gathering to support all of these plans.

The sample business recovery plan from the supplementary materials serves as a reference model for the type of structure and contents of such a document. This example is based on an original which was developed for a medium-sized, multi-site company. The prototype behind that working version was a standard template which had evolved within a consultancy practice that covered a wide range of BC work.

The original of this plan was developed for a company with a relatively straightforward business operation. Therefore, it was possible to take advantage of the modular approach and produce a BC plan which embraced all of the core activities. The scope of this plan covers the four lower areas of the hierarchy triangle shown in Figure 11-3.

11.3.1   Document Control Information

The version, source, and date should clearly be displayed on the cover page. You might also include information about where the original can be found in the corporate database, e.g., *document id = c/bcm/reports&plans/bcp.version1.doc*. Each page has *page xx of yy* in the footer together with the date of the last modification. On the cover page, the header says this document is confidential. (If your document control system places restrictions on the use of such a category you may prefer to use another descriptor, such as "In Confidence.")

By including this information, you assure everyone that they are working with the correct version of the plan. At the same time you are conveying the message that this is an important and valuable document which should be treated accordingly. If the author has taken care in finishing and presenting the document, that conveys respect for the subject matter and is a reflection of its value.

11.3.2 Contents

After the cover page comes the list of contents which is designed to help the reader find the section they are looking for. The level of detail is restricted to indicating the main sections and subsections. Don't direct readers to fine detail at this point since you want them to read things in context rather than isolation.

Section A is an introduction which tells the reader about the structure of the plan as well as how and when to use it. Everybody should be encouraged to become familiar with this section, even those who are unlikely to have a role within the plan. Spreading basic knowledge about the plan helps to embed BC within the culture.

> **Throughout the incident response and management process, there is a common set of critical milestones.**

Section B is a set of emergency instructions, covering the activation procedure. The following sections are the working sections, each of them dealing with a particular team's activities. Towards the end of the plan there is the support and reference information such as contact details and the maintenance schedule.

11.3.3 Layout

Every section, or module, has a title indicating what it covers and a code letter with numbered subsections. All of the working sections conform to a regular pattern. This makes it easier to understand and follow, especially if someone is transferred from one team to another, as often happens when dealing with the effects of a serious incident.

Each of the working sections starts with a full description of the roles and responsibilities of the team or its leader, together with their objectives. There is also space for identifying the team members. This can be filled in at the time of the incident, based on knowing who is actually available. Another approach is to fill in the names and assume, or hope, that your first or second choice will be on hand when needed. A third alternative is to allocate the responsibility to a particular job role. The final choice for this nomination or selection protocol will be influenced by the dynamics of the organization.

Important: You must distinguish between (a) the transient information about temporary roles and responsibilities which may be included within the working section of a plan and (b) the stable structure and contact details for important characters such as primary and alternate team leaders and members. Contact procedures and contact lists need to be robust and explicit, whereas the duty roster has to reflect current availability which can only be determined at the time. Contact details of specific pre-determined personnel, such as team leaders and members, should be held in the reference section of the plans where the information should be regularly reviewed and updated to reflect current status.

Throughout the incident response and management process, there is a common set of critical milestones. All of the teams gauge their progress against these milestones, which are derived from the business needs as determined in the business impact analysis (BIA). In this way, you are ensuring that the response and recovery activities meet the needs of the business.

There is a place within each section for an activity log where all of the decisions and actions can be recorded. A coding system to highlight the various types of entries in the log is helpful to make it easier to track and analyze what has transpired and what is still outstanding. In practice, of course, the logging system may be implemented through the use of flipcharts, whiteboards, or PCs, but the plan provides a prompt and a guideline.

It is often possible to supplement the basic type of logging system suggested here through the use of modern technology such as networks involving cell phones or tablet apps. However, these devices may not be sufficiently robust or dependable to be relied upon throughout an emergency situation when power and communications may be reduced or unavailable.

...limit your use of undiluted jargon, and provide clear definitions of specialist terms.

The implication here is that plans which are going to be used as key reference tools under emergency conditions and may be stored for considerable periods of time should be printed out as paper documents. Some, or all, of the information may be held and distributed on other devices but the primary reference source should always be a physical paper document. Other media such as laptops, thumb drives, tablets, intranet, or web sites are prone to corruption or failure in an emergency. They are fine for use as a means of distribution or as a form of backup but should be regarded as supplementary or complementary tools rather than the fundamental all-weather reference source. Thumb drives are a useful alternative, but they do require an electronic device such as a working laptop to be able to access the information which they hold. Unfortunately, this may not always be possible.

11.3.4   Organization Charts

Within the introduction, include a diagram showing how the various plans relate to each other. Another diagram can show the relationships between the various teams which will be using this plan. Clear diagrams are much easier to follow than a textual explanation, especially where relationships are concerned.

A key feature of the ongoing maintenance of your plans is the role of a BC administrator, whose duty is to maintain all of the BC plans in accordance with the testing and maintenance aspect of the management policy. The instructions can be included as part of the support and reference information, towards the back of the documents.

While this need not be a full-time role and does not require any special knowledge or training, it is an essential element of the long-term BC management program. By giving someone the specific responsibility of looking after the plans, together with scheduling the associated tests and exercises, you can be sure these routine tasks will be addressed.

11.3.5   Definitions

All of us tend to attach rather special meanings to some common words and phrases, and we are certainly inclined to use some unfamiliar titles when referring to BC ideas and concepts. Terms that are not readily familiar can lead to confusion on the part of those who are not fully engaged in the subject. Therefore, you should try to limit your use of undiluted jargon, and provide clear definitions of specialist terms. For example, you should make it clear what you mean by such similar words as *emergency*, *disaster*, and *crisis*. To the layman, they all mean pretty much the same thing. To a specialist, they take on very distinct meanings, but there is not always common agreement about which word applies to which meaning.

Include the definition you are using within the context of each of your plans. After all, they are specialist tools designed for use by ordinary people who are familiar with everyday language.

11.3.6   Scenarios

All contingency plans should give an indication of the scenarios they are designed to deal with. These scenarios should be couched in generalized rather than specific terms. If the scenarios become too specific, they tend to limit the application of the proposed solutions. The sample plan refers to the six principal scenarios described earlier in this book in Chapter 1:

1. Loss of access.
2. Loss of people.
3. Loss of supplies.
4. Loss of communication.
5. Loss of function.
6. Loss of data.

The plan also covers how to react during the build up to such a scenario, which is described as an anticipated or suspected disaster.

11.3.7   Roles and Responsibilities

Each of the working sections starts by defining the objectives of that particular team. Where appropriate, the roles and responsibilities of the team leader are also defined. In many of the teams, the roles and responsibilities of the leaders will be determined spontaneously by their seniors in accordance with the circumstances and requirements of the occasion. In other words, they will be following instructions rather than taking the initiative.

11.3.8   Activation Process

On the very first page of the introduction, a bold panel points the reader directly to the *activation* procedure. This information is intended to make it easier for anyone to find his or her starting point when opening up the plan for the first time.

The activation procedure explains who should make the decisions and how they should make their judgments in any situation which appears to be an actual or potential emergency.

Throughout the… process, there is a common set of critical milestones.

Supplementary information, including definitions of terms such as *emergency* and *disaster*, should be provided to help people come to their decisions with confidence. This subsidiary material should help them to understand the implications of each of the choices before them. It emphasizes the need for prompt decisions, even when knowledge is incomplete. Indecision causes delays, invites speculation, and usually makes the situation worse.

11.3.9   Decision Criteria

If you are expecting people to make important decisions under pressure and in difficult or unusual circumstances, you must provide them with some criteria. Otherwise, they will feel that they are being asked to guess and will tend to avoid the issue for as long as they can. Useful decision criteria are based on metrics or concrete facts rather than opinions or hearsay. For example, "a disaster should be declared if access to more than one (1) floor has been denied for more than 60 minutes." This description leaves no doubt about whether the conditions have been met.

Decision criteria should avoid any element of speculation. For example, "If the systems are unlikely to be available for another 12 hours…." poses a question that cannot be answered with any degree of certainty. It would be far better to say, "If this system has been down for more than 2 hours…." This question focuses on a particular system and a specific timeframe which can be measured and recorded as evidence of a correct call. If anyone should subsequently challenge a decision based on such a criterion, they will actually be questioning the validity of the procedure rather than accusing the individual of making a mistake. This relieves the decision-maker from apprehension about the long-term implications of making a necessary decision at the right time.

You don't have to be brave to follow a clear procedure which doesn't call for any guesswork.

11.3.10 Escalation Procedure

Throughout the incident response and management process, there is a common set of critical milestones. Therefore, whoever is in charge of the emergency should alert the crisis management team as soon as possible, whether the emergency is real or imagined. Crises are often the result of imagination, misinterpretation, or speculation rather than an actual event.

Throughout the duration of the abnormal condition there should be a clear escalation procedure coupled with regular communication and dialogue between the various teams and other interested parties.

It is vitally important that the various people who are dealing with different aspects of the response, management, and recovery of the situation are constantly aware of what is happening at all levels. They need a clear, up-to-date, comprehensive picture to be able to make rational decisions and avoid oversights and errors. This can only be achieved if everybody reports upwards without delay as the situation unfolds or changes. Within each team someone should be nominated as the liaison or communications officer, acting as a single point of contact. This person's role is to send and receive messages, routing the incoming ones to the right person within each team.

The escalation procedure should require each team or working group to report upwards on a regular basis. This ensures that pertinent information flows upwards and provides reassurance that nobody has gone missing or lost contact.

For example, in an evacuation scenario you might require search and rescue teams to report on where they are and what they have found every 15 minutes. If they have not made any progress during the past quarter of an hour their report should simply state: "Still searching store room – nothing to report." In addition they should report back immediately whenever they enter another area, discover people, or rescue someone. These reports should go to the emergency response or emergency management team who should pass any relevant information upward to the crisis response team (CRT). Again this escalation should occur on a regular basis to confirm that they are still there. The ideal frequency of regular reporting up to the CRT will depend on the scenario and the scale of the operation but every half hour would be a reasonable timing for most situations. In addition there should be provision for spontaneous messages to convey information about any significant progress, problems, or developments.

There should also be a downwards acknowledgment procedure which confirms that messages have been received. Each time a message arrives, the person responsible for communication within that team should send a reply, such as "Message received and understood" or "Please resend your message." Effective and trusted communication is a two way process; that's why we call it a dialog.

The reverse of this reporting protocol will be the command and control channel for ensuring that instructions and other relevant information are communicated downwards and properly acknowledged to recognize successful delivery. In the absence of a prompt acknowledgment the message should be repeated.

In the absence of an acknowledgment after three attempts to send a message it should be assumed that there is a problem and an investigation should be launched.

11.3.11 Action Lists

Each of the working sections of the plan will revolve around an agreed upon set of actions designed to meet the objectives of that particular team. These are the basic response, recovery, and restoration procedures of the emergency management project, which started as soon as the out-of-line situation was recognized. The project will last until normality has been restored throughout the business operation.

Action lists are constructed by those who are familiar with the functions, systems, or services which are the subject of this activity. Once the first draft has been prepared the list has to be proven or improved through testing of the procedure. An untested procedure is an invitation to chaos.

11.3.12 Reference Information

As mentioned earlier in the chapter, at the end of the plan there will be support and reference information such as contact details and the maintenance schedule. This reference information will support the teams in their efforts to return the business operation to a semblance of normality. Once the plan has been proven and improved through the initial test program, the body of it should remain more or less stable. Reference information will remain relatively dynamic throughout the life of the plan. Therefore, it makes sense to keep it all together and have a single set of regularly updated reference material to span all of the various plans.

> **…the leader of this key team holds the title of *emergency management director*…**

By having a common body of reference information, you can make it much easier to keep your plans up-to-date. At the same time, by keeping it all together in the same place, you are allowing everyone to become familiar with its location, and they will come to regard it as a useful and reliable source.

11.4   Emergency Response Plans

Often, the emergency response plan is embedded within the overall BC plan as one of the key modules. In our downloadable **Business Continuity Toolkit**, you can find a plan which follows exactly the same layout and carries much of the same information as the BC plan discussed above.

You may decide to include an emergency management plan as a supplement to the emergency response plan. This approach requires a number of assumptions but does provide your team with a broad outline which may prove helpful. Alternatively, you may allow for the emergency management plan to be developed after the event as a subsequent extension to the initial response. This approach will enable you and the management team to match the actions and intentions to the prevailing situation.

You can supplement the emergency response plan with a set of emergency manager's notes and a checklist. Examples of both of these documents can be found on the pages immediately following the emergency response procedures in the plan.

The emergency manager, who is the leader of the emergency response team, should be quite familiar with the contents of the plan and may not feel it necessary to keep referring to it. What he or she needs is a set of notes which can be used to keep track of the essential activities and provide a means of ensuring that everybody has been accounted for. Our set of model notes also includes space to record what is available for the evacuation, escape, and short-term accommodation of personnel.

If you look through the sample plan carefully, you will notice that the leader of this key team holds the title of *emergency management director*, a title that reflects the level of responsibility attached to this important post. After all, this person will be commanding and controlling the response on behalf of the whole enterprise, a job with some fairly serious implications. No matter what the outcome, the emergency management director is likely to come under careful scrutiny when it's all over. In fact, the scrutiny may begin long before the project is finished. Some people are liable to question the authority of their leader when they are under pressure, are a little unsure of themselves, or are uncertain about what is happening around them.

Experience shows that this leadership role is best placed in the hands of someone of the highest caliber and level of authority. He or she will be holding the keys to success and survival if ever called upon to respond to a major disruption. He or she will have ample opportunity to gain the respect of everyone involved during the tests and rehearsals that you will be organizing in Chapters 12 and 14.

11.5   Crisis Management Plans

Crisis management as a separate subject is covered in Chapter 13; so this chapter will be dealing only with the plan structure and layout.

Obviously the crisis management plan could follow the pattern of all of the other plans, sitting within the main BC plan as a self-sufficient module. However the very nature of the crisis management role lends itself to a different approach. It is more concerned with what people say than what they do or how they do it. The activities are far less prescriptive, but they do require a high degree of skill which can be developed only with plenty of practice.

Because the crisis managers do not require long and detailed task lists or reference information, the plan should be relatively simple. Furthermore, regular practice should familiarize them with the contents and intentions of their plan.

Our sample crisis plan in the downloadable **Business Continuity Toolkit** takes the form of a convenient pocket-sized checklist. The original was printed on colored card and folded to form a pocket-sized reference which the directors could carry with them at all times. It contains a brief task list together with some hints and tips about preparing and delivering a press statement. There is also some space for them to make a note of key contacts, including the rest of their team.

The concept behind this tri-fold crisis management plan was, in fact, developed in conjunction with the directors of a large newspaper chain.

11.6   Function Restoration Plans

Function restoration plans are normally devised as sections or modules within the overall BC plan. While those employees involved with functional recovery need to be familiar with the overall plan structure, they would need to have access only to those sections which apply to their particular responsibilities and task sets. Their material would also include all of the reference information.

You will need a restoration plan of some sort for each of the critical business functions determined during the BIA or functional analysis phase of the business continuity management program. In addition, you will need a salvage plan covering the cleaning up and reinstatement of buildings, equipment, and resources. The support services, such as administration, reception, and switchboard, are also a critical function, covered in a separate module. The **Business Continuity Toolkit** contains modules which cover these important areas.

11.7   Disaster Recovery (DR) Plans

The term *disaster recovery plan* applies specifically to the recovery of information technology (IT) and its associated services such as telephony, Internet, and intranet. The acronym DR for disaster recovery is widely used.

The distinguishing characteristic of these plans is the level of technical detail which is required and the precision of the procedures. In all other types of plan, the procedures are intended as guidelines to be interpreted according to the needs of the day, but in a DR plan, the procedures are prescriptive. Recovery procedures are developed and refined over time through trials and tests, and any deviation is liable to cause problems and delays.

Data recovery is impossible without backup, and backup is pointless without a data recovery capability.

The level of detail has to be such that anyone with the right technical background can apply the procedures even under the most difficult circumstances. You will do well to eliminate all assumptions about "routine tasks." In an emergency, even the most experienced technicians are likely to forget or make mistakes. For example, "Power up the system" is too vague under these circumstances. A better, explicit instruction is, "Power up the system by pressing and holding the red 'Power On' button for 3 seconds."

In this type of plan, you need to include full information about the type and size and specification of all of the equipment required. Because of the dynamic nature of systems and technology and the plans and the procedures within them, these plans need to be tested and amended on a regular and frequent basis.

11.7.1   Disaster Recovery Modules

Within the DR strategy and plans, there will be three key modules. Each module addresses a different aspect of presenting and manipulating data, which is the critical information that supports the core business operations. The technology arranges and presents the data to the users, while backup makes sure that the data can be made available at all times.

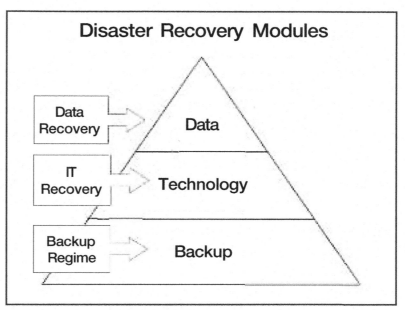

The top and bottom modules in Figure 11-4, i.e., data recovery and the backup regime, are interdependent. Data recovery is impossible without backup, and backup is pointless without a data recovery capability.

Backup Regimes: You reviewed the backup regime as a key aspect of DR in Chapter 10. Here you are simply concerned with how it fits within the

Figure 11-4. Three Key Modules in Disaster Recovery Plan

hierarchy of the DR plan. The backup and retrieval procedures are a critical module within the DR plan. Retrieval procedures are particularly relevant because they provide essential input to the data recovery process. Data can be recovered only from backup – there is no other way.

Data Recovery Procedures: The data recovery procedures describe precisely how the data should be put up onto the system and prepared for release to the users. Where there are options, alternatives, or shortcuts available, these are explained fully, together with any caveats about their use or viability.

IT Recovery: A major part of the DR plan will be devoted to the technology which can be acquired, restored, or rebuilt. Each of these options should be documented together with some hints and tips, or areas of consideration, about the final choice of method. Clearly, if you have a contract with a DR service provider, the preference would be to make use of the provider's facilities and expertise. On the other hand, if you intend to be self-sufficient there will be a wider choice and more implications to be aware of. In any case, your final plan does need to be very specific about the recovery or rebuild process so as to eliminate errors and frustration. The sample DR plan in the downloadable **Business Continuity Toolkit** is an example of a draft disaster recovery plan.

11.8   The Use of Commercial Planning Tools

Many software tools are available on the market to help you with various aspects of preparing BC plans. They range from simple word processing templates to sophisticated database tools. Some of these tools have been used successfully by large organizations over the last 25 years. If you have a contract with a disaster recovery service provider, that company may offer a software tool (as well as training and support) as part of its services. Each product has features designed to appeal to a broad public. Some are user friendly, others can produce flexible plans, and many will be able to accommodate your existing plans and documentation. Most of them will help you to manage your plans, and many will provide you with templates which form the basis of the plans they generate. Other, more sophisticated packages, can perform calculations and planning that could be difficult for you to manage in-house.

> **Where there is going to be a large portfolio... software tools can be very beneficial in plan maintenance.**

If you should decide to invest in one of these tools, think seriously about what you want the tool to do for you, and what you are prepared to do in return. Whichever one you choose, it may entail a steep learning curve before you can take advantage of its benefits. It can require time and effort to get to grips with the new tool. All too often, people fail to complete this stage and the tool doesn't deliver to its full potential. Sometimes the software project gets abandoned out of frustration or neglect.

Software tools should allow you to make changes easily and swiftly. The principal advantage of such tools is they can eliminate much of the long-term drudgery once all the original data has been captured and the draft plans have been developed. On the downside, it may take longer to install and implement such a system compared with using standard and familiar word processing techniques. Where there is going to be a large portfolio comprising many plans or modules, software tools can be very beneficial in plan maintenance.

Before making a decision about the use of such tools, have a demonstration of the product, preferably followed by a trial run. The opinion of your technical people is essential, since they will be involved in the implementation of the new application.

Table 11-1 shows the typical strengths and weaknesses of commercially available BC software. To assist your thinking in your selection process, it is based on general concepts rather than in-depth research or any specific products.

Table 11-1. Strengths and Weaknesses of Commercial BC Software

Possible Strengths	Possible Weaknesses
Top products represent current best practices.	You get what you pay for, and getting the best may require a considerable investment.
Easy to maintain.	Difficult to adapt to your particular kind of company.
Can handle large volumes of plans and data.	Full benefits require installation, training, and practice.
Built-in version control.	May differ from corporate standard.
Standard formats.	May not align with your other documentation.
Simple distribution of plans and reports.	Requires initial effort to set up lists.
Automated import and update of variable data.	May require other records to be converted to suitable layout and format.
Automated history logs.	May not account for all eventualities.
Can handle multiple locations.	All treated similarly – may not be flexible.

11.8.1 Evaluation Considerations

When you are assessing a particular product, or choosing between products, you and your technical people should consider the answers to the following questions:

- Was the demonstration convincing as a practical and suitable solution, or was it a slick sales pitch?
- Is the product fully compatible with your technical environment?
- Who maintains the software and at what cost?
- Who installs the software and at what cost?
- Is there an education package or training course? If so, is it included in the purchase price?
- Is it a one-off purchase, or is there an ongoing rental or subscription charge? Are there additional charges for multiple uses?
- Do you have recommendations from other users? If so, are they from the same industry sector?
- Does the product comply, or align, with BC standards?
- Does the product comply, or align, with industry standards or regulations?

11.9   Scaling to Fit

No two organizations are the same in size and shape, which suggests their BC programs and plans will also differ considerably. This leads to the obvious question of how to adapt the basic concepts and tools to differing sizes of enterprise. One size cannot fit all, but you do need to have a uniform approach that will allow for the differences while building upon the similarities. If you can do this, then you can feel more confident that the approach will lead to a useful outcome and the process will be easier to monitor and audit.

The first step towards scaling your BC is to regard all organizations as a grouping of business units and to use those units as your building blocks. Over time, as a business grows, it will add more and more of these business units as the natural means of expansion. The other concept which you can use as a basis for your planning is the business functions. You have already come across them in the impact analysis stage where you sought to identify the business critical functions.

By working with these relatively small business entities, you can develop resilience at the micro level. Then your overarching emergency response plans can embrace a whole location and coordinate the various activities which are outlined in the lower level function or unit recovery plans.

Sitting above this is the crisis management plan, which spans the whole of the enterprise. As the number of teams and locations gets larger and their activities more disparate and far flung, you will need to set up a more robust communication network. Communication involves the appointment of liaison officers whose principal duty is to ensure that everybody is singing from the same hymn sheet. In addition, you will need a liaison officer appointed for each of the gold, silver, and bronze level teams to maintain a close dialogue with their equivalent numbers in the other teams that are engaged in dealing with some aspect of the emergency.

These people should get to know each other prior to an event.

11.10   Preparation and Delivery of a Draft Plan

By now you will have decided on the basic type, structure, and content of your first plan. This may be based on an adaptation of one of our sample or model plans. That adaptation will take account of the corporate style and reflect your own interpretation of our guidelines and recommendations. Alternatively, you may use a commercially available planning tool which will largely dictate what your plan covers and what it will look like. The third possibility is that there may be an existing template that is already in use within your organization.

Where you have freedom of choice, the final selection will depend to a large extent on which document development tools you are familiar with and have access to. The commonest and most popular tool seems to be Microsoft Word, although some people do make use of spreadsheets. The other factor will be the availability or choice of suitable templates. Here the selection will probably be governed by the overall appearance of the resulting documents.

11.10.1 Points to Look for in Template or Format

When selecting or developing a template for any kind of BC plan you should bear in mind the following points:

- ▸ They must be easy to read.
   - ❏ Clear typeface, large print, and black ink on white paper.
- ▸ Eliminate unnecessary information like BIA results.

- Ensure that specific information is easy to find.
  - ❏ A clear index with page and paragraph numbering.

- Make sure that version control is included and made evident.
- Include clear objectives and responsibilities.
- Include a set of "milestones," describing key activities and target times.
- Define the purpose in terms of activation scenarios.
- Include clear definitions of any special terms.
- Describe the requisite roles and responsibilities.
  - ❏ Allow space to insert names and contact details.

- Include an emergency organization chart showing the relationship between teams.
- Describe escalation procedures and decision criteria.
- Include a history log to ensure that accurate records are kept.
- Include action plans for each area of responsibility.
- Include internal and external contact lists.
  - ❏ Ensure that these lists are kept up-to-date.

> **...development of all your BC plans needs to be a collaborative effort.**

11.10.2 Preparing the Final Draft

Completing the draft consists largely of entering the details which you will have collected during the investigation and analysis stages, which were covered during Part I and Part II of this book. The plan template will govern the sequence and layout of the information, although you may want to adapt the template to suit your needs and circumstances. Some caution is needed here. If the template comes from a sound source, then its design probably represents good practice which has evolved from experience gained over the years in a wide range of scenarios.

Remember that the development of all your BC plans needs to be a collaborative effort. The whole data collection and validation process should be transparent and communicative. Work together with some of the individuals who are likely to be called upon to use the plan to ensure that it all seems to make sense to them. They need to be comfortable with the layout, style, and content of the plans which you are developing on their behalf. These people were probably contributors during your data gathering, and so they should be familiar with what you are trying to achieve. Once they are happy with your draft plan, you should pass it on to your sponsor who can then release it for general review and comment.

When you have received and dealt with the resulting feedback, you should be in a position to release and circulate the working version of your draft plan. Again, the distribution should be carried out under the auspices of your sponsor to emphasize the importance and value of these documents.

Self-Examination Questions

1. The format of an organization's BC plans should be
   A. consistent across all the plans to facilitate movement of tasks and resources from plan to plan.
   B. different from plan to plan to accommodate differences among business locations or units.
   C. highly complex because BC planning is complex.

2. If there is a major threat to the premises, the number one priority at all levels of the organization is to
   A. protect the brand, image, and reputation of the enterprise.
   B. evacuate everyone safely.
   C. resume business operations that impact customers.

3. Which of the following statements describes the purpose of the disaster recovery plan?
   A. It enables technicians to repair or restore the systems and services that support critical business functions.
   B. It provides managers with a means of resuming core business operations.
   C. It supports directors in getting the right message across, at the right time.

4. Which of the following is true of BC plans?
   A. They should be printed in color, and a number of different colors should be used to distinguish the many elements.
   B. They should be shared with the public and the media to reinforce the organization's image as a prepared organization.
   C. They should contain version control information, such as the release number and/or date.

5. How should a plan be best written to take into account the five key role types (director, executive, manager, operator, technician) in an organization?
   A. It should focus on a particular area of vertical interactions across the five role types.
   B. It should address a given horizontal level in the organization and take into account that level's vertical interfaces with other levels.
   C. It should address all five role types as horizontal levels and all of their vertical interactions with each other.

6. Which of the following is NOT included in a BC plan?
   A. An activity log, where decisions and actions are recorded
   B. Definitions of key terms
   C. Specifically detailed disaster scenarios

7. Compared to other plans, the crisis management plan should
   A. be relatively complex and provide specific lists of activities.
   B. be relatively simple and break down each activity into specific steps.
   C. be relatively simple and provide more general guidance.

8. When investing in a commercial planning tool, which of the following is the most important consideration?
   A. What the organization needs in a planning tool and how much time and other resources it wants to invest in using it
   B. Price, because most planning tools do essentially the same thing in the same way
   C. Features, because the best tools can handle many plans and data and perform sophisticated calculations

Food for Thought

This chapter has looked at preparing the plans which are at the heart of BC. These documents will be key elements in the education and training of all those who are likely to be engaged in dealing with the results of a business disruption. Your plans will be their guidelines and sources of reference in times of difficulty. Before you move on, it might be useful for you to reflect upon whether you are ready for this stage of the BC program and have a clear grasp of what is involved.

As in previous chapters, I suggest that you consider how you would carry out this work in an organization that you are familiar with such as your school, college, or place of work. Concern yourself with the strategic implications at this stage; the tactics will emerge as you work with the people to develop their specific needs and expectations. Once again, it would be helpful if you were to look through the downloadable **Business Continuity Toolkit**, which includes examples of various types of plan.

Exercises

1. Think about the number, purpose, and type of plans that your organization will need. It is especially important to work out what teams will be required to deal with various types of events.
   - How many types of plan will they need?
     - What is the purpose of each of these plan types?
     - What are the roles and responsibilities?
   - What should they be called?

2. Develop an infrastructure for those plans.
   - How do these plans relate to each other?
   - How does reporting work within your structure?
   - How does the command structure work?

3. Consider the communication structure.
   - How will these teams communicate with each other?
   - How will they communicate with the emergency services?
   - How will they communicate with the outside world?

4. Think about who should be on each of these teams.
   - Roughly how many people would you want in each team?
   - Who would you nominate as leaders and deputies?

5. Think about the sequence of development and delivery of these plans.
   - Where would you start and why?
   - What sort of timescale do you have in mind?

Looking Forward

You are now ready to start developing and delivering a full set of BC plans for your organization. The next step will be to start testing and exercising, which is where you develop the competence and confidence among your teams to ensure that they are fully prepared to cope with whatever might happen.

Downloadable Business Continuity Toolkit

The complementary downloadable **Business Continuity Toolkit** includes some sample plans which you can adapt for use as templates within your own organization. Make sure that you take full account of your house style when adapting these model plans. House style is typified by such features as layout, font face and size, language, and paper size.

For Additional Reading

A number of organizations offer various tools, services, and advice in connection with BC planning, including many local authorities. However, here only relevant national authorities are listed.

In the UK, the Cabinet Office published the *Business Continuity Management Toolkit* available at www.gov.uk/government/uploads/system/uploads/attachment_data/file/137994/Business_Continuity_Managment_Toolkit.pdf

In the UK, the Centre for the Protection of the National Infrastructure (CPNI) provides advice and guidance on BC planning at www.cpni.gov.uk/Security-Planning/Business-continuity-plan/

In the US, the Ready campaign is run by the Department of Home Security (DHS) on behalf of the Federal Emergency Management Agency (FEMA). Their BC planning advice is available at http://www.ready.gov/business/implementation/continuity

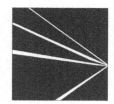

12

Exercise Preparation

Once a business continuity (BC) draft plan exists, you can move on to the ongoing testing, training, and maintenance routines. While the development and delivery of the initial draft plan can be seen as a project with distinct timeframes and outputs, the possession of a plan implies an ongoing program or set of processes. Until the elements of that plan have been tested, nobody can be sure of their effectiveness. Without proper exercising, your people will not be ready to recognize and deal with an emergency or disaster if the need should ever arise.

As Philip Jan Rothstein, FBCI points out, "An unexercised contingency plan can be more dangerous than no plan at all."

This chapter will help you to:

- ☑ Use the five-stage growth path to train your people to conduct different kinds of exercises.

- ☑ State the objectives and purpose of your exercise.

- ☑ Understand the difference between a *test* and an *exercise*.

- ☑ Identify the eight main elements in the development and delivery of a BC exercise.

- ☑ Create realistic scenarios and scripts for exercises.

12.1   Getting Started with BC Exercises

Often, there will be a change of personnel at this point where the BC program starts to move away from the short-term challenges of development and delivery projects towards the longer-term practice of an education and maintenance program. In some cases, an external consultant has been employed to lead or assist in the launch and implementation, and it will be normal for the consultant to step back and hand over control to the resident BC manager at some point, perhaps staying in the background in an ad hoc support or advisory role. Alternatively, a member of staff has led the way so far but may have second thoughts about the way forward. Is this staff member ready to adopt a rather less dynamic attitude, or should he or she consider handing over to someone else who is more suited to the long-term maintenance and administration that is required from now on? This is a question which you might like to consider in due course, but first you need to know what the future might hold.

> **...effective training methods...enable the participants to help each other through the difficult patches.**

I am going to assume you will be developing the plans and checking out (or testing) the procedures and techniques while you are also developing the skills and competence of the participants. This is the normal and most practical approach. Some of the larger generalist consultancies tend to separate plan development from education and training; I suspect this is a consequence of the way in which their own skill sets are divided. Their BC specialists don't do training, and their training specialists don't do planning. The end result can be a "standard" plan with very little customization and some fairly routine exercises that rarely manage to generate a great deal of enthusiasm for the subject.

In my experience, exercising to develop the emergency response and management skills among the various teams is the most important aspect of BC. It is vital to the success of their response to any kind of disruption. However, the style of the first venture into the realms of BC by the team members has to be appropriate. An exercise should present them with problems which are challenging but realistic, problematic but solvable.

12.1.1   Capability and Confidence: Educating Personnel

Terminology varies considerably and there are many variations in the manner in which tests and exercises are developed and delivered. In the same way, there will be considerable differences in teaching techniques and methods within any training program. Personal preferences of the trainers, tradition, local culture, and the facilities available have a strong influence. However, the basic principles and concepts should remain the same across the board. Once you understand the basics, then you can apply them to your own particular situation.

All group learning has to be organized in a sensible sequence which gradually builds towards the finished product: a competent and confident team. The same is obviously true for individuals, where pace and content can be managed to suit their progress as measured by means of tests, or examinations. However, group learning has to take into account a wide range of participants. The most effective training methods set up a steady learning curve, or *gradient*, which will enable the participants to help each other through the difficult patches. Your goal is a foolproof system which will work with a team of people with different backgrounds and experience.

At the same time, this training system has to check out and improve the plans and procedures so that you end up with a robust capability. Almost without exception, BC practitioners (and standards, where they apply) seem inclined towards a five-stage growth path in their exercise and test programs. Where there are exceptions, they are either variations on the theme, or they can be aligned easily with these five stages.

12.2   The Five-Stage Growth Path

Figure 12-1 shows how, through a series of steps in a gentle gradient, you can expect the people you are training to grow in stature, competence, and confidence as they build upon the lessons learned at an earlier stage. By the end of the program, they are prepared for any eventuality but at no time are they put through an overwhelming or unhappy experience. Each step is another challenging extension of their capability.

1. Stage One: Desktop Exercise.
2. Stage Two: Walkthrough.
3. Stage Three: Active Testing.
4. Stage Four: Command Post Exercise.
5. Stage Five: Full-Scale Exercise.

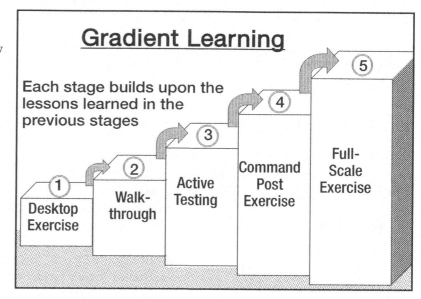

Figure 12-1. Gradient Learning: The Five-Stage Growth Path

12.2.1   Desktop Exercise

Stage One is the *desktop exercise* which is designed to familiarize the exercise participants with the plan and their role within it. A Chinese philosopher once said, "Tell me and I will forget; show me and I may remember; involve me and I will understand." Bear this in mind as you initiate your players into BC.

When you first introduce the plan, allow plenty of time to involve them in discussing the relevance of the plan and its purpose. Without getting into the detail of particular procedures or individual responsibilities, you should encourage them to comment on the layout, logic, and structure of the plan. This will help them to develop their understanding.

The key focus of this first desktop exercise should be to try and spot weaknesses or areas for improvement in the plan as a whole. By looking for faults and limitations, they will become involved and begin to understand what might be expected of them in due course. This is a good time for you to show and explain the gradient learning curve from Figure 12-1. They will find it reassuring to know that the training program will allow them the time and opportunity to learn to play this interesting new game, with the incentive that maybe one day they may be called upon to face up to the real thing, supported by the inner confidence which springs from a successful education and development program.

If there is time, the ideal way to conduct these desktop exercises is on a one-to-one basis, or with a number of relatively small groups. This allows the participants to become fully engaged in the process, although this approach can be rather time-consuming. Larger groups require more adroit handling to derive the best benefit, but with an accomplished facilitator they can be very effective as long as you capture all of the feedback. Having someone there to make notes on a flip chart can be very helpful; it shows that you take their views seriously and it encourages further reflection and comment.

The style of a desktop exercise is introduction and familiarization, with a focus on the plan and its contents. The players should go away with a basic understanding of the plan and its contents while being given the opportunity to comment on the logic and the layout.

Once they have had time to thoroughly digest what they have learned, and you have had the opportunity to adjust or amend the plan in accordance with their feedback, it is time to organize the next stage of development and learning.

12.2.2 Walkthrough

Stage Two, the *walkthrough*, is a more advanced version of the desktop exercise, in which you get the participants to spot and challenge any assumptions. At the same time you need their help to identify the *dependencies* (which you reviewed earlier in Chapter 5) and verify them. Any key dependencies which cannot be guaranteed will need to be checked out during the testing stage. So, be prepared to make a list of those components and dependencies which should be tested. Where there is any doubt about the need to check something out, base your judgment on the opinion of the participants. After all, you are trying to boost their confidence and they will be working with the end result of this development process.

> **At this stage, it is even more important to… capture and record information in real-time.**

At this stage, it is even more important to demonstrate the need to capture and record information in real-time. A walkthrough is a group process with all the players contributing in a dynamic discussion. In this atmosphere ideas will flourish and there will be several cross currents in the patterns of thought. Without a formal data capture process many of the messages can be overlooked or forgotten. It is worth making the point to the group that this is a demonstration of how the words, ideas, questions, and suggestions might flow in a real-life emergency response situation. The walkthrough will introduce them to reality in this respect, and the information logging should be formalized in accordance with the plan.

The style of a walkthrough exercise is a group-based facilitated discussion, taking the team through the activities and procedures of the plan. The participants are invited to review and discuss the plan and should go away with a feel for the way they would act as a group in response to an incident of some sort. The focus is on how they might deal with the effects of an incident.

With this experience behind them, the participants should have a fairly clear understanding of how the plan might work in practice. As a result, you may identify some improvements to be made to the plans, together with a list of the things which need to be checked out. Armed with this feedback, you can begin to prepare for the next stage.

12.2.3 Active Testing

Stage Three, *active testing*, may be tackled in bite-sized chunks rather than an all-out attempt to do everything at once. Some of the highlighted procedures and routines will need to be checked out by those responsible. In this type of testing, the emphasis is on questioning the procedures, techniques, and resources. It is not designed to test the skills and knowledge of the technicians. Rather, it is a research project in which viable solutions are being sought. There is no question of failure, simply lessons learned and alternatives explored. No one should come away from any of these component tests with a sense of defeat. If it doesn't work, they have discovered something very useful: the plan, the strategy, or the technology needs to be changed or improved before you move on towards your goal of a resilient organization.

The focus throughout this stage will be on preventing, or dealing with, the consequences of an incident. There are, in fact, two distinct styles of exercise at this stage, although it is possible to combine them into a single comprehensive rehearsal.

> *Component testing* is a rigorous proof of the methods and solutions with a focus on feasibility, suitability, timings, and costing. Output from these tests will be technical improvements together with useful data which can be fed into the decision-making process.

> *Active exercising* is a scenario-based opportunity for the participants to interpret the plans and information available in order to experience decision-making under abnormal conditions. They must be allowed to succeed and earn your congratulations; this is a vital requirement. If necessary, coach or guide them towards success.

You will also observe the beginnings of a vibrant team spirit...

Once the components have been tested, you can run a team exercise to provide the participants with some practical experience. These early exercises should be based on a relatively simple scenario: not too challenging from a decision-making point of view. The emphasis should be on the practicality and workability of the technical aspects of the recovery procedures. However, they should be expected to work with the plan in a realistic situation, preferably in the actual recovery environment. There may even be an opportunity to include some actual recovery procedures, so long as the live business operation is not put at risk.

The active exercise needs to be facilitated according to a proper script, with observers providing feedback. While providing a learning environment for the participants and a test bed for the components, it is also an opportunity for the BC management to flex their muscles in the creation and delivery of a scenario-based exercise. In other words, both sides will be building up their skills and confidence at the same time.

Active exercising should be repeated a number of times so all the various combinations of players get an opportunity to be involved in at least one such episode before moving on to the next stage.

By the time the active testing and exercising program has been completed, the participants will have gained some practical experience, the plans will be robust, and people will be familiar with their roles. You will also observe the beginnings of a vibrant team spirit because they will have shared a common set of challenges and won through. Hopefully, they will have bonded and learned to trust each other and work well together under unfamiliar circumstances. Confidence will begin to emerge; now they know the sort of thing they might have to face one day, working together as a team.

12.2.4 Command Post Exercise

Stage Four, the *command post exercise*, begins once all the feedback has been translated into changes and improvements and everybody has been congratulated on their success. The command post exercise is where you begin to refine techniques and polish skills through a realistic simulation with several groups or teams dealing with different aspects of the unfolding scenario. The emphasis here is more on the coordination and communication between the various parties which include external interests, as well as the internal teams that will be working independently.

Preparation for this level of exercise will entail the development of a more detailed script. The activities and the buildup will need to be managed to ensure everything runs smoothly. The development and delivery of such an exercise is covered in more detail in Chapter 14. On the day of the exercise, you may need to adjust the pace of the scenario to match the participants' performance. The exercise should not be too easy, but neither should it be beyond their capability. The idea is to stretch them but not to break them.

This type of exercise should be run on a regular basis, say once a year. Each time, you will need to pull together a different script with at least a few variations on the theme in order to maintain their interest and to explore different areas of exposure and response. During the command post and full-scale exercise stages the focus is on the whole scenario, the way it unfolds and how they deal with any surprises or an unexpected turn of events.

12.2.5 Full-Scale Exercise

Finally, Stage Five in the learning and development process is to conduct a *full-scale exercise*, but not before the participants have gained enough confidence in themselves, each other, and the process through the command post type of exercise. At this level, you are aiming to combine skills acquired from earlier exercises into a solid capability. You are also expecting them to demonstrate their competence, which will boost their confidence and the confidence of others. While the core teams should have some previous experience behind them, you could bring one or two beginners into the group at this stage. Plunging them in at the deep end is fine providing the other members of the team are good enough to be able to let these new people find their feet. This is exactly the sort of situation they will need to deal with in an emergency; there will be varying degrees of expertise within the group and the leaders will have to allocate the roles and tasks in a sensitive but pragmatic manner.

You can also have one or more individuals sit out the exercise, either preplanned or as a surprise, as if they are out of town or out ill. In this way, you can build the participants' resilience. So as not to waste the time of the skipped individuals, they can serve in an external role such as an observer.

The style of a full-scale exercise is one of simulation and realism. It is simulation in the sense that everything gets checked out and used – as appropriate to the scenario – and realism in the sense that the scenario is credible, believable, and relevant. Ideally, the participants should go away with a sense of relief and pride. The relief stems from the fact they have been put through a challenging examination and the pride comes from the fact they did quite well. They should walk away looking forward to the next one but hoping it won't be too soon.

The principal difference between the command post exercise and a full-scale one is simply a matter of size and scope. While the command post tends to concentrate on the work of the key decision-makers, the full-scale exercise embraces the full range of roles and responsibilities as well as their audiences. It is as close to the real thing as can be achieved without actually endangering the business or any of its people. Of course, you have to remain sensible with regard to costs and the degree of realism. Table 12-1 reviews the five stages. The normal progression would be to start at the bottom with the desktop exercise and work up towards the full-scale exercise at the top.

Table 12-1. Summary of the Five Stages and Their Characteristics

	Stage	**Purpose**	**Style and Focus**
Five	Full-Scale Exercise	Develop the capability. Demonstrate competence.	Simulation & Realism. Scenario-based.
Four	Command Post Exercise	Acquire the skills. Develop the techniques.	Coordination & Communication. Scenario-based.
Three	Active Testing	Practical experience. Test the components.	Participation & Interpretation. Consequence-based.
Two	Walkthrough	Challenge the assumptions. Verify the dependencies.	Review & Discussion. Effect-based.
One	Desktop Exercise	Validate the logic. Spot the weaknesses.	Introduction & Familiarization. Plan-based.

12.2.6 Frequency of Testing

▸ Stage One and Stage Two need to be repeated only in the event of major changes to the plans and strategies or significant changes to the personnel.

▸ Stage Three should comprise a regular testing regime with quarterly technical trials plus occasional exercises for the various response and recovery teams.

▸ Stage Four exercises should be held at least once a year in order to maintain the levels of confidence and capability, preferably twice each year.

▸ Stage Five exercises should be held annually, preferably at different times of the year. Where command post exercises are held on a regular and frequent basis, there is a case for the full-scale exercises to be held twice each year.

At this point, it's important to understand the difference between an *exercise* and a *test*.

12.3 Testing Plans and Procedures

When the word *test* is used, it tends to be taken to imply the possibility of either pass or failure; therefore, you should never apply the term to people. In general, they do not want to be viewed in such a judgmental manner, although some of them may see a test as an exciting challenge and want to continuously prove themselves. However, these are the kind of risk-takers to be avoided in recovery and continuity situations. Thus, you should restrict your testing to the inanimate aspects such as plans, procedures, and technology.

At this point, it's important to understand the difference between an *exercise* and a *test*. In the *actual test activity*, the focus needs to be on the purely technical issues, whereas *exercises* are used to explore and develop skills, interpretations, and tactics.

The decision-making and invocation aspects of the disaster recovery (DR) plans should be checked out as part of an exercise, rather than brought into question during a test. For example, in an exercise you might reasonably expect participants to make their own arrangements for food and drink because they need to build such considerations into the procedures. On the other hand, in a test you should make those arrangements for them because you want them to feel comfortable about getting on with the tasks before them. In an exercise, you are teaching valuable lessons, but in a test you are asking them to follow the procedures.

You should carry out regular tests of your plan components to check:

▸ Timings.

▸ Accuracy.

▸ Suitability.

Testing is particularly concerned with data recovery, technology recovery, and service recovery plans, although the principles of testing should be applied to all types of plans when they are first developed. However, once a management plan has been proven, its ongoing maintenance and improvement should be driven by the feedback from regular exercises.

12.3.1 Disaster Recovery Testing

Disaster recovery (DR), which includes the rebuild or restoration of technical services such as telecommunications and information technology (IT) – which you reviewed in Chapter 10 – needs to be tested in order to prove the procedures. There is also an implicit need for specialist skills which can also be enhanced through a regular test program.

Generally speaking, this type of plan assumes a certain level of technical knowledge. Where there is no expectation of technical skills, the plan will need to provide detailed instructions for precisely recovering and restoring the technology and systems. In either case, this type of plan will require regular, detailed testing and updating because technology is constantly changing and so the recovery skills need to be challenged.

Recovery of technology and its applications requires a considerable amount of skill which can be derived only from practice. Systems recovery is a very different art from that of systems management. The associated skill set is unique and it needs to be forged in the heat of battle where the enemies are time and complexity, in a region which everybody prefers to avoid.

There is little need to invent scenarios and plots for these tests which are independent of imaginary information about the circumstances or events leading up to the decision to invoke the plans and procedures. "Let's test the recovery plan" is the only challenge to be posed at the start of a test. Test conditions will steer the event towards certain facets of the plan, and so it is this aspect which you need to examine briefly.

Before you carry out a recovery test, decide on the test conditions. This means deciding what assumptions you are allowing participants to make about the prevailing circumstances for the test. The conditions need to be realistic but don't have to be complex or devious. The background information should include brief details about the time of day when the system failed, as this may affect the state of the systems and backup. The other key piece of information they will require is what will be available to them in the way of facilities, equipment, and resources.

Once team members know where they can go, and what resources they can expect to find, they should be able to rebuild or recover the systems, applications, and data to the business recovery point in accordance with the recovery procedures. The feedback should be captured by at least one technically competent person with a focus on the quality and usability of the procedures. The recorder should also make a careful note of any problems which were encountered and how they were resolved. It is also very useful to record how long it took to accomplish each of the key tasks and how and where time was lost in resolving problems. This provides management with vital information about the time taken to reestablish vital services to the business users.

12.3.2   Systems Recovery Checklist

A systems recovery checklist – designed to help technical personnel prepare for a DR test – is included in the accompanying downloadable **Business Continuity Toolkit**. It describes the test as a four-stage exercise:

- A compatibility checkout.
- Test preparation.
- Actual test activity.
- Test feedback.

Each of these stages should be carried out by the technical team, although you, as the BC manager, may want to be involved in some capacity. Your involvement should be limited and should not lead to interference. Let them tackle the tasks and adjust the plans and procedures where it is deemed necessary.

A *compatibility checkout* is conducted to ensure the standby resources are suitable for a full recovery. Where there are no alternative resources available, the only way of testing the recovery procedures is to attempt to rebuild the live system and this is not a practice I would condone.

Test preparation would normally include developing one or more objectives so that the degree of success can be measured in an objective rather than a subjective manner. This is where the BC manager will have a constructive contribution because these objectives need to be related to the business need.

Another important input from you will be the *test conditions*, which may be derived from a long-term testing strategy or a recent exercise. This means deciding, or helping them to decide, when the trigger incident is supposed to have occurred; when and where they are expected to carry out the recovery; and what resources and support they can call upon on this occasion.

The eight elements of exercise development and delivery can be broken down into two phases: *preparation* and *action*.

Once the test has been completed, the *feedback procedure* follows pretty much the same pattern as for an exercise, except the focus is purely on the technical issues. Debriefing should be carried out at the end of the test and someone has to be tasked with returning the alternate systems back to their normal status. This would usually involve deleting all of the recovered data and may include the removal of applications and software. If the equipment is dedicated as standby to a particular client or business function, then you may decide to leave the system in its newly recovered state until the next test. However, there is a security exposure with this approach if sensitive data is left on an unprotected system.

12.4   Elements of Exercise Development

An *exercise* is a lesson, or rehearsal, for the plan's users to show how it works. It is also an opportunity for participants to build up their recovery skills and boost their confidence because success removes doubt. Feedback from the exercise should lead to a better plan. The basic reasons for exercising are to:

▸ Prove that the plans and practices are sound.

▸ Demonstrate the BC capability.

▸ Establish certainty that the business can continue.

While the size and scope may vary, as a general rule, there are eight main elements in the development and delivery of a BC exercise, as illustrated in Figure 12-2. The eight elements of exercise development and delivery can be broken down into two phases: *preparation* and *action*. Before the event, the preparation phase is concerned with the development of the exercise materials and is composed of:

1. Background.
2. Buildup.
3. Quality.

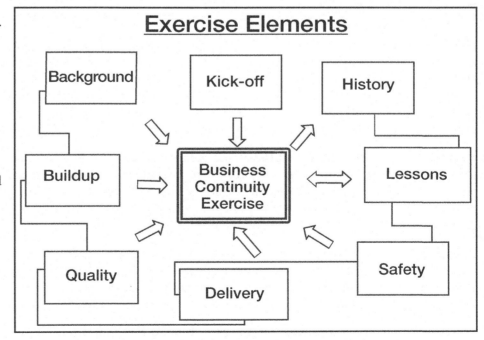

Figure 12-2. Exercise Elements

The action phase is concerned with the subsequent delivery of those materials as a useful exercise with beneficial results and includes:

4. Delivery.
5. Safety.
6 Lessons.
7. History.
8. Kick-off.

The emphasis may change according to the scale and complexity of the exercise but the principles are the same. While most of these elements are a direct or an indirect input to the exercise, history is an outcome, and lessons are both learned and applied. The first three elements – background, buildup, and quality – will be addressed in this chapter, with the others covered in following chapters.

This chapter deals with the preparation phase, while Chapter 14 will deal with the action or delivery phase.

Background: Before setting out to develop and deliver an important part of any program, you need to establish the context. Background is about understanding what you are trying to achieve and why, whom you are going to be doing it with, and how you should approach the task. Your approach should take account of the organization's view, expressed as policy, together with good practice derived from your knowledge of the subject.

Buildup: Once you have established the background, you can begin to get ready to deliver a useful and relevant exercise. Buildup is mostly about preparing: creating or acquiring all the materials, arranging the venue, and organizing the facilities. The other aspect of buildup is matching the intentions to the requirements, ensuring that the storyline and the scenario are appropriate and credible.

Quality: It is important for you to ensure that quality is maintained throughout the buildup and the subsequent stages. This attention to quality is to ensure that the exercise will be taken seriously, its results will be credible, and it represents good value. The long-term outcome of enhanced, proven performance can be achieved only through a considerable investment in time and effort as well as a focus on quality.

Delivery: Once all the preparations are complete, you can focus on the exercise delivery, a training event where you have to coordinate and manage all of the activities to ensure a smooth and safe experience for all those involved. It is an important occasion where you, and your delivery team, have to retain control across the whole board. Of course, good and thorough preparation will stand you in good stead. You will also benefit from working on the gradient shown in Figure 12-1. This means starting with small, simple events, expanding the size and complexity as you develop confidence in yourself and your team.

Safety: It is very important that the whole exercise is carried out with safety in mind. You must ensure throughout the development and delivery that both the participants and the business operation are protected from risk. This includes the avoidance of accidents through physical risks and the avoidance of consequences through technical or conceptual risks. As the person in charge, you must assume responsibility for this aspect of the whole project.

Lessons: The primary purpose of a BC exercise is to learn and to apply the lessons gained from practical experience. In order to ensure that the full benefit is derived from these lessons, you have to make sure that they are noticed, noted, and applied properly. This might imply changes or improvements to the plans or it could mean changes in attitude or behavior. Your job is to make sure that the learning is recorded and applied.

History: A long-term objective is to have a complete and accurate record of the BC exercise program. Such a history provides tangible evidence that the program is working. It is also a reference source which can help you in the selection and planning of subsequent exercises. Each exercise should be developed against a background which includes the scale, type, and scope of previous events. You also need to take account of the experience and capability of the participants.

Kick-off: Open each exercise with a kick-off in which you introduce the delivery team to the participants and outline the rules of the game. (Chapter 14 covers the process of assembling your delivery team.) You establish control and set the boundaries so that the participants know where they stand in relation to the events which are about to unfold. This is also an opportunity for you to give hints and tips to them about dealing with such a situation. Perhaps you will want to offer reminders about lessons from the past or warnings about potential difficulties.

12.5   Background: Objectives and Purpose

The statements of objectives and purpose must be developed in reference to your BC policy and agreed upon by the sponsors. A typical set of objectives is as follows:

This exercise is designed to:

▸ *Develop our BC management skills.*

▸ *Evaluate the effectiveness of our BC plans.*

▸ *Instill confidence in the BC management team.*

▸ *Identify areas for improvement in the plan, strategy, procedures, and resources.*

▸ *Establish accurate timings for activities outlined in the BC plan.*

> **…prove, demonstrate, and establish key aspects of the BC management set up and capability.**

12.5.1   Stating the Purpose

In general, your purpose will create three main reasons to prove, demonstrate, and establish key aspects of the BC management set up and capability. These might be expressed in a purpose statement similar to the following:

This exercise aims to:

▸ *Prove*

  ❑ *The plans and practices are sound.*

▸ *Demonstrate*

  ❑ *The need for, and the value of, BC plans.*

  ❑ *The capability for BC exists.*

  ❑ *Compliance with rules and regulations.*

▸ *Establish*

  ❑ *Certainty that the business can continue.*

Since you must relate your purpose to the policy and strategy, you should use them as the basis of the purpose, because you are about to prove and demonstrate their practical outcome.

Bear in mind the nature of your audience and take their expectations and capabilities into account. Try to avoid demanding too much of them. If you overwhelm them it will become a regrettable experience for them, and you might do irreparable damage to everybody's confidence, yourself included.

12.6 Buildup

The buildup should be based on the agreed upon objectives and purpose, translating them into action. From the objectives you can determine what needs to be covered in the exercise. They are a set of guidelines. A clearer idea of the design comes from understanding the purpose of the exercise. As the plot begins to take shape, it might be necessary to refine the objectives to meet the needs of the organization. On the other hand, you may need to stick with the original objectives and modify the plot accordingly. There is no right or wrong way to approach the creative process; we each have our own way of working, but we all have to stay within the limits set by the objectives and scope of the exercise.

Figure 12-3 shows how the purpose of an exercise demonstrates and proves, while providing a learning experience for the participants.

Posing of a few problems of the right scale leads the participants to develop solutions by interpreting the plan and deciding on a line of actions to resolve those problems. It is your responsibility to make sure that they are able to deal with those problems and to come up with workable solutions.

Scripting is the process of developing the exercise scenario, generating the story or plot, and creating the texts. It means turning the objectives and purpose into a set of deliverables for use during the event. It is about getting ready in the technical sense – gathering information, formulating ideas and concepts, preparing the words, and acquiring the expertise to support the whole show.

On the other hand, *preparation* is the process of managing the logistics, organizing the facilities, and setting up the equipment. It means ensuring the exercise can be run at the right time and place with the right people. It is getting ready in the practical sense: preparing the location, organizing people, arranging transport, managing the equipment, and co-coordinating the timings.

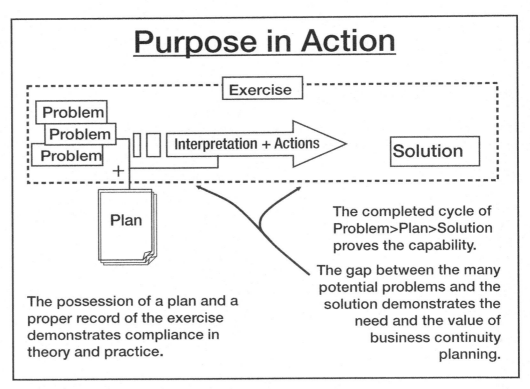

Figure 12-3. Purpose in Action

12.7　Developing the Script for the Exercise

The development process is relatively simple:

- First you choose a plot, which is a credible incident that will support the objectives.
- Then you build the scripts and a timetable.
- Various messages, instructions, checklists, and reference materials are then developed to support the script.

Perhaps the first hurdle to be overcome is the choice of a scenario or plot line. The plot must be realistic and credible which means you may need to do some research. You can find further guidance on the various possibilities, and their usefulness as plot lines, in the specially prepared plot development aid in the downloadable **Business Continuity Toolkit**.

There are two distinct kinds of exercise:

- **Case study.** This approach is based on a situation which is outside of the normal experience or expectations of the participants – based on things that have happened to other organizations or imaginary events. This provides the participants with a form of indirect learning through an example which is parallel to real life.
- **Line of business.** This approach is based on a situation that participants might encounter, based on things that have happened or could very well happen in their own organization. This provides them with a form of direct learning through an experience directly related to their own situation.

Case studies can be based upon real life events, in which case the plot is pretty well pre-determined. You can also compare the original outcome with the way in which your team deals with the scenario. There will also be two sets of lessons to be learned, one from the harsh reality of an actual incident and one from the comfort of a well-orchestrated exercise.

…it might be best to start off with some case studies to get the basic ideas across…

You can also mock up case study exercises. This is where you might invent the whole thing, including the company and its environment. Through this imaginary technique you can introduce all sorts of interesting problems in order to highlight particular aspects of BC management.

The principal advantage of the case study approach is that much of the material can be used over and over again. On the other hand, it does not focus on the actual issues of the real world. So it might be best to start off with some case studies to get the basic ideas across, and then move up to the line of business approach as the competence and capability of the participants matures.

12.7.1　The Script Process Deliverables

In order to run a successful exercise, you may need to prepare all of the documentation shown in Figure 12-4. For a simple first time exercise you may be able to get away without the full set of supporting materials but you should get into the habit of thinking about the need for them. It is far better to leave something out by judgment than through oversight.

The main inputs to the script development process are the purpose and objectives. Obviously these will be supplemented by considerations about the company and its working environment. From this background, you need to come up with a series of deliverables. I describe them as a series because one does lead to another, if you follow the process. You will need to produce:

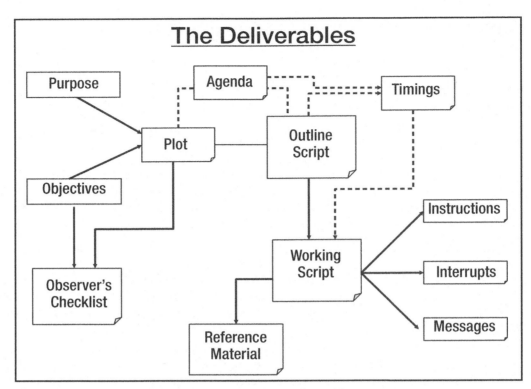

Figure 12-4. The Deliverables

- A plot or story line.
- An agenda or time table.
- An outline script.
- A working script.
- Instructions for assistants, who are part of the exercise delivery team.
- Messages – inputs to the scenario which simply pass information to participants.
- Scripts for interrupts – interactive inputs to engage one or more of the participants in a realistic interactive dialog to interrupt the participant's train of thought.
- Reference material.
- An observer's checklist.

Some of these, like the observer's checklist and assistants' instructions, can be re-used or copied; they don't have to be original or unique to a specific exercise or occasion. You may want to accumulate a small toolkit of reusable pages and paragraphs for use in economy-scale exercises or *cabaret testing*, which will be covered in Chapter 14.

The layout and structure of the exercise scripts should make the documents easy to use. A good structure means you can find things easily; this is especially important when you are running the exercise and trying to keep track of everything that's happening around you while figuring out what comes next and when, and if, to introduce it. Remember that the style of each of the documents has to suit the purpose and meet the expectations of its audience.

The script may be put together as one document or more. It may go through several stages and grow with the process, or you may prefer to work with separate papers for each stage of development. This might leave you with a better paper trail if you want to review the process later or if you might be called upon to explain the growth path.

Script development starts with looking at the purpose and objectives and choosing a plot line which is likely to make the participants meet those targets. The plot is an incident which will explore the objectives; from this you can then develop the scripts and timetable. Messages, instructions, checklists, and reference material are added as required by the script. Sometimes, it may take more than one trigger event to cause the players to fully explore a particular aspect of their response or recovery strategies. This could make for a more interesting scenario.

An outline script tells you what is there within the working script, and it also says what might be needed and when. The structure should be logical and sequential, so start with the big picture first and then add the finer details. Once you have the basic ideas worked out, arrange them in sequence. Figure out what you plan to happen and what you plan to tell the players, which may not be the truth or the whole truth.

For ease of control and delivery, it is best to keep separate items on separate documents, i.e., only one message on a page.

Please remember to mark every page as "Test Only" to prevent confusion. You do not want anybody mistaking the details of your exercise for a real threat or a credible story.

12.7.1.1 Script Content

Apart from the main story, the exercise script should have:

- Background information, to set the scene at the start.
- Agenda and timings, so the players know what to expect.
- A description of the scenario, or what has happened so far.
- Rules of engagement, so the players know what you expect of them.

This is the minimum amount of information that you should be giving to the participants in any form of exercise.

In more advanced exercises the script may also include:

- Scripts for the supporting cast, where you are expecting them to engage in some form of role play.
- Reference information, which may be helpful when answering any questions arising from the scenario.
- Messages to be passed to the players. These may take the form of imitation notes, faxes, reports, newspapers, or broadcasts to add to the realism.
- "Noise input" to divert their attention. This is where you or your team pass on messages which are spurious, misleading, or irrelevant. Only impose this additional burden on those team members who are already somewhat competent. It will stretch their information management techniques and introduce a heightened sense of realism, especially where there are several conflicting messages from different sources.

The style of the various parts of the script needs to match its purpose and audience. Those parts which are intended to be read aloud must use the words and language of the role. While some of the inputs may be incomplete or contradictory, you and your delivery team must know the full story, which includes understanding why the inconsistency has been introduced. In real life, we often get conflicting, inconsistent, or incomplete information, yet we still have to go ahead and make decisions. This includes trying to verify the truth and making the most reasonable assumptions – good practice for your target teams.

The working script for the delivery team must indicate timings and the intentions behind the nuances of the script. If you are expecting members of the delivery team to improvise you must explain the role clearly so they can match up to your intentions.

12.7.1.2 Interrupts

Interrupts that change the flow of the conversation and interaction are useful for adjusting the pace and direction of an exercise. If participants are making good progress, an interrupt can slow them down or change their focus.

Use interrupts with discretion, since you don't have to use them, and you can always use them another time. Plan and practice them so they flow smoothly and fit in with the evolving scenario. Make a point of planning when to use them, and also make up your mind about how you are going to judge whether to use them.

12.8 Quality

12.8.1 Realism

In order to be convincing, and engage participants' full attention, exercises must be realistic. Realism may mean research for it depends on knowing what can happen and how it might happen. Be convincing, otherwise you lose control!

So, if you are introducing any special effects, take the time to research the facts. In this way, you can build up your certainty and gain the confidence to be convincing.

For example, in one exercise that I led, an explosion was the trigger for an exercise and the extent of the damage to the surrounding buildings was described in some detail. However, one participant suggested the pattern of the damage would have been different. His view was that there would have been a large crater and widespread damage. On this occasion, we fully expected a challenge because this one particular participant had a tendency to tease out the detail of the script rather than focus on dealing with the problem as presented. So we prepared a small PowerPoint presentation to support our explanation, based on information supplied by explosive experts.

> **Realism... involves creating and developing imaginary scenarios which are credible to those taking part.**

I was able to explain to him and the other participants exactly how our damage was caused and why he expected different effects. Obviously, he had assumed an explosion on open ground, whereas, in our exercise, the device had been placed in a container. We had studied the possibilities and were able to use the diagram in Figure 12-5 to show him how the blast cone of an explosion is shaped by the position of the explosive.

Realism, which is an essential ingredient in any exercise, involves creating and developing imaginary scenarios which are credible to those taking part. One simple test is to ask yourself whether you would believe the story if it were told to you. Another way is to ask the delivery team members whether they would accept it as plausible.

Realism makes the participants take it seriously. Nobody argues with real life; they just accept it, work their way through the difficulties, and try to do better next time.

If any part of the plot seems unrealistic, participants will question the credibility and value of the exercise rather than try to solve problems. They may challenge your ideas and authority which will lead to frustration and disappointment on both sides.

Avoid exaggeration and try to make the whole thing seem believable. On the one hand you must make it difficult so they have to work at it; but you must also make it possible so they can start with a certain amount of confidence.

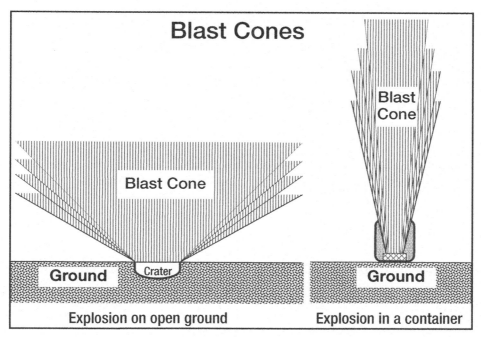

Figure 12-5. Blast Cones

12.8.1.1 Methods for Achieving Realism

You have a number of options for achieving realism in your exercises:

- External support may be available from the emergency services or from your loss adjusters. People of this caliber can add realism through their experience of many similar events and the way they were handled.

  - ❏ It is possible that the emergency services may be willing to act as advisers during the exercise itself but don't expect this because their primary and overriding duty is protecting the public, which means being ready to respond at a moment's notice.

  - ❏ You can contact your loss adjusters through your insurance company. They are much more likely to make themselves available because they are not subject to the same instantaneous demands and can plan ahead.

- Fire engineers often give live demonstrations of firefighting which can include some useful discussions about the practicalities of dealing with fire. Do not attempt to do this on your own!

- Internal support should be available from your security staff, fire wardens, facilities managers, first aiders, and maintenance workers. Familiar faces add a degree of realism and their expertise adds value to the exercise. Using your own people raises awareness and adds to the reality while you get some practical help. Usually, the members of your security team will have useful and interesting backgrounds and relevant war stories. These internal people can act as a link to the relevant external agencies. It is also a good idea to get them to act out some of their emergency duties during the exercise. For example:

  - ❏ You can give the fire wardens a chance to get some useful practice. Use them to spot things or to carry out roll calls and report whether anybody is missing. They can also help you work out what might happen within the plot.

  - ❏ Facilities people have a lot of practical experience because they manage the working environment on a daily basis.

❏ Maintenance people know what fails and how to fix it; their input can be very useful.

‣ Photos, film, and video can be also be used to add realism and color to your exercise as long as they are used wisely and sparingly. The images have to be relevant and you don't want to waste time setting the scene. The emphasis should be on getting participants to analyze the situation and start making decisions.

12.8.2 Scope

Defining the *scope* is about what the exercise covers and what is excluded. Everybody needs to be given a clear indication of the limits, and boundaries must be set for all aspects of the event such as:

‣ Who is to take part?

‣ What can they do? What can't they do?

‣ What is available to them and what isn't?

‣ What communication and support is available?

The scope of an exercise defines the physical, technical, and logical boundaries...

The scope of an exercise defines the physical, technical, and logical boundaries, relating these boundaries back to the objectives. It is where you say what you will be covering, and it sets the stage for the exercise. You need to get agreement from senior management on this aspect. They must have confidence in your approach; so it is best to let them tell you what they want. Their input ensures their support. Once they have explained what they would like to see, you can interpret their views and define the scope more fully.

Explain which general business areas are going to be covered and how the exercise will affect the people and processes involved.

Define support limits which make clear what the participants can expect and what you will need during the course of the exercise.

Areas of consideration for the scope of an exercise include:

‣ Physical aspects.
  ❏ Location and extent of the trigger event.
  ❏ Where the exercise is to be held.

‣ Communications.
  ❏ Some communication rules for the exercise could be:
    ◈ Communications kept separate from regular business traffic.
    ◈ No inbound messages, except for your input.
    ◈ Restrict or prevent outbound messages.

‣ Areas or functions with a primary role.

‣ People who have an indirect role, e.g., providing advice or data to the primary function(s).

‣ Level of representation.
  ❏ Who should attend, e.g., directors, department heads, managers, or supervisors.

Self-Examination Questions

1. Which of the following reflects the five-stage growth path of BC training?

   A. (1) Command post exercise, (2) desktop exercise, (3) walkthrough, (4) active testing, (5) full-scale exercise

   B. (1) Desktop exercise, (2) walkthrough, (3) active testing, (4) command post exercise, (5) full-scale exercise

   C. (1) Desktop exercise, (2) walkthrough, (3) command post exercise, (4) full-scale exercise, (5) active testing

2. The focus of the first desktop exercise should be on

   A. identifying areas of improvement.

   B. verifying dependencies.

   C. questioning procedures.

3. During the active testing stage, component testing may be conducted. Which of the following describes component testing?

   A. It is a scenario-based opportunity to interpret the plans and information available in order to experience decision-making under abnormal conditions.

   B. It is a rigorous proof of the methods and solutions with a focus on feasibility, suitability, timings, and costing.

   C. It is a demonstration of a formal data capture process with the purpose of capturing and recording information in real time.

4. The realistic simulation of a command post exercise

   A. should be conducted frequently at first, then less frequently, and drill the same script each time.

   B. should be conducted every few years, depending on organizational need and capability, and sometimes include variations in the script.

   C. should be conducted regularly, usually once or twice a year, and include variations in the script each time.

5. In contrast to an exercise, a test focuses on

   A. technical issues such as timings, accuracy, and suitability.

   B. learning lessons about decision-making and invocation.

   C. evaluating people's skills, interpretations, and tactics.

6. The development and delivery of a BC exercise includes eight main elements, which can generally be thought of as belonging to a preparation phase and an action phase. Which of the following are the three elements of the preparation phase?

   A. Background, buildup, and quality

   B. Background, quality, and safety

   C. Background, history, and kick-off

7. When developing a script for an exercise, why might one choose a case study approach?

   A. Participants learn through an experience directly related to their own business operations.

   B. Participants can learn from both their exercise of the scenario and the actual event on which it is based.

   C. Participants' competency and capability have matured through exercises based on line of business scenarios.

8. Which of the following is a good way to achieve realism during a BC exercise?

   A. Have participants brainstorm possible disruptive situations.

   B. Include emergency services personnel or insurance adjusters.

   C. Emphasize that participants should accept every detail of the scenario as real.

Food for Thought

Earlier chapters built up the case for engaging in a BC program and looked at what you need to know before exploring how to gather that information. You looked at how you should develop and deliver the plans together with ensuring that the right resources will be available as and when they are needed.

Now it is time to start thinking about how your people are going to put all those good ideas into practice. This means getting ready to test the plans and preparing exercises which are going to help your people develop their skills and confidence.

Exercises

Think about how you might apply the knowledge you gained from this chapter in practice. As usual, use your place of work, study, or residence as your case to study.

1. Sequence and style of events.
   - Prepare an outline test and exercise program.
     - What types of test and exercise do you suggest?
     - Why these and not others?
     - In what sequence would you arrange them?
       - Bear in mind the gradient from the perspective of the participants.

2. Frequency and timings.
   - Develop an outline schedule for those tests and exercises.
     - What time of the day, week, month, or year?
     - How long should these various events last?
       - Bear in mind the business calendar and seasons of the year.

3. Objectives and purpose.
   - Produce a possible set of objectives and purpose for each of these event types.
     - What might management want and what might the participants expect?
     - How will you measure or evaluate those objectives?

4. Deliverables.
   - List what will be needed for each of these event types.
     - Who will prepare scripts, instructions, resources, and reports?

5. Scenarios.
   - Decide which scenarios you would suggest for this training program.
     - Are these scenarios relevant to your location and environment?
     - Which ones are the most likely?
     - Which might produce the most important lessons?

Looking Forward

You want to plan successful testing that appears to be properly organized and meets everybody's expectations. You also want it to be effective, which means developing some of the required skill and confidence which is necessary for people to be able and willing to face up to a major disruption. Obviously, you are not going to turn them into battle-hardened troops in one encounter. The test and exercise program is a regular, ongoing set of actions.

Downloadable Business Continuity Toolkit

The downloadable documents from the **Business Continuity Toolkit** are useful in connection with developing scripts and plots for your exercise.

For Additional Reading

You will find a useful example of a BC walkthrough exercise template at
http://www.manchester.gov.uk/downloads/file/5591/business_continuity_plan_exercise_template_pandemic_flu_scenario_ppt

Some thoughts about choosing an appropriate exercise scenario can be found at
http://www.continuitycentral.com/bcte.htm

13

Crisis Management and Communications

Clearly, the framework for decision-making and managing a crisis should be in place long before an emergency occurs. It should be a practiced part of the business continuity (BC) plan. Once the event has actually occurred, it is far too late to develop the framework and figure out how to manage. Indeed, lack of forethought will likely be seen as the cause of, or at least a major contributor to, the failure of the organization.

Ideally, the urgent action regarding control and management of the crisis situation will be dealt with by a team of practical people (for example, if the crisis is caused by a natural disaster, it would be the emergency management team), while the questions, analysis, interpretation, and speculation – from both inside and outside the company – are handled by the crisis communications specialists. Separation of these two principal aspects of a crisis makes it easier to select, prepare, and train the right people. Members of each team can then focus on their own area of expertise, knowing they can rely on others to deal with everything else.

This chapter will help you to:

- ☑ Prepare for the variety of emotional responses to a crisis.

- ☑ Recognize the importance of information during times of apparent difficulty.

- ☑ Deliver appropriate messages and communications to the staff.

- ☑ Deal effectively with the media, customers, and competitors via traditional and social media.

- ☑ Understand and implement the rules of crisis communications.

13.1   Understanding the Dimensions of a Crisis

The British Standards Institution (BSI) and the International Organization for Standardization (ISO) define a *crisis* as "a situation with a high level of uncertainty that disrupts the core activities and/or the credibility of an organization and requires urgent action" (International Organization for Standardization, 2012).

> ... a wide range of reactions to a crisis is perfectly normal....

Bruce T. Blythe defines a crisis as "a critical incident or situation that threatens the core assets of an organization, e.g., people, reputation, brand, trust, financial wellbeing, shareholder value, ability to operate, physical property, intellectual property, or key relationships" (Blythe, 2014, p. 400).

While the term *crisis management* has more than one meaning in different contexts, within the BC community, it has traditionally been taken to mean "protection of the brand and image."

For purposes of this book, concentrating on the principles and practices of BC, I intend to focus on the credibility aspect of crisis – how to protect and manage the company image and reputation. Although the definition makes it sound as though it should be easy to recognize a crisis, the reality is that you need a much clearer idea of its character and scale before you can think about bringing a crisis under control and arranging a satisfactory resolution.

There are four dimensions, or aspects, of crisis which you need to recognize. They are the elements of:

1. Surprise.
2. Uncertainty.
3. Exposure.
4. Urgency.

Each one of these aspects can affect our way of thinking and behaving.

As a BC planner, bear in mind that a wide range of reactions to a crisis is perfectly normal, especially for those who have little or no previous experiences of such things. Anyone who is properly prepared and trained should be able to accept the first two stages, surprise and uncertainty, fairly quickly and move on into the stages of exposure and urgency almost immediately. Their training will have prepared them to meet the need for urgent action while dealing with the atmosphere of interest and speculation.

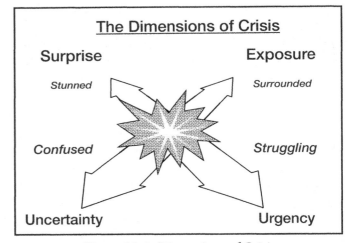

Figure 13-1. Dimensions of Crisis

13.1.1   Surprise

Anything which comes as a *surprise* is a shock to our rational thinking system. Until then we have been able to convince, or delude, ourselves that the world is predictable and controllable, providing we follow the rules. We are also pretty confident that we have figured out the rules and learned to master them. In a business situation your confidence is further boosted by the sense of strength in numbers. All of your fellow team members will have contributed to the group's confidence in their ability to deal with the environment which surrounds them.

Then, quite suddenly, that confidence is betrayed and we are stunned by the unwelcome realization that we are no longer in control. It isn't just about this situation but all those other situations which might also elude our grasp in the foreseeable future.

13.1.2 Uncertainty

Because you are now bewildered, it is difficult to think constructively about the situation and develop a suitable response. You are stuck like a rabbit caught in the glare of a car's headlights, fascinated by the strange situation and unable to see a way forward.

With no previous experience of this sort of situation, you are faced with *uncertainty*. Suddenly the old rules no longer apply; there hasn't been enough time to work out the new rules. It's confusing; you don't know what to do or to whom to turn. Guidance or leadership is desperately needed, but there are conflicting messages. There isn't enough information to be able to decide what to do or say.

...a crisis is all about perception rather than actual occurrences.

Some people will refuse to budge until they can get a much clearer idea of what happened, why it happened, and what are the implications. Others will want to be led out of this situation and be happy to trust anyone who shows initiative, simply because they are unable to figure things out for themselves.

13.1.3 Exposure

You feel *exposed*, suddenly surrounded by people who will either be criticizing your every action or exaggerating the circumstances. There will also be many people depending on you to resolve the situation on their behalf. In other words, there are lots of interested parties but very little assistance or guidance. Everybody seems to be watching and listening or getting in the way, both mentally and physically.

The sense of surprise and the accompanying uncertainty tend to make people feel helpless and useless, causing inactivity and denial. This is quite stressful. However, they soon begin to realize something needs to be done and will want to take some positive action. The adrenalin begins to flow, they regain their energy, and everything seems to speed up again. This is the start of the driven phase of the crisis as opposed to the earlier frozen moments of the initial reaction.

13.1.4 Urgency

With those around you showing an interest of one sort or another and your own desire to get things sorted out, there is a tremendous sense of *urgency*. You're struggling, nothing seems to go right, everything seems difficult or impossible, and yet you are making a superhuman effort. Progress seems to be slow and behind; at every step forward there appears to be another problem or set of problems. The harder you try, the slower the progress, or at least that is how it feels.

However, once you begin to address some of the problems and start to regain confidence, you can move out of the initial deep mood of crisis and recover the ability to think things through. You are ready to take action.

13.2 Communicating with Internal and External Groups

By acting proactively and providing factual information, you can help to ensure an accurate and balanced view of what happened and the company's response. If you are seen to be open and honest about the matter, you can establish yourself as the primary source of information about the company and its actions relating to the emergency. You can also aim to be regarded as the principal source of all information about the incident.

As soon as something has happened which might be, or could become, a crisis, the company should invoke its *crisis management plan*. Even if it turns out to be a false alarm, the *crisis communications team* (discussed in Section 13.3 below) needs to be activated because a crisis is all about perception rather than actual occurrences. The established decision-making framework should then be used to develop a specific strategic response based on the incident and the context in which it has occurred. Although there may be some confusion and all of the information may not be available, the crisis communications team members will need to prepare to meet the demand for a story within a fairly short period of time. They will need to take a number of factors into account, such as:

- The contextual environment at the time.
- The type and scale of the event.
- Likely media interest in the event.
- Public, political, and media reaction to the event.
- Potential interest and reaction by other stakeholders.

Members of two principal groups will be anxious to hear about the incident and its implications:

- *Internal* – those who are in some way directly connected to the organization.
- *External* – those whose only connection is via the media.

13.2.1   The Corporate Statement

All internal and external communications should be derived from a corporate statement that represents the official corporate view of the situation. The crisis communications team should prepare this statement which would then be approved, or endorsed, by the president. In some instances, the board may need to be involved in the approval process. Without a corporate statement no individual should be talking to outsiders about the situation or its implications. Corporate statements should be reviewed, revised, and re-issued on a regular basis until the situation has stabilized and normal operations have been re-established. The frequency of these reviews should reflect the pace and scale of the incident and subsequent developments.

To avoid the possibility of oversights, assumptions, and biases distorting the message, at least three people should be involved in the development of corporate statements. Typically this would be the author aided, or supported, by someone acting as editor or adviser and a third person acting as arbitrator or final authority.

13.2.2   Internal Groups and Staff

The internal group requiring information will include members of staff, associates, suppliers, regulators, stakeholders, and customers. They can be described as identifiable individuals or organizations with a particular interest and a bias towards support and sympathy. The extent of the bias will be determined by the previous relationship and your performance to date. In any case, they will certainly expect to be told what happened and how you are dealing with it *before* they read about it in the newspapers. As soon as it has been established what happened, these people should be given the full facts and an outline of the organization's response.

For internal inquiries, staff briefings should be held at the affected location as soon as it is safe to do so. In any event, this must take place before any information is released to outsiders such as members of the press. The briefing should be delivered by the most senior person available or the person responsible for human resources. Ideally, both of these senior people should be available to answer any questions. Everybody should also be given clear instructions about when and where to report for work or how to keep in touch. It may be necessary to reassure members of staff about the future of the company and their employment. All sorts of rumors might be flying around, especially once the press start sniffing around for an exclusive angle.

Staff members should also be reminded about the need for a single point of contact for all external inquiries. You should instruct them to respond to all external inquiries with this type of statement: "I am not in a position to say what happened. We have a company rule that requires me to refer you to the company spokesman who can be contacted at our head office."

13.2.3   External Groups and the Media

The trade press can be fairly cooperative, especially when advertising revenue is one of their aims. However, news reporters tend to be unsympathetic when seeking an "interesting angle" in the wake of a routine disaster. What is routine for them may be quite disturbing for your spokesperson who gets only one shot at getting the story out correctly.

Unlike your sympathizers and supporters, the media will be concerned only with their own self-interests which are to do with creating, telling, and selling a story. They have no vested interest in your survival, although their readers, listeners, and viewers may include some or all of your friends and allies. Almost certainly their audience will include most, if not all, of your enemies.

Among the new challenges…is *social media…*

While many companies have a marketing or public relations (PR) department responsible for putting across the corporate message under normal conditions, that department may not have a suitable mechanism in place for dealing with an out-of-line situation. If your PR department has not yet been tested by a crisis, part of your BC framework will be putting the structures in place that will prepare your communications experts to handle this new challenge.

Among the new challenges for your in-house communications staff is *social media* – unregulated electronic applications that let users create and share information to a wide audience almost instantly. As Blythe observes, "Any organization of the future that hasn't fully embraced and participated in social media with expertise will do so at their own peril" (Blythe, 2014, p. 347).

13.2.3.1 Media Policy

In general, the corporate media policy should be one of:

▸ Cooperation with the media, where it is of mutual benefit.
▸ Prompt dissemination of information to the public.
▸ Provision of timely responses to all inquiries.
▸ Using the media to propagate key corporate messages.

13.2.3.2 Ground Rules for Dealing with the Media

Wherever possible, the crisis communications team should build on the existing organizational systems rather than try to invent something new or bypass what already exists. This means making use of all the available known contacts which will probably have been established during the course of normal PR. Mistakes in releasing information about an incident can damage your business and increase your losses very quickly; thus, a clear media policy should be an important part of your BC plan.

Be prompt and proactive: By being proactive, PR will be demonstrating the company's willingness to communicate, which is a tacit sign of having nothing to hide. A prompt and proactive response to external interests actively demonstrates the company's firm commitment to the response. It is also an opportunity to assure the public, before gossip starts and rumors spread, that all possible mitigating actions are being taken. By taking the lead and offering accurate and realistic information it is possible to reduce and even correct any negative speculative reporting. In this manner, the crisis communications team can take positive steps to protect the company's longer-term interests. The spokesperson should be as professional as possible in approach, providing the media with written copy, using appropriate language, and stating the facts as they are known at that point in time.

> It is important for the organization to "speak with one voice,"…

Be an authoritative source of facts: The team needs to become established as the prime authoritative source of information about the company and its actions relating to the emergency and, if possible, to be the authoritative source of all information about the incident. This can be achieved by presenting a consistent and accurate account of the facts of the emergency itself, as well as the resultant events and the response to date. The team's response should describe what the company is doing to bring the emergency under control and to support the personnel and families involved. It is best to refrain from outlining what the company plans to do; simply report the facts without trying to predict the future or the outcome of the current activities.

Where it is appropriate, reference should be made to the company's excellent track record in this connection. Reference should also be made to the BC program, which has prepared and trained an emergency response team, ready to deal with just such an eventuality.

Be the single contact: It is important for the organization to "speak with one voice," which means a single point of contact for all external inquiries. You should also aim to align the needs and interests of the media with those of the organization itself.

13.3   Crisis Communications Team

Your crisis communications team is the small group of senior executives or directors who act as the voice and personality of the enterprise in protecting the corporate brand, image, and reputation. The members of this team and their responsibilities need to be detailed in your BC plan and the communications team should participate fully in all BC drills and exercises.

The team may also be responsible for informing, reassuring, and liaising with various interested parties such as:

- Regulators.
- Investors.
- Families.
- Business partners.
- Customers.
- Suppliers.

13.3.1   Creating the Team

During a crisis, the team works best if membership is limited to a relatively small number of people who can handle everything between them. This means they should be of the highest caliber, trained well, and have skills and knowledge that complement each other rather than duplicate or overlap. At a minimum, the team would consist of a spokesperson and a media adviser, supported by an administrator to type up the draft messages and manage the logistics, enabling the other members to focus on what to say and how to express it. If the team should ever get to be larger than six it is liable to be slowed down and its messages diluted.

The requisite team should be drawn from a cadre of trained specialists which would include:

- Company spokespersons.
- Legal advisers.
- Media and PR advisers.
- Financial advisers.
- Operational advisers.
- Administrative support.

A consistent message to all parties is very important...

You will probably need only one person from each discipline active on the crisis team, although you may want to designate alternates. Indeed, it may not always be necessary for all of these disciplines to be represented. A lot depends on the actual circumstances of the day. The actual composition of the team would be determined by the *crisis director*, based on availability and the needs of the moment.

A small team of high grade specialists is likely to respond more effectively and efficiently than a larger group with wider experience and differing opinions. In some ways, a team of one would be ideal, but it would be an onerous burden to lay upon a single person, no matter how competent or important the person might appear to be.

A consistent message to all parties is very important and the need to maintain good corporate relations, at all times, must not be overlooked in the rush to prepare a press release. The linkages and systems within an organization that deliver information and messages during an emergency do not spontaneously occur; they have to be defined, tested, and rehearsed well in advance of the need to put them into practice.

13.3.2 Responsibilities

The responsibilities within the crisis communications team are to:

- Develop and deliver a corporate statement.
- Handle journalists' inquiries.
- Prepare and distribute press releases.
- Issue background information.
- Anticipate questions from, and prepare answers for, all potential stakeholders.
- Deliver key messages, drafted under guidance from advisers.
- Brief the spokesperson and support him or her during delivery of the key messages.
- Coordinate outgoing communication with the emergency response team.

While the crisis communications team is handling its issues, the members of the intelligence section of the emergency response team should also be monitoring the media in its various forms. They should summarize the reporting, including the tone and attitudes, to the crisis communications team on a regular basis, together with updates on the incident itself. This will ensure that the spokesperson and his or her support team are fully aware of the facts, emerging opinions, and reactions.

While it is useful for the emergency response team to organize and coordinate company press conferences and arrange company participation in joint conferences with outside groups, such as emergency services, that team does not normally do the talking. The actual delivery is the exclusive territory of the crisis communications team.

13.4   Managing the Media During a Crisis

It helps to ensure a satisfactory outcome if your people follow this simple protocol when attempting to manage or control communications during a crisis:

1. Always act responsibly and ethically.
2. Always act quickly and effectively.
3. Always communicate openly and honestly.
4. Always work together as a team.
5. Keep staff informed at every step of the way.

It can also be very helpful to prepare *position papers* on any skeletons which might be in the closet and to document any near misses and how they were handled. This work should be carried out as part of the preparation and training for the crisis communications team members so they are familiar with the history and ready to deal with whatever might happen in the future.

Because it is their line of business, the media have very effective communications systems and information management systems. Their constant aim is to gather and disseminate information, illustrating and commenting as necessary, within their relevant deadlines. They will use all of the many available sources to build their story and it is best if they get information from the company quickly and easily since other sources may not necessarily have the company's best interests at heart. One of their regular sources of background information is a *clippings file* where they hold a copy of everything that has been published, and not retracted, in the past. This enables them to prepare the basis of a story before their reporter has even arrived on the scene.

> **...bear in mind that the Internet as a news channel observes few of these rules....**

The media will all be competing to be first with the news and meet their deadlines. Ideally, they will want to witness and describe the facts of the incident as they develop. Meanwhile, they will be gathering information on casualties and other human interest issues.

Wherever possible, media writers will want to include *human interest stories* based on particular individuals, bringing the stories to life with interviews and quotes in combination with their version of the background information. They will certainly want to show dramatic pictures if they can. They will be looking for a unique and exclusive angle on the story, interpreting the facts for the benefit of their audience. This will lead them to try to establish, and speculate on, the cause and the contribution of those whom they deem to be responsible.

The media also have a tendency to try to link the story to any other items which might be on their agenda.

Take account of deadlines when timing your press releases, interviews, and conferences. Generally speaking, radio broadcasters will need less than half an hour to prepare to go to air. Television, on the other hand, prefers to have about an hour to finalize news items. Although radio news items are often broadcast direct to air, TV is reluctant to take such chances unless the story warrants it. Some newspapers will work to tight deadlines, but their overall process tends to be rather slower and the focus will tend to be on covering the story in more depth for tomorrow's readership. This means they will want to capture more detail and are prepared to spend more time on elaborating the story. However, bear in mind that the Internet as a news channel observes few of these rules, and you need to be prepared for the "news" to be posted on social media by employees, observers, and others. Thus, it is important to make the website and social media part of your media strategy. (See Section 13.4.2.3 below.)

Answering the basic media questions: Journalists are trained to seek out the answers to five basic questions – the five Ws – when working on a story. This is their way of ensuring they have covered the facts before they start to embroider and weave their own variations or fantasies. These key questions are:

1. Who?
2. What?
3. Where?
4. When?
5. Why?

– And a final sixth question: How?

Once reporters have covered the basics and a clearer picture of the incident emerges, they will move on to drilling down for more detail with their follow-up questions, something like:

- What action has been taken so far?
- What are the effects and the implications – both in the short-term and long-term?
- What are the historical facts about the location, the company, and how it works?
- Can we have some basic statistics on this type of event, this company, and this industry?

13.4.1   Controlled Media Response

As far as possible, the crisis communications team needs to control the manner, style, and contents of the reporting of any incident. This means understanding the needs of the media and playing the game accordingly. There are several useful tactics which can be employed to advantage. At the very outset it is likely that no one will have a clear idea of exactly what happened, and so it would seem reasonable to try to buy a little time immediately after the incident. However, the media will want to have further details as soon as possible. If they don't get more details from you, they will use whatever they can obtain from other sources, such as social media.

Calls from the media must never be taken in operational command and control rooms.

13.4.1.1 Holding Statements

A holding statement is a simple acknowledgment of the fact that an incident has occurred. It can be based on a pre-formatted statement for completion immediately after an incident has occurred. Because of its simplicity, it can be ready and available for use as the basis of the initial response to any telephone inquiries from stakeholders or the media. It is a means of buying time while the situation is being assessed and the full media response is activated. (You will find a suggested layout for a suitable holding statement in the downloadable **Business Continuity Toolkit**.)

13.4.2   Handling Media Telephone Calls

Where possible, media calls are best taken by experienced PR people who are able to handle any questions with a degree of confidence based on their experience and knowledge of the company. Where this is not possible, then any call handlers must be trained or specialist consultants should be engaged. Consultants will need some induction training or briefing so that they can understand the corporate background and the particular company needs.

Calls from the media must never be taken in operational command and control rooms. Inquiries should be redirected to dedicated media response people working in a separate room. If calls are received before any of these people are in place, then the holding statement should be used as the basis for dealing with such calls.

13.4.2.1 Preparation for Media Calls

Before people at your site can be expected to handle calls from the media or any other interested parties, they need to be briefed properly and prepared for the task.

They should be given the opportunity to think about, and discuss with other team members, the types of questions to expect and how they should answer them. Perhaps they might even practice their responses by role playing – taking it in turns to act as both inquirer and responder. This will give them the chance to get a feel for the lines of questioning they might have to deal with.

It is important for everyone to be working from the latest press release. They should be given the time to read the press release carefully, making sure they understand its contents before attempting to answer any inquiries. All replies to inquiries must be based on information prepared and cleared by the crisis management team or the press office. This information might be available in the form of messages on status boards, press releases, or background information.

All those who are likely to be engaged in this type of activity should be given a clear understanding of scope of the stakeholder inquiries they are expected to deal with and instructions about what they should do if they receive inquiries which are outside that scope.

13.4.2.2 Response Protocol

All calls into the media response team should be answered politely with a clear, but anonymous, indication of the department and a willingness to help the inquirer; for example, "Good morning/afternoon/evening, this is the Company Press Office, how can I help you?"

Here are some basic instructions which should be followed by all those who are engaged in media response over the telephone:

- Make a note of who is calling and whom they represent. It is all too easy to forget people's names and details when you are dealing with a series of similar calls.
- Always try to be and sound helpful and positive.
- Keep calm, polite, and courteous, even if the caller seems hostile.
- If anybody asks, say you are an authorized company spokesman. You may give them your name, but you should not reveal your normal job, even when pressed.
- Think carefully about what you say and assume everything you say is liable to appear in print or be broadcast.
- Defend your colleagues and the company at all times without giving away information which has not been cleared for release.
- Refer all inquiries from relatives to the HR or personnel team.
- If you are at all unsure, put the caller on hold while you check the facts or ask for help from the team supervisor.
- Use the background information which has been provided to assist you if you are short of incident information.

▸ Log each call carefully with name, organization, type of inquiry, time, and contact number if given.

▸ Avoid offering to call back unless it is absolutely necessary.

▸ Don't offer or use any unofficial information.

▸ Never say anything "off the record."

▸ Never get angry, even if the caller seems rude or hostile.

▸ Don't answer if you are unsure.

▸ Do not speculate.

▸ Do not give your personal views or opinions.

▸ Do not answer hypothetical questions.

▸ Do not comment on any other company's business or the role of other organizations such as the emergency services.

▸ Make sure that you call back anyone where you promised to do so. Obviously, it is best to avoid making the offer wherever possible, since follow-up calls can become a huge undertaking.

▸ Brief your supervisor on any difficult or unusual calls.

▸ Ensure that any inquiries which you believe to be beyond your scope are redirected appropriately.

News on social media is transmitted instantly.

13.4.2.3 Social Media

While traditional legacy media – newspapers, magazines, radio, television – offer well organized schedules, formats, and deadlines, those traditional rules do not apply to social media, such as Facebook, Twitter, blogs, and websites. The differences you will find in dealing with social media are that:

▸ News on social media is transmitted instantly.

▸ The "reporter" is often an ordinary person, not a professional journalist. Because the person is not a professional journalist, the average citizen may find this news more believable.

▸ The news is not necessarily edited or checked before it is posted.

▸ The news goes out to a worldwide audience on the Internet, where it is also picked up by reporters from the traditional media as a source material for their "stories."

Not only will you need to monitor social media carefully, but part of your social media strategy will be to make sure the correct story is released as quickly and widely as possible. Lukaszewski recommends a blog with links to your social media site (e.g., Facebook page) attached to your website to hold your news releases (Lukaszewski, 2013, p. 226).

13.4.3 Press Releases

Press releases are used to provide information to the media and other interested parties who do not merit a personalized response to their inquiries. Press releases are a formal statement issued by the company and as such they represent the company; therefore, they must be clear, accurate, and timely.

All messages of this nature should be drafted in conjunction with the corporate legal department, or at least approved by it, before release or distribution. Clearance with third parties should also be considered whenever their names are specifically mentioned and you must obtain clearance with the police if there are any casualties.

As a general rule, the early press releases should simply be confined to statements of fact and can therefore be authorized at a local level. Any subsequent press releases attempting to express the corporate view or describe the corporate response may be drafted at the local level but they should be approved at a higher level.

13.4.3.1 Preparation and Content

The basic requirement of the media will be to obtain some facts and this is what the release should provide them with. There is no need for fancy or elaborate prose; the language should be accurate and concise. The tone should be professional, indicating concern about the damage and any danger to the health and safety of staff, clients, or members of the public.

Firstly, the release should explain the nature of the incident which has led to the crisis. Provide them with facts about the location and the date and time the incident occurred or started. The extent of the damage or the areas affected should be described but only so far as the facts have been established. If the details have not been confirmed then they should not be released. In the unfortunate circumstances where people have been injured, the number of casualties should be stated but no other details should be given.

The press release should go on to describe the actions being taken by the company to limit the damage and contain the effects of the incident. This should take account of the dangers and consequences with regard to people, property, and the environment.

The final part of the press releases should report on the progress of the response and explain the effect this incident will have on the regular business operations or services provided to clients.

Reference should be made to any third parties who are affected by the incident and how the company is working with them to meet the common needs and interests. It is also important to acknowledge the cooperation and support which is being received from other parties such as the emergency services.

Any statements which have been issued by other parties should be included or referenced.

13.4.3.2 Layout and Style

Traditional printed press releases – whether printed on paper or delivered electronically – should be timed, dated, and printed on headed stationery, or equivalent electronic format, with a press release number shown as the heading or part of the heading. Subsequent press releases should all be identified and numbered in the same way.

The basic rules apply, whether your releases are on paper or posted on your company website and distributed via the Internet. As Noël Francine Kepler advises, "Your social media strategy shouldn't be like reinventing the wheel. It should look and feel like the community materials you are already using. Use the same logos, colors, and fonts. This way your 'brand' is recognized and people can easily connect your community efforts to your web presence" (Kepler, 2010).

All press releases should be complete and make sense without reference to previous releases or other documents. Successive releases should include what has been said previously and go on to expand on that information. Anyone should be able to pick up the full history and the current situation from the latest press release.

Obviously, it is important to express regret or concern where appropriate, but there is no need to appear to be groveling or weak. Acknowledge the sterling work of the emergency and rescue services and any others who may have been involved in dealing with the incident and its effects.

Press releases should be written in the same kind of language as you would expect to find in the newspapers. Don't try to write the headlines; other people are paid and trained to do that. Stick with a bland and simple description, such as "Office Fire" or "Store Closed."

If you are going to mention other organizations (e.g., partners, contractors, authorities), it is polite, and sometimes contractually important, to advise them first and pass them a copy of the release.

The key facts and messages should always appear at the top of the press release. When publications are working to a tight deadline, there is tendency for sub-editors to cut from the bottom upwards, seeking to reduce the copy to the right number of words, rather than spend time exploring alternative wordings and trying to distill the essence of the unfolding drama. They want to be able to cut straight to the facts.

13.4.3.3 Points to Avoid

▸ At all costs, avoid any form of speculation or prediction about what might happen in the future. The same is true of any estimates of costs or timeframes.

▸ Do not give the names or details of any casualties.

▸ Do not refer to the cause or reasons for the incident. It is sufficient to say that inquiries are being conducted and to name who is carrying out those investigations.

...stick to the delivery of key messages and facts...

▸ Avoid making any statements or references concerning liability or negligence. Also make sure there is nothing which can be interpreted as such.

▸ Especially avoid any suggestion that another party might be, or should be, held to account.

▸ Make sure the language used is unemotional, couched in everyday layman's terms. Avoid using technical phrases, jargon, or acronyms. If acronyms have to be used, they must be explained, e.g., "Business Continuity Plan (or BCP for short)."

13.4.4 Interviews

Sometimes, it may be useful for a senior spokesperson to represent the company in an interview with the media. Interviews may be held face-to-face with the journalist before the cameras or they may be remote conversations over a radio or telephone link. Television and radio interviews are normally recorded and edited before release, but occasionally they may be broadcast live.

The strategy in such interviews must be to stick to the delivery of key messages and facts rather than be driven or manipulated by the interviewer's questions. There will only be time to talk about two or three things which need to be those key messages, prepared and agreed upon in advance. Before the interview the spokesperson should write down the positive and the negative aspects of the incident and their implications. It is important to know what *not* to say.

An interview might take the form of a short holding statement or it could be a more extended statement but with no questions. Sometimes there will be a need, or opportunity, for a full statement followed by a question and answer session. In this case, the spokesperson must be trained and prepared to deal with any questions which may be asked. Basically, this type of in-depth interview is an *ad hoc* press conference.

The communications team should always be prepared with key messages which spokespersons need to get across to the media and the general public on behalf of the company. Key messages must be developed early in an emergency as part of the media response strategy and should be supported, wherever possible, by tangible evidence.

Your spokespersons should become fluent at what is known as "bridging," which is moving the conversation towards another subject area such as a key message. Consider these examples:

"Yes ... and in addition ... *key message.*"
"No ... let me explain ... *key message.*"
"I don't know that ... but what I do know is ... *key message.*"
"It used to be like that ... but nowadays ... *key message.*"

It is also important to be able to flag or emphasize the key messages with statements like, "The most important fact is ...." or "It boils down to this ...." or "This is the real issue ...."

13.4.4.1 Press Conferences

The ultimate form of engagement with the media is the full blown press conference which may, perhaps, be organized by someone in the emergency services. Press conferences provide an excellent opportunity to demonstrate the company's willingness to engage in communication with the rest of the world about what has happened and how they are dealing with it. It is a means of promoting a positive image to all of the media outlets simultaneously. This can certainly reduce the pressure on the telephone response team.

The press conference itself should be message-driven.

Several factors can influence the decision to hold a press conference, but the key consideration is the amount of media interest being shown. You will also need to think carefully about the amount and the accuracy of the information which will be available in time for the press conference. This availability will be influenced by the timing of the event in relation to the media's deadlines.

It is also important to realize that journalists will press for a good story without mercy. So the potential benefits do have to be weighed against the possible downside if the situation gets out of hand and they get more than you bargained for.

The venue should be separate from, but reasonably close to, the company's premises in order to prevent journalists from gaining access to areas where they may see or hear more than they should. The press conference must be advertised in sufficient time for the journalists and their camera crews to get there and set up.

The press conference itself should be message-driven. The spokesperson should be carefully selected and rehearsed by the use of some prepared questions and answers before he or she is exposed to any interrogation by the members of the press.

13.4.4.2 Guidelines for Spokespersons

A number of preparatory steps take place before a spokesperson is ready to speak on behalf of the company.

The spokesperson needs:

- To be fully briefed on the facts of the incident and the key messages.
- To be fully aware of the company's safety and BC policies and track record.
- A carefully prepared opening statement.
- To know the areas in which the media can help, such as broadcasting contact numbers or warnings.
- An appropriate attire. For TV appearances, it is always best to avoid wearing white or red and anything with strong stripes. It also helps if the spokesperson can manage without glasses to avoid reflections from the lighting.

Once the spokesperson is prepared and properly briefed, the spokesperson should try to be clear in his or her own mind regarding what needs to be said and be ready to handle any awkward questions.

When in front of the assembled press, the spokesperson needs to remember these instructions:

> ▶ Be aware that what is said is important but *how* it is said is critical.

> ▶ Speak in ordinary conversational tones and be brief. Long sentences and complex arguments must be avoided. Otherwise, audience members may think they are being blinded with science in an attempt to cover up something. Never assume the interviewer is either well informed or ill informed.

> ▶ Be authoritative, remember that you are the expert, and try to keep it interesting and positive.

> ▶ Summarize the facts briefly, stating what has happened, what the company is doing about it, and how you personally feel about the incident.

> ▶ Show human concern. Any facts about fatalities, casualties, and missing people are very sensitive, and must be presented with extreme care.

> ▶ Deliver any key messages early in the interview, pausing between statements to improve the chance of them remaining in as part of the broadcast.

...use of the corporate website to distribute information is important...

> ▶ Be seen to be open, helpful, and caring, but not emotional. Always stick to the truth and never lie.

> ▶ Provide praise wherever it is due, e.g., emergency services, response teams, and members of the public.

> ▶ Stall if necessary, but don't speculate or answer hypothetical questions.

> ▶ Provide assurance that you are doing everything you can in conjunction with other responders to respond to the emergency.

> ▶ Provide background information to fill any void until accurate information is available.

> ▶ Use simple language and avoid technical and industry jargon. Don't use acronyms.

> ▶ In response to any criticism of the company's safety record, be prepared to accept the criticism with a response such as, "Yes, we have obviously had a clear breach of our own safety standards. We work hard to improve our performance and have succeeded until now; so we are especially concerned at what has happened today. We have already started our own investigation into the causes, and that is a matter of the greatest urgency for us."

> ▶ Never attempt to place or accept blame, accuse anyone of negligence, discuss liability, or prejudge the situation in any way.

> ▶ Never say "No comment" or use one-word answers. Such responses are unhelpful and antagonize journalists. In response to questions, you should always try to be courteous and helpful. Never get angry in the face of hostile questioning.

> ▶ Never discuss anything "off the record." All conversations are liable to be quoted even if the camera or the tape recorder has been switched off.

> ▶ Stop any line of questioning which is not directly relevant to the issue at hand.

If the company is clearly at fault in some way, go public with the facts as soon as you are sure of them and demonstrate positive plans to rectify the situation. Ensure what you have said is relayed quickly to any other company spokespersons.

13.4.4.3 Make Use of the Internet

The use of the corporate website to distribute information is important since it gives the opportunity for journalists to build their stories from pre-packaged information. It also provides access for a wider stakeholder base to get the information directly from the source. Stakeholders can be directed to the website.

Items which can be posted include:

- Press releases.
- Fast facts relating to the company.
- Photographs of the incident taken by the company.
- Video clips of statements given by company spokespeople.
- Audio statements made by company spokespeople.

The material and format for posting on the Internet is a derivative of the press statement but not necessarily a direct copy. Lukaszewski advises that you be prepared in advance with a "dark site," a special page that can be opened from the primary website's home page. This is a site that is fully populated with necessary information – such as emergency information and contact lists – and kept "dark," only to be brought online in an emergency to be the source of accurate information on fast-breaking events (Lukaszewski, 2013, pp. 135-138).

13.4.4.4 Prepare Fast Facts for Background

The following are examples of the type of fact sheets (or "backgrounders") that should be pre-produced for issue to the media when appropriate:

- History of the company.
- The company corporate structure.
- Location diagrams.
- Location photographs.
- Facts and figures.
- The company safety and environmental policy statements.
- The company safety and environmental records.
- CVs of corporate executives.
- Photographs of corporate executives and key managers looking serious, *not* smiling or laughing.

13.4.4.5 Avoid Door-Stepping Journalists

Sometimes, journalists will gather outside and try to engage people in conversation as they go in and out of the building. If your spokesperson has to deal with this type of situation, he or she should stay close to the front door to make it easy to just step back and retire behind the door once the interview is over. Anyone else who is caught by the press should refrain from making any comment, assuring the journalists that an official spokesperson will be making a statement as soon as information becomes available.

Self-Examination Questions

1. A crisis has four dimensions: surprise, uncertainty, exposure, and urgency. What are the implications of uncertainty for leadership during a crisis?

   A. It is necessary to wait until all the facts are in before making a decision.

   B. It is necessary to step back from leadership, deferring to those who have more information.

   C. It is necessary to make decisions even when information is incomplete.

2. When a crisis has occurred or may have occurred, what is the most important reason to activate the crisis communications team?

   A. By proactively providing factual information, the team establishes itself as the primary source of information and can manage how the organization is perceived.

   B. By implementing a lockdown on communications to internal and external stakeholders, the team ensures that information about the crisis is kept confidential.

   C. By developing a believable story about what happened, the team can present a version of reality that will represent the organization in the best possible light.

3. Which of the following statements is true about the corporate statement during a crisis?

   A. The corporate statement should be written by a single individual.

   B. All internal and external statements should be based on the corporate statement.

   C. Once the corporate statement is issued, it should not be revised.

4. The crisis communications team should be

   A. as large as possible in order to include people with all the information about the situation.

   B. a team of one, ideally the CEO, in order to avoid the possibility of departures from the message.

   C. a small team of highly trained specialists in PR and other fields in order to respond more effectively and efficiently.

5. What is a primary concern that members of the news media have when covering a story?

   A. Reporting facts with a minimum of drama

   B. Presenting a discrete event, separate from past events or current trends

   C. Meeting their deadline for producing or publishing the story

6. A press release should

   A. include facts about the incident but not describe the company's position or response.

   B. be written in a professional tone and confine itself to known facts.

   C. not be vetted by the legal department, law enforcement, or company officials who are named.

7. When a spokesperson communicates to the media, he or she should be adept at "bridging." What is bridging?

   A. Using technology to send a message to multiple social media platforms

   B. Using speculation to make the news story more interesting and ensure coverage

   C. Using phrases to transition from the question asked to a key message

8. During a crisis, the organization should

   A. use its website to post press releases, fact sheets, and audio-video produced by the organization.

   B. establish a newsgroup on its website to allow people to post eyewitness reports and chat about the incident.

   C. keep all information about the incident and the organization's response off its website.

Food for Thought

Previous chapters looked at how you plan for, prepare for, and deal with aspects of a business disruption. Before you move on to other aspects, take a few moments to reflect on the substance of this chapter.

Exercises

As in our previous practical exercises, imagine how you would expect your colleagues to deal with a potential crisis, using your place of work, study, or residence as the target of the world's attention.

1. The crisis communications team.
   > Who would you put on your ideal crisis communications team?
      ⌁ Include a selection of alternatives to allow for absences, relief, and support duties.

2. Training and preparation.
   > How would you train and prepare these people?
      ⌁ What tools or props would you offer them?

3. Guidance and templates.
   > Can you prepare a set of guidelines for your crisis communications team?
      ⌁ Who are its audiences?
      ⌁ What are its responsibilities?

4. The emergency response team might come under attack or criticism.
   > Can you make a short list of what the issues might be?
   > Can you suggest what the responses should be?

5. The crisis communications team will benefit from some draft statements.
   > Can you offer a draft holding statement for its first response?
   > Can you offer a template for a proper press release?

Looking Forward

You should now be in a position to play a leading role in the development and delivery of an effective BC program. Next, this book will focus on how to deliver effective exercises and refine your plans and preparations through good governance.

Downloadable Business Continuity Toolkit

Included in the downloadable **Business Continuity Toolkit** are support materials for this chapter, including samples and guidelines that you may adapt for your own use.

References

Blythe, B. (2014). *Blindsided: A manager's guide to crisis leadership* (2nd ed.). Brookfield, CT: Rothstein Publishing.

International Organization for Standardization (2012). *ISO 22300:2012 Societal security. Terminology.* Geneva, Switzerland: International Organization for Standardization.

Kepler, N. F. (2010). *Social media strategy for emergency management.* Retrieved from http://content.yudu.com/Library/A1nnfk/SocialMediaStrategyf/resources/index.htm

Lukaszewski, J. E. (2013). *Lukaszewski on crisis communication: What your CEO needs to know about reputation risk and crisis management.* Brookfield, CT: Rothstein Publishing.

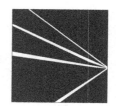

14

Exercise Management and Delivery

Previous chapters covered the steps for you to prepare a draft plan. You have learned about development and delivery of a full set of business continuity (BC) plans together with the requisite resources. You have also learned who should be involved in responding to a business disruption and have seen the need for these people to gain some practical experience.

In Chapter 12, you saw what it would take to develop a suitable exercise. Until the elements of that plan have been tested properly, your people will not be ready to recognize and deal with an emergency or disaster if the need should ever arise. Now it is time to look at how you should organize, manage, and deliver such an event.

This chapter will help you to:

- ☑ Organize an exercise delivery team.

- ☑ Prepare all the exercise delivery materials.

- ☑ Manage and control an effective BC exercise.

- ☑ Provide feedback and apply the lessons to be learned.

14.1   Exercise Delivery

The eight elements of exercise development and delivery that were discussed in Chapter 12 are shown in Figure 14-1. Before the event, the preparation phase is concerned with the development of the exercise materials and is comprised of *background, buildup,* and *quality,* covered in Chapter 12. The action phase, covered in this chapter, is concerned with the subsequent delivery of those materials as a useful exercise with beneficial results and includes *delivery, safety, lessons, history,* and *kick-off.*

The delivery of a realistic and meaningful exercise is probably the most important and demanding set of tasks in the whole of the BC program. Such an event depends upon good preparation, teamwork, timing, and direction. Here we are using the term *direction* to imply good management and facilitation as the story unfolds. As leader of the exercise, you can't expect to remain invisible; however, the participants should be more concerned with the problems they are facing than what you are doing or thinking.

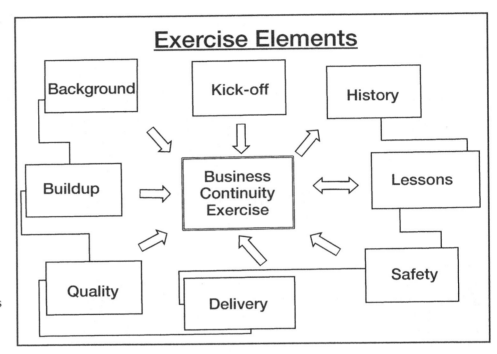

Figure 14-1. Exercise Elements

14.1.1   Exercise Coordination and Control

Good coordination and control is the secret to the successful delivery of a valuable and rewarding exercise. An exercise should be approached as a friendly contest between the two teams.

Delivery team: This group is responsible for the development, delivery, and control of the exercise. Group members should also ensure that no unnecessary risks are introduced and that health and safety are not compromised.

Response team: This group is expected to respond to, and deal with, the scenario which is presented by the delivery team. Group members should work together using the plans, procedures, and facilities which are available to them.

> **...allocate the roles and tasks to those who are best suited for the part.**

At the end of the day, the prize for both teams is more skill, more confidence, and an improved plan. The scale and complexity of the event will help to determine the size of the delivery team. The size of the response team depends largely on the plan and the scope of the exercise.

» *Coordination* is all about making sure everything and everyone work together, all in the right place, at the right time, according to the script. It involves paying attention to the details and maintaining good liaison between the various groups and individuals.

▶ *Control* is all about managing the whole affair so the event runs smoothly, correcting any problems as they occur. Good control looks easy because it hides the difficulties. Bad control looks hard because it highlights the difficulties.

Figure 14-2 shows the typical setup of teams and supporting cast.

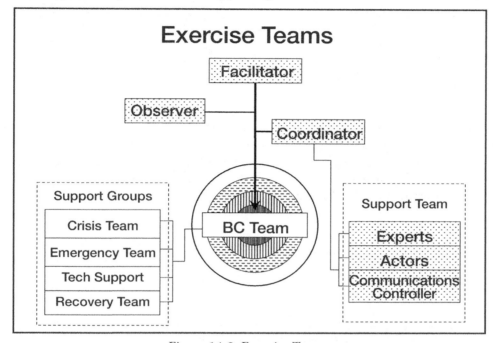

Figure 14-2. Exercise Teams

Look at each of the following roles and notice how they work together to deliver the final product. If you understand the role and the ideal characteristics associated with it, you will be able to allocate the roles and tasks to those who are best suited for the part.

Facilitator: This should be someone who is knowledgeable and self-confident. He or she needs to be a good leader and able to improvise without showing any outward signs of concern. This person is the central figure who has the whole picture and can be likened to the conductor of the orchestra: someone who knows the score and brings it to life. Often the facilitator will take the title of exercise director or exercise controller; these are descriptions which reflect the level of responsibility and empowerment for this key job.

> The coordinator... sets the tone and makes sure everyone is playing to the same tune.

The role of the facilitator is to manage the delivery team and direct the exercise on the day and take charge of the overall project. More specifically, the facilitator's duties include overall responsibility for:

▶ Objectives and purpose.

▶ Plot and script development.

▶ Selection of venue.

▶ Security of the event.

▶ Delivery and feedback.

Coordinator: This should be someone who understands what is expected and helps to make it happen. This person needs to be familiar with the organization and its environment. The coordinator is the principal support for the facilitator and, like the leader of the orchestra, sets the tone and makes sure everyone is playing to the same tune.

The coordinator's role is to organize and arrange things, such as notifying and assembling all the people, together with the necessary facilities and resources. He or she will be expected to liaise between the various teams, resolve any minor problems, and act as principal support for the project. On the day of the exercise, the coordinator is there to aid the smooth running of the event. Specific duties include:

- Managing the logistics.
- Communications.
- Prompts and props.
- Coaching the players where necessary.
- Ensuring harmony and progress on the day.

Observer: The observers (usually more than one person functions in this role) are another important part of the delivery team. They are expected to play a passive role, watching how the response teams react and work together. In effect, they are like talent scouts, or critics, comparing today's performance with the ideal. Their role is to provide an independent, unbiased viewpoint, report on how the objectives were met, capture any learning points, and make you aware of any areas for improvement.

An observer's duties include:

- Noticing what happens.
  - ❑ Discussion subjects and relevance.
  - ❑ Decisions made or orders given.
  - ❑ Achievements and progress.
- Comparing the results with the objectives.
- Providing positive feedback at the end of the exercise.
- Reporting on the overall performance.

Observation is a simple yet demanding role. The correct approach is for observers to understand what is happening and why; record what is happening and why; and, report what is relevant or important.

Therefore, observers need to know the purpose and objectives of the exercise and understand the script. Ideally, they should be working with a checklist which has been derived from the objectives.

Observers should know what is happening throughout the exercise but often there will be multiple streams of activity as different teams or groups grapple with separate problems or issues. You may need several observers to cover all of these discussions. It is better to have too many than too few people watching and listening. If an observer is unclear about something, he or she should make a note or ask a question discretely without interrupting the flow.

Support Groups: There are many people you might call on to join the supporting cast, playing their normal role such as:

- Members of the press.
- Customers and suppliers.
- Salvage, repair, and property advisers.
- Authorities, regulators, and inspectors.
- Emergency services.

However, it is often easier, and perhaps preferable, to ask people from other departments to play these parts.

They can also act as representatives of other companies, members of the public, customers, staff, or shareholders.

Where there is a need for expert advice on any particular subject you have a number of choices. You can research the matter and pretend to be an expert or have one of your team do this for you. Another way of presenting the answers is to prepare an expert's report which can be provided to the participants at the right time. If you want to allow the participants to have a live discussion with an expert, you can arrange to call someone who has been properly briefed. To add a further touch of realism, you can allow the participants to call a nominated expert using an agreed upon password in order to ensure there is no confusion with reality. Be very careful with this approach and make sure the expert is properly briefed beforehand.

14.1.2   Potential Problems

During the course of the preparation and delivery of an exercise you can anticipate several potential problems which you should identify in advance and be ready to react. Forewarned is forearmed, as the saying goes.

Challenges to Realism or Value: The possibility of challenges about the realism or the value of the event was covered earlier. To deal with this, research the facts in order to maintain credibility with regard to the realism of the scenario and refer the challenger back to the purpose of the event. If the event meets its purpose, then there can be no argument about the value, which has, after all, been endorsed by senior management.

> If the event meets its purpose, then there can be no argument about the value....

Substitute for Key Player: Another apparent difficulty you might encounter is when one of the participants sends a substitute. However, once you stop to think about it, this isn't a problem, since it is a realistic possibility. This deputy may be the one who is available on the day – so he or she also needs the training. Hopefully, the key player will attend the next exercise. It is worth making a note in your report that while a number of substitutes have been trained, not all of the key players have been exposed to the practical experience of an exercise. You might recommend that there is an obvious need for another exercise in the near future.

Absenteeism: A more worrying problem is absenteeism, when some people are unable or unwilling to attend. Your first question has to be about whether the plan actually allows for this. If the plan does allow for certain people to be missing at the time of an incident, then you need to be sure these absences are adequately covered, in terms of numbers and areas of responsibility. However, if these absences mean the plan may not work, then you have to address the mismatch somehow. In your report, you should include a list of those who were invited and those who were absent.

Dominating Players: Sometimes one participant tends to dominate the exercise; this person seems to have all the answers, all of the time. Try to accept this enthusiasm as a good thing; praise the person's expertise and willingness to help. Explain how valuable this person might be in a real emergency, but in a training situation it might be better if he or she were to allow the others to try to solve the problems first. If you can encourage such participants to act as mentors to the rest of the team, they may feel more comfortable and allow the team to work things out for themselves. Because you have recognized their status as potential saviors and have asked them to act as counselors or advisers, they will be more relaxed and less inclined to have to prove themselves.

14.1.3   Preparation and Practice

Preparation is an ongoing activity throughout the buildup; it is not just a quick look around before starting. By paying attention to the details and checking everything more than once you are going to be properly prepared, both physically and mentally. Each time you check something you are becoming more familiar with the way you are going to manage, control, and deliver a good product.

No matter how experienced you are, it is always a good idea to use *checklists* to make sure everything is ready. During the buildup, and especially on the big day, allow plenty of time to get ready and deal with any last minute snags.

Know the Script: All the members of the delivery team need to know the script and the intention behind it. They should know what is relevant, what is in there as window dressing, and what is hidden. Practice your roles together until you are quite comfortable and confident. Take the time to consider how you will try to deal with any unexpected reactions or awkward questions. Also, think about who should handle these small but important matters. It might be quite helpful to brainstorm the types of questions you might get from various individuals and figure out how you will deal with them and keep the momentum going. By thinking things through in advance, you may avoid losing momentary control which is not very good for your confidence or theirs.

Quality Control: From a quality control perspective, make sure everything is ready before the event to enable a successful exercise. Obviously, quality remains a key concern both during and after the event itself.

Before the event, there are some basic questions to be asked:

- Is your exercise fit for purpose?
- Can your design meet all the objectives?

Before the event, there are some basic actions to be taken:

- Ensure there is no risk or danger.
- Proofread the scripts and check them for consistency.
- Check that the deliverables are on track.
- Make sure that scripts and other items are labelled properly.

During the event you should:

- Stick to your timings.
- Stick to your script.

After the event you should provide:

- Prompt and accurate feedback to the participants.
- Comprehensive reports to management.

14.2   Safety: Isolation and Security

Rehearsing BC can seem like a game, but it must be safe and affordable. Isolation and security make sure of this by preventing or containing any potential effects and impacts.

Isolation means separating the training exercise and its confusion from the everyday operation of the business. It is a way of providing the participants with a private, risk-free learning environment.

Security means preventing the exercise from affecting the normal regular business operation by ensuring there is no additional risk to the business. Security is also concerned with the health and safety of the participants.

The protection works both ways:

- To protect the regular operation.
- To enable learning.

- To maintain control.
- To see how people and processes perform.
- To check that the plan works.
- To allow experimentation.

14.2.1   Creating Isolation

Isolation from routine affairs gives the event a special meaning since you have complete control over what participants see and hear. Furthermore, you can make noise without disturbing or alarming others.

A change of circumstance promotes a change of role and behavior; it becomes an escape from the chores and interruptions of daily life. Away from their normal surroundings, the participants can focus on what's before them and behave naturally rather than play their routine business role.

Some ways in which you can achieve this isolation include:

- Create a sense of separation from the normal. Use a separate room or building such as a training center, meeting room, board room, or hotel room. Restrict all communications except those between the exercise teams; any external communications should be made through your delivery team.
- Exercise at a distance to automatically give a sense of isolation. This means going to a remote location to achieve effective isolation, although the additional cost of time and travel should be considered.

As far as is practical, choose an exercise venue which would be similar to the emergency situation, with similar facilities and resources available.

14.2.2   Setting Up Security

Safety is largely a matter of being careful in the temporary accommodation, bearing in mind that people will be engaged in unusual activities in unfamiliar surroundings.

Security measures should be implemented as a part of the exercise. From a health and safety perspective, protect participants from anything which could be triggered by the exercise. Also, protect the business as some very strange messages could get out and cause confusion.

Your exercise is also an opportunity to demonstrate emergency security arrangements which should be covered in your BC plans.

- Practice good risk management.
- Restrict or control communications and use codes or passwords to prevent confusion between the needs of the exercise and live business operations.
- Properly label all exercise-related documents to ensure they are obviously and easily distinguished from all working documents.

14.3   The Ideal Scene

From a practical point of view, the location for an exercise should be convenient to get to and properly equipped with suitable resources. This means phones, faxes, flipcharts, whiteboards, catering, etc. There should also be enough space for the control and response teams to work in and somewhere they can hold press and staff briefings if this type of activity is called for in the script.

You may well find yourself in a debate about whether to hold an exercise onsite or offsite. In the early stages of the program, when you are doing a desktop or walkthrough event, the location is relatively unimportant. However, once you are past this beginning stage, an offsite location is required because most disaster scenarios involve evacuation of the normal premises. Wherever you are blessed with your own emergency management or command and control center, then you should use it. At the start of the exercise, the participants should go through the motions of commissioning or opening up the command post, especially if it has to be converted or reconfigured in some way. Very few organizations have dedicated command and control posts; they are usually set up and used for other purposes most of the time. In all other cases, it is preferable to have the emergency response teams assemble at an offsite location because it does provide a more realistic and challenging environment. Working offsite also represents what would probably happen at the start of a real business interruption.

Like little children, good observers should be seen but not heard….

If you have an offsite recovery service provider, ask the provider to host the exercise. Not only will the provider be able to let your people practice within a real disaster recovery workspace, but the provider's skills and knowledge could prove useful. Get to know the provider's staff members and develop a working relationship with them well before the need arises.

14.4   Lessons: The Feedback Stage

Feedback is all about noting and delivering the key learning points back to the players. It includes suggestions for improvement based on the exercise. Like little children, good observers should be seen but not heard – until afterwards. They should be watching the event, understanding it, and capturing the key learning points for the players. Observers should also make a note of any areas for improvement in the plans and procedures.

The reason to appoint observers is that they can offer an objective external viewpoint. They will be able to see the whole picture, have a consistent approach, and know what to record. Everybody else will be too busy to monitor what is happening, and key messages could be lost.

After the exercise has been completed you move into the feedback stage which consists of three distinct parts, each of which has its own particular value and audience.

> ‣ The *exercise debrief* takes place immediately after the event.
> ‣ The *exercise report* is written and circulated.
> ‣ The *exercise review* follows after everyone has seen the report.

14.4.1   Exercise Debrief

The debriefing should be restricted to the delivery and response teams only. It is a private opportunity for informal comments and acknowledgments while everything is fresh in everybody's mind.

Whenever you conduct a debriefing it is important that you follow these rules of debriefing:

> ‣ Always end with positive comments about the performance of the response teams. If they did not do well, it is the exercise controller, or the script writer, who should be criticized, not the participants. Encouragement will improve the teams' attitude and enhance their performance.
> ‣ Any evaluation should take the form of comparison rather than criticism. Team members will be happy to be told they compared favorably to some others but might be discouraged to be told they were not the best. They can figure that out for themselves and don't need you to remind them.

- Talk about their achievements or improvements. Again, if there is no positive outcome, the fault lays with the delivery team, not the response teams. There are bound to be a number of achievements or improvements, though perhaps not the ones you were hoping for. There will be lots of learning points and each one is an achievement as well as an opportunity for improvement.

- Give participants some idea of the amount of improvement. Don't exaggerate, but do put the message across in positive terms. Remember that the primary objectives are to boost their confidence and enhance their competence.

- Relate their response and their achievements back to the stated objectives and purpose. This proves to them that the whole thing was worthwhile.

- Explain to them how and why the plot unfolded the way it did. You can point out what was relevant, and what was put in to divert their attention, so they can get a better understanding of how things might have turned out if they had responded differently.

- Finally, thank the participants for their participation, their enthusiasm, and their contribution to BC. I usually sum up by saying something like, "Let's hope you will never be called upon to deal with a real disaster, but I feel sure some of today's lessons may help you to deal with the everyday problems and situations you are likely to meet in the normal workplace."

14.4.2   The Exercise Report

Soon after the event you will need to draw up a report which is the formal vehicle for delivering the results and recommendations. This will be for wider distribution to all interested parties and, amongst other things, will act as the starting point for the exercise review.

In order to provide a benchmark, to judge your capabilities against best practice, the regulations, or some other norm, it can be useful to measure something. Basically there are two forms of measurement: absolute and comparative.

Absolute measurement records the actual achievement without relevance to circumstances or context and would be expressed in simple terms such as time, distance, or number of goals.

Comparative measurement, on the other hand, considers the achievement in context and would be expressed in relative terms such as position, personal best, or track record. It will be related to something personal and meaningful rather than something like time or distance.

In this context we can use both forms of measurement. Absolute measurements could take the form of the time taken to complete certain actions, or the amount of time lost, or wasted, through inactivity or indecision. Perhaps, you might count how many people were able to return to work after a particular period of time.

Senior management will want to know if the exercise met the purpose....

Comparative measurements could take the form of comparing the current performance against previous or the actual versus the planned recovery time.

Both types of measurement have their uses, but do not place too much reliance on such figures. The real purpose is to learn and improve, not to chase statistics. If you are going to measure things, make sure you have a valid reason. Consider what you are going to measure as well as why and how.

On the other hand, if you decide not to measure, you need to be able to defend your position. So you need to think about what you might have learned by measuring something. If there is no advantage to be gained, then there is no real purpose in making the additional effort simply to learn nothing of any real value.

14.4.3   The Exercise Review

Exercise reviews should be held soon after the event, while the memories are still fresh in everybody's mind. They are the basis of any improvement and are an ideal opportunity to gain, or retain, commitment from the key players. It is important to include representatives from all levels to get a multi-dimensional view and everyone feels they are a part of the team with a valued opinion.

Senior management will want to know if the exercise met the purpose and objectives, what progress has been made, and what further progress needs to be made.

14.4.4   Full Sequence of Feedback

The full sequence of the feedback might be something like:

Initial Review: This review is held immediately after the event. The primary purpose is to praise and thank the participants but it is also a good opportunity to capture some of their thoughts and deal with any questions they might have.

Exercise Report: The exercise controller then amalgamates all of the delivery team's notes into an exercise report. This report should include all the constructive suggestions and recommendations as well as any scores or measurements which might have been taken. It should be distributed to all those people who might, or should, have an interest in BC. Because it is the formal record of the event it should be retained for future reference.

Formal Management Review: Once everybody concerned has had an opportunity to read and digest the report, you should arrange for a formal management review to discuss the outcome. All recommendations should be listed as action points, and someone should be made responsible for completing each of those actions. A management review should be held as soon as you can, while the memories are still fresh in everybody's mind. Start off with looking back at the purpose and objectives before covering the issues arising. Then, consider the progress that has been made and decide how to address the various learning points and recommendations.

Final Report and Plan of Action: The outcome of the review meeting should be a final report, together with a plan of action which will be the basis of the future BC management and exercise programs. The output from this review meeting should be an action list with responsibilities allocated for each of the tasks to be carried out. Get everybody's commitment to this action plan before you close the meeting. There can be no argument about who agreed to do what because they are all witnesses to the proceedings.

Ensure continuity throughout the program by linking it all back to previous events (or the uncertainty of the past). Don't treat it as an isolated event; link it forward to future events and make everyone aware of the next steps in preparation for another exercise. It is also a very good time to get their agreement, and commitment, for the next exercise.

14.5   Tracking the History

14.5.1   Records and Reports

An important element of the exercise is the history. You can choose one of two broad ways of capturing historical information: records and reports.

A *record* is an informal note of what happened and what was said or done at the time and it can take many forms. Records may include such items as a history log or an event diary, personal notes, flipcharts, whiteboards, photos, tape recordings, or video recordings. Records are actually made during the event; they may be crude, but they have the advantage of being original and contemporaneous.

A *report* is a considered view, where you compare the outcomes and performance against the stated objectives and highlight areas for future enhancement. Reports are a permanent account of the event and its proceedings that include recommendations for improvements. Reports are made after the event; so they will tend to be more organized and structured and represent the official view.

14.5.1.1 Records

Everybody will make some sort of record, but what they record and how they do it will depend on their reason, their purpose, and the audience. The intended audience (or readership) and the purpose will determine the style and, perhaps, the medium.

People will keep various types of records according to their diverse needs and purposes. There are spontaneous personal notes, intended as short-term memory aids or reminders. Then there are temporary references, or tools, such as group notices or history logs designed for information sharing and consistency. Temporary references should

> **Aids in the form of group records are to be encouraged...**

form a reference point for the whole team, and their value depends on how they are used. They may serve as a key learning point for the players. Because such informal notes are usually hand written without a clear format, they can be hard to follow. Such notes can be much more useful if you provide participants with a prepared layout in advance.

Aids in the form of group records are to be encouraged as an integral part of the BC procedures, providing they add value or serve a purpose. Apart from anything else, they help to establish a routine which is easy to settle into and add a degree of comfort when everything appears to be in turmoil. However, they do need to be legible and informative. A systematic approach using codes, symbols, and colors may help. Such aids can be useful for both the delivery team and the response team.

After the event, permanent records, which are a formal account, will be derived from a mixture of the above together with the writers' memories of what happened and the various pre-event materials.

14.5.1.2 Reports

Your delivery team's task is to prepare and distribute the exercise report.

Permanent accounts such as the exercise report should follow the house style and layout and should be aimed at those with no specialist knowledge. Reports should be easy to read and the key messages should be easy to spot. They should be laid out in a logical sequence, starting with a short management summary followed by an account of the event. Finish with a list of recommendations, together with the key learning points. Since many of your readers will not have been at the exercise, they will need to know about the background. Avoid technical terms or jargon.

During the exercise itself, it is helpful to have checklists of the objectives or specific tasks for the response teams. This, of course, should be outlined in the plans. The delivery team can also make use of checklists to track areas of interest. The controller can make a note of timings and sequences on the script. Observers should have specially prepared checklists, covering what they are supposed to be looking for. If you expect observers to make subjective judgments, you must give them some guidelines; otherwise they may be inconsistent in their interpretation of your intentions or requirements.

It is always a good idea to have a whiteboard or flipchart to track the overall activities and responses throughout the event. Again, this should really be part of the continuity plans.

14.5.2 Recording

A video camera can provide an accurate record of what happened and can be useful for debriefing and analysis. However, it can be overwhelming for the players, and the playback may seem to come over like harsh criticism for some of them. Recording certainly puts additional pressure on them, and many people are notoriously camera shy. In some scenarios, it would be realistic to expect the media to be filming the event. However if you are at all unsure, don't do it.

...your announcement could be accompanied by a *preparation pack*....

One alternative is to make a voice recording of the exercise. Recording all phone calls gives the advantage of capturing both ends of the conversation in those complex exercises that make extensive use of the phone for delivering messages or interrupts.

Recording all of the sounds in the room captures the spirit and some of the dialogue. The only drawback is that a simple recording set-up may not pick up all of the conversations and remarks. There may be several different conversations at any one time. Some comments and remarks will be too quiet and the acoustics of the room may affect the sound quality; so it is worth experimenting beforehand to make sure the equipment is up to the task.

Photography is another way of capturing additional information. Visual images can be used as support material in the exercise report. They can also be used to raise awareness, but do not make use of any embarrassing photos. During the exercise, try to be discreet and to avoid being intrusive.

For some exercises, you may want to simulate a press photographer on the scene. In this case, you are not particularly concerned with the quality or content of the actual photographs. Rather, your goal is for participants to experience carrying out their tasks under the eye of the media. In fact, to create these conditions, I have often used a camera and flash gun to good effect without even having any film in the camera.

14.6 Kick-Off

In the kick-off you introduce the delivery team to the participants and outline the rules of the game. It is where you establish control and set the boundaries so that the participants know where they stand in relation to the events which are about to unfold.

14.6.1 Announcement and Notice

Give everybody plenty of notice and make it clear who should be there and why; refer to the BC policy and any other drivers such as regulations or legislation. Explain the purpose and objectives behind the exercise and tell them how long it is planned to last. You should describe the catering arrangements, if any. You may want them to make their own arrangements as described (or not described) in the plan, in which case there might be a number of interesting learning points to come out of the exercise. To make things very clear to all those who have been invited, including first-timers, your announcement could be accompanied by a *preparation pack*, including details of the venue, timings, what they can expect, and what will be expected of them.

It is important to gauge the period of notice correctly. Some people have their calendars fully booked months ahead, whereas others may only have a relatively short time horizon. You may even need to give notice up to six months in advance with reminders every month.

Your announcement should make it quite clear when and where the exercise will start and what is expected of participants.

> ▸ Should they remain at their desks until notified by the callout procedure or do you expect them to gather as if that part of the plan had already started?
>
> ▸ What should they bring with them, if anything? Perhaps you expect them to bring a copy of the plan with them simply because it is a BC exercise. However, don't place too much reliance on this type of "automatic" behavior since they are still learning.

A key requirement in the kick-off is to establish the scope of the exercise....

At the start of the exercise proper, you should explain the *rules of engagement* (see Section 14.6.3 below), even though you may have already sent them as part of their preparation pack.

14.6.2   Cautions

Here are a few words of warning about what to do and what not to do.

DO NOT

> ▸ Pull the plug, i.e., disable or interfere with normal business processes or facilities.
> ▸ Cry wolf, i.e., pretend there is a real emergency, except when everyone knows that it is part of a planned exercise.
> ▸ Spring surprises.

You will gain nothing by such things, but you might lose a lot of support.

DO

> ▸ Be safe.
> ▸ Remember that the people may be under stress in unfamiliar circumstances.
> ▸ Be realistic.
> ▸ Coach for success.
> ▸ Make sure participants get a positive result.
> ▸ Help participants and encourage them to make the right decisions.

14.6.3   Rules of Engagement

A key requirement in the kick-off is to establish the scope of the exercise and the rules of engagement so that the participants know what they can and cannot expect. You make these rules clear at the beginning to avoid any misunderstanding and to set the scene before the actors take to the stage. For example, the rules of engagement for a walkthrough exercise might be:

> ▸ Exercise conditions apply from when the exercise controller says "Start of exercise" until he or she announces "End of exercise."
> ▸ All communications with other parties are to be made via the exercise controller or exercise coordinator.
> ▸ All staff and press briefings are to be written and retained for record purposes.
> ▸ No external communications are to be made outside of the exercise to avoid confusion with live business operations.

- The exercise will be a tabletop walkthrough only, and no actions are to be taken outside the exercise room.

- All activities are to be logged and noted for discussion during the exercise debriefs.

- Guidance will be given by the exercise control staff when necessary.

- All information within the exercise is deemed confidential and will be treated as such.

- Any assumptions may be challenged and proved to be false as the script unfolds. If you are uncertain, please ask someone.

- There are no wrong decisions.

- Your press office will expect a briefing about the emergency and your response to it.

- You should also conduct a staff briefing prior to the release of any information to the press. This should be based upon a written statement which can be retained for reference purposes.

- The BC plans will be developed or refined as a result of this exercise; therefore, any thoughts or ideas about the content, style, or structure of such plans should be noted and fed back into the BC planning process.

- The exercise delivery team will play the role of the general staff at any briefings during the exercise.

14.6.4   Keeping It Going

One perceived difficulty is the problem of keeping the exercise going when participants have managed to deal with all the problems in a much shorter space of time than anticipated. Well, the answer is that you don't really have to keep it going. If you (or rather they) have achieved all of the objectives, then you can either change your strategy to make use of the opportunity or you can close early.

Don't keep it going just for the sake of it; an early debrief is a sign of success deserving congratulations all around.

Obviously, you need to pace your input so the scenario unfolds in such a way as to fill the time allowed. You also have to have enough material to keep them fully engaged with problems of varying magnitude and relevance. Another option is to have prepared additional, optional materials you could weave into the exercise if you are running ahead of schedule.

However, if you do have a few minutes to spare and they are willing to get involved, then you could simply challenge the participants to find any holes in the plan and talk about the areas where it might be improved. Alternatively, you could ask them to go back and rethink their initial reactions and decisions. Was there another, not necessarily better, way of dealing with it?

Generally, it is better to let them celebrate their victory rather than for you to risk outstaying your welcome.

14.7   Advanced Techniques

Over the years I have experimented with a number of different ways of delivering the type of incident-based training which is necessary to develop and sustain the capability to deal with an unexpected business disruption. This has resulted in the development of some original approaches which you might find useful. For example, "Cabaret Quizzing" is a fast-path method of involving the participants in thinking about incident response and management. On the other hand, "The Bang and Echo Program" is a rather more comprehensive training program which seeks to extract the maximum benefit from the effort invested in developing a full set of exercise delivery materials.

14.7.1   The Command and Control Exercise Scale

Emergency response and crisis management skills need to be built up over time without overwhelming the participants or incurring unnecessary overheads. Therefore, in my consultancy we construct our exercise scenarios on the basis of five distinct levels of complexity, shown in Table 14-1, which are intended to be delivered and tackled in sequence as the participants improve their skills and develop their confidence.

Table 14-1. Five Levels of Command and Control

Level One	**Single site; simplex scenario**
	This is where the scenario involves a single location which is affected by a single impact on its premises, infrastructure, or systems. There are no prerequisites for this level of exercise; it is the normal entry point for participants in a BC training program.
Level Two	**Single site; complex scenario**
	This is where the scenario involves a single location which is affected by more than one impact on its premises, infrastructure, or systems. Usually an initial incident is later followed by other circumstances or factors that may cause earlier decisions to be called into question or conflicts to arise regarding the best response.
	The prerequisite is that the response team should have been involved in at least one Level One exercise. This does not mean every single individual but the team as a whole should have some experience.
Level Three	**Multiple site; simplex scenario**
	This is where the scenario involves multiple locations which are affected by the same single impact incident or its ramifications. More than one response team is likely to be involved at this level.
	The prerequisite is that the response teams should all have been involved in at least one Level Two exercise. This does not mean every single individual but the team as a whole should have the benefit of previous experience to draw upon.
Level Four	**Multiple site; complex scenario**
	This is where the scenario involves multiple locations which are affected by the same complex incident or its ramifications. Several response teams are likely to be involved at this level.
	The prerequisite is that the response teams should all have been involved in at least one Level Three exercise. This does not mean every single individual but the team as a whole.
Level Five	**Multiple site; multiple scenario**
	This is where the scenario involves a number of incidents, occurring at a number of sites during the period of the exercise. These incidents may occur more or less simultaneously in different countries and in differing time zones. Many teams are likely to be involved in an exercise of this scale.
	The prerequisite is that the response teams should all have been involved in at least one Level Four exercise. This does not mean every single individual but the team as a whole.
	This is the ultimate scenario in terms of complexity and is therefore an extreme test of the capability to respond to emergencies. However relatively few organizations feel it necessary to strive to demonstrate this level of capability.

14.7.2   Cabaret Exercising

Once you have gained some experience in setting up and running exercises and developed some confidence in your capability to think on your feet, you might want to step up to the challenge of what I call cabaret style exercising.

Cabaret exercising is an interactive approach which relies on specialist skills and tools rather than prepared scripts. Because not much preparation is involved, these spontaneous tests can be a very cost-effective way of getting some quick results, especially at the operational level. Another advantage is the fact that this type of exercise is particularly practical because it deals with situations which are bound to be real to the participants.

The main thrust of this technique is for the exercise controller to actually develop the scenario as the exercise proceeds. This instantaneous style of delivery draws upon previous experience, supported by a collection of ideas and props.

Your "cabaret collection" is a compilation of random notes from previous exercises, newspaper clippings, memories of past incidents, and some prepared messages purporting to be from various likely sources such as the police, salvage engineers, insurers, builders, and customers. For example, you might make up a realistic-looking fax from someone like a key client with some blank spaces to fill in the actual details of the message. Then you can quickly mock up a fresh message for immediate delivery during the exercise.

A lively imagination is the key to success in building up one of these collections. The actual delivery process is quite straightforward.

Step 1: Conduct Workshop with Key Players to Identify Threats – All of the key players are invited to attend a BC workshop at which they will be taking part in some practical exercises. The invitation suggests that these exercises will be based on the real threats and problems the business might face on a daily basis and goes on to pose the question, "Do we actually know what these risks are?" Schedule the meeting to last about 45 minutes.

At the start of the meeting, you can update them on the current status of the BC program. The next step is to ask each of them to suggest one or two scenarios in which the plan might be invoked. Use a flipchart or whiteboard to make a note of the ideas they come up with. You need to capture only the main headings, such as "Basement Flood," "Factory Fire," or "Road Accident." All you need is half a dozen alternatives, but the actual number isn't important.

If you get a member of the audience to act as the official scribe, making the notes on a flipchart, it will give you the opportunity to scribble some notes and begin to figure out some of the plot possibilities while the key players are engaged in the discussion about the potential trigger events. In the first round of the game, capture all of their suggestions without thinking about the likelihood or the impact.

Step 2: Create a Scenario – Once you have a sufficient number of suggestions you ask the audience which of these incidents are the most credible. Perhaps they can rank them in the order of credibility with the most likely ones being given a star rating: one star for "believable," two stars for "quite likely," and three stars for "could be happening right now."

Now you have a short list of credible scenarios and it is time to choose one as the basis of an exercise. You can either select one at random, or you can go along with their preference as the scenario they would like to explore. If you are going to select at random, you could use a set of dice, toss a coin, or pull a number out of a hat.

The outcome of this process is the basis of a realistic emergency situation which they have already bought into. Thank your helper for his or her assistance and ask him or her to rejoin the group.

Step 3: Conduct a Scenario-Based Exercise – Now the first actual exercise can begin. Start off by giving the players some rules of engagement to set the scene and to help them recognize when one discussion has ended and the next game is starting. For the next 20 minutes or so, you can run a mini exercise. The primary focus of one of these sessions will be their initial reactions and the first few minutes of the incident. Once they have gotten their act together, invoked the plans, outlined their strategy, and developed an action plan, you can call a halt to this first exercise session. After a short debriefing, you can move to one of the other triggers and run a second scenario in exactly the same manner.

> ...three exercises and three workshops spread throughout the year....

Obviously, these are relatively simple exercises and they are of fairly short duration, but they are a very useful way of introducing the players to the early stages of emergency response. There is no need for any observers and relatively little preparation to be done; so you can run a cabaret session at almost any time without imposing a strain on the workload or the budget.

14.7.3   The Bang and Echo Program

I created this approach when I was asked to develop a comprehensive exercise and training program for a large telecommunications company. They wanted their chief executive and his peer group to lead the way in preparing to face up to an emergency, but they also wanted to make sure that an equivalent level of expertise would be developed throughout the organization.

My solution was to suggest the development of a really good plot and supporting material – featuring a dramatic and attention-getting explosion – and, in order to extract the maximum benefit, to re-use some or all of the prepared material in a series of subsequent events spread throughout the year.

To create realistic looking explosive devices, we used whole meal flour mixed with walnut oil to simulate Semtex, a plastic explosive material commonly used by terrorists because it is difficult to detect and relatively easy to handle. We also mocked up other terrorist's tools such as envelopes filled with talcum powder to simulate anthrax.

The delivery program involved a series of three exercises and three workshops spread throughout the year, followed by an open discussion at the end of the year. We started in the spring with an exercise called "Big Bang" aimed at the top executives and their support team. In the summer and autumn we ran "Little Bang" and "Baby Bang" for their alternates and deputies, using the same exercise materials. After each exercise we ran an "Echo" workshop in which we discussed the implications of the decisions made during the exercise. The participants in these "Echo" workshops were the managers and technicians who would be involved in the recovery and restart procedures.

Although there were full debriefings at the end of each exercise for those involved, we did not circulate any information about the responses and outcomes until the program was completed. This was to ensure an even playing field throughout, everybody basing their thinking on the plans and the scenario rather than someone else's experience. At the end of the year, we brought everybody together for a full and frank final discussion before releasing and distributing our findings. The same pattern of seven events was repeated the following year with a different scenario, based on suggestions made during the final discussion with the participants. I have successfully repeated this formula a number of times with other clients and the results have been very satisfying.

Self-Examination Questions

1. During an exercise, the delivery team
   A. is responsible for testing the response team to the limits of its capability and beyond.
   B. is responsible for using the plans, procedures, and facilities provided by the response team.
   C. is responsible for the safe development, delivery, and control of the exercise.

2. The role of the exercise facilitator is
   A. to manage the delivery team and direct the exercise.
   B. to manage logistics and liaise between teams.
   C. to play a passive, independent role and observe other people.

3. If an exercise participant challenges the realism of the scenario, what is an effective response?
   A. Remind the challenger of the purpose of the event and point out that the exercise is fulfilling that purpose.
   B. Tell the challenger that he or she is incorrect and should not be voicing objections.
   C. Educate the challenger that realism is irrelevant to the purpose of exercising the BC plan.

4. It is important that members of the delivery team know the script. This means
   A. they practice individually and not as a group to ensure they have really mastered it.
   B. they know what elements are relevant and which ones are window dressing.
   C. they will be able to refer unexpected responses to or questions about the scenario to the correct person.

5. The purpose of isolation during the exercise of the plan is to
   A. provide participants with a private, risk-free learning environment.
   B. ensure the health and safety of the participants.
   C. prevent the exercise from posing risks to normal regular business operations.

6. Which of the following statements about the exercise debriefing is true?
   A. The evaluation should be posted where all employees can review it.
   B. The evaluation should focus primarily on opportunities for improvement.
   C. The evaluation should have an overall positive and encouraging tone.

7. During the kick-off, which of the following should the delivery team NOT do?
   A. Ensure that participants achieve a positive result.
   B. Remember that participants may feel stress.
   C. Tell participants that there is a real emergency.

8. Which of the following statements correctly describes cabaret-style exercising?

   A. It usually features crisis events that are unfamiliar to participants.
   B. It is a spontaneous, interactive approach best used by people with experience in running exercises.
   C. It is an advanced and relatively expensive approach that requires extensive preparation.

Food for Thought

BC is an intriguing mixture of art and craft, and in previous chapters you have explored the craft aspect and learned about the techniques required to develop, implement, and check out a BC plan together with the requisite supporting materials and systems. Now it is time to consider whether you have a full understanding of the art of developing the essential skills and competence in those who will be in the front line when things go wrong.

As before, consider how you would apply the lessons from this chapter to an organization that you are familiar with such as your school, college, or place of work. Concern yourself with the strategic implications at this stage; the tactics will emerge as you work with the others to develop their specific needs and expectations.

Exercises

1. Think about organizing an exercise and training program for your organization, assuming that they now have a suitable set of BC plans.
   - What types of exercise would you consider using?
   - What would the first year's schedule look like?
   - How many, how often, and when?

2. Consider who should take part in these exercises. Think in terms of roles or titles rather than actual names.
   - Make a list of who should be invited to each exercise in your schedule.

3. Prepare invitations to send out to these people.
   - When and how would these messages be delivered?
   - Give them adequate notice and good reasons to attend.

4. Consider who should be on the delivery team. Here you can think of real individuals with whom you would be comfortable working.
   - Make a list of the people and their roles.
   - Which role will you be playing?

5. Consider how you would open up one of these events: introductory remarks to set the scene before the start of the actual exercise.
   - Share your proposed opening remarks with a friend or colleague.
   - Rewrite your introduction if necessary.
   - Will you try a dress rehearsal or are you sufficiently confident?

Looking Forward

By now you should be ready to arrange the testing and exercising of the BC plans which have been developed and delivered under your guidance. What you have achieved will prepare your people to confidently respond to an emergency situation in readiness to recover and restart the key business activities. The next stage in the BC process is to look at the longer-term aspects of the program and how you sustain the progress that has been made.

In the next part of this book we shall be discussing how you can keep the momentum going and ensure that your plans remain fit for purpose in an ever-changing world.

Downloadable Business Continuity Toolkit

There are some useful documents in the downloadable **Business Continuity Toolkit** which might help you with your exercise delivery work.

For Additional Reading

Phelps, R. (2010). *Emergency management exercises: From response to recovery.* San Francisco, CA: Chandi Media.

Rothstein, P. J. (2007). *Disaster recovery testing: Exercising your contingency plan.* Brookfield, CT: Rothstein Publishing.

In the UK the government offers advice on testing and exercising at www.gov.uk/government/uploads/system /uploads/attachment_data/file/61086/exercise-guidance-good-practice.pdf

In the US the Ready campaign of the Federal Emergency Management Agency (FEMA)/Department of Homeland Security (DHS) offers advice on testing and exercising at www.ready.gov/business/testing

Part

V

Long-Term Continuity

Part I: Preparation and Startup
Part II: Building a Foundation
Part III: Responding and Recovering
Part IV: Planning and Implementing
Part V: Long-Term Continuity

Now that you have a grasp of all the basics, this book will explore some of the more advanced issues so that you have a complete understanding of the principles and practices of our subject and its implications. The more advanced concepts will help give you a full understanding of the principles and practices of business continuity (BC) and its implications.

Chapter 15 – Auditing and Maintaining Your Plans

▸ Describes how to make sure your tools, techniques, and preparations remain fit for purpose.

Chapter 16 – Governance in the Resilient Organization

▸ Explores how BC experience could be used to enhance the way you organize your company for better governance and increased resilience.

Chapter 17 – Your Future in Business Continuity

▸ Presents information about the future of the profession and your career.

15

Auditing and Maintaining Your Plans

So far in this book, you have discovered how to launch a business continuity (BC) program, gather all the requisite data, and develop a set of plans. To ensure that your BC plans, procedures, and techniques are up-to-date and effective, you will need to conduct regular reviews and audits. These audits will permit you to check that the process has been properly applied and its outcomes are fit for purpose. Of course, your organization's actual readiness to cope with a disruptive scenario can be proved only through practice, which we covered earlier in chapters 12 and 14.

This chapter will help you to:

- ☑ Understand why you need to conduct regular reviews of your plans and procedures.

- ☑ Prepare to conduct your own reviews.

- ☑ Develop effective reporting procedures and techniques.

- ☑ Appreciate how auditing provides an independent, unbiased view to be taken seriously.

- ☑ Ensure that your BC auditing is effective.

15.1   Terms of Reference for Review

Before you can set out on a formal review or an audit, make sure that you have the authority to proceed, which will probably take the form of some *terms of reference*. The terms of reference set out the scope of the review or audit together with what is expected. Gaining the authority to proceed will involve your BC sponsor, who will provide you with that authority and supply, or at least sign off on, your terms of reference.

Your terms of reference should provide you with a clear indication of:

- The aim and purpose of the assignment.
- Your objectives.
- The scope of the inquiry.
- The recipient's expectations or anticipated deliverables.
- Any assumptions or constraints.
- Budgetary limitations that might apply.
- Anticipated timescales.
- Reporting structure.

The terms of reference may also mention the preferred approach or method to be used which might reflect standard practice for other disciplines or activities within the organization.

15.2   Steps in Review Process

Reviewing is the *internal quality control process* which looks for a practical and effective capability, checks that nothing has been overlooked, reviews the past, considers the future, takes note of changing circumstances, and makes recommendations where appropriate. It is internal in the sense that it is carried out by those who are directly involved in the BC program and hence may be somewhat subjective at times. The output might include wish lists as well as shortfalls and inadequacies.

> **The main activities of the review process are gathering information ...and reporting on its effectiveness.**

The review is also a way of reassuring everyone that their interest in the organization is protected because you are able to show you are well prepared to deal with the unexpected.

The main activities of the review process are gathering information about the BC program and reporting on its effectiveness. Review is the quality control mechanism you will use to ensure everyone is doing an effective job with the right tools. *Audit*, on the other hand, ensures everyone is doing an honest and thorough job. That will be covered later in the chapter.

The review process is shown in graphic form in Figure 15-1. All of the activities center on the three key areas of interest which are:

1. Facilities.
2. Resources.
3. Plans.

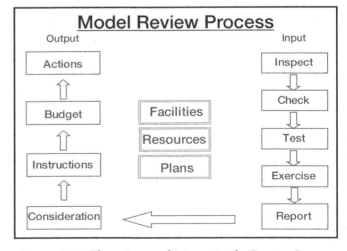

Figure 15-1. Three Areas of Interest in the Review Process

Regular input to the process is gathered by inspecting, checking, testing, and reporting. The report then goes to whoever is responsible for the BC budget and actions.

The output from the process is then generated through instructions, leading to the development of the budget and a set of action plans. Subsequent reviews would then take account of whether those instructions have been implemented and the effectiveness of the actions in enhancing the BC capability. Thus, the review process is cyclical, following the progress and development of the ability of the organization to respond to, and deal with, an emergency situation.

The review process should be ongoing, ideally with quarterly or monthly inspections, during which you would carry out static checks or straightforward inspections. Tests and exercises (covered in Chapters 12 and 14) should be conducted at least once a year.

15.2.1   Facilities

In this context, we use the term *facilities* to cover all of those items of equipment or accommodation which have been reserved or allocated for BC purposes. They may be rented, purchased, or subject to some form of service contract. They may be dedicated to your BC program or shared with others for the same, or different, purposes.

The reviewer's task is to make sure these facilities:

- Will be available whenever they may be needed.
- Will be fit for use when they are needed.
- Are suitable for use as described in your plans.
- Are adequate to support your business needs.

You should visit and inspect each BC accommodation at least once a year. The inspection will allow you to make sure that:

- The accommodation is still there.
- The capacity is adequate (floor space, number of desks, equipment, etc.).
- The condition of the property is acceptable.
- The requisite services are available.
- The accommodation corresponds with what is described, or expected, within the BC plans.

Get to know the facilities manager (if there is one), since this will make your inspection more effective. Check on the status of all of the equipment reserved for, or allocated to, your BC purposes. At the same time, you are actually checking that it is in fact still there. If it is missing, you should make a few inquiries before reporting it as "missing." Someone may have borrowed or moved it, perhaps without realizing the significance of such actions.

Make sure any technical equipment has all of the right features and accessories. A member of the information technology (IT) group should be on hand to help you identify and qualify the technical equipment.

15.2.1.1 Facilities Testing

There should be a regular series of tests designed to prove the suitability of the recovery procedures, etc. These tests are also useful for training and familiarizing the recovery teams with the working environment.

Your review should check that these tests have been carried out and whether they were successful. Ask to see the test results and make a note of any problems encountered, whether the problems were resolved, and how much effort was involved. If any of the tests were aborted, cancelled, or postponed, you need to find out why and whether the test has been or will be rescheduled.

Every BC program should also include regular exercises or rehearsals, involving the end users in checking out the recovery capability. They are a chance to make sure the facilities are effective in supporting the recovery procedures. Your review should include a summary of the objectives for these exercises and whether those objectives were met. All of this information should be found in the exercise reports. (See details about conducting exercises and recording and applying the results in Chapters 12 and 14.)

You should also report on the frequency of these exercises and whether they have all been carried out. Include in your report any lessons which have been learned and make a note of any problems encountered. If a solution has been suggested, include that in your report, noting who suggested it for follow-up.

15.2.2   Resources

Resources in this context means the goods, supplies, or devices which are reserved or allocated for BC purposes. They are essential for any recovery operation. People and information are also key resources in this context. Basic emergency resources may be held in reserve to support the immediate needs of the business. Further supplies should be available on demand.

Your task is to make sure these resources:

> ▸ Are available whenever they may be needed.
> ▸ Will be fit for use when they are needed.
> ▸ Are suitable for the use described in your plans.
> ▸ Are adequate to support your business needs.

Check that all of the emergency supplies held in stock are actually available in the right quantities and in the right place.

Check whether the business requirements for these resources have changed, since they may no longer be adequate or needed. Ensure further supplies or special emergency supplies will be available if, and when, they are needed. Check whether proper contracts and procedures are in place to acquire these additional resources at short notice.

Tests, exercises, or rehearsals should confirm whether the emergency resources do actually satisfy the immediate needs...

It may be necessary to test some items which are held as emergency supplies. This testing should all be covered in your regular maintenance scheme. The users should be able to tell you what needs to be tested and how to test it. However, it would be more useful to get them to do these tests as part of their training and familiarization program. Record the results of any tests in a history log as part of the maintenance scheme.

Make sure that any items which fail a test are repaired, replaced, or replenished and re-tested. Highlight any failures or concerns in your report.

Tests, exercises, or rehearsals should confirm whether the emergency resources do actually satisfy the immediate needs of the business in an emergency. On the other hand, these events might suggest that the needs of the business have changed and different emergency supplies are now required. This could mean changes to the range, or the quantity, of items held.

Check through the test and exercise reports to see whether any changes were proposed. If so, find out if, and when, those changes were carried out.

Your report should mention any significant changes, when they were carried out, what was disposed of, and the cost.

15.2.2.1 Resources Testing

Exercises or rehearsals are the most valuable aspect of any BC program and should be the main focus of your reviews. You must report on the quality and frequency of the exercises and rehearsals.

The key questions would be:

- Did they run these events according to the agreed schedule?
- Were they properly organized?

You must also report on the outcome of these events:

- Did they meet the objectives?
- Were there any lessons to be learned or applied?

Include a reference to comparative progress.

- Is the BC capability improving?

15.2.2.2 Reviewing Dynamic and Stable Plan Content

Plans and their contents are considered to be at the core of BC. This makes them important items for your review. They describe what should be done, how it is done, and who will do it. If the plans are wrong then the whole process is likely to fail. Your review of the plans is a key indicator of the way in which BC is being implemented. Up-to-date plans suggest BC is being taken seriously; out-of-date plans show it is not being taken seriously enough.

Two key aspects of a plan need to be reviewed. Ideally, they should be in separate sections, or modules, for ease of maintenance and review.

Dynamic content is the variable, detailed information about people, equipment, and processes. It will consist mostly of lists, such as contact lists with names and addresses or lists of equipment needs and requisite features.

The dynamic content should be checked every time a plan is reviewed. The main concern is whether the contents have been kept up-to-date. It should only be necessary to check out the specific details when you suspect the plan is wrong, or out-of-date.

Stable content is the basic stuff which is likely to remain the same unless there are major changes to the business operation. It will consist mostly of procedural information such as task lists, or action plans, procedures, and instructions. The basic layout of the document should also be quite stable; it is only the detail which needs to be changed.

The stable content needs reviewing only when the plan is new or there have been major changes. A full plan review considers whether the basic layout, requirements, policies, and procedures are reasonable; it also makes sure that the dynamic content is accurate. A simple change review focuses on whether the changes were applied properly, assuming the rest is still acceptable.

15.2.3   Output Phase

One purpose of your review is to inform senior management. Their main concern will be effectiveness of the preparations designed to protect business operations. Their considerations will lead them into confirming their commitment, issuing new instructions where necessary, and allocating budgets. This process leads naturally into the ongoing actions required to sustain the BC program.

15.2.3.1 Status Reports and Activity Reports

You will need to prepare two different types of reports in order to complete the review process.

1. A **status report** provides a high level view for consideration by the executive group in connection with long-term policy.
2. An **activity report** gives a more practical view to the management team as an assurance of the capability and justification of the expenditure.

A status report should be prepared and submitted to the executives on a regular (e.g., quarterly) basis and should give an overview of the whole BC program. It should explain the strengths and weaknesses of the BC program and report on progress since the last report. A status report should include any recommendations which have emerged together with some statistics such as:

- The number of plans that have been reviewed.
- The number of tests, exercises, or rehearsals that have been done.
- The number of tests, exercises, or rehearsals that are planned.

Activity reports should include reviews of the plans with feedback on each test, exercise, or rehearsal. All BC plans should be reviewed regularly to determine their currency and accuracy. An activity report should include information about:

- The specific plans that have been reviewed.
- What those reviews revealed.

You should also report on all tests, exercises, and rehearsals that have been carried out, giving details of:

- What has been tested and what the test proved.
- Any lessons that have been learned.

An **emergency incident report** should be prepared and submitted to both management and executives whenever an incident causes an invocation or puts any of your response teams on standby. This report should include:

- What happened and why (if the cause is known).
- The actions that were taken.
- Whether the plans were followed.

- Whether the resources were adequate.
- Any lessons that have been learned.
- Any further actions that should be taken.

You should always suggest acknowledgment or recognition of those who took part in the emergency.

15.2.4 After the Reports

When the managers and executives receive your regular status or activity report, they have the responsibility to consider whether to confirm their support for the BC program. The same is true for an emergency incident report, although the circumstances will have changed and there should no longer be any doubt about the value and future of the BC program. Your report should give the decision-makers the confidence to continue to offer their support.

...your reports are an essential element in ensuring the BC program is properly funded.

These decision-makers will also be considering whether the program needs to be modified in some way. Does it need to be expanded or enhanced or should they adopt a different strategy in some areas? Include any ideas or recommendations about areas for expansion, improvement, or enhancement within your reports.

If the executive or management teams conclude that the program would benefit from a change, then they will issue instructions about what they want to be done. This may simply be an endorsement of some of your recommendations, or it might be a variation on the same theme. Their response may also be prompted by some other advice, a different evaluation of the facts, or it may represent a change of policy or of the business environment. In any case, it will be your reports which prompt these changes and instructions.

Whenever the executive or management teams issue some fresh instructions or endorse the current policies and procedures, they will have to recognize the need for a budget to support the activities. Therefore, your reports are an essential element in ensuring the BC program is properly funded. You should be able to assure them that these funds are being used wisely in a practical and valuable cause.

Once the executive or management teams have considered the situation, given their instructions, and allocated the budget, they will expect someone to be taking action. This may not appear to affect you directly as the instructions may be aimed at other people or other departments. Take note of those actions so you can track and review them in your next report. This gives continuity to your review process and shows you are alert to their expectations.

15.3 Auditing

Much of what has been said about the review process will apply to the more formal and objective process of auditing. Here we are concerned with the role of the BC auditor rather than the company auditor, but the principles of audit remain the same whatever the subject. Perhaps your regular internal auditor may be the right person to carry out this work for you.

While review is internal, *auditing* is an *external* process which looks for evidence of compliance with policy, financial prudence, achievement of purposes, and justification of any claims. The auditor also highlights any other areas of concern which are revealed by the process. It is external in the sense of independence from the function in question rather than external in the sense of an outsider, or third party, being involved. Independent means that the viewpoint is balanced and unbiased. Audit is somewhat similar to the review process, but it is rather more formal and has different objectives; it is normally carried out annually.

The reviewer seeks to develop and offer an opinion, based upon a cooperative dialog and reference to corporate policy, while an auditor aims to provide a judgment based on an investigation and reference to recognized standards.

Internal audit: Audits, as a basic procedure, may be carried out by internal people who are familiar with the organization and its aims; they will be seeking to reassure top management that key business areas appear to be following the relevant corporate policy. At this level, they will be seeking evidence that the principles of good practice are being adhered to. Internal audit is commonly used as a means of maintaining and demonstrating good governance, providing reassurance to the stakeholders. An internal auditor will tend to use company policy and culture as a yardstick; their acquaintance with BC will depend upon the maturity of the BC program.

A BC practitioner may be expected to carry out an internal audit either as a precursor or dress rehearsal for a more detailed and independent audit which might be carried out subsequently. In the same way, a trained auditor may be asked to offer a verdict and recommendations as an integral part of the preparation for certification.

External audit: External audit is a rather more rigorous version of the same process, but the accent is more on finding proof that the program or process under examination complies with standards and regulations. Professional external auditors will want to be able to find proof that would stand up in court if necessary. External audit is often a requirement imposed by regulatory or legislative dictates. An external auditor will tend to rely on published standards and regulations as a benchmark; they may not be conversant with BC as it is typically practiced.

BC professional's role: Occasionally, a BC professional may be invited to conduct, or assist with, an audit. In this case the main aim of the audit is to establish whether or not the BC plans, procedures, and facilities are likely to enable a successful response to, and recovery from, any likely form of disaster scenario. The reason for bringing in a BC professional is to gain assurance that the solutions which are in place, or proposed, are realistic and likely to prove to be effective. This professional will tend to rely upon knowledge and experience together with recognized standards of good practice; his or her emphasis will be on the practicality of the solutions which are in place.

The most rigorous style of audit is employed during the certification process in which an organization is evaluated for accreditation against a national, or international, standard such as ISO 22301. Clause 9 of the ISO 22301 standard requires "permanent monitoring of the system as well as periodic reviews" (Professional Evaluation and Certification Board, 2015, p. 6).

In this type of analysis, an independent BC professional is usually engaged to join the investigative team as a subject matter expert. His or her role is to interpret the applicant's plans and procedures and advise the lead investigator regarding their quality, suitability, and conformity with the guidelines associated with the standard in question. The investigator will be a trained auditor who is familiar with the language and meaning of the standard itself.

In this book we are simply offering some basic guidance for those BC professionals who may be asked to participate in, or provide advice during, an audit of their business area. Our focus is on relating the audit process to the BC environment; we do not suggest that we are in position to tell the auditor how to approach his or her job. We also think it is important for the BC professional to know what to expect from, and how to prepare for, the various forms and levels of audit.

Case Study: Review and Audit in Practice

A supplier of components to the motor industry employs about 300 people across two sites in central Germany. In autumn 2012, a group of car manufacturers decided to require business continuity management (BCM) in line with ISO 22301. Customer A told the operations director that BCM was to be "a requirement in all future contracts." Customer B told the sales director that they "expected BCM in all key suppliers." A and B were separate divisions of a large corporate entity, operating under several brand names.

Arnold Schmidt from quality assurance started a BCM program in accordance with ISO 22301 at Site A. At about the same time, Alfred Schmidt from production control initiated ISO 22301 at Site B.

Quarterly *reviews* in February and May found and reported "steady progress in the BCM program across the company under the lead of Herr Schmidt." This was good news that reassured the board of directors. Review seems to have focused on results rather than the details of the development and delivery process. It was not concerned, or didn't even realize, that there were two leaders with similar names engaged in similar but separate assignments.

However, an internal audit report in September found "two separate projects, separate budgets, and separate leads, but parallel progress against the required standard. All compliant, but there is some inconsistency in terminology and layout. Recommend that Arnold Schmidt confer and collaborate with Alfred Schmidt to resolve inconsistencies and duplication of effort." *Audit* appears to have visited both sites, recognizing that there were two distinct but parallel processes. This realization led to further investigation which revealed the differences, leading to the conclusion that collaboration could probably produce better value with less effort.

While *review* found acceptable results, it took *audit* to realize that there were some inconsistencies and duplication. These different conclusions were because they had different purposes and were concerned with differing levels of detail. *Review* was reassuring; there were no major problems and progress was being made. *Audit* was concerned about the process behind the outcomes which led to constructive enhancement.

Lessons Learned: BC is now proceeding in this company under a single budget with board level reporting via the director of operations. The lighter touch of the *review* process came to a reasonable conclusion:

> There was nothing to worry about.
> The results were acceptable.

A relatively small amount of effort revealed that the primary objective was being met.

The heavier hand of the *audit* process looked much deeper and discovered some additional facts. These facts were not at odds with the earlier conclusion; they simply provided more detail which led to a better understanding and suggested areas for improvement.

The extra effort revealed that:

> The primary objective was being met.
> But there was a better way of doing things.

This led to a substantive improvement in the BC program.

If the two halves of the BC effort had been at odds with each other, the review would have raised concerns that warranted further investigation and the final conclusion would have been reached much earlier. However, because both projects were in line with requirements, there was no cause for concern at *review* level.

Audit proved its additional worth by spotting the anomalies and recommending a more efficient approach.

15.3.1 The Audit Process

The principal activities of the audit process are inspection and investigation. Effective audit operates on two levels of inquiry. Normally, it is a routine inspection, checking to see whether official policies and strategies are being followed. It is also an opportunity to investigate wherever there is doubt.

1. **Inspection** simply means looking around, with a wary and inquisitive eye.
2. **Investigation** implies asking questions and evaluating the answers against the rules of audit and corporate policy.

Checklists and questionnaires are often used at the inspection level because they help you to maintain your consistency and objectivity while ensuring that you cover the ground properly without oversights or omissions.

When the initial inspection raises suspicions, or fails to give complete assurance, then you investigate or probe deeper to obtain additional information or evidence. You start to ask some searching questions like, "Can you show me what you do (or did)?" or "Can you show me how?" or "Can you show me where?"

The audit process is shown in graphic form in Figure 15-2. All of the activities center round the five key areas of interest, which are:

1. Policy.
2. Facilities.
3. Resources.
4. Plans.
5. Budgets.

Regular input to the audit process is gathered through visiting people and places, inspecting, and making notes. Occasionally, this will be supplemented by interrogating to obtain an extra level of detail. Here we are using the term *interrogating* to indicate questioning those responsible for the area concerned.

You will note that the areas of interest have been extended from the focus of the review, discussed above, to include policy and budgets as well as the facilities, resources, and plans.

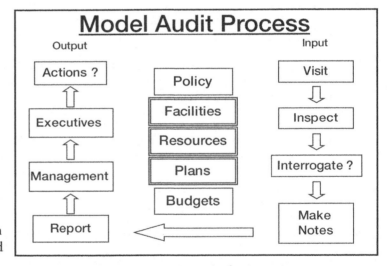

Figure 15-2. Major Audit Activities

The output of your audit will be a report to management and the executives who then decide whether to call for any actions. Usually those decisions will be prompted by the recommendations included in the auditor's report.

15.3.2 Rules of Audit

Some of the rules of audit include:

▸ As a BC auditor you need to be satisfied that people have carried out their duties properly according to instructions or policy, in an honest and safe manner.
▸ An auditor should establish whether the policies, strategies, and instructions represent best practice and are suited to the needs of the business.

- Opportunities for fraud or theft should be minimized due to the practice of regular and thorough audits.
- Where you are not satisfied, you should investigate further to establish the facts beyond reasonable doubt.
- An auditor has a duty to ensure his or her findings are reported honestly and accurately to those responsible.
- Important: A person *cannot* audit his or her own area of responsibility.

Indicators…become the basis of your audit on matters of policy.

15.3.3   Policy

In order to conduct an audit of BC policy you need to become familiar with the policy. Your first step is to read it through and discuss it with someone to make sure you have a clear idea of what it says and its intentions. Once you have a thorough grasp of the policy, you can then summarize its main points to form your own set of policy indicators.

Indicators are the things that you look for in your audit. These indicators then become the basis of your audit on matters of policy. For example, if there are three main points in the three questions about compliance with that policy you will thus be able to make an objective judgment about the application of the policy.

15.3.4   Compliance

In order to assess *compliance* with policy, you need to turn the main points of the policy into questions, or lines of investigation, about how current practice complies with the intention of the policy. If you are not convinced by the answers you get to your high level, or first, question, then you must be prepared to follow up with an investigative question designed to dig below the surface.

While it is acceptable to make up your investigative questions as you go along, it is worthwhile to prepare a few in advance. This will make it easier for you to be able to move over into the probing style of questioning which might be required. Some people find it difficult to adopt this more inquisitive stance without appearing to be confrontational. A little practice may help you to get the tone right.

For example, a business company has a policy which says:

It is the policy of this company to ensure its customers should always be able to contact their sales representative by phone or email with a minimum of fuss or delay.

You might turn that into an indicator statement: Instant access from customer to sales.

So your audit procedure might include the question, "How do you make sure customers can always get through to the sales people?"

If not satisfied or convinced by the answer, you then ask some investigative questions such as "Can you show me how you would recover the service?" and "How long would a customer have to wait in the worst case?"

15.3.5   Finance

The prudent and proper use of money is essential to the success of any organization. It is also a very precise aspect of business. Financial accounting does not leave room for errors or opinions. Thus, people will want exact answers and will expect auditors to assure them that these answers are accurate.

As a BC auditor you are concerned with all aspects of BC and making sure that:

- Capital investment is used wisely.
- Expenditures are properly controlled without waste.
- Proper records are kept of all financial transactions.

15.3.6 Investment

Your audit will probably cover investments such as real estate, which is land and buildings that may be owned or rented. You need to make sure they haven't been abused or misappropriated.

> **...you want to be able to report that people have not been reckless and wasteful.**

Where items have been acquired by purchase order, be sure each item was properly ordered and is being used for its intended purpose. Where items have been acquired by board decision, ensure the items have been put to the proper use in accordance with that decision. Where contracts are in place for the supply of goods, services, or support make sure everything is in order with each contract and its commission. Are the terms and conditions suitable to meet the emergency needs of the business?

15.3.7 Expenditure

Your audit will also cover ongoing expenditure such as maintenance costs, which leads to questions about whether all the maintenance has been carried out and accounted for in a proper manner. Where regular running costs have been incurred, check whether these costs are reasonable and recorded properly.

Occasionally, maintenance will involve repairs and replacements. Ensure these were necessary and reasonable. It is also worth asking what became of the original items in the case of replacement. Were they disposed of as waste, or redeployed, or did somebody benefit inappropriately from the transaction?

You must also check that the operation has stayed within budget.

15.3.8 Prudence

Prudence is all about making wise choices regarding the way money and resources are used. As an auditor, you want to be able to report that people have not been reckless and wasteful. The questions you need to ask of yourself and others are: "If it was your money, would you spend it that way?" "If you had spent your money that way, would you be satisfied with what you got for it?" "Has it all been properly accounted for?"

15.3.9 Purposes

As an auditor, check that the BC program is achieving its purposes. You have to be clear about what those purposes are. You will need to summarize the purposes, just as you did with the main points of policy. Your summary can then be used as the basis of your audit on the achievement of purposes.

When asking about basic purposes and their achievement, you need to aware of and avoid involvement in any hidden agendas or company politics. People often try to achieve their own objectives rather than the group's original purpose. Where this seems to be happening you should investigate and report on the matter.

15.3.10 Achievement

Once you have established what the purposes are, it should not be difficult to find out whether they were actually achieved. It is especially easy where the purpose is something precise and has been tested. For example, a test certificate would prove an IT recovery test had achieved its purpose of "recovery capability within x hours." In other instances, you may have to think about how you can estimate or measure the degree, or extent, of achievement. Often, this means you have to recommend regular testing or exercising in order to prove or demonstrate achievement of purpose.

15.3.11 Claims

Well intentioned people may make a number of claims about what they, or parts of the BC program, have done or could do under various circumstances. They may make these claims to inspire confidence or to deceive themselves and others. As an auditor, you need to discover what those claims might be and the underlying purpose of such claims.

Your questioning might take the form of: "How confident are you that you could achieve a complete recovery of your part of the business?" and "What makes you so confident?"

Usually your concerns will be about *gaps*... in the way things are organized or managed.

When you are looking for justification of such a claim, you need to see some proof or evidence. If they have demonstrated they can do something, there should be a record of it. Without any record, the claim is unjustified. Your recommendation therefore would be for a proper test or demonstration.

If the claim is intended to boost people's confidence, then inviting them to come along and see for themselves could be a great help in this direction.

15.3.12 Concerns

As you carry out your audit, meeting people, asking questions, making notes, and preparing to write a report, you may come across some concerns. Usually your concerns will be about *gaps* – either a gap in your knowledge or a gap in the way things are organized or managed. For example, the security guard may stop strangers coming through the front door, but who, or what, stops them coming through the back door?

You might also ask people whether they have any particular concerns. Most of the time, you will find the answer to the gap in your knowledge and the concern will go away.

Where you come across a concern and cannot account for the gap, then highlight the concern in your report. A separate section of your report should give details of any concerns emerging from your audit. Because you may not have the full picture, it is normal to phrase your concerns in a cautious manner. For example, "There does not appear to be any means of preventing unauthorized access at the rear of the building."

15.4   Completing the Audit

15.4.1   Audit Checklists

As an auditor, you need to prepare and use a formal checklist for your inspections. This ensures that you cover everything and that you can demonstrate the thoroughness of your audit.

▸ Do not rely on memory for your questions.

▸ Do not rely on memory to capture the answers.

The checklist is a valuable tool for the high level inspection and should also provide prompts for a fuller investigation where necessary. Once you have developed a proper checklist it can be used on a regular basis and so trends can be monitored and progress recognized.

For each area of interest you need a similar set of questions. The first question is a broad one about the subject and the other questions probe for detail. For example, Question 1 would be of the type: "Do we comply, are we prudent, have we achieved, or is it justified?" This would then be followed by questions about how you can test the answer to Question 1. The next question would be something like: "How can you show that we are compliant?" or "Where is the evidence?"

You also need to consider how you would rate the degree of achievement in that area since the last audit and whether there has been an improvement. Don't try to get too complex; a score of 1 to 5 is probably sufficient, although you may prefer to extend that range up to 10 if that better suits the corporate culture. Finally, you need to ask whether you (or they) have any particular concerns in that area.

Policy	Finance	Purpose	Claims
Compliance?	Prudence?	Achievement?	Justification?
Can I test?	Can I test?	Can I test?	Can I test?
Rating?	Rating?	Rating?	Rating?
Improved?	Improved?	Improved?	Improved?
Concerns?	Concerns?	Concerns?	Concerns?

Figure 15-3. Typical Types of Questions

15.4.2 Checklist Construction

Your audit checklist should address each area of interest and list the type of questions you intend to ask. For examples, see Figure 15-3.

Generally, you will have no need to audit every single aspect of the BC program each year. You would need to do this only where there were some serious doubts to be addressed.

Normally, you would select one or two areas at random and carry out a sample inspection. A reasonable sample size would be 5-10%. Keep a record of the areas you have audited and ensure that all important areas are covered in due course. This suggests that a long-term schedule would be useful as a reminder.

If you are satisfied that there is no cause for concern in those areas, then you may be able to assume other areas would produce a similar satisfactory result. Where you think there is some cause for concern, it would be wise to explore a bit further in some other areas, especially those which are related in some way. Normally, 10-20% would be a sensible size for an extended sample.

15.4.3 Audit Reports

Audit reports are formal documents and should follow the corporate standards for such documents. They should be distributed to managers for consideration before they are sent to executive management.

Follow the proper process throughout the audit. Within the report, include a summary of how the process works. This will ensure everyone understands how and why you have come to your conclusions. Once it has been written, the description of the audit process can be included as a standard paragraph in future audit reports.

Note that all of your audit notes, records, and reports are confidential documents and should be treated as such.

Self-Examination Questions

1. In business continuity, what is the review process?
   A. An internal quality control process that evaluates capability and makes recommendations as needed
   B. An external process that looks for evidence of compliance with policy and financial prudence
   C. A thorough test of every BC plan to ensure all risks are comprehensively addressed

2. The three key areas of interest in a review of a BC program are facilities, resources, and plans. Which of the following is an accurate statement about resources?
   A. Resources should be available and fit for use when needed.
   B. Resources are materials but not people or information.
   C. Once resource needs have been documented, only resource availability requires review.

3. Dynamic content in the BC plans
   A. is unlikely to have changed and only needs review when the plan is new or has undergone major changes.
   B. should be verified in detail during every plan review, even if maintenance records indicate that it has been kept up-to-date.
   C. should be checked to ensure it is up-to-date and verified in detail if it may not have been maintained.

4. Which of the following is true about a status report?
   A. It gives feedback on each test, exercise, or rehearsal that has been conducted.
   B. It provides regular updates on the strengths and weaknesses of the BC program.
   C. It is generated whenever an incident triggers an alert or an activation of the plan.

5. What is an audit of business continuity?
   A. The audit is an internal process carried out by the organization's BC professionals.
   B. The audit is a formal process carried out by someone independent of the BC function.
   C. The audit consists in part of an exercise of the most critical parts of the BC plans.

6. During an audit, the auditor will
   A. inspect to see whether official policies and strategies are being followed and investigate where there is doubt.
   B. only inspect to see whether official policies and strategies are being followed, as investigation lies outside the purview of an audit.
   C. inspect to see whether official policies and strategies are being followed and investigate a predetermined percentage.

7. When auditing BC program achievement, the auditor
   A. first identifies what achievement has been objectively demonstrated and then defines the purposes of the program in terms of those achievements.
   B. first identifies the program's purposes and then solicits BC practitioners' opinions as to what extent those aims have been achieved.
   C. first identifies the program's purposes and then looks for objective demonstration of achievement of those aims.

8. During an audit, which of the following is NOT a purpose of using a formal checklist?
   A. To ensure that everything is covered to demonstrate the audit's thoroughness
   B. To provide a means of monitoring trends and tracking progress
   C. To allow employees in the BC function to conduct as much of the audit as possible

Food for Thought

Previously you found out how to lay the foundations, set policy, determine strategy, gather data, agree on tactics, and deliver plans. Now it is time to look back, compare the output, and check that it appears to meet the expectations which were laid out in the policy. A regular review provides an ongoing, comforting overview; the occasional audit is a more rigorous way of checking that everything is in place, fit for purpose, and compliant with regulations or standards. In review mode you are seeking assurance and want to hear the right answers. In audit mode you should be seeking certainty and want to see evidence or proof.

Exercises

This exercise is mostly about review because it gives you an informal introduction to the more formal audit process. As before, use your place of work, study, or residence as your case to study. Prepare to check out what BC planning and preparation is in place and verify whether that is adequate.

1. Review checkpoints.
   - What key indicators would you look for?
   - Which areas would you want to check?
     - How would you prioritize them?
     - Which are the top three?

2. Review questions.
   - What questions would you ask?
   - Whom would you approach?
     - Roles or titles rather than real names?

3. Uncertainty about plan maintenance.
   - What would you do if you were not sure about its effectiveness?
   - What would you do if you found a problem?

4. Uncertainty about the recovery service referred to in the plan.
   - What would you do if you were not sure about its effectiveness?
   - What would you do if you found a problem?

5. Audit program.
   - How would you plan your audit program?
     - A shotgun approach or a steady progression – i.e., a big annual effort or a regular section-by-section coverage?
   - What outline process or methodology would you follow?
     - Checklists? Interviews? Spreadsheets? Web-based questionnaires? Outside help?

Looking Forward

Review and audit or inspection and introspection are, of themselves, cause for reflection. They are passive techniques for gaining reassurance. When combined with testing and exercising, audit gives you active ways of making certain, bolstering confidence, and developing competence.

Downloadable Business Continuity Toolkit

There are several complementary documents available for downloading which might help you with your review and audit activities.

References

Professional Evaluation and Certification Board (2015). *ISO 22301 Societal security business continuity management systems* [White paper]. Retrieved from https://pecb.com/pdf/whitepapers/pecb.whitepaper_iso-22301.pdf

For Additional Reading

Disaster Recovery Institute (2015). *Become a certified business continuity auditor.* Available at https://www.drii.org/certification/cbca.php

Hiles, A. (Ed.). (2011). *The definitive handbook of business continuity management* (3rd ed.). Chichester, West Sussex, UK: John Wiley & Sons.

You could become a qualified BC auditor by taking the British Standards Institution's ISO 22301 internal auditor training course. See www.bsigroup.co.uk/en-GB/iso-22301-business-continuity/iso-22301-training-courses/iso-22301-internal-auditor

16

Governance in the Resilient Organization

In this book, you have looked at how and why you might approach the development and delivery of a successful and effective business continuity (BC) program. This process has involved exploring the tools, techniques, and products. By now, you should be in a position to practice this discipline in a professional manner, and this book has focused on the detail level at which BC is expected to operate and prove to be beneficial. Now, in this chapter, intended for both the experienced BC practitioner and a person entering the profession, you have a chance to look upwards and outwards to see where BC fits within your organization's hierarchy and how it might filter upwards and penetrate downwards, as BC is integrated into your corporate culture.

This chapter will help you to:

- ☑ Maintain a permanent response capability.

- ☑ Manage major organizational changes.

- ☑ Understand what it takes to achieve ongoing resilience.

- ☑ Develop resilience as an integral part of the culture of your organization.

- ☑ Integrate BC into corporate governance.

16.1   Horizon Scanning

In this book, I strongly advocate that you take a long-term view as a companion to the shorter horizons. While viewing the broader horizon is not a substitute for your necessary close-range thinking, it is a long-sighted approach that will allow you to face up to the challenges and figure out how to deal with them.

16.1.1   Future Potential Moments of Vulnerability

One way to extend your horizon is to look into the future and develop a better understanding of the potential moments of vulnerability. If you know when the business, or a particular part of it, is going to be engaged in periods of intense activity or major change, then you can avoid imposing additional workloads or allowing diversions at these times.

The idea is to create a simple *profile of risk* over time, which charts the anticipated periods of intense activity or heavy engagement. Such a chronogram of vulnerability will enable you and your colleagues to select the most appropriate time for all those tasks and projects which are necessary but not tied to a particular date or season.

BC management should spot, and track, the perils which might be out there and alert those in charge....

Obvious examples of these movable feasts would be your tests and exercises. Vulnerable moments would include such occasions as end of year accounts, seasonal sales, takeovers, mergers, or the launch of a major project or campaign.

Your timeframe for consideration in this context will be determined, to a large extent, by the nature, size, and pace of the enterprise. However, a good practice is to take a monthly view, covering at least a year into the future, while planning for a two-year horizon. As BC manager, you do not have to be given details or confidential information about future plans. You need to know only when it is best to be careful – the precise reason behind such periods of caution is interesting but superfluous information.

16.1.2   Geographic and Economic Horizons

Apart from looking forward to moments of significant change in the future, you should be considering the other dimensions of your field of operation and interest: the geographic and economic aspects.

16.1.2.1 Geographic Horizon: Locations and Marketplaces

Geographic horizon means looking at the spread of an organization's activities, which might span a number of working locations and marketplaces. Each of these arenas will have its own advantages, limitations, and perils. Obviously, the business will have moved into these locations because of the advantages and sought to overcome the limitations. As ever, the secret is to establish a balance in which the rewards outweigh the drawbacks. Over long periods of time, subtle or even dramatic changes will occur, which may or may not be to your advantage. Conduct a regular risk review – carried out as a BC activity – that includes scanning those distant horizons such as your outposts and agencies. BC management should spot, and track, the perils which might be out there and alert those in charge whenever you spot signs of distant clouds or storms.

16.1.2.2 Economic Horizon: Supply Chains and Value Chains

The economic horizon means looking at supply chains and value chains. Does your organization check whether its key suppliers have workable plans guaranteeing continuity of supply? In the same vein, you should be checking the distribution chain. Can key distributors continue to deliver your products and services to your end users? If not, are there alternatives within the distribution chain?

You have already looked at alternate sourcing as a continuity strategy, but here I am advocating applying the same principle to your outbound value chain. The important message for the longer term is to revisit these areas regularly and challenge the implications of any changes. While keeping your eyes open for potential problems, you could also spot opportunities which your sales and marketing people may not pick up on. An extra pair of untrained eyes sees things from a fresh perspective. The layman will also tend to ask more questions which can lead to additional insights.

> **Looking ahead to this potential interruption means applying the basic BC principles....**

16.2   Disruption from Relocation or Expansion

Certain disruptive events that are a normal part of business life bring opportunities to employ BC tools and techniques. Whenever there are projects which involve relocation or expansion of facilities and systems or imply the relocation of personnel or services, view these as potential interruptions, or even a series of interruptions. Looking ahead to this potential interruption means applying the basic BC principles of risk assessment, impact assessment, and continuity strategies – followed up by concrete plans for managing any emergencies or crises which might arise.

Hopefully, these preparations will serve only to ensure that everything goes smoothly because the wrinkles will all have been ironed out before the event. Ideally, you should also try to encourage others to rehearse in advance, wherever it is practical.

> **If BC is properly embedded...its proponents will be regarded as the guardians of change....**

Another very sound piece of advice is to avoid over-commitment. For example, if you need to set up a fresh system, then the old system should be left running until well after the moment of commitment to the new system. If practical, workloads should be transferred gradually rather than all at once. Even when the full workload has, apparently, been transferred successfully there is always the possibility of an early-life failure with any new setup. Until the new operation has stabilized and taken the full brunt of peak activities, be prepared to invoke the *exit plan*, which allows for a safe return to the old tried and tested working environment of the past. Better to be safe than sorry.

A small team of emergency managers or troubleshooters on standby during such a major disruption can literally save the day. Their input during the buildup might avert some, or all, of the problems and embarrassment. However, if something goes dramatically wrong, they can deal with the problem while the main project team members continue their efforts to complete the move on time, as planned. If the disruption goes beyond the confines of the exercise and represents a threat to the company, then emergency or crisis teams would be put in action.

16.2.1   Reorganization or Restructuring

Whenever there are any significant alterations to the way in which the business is run, or its products or services are delivered, you can help to smooth the path of change. If you are involved in the preparations, you can also act as the protector of the process. You can be dealing with any unexpected failures and threats while everybody else remains focused on a successful implementation.

If BC is properly embedded within the corporate culture, then its proponents will be regarded as the guardians of change whenever the agents of change seek to conspire against the routine of regular business.

16.2.2 Survival of BC in Times of Economic Downturn

Obviously, you can maintain an effective BC capability only with the full support of top management. Budgets may be reduced, or cut, when money is tight and they are looking to make savings in an attempt to balance the books. This common mistake only adds to the very risks that BC was set up to deal with.

By mirroring the normal management structure, you automatically instill a sense of continuity.

BC has to be regarded as a long-term ongoing investment that is an essential aspect of good governance. It is a necessary fixed overhead like security, HR, risk management, or insurance. It is not a temporary optional extra. At the start of your BC program you convinced them by proving that the return on this investment would be worthwhile. In times of hardship that business case makes even more sense. When a business gets close to the brink, BC is one of the few lifelines available. If the world is turning its back on you, you need to be sure that you can help yourself when something unexpected and unwelcome happens.

Behind your all efforts is a company policy; that policy justifies the ongoing investment in time, money, and resources. Furthermore, there may be regulatory requirements, depending on the type of business and where you operate. The watchdogs who may help you to preserve your budgets will be the auditors, who should be making sure that policies and standards are adhered to. These people do have the ear of all those who make high-level decisions. It is worth talking to your auditors to make sure that they understand the importance and value of BC together with the implications of not being able to respond effectively to a disruption. Working with internal and external auditors was covered in Chapter 15.

During your conversation with auditors you should refer to the hidden benefits of BC and the board-level motivators, which were discussed in Chapter 3.

16.3 Tiers of Governance

If you expect BC to be able to protect your organization effectively it must become an integral part of the corporate culture. This means that BC plans and processes must be absorbed into the governance structure of your organization.

As you have seen from the previous chapters, BC plans cannot be standardized because they need to be tailored to fit the enterprise and its environment. Indeed, I recently heard someone suggest that the motto of BC professionals should be "Keep It Simple and Make It Fit" or "KISMIF" for short. However, this book can generalize and provide guidance about the basic concepts and how they can be adapted. Organizations vary enormously due to many factors, but one can assume they will be governed, directed, managed, and supervised through a typical four-tier hierarchy. This hierarchy needs to be reflected in your plans which are about directing and managing operations under atypical conditions. By mirroring the normal management structure, you automatically instill a sense of continuity.

Almost every enterprise which has grown beyond the bounds of a family business or a loose cooperative of like-minded individuals will need to have evolved some form of management hierarchy. This means that different individuals, groups, or teams are assigned to their particular responsibilities and duties. Over time, as the organization grows in size and stature, these demarcations and the associated duties tend to become more distinctive and, perhaps, more separated.

The mature model will tend to have four tiers, perhaps with several sectors or divisions in the lower tiers. Regular communication and a common understanding between these tiers and sectors is a key factor in the long-term success of any enterprise. Understanding these tiers and how they interrelate on a practical day-to-day basis is essential to the success of your BC program.

The demarcation between the four tiers may not always be clear and the boundaries may be quite flexible. On the other hand, the boundaries and demarcations may be quite distinct and inflexible. You need to take these considerations into account when putting forward emergency response plans. Throughout the planning and implementing of your BC program, you should also be sensitive to any underlying issues of status, rank, or dignity when empowering (or restricting) the response teams.

A fully established hierarchy of governance and management should comprise four distinct but interdependent levels of people and responsibilities. Each of these groups serves a distinct purpose and it is their combined powers and efforts which enable the long-term success of the enterprise. Orders, commands, or directives come down from the layer above while reports, news, and intelligence go up from the layer below to form the regular command and control dialogue. The BC relationships which we covered in Section 4 of Chapter 2 are also shown here.

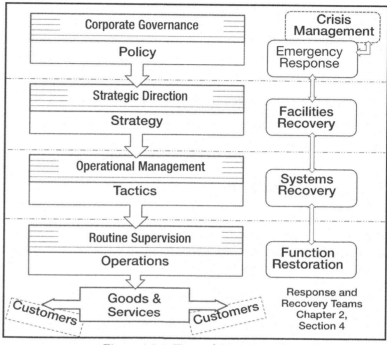

Figure 16-1. Tiers of Governance

1. **Corporate governance** is made up of the corporate governors who define principles and give direction by deciding the policy.

2. **Executive strategic direction** interprets principles and provides control by developing the strategy.

3. **Operational management** is by the line managers, who power the core functions of the company, organizing supply and production by settling the tactics.

4. **Routine supervision** is by supervisors who steer the daily functions of the company, achieve output, and arrange delivery by issuing instructions.

Looking at these layers and their roles and style of working, you should also be able to see how they contribute to the success of the enterprise – providing that they are all working in harmony and covering their full range of duties.

The core characteristics of these tiers, or layers, of governance are summed up in this simplified version of the previous diagram which reduces each concept to a single word. Later on in this chapter the book will be using this interpretation to relate the tiers of governance to the BC disciplines which were covered in previous chapters. The aim is to bring all these interesting ideas together into one comprehensive model making sure that it is also comprehensible which means explaining each of the new facets before merging them with what should already be familiar.

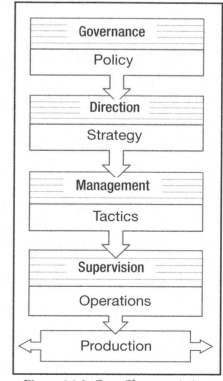

Figure 16-2. Core Characteristics

16.3.1   Corporate Governance

Corporate governors in this high-level executive group provide enterprise level leadership and, in the final reckoning, take full responsibility for everything that is done in their name.

Their duties will include:

- Setting corporate policy which guides all activities and operations.
- Obtaining and investing capital to fund the workings of the enterprise.
- Satisfying stakeholders in order to retain their support.
- Accepting risk, which means knowing what is involved.
- Ensuring the respectability of the enterprise and its endeavors.
- Keeping up the position in the market place.

16.3.2   Strategic Direction

The executive group imposes control on behalf of the corporate governors, interpreting their directions into suitable strategies and reporting progress. The directors are responsible for dealing with any issues raised by the managers or escalating them upwards. In any case, they will track progress of such issues, report upwards, and advise downwards as appropriate.

Their role or set of duties will include:

- Interpretation of policy into suitable strategies.
- Compliance with standards, rules, and regulations.
- Establishment of core business operations and processes.
- Development of the range of products or services.
- Developing and maintaining demand for the products and services.
- Acquisition and allocation of resources, supplies, and materials.

16.3.3   Operational Management

Operational management organizes and oversees the daily operation, ensuring the delivery of results in the form of goods and services to the client base. These managers report regularly to the executives on progress and achievements against plans or targets, together with any relevant market or industry intelligence.

These managers will also be expected to provide specialist advice as, and when, required. This means they should be able to draw on their own experience or have access to subject matter experts, perhaps both.

Their duties will include:

- Risk management through awareness and mitigation measures to avoid and reduce risks.
- Financial prudence through appropriate accounting and auditing.
- Customer contact, sales, and invoicing.
- Quality control of supplies, goods, and services.
- Running a cost-effective business operation.
- Maintenance of standards throughout the business.

- Delivery of products, goods, and services.
- Satisfaction of customer demand.
- Effective use and maintenance of resources.

16.3.4   Routine Supervision

Supervisors engage with, and run, the daily routine of production and delivery. They are responsible for identifying and resolving problems which occur within the business operation. Any problems which are either beyond their capability or above their budgetary limits should be escalated as issues, together with any long-standing unresolved difficulties.

Their duties will include:

- Progress monitoring, tracking, and chasing.
- Inspection and measurement, including calibration.
- Delivery of supplies and services to distributors or customers.
- Record keeping, which includes accounting and billing.
- Scheduling of activities, including working and standby rosters.
- Store keeping, including stock levels and replenishment.
- Health and safety, including fire prevention and protection.
- Personnel management including training, recruitment, and induction.

Managing Management at Broad & Leaf Financial: A Case Study

Background: Broad & Leaf is a growing, medium-sized, financial services organization with close to 1,000 employees in two principal locations in the US. For about four years, the information technology (IT) department has had a disaster recovery (DR) plan in place, sponsored by the CFO, tested about twice yearly, and generally well maintained. Recently, the company more than doubled in size and revenue, acquiring two smaller companies which depend heavily on corporate IT. Broad & Leaf moved from mainframe, terminal-based systems to client-server applications and numerous LANs. With higher degrees of sophistication, protection, and control came more recovery costs. Meanwhile, management remained complacent about IT recovery, assuming they could recover fully from virtually any disruption in a matter of hours. This complacency changed when IT submitted a request for renewal of the multi-year recovery site agreement and associated investment, with a significant cost increase.

The Issue: At a management meeting, the CIO listed DR needs for recovering the client/server and LAN environments, telecommunications, Internet, and external networks. He asked for interim processing strategies for critical business units to cope while IT was recovering the infrastructure and to further broaden the scope to work area recovery, web servers, and telecommunications. After a stunned silence, the COO finally broke the ice by questioning the need for any DR: "After all, we've never had a disaster." A business unit manager objected to additional work for her already overloaded group. The CFO, an original supporter of DR, was concerned about the expense, noting the company's financial position. The CIO, quite pale by this time, went back to his staff to reexamine issues and options.

The Trap: Broad & Leaf was operating on the basis of assumed expectations. While the CIO's recommendations were probably on target, his audience was unable to reconcile these with the assumptions they had lived with for four years.

> Assumption 1: IT was somehow populated by wizards who could instantaneously handle any crisis with minimum impact on business units. *In reality,* recovery from a major disruption would take 30-36 hours at best and could lose transactions.

> Assumption 2: IT had automatically integrated four years of diverse new technologies and platforms into the DR program. *In reality,* IT did not implement or operate all of these platforms.

> Assumption 3: No matter the cause or scope of disruption, IT would recover all data accurately to the point of failure. *In reality,* recovery would be to the prior night's backup, at best, and, most probably, to a point at least three to four nights prior.

> Assumption 4: Recovery capabilities were based on the impact of a potential outage. *In reality,* it had been four years since the last business impact analysis (BIA), meaning company contingency plans were outdated and no longer aligned with current critical exposures.

Lessons Learned: BC can work *only* when top management signs on from the start; without explicit commitment, BC plans *will* fail. After delicate negotiation and outside consulting assistance, Broad & Leaf's management approved the CIO's proposal and established a steering committee to address company-wide BC – something that should have been in place all along.

To manage management in BC, you need to:

> Document explicit service level agreements to spell out the limitations and exclusions as well as the promises – don't rely on assumptions made by top management, clients, or other stakeholders about your ability to deliver salvation from disruption.

> Communicate regularly to stakeholders any technological, business, or operational changes which impact recoverability – don't wait until there is no practical alternative, or until management has already acted on the basis of out-of-date assumptions.

> Present BC options, constraints, and alternatives to business unit managers and to top management early in their decision cycles – don't wait until they are committed to a course of action which impairs disaster recoverability.

– Philip Jan Rothstein, FBCI

16.4   Creating the Integrated Infrastructure

Now it's time to see how these four tiers of governance can be aligned with the BC arrangements to form an integrated command, control, and management infrastructure which you can adapt to fit your own organization. The resulting model of robustness has three distinct facets which show differing perspectives of

> **...there will always be a hierarchy, and everyone should know and respect his or her place within that hierarchy.**

how to set about managing and protecting the best intentions of the enterprise, which is to be able to continue to deliver goods and services to the customers.

The ongoing supply of goods and services is the final outcome of the business set-up and is shown in this model as the basement layer. You could also describe it as the service layer because it is the one which directly serves the interests, needs, and requirements of the customers. From the corporate perspective it represents the company's position and presence in the marketplace. As a BC practitioner, your interests lie in the four tiers which lead down towards the customer base. These tiers empower, motivate, and enable the production and delivery that is the embodiment and purpose of the overall business operation.

Down the left side of Figure 16-3, you can see how the BC response and recovery levels, which you looked at in Chapter 2, relate to the governance structure. This facet shows the BC activities which these people are expected to perform in accordance with their respective skills and capabilities. Down the right hand side you can see the command and control levels which were covered in Chapter 7. This aspect is a reflection of their BC management responsibilities which are related to their levels of authority.

So, as you can see, the center column of this integrated infrastructure model shows the normal governance hierarchy of a business, while the two side columns show how groups of people engage with and support the BC program.

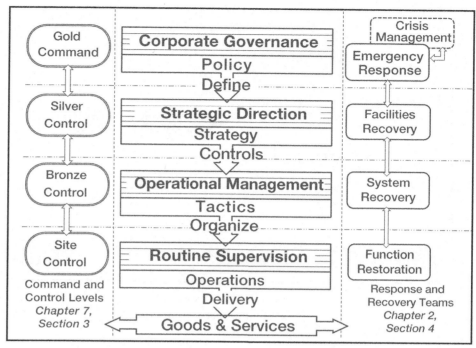

Figure 16-3. An Integrated Robust Business Infrastructure

Although the broad picture of these levels of control, management, and responsibility is typical of business operations around the world, you can expect to see many variations, especially at the detail level. It is best to regard this overview as an outline rather than a blueprint. However, you will find that the principles of tiered governance will apply wherever you are. The lesson to be learned here is that there will always be a hierarchy, and everyone should know and respect his or her place within that hierarchy. To avoid conflict, frustration, delay, and possible failure, your BC arrangements and plans must take full account of, and match, the existing infrastructure in your organization.

16.5   Relationship Between Governance and Business Continuity Standards

You were introduced to the concept of standards in Chapter 1, and Chapter 3 gave you an overview of standards in different countries that will have bearing on your work as a BC manager. In many organizations, governance and BC standards are included in a larger part of the organization known as governance, risk, and compliance (GRC).

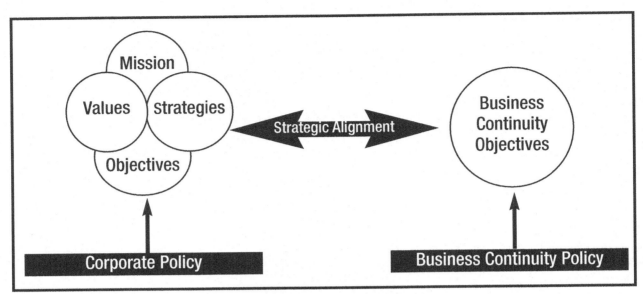

Figure 16-4. Business Continuity and Strategic Alignment
(Source: Professional Evaluation and Certification Board, 2015)

16.5.1   ISO 22301

ISO 22301, *Societal security – Business continuity management systems*, covers all phases of BC, but this chapter will address the relationship to governance.

According to the BSI Group, compliance with this standard brings with it many advantages:

> ISO 22301 will provide you with a framework for assessing critical suppliers and their associated risks, assessing current business practices and planning contingency measures. So when incidents happen, you'll be prepared and able to respond effectively. You'll also be able to reduce downtime having identified alternative arrangements. With ISO 22301, you will not only significantly help reduce the risks to your business, you will help achieve operational resilience (BSI Group, 2015, p. 5).

Andrew Hiles notes that the advantages of the standard include maximum quality and efficiency, resilience, reputation, competitive advantage, and business improvement (Hiles, 2014).

A compelling starting point...is everything starting with "Understanding the business."

Within the standard, "Clause 4: Context of the Organization" addresses governance issues directly, looking at all of the organization's activities and relationships, the links between the BC policy and other company objectives and policies, and applicable legal and regulatory requirements (Professional Evaluation and Certification Board, 2015). According to Hiles, "This section translates into understanding the organization's needs, both internal and external and establishing the clear scope of the management systems. It includes understanding the needs and expectations of key interested parties" (Hiles, 2014).

Steve Mellish, in regard to the applicability of the standard to corporate governance, notes, "A compelling starting point, and one that I consistently remind the business about, is everything starting with 'Understanding the business.' It is a very profound statement of intent that shows how a good BCM program should operate" (Mellish, 2011, p. 355).

Self-Examination Questions

1. Over the longer term, the organization would be most vulnerable at which of the following times?

   A. When no major product launch is planned

   B. When no site relocations are planned

   C. During a seasonal peak in workload

2. Scanning the economic horizon for risk should include

   A. suppliers and distributors.

   B. suppliers only.

   C. distributors only.

3. What should the role of business continuity be in an organizational restructuring?

   A. BC should be involved to identify and protect against potential threats.

   B. BC should be involved because a successful implementation means "all hands on deck."

   C. BC should not be involved until after the restructuring is complete.

4. Organizations of any size tend to be divided along four tiers of governance. What is the responsibility of the strategic direction tier?

   A. These line managers organize tactics for achieving the organization's objectives.

   B. These executives interpret the organization's vision and mission and develop the plan for achieving them.

   C. These senior leaders and board members establish the organization's vision and mission.

5. BC programs must be aware of the different roles within an organization since job scope impacts how empowered or restricted team members can be. Which of the following is typically a task for line supervisors?

   A. Compliance with standards, rules, and regulations

   B. Risk management through awareness and mitigation measures

   C. Health and safety, including fire prevention and protection

6. To ensure executive understanding of and support for BC, which of the following is advisable?

   A. Do not challenge executives' assumptions, especially if they are positive assumptions about your abilities.

   B. Proactively communicate any technological, business, or operational changes that impact recoverability.

   C. Wait until late in the decision cycle to begin to incorporate BC, because at that point you will know as much as possible about constraints and alternatives.

7. Which of the following accurately reflects a typical correspondence between BC and an organizational hierarchy?

   A. Governance – functional restoration; Direction – systems recovery; Management – facilities recovery; Supervision – emergency response

   B. Governance – functional restoration; Direction – facilities recovery; Management – systems recovery; Supervision – emergency response

   C. Governance – emergency response; Direction – facilities recovery; Management – systems recovery; Supervision – functional restoration

8. ISO 22301: Societal security – Business continuity management systems

   A. explicitly links BC with internal and external stakeholders' needs.

   B. addresses BC in isolation from other organizational objectives and policies.

   C. does not address linkages between BC and management structures.

Food for Thought

To reinforce what you have learned in this and previous chapters think about how the theory might evolve into practice. Consider how you see these ideas of infrastructure being applied to an organization you are familiar with such as your school, college, or place of work.

Exercises

1. You looked at the tiers of governance and the associated roles.
   > How would you populate those tiers and who should be in the various roles? Use real people if you can; otherwise try to develop their specific characters as if you were about to recruit for those roles.

2. An important aspect of long-term BC is the supply chain.
   > How would you suggest ensuring that your supply chain is robust enough to support the core business under all circumstances?

3. Equally important is the outbound distribution chain.
   > How would you suggest ensuring that your distribution chain is robust enough to support your business and its customers under all circumstances?

4. In the event of a planned relocation or the opening of a new location, how would you employ BC tools and techniques to ensure that the project runs smoothly?
   > Imagine your organization plans to move to a site you are familiar with.
      ⌁ Would you prepare some specific plans or adapt the existing ones?

5. How do you see the risk profile of your organization changing over time?
   > Prepare a short report covering the company's history.
   > Prepare a short report covering the foreseeable future.
      ⌁ Is there any connection or disparity between these two views?

Looking Ahead

You should now be fully prepared, at least from an intellectual perspective, to engage fully with the subject of BC, developing, delivering, and promoting the art, craft, and science of this fascinating subject.

Downloadable Business Continuity Toolkit

In the downloadable toolkit you will find documents that might help you to anticipate or even influence the way in which the profession continues to develop and grow.

References

BSI Group (2015). *ISO 22301 business continuity management.* Retrieved from
http://www.bsigroup.com/en-US/ISO-22301-Business-Continuity/

Hiles, A. (2014). *Business continuity management: Global best practices* (4th ed.). Brookfield, CT: Rothstein Publishing, Appendix A.

Mellish, S. (2011). BC strategies in the retail sector. In A. Hiles (Ed.), *The definitive handbook of business continuity management* (3rd ed.) (pp 352-361). Chichester, West Sussex, UK: John Wiley & Sons.

Professional Evaluation and Certification Board (2015). *ISO 22301 Societal security business continuity management systems* [White paper]. Retrieved from
https://pecb.com/pdf/whitepapers/pecb-whitepaper_iso-22301.pdf

For Additional Reading

Alfred P. Sloan Foundation (2008). *Framework for voluntary preparedness.* Available from
http://www.sloan.org/fileadmin/media/files/olsiewski/frameworkforvoluntarypreparednessfinalreport.pdf

MIR3 (2012). *The concise guide to business continuity standards.* Available from
http://info.mir3.com/the-concise-guide-to-business-continuity-standards.html?Isdet=Resource+Center

Protiviti (2013). *Guide to business continuity management: Frequently asked questions* (3rd ed.). Available from
http://www.protiviti.com/en-US/Documents/Resource-Guides/Guide-to-BCM-Third-Edition-Protiviti.pdf

17

Your Future in Business Continuity

By now you should have gained a clear impression of what business continuity (BC) is, what it can do, and how to manage it. You are now ready to take that knowledge forward with you into the real world of corporations which have or need BC programs. In some cases, you may be asked to combine BC with other related responsibilities or you may be expected to engage with it as a full-time occupation.

This chapter will help you to:

- ☑ See what to expect as you apply the materials in this book to your BC career.

- ☑ Appreciate the career opportunities for you in the profession.

- ☑ Identify the professional certifications available to you.

- ☑ Glimpse the possible future of the profession.

17.1   The Long-Term Management of Your BC Plans

Be aware that BC can be neglected quite easily if there is not someone or something there to sustain it. In my experience a common problem is the decline in BC that can occur in those organizations which fail to set up a robust and sustainable program. There seem to be five BC scenarios in companies; the first four are likely to be scenarios in which the BC program remains fairly stable, but the last is a matter for concern. These scenarios are:

1. BC is driven by legislation or regulation.
2. BC is in common usage.
3. BC is managed by a central team.
4. BC is a collaborative effort.
5. BC is dependent on an individual manager.

Wherever your activities are governed, controlled, or driven by *legislation*, there is little choice. BC has to remain functional, although it might become a tick-in-the-box solution. Most regulators will insist upon regular exercising to ensure that your plans and solutions remain valid.

Due to the very nature of their business, some organizations have BC in *common usage*. They experience regular disruptions which emphasize the need for some form of planning and preparation to deal with these difficulties. For example, those service industries which supply water, oil, or electricity are prone to such failures, and BC practices become an integral part of their standard operating procedures.

There is no continuity in a program which depends entirely on one key player.

If BC is managed by a *central team*, there is likely to be a certain amount of stability. However, when a key player moves on for whatever reason, some of the skill and drive will be lost, and over time BC can become stunted. Good handover procedures will help and high-level support and recognition are important.

In an organization in which BC is a *collaborative* effort, the skill base and enthusiasm for the subject is spread across a number of departments or locations. In such an organization, BC administrators are trained and coordinated by a central team or leader. This usually results in a robust BC program which is more or less self-sustaining. In this case, the loss of one individual does not cause the program to collapse. There may be some variation across the whole organization, but at least something is in place in all the critical areas.

The most vulnerable version of BC management is where it is the responsibility of *one individual*. It is true to say that this person is a single point of control, but that implies a single point of failure. When a leader moves on – unless a very well organized handover program is in place – the successor may or may not continue with the same level of enthusiasm or knowledge. I have often noticed the virtual collapse of a BC program whenever the hierarchy changes in such cases. There is no continuity in a program which depends entirely on one key player. The only hope in such circumstances is if the leader has managed to embed BC in the corporate culture to the extent that the organization is able to recover from the loss.

17.2   Challenges

However you are placed, you will find that BC activities do give you a thorough appreciation of how the enterprise works and the risks it faces. You will develop a broad understanding of all the many and varied functions within the enterprise. This knowledge may open the way for all sorts of career opportunities or it may convince you that BC is a fascinating and rewarding subject of itself.

17.2.1   Lack of Understanding and Appreciation

At times it may seem a bit tough; not everybody will be on your side all of the time. You will have to be patient and persistent to win over those who don't support BC. Many of them will be too busy to fully engage with your program because they don't appreciate its importance and value. You will also come across those who seem to be convinced that BC is an unnecessary extravagance through shortsightedness or disbelief. "It won't happen here" is their equivalent of the ostrich who sticks its head in the sand to avoid seeing danger. However, you should have the backing of top management and will be able to refer them to corporate policy, industry regulations, local legislation, or recommended good practice in the form of standards or guidelines.

17.2.2   Change of Ownership or Leadership

Another potential hurdle is a change of ownership or leadership which often leads to a change of heart. The protection against this possibility has to be a corporate culture which accepts and embraces BC as a key component in its risk prevention and management arrangements. Where BC planning, testing, and exercising are seen as regular worthwhile events the BC program should survive the handover period because it has become an essential element of a business which seeks to be robust and reliable. In those cases where BC has not been thoroughly embedded into the corporate culture there is a strong chance that a change of leadership could lead to a compromise which might weaken or close the existing program. This could occur through a change of emphasis, budgetary constraints, or even a reduced headcount.

...you need to make your voice heard whenever you have something important to say.

You must plan for this as a possibility and make sure that you get the opportunity to get to the new leaders and convince them about the wisdom and value of your BC arrangements before they start to impose their views and ideas as part of what they might see as a superfluous rescue package. In reality, of course, this approach is shortsighted and fraught with danger – if there is a weakness in the way the business is being run then the absence of valid recovery and restoration procedures will only hasten its descent into further difficulties and subsequent failures.

17.2.3   Lack of Priority

In a busy, high-pressure enterprise (and almost everybody will claim to be included here) BC is often seen as a low priority or superfluous burden so it tends to get delayed or interrupted and consequently your good intentions may never come to fruition. Be prepared to keep prompting and reminding people until they do eventually engage with their part of the process. Stay patient, remain persistent, and communicate frequently but politely.

17.3   Opportunities

In your role as a BC specialist you will absorb a good deal of knowledge about some of the more obscure aspects of the many activities that make up the overall business operation. You will also be bringing an external perspective to each of those areas. Sometimes this will give you an insight which none of the locals seem to have noticed. This is because they may be too absorbed in the daily routine to step back and take a good look at what they think they know so well. So, be prepared to spot opportunities and improvements which are above and beyond the BC intention to prevent problems and deal with the unexpected.

Potential solutions to possible issues can easily become improvements to routine procedures, especially when seen through the eyes of a comparative stranger. This leads to an important aspect of your role as a BC practitioner: you need to make your voice heard whenever you have something important to say. You need to work out for yourself how to escalate your concerns and findings. Consider how the reporting chain works in your organization and where you and your team fit within that chain. There should be some sort of fast path route to the top, or near the top, for issues connected with BC which management should perceive as a permanent monitor for alarms and danger signals. If that route does not exist, then you must develop it.

Some years ago when I was working for IBM we had an "Open Door" policy which meant that if you were concerned about something in your department you could bypass your immediate manager and go straight to his or her boss without any fear of recrimination or rebuff. If there is a similar policy within your organization, do not hesitate to use it but do be careful about abusing it. It is not a mechanism for dealing with petty squabbles. If there is not such a policy in place I would be inclined to assume that the route is open for such a mechanism to be discovered. This means knocking on a higher manager's door and politely requesting a moment of his or her time when, and if, the occasion demands it. Be brave and set a precedent; if it backfires then you are probably in the wrong place at the wrong time and now may be the time to move on.

You could also think about how you can apply the principles of BC to your home life and prepare yourself to be able to respond to whatever might happen. As a child I joined the Boy Scouts. Our motto was "Be Prepared" and that concept has stuck with me ever since. My wife and I have developed contingency plans with two other couples. We all have copies of each other's keys, we have temporary sleeping arrangements in each other's homes, and we often eat together. A few weeks ago, one of the couples had a power failure so they came to our house for a cooked meal and a night's rest.

17.4   Professional Certification

Over the years those of us who conscientiously practice and preach BC have established ourselves as members of a valuable and much-needed discipline with high standards and sound practices. In the process, we have sought to distinguish ourselves from those who have little or no practical knowledge of the subject and its many nuances. As a result, there are now a number of professional bodies who can offer you some form of evidence that you are competent. This certification of competence implies a basic understanding of the subject, familiarity with some (or all) of the techniques, and the requisite skills to apply that knowledge.

BC is now recognized around the world as an essential protective discipline. Employers, regulators, and organizations tend to require their BC professionals to have some form of certification. Even where there is no specific requirement, there will certainly be respect for such a distinction.

Certification also indicates membership in an organization that will provide you with the opportunity to develop and improve your knowledge of the subject and to network with your peers.

Perhaps the most important aspect of certification is that it does give you the right to put letters after your name. These post-nominal letters demonstrate to the world that you are a skilled professional following a formal code of practice.

17.4.1 The Business Continuity Institute (BCI)

The Business Continuity Institute (BCI), founded in 1994, offers a wide range of resources for business professionals who are concerned with raising levels of resilience within their organizations or considering careers in BC. The BCI has over 8,000 members in more than 100 countries worldwide, working in an estimated

3,000 organizations. The BCI Partnership, through corporate membership, offers organizations the opportunity to work with the BCI to promote best practice in BC.

BCI Certifications

CBCI: The Certificate of the BCI (CBCI) is an assurance that professionals have the full knowledge and understanding of the theory of global good practice BC. This theory is based on the *Good Practice Guidelines* (aligned to ISO 22301), the global guide to good practice in BC.

Certification is achieved by passing the CBCI Examination. Preparation is via instructor led courses – in a classroom or online – comprising approximately 32 hours of training and covering a step-by-step study of the complete Business Continuity Management (BCM) Lifecycle.

Certification is valid for 3 years, during which time an annual maintenance fee is payable. When the 3-year period expires, the member must re-take the exam to demonstrate that knowledge is up-to-date.

Other certifications include: **MBCI**, member of BCI for those who pass the test with merit; **AMBCI**, associate certification for those with less experience in the field; and **ABCI,** associate membership for students and those in other fields wishing an entry-level membership. For full details of current certification levels and requirements, please see: http://www.thebci.org/

17.4.2   Disaster Recovery Institute International (DRII)

Disaster Recovery Institute International (DRII), founded in 1988 as Disaster Recovery Institute, is a nonprofit organization dedicated to helping organizations prepare for and recover from disasters. DRII has trained more than 12,000 active certified professionals from more than 100 countries worldwide, offering training in more than 50 of those countries.

DRII Certifications

DRII certification is for individuals who have demonstrated knowledge and working experience in the BC/disaster recovery industry.

ABCP: For those new to the industry or who have expertise in another field, the Associated Business Continuity Professional (ABCP) level is for individuals with less than two years of industry experience, but who have minimum knowledge in BC management, demonstrated by successfully passing the qualifying exam. ABCP is for individuals with some knowledge in BC planning, but who have not yet acquired the necessary experience for certification at a higher level.

As the holder of the ABCP certification gains experience and knowledge, he or she may enhance his or her certification to CBCP or one of the other levels by completing the test and work requirements. At the ABCP level, no recertification required other than payment of annual fee.

CBCP: The Certified Business Continuity Professional (CBCP) level requires more than two years of experience. Applicants must be able to demonstrate specific and practical experience in five of the subject matter areas of the Professional Practices. Regular recertification requires an ongoing commitment to continuing education and industry activities.

Other certification levels include **MBCP** and **CFCP**. For full details of these and other certification levels and requirements, please see: https://www.drii.org/certification/cbcp.php

17.4.3   International Consortium for Organizational Resilience (ICOR)

The International Consortium for Organizational Resilience (ICOR) is a not-for-profit education and credentialing organization that provides professional development, certification, thought-leadership, and the latest in research and industry trends. ICOR's vision is to enable organizations across the globe to understand all of the elements that must be considered in order to enable them to embed the culture and systems they need to provide goods and services in all conditions and situations. Training is offered through a variety of educational institutions in the public and private sector.

ICOR Certifications

CORS: The Certified Organizational Resiliency Specialist (CORS) in BCM certification may be achieved through the completion of a curriculum that includes multiple courses and an eight-question written examination. Completion of the entire series earns the participant seven CEUs (certified education units) or 70 hours of credit (generally, one CEU is awarded for each 10 hours of instruction time). ICOR awards credit for existing credentials earned through the BCI and DRII.

This certification process requires the following: a minimum of two years of experience; a minimum of 3.5 CEUs in the BCM discipline (from the 10 courses available); a passing score (80%) on each of the individual course exams; and a passing score (80%) on the written certification exam.

ICOR awards a wide range of certifications in different areas of organizational resilience. For details, see www.theicor.org

17.4.4   Other Professional Certifications Available

ARM: Associate in Risk Management, granted by The Risk Management Society (RIMS), www.rims.org

C/DRE: Certified Disaster Recovery Engineer, granted by Mile2, www.mile2.com

CEM: Certified Emergency Manager, granted by the International Association of Emergency Managers (IAEM), www.iaem.com

CFM: Certified Facility Manager, granted by International Facility Management Association (IFMA), www.ifma.org

CISA: Certified Information Systems Auditor, granted by Information Systems Audit and Control Association (ISACA), www.isaca.org

CISSP: Certified Information Systems Security Professional, granted by the International Information Systems Security Certification Consortium ((ISC)²), www.isc2.org

EDRP: EC-Council Disaster Recovery Professional, granted by EC-Council, www.eccouncil.org

17.5   What's Next for Business Continuity

As BC practitioners, it is incumbent upon us to contemplate the future because that is where our value, intentions, and responsibilities lie. Can we learn from past history, and if so how do we apply the lessons? We should certainly be scanning the horizon for forthcoming events and changes which might have an impact upon our business operations. Some would say that this is just a matter of being observant but that raises the questions: "What are the signs that we should be looking for?" and "How do we interpret those signs?" These are interesting questions, which we all need to continue asking.

Perhaps it is easier to predict what might happen in those areas where we can exert a certain amount of control or influence like, "Where is our profession going?" There is no doubt that BC is now established in the sense that it is likely to persist and endure for many years to come. However we don't know for sure whether it will come to be a dominant feature of future corporations or whether it will be absorbed into, or overtaken by, another discipline. It could flourish under another name. After all, we have seen several changes in terminology in the past, although we have retained many of the original terms to indicate subsidiary or support disciplines or techniques.

> **…BC is now established in the sense that it is likely to persist and endure for many years to come.**

I see our profession moving onwards and upwards and in the process it will need to absorb or generate new ideas, new relationships, new interpretations, and new causes. There will be changes in legislation, regulations, and standards. Perhaps you will be able to influence those changes to ensure that they reflect our needs based upon our real life experience and knowledge of what is happening in the world. I suspect that we shall see evolution rather than revolution, but we must be prepared to allow for those who would seek drastic change rather than incremental progress. We are at the start of a long and winding road and must avoid getting lost or left behind.

17.6   A Parting Word

This book has often pointed out what it takes for BC to become an integral part of the corporate culture for it to be fully effective. This is where the importance of acknowledgment comes into play. Whenever people do something which is above and beyond their regular range of duties they expect some form of closure; otherwise, they tend to doubt the value and importance of that piece of work. Consequently, they will be reluctant to get involved again. However, if they are properly acknowledged they will be much more positive about the matter. The best form of acknowledgment is a public recognition; so please remember to say "Thank you," preferably in a positive and meaningful format. It will make them feel better about themselves, you, and whatever you have asked of them.

Dear Reader,

Thank you for showing an interest in the subject and making the effort to study it thoroughly. Having read this book and engaged in some of its exercises, you should now be familiar with the basic principles of business continuity and ready to engage in its practice, using my tools and techniques. I wish you every success in the future.

Jim

BC is still a relatively young and developing discipline that has benefitted from its practitioners and advocates who have come from all walks of life. It will continue to evolve with your help and support. Think about what you can contribute to the growing bank of knowledge. Perhaps you can come up with some new techniques, import them from other areas, or simply improve upon the old ones.

Networking among fellow practitioners is an important way of staying ahead of the game, as are horizon scanning and socializing. I suggest that you join a professional association such as the BCI. This would also offer you an opportunity for a formal qualification.

You could link up with DRJ (Disaster Recovery Journal), publisher of a quarterly magazine and host of two major conferences each year. At the end of this chapter is a list of BC networks you may wish to join. You should consider networking within your industry sector(s) through local or regional trade associations, regulatory bodies, and government initiatives. Keep an eye out for new and evolving standards which are relevant or related to BC and other parallel disciplines.

Your motto should be, "Don't be surprised to be surprised." We live in a dynamic, changing world so it is best to remain alert and be prepared to revise your opinions, options, and intentions.

Food for Thought

To reinforce what you have learned in this and previous chapters think about how the theory might evolve into practice. Consider how you see these ideas of infrastructure being applied to an organization you are familiar with such as your school, college, or place of work.

Exercises

1. This book has discussed how the profession has evolved over the years and how the name of the game has changed from time to time.

   > Can you develop your own descriptive name for what the profession could or might become?

   >> Start with an outline description describing what and why. Then refine that sentence down to a short phrase before distilling it further to arrive at a short name using only two or three words.

   > How might that name or phrase resonate with people within your organization?

2. How do you see BC and related disciplines evolving in your organization over the next few years?

   > What influence or impact might you have on this?

3. Think about how your relationship with BC might evolve or change over the next few years.

   > Will it become your full time career, a stepping stone to something else, or something useful to have in your toolkit?

Looking Ahead

To be fully prepared for the future, you need to be fully informed about the future. The best way to do this is to know what others are thinking and saying about what is happening, what might happen, and what you can do. Here are a number of useful networking organizations through which you might benefit from other peoples' views and news.

Organizations and Journals

Continuity Central is an international business continuity information portal which can be found at
www.continuitycentral.com

Continuity Forum is a forum for sharing knowledge about business continuity and resilience which can be found at www.continuityforum.org

ACP, the Association of Contingency Planners, is a membership group that operates throughout the US, Mexico, Central America, and the Caribbean which can be found at www.acp-international.com

The Business Continuity and Resiliency Journal is a quarterly journal which is available online at
www.businesscontinuityjournal.com

For Additional Reading

The following is a selection of the many books available on BC and related subjects:

Blythe, B. (2014). *Blindsided: A manager's guide to crisis management* (2nd ed.). Brookfield, CT: Rothstein Publishing.

Burtles, J. (2013). *Emergency evacuation planning for your workplace: From chaos to life-saving solutions.* Brookfield, CT: Rothstein Publishing.

Cabinet Office (2012). *Business continuity for dummies.* Chichester, West Sussex, UK: John Wiley & Sons.

Graham, J. & Kaye, D. (2006). *A risk management approach to business continuity: Aligning business continuity with corporate governance.* Brookfield, CT: Rothstein Publishing.

Hiles, A. (Ed.). (2011). *The definitive handbook of business continuity management* (3rd ed.). Chichester, West Sussex, UK: John Wiley & Sons.

Hiles, A. (2014). *Business continuity management: Global best practices* (4th ed.). Brookfield, CT: Rothstein Publishing.

Hotchkiss, S. (2010). *Business continuity management: In practice.* London, UK: BCS.

Phelps, R. (2010). *Emergency management exercises from response to recovery: Everything you need to know to design a great exercise.* San Francisco, CA: Chandi Media.

Appendix A

Making Decisions Under Pressure

You looked at the development, delivery, and exercising of business continuity (BC) plans and procedures. You also reviewed how to protect the brand and image by dealing with the communications issues during a period of real, or imagined, crisis. Now you may find it useful to understand how your response and recovery teams can best approach decision-making under stressful and demanding conditions.

A.1   Decision-Making Protocols

In any situation which is likely to be construed as a significant turning point or a lost opportunity, it is important that key decisions and the decision-makers can be robustly defended. If it all goes awry, there will certainly be an inquiry, and this could be followed by a court case. Your emergency decision-makers will then be asked to explain and justify their actions. Their best defense will be to claim that they followed a reasonable set of procedures and offer evidence to support that claim. Thus, you need to have a protocol, or formal process, in place to ensure that they reach their conclusion after due consideration and that the whole process is recorded in accordance with your BC plans, which should call for a history log to be maintained.

Since there are many ways of making a decision, you need to examine those which are appropriate to the circumstances of a business disruption when time is at a premium, knowledge is incomplete, and a great deal is at stake. In this appendix you will look at seven decision-making techniques which are relevant to the emergency management aspect of your BC program.

The first three methods are included here as background information and act as an introduction to the subject. They do not really qualify as "protocols."

1. "Fight or Flee" which is based upon a perceived threat.
2. "Black Swan" which is based upon a surprise.
3. "Routine Mission" which is based upon regular exposure.

The final four are "practical" options that would, or could, work in practice. However, only the final one is actually designed to be truly defensible in a subsequent court of law, which is why it occupies the second half of this appendix.

4. "Dark Serpent" which is based upon a problem.
5. "Carousel Solution" which is based upon group thinking.
6. "Foxy Thinking" which is based upon knowledge.
7. "The DICE Model" which is based upon a formal protocol.

A.2　Fight or Flee

The common tendency to fight or to flee is a natural reaction to a perceived threat to survival, first described by Walter Cannon (Cannon, 1929). In our context, it refers to the momentary state of confusion that we all experience when something dramatic occurs in our environment. Our survival instinct prompts us to flee from danger, but a desire to protect territory and family urges us to stand our ground. In the typical business disruption scenario it is not very clear whether the danger outweighs the desire or the other way around. Confusion steps in and the victim is overwhelmed, struck down by indecision.

…ensure that your people are not caught up in this numbing trap of indecision.

Obviously, such awkwardness is not a useful outcome; in the long run it benefits no one and imposes more responsibility on those who are in the same situation but affected to a lesser degree. You must take steps to ensure that your people are not caught up in this numbing trap of indecision. You can do this by making sure that they have the confidence to follow your plans and procedures through suitable training or exercising.

A.3　Black Swan

Occasionally, something occurs which takes the world by total surprise and we find ourselves having to re-think the way we look at things. According to Nassim Taleb, these unforeseen happenings can be called *black swan* events, so named because until recent times it was always assumed that all swans were pure white. Because such events bring a whole new range of meanings and implications, it takes us a considerable amount of time to absorb the fresh knowledge, integrate it with what we already know, and extract the full range of probabilities in connection with future decision-making (Taleb, 2007).

Clearly, in an emergency or crisis situation, you have no time to ponder on all of the possibilities that an intriguing black swan can offer. You have to get your people to deal with the symptoms or effects of such an event rather than try to speculate on the cause or what might be over the horizon. Your plans and your instructions should get them to focus on sustaining the business essentials and dealing with the scenarios of disruption (as discussed in Chapter 1).

A.4　Routine Mission

The ideal reaction to a difficult or disastrous situation is demonstrated regularly by members of the military or emergency services (such as fire-fighters and rescue workers) who seem to be able to regard the whole episode as a routine mission. Because of months or years of practice, they exhibit what appears to be an effortless but instantaneous thought process. Because they are practicing this type of behavior daily, they are able to approach the situation in a detached, apparently emotionless frame of mind. Their range of experience enables them to assess and evaluate the situation as soon as they arrive. By the time they have parked their vehicles and gotten to their feet, they will already know what needs to be done and will be in the process of selecting the best place to start. Decisions are made so well and easily as to be almost invisible; they just seem to know what to do. It all goes so smoothly that it looks like they are following a script.

To the onlooker who is scared and confused, it all seems to happen without pause. A truly professional approach can come only from a wealth of experience. However, your people don't have the time or the need to acquire the depth of knowledge or develop the competence to perform at this level, although you can use this pattern of behavior as an example to illustrate the value of the plans you have provided and the exercises in which your participants will engage.

While the "routine mission" approach is an ideal way to make emergency decisions, you have to accept that it is impractical for BC personnel, simply because they do not get enough regular exposure to be able to regard a disaster as a routine mission. I have come across a couple of instances in which the nature of the business has required frequent exposures to emergency thinking and, as a result, these people are able to deal with such events as routine; however, they are far from typical.

A.5　The Dark Serpent

These first three "introductory" ways of reaching a decision, described above, provided you with an insight into how the human mind works, but they are neither practical nor dependable enough for you to use as a formal BC procedure. The following four "practical" approaches are methodical ways of reaching conclusions regarding a course of action.

The first, the Dark Serpent dilemma, was first described in relation to the development of counseling procedures for those individuals who had been involved in, or exposed to, an emergency situation (Burtles, 2007). It is relevant here because it explains the manner in which untrained and unprepared people deal with the unexpected such as a BC incident.

For example, imagine that you come across a dark serpent lying on your garden path, and you want to get back into the house. What may appear to be an infinite number of choices may be reduced to five basic strategies that are shown in Figure A-1.

1. **Attack.** You could attack the serpent, hoping to defeat it.
2. **Retreat.** You might take fright and run away.
3. **Evade.** You might consider taking a roundabout route trying to avoid it, hoping it will either leave you alone or fail to spot you.
4. **Ignore.** You can turn around and ignore the serpent, pretending it is not there.
5. **Succumb.** You may be rooted to the spot.

A.5.1　Attack

One approach to any kind of problem, including the dark serpent, is a direct frontal attack. We hope to solve the problem by recognizing it for what it is and using our mental and physical resources to confront the difficulty, overcoming it. This approach often takes a degree of confidence or bravery, as well as some skill in implementing the solution.

You might try beating the serpent with a stick – brutal but effective. You could threaten it with the stick, perhaps throwing in a few aggressive noises for good measure – braver but less certain. You could grab the snake by the tail and toss it over the garden wall. This would require considerable skill and bravado, although it may not be in the best interests of your neighbors. An expert might well recognize the serpent as a harmless species or might know how to drive it away by blowing smoke at it. This would, of course, require specialist knowledge and equipment.

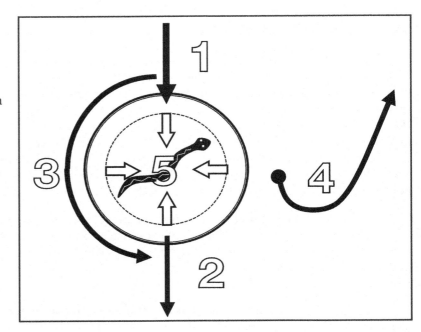

Figure A-1. The Dark Serpent

These typical options within the attack strategy imply going straight ahead and dealing with the problem in an appropriate manner. However, what is appropriate on one occasion may be reckless in many other situations.

A.5.2   Retreat

The opposite of the attack strategy is to assume the problem is not likely to be overcome, and simply run away from it. In the case of the dark serpent, this would mean running or walking away from the serpent, an action justified by the common thought that it is better to run away and fight another day. Unfortunately, the result may be to accumulate a whole series of defeats without ever having fought a battle. The end result is a poor insecure character, afraid of everything and everyone. The retreat strategy can take a number of forms and often leads to some involved reasons, excuses, or justifications for taking the easy way out or the soft option. Do not be deceived – this is not the route to success; it is a loser's strategy.

An expert whom you consult might suggest that this particular species of serpent is indestructible, highly venomous, and has caused thousands of deaths. Another might claim that he does not handle such cases because of an allergy to snakes. However, very few professionals will admit that they run away from problems as a matter of habit.

A.5.3   Evade

The third option is to avoid any direct conflict with the problem. In the case of the dark serpent, this might involve tiptoeing around the back of the bushes, going out of the back gate, and going around the block to enter the house by the front door, or even climbing a tree and entering through an upper story window.

This route would be explained away as "I didn't want to disturb the snake. It looked so happy" – or "frightened," "pregnant," "asleep," or even "an endangered species."

In a real-life situation, the evader would probably rationalize inaction with the excuse that there is no real need to invest too much time and effort on a problem which is infrequent. The avoidance route can often be quite complex and might even be justified by virtue of the fact that it is "more interesting," "more scenic," "more safe," or whatever. The end result is a devious character, one who pretends to himself as well as others. This deviousness may become a habit to the extent that the person may no longer be capable of seeing things as they really are, let alone using simple straightforward solutions.

A.5.4   Ignore

The fourth option is for the person to turn his back on the problem and try to pretend it is not there. For example, he would carry on gardening in the presence of the dark serpent, perhaps mistaking it for a hosepipe. Conceptually, the person is turning his back and not recognizing the fact that there is a problem.

The classic way of dealing with a problem by ignoring it is simply to let all the difficulties mount up and take no action until forced to do so by outside circumstances. A common example is those people who have difficulties with confronting their bills or accounts and consequently get behind in all their payments until someone takes them to court – even then, they pretend all is well. All is well, except for a slight oversight because they have been "so busy" (on holiday, away on business, off sick, etc.) and they will offer to pay off all of their debts by the end of the week, even though there is nothing in their bank account. The true evader does not even know how much money is there, for this person doesn't believe in reading bank statements because they are "so complex," "unreliable," "boring," or even "depressing."

This type of exercise will enhance your team's ability to deal with life and all its attendant problems....

A.5.5   Succumb

The final way of dealing with the dark serpent is simply to stay put and wait for it to bite or possibly move away of its own accord. In any case, there is nothing that the victims can do about it except perhaps to pray or cross their fingers. People who tend to succumb are often highly superstitious, hoping their rabbit's foot, four leaf clover, wooden cross, clove of garlic, or whatever will ward off the evil spirits.

Such people are at the mercy of their environment and will not be able to cope with walking under a ladder in the presence of a black cat, except when there are three magpies in sight, or there is a G in the month. Once one has learned how easy it is to succumb (the trick is to be able to blame someone or something else, e.g., "circumstances," "fate," "the weather," "the season," or "the economy") it is tempting to succumb again, and again, and again. The end result is an apathetic approach to the challenges of life. The ultimate succumb is a coma.

A.5.6   Taking Advantage of the Dark Serpent

The dilemma of the dark serpent can be turned into a useful tool, once you understand the underlying mechanism, which is the basis of solving all of life's problems. You can get your people to practice using the mechanism as a game-plan. Ask them to identify some imaginary problems and then work out how they might solve them with the most appropriate strategy.

This type of exercise will enhance your team's ability to deal with life and all its attendant problems, without exposing them unduly to real life and potentially stressful situations. It is an educational process based on using the imagination within a safe environment rather than a learning exercise based on hard experience out in the field.

The dark serpent dilemma is a useful training and awareness tool which can help people to understand that there is usually a wide range of options and the secret of success is to select the solution which will lead to the most favorable outcome. Its primary purpose is to support the selection of a broad strategy rather than the development of tactics or action plans which require a more detailed approach.

A.6   Carousel Solution

I first came across this simple but effective technique during an exercise which I facilitated on a university campus. The emergency response team was made up of a mixture of lecturers, researchers, and administrators. This decision-making technique appeared to evolve as a natural progression from their normal management style, which they were able to adapt for use in an emergency situation. Subsequently, I have invited other groups to follow a similar team-based approach to decision-making.

When the group is faced with a problem which requires a strategic or a tactical decision to be made, the leader brings them together for an interactive decision-making session. First the leader describes the situation and the need for a decision to the group. The problem is then summarized as a statement on a flipchart or whiteboard, and the leader invites comment regarding the accuracy or validity of this initial premise. If necessary, the group re-words the original statement. The whole purpose here is to ensure that everybody has a thorough understanding of the problem; however, it needs to be kept on track and not be seen as an attempt to explore the nuances of the English language.

Once the group has defined the problem, each person, in turn, suggests a possible solution. No one is allowed to pass, although a participant is allowed to rephrase a previous suggestion or merge two or more into an alternate or improved offering. The essence of each of these ideas is captured on a flipchart. After a short pause for reflection, each person, in turn, is invited to challenge one of the suggestions. This gives the group a chance to look at the answers from an alternate perspective. To ensure that everyone remains focused on the main issue, no one is allowed to make more than one challenge. This is a decision-making group, not a debating society.

After a brief discussion the group is asked to vote and the overwhelming majority indicates the solution to be adopted. If there is no clear winner, then those who proposed the leading contenders are invited to "sell" their ideas before another set of votes is cast. In the unlikely event that they still fail to reach agreement, the leader makes the final decision, taking account of all that has been said.

Sometimes one member of the group makes a suggestion which seems to tick all the boxes right away and no one can come up with a realistic alternative or improvement. The group members immediately recognize that they have the right answer and there is no need for any further discussion. I have noticed that this tends to happen more frequently when the team has been through the exercise a few times before and a kind of group consciousness begins to emerge. In this situation, it seems as though they have all absorbed something of each other's way of seeing and judging things, which gives them a common group perspective.

In the UK, this approach for emergency response teams was adopted by the Highways Agency, a government department responsible for the construction and maintenance of all the main roads. The agency has a dozen regional offices, each with its own BC plans and teams. I proposed the use of this decision-making procedure during a BC training exercise because the facilities manager seemed to be dominating the conversation. He had all the right answers to the questions posed by the unfolding scenario because he had been at the job a number of years and was able to draw on his experience, a perfect example of someone who could view an emergency as another routine mission. I thought that the carousel system would give everyone else a chance to express themselves.

The group soon realized that this rather more democratic approach made a better use of their combined knowledge and expertise. They called it their *round robin thinking system*. The major benefit was that all team members were engaged fully in the exercise so their learning was enhanced. In addition, their knowledgeable manager was able to relax while the debate took place and then chip in at the end if they failed to come up with what he regarded as a sound solution.

Subsequently, the technique was adopted in the other regions and became common practice in much of their committee work outside of the BC context. As you can imagine, these people are confronted regularly by difficult or emergency situations. The pace of response to the majority of their problems can be measured in days rather than hours or minutes; thus, they are not usually working under extreme pressure. Also, they often have a number of alternative solutions with some subtle variations, and this method of decision-making is well suited to their needs in such circumstances.

Confidence to confront the future…is the hallmark of BC preparedness.

This technique was also adopted by a property development and management company which specializes in high-rise office blocks. So far, the company has used the system only in BC exercises and non-urgent situations. However, managers are confident that they are well prepared should the occasion ever arise in which they have to deal with a major emergency. Confidence to confront the future, no matter what it holds, is the hallmark of BC preparedness.

This carousel approach to problem solving and decision-making introduces the concept of a protocol which clearly demonstrates cooperation and collaboration. In other words, group members have reached a conclusion through shared responsibility, full engagement, and a democratic process.

A.7   Foxy Thinking

I was first introduced to this line of thought in 2001 when I was asked to speak at a BC conference in South Africa. One of the other presentations was given by Chantel Ilbury and Clem Sunter who were promoting their book, *The Mind of a Fox* (Ilbury & Sunter, 2001). Their basic premise was that foxes think very carefully before making a decision, in contrast to hedgehogs, which are inclined to make "snap" decisions that are not necessarily the wisest.

According to the authors, whenever a fox spots what might be an opportunity, she will carefully weigh all the information available. Then she will look at the options and consider how those choices might pan out before choosing what to do. Her final choice will be based upon the scenario which is most likely to prove profitable. Profit could take the form of a pleasurable or beneficial outcome; it could also be a reduction of risk or the avoidance of pain or danger. The type of profit chosen will depend upon the situation and the opportunities which present themselves.

The other creature which they used to illustrate the value of their scenario planning approach was the poor old hedgehog, a creature that lacks the refined intellectual capacity of his friend the fox. We assume they are good friends because they share the same territory and don't spend their time squabbling. On the other hand, this may be another example of the fox thinking things through; there is no point in wasting time and energy arguing or fighting with someone so slow and so spiny.

If a hedgehog smells food, he will simply "follow his nose" and might end up in the middle of a country road, exposed to the occasional car. He might end up with a full tummy, but at what risk? A fox faced with the same situation will "use her nose" to locate the food, use her eyes to spot trouble, and use her ears to listen for traffic. She wants to understand the risks and benefits before committing herself with a particular outcome in mind.

When I returned to the UK I reflected on what I had seen and heard. This led to the preparation of my own version of this decision-making model in which I used the wise old owl and the ostrich. These two also have very different approaches to their interpretation of the world around them.

A.7.1   Foxy Scenario Planning

Basically, two key dimensions of any given scenario should influence our decision-making because these aspects govern the likely outcome.

- The degree of *control*, or power.
- The amount of *knowledge* available.

There are varying degrees in many of the factors within either of these two dimensions. However, the principle remains the same. There are aspects of the situation which you can or can't control, and there are things which you do or don't know. Scenario planning aims to take all of these factors into account whenever you are making an important decision. Of course, in practice, we often take a few obvious factors into account and assume that everything else will either have no effect or a benign influence.

Ostrich: The ultimate version of this strategy is to base our decision on the first factor we come across, which is how the ostrich usually operates. He hears a strange noise, takes fright, turns his back, and runs away.

Owl: Our wise old owl would want to know where the sound comes from and think about the implications before working out the options; then she would decide whether to take any action.

Scenario planning is a four-step process, shown in Figure A-2, that requires us to consider what we can, or cannot, control and balance that information against what we know, or don't know, before making a decision in any given situation. Obviously there will be some doubts about the information we have or the assumptions we make, so there is some introspection involved. This reflective aspect of the process should improve the chances of reaching a desirable outcome or at least avoiding the worst result.

Although this technique is specifically intended as a problem solving process, you could use it when facing an opportunity or simply choosing what to do or where to go.

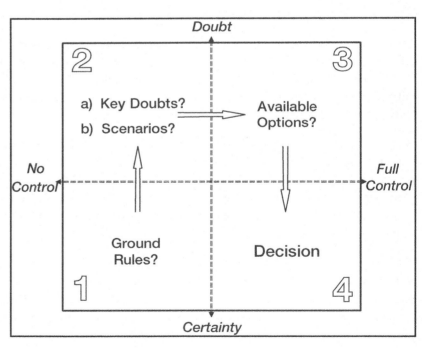

Figure A-2. Scenario Planning

If you plot the degree of control against the degree of certainty you end up with four areas of concern.

1. The first concern is to establish the ground rules of the game. This is the area where you have no control but there is a degree of certainty.

2. The second thing to look at is the area where you have no control and there are some doubts. It is easier to compare the various possibilities by looking at the likely scenarios. In other words, what are the likely outcomes, or how might the future develop?

3. The third area is where you begin to assume, or at least look for, a degree of control. To exercise control, you need to weigh the options which are available to you. Each option is likely to develop into one of the scenarios which you looked at. Some of those scenarios will be more attractive than others; you will need to think things through so that the decision you make leads towards the certainty of a positive outcome. In other words, you need to shoot for the best scenario or make the decision which is most likely to lead towards a good result. This is often described as "weighing the odds."

4. The fourth area, of course, is the decision.

It does help if you come up with a graphic name for each of the possible scenarios because it invests the outcome with a meaningful image rather than a mere statistic like "yes" or "no," "good" or "bad." If you labelled one of the possibilities as "9/11" there would be no doubt about its unattractiveness whereas "Eureka" might signify that there is the strong possibility of a rather more pleasurable or positive outcome.

Review of recent real history prepares us to face the future with more confidence and competence.

In any ongoing event, it is wise to go around the loop again to review your thoughts, knowledge, and outcomes as the situation develops. This will enable you to apply other decisions which could help to deliver a positive result. The other benefit of reviewing the whole process is to spot errors, noticing where you missed something and recognizing the benefits which sprang from your actions or thoughts. Review of recent real history prepares us to face the future with more confidence and competence.

This approach to decision-making is quite deliberate and very well suited to long-term strategic planning. It hasn't been adopted within the BC community because it doesn't seem to suit an erratic or volatile scenario, but it is generally accepted as a useful long-range planning tool within the corporate world. For information about the latest developments in regard to foxy thinking you could visit the authors' website (www.mindofafox.com).

A.8   The DICE Model

These first three "practical" approaches – The Dark Serpent, Carousel Solution, and Foxy Thinking – are a step in the right direction; they provide sensible, useful ways of reaching rational conclusions. However, they do not appear to withstand harsh retrospective inspection. In the BC world, you need to have a robust decision-making system which will stand up to interrogation in a subsequent court of law. Although that is an extreme situation, it must also be regarded as a likely situation because most significant emergencies warrant some form of post-event investigation. Without evidence that decisions were assessed and managed in a reasonable manner under the circumstances existing at the time, the organization and the individuals involved could be deemed to have acted in a reckless manner.

The final offering in connection with decision-making is a protocol which has been specifically developed for use in an emergency situation. The original version was developed in the UK for use by senior police officers. It sought to provide them with a logical, evidence-based approach to making important policing decisions. This approach meant that their decisions would stand up to scrutiny and investigation in the event of a subsequent inquiry or court case.

The version offered here was developed for members of the Business Continuity Institute (BCI) to be used as a decision-making process during a crisis or an emergency situation. It has been given the title of DICE, an acronym which is derived from "**D**ecisions **I**n **C**rises or **E**mergencies." The phrase itself is a description of the model's basic purpose while the abbreviated title hints at the uncertain nature of those circumstances where it might be employed (Higgins & Burtles, 2013).

DICE is a model process which is designed to help top managers and their teams to be able to develop, and subsequently demonstrate, the professional judgment which is deemed necessary to make effective, realistic decisions when dealing with a crisis or an emergency situation, its subsequent effects, and the ensuing consequences.

Adoption and use of this protocol will enable decision-makers to demonstrate that their decisions were arrived at, and managed, in a reasonable and professional manner under the circumstances which prevailed at the time. In retrospect, this should provide them with a sound defense even if some harm resulted from their decisions and actions.

A.8.1   The Six Key Elements

The six key elements in the DICE model, shown in Figure A-3, are the sequential elements of the decision-making process: Values, Information, Strategy, Authority, Tactics, and Actions. Each component provides the user with an area for focus and consideration. The model is intended for use during a crisis and the subsequent response, recovery, and restoration activities.

The inner circle represents the mission and value statement for the organization. This statement needs to be tailored to suit the needs, aims, and culture of the organization. It should be related to, embedded in, or at least aligned with, the organization's BC policy. For example:

▶ *The mission of this business is to provide high quality goods and services to its customers through ethical dealing, fair trading, and honest behavior. At all times we shall endeavor to act to the benefit of the community in which we operate and at no time will we knowingly act to endanger the lives or the safety of our personnel, the emergency services, or the public.*

▶ *We will use discretion, professional judgment, and common sense to guide us and will be accountable for our decisions and actions.*

▶ *The reputation, brand, and image of this organization, together with its products and its services, are of paramount importance and should be borne in mind whenever our decisions, words, or actions are likely to come to the attention of our staff, customers, suppliers, regulators, or the public.*

In a fast-moving incident, it may not always be possible to segregate the thinking....

It is the constant reference back to this mission and value statement together with its integral recognition of the necessity to take calculated risks during an emergency that differentiates this model from other decision-making models. The inner circle connects to, and supports, the five active stages of the decision-making process. While one step logically follows another in a predetermined sequence, the model does allow for continual reassessment and returning to earlier steps when deemed necessary.

A.8.2   Application

This decision model is suitable for making all types of decisions. It can be applied to spontaneous incidents or planned operations, by an individual or teams of people, and to both operational and non-operational situations. It can be used by decision-makers to structure a rational explanation of what they did during an incident and why, and by managers and others to review decisions and actions taken. The inherent flexibility of the model means it can be adapted easily to various situations and scenarios. In every case, the model stays the same, but the users decide for themselves what questions and considerations they apply at each stage.

In a fast-moving incident, it may not always be possible to segregate the thinking or the response according to each phase of the model. In such cases, the main priority of decision-makers is to keep in mind their overarching mission.

A.8.3   Values

Throughout the developing situation, particularly when moving forward to the next stage of the process, the decision-makers should ask themselves:

▸ Is what I'm considering consistent with our mission and value statement? (Decisions should reflect an understanding of the decision-maker's duty to act with integrity, avoid any unnecessary risks, and consider the interests of others.)

▸ What would an official inquiry expect of me in this situation?

▸ What would any victim(s), the affected community, and the wider public expect of me in this situation?

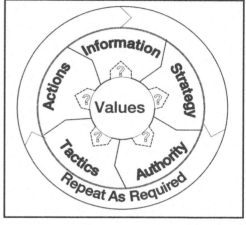

Figure A-3. The DICE Model

A.8.4   Information – Gather Information and Intelligence

During this stage, the decision-makers define the situation (i.e., what is happening or has happened) and clarify matters relating to any initial information and intelligence that is available at the time. Questions include:

▸ What has actually happened?

▸ What is happening now?

▸ What do we know so far?

▸ What further information (or intelligence) do we want or need?

▸ How might we obtain further information?

A.8.5   Strategy

This stage involves assessing the situation, including any specific threat, the risk of harm, and the potential for benefits. Questions include:

▸ Do we need to take action immediately?

▸ Do we need to seek more information?

▸ What could go wrong? What could go well?

▸ What is the risk of further damage or harm? How serious would it be? Is that level of risk acceptable?

▸ Does the situation require that emergency services (i.e., police, fire, or ambulance services) be involved?

▸ Are we the appropriate people to deal with this?

Develop a working strategy to guide subsequent stages by asking yourself:

▸ What are we trying to achieve?

A.8.6 Authority – Powers and Policy

This stage involves considering what powers, policies, regulations, and legislation might be applicable in this particular situation. Questions include:

- What particular powers might be required?
- Is there any guidance from the emergency services, regulators, head office, or others covering this type of situation?
- What does our BC plan suggest?
- Do any local organizational policies or guidelines apply?
- What legislation might apply?

Providing there is a good rationale for doing so, you may find it reasonable to consider acting outside the boundaries of policy.

- If you do choose to stray from standard policy, be sure to record your decision and make a note of the reasoning behind it.

A.8.7 Tactics – Options

This stage involves considering the different ways in which a particular decision regarding incident response, recovery, or restoration can be made (or the situation resolved) with the least risk of harm or loss to people, property, or the corporate image.

The question at this stage is: What options are open to us?

Then the decision-makers should identify suitable responses, taking into consideration:

- The immediacy of any threat.
- The limits of information at hand.
- The amount of time available.
- Available resources and support.
- Their own knowledge, experience, and skills.
- The impact of potential actions on the situation, staff, customers, and the community.

If they have to account for their decision, will they be able to say it was:

- Proportionate, legitimate, necessary, and ethical?
- Reasonable in the circumstances facing them at the time?

Contingencies to be considered include:

- What will we do if things do not happen as we expect?
- Are there any alternatives to which we might turn?

A.8.8   Actions and Review

A.8.8.1 Actions

This stage requires the decision-makers to make and implement appropriate decisions. It also requires them to review what happened once the incident is over.

Respond

- ‣ Implement the option you have selected.
- ‣ Does anyone else need to know what you have decided?

Record

If you think it appropriate, record what you did and why. Records are more dependable than memories.

Monitor

- ‣ What happened as a result of your decision?
- ‣ Was it what you wanted or expected to happen?

If the incident is continuing: Go through the model again as necessary.

A.8.8.2 Review: Recording What Was Done and Why

If the incident is over, review your decisions using the model as a guide, asking:

- ‣ What lessons can you take from how things turned out?
- ‣ What might you do differently next time?

Decision-makers are accountable for their decisions and must be prepared to explain the logic of what they did and why. In some circumstances the need for them to document their decisions is:

- ‣ Prescribed by regulations or legislation.
- ‣ Required by organizational strategies, policies, or local practices.
- ‣ Left to the decision-maker's discretion.

Since it may be impossible or impractical to record every single decision – and not all decisions need to be recorded – professional judgment should guide whether or not to record the rationale as well as the nature and extent of any explanation. What is recorded should be proportionate to the seriousness of the situation or incident, particularly if this involves a risk of harm.

Just as decision-makers can rely on the decision model to guide their actual decisions and actions, they may also find it useful when explaining their logic after the event.

Questions and Considerations to Examine Decisions

The DICE decision model is ideal for examining decisions made and actions taken, whether by a manager, a supervisor, an informal investigation, or a formal inquiry. Examples of questions and considerations are:

Values

> How were the organization's mission and values, risk, and the protection of others kept in mind during the situation?
> Are those values still relevant to the organization's aims, ideals, and purpose?

Information

> What information/intelligence was available?
> What information/intelligence should have been available?

Strategy

> What factors (potential benefits and harms) were assessed?
> What threat assessment methods were used (if any)?
> Was a working strategy implemented? Was it appropriate?

Authority – Powers and Policy

> Were there any other powers, policies, or legislation that should have been considered?
> If policy was not followed, was this reasonable in the circumstances?

Tactics – Options

> How were the feasible options identified and assessed?

Actions and Questions

> Were the decisions proportionate, legitimate, necessary, and ethical?
> Were the decisions reasonable in the circumstances facing the decision-makers?
> Were the decisions communicated effectively?
> Were the decisions and explanations recorded as appropriate?
> Were the decisions monitored and reassessed where necessary?
> What can be learned from the outcomes and how the decisions were made?

Questions for Top Management

> Did you recognize and acknowledge instances of initiative or good decisions (and pass to the decision-makers' managers where appropriate)?
> Did you recognize and challenge instances of poor decisions?
> Did you show support for your staff members even where the outcome was not what you hoped for if the decision taken by them was reasonable under those circumstances?

A.9   Learning from Hindsight

In a post-event situation you might consider reviewing the steps in reverse order in order to obtain the maximum benefit in the form of lessons learned and improvements which could be made to the process, its interpretation, or its basic assumptions.

Start off by looking at the outcomes and subsequent consequences. How do they relate to the ideals of the organization?

Continue to examine the decisions and the process behind them in reverse sequence. Reflect on the outcome and then consider the actions taken, options (tactics) available, powers (authority) available or needed, selected strategy, and information which was available or used. Finally, you should mull over the underlying values and whether they still relate to, or represent, the aims, ideals, and purposes of the organization.

References

Burtles, J. (2007). *Coping with crisis: A counselor's guide to the restabilization process.* Ann Arbor, MI: Loving Healing Press

Cannon, W. B. (1929). *Bodily changes in pain, hunger, fear, and rage* (2nd ed.). New York, NY: Appleton-Century-Crofts.

Higgins, D. & Burtles, J. (2013). *DICE: The decision model.* London, UK: BCI World Conference.

Ilbury, C. & Sunter, C. (2001). *The Mind of a fox: Scenario planning in action.* Cape Town, South Africa: Human & Rousseau, Tafelberg.

Taleb, N. N. (2007). *The black swan: The impact of the highly improbable.* New York, NY: Random House.

For Additional Reading

Disaster Recovery Journal can be found at www.drj.com

The International Consortium for Organizational Resilience (ICOR) can be found at www.theicor.org

Acknowledgment

The DICE model procedure was inspired by, and is derived from, the National Decision Model (NDM) which is used throughout the United Kingdom by members of the Association of Chief Police Officers (ACPO). It was originally developed by the ACPO Ethics Portfolio and the National Risk Coordination Group as a logical, evidence-based approach to making policing decisions. The BCI version was prepared by Deborah Higgins MBCI and Jim Burtles Hon FBCI and presented at the 2013 BCI World Conference in London. The original paper is included in the downloadable **Business Continuity Toolkit**, together with the slides which were used.

Since its introduction at the World Conference in 2013 the DICE decision-making model has had a favorable response from BCI members around the world. In 2014, Higgins subsequently presented it to the US audience at *Disaster Recovery Journal's* DRJ Spring World in Florida where it was well received. Practitioners appreciate its sound pedigree and the transparency which it brings to the proceedings.

The DICE model is now included in the BCI's Crisis and Incident Management course and the BCI's knowledge bank, accessible through its website. Higgins' presentation is available in the DRJ Live Learning Center as well as the ICOR's library of resources.

This decision-making protocol is steadily gaining ground as a recognized methodology which meets the needs of an emergency response or crisis management team whose members might be called to account for their actions.

Appendix B

Case Study: Organic Resilience at Rushmore Enterprises

One means of achieving and maintaining survival capability is *organic resilience*. Any working organization is made up of a number of specialized functional units, each of which contributes to and benefits from the performance and protection of the overall structure. As indicated in the model shown in Figure B-1, performance of the whole arrangement is derived from the outputs or achievements of the functions rather than from the actual functions themselves. An ongoing example in this section will be the experiences of "Rushmore Enterprises," a specialized provider of garden gnomes which are made from cast concrete. It offers a range of styles and sizes to fit all tastes and types of gardens.

B.1   Organic Resilience Approach

This approach could prove to be important in the development and implementation of your business continuity (BC) plan. It will enable you to embed the principles here into the operational structure of your organization, ensuring that BC becomes an integral part of the corporate culture. Once BC has become accepted as an intrinsic part of the overall operation it will become self-sustaining, meeting your objectives of permanence and resilience.

As shown in Figure B-1, any of those functional units could be replaced (or simulated) to enable the overall organization to perform in support of its mission. The quality of the simulation will affect the quality of the overall performance in just the same way as the original function would.

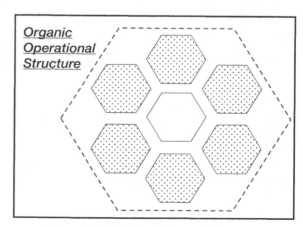

Figure B-1. The Basic Organic Structure

From the standpoint of security, these functional units are essential to the wellbeing and performance of the overall organization and therefore must be safeguarded.

These key functions are interdependent: each depends on the others to receive supplies, goods, or services, and in turn, the purpose of each is to provide supplies, goods, or services to other functions. Whether some of these functions are internal or external to the enterprise makes little or no difference to this discussion, which is about the relationship rather than the ownership. A *process* function carries out a process on a supply of materials or information which comes from a *source* function. This functional relationship is called a *request/response relationship*, an arrangement in which the local requirements have to be met in response to the overall business needs, and services must be properly requested and accounted for.

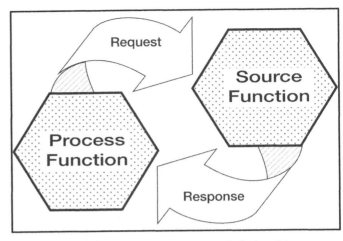

Figure B-2. Request/Response Relationship

Good management is critical to the processes of this basic relationship, both to achieve overall efficiency and to reduce or eliminate waste. For example, the quantities of raw materials on site must match anticipated demand without exceeding their shelf life or breaking the bank. The volume held in storage has to be balanced against the cost of investment and obtaining the best price from suppliers.

Before moving on, take a moment to review a hypothetical business operation. At the core of this imaginary enterprise is the *sales* team which organizes or instructs *production* and *shipping*; it also maintains a dialog with the *accounts* people who look after the finances. The main business operation starts with *stores* which obtains and holds the raw materials that feed the *production* unit. Once the goods are produced they are passed on to *packaging* which prepares them for dispatch and delivery.

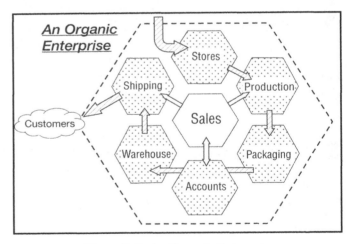

Figure B-3. An Organic Enterprise

Finished goods are held in the *warehouse* until the *sales* team issues instructions for *shipping* to forward them to one of its *customers*. *Accounts* deals with the payment arrangements and gives the OK to *sales* when appropriate. The continuing success of the overall business depends upon the combined efforts of all these elements.

B.2   The Basic Processes in Functional Relationships

To follow on from the basics reviewed above, each function within the organization relates to the others (and thereby contributes to the whole) by one of the four basic processes, as shown in Figure B-4. In essence, these are all quite simple, although their actual implementation may be quite complex or sophisticated at the level of fine detail.

1. **Supplying** is all about the ordering of, or acting as the source for, supplies, services, or raw materials and/or arranging for them to be delivered or available.

2. **Producing** is the conversion of supplies, services, or raw materials into components, finished goods, or services.

3. **Storing** is all about the acquisition of, and holding, stocks of components, supplies, or raw materials and making them available.

4. **Communicating** is all about providing and sending or receiving data or information. It would also include the collection, assembly, manipulation, and conversion where necessary to present the information or data in a suitable format.

Each of these mechanisms can be protected, replicated, simulated, or handled for the organization at the functional level by focusing on the expected outcome of the relationship. The principal concern is the ongoing effectiveness of the overall business operation.

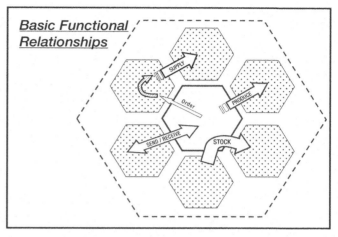

Figure B-4. Basic Functional Relationships

Case Study: Rushmore Enterprises

This case study explores how each of these mechanisms (the four basic processes) might operate in a real-life example of the hypothetical business.

Supplying. The stores department is responsible for making sure that there is a regular and sufficient supply of raw materials. This means it must keep enough cement and sand for a full week's production. Deliveries are normally made on Friday afternoons. Paints are collected as required from a nearby D-I-Y superstore. Packaging also supplies wrapped and labelled goods to the warehouse, ready for shipping.

1. **Producing.** The workshop (i.e., the production unit) is responsible for converting the raw materials into finished products in the right size, shape, and color. There are a number of subsidiary activities which contribute to the overall production process. These include selecting and preparing the molds, mixing the concrete, casting the gnomes, and decorating them once they are dry and hard.

2. **Storing.** There are two functions which are engaged in storing. The stores department holds a stock of raw materials, which means it has to manage and maintain the stock levels. The warehouse keeps the finished and packaged products awaiting instructions for shipment. These instructions are dependent upon sales and accounts completing the deal with the customer. Warehousing has also to keep track of all the individual items to ensure that customers receive the right gnome.

3. **Communicating.** All departments are engaged in communicating to some degree, otherwise chaos would ensue. The main communicators are the sales team members who sell to the customer, report the sale to accounts, and issue instructions to the workshop. Subsequently they get the okay from accounts when the customer has paid and forward delivery instructions to the shipping group. Regular communication between the workshop and stores ensures that the right materials are in the right place at the right time. In the accounts department information about the customer must support invoicing; shipping needs to know the delivery address; sales probably needs names and telephone numbers; and the workshop needs to know how many are needed of each type and color.

You can look at these organic relationships and consider how you might support those relationships in an emergency situation. Those support mechanisms will form the basis of your BC strategy at the tactical level. As you go through the options think how Rushmore Enterprises might approach this aspect of its BC preparations.

B.2.1   Emergency Supplies

In the event of an emergency, when one function is dependent on another for supplies, direct purchasing can form the basis of a practical emergency service.

Supplying requires direct access to the supply chain. In an emergency, the required supplies are ordered directly from within the function, making use of suitable resources, perhaps even retaining the services of the same supplier.

Compared with normal operations, you may experience some loss of purchasing skills and controls. While supplying in this way may impact costs, quality control, and logistics, it has the advantage of being a means of sustaining the operation.

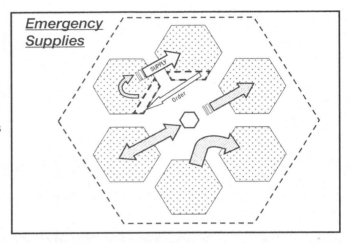

Figure B-5. Emergency Supplies

Emergency direct purchasing does need careful planning in advance of the event. Last-minute changes to the purchasing procedure are fraught with potential problems. For example, a provider of emergency goods and services may see this as an ideal opportunity to renegotiate terms and prices. For that reason, contact details, specifications, contract terms, and other relevant information need to be available and kept up-to-date.

On the other hand, this approach does ensure that the purchaser (the dependent function) is the ultimate user of the product or service and knows exactly what to require and expect from the supplier.

Case Study: Rushmore Enterprises

Rushmore Enterprises already uses direct purchasing for the acquisition of paints and has an account at the local D-I-Y superstore. If its normal suppliers were unable to provide cement or sand, it would have to order some from one of the local builder's merchants at a slightly higher price. Rushmore Enterprises might not be able to get more than two days' supply from such a source at short notice so it is prepared to use several alternate emergency suppliers. The accounts department keeps track of the price of both sand and cement from local sources.

B.2.2   Emergency Production or Acquisition

In the event of losing a production function, apart from closing down, you have two choices:

1. **Emergency Acquisition**, that is, outsourcing all or part of the function, is an option but it could lead to problems with capacity, delivery, quality control, costs, and perhaps image.

2. **Emergency Production** from within the function, on the other hand, contains the problem but it may require a considerable amount of prior planning and investment. The main questions which need to be addressed are those of:

▸ Capacity to meet the demand.

▸ Skills to perform the operation.

▸ Quality control.

Some consideration must also be given to the commissioning (or invocation) process which might introduce delays or other concerns.

A combination of these two approaches might provide a more flexible solution or perhaps be the basis of a phased strategy. If your organization intends to invest in the development of an emergency production capability, an acquisition procedure might serve as a stopgap while it is being developed or commissioned.

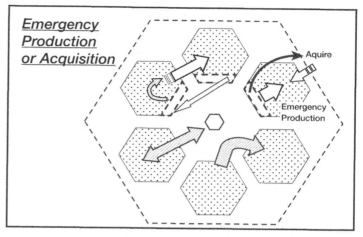

Figure B-6. Emergency Production or Acquisition

Case Study: Rushmore Enterprises

Rushmore Enterprises has identified a couple of suppliers which might be able to supply the company with a limited number of ready-made gnomes in an emergency, but this would be a stopgap measure that would be expensive and might not meet the needs of particular customers. This would be an acquisition strategy, but the company's preferred approach would be to model its gnomes by hand if necessary using old-fashioned methods. Such an emergency production program would be carried out by its modelers and an artist, working at home in their garden sheds. This has been proven to work in a recent BC exercise, so the company is confident that it is an effective strategy.

B.2.3 Emergency Stores or Inventory

Two basic strategies can be taken to cope with the unexpected loss of an internal or onsite stores or inventory function. Your dependent function may be able to cope for some time by revising its operational mode as a temporary measure, but your truly resilient choice is between emergency stock and emergency purchasing.

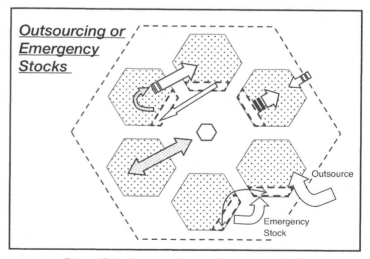

Figure B-7. Outsourcing or Emergency Stock

▸ **Emergency Stock.** Maintaining and storing emergency stock raises a number of warehousing questions such as accommodation and capacity, shelf life, stock control, stock rotation, security, stock volumes, and capital investment. In some cases, the sheer variety of items that may be required is a deterrent. On the other hand, it may be the only way to ensure the continuity of supply to other key functions.

On the positive side, emergency stock can act as a buffer to the normal supply chain and does provide instantaneous cover for an emergency. A suitably buffered supply chain is far more resilient than any just-in-time arrangement. Unfortunately, the just-too-late or even the far-too-late scenario is the ultimate nightmare outcome of such a finely tuned dependency, especially when you are trying to recover from a major disruption.

▸ **Emergency Purchasing**, or *outsourcing*, is the other alternative to having sufficient stock in an emergency. This solution raises a number of questions about delays, quality, volumes, contracts, delivery times, and obtaining credit with new suppliers.

On the other hand, emergency purchasing may be cost-effective because no up-front investment is required other than setting up the necessary procedures. Furthermore, the effectiveness of the process can be tested from time to time whenever the normal supplies are depleted or running low.

To achieve resilience, the ability to test and prove any emergency strategy is a major advantage, especially when it can be achieved without undue disruption or costs. Confidence that the BC and recovery strategies are able to support the business in times of need is a great comfort and a distinct marketing advantage.

Case Study: Rushmore Enterprises

As you have already seen, Rushmore Enterprises does normally carry sufficient stock of its raw materials to last a week or more. This is partly due to bulk purchasing in pursuit of a lower price, and it also allows for delays in delivery. Its BC manager is currently negotiating for additional storage space so that an extra week's supply can be held as an emergency stock. Emergency purchasing plans are also in place. There is one vital item in the company's supply chain which it is unable to simulate or substitute – if the water supply fails it will have to cease production. However, this is seen as a low and acceptable risk which was revealed during the company's risk assessment and discussed during its business impact analysis (BIA).

B.2.4   Emergency Communications

In the area of communications, you face the risk of losing the services of receiving information from an information provider as well as the equally important problem of losing the ability to transmit information.

B.2.4.1   Receiving Information

Where a function loses the service of an information provider, you have four possible responses, as shown in Figure B-8.

1. **Estimate the information.** Very often the required information can be estimated based on trends and norms. Then you can act upon your estimates rather than cease activities altogether simply because of a lack of detail. However, take into account the likely margins of error and their acceptability. This technique is particularly applicable where the information is about volumes of activity, such as production quotas.

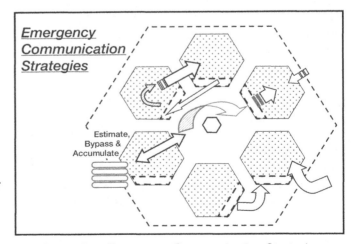

Figure B-8. Emergency Communication Strategies

Also, in the estimation process, allow for "information drift" whereby margins of error increase over time due to lack of feedback or fresh input.

2. **Bypass the function.** Another possibility is to bypass the original function, which gathers and processes information, by going directly to the source. Bypassing the function entirely may involve processing the information in another way, which will require your people to have the capacity and skill to carry out this processing.

3. **Take no action without information.** Sometimes inaction may be your preferred, or only, choice. In this context, instructions can be considered to be a form of information. This default strategy applies where there is a high risk of error or wastage without specific information at hand. For example, a tailor would not want to start cutting the cloth without knowing the measurements of the client. On the other hand, an off-the-rack garment is cut to a standard choice of sizes.

4. **Invent or assume.** In some situations, it may be possible to invent or assume some of the required information and proceed with caution on the basis that some activity is better than no activity. The costs and implications of halting and then restarting a production process may argue against a total closure of the plant. Wasted production may prove to be a cheaper option than the cost of a full restart.

Case Study: Rushmore Enterprises

Acting on any kind of guesswork requires both a high degree of confidence on the part of the decision-maker and an ability to do accurate estimates based on past performance.

The model organization, Rushmore Enterprises, tends to use the estimation route in regard to information about production. This is because there is a steady demand for its standard range of models which doesn't vary a great deal. If too many of one model are made it isn't a huge problem because concrete gnomes do have a long shelf life. The company sticks to the "No action without information" rule in regard to the shipping operation because it cannot deliver and install without the exact name, address, and delivery time.

Inventing or assuming information does not suit any part of its normal operation although some members of the sales team are inclined to stretch the truth at times to persuade a customer to place an order.

B.2.4.2 Sending Information

Where a function loses its ability to send information to another function, you also face these four possible approaches:

1. **Retain the information.** This is a reasonable strategy providing that you have enough storage capacity and the information can retain some of its value.

2. **Condense the information.** Where capacity is limited or the volumes of data are large, you may find it possible to compress the data into a condensed format that will still be of value after the event.

3. **Bypass the damaged function.** Send the raw information directly to its final target, perhaps at the expense of some degradation of the service.

4. **Ignore or delete the information.** This may be your only available option. Summaries might provide you with sufficient historical data after the event.

The model organization looked at all the issues surrounding its emergency communications when developing its BC strategies. The book covered this in Chapter 6.

Case Study: Rushmore Enterprises

At Rushmore Enterprises the actual amount of information passing through the enterprise is relatively small and easy to retain. Hardcopies are kept of all customer details and dealings; accounts still uses a largely paper-based system for work in progress, and data is captured electronically when the product arrives in the warehouse. There is no perceived need to compress information.

In the event that the sales team was incapacitated for some reason, accounts would continue to inform all functions about the status of all current work. This slight overload of information is accepted as an integral way of making sure that everyone knows what's going on. It is regarded as a worthwhile overhead, part of the corporate culture.

It isn't felt that ignoring or deleting information is appropriate to the company's line of work.

B.2.5 Protective Strategies

The loss of a key function has an impact on other functions (and therefore the whole organization) by curtailing or degrading the relationship or service. However, functional outages are often partial or temporary rather than a complete and utter chronic failure. Thus, solutions need to be capable of an instant response and immediate shutdown with minimum fuss or commitment.

In order to develop appropriate and viable protective strategies for the main functions in your organization, you will need to have a clear understanding of the overall business operation as well as a good grasp of how the individual functions work and interact with each other. Earlier you looked at how you might gain such useful knowledge. Risk assessment (Chapter 4) provided an insight into how things work and some of the potential problems. Then you were able to probe more deeply with BIA (Chapter 5), where you examined how the business operates at a grass roots level. Now you are working to develop detailed solutions to support the selected BC strategies (which you dealt with back in Chapter 6) and the emergency responses (covered in Chapter 7). At this point, you can see how it all fits together. It's no surprise that the BC practitioner often has a clearer understanding of the overall workings of the enterprise than anyone else in the business!

You can attempt to protect your organization by adopting one of four strategies:

1. **Defend the function.** Looking at all probable risks, seek to prevent the loss of the relationship by protecting it against all of the known threats. Shown in Figure B-9.

2. **Recover the function.** Be prepared to revive or restart the affected function with minimum delay. Shown in Figure B-10.

3. **Simulate (synthesize) the function.** Establish an alternate source with minimum delay, thus emulating the effect of the affected function. Shown in Figure B-11.

4. **Supplement the function.** Enhance an impoverished relationship by supplementing it from within the target function. Shown in Figure B-12.

B.2.5.1 Defense as a Strategy

When contemplating the ongoing operability of the complete organization, bear in mind the relative value of defense against that of the alternate strategies.

Since defense can be effective only as part of a long-term policy, it requires a major commitment and long-term investment. In practice, defense is only a realistically affordable protection strategy in those organizations where total impregnability is expected and cost is a relatively minor consideration (such as in the armed forces or in key components of the national infrastructure such as power stations).

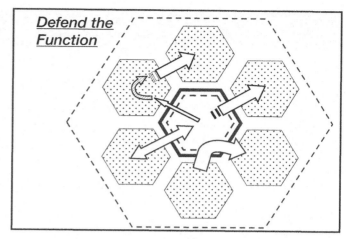

Figure B-9. Defend the Function

Purely defensive measures offer little or no side benefits; they are dedicated to their one purpose and therefore cannot be put to other uses to offset their costs. A defensive policy inevitably imposes restraints or limitations on any future developments which will need to incorporate a similar level of defense.

B.2.5.2 Recovery as a Strategy

For recovery to be an effective strategy, you will need capital outlay or prior investment. Resources and facilities will need to be made available at relatively short notice with some degree of certainty.

The recovery capability needs an ongoing commitment to training and maintenance and will be ineffective if not supported by the requisite recovery skills.

Recovery should be viewed as a medium-term strategy which needs to be reviewed regularly. Every change in the technology, materials, or products will affect the manner in which recovery works.

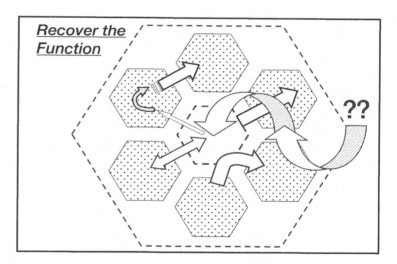

Figure B-10. Recover the Function

There may be hidden benefits. For example, the extra capacity can serve as a training environment or it might be used to carry overloads at peak periods. On the other hand, take care that the recovery facility is not regarded as extended capacity rather than a reserve capability.

You may identify an opportunity to share the cost and utilization of the recovery facility. This could be through cooperation with other similar organizations or by contracting for some form of recovery service with a specialist provider.

Case Study: Rushmore Enterprises

Rushmore Enterprises is considering the development of a hands-on art school focusing on sculpture and modeling techniques which it could use as a recovery facility. Student fees would help to fund the project and the ongoing teaching program would make sure that the facility was always operational. This is likely to be a cooperative endeavor with the local adult education college. In the unlikely event of an invocation, students might be able to act as temporary members of the workforce helping to catch up with the backlog. (See coverage of the "backlog trap" earlier in the book.)

B.2.5.3 Copycat or Simulation Strategy

The principle here is to be able to draw the activity of the source function back into the domain of the dependent function in order to simulate the service which is normally provided by the original source. It is the business equivalent of D-I-Y where you figure out how to do the work at home. Theoretically, all you need are the right tools, the proper materials, and a bit of practice. Obviously, some tasks will require much more investment in resources and skills than others. So a judgment call has to be made in regard to the feasibility and additional costs.

This strategy involves providing your process function with the means to cope independently of the original source function on a temporary basis, perhaps with some degree of compromise in terms of performance, cost, or volumes available. On the other hand, the delivery and communication lines

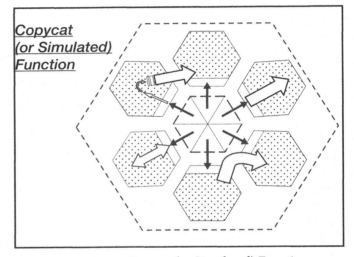

Figure B-11. Copycat (or Simulated) Function

will be much shorter because everything will be happening in-house rather than at a distance. Feedback on issues like quality or customization can be quick and direct.

This strategy does require some forward planning and investment to provide the copycat base from which the simulation can operate within the dependent function.

You also have to recognize and agree upon the degree of compromise that may be required. This copycat base may take the form of accommodation, equipment, skills, or some suitable combination. These alternative resources may either be dedicated for recovery purposes or they can be made available at short notice. You need to make sure that their availability can be relied upon.

Wherever resources are expected or designed to serve dual roles, the secondary role may become critical to some aspect of the operation and a conflict of interest may arise. This risk does need to be monitored on a regular basis.

Case Study: Rushmore Enterprises

At Rushmore Enterprises, the concept of a copycat strategy should be relatively easy to implement because the company is not dependent upon expensive or complex forms of technology and plenty of space is available for additional workbenches or desks. So far it has not been adopted as a recovery strategy simply because no one has looked at it as a serious option. Many organizations overlook some of the simplest of recovery techniques. Somehow, simple solutions seem to be the hardest for some people to accept as robust and reliable, even though simplicity itself is the key to reliability and usually offers the most affordable solution.

It could be argued that the company already uses the copycat strategy in most of its functions, referring to it as "overlapping." The workshop usually holds a supply of raw materials which overlaps the stock held in stores. Packaging and warehousing also share space where finished goods are held. The warehousing people are able to arrange deliveries on behalf of shipping. The sales team members could also do much of the accounting although they do not have access to the accounts for security reasons. This type of overlap would require a high-level decision regarding a significant change in the company's security policy.

B.2.5.4 Supplementing as a Strategy

The principle of supplementing a function is that of boosting or supporting the service available from within the dependent function. It is a subtle but distinct alternative to the synthesis strategy. A careful choice needs to be made between these two alternatives. In some instances both methods might be employed.

In the supplement strategy, each of the dependent functions aims to be able to house, assist, or control its aspect or outcome of those functions which provide it with a service of some sort.

This approach is particularly useful for coping with a diminished service situation. Emergencies often reduce or restrict the capability of a function rather than eliminate it altogether. There are times when the threat of a reduced service has a limiting effect on the

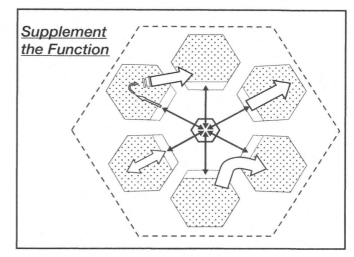

Figure B-12. Supplement the Function

dependent function because the function determines a need to reduce its exposure to an actual interruption which may have a number of undesirable effects.

This strategy also requires forward planning to provide an operating base within the dependent function. This base may be in the form of accommodation, equipment, or skills. Such resources may either be dedicated for recovery purposes or can be made available at short notice. Wherever there is a reliance on making anything available at short notice, you do need to ask some searching questions about the dependability and costs of such solutions. You may need some form of contractual agreement, perhaps with membership or investment costs required to guarantee that the benefits will be there as and when required.

The degree of compromise needs to be recognized and agreed upon. Furthermore, the boundaries of responsibilities need to be defined carefully in order to accommodate the various situations which might arise. It is wisest to challenge the assumptions and explore the likely scenarios before finalizing your strategy for the emergency supplementation of any goods or services.

At Rushmore Enterprises there is a tendency for the supplement strategy to be seen as an integral part of the way in which the company works. Its apprentices serve time in each of the different departments so they become familiar with the various functions and the working environments. Employees tend to work as a community and help each other out as a matter of course. It makes the job more interesting for everybody concerned; it improves overall productivity because no one sits around idle and they are regularly practicing their BC arrangements.

One of the keys to the success of this approach is the way in which the personnel are recruited and their terms of employment. Everybody is expected to be willing to share skills and knowledge, and nobody is treated reverentially or differently. In essence, it is the culture of the organization that allows or encourages this type of work ethic where everybody sets out to be reasonable rather than confrontational. It is also a side effect of adding BC to the culture because flexibility and reasonableness are at the heart of what everyone does.

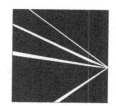

Appendix C

Working with People

People are the most important and valued asset of any organization. At the same time, they are in many ways the most vulnerable and the least understood or appreciated of its resources. Unfortunately, because of the astonishing complexity and resilience of people, much of their vulnerability lies hidden beneath the surface and is rarely revealed to anyone but the most acute or determined observer. Thus, many business disruptions are the type of events that are likely to have an impact upon people without anyone realizing until it is too late.

The key areas of concern for you as a business continuity (BC) planner would be:

- Physical aspects such as personal health and safety and emergency working conditions.
- Welfare aspects such as fatigue and isolation.
- Organizational aspects such as duties and schedules.
- Motivational aspects such as rewards and acknowledgments.
- Mental aspects such as trauma and counselling.

In this appendix, while looking at the effects on people, the term *crisis* is used rather than *emergency* or *disaster* because the concern here is mostly with images and impressions rather than the actual physical effects of the event.

C.1   Health, Safety, and Welfare

The number one priority will always be the health and safety of all concerned. Indeed a great deal of time, effort, and money are regularly invested in preventative measures to achieve this goal. In an emergency situation where people are under stress and perhaps less careful than usual you need to make sure that your arrangements and plans do not aggravate the situation. As you have already seen in Chapter 7, evacuation plans are your means of getting all of your people out to a place of safety. Obviously this will be in cooperation with, or under the control of, the emergency services people who will be expected to take the lead in such matters.

However, once workers and visitors are safely out of the building, think about how they are going to get home. In a large-scale emergency, there may be transport difficulties or travel restrictions – and many of your people may have lost, or mislaid, their personal possessions in the confusion and chaos. This means that they may be left standing around in the cold and wet without money or means of getting home (Burtles, 2013).

Representatives from the HR department, or managers, should be there to reassure people and help them to resolve their short-term difficulties. This may involve a supply of ready cash. To gain some idea of the potential sums of money involved, you could conduct a short survey asking how far your people travel to get to work and what their bus or train fare might cost. Obviously, most of them would have grabbed their jackets, handbags, and wallets before they rushed out, but several of them are likely to have abandoned everything as they fled from apparent danger.

An alternative to a supply of ready cash would be to provide transport for everybody. This could take the form of arranging for a fleet of taxis or a special bus service, but the details would depend entirely on your location, circumstances, and where most members of your staff live.

So far you have looked at protecting and supporting your members of staff, but there are probably going to be other people who will be affected by the disruptive incident. The type and numbers of visitors, clients, passers-by, and neighbors involved will depend upon a number of factors such as your line and style of business, the environment in which you operate, and the local culture. This casual population might vary according to when the incident occurs. Your evacuation plans and preparations need to take account of these issues. Although you might not have any long-term responsibility for these people, it is essential that they reach safety and come to no harm as a result of what happened on your premises. Once they are out of your premises and in a public space, it is probably safe to assume that the emergency services will take care of them. However that is an assumption and I suggest that you check with your local authority in a frank and open discussion about your premises and those who frequent them. It is not merely a question of what the law says or the regulations state; it is more about how these are interpreted by those involved when they are working under difficult or stressful conditions. You will also find it easier to work with these people if you clearly understand how they are likely to behave and what they will expect.

Many emergency situations have an impact on transportation within the area and this can make it difficult for people to get to and from their place of work. If you hold a stock of sleeping bags, it will enable staff to remain in the office overnight in the event of a major transport disruption. They will also need to have access to food and drink. Presumably there will be some simple washing facilities within the premises. Car sharing might also help to get people home.

Temporary staff or visitors to the premises are often not provided for in the BC planning. So the question arises of how to keep track of them and communicate with them, who knows about them, and if reception, the switchboard, or security would be able to locate them.

The other concern during the immediate response to any sort of alarm is the question of security. An incident often provides an opportunity for criminal activity to flourish under the cover of chaos and confusion. Indeed, many incidents have been triggered in order to divert attention and breach security. This is a common way of launching a burglary attack that reduces the risk of being apprehended; the would-be thief can claim that they were only trying to help.

C.2 Emergency Working

Often, there is a need for a major change in the work style, behavior, and scheduling of personnel during the response and recovery phases of a business disaster. There will be many unfamiliar tasks to be addressed and the working conditions may be far from normal. Protective clothing may be required to protect people from hazards such as dust, debris, water, and falling masonry. Much of the work may have to be carried out without the benefit of electricity; emergency lighting might be required. Access to some parts of the premises might be restricted or difficult. If the weather is cold, there may be a need for warm clothing because there might not be any heating available. You and your managers should make sure that anyone who is expected to help out is capable of coping under what might be rather difficult conditions.

Another common requirement of business recovery is for people to be transferred to other locations and take on different roles. This may involve significant differences in their daily travel arrangements, costing them more money and taking up more of their time. Think about how this is going to impact their personal lives and whether it may give them cause for concern or distress.

Management needs to be particularly sensitive to staff needs and reactions at this time. It is important to maintain a regular and open dialogue with all those who are involved or affected. People who are suddenly forced to work with strangers in unfamiliar surroundings can feel quite isolated. This sense of isolation also applies to many of those who are expected to work from home. They lose the sense of camaraderie which buoys them up in the regular workplace, especially if they are at home on their own.

> **In scheduling and staff rotation...bear in mind the impact on employees' family and home life.**

C.2.1 Fatigue and Isolation

The excitement and pressure of the recovery environment prompts everybody to work at full stretch for longer periods of time than they are used to. Often the work is more strenuous than their normal routine. Just the fact that they are working in a different place makes them feel slightly unsettled and nervous. This can lead to fatigue and even exhaustion. During the emergency response and recovery phases, people should be encouraged to take regular breaks and work shorter shifts. If the working day has to be extended in order to deal with a huge backlog, then a shift system should be introduced to combat the effects of fatigue and exhaustion.

C.2.2 Rotating Tasks

During the recovery and restoration phases there may be only a limited number of tasks to be performed which often means a large portion of the normal workforce remains idle while others work their socks off. Apart from the wasted opportunity, this can lead to large numbers of people feeling they aren't wanted and others feeling they are being exploited. Therefore, the tasks should be rotated among all those who are capable. This may be a rather idealistic approach, especially where the work entails specialist skills or knowledge, but the principle is worth bearing in mind.

The schedule of assignments (called a *rota* in the UK) for any particular task should allow for shorter rather than longer working hours. This adjustment should help to reduce the levels of fatigue and also give more people the opportunity to join in and do something useful, which is much more rewarding for them than sitting at home fretting about the situation in which they find themselves.

In scheduling and staff rotation, it's important to bear in mind the impact on employees' family and home life. In reality, some workers may not be able to respond effectively when called upon in a crisis because of family or other commitments – or, because the situation has affected them or their family outside of work (e.g., a regional disaster or weather situation).

C.3   Rewards and Acknowledgment

In order to retain the loyalty of all those who pitched in during the darkest hours of the crisis you must make sure that the organization recognizes and rewards their contribution towards the successful recovery of the business operation. The principal requirement for all those who have been through the stressful moments of a crisis is a proper acknowledgment of their efforts. This should take the form of a public recognition and should come from the head of the organization. Ideally, it would be a personal thank-you in front of friends and colleagues.

Without proper recognition and acknowledgment, the cycle of events remains incomplete and bad thoughts will begin to fester in some people's minds. The inevitable result will be reduced morale. In order to provide an effective closure to the incident, the recognition and acknowledgment should be carried out as soon as it is safe to do so. The longer the delay the more likely that someone will be finding it difficult to cope with the uncertainty, anxiety, and stress which often build up in such circumstances.

C.3.1   Benefits of Debriefing

Whether it is an exercise or the real thing, a debriefing is a very useful way of understanding what happened and capturing the lessons learned. The main reason for a debriefing is to derive the maximum benefit from the experience. (For more about psychological advantages of debriefing, see C.5.3.) However, there are some other benefits which you should recognize.

> ‣ It is an opportunity for all participants to share their concerns and confront their fears in a comfortable context; they will be sharing their thoughts with colleagues who have been through the same experience with them.

> ‣ Everybody gets the chance to make sure the official record is an accurate reflection of what happened and why. You should always assume there will be an inquiry into the events which led up to the incident and the way it was handled. Whether this is a public inquiry, an official inquiry, or an unofficial review is a matter of conjecture, but it is pretty certain there will be some form of inquiry at some stage.

> ‣ There is a success to celebrate. People should all be congratulated for playing their part in the response. They have won a victory against chance and deserve to be recognized; otherwise they may be reluctant to continue to support an ungrateful employer, especially if the going gets tough again.

C.4   Emotional Reactions to a Crisis

Your BC plan needs to make provisions to address the emotional issues that normally arise at the time of the emergency and provide some form of victim support. Often, the personal reactions and emotional implications of an emergency are completely ignored. Even in those cases where the problem is recognized, little or nothing is done until long after the recovery of the business processes. Procedures should be in place to spot potential distress and counselors should be available to help the victims understand and deal with the situation and their reactions to it.

One way to deal with these costly post-crisis effects is to anticipate them and train senior management to recognize the symptoms, understand the implications, and handle their people in a sensitive, constructive manner during and after the event. Such training might also help your managers to be more effective team leaders on a day-to-day basis, a relatively minor investment which could offer a major return.

> **...a few people are able to cope with a critical situation without any apparent long-term effects.**

C.4.1   The Five Discoveries of Stress

After several years of experience in BC, I began to concern myself with how the people were affected after a catastrophic event, such as an earthquake or an avalanche. These massive and violent events had an immediate and obvious effect on most of the victims. However, they were not typical of the crises with which the BC planner is normally concerned. The average business disruption is more likely to threaten jobs and profits than lives and property.

However, it did seem logical to suppose that those who were exposed to less dramatic emergency situations were probably going to be affected in a similar manner – perhaps to a lesser degree, but nevertheless affected. Thus, I began to take a serious interest in the human mind and human behavior under stressful circumstances.

From my observations, I identified five common reactions to a severe crisis, which I think of as the *five discoveries of stress*. Four of them are, in effect, self-discovery in the face of crisis, and the fifth is a kind of discovery of the unknown.

They are the discovery of:

- ▸ Fear.
- ▸ Excitement.
- ▸ Capability.
- ▸ Chaos.
- ▸ Numbness of the unknown.

Each of these reactions eventually led to the same, or similar, result. The victims began to distance themselves from the scene to some extent, either mentally or physically – often a combination of both.

It is worth noting that a few people are able to cope with a critical situation without any apparent long-term effects. Indeed, there are those who experience the phenomenon of eustress or the "euphoria of stress" as opposed to the "gloom of distress." *Eustress* is the technical term for what many of us would call the "adrenalin buzz" that comes from the excitement of the situation. Such excitement can be triggered by the pace at which things appear to happen, the strange nature of the occurrence, the sense of adventure, or the feeling of imminent danger (Burtles, 2007).

C.4.1.1 Discovery of Fear

Whenever people suddenly find they are unable to control the situation around them, they may experience fear of the unknown. Often, this perceived inability to control is simply less control than they had before. However, bear in mind, some of us do not feel that we are in full control of the scene in which we *normally* operate. Most of us have learned to cope with a certain amount of mystery and confusion around us as part of our regular operating environment.

This discovery of fear is accompanied by the recognition of fear as a most unpleasant or uncomfortable experience. Thus, when everything has returned to more or less normal, the subconscious reaction is to regard the once comfortable place of work as a place where life can become most uncomfortable. The victims may seek to change to a safer place of work, one which does not retain the ghosts and shadows of bad memories or anything which reminds them of those bad memories. For many individuals a repeating pattern begins to emerge and with each repetition they become more firmly locked into the pattern and its effects.

C.4.1.2 Discovery of Excitement

Another type of individual will react to the crisis in a totally different way. For some, the event is all rather exciting and dramatic; they find that they enjoy all this random activity around them. When everything is back to normal, these people feel let down and seek further excitement which they will either create or find. To create it they might take direct action, such as setting fire to things, or they may simply be less cautious, leaving windows and doors open or taking risks in some other way. If they do not create the danger which leads to excitement, they will probably seek alternative employment in the hope that things might go wrong elsewhere. What is more, they may set out subconsciously to become a contributory factor to the next "exciting" event. Again a pattern can emerge and become self-perpetuating.

C.4.1.3 Discovery of Capability

Whenever people are plunged suddenly into a situation where the old rules no longer seem to apply, they are often given, or they have to assume, a higher degree of responsibility. As a result they discover their innate capability to exercise more control, or make decisions, or make things happen, or whatever. In short, they discover their true worth under adversity, or at least they get closer to it.

When all the fuss has died down, these capable people are then expected to continue doing the same job as before. Gone is all the excitement and that beguiling sense of power or control. Feeling deprived of responsibility, such people may now seek more responsibility and will begin to look elsewhere to find it. They are unlikely to apply for promotion or expansion in their current environment; they will automatically assume that where there has been no growth in the past, there will be no growth in the future. This is a perfectly rational and often valid assumption.

Having outgrown their current position, they will be keen to move on to somewhere else where they feel they may get the recognition and appreciation they need and want. They will also be encouraged by the fact that they have proved themselves and the experience looks good on their revised CV.

Subconsciously, they may not have been fully motivated for some time. They might have felt bored, stuck in a rather mundane job with few challenges. This type of person needs to be stretched to feel alive. He or she is often summarized on a personnel report form as "works well under stress," "unflappable," or "capable, but lazy." The last comment reflects a situation where the evaluator had not observed the person working happily and purposefully under pressure.

C.4.1.4 Discovery of Chaos

For those who have always led and sought a stable, comfortable lifestyle, their first experience of chaos comes as a bit of a rude shock. What they have always feared and tried to avoid has now invaded their own personal territory. Suddenly they have been confronted by a situation in which there is now very little to cling to –

everything appears to be mobile and insubstantial. All the familiar soothing noises of normal activity, the comforting souvenirs and pictures of the family, seem to have been replaced by a noisy maelstrom of activity, in which nothing stays still long enough to become familiar.

After being burgled, many people say they feel invaded and unhappy rather than robbed. They themselves have feelings of guilt – guilty of being a victim. When they think about it logically, that seems like nonsense, and so they regard themselves as victims of nonsense which is ludicrous. All self-respect seems to have been lost forever.

From this unexpected experience they will have acquired some new knowledge. This new knowledge needs to be evaluated, its intrinsic value and relative truth weighed against existing knowledge. Wherever there is a conflict between existing and new information, the mind will tend to come down heavily in favor of the old knowledge, simply because it has proved workable in the past. Even if the old knowledge proved to be unworkable, at least the degree of unworkability is known and can be allowed for. Familiarity breeds a kind of comfort which is preferable to the uncertainties brought about by change. Any significant change of attitude, viewpoint, or behavior can be very difficult and requires a significant amount of effort and determination. Most of us don't feel inclined to make the effort; it's too much of a struggle. Few of us have the determination to succeed in this area.

The normal conclusion for this type of person will be that it is obviously possible to survive chaos, but it is most unpleasant. We can all benefit from a certain amount of chaos, or change, around us for the sake of learning and to avoid boredom. The problems begin when the amount of chaos exceeds our own personal threshold. Different individuals will have differing degrees of tolerance to disorder or chaos. There are those who seem to thrive on meeting the challenges posed by chaos, but most of us try to lead well-ordered lives in an attempt to limit or eliminate chaos. A stable, familiar environment is the only safe kind or environment for these steady, level-headed individuals.

For this type of person to suddenly discover, or rediscover, the effects of chaos, it must be an unpleasant experience – otherwise they would have been wrong to avoid chaos in the past. Their mind will resist all attempts to make it seem to have been wrong. Being wrong is unpalatable and unacceptable to their subconscious mind, which must always try to prove itself to be right – no matter how devious the proof.

> **Those who have retreated into numbness will now regard their old working environment as…"too dangerous."**

Having revisited and reinforced the decision that chaos must be avoided at all costs, this seeker of a stable environment will now see the current environment as potentially unstable and therefore to be avoided. One way of avoiding the place is to get sick; another way is to find another job. An even more effective combination is to get sick *and* find another job. This person can be expected to have, at least, a cold or flu after a traumatic event. In the extreme, they will even go so far as to get run over by a bus rather than return to what they define as an unbearable "scene of madness."

C.4.1.5 Discovery of the Numbness of the Unknown

There is yet another type of people who are, literally, dumbstruck by a traumatic event. They become petrified with an apparently irrational fear – their fear seems to be far greater than the situation actually warrants. Their basic underlying fear is that of knowing (or experiencing) the unknown.

These people have always assumed they would be unable to cope in a situation in which they were truly afraid. This assumption gets proved right because people of this type retreat mentally and will not confront any situation they suppose they cannot cope with.

This numbness, of course, reinforces their certainty that their mind cannot cope. As this has happened every time they have been exposed to an unusual situation, the reinforcement has conditioned them to respond with "instant incapability" in the event of a crisis or any unfamiliar situation.

Those who have retreated into numbness will now regard their old working environment as a place which has become "too dangerous." They will not be able to feel comfortable there again unless the place is quite literally altered out of all recognition. These people are often unwittingly saved by the fact that the business disruption is sometimes regarded by others as an opportunity to refurbish the premises or re-arrange the furniture, thus saving them from re-immersion in a place which is fraught with danger.

C.4.2   Post-Crisis Exit Effect

Most people will revise their viewpoint of both the job and its surroundings after a major crisis. For many it will lead, in due course, to a subconscious desire or need to move. This move will be to a new type of work, a new place of work, or a combination of both. The essential element they desire is either a change of environment or their position within that environment. Occasionally, this change can be accomplished through a change of uniform or dress style – a fresh outfit can bring about a change of viewpoint regarding one's self and such people see themselves in an entirely different light now that they have consciously made a noticeable change.

> **...delayed exit effects begin to strike just as the company looks like it is on the road to recovery.**

As they are compelled by an unidentified, subconscious desire, their conscious minds will need to invent some kind of rational explanation for the urge to seek change. The social veneer level of "thinking" will be saying something like "I don't want to be stuck in a rut," or "Perhaps I should spend more time with my kids." As some of these excuses can sound rather weak, they may be consciously restructured to be seen to be more acceptable. A whole fabric will be woven around the invented excuse to make it seem more plausible by giving it a complete context. Gradually, they will develop a watertight explanation for themselves. Discussing it with other people will help them to get it clear in their minds, thus reinforcing their need to escape into another environment.

C.4.2.1   Delayed Exit Phenomena

I have observed two *delayed exit* effects – physical and mental – and I have seen how a strong team can be soon weakened by lack of numbers and/or reduced capability. Often, these delayed exit effects begin to strike just as the company looks like it is on the road to recovery. This second, incipient calamity can be more harmful than the original, obvious event. The two delayed exit effects are described below.

- **Delayed Physical Exit.** The end result of all these emotional conflicts and potential solutions is a high proportion of the staff resigning for all sorts of apparently unconnected reasons. Much of this subliminal thinking may take weeks to surface and further days, weeks, or months to implement. Thus, there is such a lag between the true original cause (the crisis event) and the eventual consequence (job change) that the connection between the two events is disguised. This condition is a continuation of the "discoveries of stress," which can lead to a strong need to escape, as discussed earlier in this appendix.

- **Delayed Mental Exit.** Not everyone will respond to subliminal thinking by a full-scale departure – at least, not on the physical level. For some individuals these pressures will cause them to depart from the scene only in a mental sense, a large part of their attention being focused elsewhere. They will while away the hours, and make themselves feel more comfortable, by daydreaming about their aging parents, young kids, puppy dog, or dearest friends. Since their minds are not fully on the job, they will be more prone to accidents and errors than usual.

In effect these daydreamers are operating (responding and reacting) according to their fantasies – their private mental universes – almost as much as they are to the realities of the normal physical universe around them. The more fantasy-oriented they are, the more inappropriate their interpretation of (and consequent reaction to) the real world in which they are operating. They have removed themselves from reality as a form of mental protection. Thus, their minds can become attuned to the different pace, different reaction times, different values, morals, ethics, etc. of those other universes. As a result, when they need to handle what is currently happening in the real physical universe, reactions are inappropriate. The end result is a wrong solution because the mind is operating within the wrong parameters.

If, somehow, you can manage to reduce the impact of these exit effects, you will find it very worthwhile from the business point of view. Clearly, management style during difficult times, or the lack of it, can have a major influence on the way that members of staff deal with their own inner feelings. It costs very little to be kind and considerate, but many of us are locked into an unsympathetic "strictly business" approach which can prevent us from descending to the human plane.

C.5   Specific Forms of Counseling

Often, when working as a disaster support specialist, I came across the need for some form of counseling or moral support among my clients. Over the years, I studied the subject, discussed it with experts, and developed my own approach to dealing with mental and emotional problems associated with people who have been somehow involved with a business disruption. The distinguishing characteristic here is that these people have been exposed to something quite unexpected that occurred only once. They have not been subjected to an ongoing series of similar or related experiences, which is unusual in the field of psychotherapy where most sufferers are, or have been, victims of repeated attacks or disturbances. Unless you have some training and practice in counseling and are prepared for the many surprising reactions people can have to the most well-meaning attempts to help them, please seek the advice of a trained counselor before attempting to use any of these methods on your own.

C.5.1   Restabilization

Working with a couple of experts in the field of therapeutic counseling, I developed a technique I call *restabilization*, which has proved an effective therapy for those who have been impacted by an emergency situation in the workplace. Although it is a simple process, it should be applied only by those who have had training and practice as counselors. Restabilization is a four-step process: recap, review, repair, and reinforce. Each session deals with a specific aspect of the event and its consequences.

1. **Recap:** During the initial recap session, the person who has been exposed to an unpleasant experience is asked by a trained facilitator to recall what happened and how he or she reacted. This establishes a clear picture of what actually occurred and the impact it had upon this person. Although it may rekindle some of the emotions associated with the event, it does allow the person to confront those emotions. The next step in the process should follow shortly afterwards or it may even be an extension of the first session, if the person is ready to move on.

2. **Review:** In the review session, the person is asked to review his or her reactions to the situation and any misunderstanding which may have arisen. The idea here is to get the person to take responsibility for his or her reactions and compare them to his or her image of the ideal way of dealing with such a situation. Often the person will recognize a number of alternative options. For example, the reaction at the time may have been mixed emotions of anger and frustration. On reflection, the person may realize that the initial anger was not helpful and patience would have

been more constructive than frustration. This leads the person to think that harnessing anger and focusing attention on trying to be helpful would have been wiser and more productive.

3. **Repair:** Soon after, at the repair session, the person looks at how he or she might deal with a similar situation in the future, adopting the wiser and more productive approach which was recognized during the previous step. Once the person has figured out a better way of dealing with such a situation, his or her attitude will change. Instead of fearing a repeat set of similar circumstances, which would re-stimulate anxiety, he or she can look forward to meeting the challenge with a degree of confidence that he or she can turn a negative event into a positive outcome. That confidence is helpful, but it may only be short-lived and doubts could set in.

4. **Reinforce:** In the final reinforcement session, confidence for the future is built up by exploring what might happen in a number of similar imaginary situations. After a few of these introspective case studies, the person begins to be convinced that he or she is ready for anything that the future might bring. By now, participants will know themselves and have worked out how to think their way through such a situation in a practical manner rather than be overwhelmed by their emotions. Armed with that confidence, the person is no longer suffering from the traumatic after-effects of the incident.

Be aware that I do not recommend this restabilization process for those really traumatic incidents in which there are casualties or serious injuries. While restabilization might be useful as a form of first aid, deep trauma may require rather more serious psychotherapy.

C.5.2   Traumatic Incident Reduction (TIR)

A more generalized approach to counseling for people who have experienced a traumatic incident, or even a series of traumas, is *traumatic incident reduction* (TIR). Developed by Dr. Frank Gerbode, the founder of the modern *metapsychology* movement, TIR stresses counseling therapy as a way of developing the spirit for personal growth and recovery, rather than as an answer to all sorts of mental disorders (Gerbode, 2013). TIR is aimed specifically at providing relief from the after-effects of a traumatic incident. The technique is now taught and delivered around the world by members of the Traumatic Incident Reduction Association (TIRA). This professional group was formed by and is recognized by Applied Metapsychology International (AMI) as the official membership organization for those practicing TIR and related applied metapsychology techniques (TIRA, 2014). The essential elements of this style of counseling are that the counselor is trained to allow clients to develop their own understandings and resolutions to the problems which they face. The counselor quietly and patiently steers the client towards his or her own solution, does not draw any conclusions, but offers support throughout the process. Because the treatment stems from the client's self-observations and insights rather than the imposition of another person's suggestions which have to be learned, adapted, and adopted, TIR works relatively quickly and does not usually require multiple sessions for the benefits to be realized. Like the other methods described here, it should be applied only by those who have had training and practice as counselors.

> **...it is important that no one be forced to participate and that no negative professional evaluation be noted...**

C.5.3   Debriefing Sessions

Scheduled debriefing sessions need to be part of your BC plan. In the majority of business disruptions, the emotional impact on most of the people will be relatively light. After all, problems and setbacks are so commonplace in our working lives that we learn to deal with them and accept their consequences. However, there are limits to our capacity to take things in our stride; some of us are better than others, and some of us might be going through a tough patch when an incident occurs. A formal debriefing is a means of capturing the lessons, providing evidence of prudent management, and enhancing team spirit. If the process is approached in the right way, the therapeutic benefits come as a bonus. Since the facilitator of the debriefing is probably not a trained mental health professional, it is important that no one be forced to participate and that no negative professional evaluation be noted for the people who do not participate. Those who are too upset to participate should meet with a professional counselor to determine the next step they need to take to re-enter a workplace that has been disturbed for them.

A well-organized debriefing session can offer psychological benefits in the wake of a low impact, injury-free incident, although psychological assistance may not be perceived or mentioned as its primary purpose. Once you have explained to management that the purpose of the debriefing is capturing the lessons and demonstrating prudent management, the debriefings will be accepted as part of the recovery process without any further argument or justification. Your only challenge is to make sure that debriefing is handled in a manner that improves the team spirit and allows people to deal with their hidden concerns about the workplace which has become a reminder of something somber.

After the meeting, people who have shared a difficult experience together and have also had a chance to see it from each other's perspective will feel closer to each other than before. They might also feel comfortable discussing the matter among themselves as a means of dealing with any remaining bad memories. The end result will be a better team spirit and a more productive atmosphere.

The timing and the style of the debriefing or review session are important. Hold the meeting soon after the incident is over, preferably within 24 to 48 hours. Events will still be fresh in everybody's mind but no longer troubling them. If you wait longer, people may find the meeting uncomfortable and are likely to have forgotten much of the detail.

During the meeting, all participants should have a chance to air their views and express their opinions. Talking about it is the only way for them to gain release from the emotional attachment or impact. There should be a rule that nobody gets criticized or corrected at this time; otherwise you could make the situation worse for them by enhancing the bad aspect of their memory of the event. Without such a rule, some people will not feel safe to vent their feelings in case they are accused of weakness, ignorance, or stupidity.

The group as a whole should agree upon the facts which need to be recorded because that is the primary purpose of the gathering. However, opinions, emotions, and doubts do not count as facts, serve no long-term purpose, and are best left unrecorded. This should be made clear at the outset to encourage freedom of expression during the meeting.

C.5.4   Self Help

Some of your people who have lost some self-confidence through exposure to an incident and its after-shocks may be reticent to air their problems in public, open to the intervention of others. They might want to try to deal with the issues alone through a process of self-analysis. They may even be unwilling to participate in the most non-threatening debriefing. The essential element of such a process is for them to find a way to express their thoughts and reactions about the event which has affected them. Once they have put these thoughts into words, they have an opportunity to work out in their minds what really happened and what needs to be done or said to put the whole matter to rest.

Clearly, this approach is effective only in those cases where the symptoms are light or marginal and the subjects are willing and able to manage the process for themselves. A very simple and useful technique uses journaling to allow people to record their thoughts in writing and then re-read what has been written with a view to learning more about what happened and how they reacted. (While some professional teachers of this method insist that better results are achieved when ideas are expressed in longhand on paper, people who are accustomed to working on a computer may be more comfortable setting up their journaling as computer documents. If they don't have to write in longhand, they may be more likely to complete the exercise.) This process can lead to more writing and more reviewing. Eventually, by repeating the cycle, people can achieve relief from whatever was troubling them or at least put it into such a perspective that they can deal with it, possibly by seeking outside support if needed.

…the news to next of kin needs to be delivered by people who have the training and preparation…

A formal process known as *paper exploration therapy* (PET) may be of some use to your people. The PET process has been in regular use by a number of my colleagues for a few years now and is accepted by them as a useful lightweight therapy. A full description is available in the downloadable **Business Continuity Toolkit**. Make sure you understand the program and how it works – and seek the guidance of a counseling professional – before taking it upon yourself to "prescribe" to others.

C.6   A Family Contact Team

Whenever a serious incident occurs, the relatives and friends of all those who might have been involved will want to know what is happening, what is being done about it, and how it has affected their loved one. Once the news gets out that something has gone wrong, the world will want reassurance about their acquaintances, friends, co-workers, neighbors, and relatives.

Staff members who are safe and uninjured should be encouraged to call their own relatives as soon as possible to report their safety. This will reduce incoming telephone traffic, which tends to be overwhelming in the event of a major incident. It is a proactive approach which will be appreciated as a positive contribution to the community spirit.

Setting up a small *family contact team* as one of the teams in your BC plan is a practical way of dealing with worried relatives. Worried relative inquiries will probably outnumber the staff headcount by a considerable margin. This group should be tasked with calling the families of any staff members who are, or might be, affected by the incident and are unable to make those calls themselves. Appropriate contact details should be held by the HR department. If you have a computer-based BC plan, you may have already gathered all the staff contact information in a database as part of the BC plan, along with alternate numbers to reach staff members and their relatives.

Your family contact team needs to coordinate with the crisis management team to ensure that all messages to the outside world are synchronized. Team members need to be provided with a statement or instructions about what to say and not say. The basic instructions will be in your BC plan but will need to be adapted for the current situation.

If casualties or fatalities are involved, the news to next of kin needs to be delivered by people who have the training and preparation to deal with this sort of situation and to cope with the consequences. While in the UK such tasks are usually left to law enforcement, medical personnel, or the coroner's office, in the US it is often the trained "family representatives" of the organization who deliver the news. Blythe observes, "Whatever the culture, it's a mistake to assume that you can simply pass the duty of death notification on to law enforcement or medical personnel" (Blythe, 2014, p. 141). Your organization would do well to arrive at clearly stated "Family Notification Guidelines" as part of your procedures and planning (Blythe, 2014, pp. 142-143).

References

Blythe, B. T. (2014). *Blindsided: A manager's guide to crisis leadership* (2nd ed.) Brookfield, CT: Rothstein Publishing.

Burtles, J. (2007). *Coping with crisis: A counselor's guide to the restabilization process.* Ann Arbor, MI: Loving Healing Press

Burtles, J. (2013). *Emergency evacuation planning for your workplace: From chaos to life-saving solutions.* Brookfield, CT: Rothstein Publishing.

Gerbode, F. (2013). *Beyond psychology: An introduction to metapsychology.* Ann Arbor, MI: AMI Press.

Traumatic Incident Reduction Association (2014). Retrieved from http://www.tir.org/index.html

For Additional Reading

Ellis, A. & Harper, R. A. (1979). *A new guide to rational living.* North Hollywood, CA: Wilshire Book Company.

Hawkins Mitchell, V. (2013). *The cost of emotions in the workplace: The bottom line value of emotional continuity management.* Brookfield, CT: Rothstein Publishing.

Lukaszewski, J. E. (2013). *Lukaszewski on crisis communication: What your CEO needs to know about reputation risk and crisis management.* Brookfield, CT: Rothstein Publishing.

Appendix D

Emergency Evacuation and Back to Normal

Over the years, many of us have looked at emergency and contingency plans for such diverse threats as fires, floods, hurricanes, typhoons, tornadoes, earthquakes, terrorist activity, riots, demonstrations, and military coups. In all of these situations, there is a basic question of how to ensure the safety of the people. Sometimes, it is safer to remain indoors than to run out into the face of unknown danger. There may not be enough warning or information to make a carefully considered choice.

In a military context one workable solution is to harden the building to provide a permanently safe shelter for the workforce. While some elementary defensive measures are possible in the commercial world, you will be more likely to adopt evacuation as a preferred and practical choice. All of the other options seem to require capital investment or invite high running costs when they are invoked.

If emergency evacuation planning (EEP) is accepted as a sound strategy, it is worth exploring what is involved and how you might adopt, or adapt, a common approach. The process described here is offered as a starting point rather than a de facto standard. You may need to modify it beyond recognition before it suits your particular circumstances. For a more comprehensive and authoritative guide, the reader can refer to the EEP lifecycle process in my book, *Emergency Evacuation Planning for Your Workplace: From Chaos to Life-Saving Solutions* (Burtles, 2013, pp. 1-8).

D.1   Emergency Evacuation: The Starting Point

My starting point was to consider what I have learned over the years as a practitioner, review the literature, and apply some common sense. Much of the material I had access to was anecdotal or confidential and a lot of the common sense was second hand. But the acid test of these suggestions is whether you are prepared to take them on board as the basis of your approach.

There are five stages of consideration and action:

1. Site review process.

    Highlighting risks and identifying opportunities.

2. Evacuation and invacuation.

    Looking at the options and making choices.

3. Emergency assembly areas.

    Selection of safe sites and safe routes.

4. Emergency response timing.

    What is realistic vs. desirable or needed.

5. Test and rehearsal regime.

    Proving it works and preparing the people.

Emergency evacuation planning focuses on the protection and safety of people, taking no account of the protection of resources or property. It assumes that property and resources are expendable in the circumstances of such an evacuation.

Note: *Invacuation* is a specialized variant of evacuation that seeks to make use of internal refuges or safe spaces within the building. It is particularly relevant to those premises where there are people who have disabilities or limited mobility.

D.1.1   Site Review

A site review for emergency evacuation planning includes the whole of the neighborhood and the neighbors. You need to identify any risks to people's safety throughout their progress from their place of work to the probable points of safety. Bear in mind the likely circumstances that would trigger an emergency evacuation and the numbers of people involved. Many of the potential threats would apply to buildings in the immediate vicinity.

> **A safe open space will be at some distance from the home location and will not be in line of sight....**

Pay particular attention to the exit points from the building. There must be at least two emergency exits, each offering different aspects or escape routes. People should be able to exit in any direction, i.e., through a front, rear, or side exit. Where appropriate, exit points should be equipped with a stout canopy, or a covered walkway, so people are protected from falling debris as they move away from the building.

Safe Spaces

The second objective of the site review is to identify a number of safe spaces to be considered as a potential emergency assembly area.

A safe open space will be at some distance from the home location and will not be in line of sight of the likely target. This is a precaution against flying debris. The assembly area should also be a safe distance from nearby buildings to avoid the hazard of falling debris. In practice, the area should be at least 500 meters away or within about 5 minutes of walking distance.

Once you have identified some safe spaces you need to plot some safe escape routes from the exit points to the external assembly areas. There should be at least two alternative routes to each assembly area to avoid unexpected crowds, obstacles, or additional dangers. Ideal escape routes avoid straight lines because corners provide protection.

Will We Be Safer Indoors or Outdoors?

"To flee or not to flee, that is the question: whether 'tis nobler to stay behind and suffer the slings and arrows of fortune or to take a chance amongst a sea of rubble?" Hamlet clearly had a dramatic moment and was unable to make up his mind. In an emergency situation, you have no time for introspection or speeches – you must decide and act accordingly without delay.

You need to establish whether your building can be considered as a safe refuge in the event of an emergency. If there is enough safe space within the building, *invacuation* might be an option. There is the advantage that nobody has to expose themselves to any external dangers as they escape. This has to be balanced against the possibility of being trapped inside the building. Clearly, if there is sufficient notice of the impending danger, then complete evacuation to a remote assembly area is usually the preferred strategy.

D.1.2   Emergency Evacuation Process and Timing

In order to develop a rational process for emergency evaluation and evacuation you have to make some assumptions or set certain parameters. These parameters will need to be tested, reviewed, and revised at the earliest opportunity. Here are some typical parameters you might use as a starting point:

- There will be an evacuation window of up to 20 minutes.
  - ❏ That is the time from the first alarm to the incident occurrence.
- The emergency assembly areas are within a 5-minute walk.
- Exit time is 4 minutes.
  - ❏ That is the time it takes to get everyone out of the target building.

You cannot verify or influence the duration of the evacuation window, but you can take steps to check the other two parameters. If you cannot meet either of these limits, then one has to question the wisdom of occupying that particular building.

The emergency evacuation procedure will be something like this:

1. An alarm message is received and passed directly to the security officer, the person responsible for security and safety.

   Target = 2 minutes from ET Zero   (ET Zero = Start of Emergency Time)

2. A staff warning is issued advising everybody that an emergency is being investigated and that they should have their personal belongings with them. Meanwhile the security officer tries to verify whether it is a genuine emergency. This may be a call to the police or a quick review of the known facts and the current state of alert.

   Target time = 4 minutes from ET Zero

3. Security officer then confirms the message and invokes the emergency evacuation procedure or selects stand-down.

   Target time = 5 minutes from ET Zero

4. Security officer selects the assembly area and escape route based on information available. The default area should be indicated in the plan.

   Target time = 6 minutes from ET Zero

5. Evacuation, or stand-down, is announced by the most appropriate means. If there is no PA system the message may be cascaded via floor marshals. The message clearly states which exits, routes, and assembly area to use.

    Target time = 8 minutes from ET Zero

6. Everybody leaves the building via the selected exits and proceeds to the emergency assembly area using the selected route. Security staff or floor marshals check that the building is clear before leaving.

    Target time = 12 minutes from ET Zero

7. Everybody gathers at the emergency assembly area awaiting further instructions. All heads of departments, or specially appointed marshals, conduct a head count or identify anyone missing from those who were known to be in the building. Everyone else should try to meet up with the rest of their department and make their presence known.

    Target time = 18 minutes from ET Zero

Exceptions

If the original alarm message is from a trusted official source, such as the police or fire service, the security officer should immediately invoke the emergency evacuation procedure (step 5), as there is no need to verify that the alarm is genuine.

Once you are reasonably confident the plans should work, you must carry out a dress rehearsal....

If the original alarm is not confirmed as a genuine emergency situation, the security officer should issue a stand-down message so everyone can return to their normal duties with confidence.

This is a simplistic outline of the basic process and should be tailored to suit any particular organization and its circumstances.

D.1.3   Test and Rehearsal Regime

No plan of action has any value until it has been proven. Even then it has precious little value until all of the actors have practiced their performance. There is no question that Shakespeare wrote good plays but I can't imagine any drama company wanting to stage one of them without a few rehearsals. Remember, our actors are not accomplished professionals, and perhaps you should not put too much faith in a plot that has not yet stood the test of time.

Seriously, you must test your plans to see how well they work. You must also challenge the assumptions about timings. Once you are reasonably confident the plans should work, you must carry out a dress rehearsal to make sure everyone knows what to do and how to do it. Over time they will either have forgotten what they were told, lost confidence in the process or their recollection of it, or they will have been replaced. This means you have to carry out practice evacuations on a fairly regular basis; otherwise, your plans could cause chaos rather than save lives and, after all, saving lives is the whole point of the exercise.

Explanations, diagrams, and presentations are not enough to convince people about the wisdom and practicality of the company scheme to get them out of the building and to a place of safety. It is essential that they are given the opportunity to explore the whole of the route. This has two benefits. First, they will have a clear picture in their minds of the routes and assembly areas which means they will be able to understand and follow the emergency evacuation instructions. Second, they will become confident that there really is a route to safety, which is very reassuring in an emergency situation.

D.2   Back to Normal: Reverse Recovery or "Revacuation"

After evacuating your normal place of work, establishing yourself in some temporary accommodation, and catching up on the backlog, it is soon time to think about *revacuation*, or the return journey. The only problem is it might not be a return journey in the sense that you simply go back to where you came from. It could all be very different – in fact it will probably be very different even if it looks the same. A lot has happened while you have been away. Days have come and gone. Databases and applications have been updated and changed. Services and products have been delivered – or not delivered. Customers have been served, misled, confused, or disappointed.

How can you make this return journey any easier than the sudden unplanned retreat which proved the need for continuity plans, recovery services, and plenty of practice? Well, the first thing to remember is that you can return at a time of your choosing. The second thing to remember is what you have learned from the review of the exodus. You can also adopt a rather different attitude to the homecoming: it is a welcome opportunity rather than a dreaded possibility.

Don't view this as a step back, rather as a step forwards. It is a *relocation project* and needs to be approached in that light. Maybe there is an opportunity, or even a need, for refurbishment or redecoration. Perhaps there is even some new equipment. It should be something for people to look forward to. Is it worth considering whether the old layout was the best layout? Maybe there is a case to be made for looking at who, and what, goes where. It's not a requirement to make changes, but you should

> **Very few BC plans cover this return phase, or reverse recovery, as a part of the long-term strategy....**

at least ask the question. Now is an ideal opportunity. On the other hand, if there has already been enough chaos, perhaps a bit of stability will make a nice change.

D.2.1   The Timing

The reverse recovery operation should be attempted during a quiet period rather than a peak period of activity or change. Avoid busy times like the end of a month, quarter, or year. You may also want to avoid peak holiday periods or any other occasions when you are likely to be short of staff; on the other hand, a holiday period may be the quietest time. A good business continuity (BC) manager knows when the business is at its most stable point and when its vulnerability or exposure is high. In any case, allow everyone time to recover, mentally and physically, from the recent emergency situation.

D.2.2   Migration and Commitment Points

Regard this next adventure as a migration rather than a leap in the dark. Do things in a planned and phased manner – there is no need to cut and run. You can overlap your operations, bring up the home systems, and gradually move them across, a section or group at a time. If things start to go pear-shaped, you can back out of the commitment to the old systems and stay with the recovery system. This applies to data processing and all other sorts of business operations. Figure out where your commitment points are and make sure everyone knows how to spot them. Do not burn any bridges, since you want to keep the choices open as long as you can.

You will need a proper project plan for this move. The regular BC plan may work backwards or it might have a reversing mechanism built into it. Only you can know about that.

Very few BC plans cover this return phase, or reverse recovery, as a part of the long-term strategy, although they should. Usually the return to normal is arranged as an afterthought, and people tend to have a strong feeling that once they have survived a disaster, they will be in a much better position to deal with another disruption. However, it is far better to invest in some real preparation than to place any reliance on the romantic notion of inspiration somehow saving the day.

D.2.3   Stumbling Blocks to the Return to Normal

If you have come this far, it must be worth making the extra effort to develop at least some guidelines for the return to normal. The return phase may not be as simple as merely reversing the recovery procedures. The timeline of continuity only moves forward; it can't be forced to go backwards. Therefore, you must figure out an equally robust return capability to which the business can turn with some confidence. For both participants and upper management, the successful recovery will have gone a long way to underpin their confidence and trust in the therapeutic powers of BC. Some of the stumbling blocks you might encounter during this seemingly innocuous but equally precarious set of maneuvers can include:

  ▸ Overconfidence causing carelessness.
  ▸ Apprehension leading to diffidence.
  ▸ Bravado in the face of a challenge.
  ▸ Insufficient recuperation.
  ▸ Catching up and forward loading.

D.2.3.1 Overconfidence

People will feel weary if they are not given a few days in which to settle back into their routine…

After overcoming one set of hurdles quite successfully there is a natural tendency towards a sense of invulnerability. In practical terms this can lead to silly mistakes caused by lack of attention to detail. Just because the big picture looks rosy there is no reason to allow people to take their eye off the ball. Indeed, now is the time to be ultra-cautious because the battle is not yet over; there is at least one more skirmish to come.

D.2.3.2 Apprehension

While over-optimism can cause a degree of recklessness, the opposite approach can be equally damaging. You must not allow judgment to be impaired by low expectations inspired by the experience of recent events. Waiting too long, suspecting the worse, and acting nervously can be demoralizing. Not only that, but the resultant blinkered view may cause your people to lose sight of the big picture. Focusing on the negative can obscure the positive.

D.2.3.3 Bravado

Bravado is also known as the "Rambo" effect. Here the concern is with those individuals who are inclined to become rather reckless once they are let loose. They actually enjoy chaos and will do whatever they can to introduce it and turn the whole process into an exciting adventure. Their dream of performing heroic deeds can easily become a nightmare for those who become their unwitting victims.

D.2.3.4 Insufficient Recuperation

Once all the excitement and activity associated with emergency response and recovery of the operations is over, fatigue is likely to set in. People will feel weary if they are not given a few days in which to settle back into their routine and catch up with themselves. Do not be in too much of a hurry to impose another upheaval upon them; let them have a chance to regroup and recuperate.

Staggered "Unrecovery"

It is worth bearing in mind that the return to base does not have to be achieved all in one swift move. There is a case to be made for staging, with a respite in between stages. Take a breather from time to time and let the dust settle. Then you can tackle the next step with a lighter heart. Naturally, you will feel a lot of pressure to get the job over and done with, but it does need to be managed and controlled in conjunction with all the other activities of the normal routine.

D.2.3.5 Catching Up and Forward Loading

Perhaps the most treacherous pitfalls you are likely to encounter during the reverse recovery are the *backlog trap* and its cousin, the *forward workload*. This is the biggest, and most complex, of the stumbling blocks. Once a recovery has been accomplished successfully, there is always a lot of catching up to be done. This phenomenon was explained in Chapter 2, where the concept of the backlog trap was introduced. The forward

Lower morale reduces efficiency, and so the backlog may never go away.

workload is another aspect of how work accumulates whenever our time and attention are absorbed by abnormal activities. It is, in effect, the backlog of the future which can be avoided, or at least reduced, providing that you recognize the menace and take its effect into account.

Backlog Trap

When you first go into emergency mode there will inevitably be a backlog to be dealt with. Much of your response strategy will be focused on reducing the scale of the backlog by spotting the problems early and responding quickly. However, there will be an abnormal workload which will last for quite some while after the initial recovery. From an operational point of view, the business is still in danger until that outstanding workload has been dealt with. Then you may want to give people a chance to gather their breath before being plunged into another period of hectic activity.

Forward Workload

Once the decision has been taken to move back to the original mode of operation at the home site, preparations should begin for dealing with the forward workload. For example, there may be certain routine tasks which have to be carried out every day. One of these tasks might be an end-of-day run which tidies up the system before closing down and taking the overnight backup. If the migration takes two days it might be necessary to run this procedure three times before the operation is synchronized with the calendar. For example, if the migration takes all of Monday and Tuesday, then you might have to carry out Monday's and Tuesday's end-of-day procedures before you can close down the system on Wednesday.

It might be worth considering carrying out some, or all, of these scheduled tasks in advance of the actual move. Why not put in some extra work in advance so that you can get ahead of the game before moving? If you plan to move back on Sunday then try to do as much of Monday's work as you can on the Saturday. Building up this forward workload is a way of avoiding the backlog trap. If anything untoward happens during this period you can always postpone the return journey without endangering the business.

Remember, the backlog can be handled only by applying spare capacity, if you have any. An organization running at 95% efficiency will find it difficult to get up to 98% efficiency and that only allows you to whittle away at the backlog with 3% effectiveness. It could take a very long time to reduce the backlog to zero. It is always demoralizing for people to have more work than they can possibly handle. Lower morale reduces efficiency, and so the backlog may never go away. What was to be a three-day turnaround becomes a five-day turnaround, and before long the cash flow and the balance sheet reflect this sad state of affairs.

D.2.4   Reverse Criticality

Reverse criticality is a logical aspect of reverse recovery, except everything happens in reverse order, including how you handle the most critical issues. When you are carefully re-establishing your operations rather than frantically recovering them, the priorities are distinctly different. On the outbound journey it was essential to restore the most delicate and critical functions as quickly as possible. Now, on the inbound journey, those same critical functions need to be transferred to their original home as safely as possible. While everything is performing properly in a safe environment, it is wise to concentrate on moving the more robust, less critical functions back to the home base. Once the basic services and functions have settled in, then you can focus on returning the more critical and sensitive functions.

In many ways, the priorities should be reversed during the return to normal. It is a time to be cautious and protective rather than urgent and reactive.

D.2.5   Troubleshooting

The reverse recovery period of activity, like the evacuation, is a time of change and added risk. A team of people will be managing and controlling the whole exercise to a fairly tight schedule and budget. They need to be protected from involvement with side issues so they can focus on the logistics, etc.

It is a good idea to appoint someone to act as your *troubleshooter*. Then if anything goes wrong with the move, he or she can step in and handle the problem while the members of the main team continue with their work. If nothing goes wrong, then the troubleshooter's observations at the debriefing will provide a useful, independent perspective. And if something does go wrong, you may be very glad that someone was there to deal with the unexpected.

If serious trouble occurs during the reverse recovery process, any development that puts the brand and reputation of the company at risk could be regarded as a "potential crisis" and aspects of the *crisis management plan* (which you have as a subset of the BC plan, as described in Chapter 11) would be called into play.

D.3   Back to Normal

As you move out of your recovery center, looking forward to returning to familiar surroundings, it is all too easy to simply close down, walk away, and put the whole experience out of your mind.

D.3.1   Exit Housekeeping

Bear in mind that your recovery center may need to be opened up and put into service again in a hurry. Now is the time to tidy it up, put everything safely into storage, and replenish all the stores and supplies. If you don't do it now, it may never get done. Leave the place just as you would expect to find it.

D.3.2   The Debriefing Process

Soon after the emergency has been dealt with and the business has been stabilized, everybody should be involved in the debriefing process during which the incident is analyzed and any lessons learned are captured for the future. This achieves two objectives:

▸ Everybody gets to understand what happened and why.

▸ Everybody gets the chance to air fears and doubts, which helps everyone deal with any unpleasant or disturbing memories. Time will also help them to get everything into perspective.

As an integral part of the debriefing process, everyone should be properly acknowledged for their efforts during a time of stress and confusion. A tangible token of gratitude coming from the chief executive will go a long way to restoring confidence and reinforcing the sense of loyalty and comradeship which comes from sharing a traumatic experience together with the other members of the group.

Perhaps they should have a certificate, or some other acknowledgment, to act as a permanent reminder of the fact that their contribution to the recovery effort was appreciated at the highest level. If they have done a really splendid job then a party, a weekend away, or a bonus, would be in order. After all, they did save the company.

If the leaders fail to show their gratitude after all that hard work, the team spirit will vanish....

If the leaders fail to show their gratitude after all that hard work, the team spirit will vanish, together with many members of the staff. Morale often flags after all the excitement has died down and everybody is settled back into the same old routine. Strangely enough, it didn't seem dull until a brief moment of chaos revealed another side of life.

This is also an appropriate time for a review to figure out what has been learned, and to begin to apply the lessons. Otherwise, the details are soon forgotten and the whole experience will have been an expensive waste of time and effort.

Depending on the nature of the event, some people may need to be comforted, counseled, or reassured. You must recognize that it is perfectly normal for someone to be affected by a traumatic incident. Indeed, it is those who appear to remain unaffected who often show signs of abnormality. There will be lots of doubts and questions. It is time for open discussion to deal with questions like: "What happened and why?" "Who did what, when, and where?" "What have we learned?" "How do you feel?" "Will it happen again?" "Is my job secure?"

D.3.3   Inventory Check

Soon, it will be time to count the cost and figure out what is missing. It is always wise to run an inventory check soon after a recovery and an even better idea after you have had two consecutive recoveries (one out and one in). Inevitably, things get lost or go astray during all the upheaval. There is also the possibility that opportunists will have benefited from these occasions. If you find out what is missing early enough, it might be possible to retrieve the missing items. But once things start to wander, they seem to have a habit of straying further and further from their old home. In the end, someone will offer them a new home.

D.3.4   Prevent a Recurrence

If a business disruption has happened once, requiring relocation, it could happen again. You now have the evidence that it can and does happen. You also have the experience of how it happened. If it was an avoidable disruption, to allow it to happen again might be considered to be careless. Everybody will need to be reassured that you have taken steps to prevent a repeat performance. Unless it was a genuine act of God, you should be able to reduce the risk of a repetition. Make everyone aware of what has been learned about how and why it happened. At the same time, tell them what you have done about managing that risk or set of risks.

D.3.5   Opportunity

Once everybody is out of the way, working in recovery mode, there is a chance for some reflection on how the operation was run and to consider conditions in the old working environment. Obviously, there may be a need for repairs and reinstatement, but there is also an opportunity to carry out a few improvements. These enhancements might include such options as a major refurbishment, re-engineering processes, relocating to somewhere else, or even re-branding.

While it is important to reflect on how things could be improved and to consider taking advantage of the post-event situation, it is equally important to bear in mind that any improvement involves change. Change imposes additional risk; the more changes you make the more risks you run.

D.3.6   Public Relations

A good recovery story is a valuable asset, so it must not be wasted. Tell your customers, shareholders, and competitors how well your plans and people worked to make sure no single business opportunity was lost. It is a time to be proud of your staff, and they will appreciate it if the world is told about their success, energy, willingness, and sheer brilliance.

References

Burtles, J. (2013). *Emergency evacuation planning for your workplace: From chaos to life-saving solutions.* Brookfield, CT: Rothstein Publishing.

Glossary

Note: *Glossary produced as an initiative of the Editorial Advisory Board of Disaster Recovery Journal (DRJ). Used by the kind permission of DRJ. Edited for clarity.*

ABCP Associate Business Continuity Professional. The ABCP certification from DRI International is designed for individuals with less than two years of continuity management experience, but who have minimum knowledge in continuity management, and have passed the qualifying exam from DRI International.

alert Notification that a potential disruption is imminent or has occurred; usually includes a directive to act or standby.

alternate site A site held in readiness for use during/following an invocation of business or disaster recovery plans to continue urgent and important activities of an organization.

alternate work area Recovery environment complete with necessary infrastructure (e.g., desk, telephone, workstation, and associated hardware, equipment, and communications).

AMBCI Associate member of the Business Continuity Institute. This entry level certification is for those with at least one year's general experience within BCM across all six business continuity competencies. Applicants need to obtain a pass in the BCI certificate examination or hold other recognized credentials.

annual loss exposure/expectancy (ALE) A risk management method of calculating loss based on a value and level of frequency.

application recovery The component of disaster recovery that deals specifically with the restoration of business system software and data after the processing platform has been restored or replaced.

assembly area The designated area at which employees, visitors, and contractors assemble if evacuated from their building/site.

asset Anything that an organization signifies as important or valuable. This could include technology equipment, real estate, operating equipment, intellectual property, reputation, and financial resources.

backlog (1) The amount of work that accumulates when a system or process is unavailable for a long period of time. This work needs to be processed once the system or process is available and may take a considerable amount of time to process. (2) A situation whereby a backlog of work requires more time to action than is available through normal working patterns. In extreme circumstances, the backlog may become so marked that the backlog cannot be cleared.

backup (data) A process by which data (electronic or paper-based) and programs are copied in some form so as to be available and used if the original data from which it originated is lost, destroyed, or corrupted.

backup generator An independent source of power, usually fueled by diesel or natural gas.

business continuity (BC) The strategic and tactical capability of the organization to plan for and respond to incidents and business disruptions in order to continue business operations at an acceptable predefined level.

business continuity coordinator A role within the BCM program that coordinates planning and implementation for overall recovery of an organization or unit(s).

Business Continuity Institute (BCI) A global membership institution for business continuity professionals. The overall purpose is to promote the art and science of business continuity worldwide.

business continuity management (BCM) The process that organizations use to ensure business continuity is maintained across their organization.

business continuity management program Ongoing management and governance process supported by top management and appropriately resourced to implement and maintain business continuity management (*ISO 22301:2012*).

business continuity management team A group of individuals functionally responsible for directing the development and execution of the business continuity plan, as well as responsible for declaring a disaster and providing direction during the recovery process, both pre-disaster and post-disaster. Similar terms are *disaster recovery management team* and *business recovery management team*.

business continuity plan (BCP) Documented procedures that guide organizations to respond, recover, resume, and restore to a pre-defined level of operation following disruption. **Note:** Typically this covers resources, services, and activities required to ensure the continuity of critical business functions (*ISO 22301:2012*).

business continuity plan administrator The designated individual responsible for plan documentation, maintenance, and distribution.

business continuity planning The process of developing prior arrangements and procedures that enable an organization to respond to an event in such a manner that critical business functions can continue within planned levels of disruption. The end result of the planning process is the BC plan (Business Continuity Institute (BCI) *Dictionary of BC Management Terms*).

business continuity steering committee A committee of decision-makers (e.g., business leaders, technology experts, and continuity professionals) tasked with making strategic policy and continuity planning decisions for the organization, and for providing the resources to accomplish all business continuity program goals.

business continuity strategy An approach selected by an organization to ensure its recovery and continuity in the face of a disaster or other business disruption.

business continuity team Designated individuals responsible for development, execution, rehearsals, and maintenance of the business continuity plan.

business impact analysis (BIA) A process designed to assess the potential quantitative (financial) and qualitative (non-financial) impacts that might result if an organization were to experience a business disruption.

business interruption Any event, whether anticipated (e.g., public service strike) or unanticipated (e.g., blackout) which disrupts the normal course of business operations at an organization's location. Similar terms are *outage* and *service interruption*.

business interruption costs The impact to the business caused by different types of outages, normally measured by revenue lost.

business interruption insurance Insurance coverage for disaster-related expenses that may be incurred until operations are fully recovered after a disaster. Business interruption insurance generally provides reimbursement for necessary ongoing expenses during this shutdown, plus loss of net profits that would have been earned during the period of interruption, within the limits of the policy.

business recovery coordinator An individual or group designated to coordinate or control designated recovery processes or testing.

business recovery team A group responsible for relocation and recovery of business unit operations at an alternate site following a business disruption, and for subsequent resumption and restoration of those operations at an appropriate site.

business recovery timeline The approved sequence of activities required to achieve stable operations following a business interruption. This timeline may range from minutes to weeks, depending upon the recovery requirements and methodology.

business unit recovery A component of business continuity which deals specifically with the recovery of a key function or department in the event of a disaster.

call tree A document that graphically depicts the calling responsibilities and the calling order used to contact management, employees, customers, vendors, and other key contacts in the event of an emergency, disaster, or severe outage situation.

cascade system A system whereby one person or organization calls out/contacts others who in turn initiate further call-outs/contacts as necessary.

CBCP Certified Business Continuity Professional. The CBCP certification from DRI International is for individuals with a minimum of two years of enterprise continuity management experience in 5 of the 10 professional practice areas, who have passed the qualifying exam and have had their DRI International certification application approved.

CFCP Certified Functional Continuity Professional. The CFCP certification from DRI International is designed for individuals with a minimum of two years of continuity management experience in 3 of the 10 professional practice areas, who have passed the qualifying exam and have had their DRI International certification application approved. This certification provides a certification opportunity for those individuals with continuity management experience in specific functional or vertical areas vs. enterprise-wide.

checklist (1) A tool to remind and/or validate that tasks have been completed and resources are available, to report on the status of recovery. (2) A list of items (names, or tasks, etc.) to be checked or consulted.

checklist exercise A method used to exercise a completed disaster recovery plan. This type of exercise is used to determine if the information such as phone numbers, manuals, equipment, etc. in the plan is accurate and current.

cold site An environmentally equipped facility that provides only the physical space for recovery operations while the organization using the space provides its own office equipment, hardware and software systems, and any other required resources to establish and continue operations.

command center The (facility) location, local to the event but outside the immediate affected area, where tactical response, recovery, and restoration activities are managed. There could be more than one command center for each event reporting to a single emergency operations center.

communications recovery The component of disaster recovery which deals with the restoration or rerouting of an organization's telecommunication network, or its components, in the event of loss.

consortium agreement An agreement made by a group of organizations to share processing facilities and/or office facilities if one member of the group suffers a disaster.

contact list A list of key people to be notified at the time of disruption or as needed.

contingency plan An event-specific preparation that is executed to protect an organization from certain and specific identified risks and/or threats.

contingency planning Process of developing advanced arrangements and procedures that enable an organization to respond to an undesired event that negatively impacts the organization.

continuity of operations (COOP) Management policy and procedures used to guide an enterprise response to a major loss of enterprise capabilities or damage to its facilities. It defines the activities of individual departments and agencies and their subcomponents to ensure their essential functions are performed. The term is primarily used in the public sector.

continuous availability A system or application that supports operations which continue with little to no noticeable impact to the user. For instance, with continuous availability, the user will not have to log in again, or to resubmit a partial or whole transaction.

continuous operations The ability of an organization to perform its processes without interruption.

corporate governance The system/process by which top management of an organization are required to carry out and discharge their legal, moral, and regulatory accountabilities and responsibilities.

corporate risk A category of risk management that looks at ensuring an organization meets its corporate governance responsibilities, takes appropriate actions, and identifies and manages emerging risks.

cost benefit analysis A process (after a BIA and risk assessment) that facilitates the financial assessment of different strategic BCM options and balances the cost of each option against the perceived savings.

crisis A situation with a high level of uncertainty that disrupts the core activities and/or credibility of an organization and requires urgent action (*ISO 22300*).

crisis management The overall direction of an organization's response to a disruptive event, in an effective, timely manner, with the goal of avoiding or minimizing damage to the organization's profitability, reputation, and ability to operate.

crisis management team A team consisting of key leaders (e.g., media representative, legal counsel, facilities manager, and disaster recovery coordinator), and the appropriate business owners of critical functions, who are responsible for recovery operations during a crisis.

critical business functions The critical operational and/or business support functions that could not be interrupted or unavailable for more than a mandated or predetermined timeframe without significantly jeopardizing the organization.

critical data point *See* recovery point objective.

critical infrastructure Physical assets whose incapacity or destruction would have a debilitating impact on the economic or physical security of an organization, community, nation, etc.

critical service A service without which a building would be "disabled." Often applied to the utilities (water, gas, electric, etc.), it may also include standby power systems, environmental control systems, or communication networks.

damage assessment The process of assessing damage to computer hardware, vital records, office facilities, etc., and determining what can be salvaged or restored and what must be replaced following a disaster.

data backup strategies Approaches that determine the technologies, media, and offsite storage of the backups necessary to meet an organization's data recovery and restoration objectives.

data backups The copying of production files to media that can be stored both onsite and/or offsite and can be used to restore corrupted or lost data or to recover entire systems and databases in the event of a disaster.

data center recovery The component of disaster recovery which deals with the restoration of data center services and computer processing capabilities at an alternate location and the migration back to the production site.

data mirroring A process whereby critical data is replicated to another device.

data protection Process of ensuring confidentiality, integrity, and availability of data.

data recovery The restoration of computer files from backup media to restore programs and production data to the state that existed at the time of the last safe backup.

database replication The partial or full duplication of data from a source database to one or more destination databases.

declaration A formal announcement by pre-authorized personnel that a disaster or severe outage is predicted or has occurred and that triggers pre-arranged mitigating actions (e.g., a move to an alternate site).

declaration fee A fee charged by a commercial hot site vendor for a customer-invoked disaster declaration.

denial of access The inability of an organization to access and/or occupy its normal working environment.

dependency The reliance or interaction of one activity or process upon another.

desk check One method of validating a specific component of a plan. Typically, the owner of the component reviews it for accuracy and completeness and signs off.

desktop exercise *See* table top exercise.

disaster (1) A sudden, unplanned catastrophic event causing unacceptable damage or loss. (2) An event that compromises an organization's ability to provide critical functions, processes, or services for some unacceptable period of time. (3) An event where an organization's management invokes their recovery plans.

disaster recovery (DR) The technical aspect of business continuity. The collection of resources and activities to re-establish information technology (IT) services (including components such as infrastructure, telecommunications, systems, applications, and data) at an alternate site following a disruption of IT services. Disaster recovery includes subsequent resumption and restoration of those operations at a more permanent site.

disaster recovery plan The management approved document that defines the resources, actions, tasks, and data required to manage the technology recovery effort. Usually refers to the technology recovery effort. This is a component of the business continuity management program.

disaster recovery planning The technical component of business continuity planning.

DRI International A nonprofit organization that offers premier educational and certification programs globally for those practitioners within the business continuity management field.

drop ship A strategy for (1) delivering equipment, supplies, and materials at the time of a business continuity event or exercise, and (2) providing replacement hardware within a specified time period via prearranged contractual arrangements with an equipment supplier at the time of a business continuity event.

electronic vaulting Electronic transmission of data to a server or storage facility.

emergency An unexpected or impending situation that may cause injury, loss of life, and destruction of property, or cause the interference, loss, or disruption of an organization's normal business operations to such an extent that it poses a threat.

emergency control center (ECC) The command center used by the crisis management team during the first phase of an event. An organization should have both primary and secondary locations for an ECC in case one of them becomes unavailable or inaccessible. It may also serve as a reporting point for deliveries, services, press, and all external contacts.

emergency coordinator The person designated to plan, exercise, and implement the activities of sheltering in place or the evacuation of occupants of a site, with the first responders and emergency services agencies.

emergency operations center (EOC) The physical and/or virtual location from which strategic decisions are made and all activities of an event/incident/crisis are directed, coordinated, and monitored. **Note:** EOC is different from command center. *See also* command center.

emergency preparedness The capability that enables an organization or community to respond to an emergency in a coordinated, timely, and effective manner to prevent the loss of life and minimize injury and property damage.

emergency procedures A documented list of activities to commence immediately to prevent the loss of life and minimize injury and property damage.

emergency response The immediate reaction and response to an emergency situation commonly focusing on ensuring life safety and reducing the severity of the incident.

emergency response plan A documented plan usually addressing the immediate reaction and response to an emergency situation.

emergency response procedures The initial response to a critical event, focused upon protecting human life and the organization's assets.

emergency response team (ERT) Qualified and authorized personnel who have been trained to provide immediate assistance.

enterprise-wide planning The overarching master plan covering all aspects of business continuity within the entire organization.

escalation The process by which event related information is communicated upwards through an organization's established chain of command.

evacuation The movement of employees, visitors, and contractors from a site and/or building to a safe place (assembly area) in a controlled and monitored manner at time of an event.

event Any occurrence that may lead to a business continuity incident.

executive management succession plan A predetermined plan for ensuring the continuity of authority, decision-making, and communication in the event that key members of executive management unexpectedly become incapacitated.

exercise A people-focused activity designed to execute business continuity plans and evaluate the individual's and/or organization's performance against approved standards or objectives. Exercises can be announced or unannounced, and are performed for the purpose of training and conditioning team members, and validating the business continuity plan. Exercise results identify plan gaps and limitations and are used to improve and revise the business continuity plans. Types of exercises include table top exercise, simulation exercise, operational exercise, mock disaster, desktop exercise and full rehearsal.

exercise auditor An appointed role that is assigned to assess whether the exercise objectives are being met and to measure whether activities are occurring at the right time and involve the correct people to facilitate their achievement. The exercise auditor is not responsible for the mechanics of the exercise. This independent role is crucial in the subsequent debriefing.

exercise controller *See* exercise owner.

exercise coordinator A person responsible for the mechanics of running the exercise. The coordinator must lead the exercise and keep it focused within the predefined scope and objectives of the exercise as well as on the disaster scenario. The coordinator must be objective and not influence the outcome. He or she makes sure appropriate exercise participants have been identified and that exercise scripts have been prepared before, utilized during, and updated after the exercise.

exercise observer A person who has no active role within the exercise but is present for awareness and training purposes. An exercise observer might make recommendations for procedural improvements.

exercise owner An appointed role that has total management oversight and control of the exercise and has the authority to alter the exercise plan. This includes early termination of the exercise for reasons of safety or the objectives of the exercise cannot be met due to an unforeseen or other internal or external influence.

exercise plan A plan designed to periodically evaluate tasks, teams, and procedures that are documented in business continuity plans to ensure the plan's viability. This can include all or part of the BC plan, but should include mission critical components.

exercise script A set of detailed instructions identifying information necessary to implement a predefined business continuity event scenario for evaluation purposes.

exposure The potential susceptibility to loss; the vulnerability to a particular risk.

extra expense The extra cost necessary to implement a recovery strategy and/or mitigate a loss (e.g., the cost to transfer inventory to an alternate location to protect it from further damage, the cost of reconfiguring lines, or the cost of overtime). It is typically reviewed during BIA and is a consideration during insurance evaluation.

FBCI Fellow of the Business Continuity Institute. This senior membership grade is currently held by more than 125 BCM practitioners. Applications or nominations to this grade are considered from very experienced MBCIs or SBCIs, who can provide evidence of a significant contribution to the institute and the BCM discipline. There is no direct entry into fellowship.

floor warden Person responsible for ensuring that all employees, visitors, and contractors evacuate a floor within a specific site.

full rehearsal An exercise that simulates a business continuity event where the organization or some of its component parts are suspended until the exercise is completed.

gap analysis A survey whose aim is to identify the differences between BCM/crisis management requirements (what the business says it needs at time of an incident) and what is in place and/or currently available.

hardening The process of making something more secure, resistant to attack, or less vulnerable.

health and safety The process by which the wellbeing of all employees, contractors, visitors, and the public is safeguarded. All business continuity plans and planning must be cognizant of health and safety statutory and regulatory requirements and legislation. Health and safety considerations should be reviewed during the risk assessment.

high-availability Systems or applications requiring a very high level of reliability and availability. High-availability systems typically operate 24x7 and usually require built-in redundancy to minimize the risk of downtime due to hardware and/or telecommunication failures.

high-risk areas Areas identified during the risk assessment that are highly susceptible to a disaster situation or might be the cause of a significant disaster.

hot site A facility equipped with full technical requirements including IT, telecoms, and infrastructure, and which can be used to provide rapid resumption of operations. **Note:** Hot sites usually refer to IT and telecommunication capabilities. When used in the same context for business users they are more often referred to as work area recovery sites.

human continuity The ability of an organization to provide support for its associates and their families before, during, and after a business continuity event to ensure a viable workforce. This involves pre-planning for potential psychological responses, occupational health and employee assistance programs, and employee communications.

human threats Possible disruptions in operations resulting from human actions as identified during the risk assessment (e.g., disgruntled employee, terrorism, blackmail, job actions, or riots).

impact The effect, acceptable or unacceptable, of an event on an organization. The types of business impact are usually described as financial and non-financial and are further divided into specific types of impact.

incident An event which is not part of standard business operations which may impact or interrupt services and, in some cases, may lead to disaster.

incident command system (ICS) A standardized on-scene emergency management construct specifically designed to provide for the adoption of an integrated organizational structure that reflects the complexity and demands of single or multiple incidents, without being hindered by jurisdictional boundaries. ICS is the combination of facilities, equipment, personnel, procedures, and communications operating within a common organizational structure, designed to aid in the management of resources during incidents. It is used for all kinds of emergencies and is applicable to small as well as large and complex incidents. ICS is used by various jurisdictions and functional agencies, both public and private, to organize field-level incident management operations (Federal Emergency Management Agency (FEMA) *ICS Glossary*).

incident management The process by which an organization responds to and controls an incident using emergency response procedures or plans.

incident management plan A clearly defined and documented plan of action for use at the time of an incident, typically covering the key personnel, resources, services and actions needed to implement the incident management process.

incident manager A person who commands the local emergency operations center (EOC), reporting up to senior management on the recovery progress. He or she has the authority to invoke the recovery plan.

incident response The response of an organization to a disaster or other significant event that may significantly impact the organization, its people, or its ability to function productively. An incident response may include evacuation of a facility, initiating a disaster recovery plan, performing damage assessment, and any other measures necessary to bring an organization to a more stable status.

information security The securing or safeguarding of all sensitive information, electronic or otherwise, which is owned by an organization.

infrastructure The entire system of facilities, equipment, and services that an organization needs in order to function (Praxiom Research Group, Limited, *Plain English ISO 22301 2012 Business Continuity Definitions*).

integrated exercise An exercise conducted on multiple interrelated components of a business continuity plan, typically under simulated operating conditions. Examples of interrelated components may include interdependent departments or interfaced systems.

integrated test(ing) Examination of a plan that addresses multiple plan components, in conjunction with each other, typically under simulated operating conditions.

interim site A temporary location used to continue performing business functions after vacating a recovery site and before the original or new home site can be occupied. Move to an interim site may be necessary if ongoing stay at the recovery site is not feasible for the period of time needed or if the recovery site is located far from the normal business site that was impacted by the disaster. An interim site move is planned and scheduled in advance to minimize disruption of business processes. Equal care must be given to transferring critical functions from the interim site back to the normal business site.

internal hot site A fully equipped alternate processing site owned and operated by the organization.

key tasks Priority procedures and actions in a business continuity plan that must be executed within the first few minutes/hours of the plan invocation.

lead time The time it takes for a supplier, of either equipment or a service, to make that equipment or service available. Business continuity plans should try to minimize this time by agreeing to service levels with the supplier in advance rather than relying on the supplier's best efforts. *See also* service level agreement (SLA).

logistics/transportation team A team comprised of various members representing departments associated with supply acquisition and material transportation, responsible for ensuring the most effective acquisition and mobilization of hardware, supplies, and support materials. This team is also responsible for transporting and supporting staff.

loss Unrecoverable resources that are redirected or removed as a result of a business continuity event. Such losses may be loss of life, revenue, market share, competitive stature, public image, facilities, or operational capability.

loss adjustor Designated position activated at the time of a business continuity event to assist in managing the financial implications of the event and should be involved as part of the management team where possible.

loss reduction The technique of instituting mechanisms to lessen the exposure to a particular risk. Loss reduction involves planning for, and reacting to, an event to limit its impact. Examples of loss reduction include sprinkler systems, insurance policies, and evacuation procedures.

loss transaction recovery Recovery of data (paper within the work area and/or system entries) destroyed or lost at the time of the disaster or interruption. Paper documents may need to be requested or re-acquired from original sources. Data for system entries may need to be recreated or reentered.

manual procedures An alternative method of working following a loss of IT systems. As working practices rely more and more on computerized activities, the ability of an organization to fall back to manual alternatives lessens. However, temporary measures and methods of working can help mitigate the impact of a business continuity event and give staff a feeling of doing something.

MBCI Member of the Business Continuity Institute. Those wishing to attain this well respected certification need to demonstrate experience of working as a BCM practitioner for 3+ years across all 6 business continuity competencies and have passed the BCI certificate examination with merit or hold other recognized credentials.

MBCP Master Business Continuity Professional. The master level certification from DRI International is for individuals with a minimum of 5 years of enterprise continuity management experience in 7 of the 10 professional practices, who have passed both the qualifying exam and the master's case study, and have had their DRI International certification application approved.

mission-critical activities The critical operational and/or business support activities (either provided internally or outsourced) required by the organization to achieve its objective(s), i.e., services and/or products.

mission-critical application Applications that support business activities or processes that could not be interrupted or unavailable for 24 hours or less without significantly jeopardizing the organization.

mobile recovery A mobilized resource purchased or contracted for the purpose of business recovery. The mobile recovery center might include computers, workstations, telephone, electrical power, etc.

mobile standby trailer A transportable operating environment, often a large trailer, that can be configured to specific recovery needs such as office facilities, call centers, or data centers. This can be contracted to be delivered and set up at a suitable site at short notice.

mobilization The activation of the recovery organization in response to a disaster declaration.

mock disaster One method of exercising teams in which participants are challenged to determine the actions they would take in the event of a specific disaster scenario. Mock disasters usually involve all, or most, of the applicable teams. Under the guidance of exercise coordinators, the teams walk through the actions they would take per their plans, or simulate performance of these actions. Teams may be at a single exercise location, or at multiple locations, with communication between teams simulating actual "disaster mode" communications. A mock disaster will typically operate on a compressed timeframe representing many hours, or even days.

N + 1 A fault tolerant strategy that includes multiple systems or components protected by one backup system or component. (Many-to-one relationship.)

network outage An interruption of voice, data, or IP network communications.

offsite storage Any place physically located a significant distance away from the primary site, where duplicated and vital records (hard copy or electronic and/or equipment) may be stored for use during recovery.

operational exercise *See* exercise.

operational risk The risk of loss resulting from inadequate or failed procedures and controls. This includes loss from events related to technology and infrastructure, failure, business interruptions, staff-related problems, and from external events such as regulatory changes.

orderly shutdown The actions required to rapidly and gracefully suspend a business function and/or system during a disruption.

outage The interruption of automated processing systems, infrastructure, support services, or essential business operations, which may result in the organization's inability to provide services for some period of time.

peer review A review of a specific component of a plan by personnel (other than the owner or author) with appropriate technical or business knowledge for accuracy and completeness.

plan maintenance The management process of keeping an organization's business continuity management plans up-to-date and effective. Maintenance procedures are a part of this process for the review and update of the BC plans on a defined schedule.

preventive measures Controls aimed at deterring or mitigating undesirable events from taking place.

prioritization The ordering of critical activities and their dependencies as established during the BIA and strategic-planning phase. The business continuity plans will be implemented in the order necessary at the time of the event.

qualitative assessment The process for evaluating a business function based on observations and does not involve measures or numbers. Instead, it uses descriptive categories such as customer service or regulatory requirements to allow for refinement of the quantitative assessment. This is normally done during the BIA phase of planning.

quantitative assessment The process for placing value on a business function for risk purposes. It is a systematic method that evaluates possible financial impact for losing the ability to perform a business function. It uses numeric values to allow for prioritizations. This is normally done during the BIA phase of planning.

quick ship *See* drop ship.

reciprocal agreement Agreement between two organizations (or two internal business groups) with similar equipment/environment that allows each one to recover at the other's location.

recoverable loss Financial losses due to an event that may be reclaimed in the future, e.g., through insurance or litigation. This is normally identified in the risk assessment or BIA.

recovery Implementation of the prioritized actions required to return the processes and support functions to operational stability following an interruption or disaster.

recovery management team *See* business continuity management team.

recovery period The time period between a disaster and a return to normal functions, during which the disaster recovery plan is employed.

recovery point capability (RPC) The point in time to which data was restored and/or systems were recovered (at the designated recovery/alternate location) after an outage or during a disaster recovery exercise.

recovery point objective (RPO) The point in time to which data is restored and/or systems are recovered after an outage. **Note:** RPO is often used as the basis for developing backup strategies and determining the amount of data that may require recreation after systems have been recovered. RPO for applications can be enumerated in business time (i.e., "8 business hours" after a Sunday disaster restores to close of business Thursday) or elapsed time, but is always measured in terms of time before a disaster. RPO for systems typically must be established at time of disaster as a specific point in time (e.g., end of previous day's processing) or software version/release.

recovery services agreement/contract A contract with an external organization guaranteeing the provision of specified equipment, facilities, or services, usually within a specified time period, in the event of a business interruption. A typical contract will specify a monthly subscription fee, a declaration fee, usage costs, method of performance, amount of test time, termination options, penalties and liabilities, etc.

recovery site A designated site for the recovery of business unit, technology, or other operations, which are critical to the enterprise.

recovery strategy *See* business continuity strategy.

recovery teams A structured group of teams ready to take control of the recovery operations if a disaster should occur.

recovery time capability (RTC) The demonstrated amount of time in which systems, applications, and/or functions have been recovered, during an exercise or actual event, at the designated recovery/alternate location (physical or virtual). As with RTO, RTC includes assessment, execution, and verification activities. RTC and RTO are compared during gap analysis.

recovery time objective (RTO) The period of time within which systems, applications, or functions must be recovered after an outage. RTO includes the time required for assessment, execution, and verification. RTO may be enumerated in business time (e.g., one business day) or elapsed time (e.g., 24 elapsed hours). **Note:** Assessment includes the activities which occur before or after an initiating event, and lead to confirmation of the execution priorities, time line and responsibilities, and a decision regarding when to execute. Execution includes the activities related to accomplishing the pre-planned steps required within the phase to deliver a function, system or application in a new location to its owner. Verification includes steps taken by a function, system, or application owner to ensure everything is in readiness to proceed to live operations.

recovery timeline The sequence of recovery activities, or critical path, which must be followed to resume an acceptable level of operation following a business interruption. The timeline may range from minutes to weeks, depending upon the recovery requirements and methodology.

resilience The ability of an organization to absorb the impact of a business interruption, and continue to provide a minimum acceptable level of service.

resilient The process and procedures required to maintain or recover critical services such as "remote access" or "end-user support" during a business interruption.

response The reaction to an incident or emergency to assess the damage or impact and to ascertain the level of containment and control activity required. In addition to addressing matters of life safety and evacuation, response also addresses the policies, procedures, and actions to be followed in the event of an emergency.

restoration Process of planning for and/or implementing procedures for the repair of hardware, relocation of the primary site and its contents, and returning to normal operations at the permanent operational location.

resumption The process of planning for and/or implementing the restarting of defined business processes and operations following a disaster. This process commonly addresses the most critical business functions within BIA specified timeframes.

risk Potential for exposure to loss which can be determined by using either qualitative or quantitative measures.

risk assessment/analysis Process of identifying the risks to an organization, assessing the critical functions necessary for an organization to continue business operations, defining the controls in place to reduce organization exposure, and evaluating the cost for such controls. Risk analysis often involves an evaluation of the probabilities of a particular event.

risk categories Risks of similar types grouped together under key headings. These categories include reputation, strategy, financial, investments, operational infrastructure, business, regulatory compliance, outsourcing, people, technology, and knowledge.

risk controls All methods of reducing the frequency and/or severity of losses including exposure avoidance, loss prevention, loss reduction, segregation of exposure units, and non-insurance transfer of risk.

risk management The culture, processes, and structures that are put in place to effectively manage potential negative events. As it is not possible or desirable to eliminate all risk, the objective is to reduce risks to an acceptable level.

risk transfer (1) A common technique used by risk managers to address or mitigate potential exposures of the organization. (2) A series of techniques describing the various means of addressing risk through insurance and similar products.

roll call The process of identifying that all employees, visitors, and contractors have been safely evacuated and accounted for following an evacuation of a building or site.

salvage and restoration The act of conducting a coordinated assessment to determine the appropriate actions to be performed on impacted assets. The assessment can be coordinated with insurance adjusters, facilities personnel, or other involved parties. Appropriate actions may include disposal, replacement, reclamation, refurbishment, recovery, or receiving compensation for unrecoverable organizational assets.

SBCI Specialist of the Business Continuity Institute. This membership grade was developed to allow certification to those practitioners who specialize in aspects of BCM or who work in associated disciplines. Two years of specialist experience, a pass in the BCI certificate examination, and a professional qualification from another awarding body will enable the applicant to enter one of the six specialist faculties.

scenario A pre-defined set of business continuity events and conditions that describe, for planning purposes, an interruption, disruption, or loss related to some aspect(s) of an organization's business operations to support conducting a BIA, developing a continuity strategy, and developing continuity and exercise plans. **Note:** Scenarios are neither predictions nor forecasts.

security review A periodic review of policies, procedures, and operational practices maintained by an organization to ensure that they are followed and effective.

self insurance The pre-planned assumption of risk in which a decision is made to bear loses that could result from a business continuity event rather than purchasing insurance to cover those potential losses.

service continuity The process and procedures required to maintain or recover critical services such as "remote access" or "end-user support" during a business interruption.

service continuity planning A process used to mitigate, develop, and document procedures that enable an organization to recover critical services after a business interruption.

service level agreement (SLA) A formal agreement between a service provider (whether internal or external) and their client (whether internal or external) which covers the nature, quality, availability, scope, and response of the service provider. The SLA should cover day-to-day situations and disaster situations, as the need for the service may vary in a disaster.

service level management (SLM) The process of defining, agreeing, documenting, and managing the levels of any type of services provided by service providers whether internal or external that are required and cost justified.

simulation exercise One method of exercising teams in which participants perform some or all of the actions they would take in the event of plan activation. Simulation exercises, which may involve one or more teams, are performed under conditions that at least partially simulate "disaster mode." They may or may not be performed at the designated alternate location, and typically use only a partial recovery configuration.

single point of failure (SPOF) A unique pathway or source of a service, activity, and/or process. Typically, there is no alternative and a loss of that element could lead to a failure of a critical function.

stand down Formal notification that the response to a business continuity event is no longer required or has been concluded.

standalone test A test conducted on a specific component of a plan in isolation from other components to validate component functionality, typically under simulated operating conditions.

structured walkthrough Types of exercise in which team members physically implement the business continuity plans and verbally review each step to assess its effectiveness, and identify enhancements, constraints, and deficiencies.

subscription *See* recovery services agreement/contract.

supply chain All suppliers, manufacturing facilities, distribution centers, warehouses, customers, raw materials, work-in-process inventory, finished goods, and all related information and resources involved in meeting customer and organizational requirements.

system Set of related technology components that work together to support a business process or provide a service.

system recovery The procedures for rebuilding a computer system and network to the condition where it is ready to accept data and applications, and facilitate network communications.

system restore The procedures necessary to return a system to an operable state using all available data including data captured by alternate means during the outage. System restore depends upon having a live, recovered system available.

table top exercise One method of exercising plans in which participants review and discuss the actions they would take without actually performing the actions. Representatives of a single team, or multiple teams, may participate in the exercise typically under the guidance of exercise facilitators.

task list Defined mandatory and discretionary tasks allocated to teams and/or individual roles within a business continuity plan.

technical recovery team A group responsible for relocation and recovery of technology systems, data, applications, and/or supporting infrastructure components at an alternate site following a technology disruption, and for the subsequent resumption and restoration of those operations at an appropriate site.

test A pass/fail evaluation of infrastructure (e.g., computers, cabling, devices, or hardware) and/or physical plant infrastructure (e.g., building systems, generators, or utilities) to demonstrate the anticipated operation of the components and system. Tests are often performed as part of normal operations and maintenance. Tests are often included within exercises. *See also* exercise.

test plan *See* exercise plan.

threat A combination of the risk, the consequence of that risk, and the likelihood that the negative event will take place.

trauma counseling The provisioning of counseling assistance by trained individuals to employees, customers, and others who have suffered mental or physical injury as the result of an event.

trauma management The process of helping employees deal with trauma in a systematic way following an event by proving trained counselors, support systems, and coping strategies with the objective of restoring employees' psychological wellbeing.

unexpected loss The worst-case financial loss or impact that a business could incur due to a particular loss event or risk. The unexpected loss is calculated as the expected loss plus the potential adverse volatility in this value. It can be thought of as the worst financial loss that could occur in a year over the next 20 years.

uninterruptible power supply (UPS) A backup electrical power supply that provides continuous power to critical equipment in the event that commercial power is lost. The UPS (usually a bank of batteries) offers short-term protection against power surges and outages. The UPS usually only allows enough time for vital systems to be correctly powered down.

validation script A set of procedures within the business continuity plan to validate the proper function of a system or process before returning it to production operation.

vital records Records essential to the continued functioning or reconstitution of an organization during and after an emergency and also those records essential to protecting the legal and financial rights of that organization and of the individuals directly affected by its activities.

warm site An alternate processing site equipped with minimal hardware, and communications interfaces, electrical and environmental conditioning. Capable of providing backup only after additional provisioning, software, or customization is performed.

work area facility A pre-designated space provided with desks, telephones, PCs, etc. ready for occupation by business recovery teams at short notice. May be internally or externally provided.

work area recovery The component of recovery and continuity that deals specifically with the relocation of a key function or department in the event of a disaster, including personnel, essential records, equipment supplies, work space, communication facilities, work station computer processing capability, fax, copy machines, mail services, etc. Office recovery environment complete with necessary office infrastructure (desk, telephone, workstation, hardware, communications).

work area recovery planning The business continuity planning process of identifying the needs and preparing procedures and personnel for use at the work area facility.

workaround procedures Alternative procedures that may be used by a functional unit(s) to enable it to continue to perform its critical functions during temporary unavailability of specific application systems, electronic or hard copy data, voice or data communication systems, specialized equipment, office facilities, personnel, or external services.

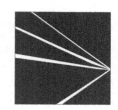

Index

Figures and tables are indicated by f and t following the page number.

A

ABCP (Associated Business Continuity Professionals), 335, 393
Abilities of emergency response personnel, 125
Absenteeism, 281
Absolute measurement, 285
Access
    to backup, 200
    to battle boxes, 148–49
    denial of, 170–73, 184, 398
    to facilities and resources, 10, 103, 130, 142
    in salvage and restoration, 170–73, 184–85, 185f
Accidental man-made hazards, 70
Accreditation, 306
Acknowledgment of personnel, 372, 391
Action lists, 225
Action plans, 40–41
Activation process, 214, 223
Active exercising, 239
Active testing stage, 237f, 238–39, 240t
Activity recovery plans, 35
Activity reports, 304, 305
Administrative teams, 42, 129

Adrenalin buzz, 373
AIDS/HIV, 175
Air conditioning, 174, 175, 191, 193
ALE (annual loss exposure/expectancy), 393
Alerts, defined, 214, 393
Alternate routing of services, 192–93
Alternate sites, 393
Alternate sourcing of supplies, 103–4, 192, 319
Alternate work areas, 393
AMBCI (Associate Member of the Business Continuity Institute), 335, 393
AMI (Applied Metapsychology International), 378
Amosite, 172
Annual loss exposure/expectancy (ALE), 393
Anti-shatter film, 173
Application recovery, 393
Application restart, 16
Application software, 198
Applied Metapsychology International (AMI), 378
Apprehension following emergencies, 388
Apprenticeships, 6
Archive records, 112–13
ARM (Associate in Risk Management), 336
Armed sieges, 171
Army Corps of Engineers (US), 160
Art paper retrieval, 179
Asbestos, 172, 173, 174, 175
Assembly areas, 44, 131, 136, 148, 384–85, 394

Assets
    defined, 394
    invisible, 69
    personnel as, 369
    reputation as, 91
    retention of, 144
Associated Business Continuity Professional (ABCP), 335, 393
Associate in Risk Management (ARM), 336
Associate Member of the Business Continuity Institute (AMBCI), 335, 393
Auditors
    collaboration with, 31
    in development phase, 54
    exercise, 400
    external, 306
    internal, 31, 306
    support for business continuity from, 24
Audits, 305–13
    on achievement of purposes, 310–11
    case study, 307
    checklists for, 308, 311–12, 312*f*
    on claims made by business, 311
    compliance, 309
    defined, 300, 305
    expenditure, 310
    external, 306
    financial, 309–10
    internal, 31, 306
    investment, 310
    policy, 309
    process for, 308, 308*f*
    on prudence, 310
    reporting on, 313
    rules of, 308–9
Australia, standards of practice in, 52–53
Auto-changers, 199
Automation, 73, 101

B

Background for exercises, 244, 245
Backlog traps
    as board-level motivators, 49
    business critical point and, 14, 15*f*
    defined, 12, 394
    development of, 12, 13*f*
    efficiency and, 14
    persistence of, 13–14, 13*f*, 389
    reduction of, 13

Backup and restoration procedures, 109–13, 194–206
    for archive records, 112–13
    for business records, 196
    corporate information, locating and cataloging, 109
    critical information, identification of, 109–10
    for critical records, 197–202
    data recovery process, 202–4, 203*f*, 227*f*, 228, 397
    defined, 194, 394
    device considerations, 199–200
    for dynamic records, 112, 200, 201, 201*f*
    Golden Rules of Recovery, 205
    information protection and replication, 110
    life cycle of, 200–202, 201*f*
    management and control of, 206
    objectives of, 194–95
    for primary records, 112, 201, 201*f*, 202
    response and recovery teams for, 27
    rotation and re-use of media, 205–6
    schedules for, 202
    for software applications, 162, 197–98
    for stable records, 112, 200–201, 201*f*
    storage considerations, 110–12, 114
    technological innovations in, 111–12, 195
Backup generators, 150, 193, 394
Backup regimes, 190, 195, 227, 227*f*
Bacterial contamination, 175
Bang and Echo Program, 290, 293
Battle boxes, 148–54
    accessibility and security of, 148–49
    characteristics of, 148–49
    checklist for, 154, 154*t*
    color coding and labeling of, 148
    in command and control centers, 131
    for command post support, 153
    contents of, 149–53
    for crisis management and public relations, 152–53
    defined, 142
    for emergency response, 152
    for health and safety officials, 152
    for inspection and assessment of damage, 149–50
    maintaining and updating, 153–54, 154*t*
    for office support, 150–51
    portability of, 148
    for rescue and recovery, 150
    for security and isolation, 151
    strategies for, 148
BC. *See* Business continuity
BCI. *See* Business Continuity Institute

BCM. *See* Business continuity management

BCM Legislations, Regulations, Standards and Good Practice (BCI), 53

BCPs. *See* Business continuity plans

BIA. *See* Business impact analysis

Black swan events, 342

Blast cones, 250, 251f. *See also* Explosions

Blogs, 267

Blue asbestos, 172

Blythe, Bruce T., 258, 261, 380

Board-level motivators, 47–51
    backlog traps, 49
    consultants, 49–50
    external influences, 47–48
    failure to exercise plans and review physical risks, 48–49
    governmental guidelines and regulations, 48
    internal influences, 48–49
    practical considerations, 49–50
    reassurance, 49
    risk of liability or negligence, 48
    as strategy for success, 24
    timing considerations, 50–51

Bomb alerts/threats, 171

Book retrieval, 179

Bound documents, 179

Brand of organization, 34

Bravado following emergencies, 388

Breakout areas, 132

Bridging, 270

Briefing areas, 132

British Association for Counseling and Psychotherapy, 162

British Standards Institution (BSI), 7, 52, 258, 326

Bronze control. *See* Gold, Silver, Bronze command and control model

Brown asbestos, 172

Buffer stock, 104, 105–6

Buildup of exercises, 244, 246–50, 246f, 248f

Burglary, reaction to, 375

Business continuity (BC)
    backlog traps and, 12–14, 13f, 15f, 49
    business case for, 47–51, 108
    business impact analysis for. *See* Business impact analysis (BIA)
    challenges in, 332–33
    collaborative networks in, 30–32, 332
    competency standards for, 4, 5, 6–7
    components of, 5–6, 5f, 100
    crisis management in. *See* Crisis management

decision point and, 14–16, 16f
defined, 394
development phase. *See* Development phase
disciplines complementary to, 30–32
disruptive scenarios in, 9–12, 11f, 43–44, 62
emergency preparedness in. *See* Emergency preparedness
future outlook for, 337
history and development of, 4–5
infrastructure for, 32–35, 32f
integration with governance structures, 324–26, 325–26f
laws and regulations for, 5, 44, 48
management structure in, 22–23, 22f, 25–29
organizational support for, 4, 5, 25
planning. *See* Business continuity plans (BCPs)
professional challenges in, 6–7
recovery plans. *See* Disaster recovery (DR)
risk assessment in. *See* Risk and risk assessment
standards of practice, 7–8, 8f, 24, 51–53
strategies for success, 24
survival in economic downturn, 320

Business continuity coordinators, 394

Business Continuity Institute (BCI)
    on business impact analysis, 82
    certifications from, 335
    defined, 394
    membership benefits, 50, 337
    objectives of, 334–35
    SMARTRisk method and, 73, 75
    standards of practice from, 4, 52

Business continuity management (BCM)
    benefits of, 53–54
    components of, 5–6, 5f
    defined, 394
    history and development of, 4–5
    planning types in, 8, 8f
    process model for, 8–9, 9f

Business Continuity Management Guidelines (Monetary Authority of Singapore), 48

Business continuity managers, 5, 10, 24, 26

Business continuity plan administrators, 394

Business continuity plans (BCPs), 213–31
    activation process for, 214, 223
    area of responsibility in relation to plan type, 216, 216f, 218–19
    for business recovery, 216, 216f, 220–25
    commercial tools for, 228–29, 229t
    components of, 5f, 6
    for crisis management, 216, 216f, 220, 226, 230, 260

defined, 394
development process for, 216–20
for disaster recovery, 103–7, 114–15, 216, 216*f*, 220, 227–28, 227*f*
drafting, 230–31
dynamic vs. stable content of, 303–4
for emergency response, 216, 216*f*, 220, 225–26, 230
for evacuation. *See* Emergency evacuation planning (EEP)
for function restoration, 216, 216*f*, 220, 226
Golden Rules for, 217
hierarchy of, 214–16, 215–16*f*
in-house ownership of, 42–43
long-term management of, 332
maintenance of, 27, 42, 404
modular approach to, 24, 51, 214, 219, 227–28, 227*f*
origins of, 4
reviewing. *See* Review process
scaling to fit, 230
structure and design of, 217–18
templates for, 230–31
testing. *See* Exercises; Testing
types of, 216, 216*f*, 219–20
Business continuity steering committees, 395
Business continuity team, 395
Business critical point, 14, 15*f*
Business cycles, 88, 94
Business drivers, 47
Business impact analysis (BIA), 79–95
data collection in, 82–85
defined, 395
dependency modeling in, 81, 90–91, 90*f*
on disruptions, 86, 86*t*
disruptive scenarios in, 80–81
facilitated, 81, 87–89
functional analysis in, 81, 89, 91–95, 92*f*, 94*f*
interactive impact modeling in, 87–89, 88*t*
interviews in, 83–84, 85
on loss exposure, 87, 87*t*
organization of projects for, 82
overview, 79, 80
reporting on, 85–87
team involvement in, 81
workshops in, 84–85
Business interruption costs, 395
Business interruption insurance, 170, 171
Business interruptions, 23, 70, 84, 90, 103, 395
Business records, 196

Business recovery coordinators, 395
Business recovery plans, 220–25
action lists in, 225
activation process for, 223
contents of, 221
decision criteria in, 223–24
definitions and terminology in, 222
document control information for, 220–21
escalation procedures in, 224–25
layout for, 221–22
objectives of, 220
organizational charts in, 222
reference information in, 225
roles and responsibilities in, 216, 216*f*, 223
scenarios requiring, 222–23
Business recovery team, 395
Business recovery timeline, 395
Business-specific skills, 146
Business unit managers, 146
Business unit recovery, 218, 395
Bypass arrangements, 106

C

Cabaret exercising, 248, 290, 292–93
Call center operations, 107, 191
Call gapping, 136
Call trees, 395
Cannon, Walter, 342
Capability, discovery of, 374
Capital expenditures, 69, 143
Carousel technique for decision-making, 346–47
Cascade system, 395
Case studies approach, 247
Cash flow, 10, 11*f*, 93
Category 1 Responders, 31
Central records, 198
Certificate of the Business Continuity Institute (CBCI), 335
Certification, 306, 334–36
Certified Business Continuity Professional (CBCP), 335, 395
Certified Disaster Recovery Engineer (C/DRE), 336
Certified Emergency Manager (CEM), 336
Certified Facility Manager (CFM), 336
Certified Functional Continuity Professional (CFCP), 335, 396
Certified Information Systems Auditor (CISA), 336
Certified Information Systems Security Professional (CISSP), 336

Certified Organizational Resiliency Specialist (CORS), 336
Chairs, 130
Chaos, experience of, 374–75
Checklists
    audits, 308, 311–12, 312f
    battle boxes, 154, 154t
    defined, 396
    exercises, 282, 287, 396
    systems recovery, 242–43
Checksums, 204
Chemical contamination, 173, 175
Chevy Truck Access Method (CTAM), 195
CISA (Certified Information Systems Auditor), 336
CISSP (Certified Information Systems Security Professional), 336
Civil Contingencies Act 2004 (UK), 5, 31, 48
Clippings file, 264
Clocks, 131
Clothing, protective, 131, 172, 175, 371
Cloud computing, 195
Coast Guard (US), 160
Coding systems, 74, 221
Cognitive marketing, 44–45
Cold site services, 102, 396
Collaborative networks, 30–32, 156–60, 332
Color coded battle boxes, 148
Command and control structures
    battle boxes for, 153
    for emergency response teams, 28, 30, 127–32
    exercises, 237f, 239–40, 240t, 241, 291, 291t
    Gold, Silver, Bronze model, 32–33, 32f, 34–35, 126, 128–29, 128–30f
    logical structure for, 128–29, 129f
    media access to, 131–32
    in military, 22, 23
    mobile, 130
    physical structure of, 129–32
    roles in, 22–23, 22f
Command center, defined, 396
Command post exercises, 237f, 239–40, 240t, 241, 291, 291t
Command skills, 146
Communication. See also Media; Social media
    alternate forms of, 136
    of business continuity professionals, 5, 7
    in business impact analysis, 82
    in command and control centers, 130
    contact information for suppliers of, 162
    in crisis management, 230, 259–63

    with customers, 131
    emergency response teams and, 127, 129, 130f, 134–36
    in escalation procedures, 224–25
    during exercises, 252
    in exercises, 283
    in functional relationships, 359
    images and, 46–47
    loss of, 11, 91
    in management support groups, 129
    organic resilience and, 362–64, 362f
    receiving information, 362–63
    sending information, 363
    telecommunications, 136, 191
Community resilience initiatives, 156
Comparative measurement, 285
Compatibility checkout, 242
Compatibility of equipment, 113, 151, 177
Competency standards, 4, 5, 6–7
Competitors, collaboration with, 157–58
Compiling process, 196
Compliance
    audits of, 309
    as functional driver, 93
    with standards of practice, 53
Compliance officers, 23, 31, 156, 196
Component testing, 239
Compression techniques, 111, 203
Computers. See also Software applications
    in command and control centers, 131
    hardware for, 162, 177
    Internet and, 191, 193, 264, 271–72
Confidentiality issues, 109, 111, 197, 313
Conflicting information, 135
Consequences of disruptive scenarios, 71, 81
Consequential loss, 169
Consortium agreements, 396
Consultants
    as board-level motivators, 49–50
    methodology and software used by, 50
    qualifications for, 50
    training for, 265
Contact lists, 131, 160–63, 161t, 163t, 221, 396
Containment measures, 73
Contamination, 172–73, 174–75, 178, 181, 182–84
Contingency planning, 4, 147, 396
Continuing education, 335, 336
Continuity of operations (COOP), 396
Continuous availability, 396
Continuous backup, 112

Continuous operations, 396
Control structures. *See* Command and control structures
Coordinators, of exercise delivery teams, 279–80, 400
Coping strategies, 122–24
Copycat strategies, 366, 366*f,* 367
Corporate chronology, 51
Corporate governance, 8, 34, 111, 321–22, 321*f,* 396.
    See also Audits
Corporate Governance Code (UK), 62
Corporate image, 34, 69, 93
Corporate Manslaughter and Homicide Act of 2007 (UK), 48
Corporate risk, 396
Corporate statements, 260
Corrosion, 171, 174, 181, 182, 183
CORS (Certified Organizational Resiliency Specialist), 336
Cost benefit analysis, 397
Costs
    of dormant difficulties, 88, 88*t*
    invisible, 68–69
    long-term capital, 143
    of loss, 64, 67–69
    of opportunity, 69
    short-term running, 143
Counseling services, 126–27, 162, 377–80, 408
Crisis. *See also* Crisis management
    counseling services following, 126–27, 162, 377–80, 408
    defined, 26, 258, 397
    delayed exit phenomena and, 376–77
    dimensions of, 258–59, 258*f*
    emotional reactions to, 372–77
    post-crisis exit effect, 376
Crisis communications team, 260, 261–63, 265
Crisis directors, 263
Crisis management, 257–72
    battle boxes for, 152–53
    communication in, 230, 259–63
    defined, 41, 219, 258, 397
    holding statements for, 265, 266
    Internet in, 271–72
    interviews in, 269–72
    media protocol during, 261–62, 264–72
    overview, 257
    plans for, 216, 216*f,* 220, 226, 230, 260
    press conferences in, 270
    press releases in, 267–69
    in reverse recovery period, 390

social media in, 261, 264, 267
    spokesperson guidelines for, 270–71
    teams for, 27, 27*f,* 28, 397
    telephone calls during, 265–67
Crisis response team (CRT), 224
Critical customers, 162
Critical functions
    agreement regarding, 93–94
    defining, 92, 397
    drivers of, 93, 94
    highly critical, 92, 92*f,* 95
    identifying, 91, 92, 92*f*
    maps of, 94, 94*f*
    protection of, 100
    super critical, 92, 92*f,* 95
Critical infrastructure, 397
Critical records, 197–202
Critical services, 192, 397
Crocidolite, 172
CRT (crisis response team), 224
CTAM (Chevy Truck Access Method), 195
Customers
    business as perceived by, 12
    communicating with, 131
    critical, 162
    expectations of, 66–67
    in functional relationships, 358
    meeting needs of, 48, 54, 106, 324
    records regarding, 197

D

Damage assessments, 148, 149, 397
Dark Serpent dilemma, 343–46, 344*f*
Dark sites, 272
Data. *See also* Backup and restoration procedures
    assembling, 204
    loss of, 11, 91
    mapping, 65, 65–66*t*
    methodology for collection of, 82–85
    recovery process for, 202–4, 203*f,* 227*f,* 228, 397
    salvage and restoration of, 176–78
    storage of, 199–200
    synchronizing, 204
Database replication, 397
Data center recovery, 397
Data deduplication, 111
Data mirroring, 397
Data protection, 54, 197, 397
Data recovery, 202–4, 203*f,* 227*f,* 228, 397

Death, denial of access due to, 172
Debriefing, 243, 284–85, 288, 372, 378–79, 391
Decision-making, 341–56
    in black swan events, 342
    carousel technique for, 346–47
    criteria for, 223–24
    in Dark Serpent dilemma, 343–46, 344f
    DICE model for, 349–54, 351f
    by emergency response teams, 127, 135
    fight or flee reactions and, 342
    foxy thinking in, 347–49, 348f
    learning from past decisions, 355
    by police, 349
    protocols for, 341–42
    review process for, 353–54
    routine mission approach to, 343
Decision points, 14–16, 16f
Decisions In Crises or Emergencies (DICE) model,
    349–54, 351f
Declaration, defined, 398
Declaration fees, 398
Defense mechanisms, 122–24
Defensive measures
    organic resilience and, 364, 365, 365f
    risk assessment of, 69–71
Delayed exit phenomena, 376–77
Delegation, 126, 128, 129
Deliberate man-made hazards, 70
Deliverables
    milestones for, 36, 41
    in scripting process, 247–50, 248f
    vision of, 24
Delivery of exercises, 244, 278–82, 278–79f
Delivery team, 278–81, 284
Denial of access, 170–73, 184, 398
Departmental deputies, 22–23, 22f
Department recovery plans, 35
Dependency, defined, 398
Dependency modeling, 81, 90–91, 90f
Desk checks, 398
Desktop exercises, 237–38, 237f, 240t
Deterioration
    of building materials, 173–74
    of storage media, 113, 114
Development phase, 39–54
    action plans in, 40–41
    auditor's role in, 54
    board-level motivators in, 24, 47–51
    for business continuity plans, 216–20
    compliance issues and, 53

    for deliverables, 41
    game plans in, 24, 34–35, 40, 41, 51
    for initial project phase, 42
    kick-off meetings in, 40
    launch argument formula for, 40, 42–47
    leadership in, 41
    overview, 39
    for permanent process, 42
    standards of practice and, 51–53
DICE (Decisions In Crises or Emergencies) model,
    349–54, 351f
Director, roles and responsibilities of, 214, 215, 215f,
    218, 219
Disaster recovery (DR), 99–115. See also Emergency
    response team (ERT)
    approaches to, 100–103
    backup procedures in. See Backup and restoration
    procedures
    business continuity plans for, 103–7, 114–15, 216,
    216f, 220, 227–28, 227f
    bypass arrangements in, 106
    characteristics of, 190
    cold site services for, 102, 396
    defined, 398
    dual systems in, 100–101
    effective process for, 195, 195f
    emergency preparedness for, 160
    harmonic recovery, 101
    hot site services for, 101, 102, 111, 401, 402
    hypothesis regarding, 12
    information recovery process, 113–14
    mobile recovery services, 101–2
    modular approach to, 227–28, 227f
    origins of, 4
    outsourcing during, 106–7
    overview, 99, 100, 190
    plans for, 216, 216f, 220, 227–28, 227f
    reciprocal agreements in, 102–3
    redeployment and relocation strategies for, 54,
    104–5, 151
    reduction of operations in, 105–6
    research stage of, 107–8
    salvage efforts in. See Salvage and restoration
    site options for, 102–3, 111, 194
    standards of practice for, 52
    strategy selection, factors influencing, 107–8, 190
    supply strategies for, 103–4
    systems recovery and, 16, 27, 27f, 29, 193–94,
    242–43
    for technology and support services, 191–93

termination and change strategies in, 106
testing plans and procedures for, 241–42
Disaster Recovery Institute International (DRII), 4, 52, 124, 335, 398
Disaster Recovery Journal (DRJ), 338
Disasters. *See also* Disaster recovery (DR); Physical disruptions
    actions and modes, 145–47, 145*f*
    decision point in declaration of, 14–16, 16*f*
    defined, 398
    evacuation planning. *See* Emergency evacuation planning (EEP)
    recent, relevant, and remarkable events, 43–44
    tangible impact, 91
Disease, precautions against, 175
Disruptive scenarios
    in business impact analysis, 80–81
    causes of, 70
    consequences of, 71, 81
    cost of loss in, 64, 67–69
    elements of loss in, 9–10, 11*f*, 71, 91
    impact of, 81, 86, 86*t*
    launch argument formula and, 43–44
    physical, 10–11, 91
    in relocation and expansion, 319
    in risk management, 62
    symptoms of, 71
    technical, 10, 11–12, 91
Documents. *See* Records and documents
Dominating players in exercises, 281
Dongles, 162, 177
Door-stepping journalists, 272
Dormant difficulties, 88, 88*t*
DR. *See* Disaster recovery
Draft statements, 131
DRII (Disaster Recovery Institute International), 4, 52, 124, 335, 398
DRJ (*Disaster Recovery Journal*), 338
Drop ship, 398
Dry powder extinguishers, 184
Dual systems approach, 100–101
Duplication of records, 110
Dust, 171, 176, 177, 178, 180, 183
Dynamic records, 112, 200, 201, 201*f*

E

Earthquakes, 10, 44, 91
EC-Council Disaster Recovery Professional (EDRP), 336

ECC (emergency control center), 398
Economic horizon, 318–19
Education. *See* Training and education
EEP. *See* Emergency evacuation planning
Efficiency, efforts to improve, 14
Electricity services, 191, 193
Electronic equipment, 180–81
Electronic vaulting, 398
Emergencies, defined, 26, 398
Emergency acquisition, 360, 361, 361*f*
Emergency call centers, 107
Emergency control center (ECC), 398
Emergency coordinators, 399
Emergency evacuation planning (EEP)
    for bomb threats, 171
    evacuation, defined, 399
    fire exposure analysis and, 80
    in hierarchy of BCPs, 216, 216*f*
    overview, 383–84
    for personnel safety, 370
    process and timing in, 385–86
    signage in, 44
    site review in, 384–85
    test and rehearsal regime in, 386
Emergency Evacuation Planning for Your Workplace: From Chaos to Life-Saving Solutions (Burtles), 383
Emergency incident reports, 304–5
Emergency management plans, 220
Emergency managers, 146, 225–26
Emergency mode, 145, 145*f*
Emergency operation center (EOC), 399
Emergency planning officers, 157–58, 160
Emergency preparedness, 141–63
    access control in, 142
    asset retention and, 144
    battle boxes for, 131, 142, 148–54, 154*t*
    collaborative networks in, 156–60
    community resilience initiatives and, 156
    competitors and, 157
    contact lists in, 160–63, 161*t*, 163*t*
    disaster actions and modes, 145–47, 145*f*
    for disaster recovery, 160
    feedback and, 144–45
    for fire, 158–59
    for flooding, 159–60
    insurers and, 156
    inventory control in, 142–43
    neighbors and, 157
    police in, 157, 158
    recovery facilities in, 155–56

regulators and monitoring bodies in, 156
resource identification and maintenance, 142–45, 146–47
for salvage and restoration, 160
skills for, 146
tools and supplies for, 104, 145–46
Emergency procedures, 100, 103, 399
Emergency production, 360–61, 361*f*
Emergency response, defined, 399
Emergency response plans, 216, 216*f*, 220, 225–26, 230
Emergency response procedures, 225, 399
Emergency response team (ERT), 121–36
  battle boxes for, 152
  capabilities required for, 126–27
  collaboration with, 30–31
  command and control structures for, 28, 30, 127–32
  communication and, 127, 129, 130*f*, 134–36
  decision-making by, 127, 135
  defined, 124, 399
  Gold, Silver, Bronze model for, 126, 128–29, 128–30*f*
  leadership on, 28
  organization of, 27, 27*f*, 28
  overview, 121
  performance concerns, 122–24
  phased incident management by, 133–34, 133*f*
  selection of personnel for, 124–25
  task sets for, 125–26
  training and education for, 125–26
  trauma and, 125, 126–27
Emergency services
  collaboration with, 157–60
  contact lists for, 160, 161*t*
  as exercise advisers, 251
Emergency supplies, 104, 302–3, 360–62, 360–61*f*
Emotional reactions to crisis, 372–77
Employees. *See* Personnel
Empowerment, of emergency response teams, 126
Encryption techniques, 203
Enhancing techniques, 203
Enterprise risk, 62
Enterprise-wide planning, 399
Entrances to command and control centers, 132
Environment Agency (UK), 31, 160
EOC (emergency operations center), 399
Equipment. *See also* Resources
  in command and control centers, 130, 131
  compatibility of, 113, 151, 177
  electronic, 180–81

loss of, 11, 91
review process for, 301
salvage and restoration of, 176–78, 180–84
ERT. *See* Emergency response team
Escalation procedures, 224–25, 399
Eustress, 122, 373
Evacuation. *See* Emergency evacuation planning (EEP)
Evacuation, defined, 399
Event history logs, 131
Events, defined, 399
Excitement as crisis reaction, 374
Executives
  roles and responsibilities of, 214, 215*f*, 216, 218, 219
  succession plans for, 399
Executive strategic direction, 321, 321*f*, 322
Exercise auditors, 400
Exercise coordinators, 279–80, 400
Exercise observers, 280, 284, 400
Exercise owners, 400
Exercises, 235–52, 277–93. *See also* Testing
  action phase of, 244, 278
  active testing stage for, 237*f*, 238–39, 240*t*
  background for, 244, 245
  Bang and Echo Program for, 290, 293
  buildup of, 244, 246–50, 246*f*, 248*f*
  cabaret exercising, 248, 290, 292–93
  checklists for, 282, 287, 396
  command post, 237*f*, 239–40, 240*t*, 241, 291, 291*t*
  communication in, 283
  coordination and control of, 278–81, 279*f*
  debriefing following, 243, 284–85, 288
  defined, 241, 243, 399
  delivery of, 244, 278–82, 278–79*f*
  desktop, 237–38, 237*f*, 240*t*
  elements of, 243–45, 243*f*, 278, 278*f*
  facilities for, 283–84, 302
  feedback on, 243, 284–86
  five-stage growth path for, 237–41, 237*f*, 240*t*
  frequency of, 241
  full-scale, 237*f*, 240, 240*t*, 241
  history of, 244–45, 286–88
  importance of, 235–36
  integrated, 402
  kick-off meetings for, 245, 288–90
  preparation phase of, 243–44, 246, 278, 281–82
  quality of, 244, 250–52, 282
  realism of, 250–52, 281
  recording, 288
  reports and reviews of, 284, 285–88

rules of engagement for exercises, 289–90
safety of, 244, 282–83
scope of, 252
scripting, 246, 247–50, 248f, 282, 400
for testing plans and procedures, 241–43
walkthrough, 237f, 238, 240t, 289–90
Exit plans, 132, 319, 385. *See also* Emergency
    evacuation planning (EEP)
Expansion strategies, 319
Expenditure audits, 310
Experts, consultation of, 107, 131–32, 173, 178, 281,
    306, 344, 377
Explosions, 170–71, 175–76, 178, 184, 250, 251f
Exposure
    in crises, 259
    defined, 400
    to loss, 80, 81, 87, 87t
External audits, 306
External contacts, 162–63, 163t
Extinguishers, fire, 159, 175, 182, 184
Extra expenses, defined, 400

F

Facebook, 267
Facilitated business impact analysis, 81, 87–89
Facilitators, on exercise delivery teams, 279
Facilities
    access to, 10, 103, 130, 142
    alternative, 162
    defined, 142, 301
    in emergency evacuation planning, 384–85
    for exercises, 283–84, 302
    functional, 155–56
    maintenance of, 142–45
    management of, 28, 30, 301
    recovery, 155–56
    recovery team, 27, 27f, 28
    review process for, 301–2
    testing, 301–2
Fact sheets, 272
Family contact teams, 380
Family representatives, 380
Fatigue, 13, 133, 371, 388–89
FEA (fire exposure analysis), 80
Fear, 373–74, 375
Federal Emergency Management Agency (FEMA), 31,
    33, 160
Feedback, 144–45, 231, 243, 284–86
Fellow of the Business Continuity Institute (FBCI), 400

FIFO (first-in, first-out) stock method, 104
Fight or flee reactions, 342
Financial audits, 309–10
Financial control of resources, 143
Fire
    alarms, 44
    contamination resulting from, 182–83
    denial of access due to, 171–72
    drills, 80
    extinguishers, 159, 175, 182, 184
    information recovery from, 114
    loss of supplies due to, 11, 91
    precautions following, 175, 183
    reigniting, 158, 159, 172, 175
    training for, 159
Fire and rescue services, 158–59, 171–72
Fire engineers, 251
Fire exposure analysis (FEA), 80
First-in, first-out (FIFO) stock method, 104
Five-stage growth path for exercises, 237–41, 237f,
    240t
Flash drives, 199
Flipcharts
    in command and control posts, 130
    in decision-making, 346
    for exercises, 237, 287, 288, 292
    in logging systems, 221
    for QwikRisk tool, 71
Flooding
    denial of access due to, 171
    emergency services response to, 159–60
    loss of supplies due to, 11, 91
    precautions following, 175, 183
    salvage and restoration following, 178
    warning maps, 31
Floor wardens, 400
Forensic investigations, 170, 171, 172
Foreseeable risks, 31
Forward workload, 389–90
Foul water, 175
Foxy thinking, 347–49, 348f
Fragmentation, 203
Freezing documents, as salvage strategy, 162, 180
Full rehearsal, 400
Full-scale exercises, 237f, 240, 240t, 241
Functional analysis, 81, 89, 91–95, 92f, 94f
Functional drivers, 93, 94
Functional facilities, 155–56
Functional improvements, benefits of BCM for, 54
Functional mode, 145, 145f

Functional relationships, 358–60, 359*f*
Functional resources, 155
Function recovery plans, 35
Function restoration
    plans for, 216, 216*f*, 220, 226
    teams for, 27, 27*f*, 29
Fungal contamination, 174
Furnishings, 131, 176

G

Game plans
    defined, 24
    Gold, Silver, Bronze structure for, 34–35
    introduction of, 40
    organizational influences on, 41, 51
    scaling to fit, 51
    viability of, 40
Gap analysis, 400
Generators, 150, 193, 394
Geographic horizon, 318
Geological Survey (US), 160
Gerbode, Frank, 378
Ghost signals, 206
Ginn, Ronald D., 4
Glass fragments, 173, 175–76, 184
Gold, Silver, Bronze command and control model,
    32–33, 32*f*, 34–35, 126, 128–29, 128–30*f*
Good Practice Guidelines (BCI), 52, 335
Goodwill, 69
Governance, risk, and compliance (GRC), 325
Governance structures, 320–26
    case study, 323–24
    compliance issues for, 53
    corporate, 8, 34, 111, 321–22, 321*f*, 396
    executive strategic direction in, 321, 321*f*, 322
    in Gold, Silver, Bronze model, 34
    integration with business continuity, 324–26,
        325–26*f*
    operational management in, 321, 321*f*, 322–23
    operational risk in, 62
    roles and responsibilities in, 214–16, 215*f*
    routine supervision of, 321, 321*f*, 323
    standards of practice and, 325–26, 326*f*
    tiers of, 320–23, 321*f*
Gradient learning curve, 236, 237, 237*f*
Grandfather, father, and son backup cycle, 111, 205
Grid impact analysis, 64–66, 65–66*t*
Group interviews, 63

H

Halon, 182–83
Hard disk storage, 199
Hardening, defined, 400
Hard hats, 131, 172
Hardware applications, 162
Harmonic recovery, 101
Harris, Norm, 4
Hawkins Mitchell, Vali, 122
Hazardous materials, 174
Hazards, natural vs. man-made, 70
Health and safety officials, 152, 172–73
Health of personnel, 370–71
Hepatitis, 175
High-availability, 4, 201, 401
Highly critical functions, 92, 92*f*, 95
High probability/high impact risk, 72, 73
High probability/low impact risk, 72, 73
High rise buildings, 173
High-risk areas, 401
Highways Agency (UK), 346
Hiles, Andrew, 52, 326
History of exercises, 244–45, 286–88
HIV/AIDS, 175
Holding statements, 265, 266
Home, working from, 105
Homeland Security Department (US), 33
Horizon scanning, 318–19, 336–37
Hot site services, 101, 102, 111, 401, 402
Housekeeping duties, 390
Human continuity, 401
Human interest stories, 264
Human resources (HR), 30, 370. *See also* Personnel
Human threats, defined, 401
Humidity, 173, 174, 182, 183
Hydrochloric acid, 174, 182
Hydrogen bromide, 182–83

I

IAEM (International Association of Emergency
    Managers), 30–31, 336
ICOR (International Consortium for Organizational
    Resilience), 336
ICS (Incident Command System), 33, 35, 401
IFMA (International Facility Management
    Association), 336
Ilbury, Chantel, 347
Image of organization
    as asset, 69

in business continuity plans, 215
as functional driver, 93, 94
industry image and, 157
protection of. *See* Crisis management
Images, communication through, 46–47
Impact, defined, 401
Impact analysis
in action plan development, 40
of disruptive scenarios, 81, 86, 86*t*
intangible, 91
interactive impact modeling, 87–89, 88*t*
tangible, 91
Imported skills, 146
Incident, defined, 401
Incident Command System (ICS), 33, 35, 401
Incident management, 133–34, 133*f*, 401
Incident response, 221, 224, 352, 402
Incremental backup, 112
Indicators, 309
Information drift, 363
Information recovery process, 113–14
Information security, 197, 402
Information Systems Audit and Control Association
(ISACA), 336
Information technology (IT)
backlog traps in, 12, 14
records storage and management in, 110
recovery systems for, 4, 227*f*, 228
Infrastructure, 32–35, 32*f*, 402
In-house ownership of business continuity plans,
42–43
Initial project phase, 42
Injuries
denial of access due to, 171, 172
from glass fragments, 175–76
Inspection
in audit process, 308
battle boxes for, 149–50
of facilities and equipment, 144, 301
of high-rise buildings, 173
Insurance and insurers
for business interruptions, 170, 171
collaboration with, 32, 156
contact information for, 162
denial of access by, 170
mitigation of loss and, 168–69
primary vs. secondary claims, 169
self-insurance, 169, 407
Intangible impacts, 91
Integrated exercises, 402

Integrated testing, 402
Intelligence section, 129, 263
Intelligent compression, 111
Interactive impact modeling, 87–89, 88*t*
Interim sites, defined, 402
Internal audits, 31, 306
Internal contacts, 161, 161*t*
Internal hot sites, 402
International Association of Emergency Managers
(IAEM), 30–31, 336
International Consortium for Organizational
Resilience (ICOR), 336
International Facility Management Association
(IFMA), 336
International Information Systems Security
Certification Consortium ((ISC)²), 336
International Organization for Standardization (ISO)
crisis as defined by, 258
*Information security – Security techniques –
Guidelines for information and communication
technology readiness for business continuity*
(ISO/IEC 27031:2011), 52
*Societal security – Business continuity management
systems – Guidance* (ISO 22313:2012), 51–52
*Societal security – Business continuity management
systems – Requirements* (ISO 22301:2012), 7, 51,
52, 306, 307, 326
Internet, 191, 193, 264, 271–72
Interrogations, in audit process, 308
Interrupts, 250
Interviews
in business impact analysis, 83–84, 85
group, 63
with media, 269–72
in risk management, 63
Invacuation, 384, 385
Inventory control, 142–43, 168, 391
Investigation, in audit process, 308
Investment audits, 310
Investment wisdom, 69
Invisible assets, 69
Invisible costs, 68–69
ISACA (Information Systems Audit and Control
Association), 336
(ISC)² (International Information Systems Security
Certification Consortium), 336
ISO. *See* International Organization for
Standardization
Isolation
battle boxes for, 151

of personnel, 371
in training exercises, 157, 282, 283
IT. *See* Information technology

J

Jackets, reflective, 131
Journaling, 379–80
Journalists, 272. *See also* Media

K

Kepler, Noël Francine, 268
Key tasks, defined, 402
Kick-off meetings, 40, 83, 85, 245, 288–90
King Report III (2009), 48
Knowledge, defined, 125
Knowledge workers, 105

L

Labeling
archive records, 113
of backup records, 200, 205
battle boxes, 148
of exercise material, 283
Launch argument formula, 42–47
cognitive marketing in, 44–45
development of, 40
in-house ownership and, 42–43
observation in, 44
reach and withdraw technique in, 45–46
realism in, 46–47
step-by-step processes and, 47
LBC (level of business continuity), 86, 89
Leadership
in business impact analysis, 82
changes in, 333
in development phase, 41
on emergency response teams, 28
Lead time, 402
Learning curve/gradient, 236, 237, 237*f*
Legal requirements for business continuity, 5, 44, 48
Leptospirosis, 175
Lessons from exercises, 244
Level of business continuity (LBC), 86, 89
Liability, 48
Lighting considerations, 130
Line of business approach, 247
Local resilience forums (LRFs), 31

Logging systems, 221–22
Logistics team, 402
Long-term capital costs, 143
Loose documents, 179
Loss
consequential, 169
cost of, 64, 67–69
defined, 402
in disruptive scenarios, 9–10, 11*f,* 71, 91
exposure to, 80, 81, 87, 87*t*
of profit, 67–68
recoverable, 404
unexpected, 361, 408
Loss adjusters, 162, 169, 176, 181, 251, 402
Loss assessors, 169, 176
Loss reduction, defined, 402
Loss transaction recovery, 403
Loudhailers, 131
Low probability/high impact risk, 72, 73
Low probability/low impact risk, 72, 73
LRFs (local resilience forums), 31
Lukaszewski, James E., 127, 132, 267, 272

M

Machine language, 196
Magnetic tape, 199
Mainframe computers, 4
Maintenance
of battle boxes, 153–54, 154*t*
of business continuity plans, 27, 42, 404
of resources and facilities, 142–45
Management skills, 146
Management structure, 22–23, 22*f,* 25–29
Management support groups, 129
Managers, roles and responsibilities of, 214, 215*f,* 216, 218, 219
Mandatory backup records, 197
Man-made hazards, 70
Manslaughter, corporate, 48
Manual procedures, defined, 403
Maps
of critical functions, 94, 94*f*
of data, 65, 65–66*t*
flood warning, 31
risk maps, 75
Marketing
BCM benefits for, 54
cognitive, 44–45
critical records regarding, 197

Master Business Continuity Professional (MBCP), 335, 403
MBCI (Member of the Business Continuity Institute), 335, 403
MCAs (mission-critical activities), 86, 89, 403
Media. *See also* Social media
    access to command and control centers, 131–32
    contact information for, 162
    controlled responses to, 265
    crisis management protocol regarding, 261–62, 264–72
    fact sheets for, 272
    holding statements for, 265, 266
    interviews with, 269–72
    press conferences for, 270
    press releases for, 267–69
    telephone calls from, 265–67
Megaphones, 131
Mellish, Steve, 326
Member of the Business Continuity Institute (MBCI), 335, 403
Memory sticks, 199
Mental exits, delayed, 376–77
Mergers, 54
Metapsychology movement, 378
Methodology
    for consultants, 50
    for data collection, 82–85
    for risk assessment, 63–64
Metropolitan Police Service (UK), 33
Microfiche/microfilm, 180, 205
Microsoft Word, 230
Mildew, 171, 175
Mile2, 336
Military, command and control structure of, 22, 23
The Mind of a Fox (Ilbury & Sunter), 347
Minimum recovery capability, 147
Minimum service level, 147
Mission-critical activities (MCAs), 86, 89, 403
Mitigation factors, 74, 75
Mobile command and control centers, 130
Mobile phones, 136
Mobile recovery services, 101–2, 403
Mobile standby trailers, 403
Mobilization, defined, 403
Mock disasters, 403
Modular approach, 24, 51, 214, 219, 227–28, 227f
Mold, 174, 178, 180
Motivators. *See* Board-level motivators

N

National Emergency Management Association (NEMA), 31, 158
National Fire Protection Association, *Standard on Disaster/Emergency Management and Business Continuity Programs* (NFPA 1600), 41, 52
National Incident Management Structure (NIMS), 33, 35
Natural disasters. *See* Crisis; Disasters
Natural hazards, 70
Negligence, 48
Network outages, 403
Networks, collaborative, 30–32, 156–60, 332
Neverfail disaster recovery service, 45
New normal, 13
Noise input, 249
Noncritical functions, 95
Non-participants, role of, 29
Non-transferable risk, 66–67
Notification of family procedures, 380
N + 1 strategy, 403
Numbness of the unknown, 375–76

O

Observation, in launch argument formula, 44
Observers, on exercise delivery teams, 280, 284, 400
Occupational Safety and Health Administration (OSHA), 172, 173
Office support, battle boxes for, 150–51
Offsite storage, 162, 403
Olympic Games (2012), 33
Online backup, 200, 201
Open Door policies, 334
Operating systems, 197–98, 204
Operational risk, 62, 404
Operations
    as functional driver, 93
    management of, 321, 321f, 322–23
    records of, 198
    reduction during disaster recovery, 105–6
Operators, roles and responsibilities of, 214, 215f, 216, 218, 219
Opportunity, cost of, 69
Optical storage, 199
Orderly shutdowns, 404
Organic resilience, 357–68
    case study, 359–64, 366–68
    communication and, 362–64, 362f
    functional relationships and, 358–60, 359f

outsourcing vs. emergency stock and, 361–62, 361*f*

production vs. acquisition and, 360–61, 361*f*
protective strategies for, 364–68, 365–67*f*
request/response relationship in, 358, 358*f*
structure for, 357–58, 357–58*f*
supplies and, 360, 360*f*
Original document retrieval, 179
OSHA (Occupational Safety and Health Administration), 172, 173
Outages, defined, 404. *See also* Power failures
Output phase of review process, 304–5
Outsourcing, 106–7, 361, 361*f*, 362
Overconfidence following emergencies, 388

P

Panic, fear of starting, 136
Paper exploration therapy (PET), 380
Paralympic Games (2012), 33
Parking considerations, 132
PAS 56. *See* Publicly available specification 56
PCBs (polychlorinated biphenyls), 172–73
Peer review, 404
Personal documents, 179
Personnel, 369–81
    as asset, 369
    backup, 27
    briefings for, 260–61
    counseling services for, 126–27, 162, 377–80, 408
    critical records regarding, 197
    debriefing sessions for, 243, 284–85, 288, 372, 378–79, 391
    delayed exit phenomena and, 376–77
    emergency working considerations for, 13, 371–72
    emotional reactions to crisis by, 372–77
    family contact teams for, 380
    fatigue of, 13, 133, 371, 388–89
    health, safety, and welfare of, 370–71
    human resources and, 30, 370
    isolation of, 371
    loss of, 10, 103
    organizational structure of, 214–16, 215*f*
    post-crisis exit effect and, 376
    rewards and acknowledgment for, 372, 391
    rotating tasks for, 371–72
    selection for ERTs, 124–25
    training exercises, 236
PET (paper exploration therapy), 380
Phased incident management, 133–34, 133*f*

The Phoenix Society, 30
Photocopiers, 131
Physical disruptions, 10–11, 91
Physical exits, delayed, 376
Physical risks, 49
Plan maintenance, 27, 42, 404
Plans and planning. *See* Business continuity plans; Business recovery plans; Emergency evacuation planning; Game plans
Police
    collaboration with, 157, 158
    decision-making by, 349
    denial of access by, 171, 172, 173, 184
Policy audits, 309
Policy statements, 34
Polychlorinated biphenyls (PCBs), 172–73
Portable battle boxes, 148
Portable cold sites, 102
Portable fire extinguishers, 159
Position papers, 264
Post-crisis exit effect, 376
Post-crisis stress, 373–76
Power, Peter, 33
Power failures, 11, 16, 44, 150, 173
Preparation packs, 288
Preparedness. *See* Emergency preparedness
Press conferences, 270
Press releases, 267–69
Preventive measures, defined, 404
Primary records, 112, 201, 201f, 202
Principles of Emergency Management (IAEM), 31
Prioritization, defined, 404
Process functions, 358
Production
    emergency, 360–61, 361*f*
    in functional relationships, 359
    reduction of, 105–6
    resources for, 142
Professional Practices (DRII), 52
Profiles of risk, 318
Profit, loss of, 67–68
Program managers, 22, 22*f*
Protective clothing, 131, 172, 175, 371
Prudence, 310
Publicly available specification 56 (PAS 56), 7–9, 8*f*, 52
Public relations, 152–53, 261–62, 265, 392
Purpose statements, 245
Pursey, Richard, 45

Q

Qualitative methods of risk assessment, 63–64, 404
Quality control, 244, 250–52, 282, 300. *See also* Audits;
    Review process
Quantitative methods of risk assessment, 63–64, 404
Questionnaires, 83, 85
QwikRisk tool, 71–73, 72*f*, 78

R

RAG (red, amber, and green) coding system, 74
RAID (Random Array of Independent Disks)
    technology, 111
"Rambo" effect, 388
Ratner, Gerald, 69
Reach and withdraw technique, 45–46
Ready mode, 145, 145*f*
Realism
    of exercises, 250–52, 281
    in launch argument formula, 46–47
Real-time backup, 112
Reciprocal agreements, 102–3, 404
Records and documents. *See also* Backup and
    restoration procedures
    business, 196
    central, 198
    critical, 197–202
    of decision-making, 353
    duplication vs. replication, 110
    dynamic, 112, 200, 201, 201*f*
    emergency response issues for, 180
    of exercises, 286–87, 288
    mandatory backup records, 197
    operational, 198
    primary, 112, 201, 201*f*, 202
    retention period for, 111
    salvage and restoration of, 178–80
    stable, 112, 200–201, 201*f*
    storage considerations, 110–12, 114
    types of, 112–13, 179–80
Recoverable losses, 404
Recovery. *See also* Backup and restoration procedures
    defined, 404
    as protective strategy, 364, 365, 365*f*
Recovery facilities, 155–56
Recovery mode, 145, 145*f*
Recovery period, defined, 404
Recovery point capability (RPC), 405
Recovery point objective (RPO), 86, 89, 100,
    112, 405

Recovery services agreements/contracts, 405
Recovery site, 100, 113, 142, 155, 194, 405
Recovery teams, defined, 405. *See also* Response and
    recovery teams
Recovery time capability (RTC), 405
Recovery timeline, 405
Recovery time objective (RTO), 86, 89, 100, 405
Red, amber, and green (RAG) coding system, 74
Redeployment strategies, 104–5, 151
Reflective jackets, 131
Refreshments, 132
Regulatory requirements for business continuity,
    5, 44, 48
Relevance, in launch argument formula, 43, 46
Reliability
    data backup technologies, 195, 199
    information duplication, 110
    phone system, 136
    RAID (Random Array of Independent Disks)
        technology, 111
    scrap or salvage decision based on, 168
    sprinkler system, 159
Relocation strategies, 54, 104–5, 151, 319
Repair work, 144
Replication of records, 110
Reporting
    on audits, 313
    on business impact analysis, 85–87
    escalation procedures and, 224–25
    on exercises, 284, 285, 286–88
    on review process, 304–5
    risk reporting, 40, 63, 75
    in salvage and restoration, 184, 184*f*
Reputation
    as asset, 91
    in business continuity plans, 215
    bypass arrangements and, 106
    of industry, 157
    organizational, 34
    protection of. *See* Crisis management
Request/response relationship, 358, 358*f*
Rescue and recovery, battle boxes for, 150
Research stage of disaster recovery, 107–8
Resilience
    community resilience initiatives, 156
    of data centers, 103
    defined, 405
    disaster recovery and, 100, 191
    ISO 22301 and, 326
    maximizing, 192

organic. *See* Organic resilience
risk management and, 62
systems recovery and, 193
Resource contingency plans, 147
Resources and supplies. *See also* Equipment; Facilities
    access to, 10, 103, 130, 142
    alternate sources for, 103–4, 192, 319
    BCM benefits for utilization of, 54
    buffering principle, 104, 105–6
    in command and control centers, 130, 131
    contact information for, 162
    defined, 142, 302
    diversion of, 155
    emergency, 104, 302–3, 360–62, 360–61*f*
    external, 162–63, 163*t*
    feedback and, 144–45
    financial control of, 143
    functional, 155
    in functional relationships, 359
    human. *See* Human resources (HR)
    identification and maintenance of, 142–45, 146–47
    internal, 161, 161*t*
    inventory control of, 142–43, 168, 391
    loss of, 11, 91
    for preparedness, 104, 145–46
    retention of, 144
    review process for, 302–4
    service and repair of, 144
    testing, 302–3
    updates and changes to, 144
Response, defined, 406
Response and recovery teams
    emergency response. *See* Emergency response team (ERT)
    in exercises, 278
    in management structure, 22*f*, 23, 26–29
Restabilization technique, 377–78
Restoration, defined, 406. *See also* Backup and restoration procedures; Salvage and restoration
Resumption, defined, 406
Revacuation planning, 387–90
Reverse criticality, 390
Reverse recovery period, 387–90
Review process, 299–305. *See also* Audits
    for decision-making, 353–54
    for exercises, 284, 286
    for facilities, 301–2
    output phase of, 304–5
    overview, 299

    for resources, 302–4
    steps in, 300–305, 300*f*
    terms of reference for, 300
Rewards for personnel, 372
RIMS (Risk Management Society), 336
Risk acceptance, 66–67
Risk and Governance Committee (BCI), 73
Risk and risk assessment, 63–75. *See also* Risk management
    categories of risk, 406
    components of, 74
    corporate, 396
    cost of loss in, 64, 67–69
    of critical services, 192
    of defensive measures, 69–71
    defined, 406
    foreseeable risk, 31
    grid impact analysis in, 64–66, 65–66*t*
    of incident management, 133*f*, 134
    investment wisdom and, 69
    of non-transferable risk, 66–67
    operational, 62, 404
    quantitative vs. qualitative methods for, 63–64, 404
    QwikRisk tool for, 71–73, 72*f*, 78
    SMARTRisk method for, 73–75
Risk controls, 406
Risk management. *See also* Insurance and insurers
    collaboration in, 31–32
    defined, 406
    disruptive scenarios in, 62
    enterprise risk, 62
    interviews in, 63
    operational risk, 62
    of physical risks, 49
    protocol for, 62
Risk Management Society (RIMS), 336
Risk maps, 75
Risk matrix, 72, 72*f*
Risk profiles, 318
Risk registers, 74–75
Risk reporting, 40, 63, 75
Risk transfer, 406
Roll call, 161, 251, 406
Rothstein, Philip Jan, 195, 235, 324
Round robin thinking system, 346
Routine mission approach to decision-making, 343
Routine mode, 145, 145*f*
RPC (recovery point capability), 405
RPO (recovery point objective), 86, 89, 100, 112, 405

RTC (recovery time capability), 405
RTO (recovery time objective), 86, 89, 100, 405
Rules of engagement for exercises, 289–90
Running costs, 143

S

Safety and security
     of battle boxes, 148–49
     of command and control centers, 130
     contact information for providers of, 163
     denial of access and, 171–72
     encryption techniques for, 203
     of exercises, 244, 282–83
     health and safety officials, 152, 172–73
     of information, 197, 402
     of personnel, 370–71
     of recovery facilities, 155
Salvage and restoration, 167–85
     access issues in, 170–73, 184–85, 185f
     defined, 406
     of documents and records, 162, 178–80
     emergency preparedness for, 160
     of equipment and technology, 176–78, 180–84
     insurance considerations and, 168–69
     overview, 167
     precautions following events, 175–76, 183
     professional assistance regarding, 169–70
     reporting structure for, 184, 184f
     scrap vs., 168
     of site and structures, 173–75
Salvage engineers, 163, 168, 169, 181, 182
SBCI (Specialist of the Business Continuity Institute), 406
Scenario planning, 348, 348f
Scenarios, defined, 406. See also Disruptive scenarios
Scripts for exercises, 246, 247–50, 248f, 282, 400
Sealing documents, as salvage strategy, 180
Second site option, 103
Security reviews, 407. See also Safety and security
Self-help, 379–80
Self-insurance, 169, 407
Senior managers, 26–27
Service, as functional driver, 93
Service continuity, defined, 407
Service contracts, 168
Service engineers, 170
Service level agreement (SLA), 407
Service level management (SMA), 407
Sewage systems, 192

Shelf life, 104, 112, 148, 153
Short-term running costs, 143
Shower facilities, 132
Silver control. See Gold, Silver, Bronze command and control model
Simulation exercises, 239, 240, 407
Simulation strategies, 366, 366f
Singapore, business continuity in, 48
Single point of failure (SPOF), 104, 332, 407
Site reviews, 384–85
SLA (service level agreement), 407
Sleeping areas, 132
SMA (service level management), 407
Small Business Administration, 31
SMARTRisk method, 73–75
Smoke contamination, 174, 178, 181
Smoke detectors, 159
Social media, 131–32, 261, 264, 267
Software applications
     backup and restoration procedures for, 162, 197–98
     for business continuity plans, 228–29, 229t
     compatibility with equipment, 177
Solid state storage devices, 199
Soundproof command and control centers, 132
Source code, 196
Source functions, 358
Source information, 196
South Africa, business continuity in, 48
Spare capacity, 163
Specialist of the Business Continuity Institute (SBCI), 406
SPOF (single point of failure), 104, 332, 407
Spokespersons, guidelines for, 270–71
Sponsors
     in business impact analysis, 82
     on emergency response teams, 28
     in management structure, 22, 22f
     role of, 22, 25–26, 34
     selection of, 23
Sprinkler systems, 159, 171
Stable records, 112, 200–201, 201f
Staff. See Personnel
Stagnant water, 175
Standalone test, 407
Standards of practice
     in Australia, 52–53
     compliance with, 53
     governance structures and, 325–26, 326f
     government guidelines on, 5, 44, 48

international, 7, 51–52
organizational influences on, 24
in United Kingdom, 7–9, 8f, 52
in United States, 52
Standby power, 131
Standby stock. *See* Emergency supplies
Stand down, 385, 386, 407
Startup teams, 42
Status reports, 304, 305
Stevens, David, 33
Storage
of critical records, 199–200
in functional relationships, 359
offsite locations for, 162, 403
of records, 110–12, 114
Stress
eustress, 122, 373
post-crisis manifestations, 373–76
responses to, 122–24
Structural damage, 171, 172, 175
Structured walkthroughs, 407
Sunter, Clem, 347
Super critical functions, 92, 92f, 95
Supervision of governance structures, 321, 321f, 323
Supplementing as protective strategy, 367–68, 367f
Supplies. *See* Resources and supplies
Supply chains, 11, 104, 105, 155, 318–19, 360, 407
Support groups, for exercise delivery teams, 280–81
Supporting documents, 198
Surprise, as reaction to crisis, 258–59
Suspicious packages, 171
System, defined, 407
System restore, defined, 16, 408
Systems recovery, 16, 27f, 29, 193–94, 242–43, 407

T

Tables, 130
Tabletop exercises, 408. *See also* Desktop exercises
Taleb, Nassim, 342
Tangible impacts, 91. *See also* Physical disruptions
Task lists, 190, 226, 303, 408
Teams. *See also* Response and recovery teams
administrative, 42, 129
business continuity, 395
business recovery, 395
crisis communications, 260, 261–63, 265
crisis management, 27, 27f, 28, 397
crisis response, 224
delivery of exercises, 278–81, 284

facilities recovery, 27, 27f, 28
function restoration, 27, 27f, 29
startup, 42
technical recovery, 408
Technical disruptions, 10, 11–12, 91
Technical recovery. *See* Backup and restoration procedures
Technical recovery team, 408
Technical specialists, 22, 22f, 23, 193
Technicians
collaboration with, 31
data recovery, 177
roles and responsibilities of, 214, 215f, 216, 218, 219
Technology. *See* Computers; Information technology (IT); Internet; Social media
Telecommunications, 136, 191
phone calls, during crisis management, 265–67
Termination, as disaster recovery option, 106
Terms of reference, 300
Terrorism, 171
Testing. *See also* Exercises
conditions for, 243
defined, 241, 408
disaster recovery, 241–42
emergency evacuation plans, 386
facilities, 301–2
integrated, 402
preparation for, 243
resources, 302–3
systems recovery checklist for, 242–43
Threats, defined, 408
Thumb drives, 199, 222
Timing considerations
for board-level motivators, 50–51
in emergency evacuation planning, 385–86
TIR (traumatic incident reduction), 378
TIRA (Traumatic Incident Reduction Association), 162, 378
Tolerance threshold, 86, 147
Toxic water, 175
Trade associations, 157
Training and education. *See also* Exercises
for business impact analysis, 82
for certification, 335–36
for consultants, 265
continuing education, 335, 336
for emergency response teams, 125–26
for fire, 159
learning curve/gradient in, 236, 237, 237f

Transient documents, 179
Transport services, 163, 370, 402
Trauma
    counseling and support for, 126–27, 162,
      377–80, 408
    management of, 408
    symptoms of, 125
Traumatic incident reduction (TIR), 378
Traumatic Incident Reduction Association (TIRA),
    162, 378
Troubleshooters, 390
Twitter, 267

U

Uncertainty, as reaction to crisis, 259
Unexpected loss, 361, 408
Uninterruptible power supply (UPS), 193, 408
United Kingdom (UK)
    business continuity requirements in, 7, 48
    Corporate Governance Code, 62
    corporate manslaughter and homicide in, 48
    counseling services in, 162
    emergency planning officers in, 158
    Environment Agency, 31, 160
    family notification procedures in, 380
    Gold, Silver, Bronze command and control
      model in, 32–33, 32f, 34–35, 126
    health and safety officials in, 172
    Highways Agency, 346
    standards of practice in, 7–9, 8f, 52
United States (US)
    Army Corps of Engineers, 160
    Coast Guard, 160
    emergency management in, 31
    emergency planning officers in, 157–58, 160
    family notification procedures in, 380
    health and safety officials in, 172
    Incident Command System, 33, 35
    standards of practice in, 52
UPS (uninterruptible power supply), 193, 408
Urgency, as reaction to crisis, 259

V

Validation scripts, 408
Value chains, 318–19
Ventilation considerations, 132
Visual aids, 46–47
Vital records, 194, 195, 408

W

Walkthrough exercises, 237f, 238, 240t, 289–90
Wall clocks, 131
Warm sites, defined, 409
Washing facilities, 132
Water. *See also* Flooding
    supplies of, 191, 192
    toxic, 175
Weatherproof command and control centers, 130
Weather-related events. *See* Disasters
Webber, Andrew Lloyd, 45
Weil's disease, 175
Welfare of personnel, 370–71
Whiteboards, 71, 130, 221, 287, 288, 292
Withholding information, 135
Work area facilities, defined, 409. *See also* Facilities
Work area recovery, 190, 409
Workaround procedures, defined, 409
Workshops, in business impact analysis, 84–85
Write Once–Read Many (WORM) format, 199

About the Author

Jim Burtles KLJ, MMLJ, Hon FBCI is a well-known and respected leader within the business continuity profession. Now semi-retired and living in West London, he can look back and reflect upon the lessons learned from a wealth of experience gained in some 40 years of practice, spread across 4 continents and 24 countries. He was granted Freedom of the City of London in 1992, received a Lifetime Achievement Award in 2001, and was awarded an Honorary Fellowship by the Business Continuity Institute (BCI) in 2010. In 2005, he was granted the rank of a Knight of Grace in the Military and Hospitaller Order of St. Lazarus of Jerusalem, an ancient and charitable order which cares for those afflicted with leprosy and similar debilitating diseases.

Working as an IBM field engineer, in the mid-70s he took on the role of a rescue engineer, helping customers recover their damaged systems in the wake of fires, floods, and bombings. This type of work was the beginning of what later became known as *disaster recovery*. During the 80s, he became an early pioneer of what was then the emerging *business continuity* profession. In 1994 he helped to found the Business Continuity Institute (BCI) and now serves on its Global Membership Council, representing the interests of the worldwide membership. His practical experience includes hands-on recovery work with victims of traumatic events such as explosions, earthquakes, storms, and fires. This includes technical assistance and support in 90-odd disasters, as well as advice and guidance for clients in over 200 emergency situations.

Over the past 40 years, Jim Burtles has introduced more than 3,500 people into the business continuity profession through formal training programs and has provided specialist training for another 800 or so through workshops covering specific subjects or skill areas. For several years he was a regular visiting lecturer at Coventry University.

Recent published works include *Coping with a Crisis: A Counselor's Guide to the Restabilization Process*, 2011, and *Emergency Evacuation Planning for Your Workplace: From Chaos to Life-Saving Solutions*, published by Rothstein Publishing in August 2013.

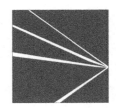

Credits

Kristen Noakes-Fry ABCI is Executive Editor at Rothstein Publishing. Previously, she was a Research Director, Information Security and Risk Group, for Gartner, Inc.; Associate Editor at Datapro (McGraw-Hill); and Associate Professor of English at Atlantic Cape College in New Jersey. She holds an M.A. from New York University and a B.A. from Russell Sage College.

Cover Design and Graphics:	Sheila Kwiatek, Flower Grafix
Typography, Layout and Graphics:	Jean King
Copy Editing:	Nancy M. Warner
Instructional Design:	Paula Fleming, Fleming Editorial Services
Index:	Enid Zafran, Indexing Partners, LLC

Title Font:	Haettenschweiler
Body Fonts:	Minion Pro and Myriad Pro

a division of Rothstein Associates Inc.
www.rothsteinpublishing.com

Rothstein Publishing is your premier source of books and learning materials about Business Resilience including Crisis Management, Business Continuity, Disaster Recovery, Emergency Management, and Risk Management. Our industry-leading authors provide current, actionable knowledge, solutions, and tools you can put into practice immediately. Founded in 1984 by Philip Jan Rothstein FBCI, our company remains true to our commitment to prepare you and your organization to protect, preserve, and recover what is most important: your people, facilities, assets, and reputation. Rothstein Publishing is a division of Rothstein Associates Inc., an international management consultancy.

THE WORLD'S LEADING INSTITUTE FOR

CONTINUITY AND RESILIENCE

The Business Continuity Institute is the leading global membership and certifying organization for business continuity and resilience professionals

MEMBERSHIP

- **Join a global** professional network of like-minded business continuity and resilience professionals

- **Achieve international recognition** and status through certified membership grades

- **Progress your career** by helping to secure jobs and consultancy work

- **Access CPD and Mentoring** programmes

- **Receive exclusive access** to a wide range of high-quality business continuity and resilience resources

- **Receive discounts** and promotions for various products, services and conferences

- **Multiple routes to membership** including CBCI Examination, DBCI Diploma, Alternative Route or Affiliate/Student

CORPORATE PARTNERSHIP

- Enables organizations to work more closely with the BCI to help raise the profile of the discipline
- Promotes the highest standards of professional competence in business continuity and resilience within organizations worldwide
- Has over 125 corporate partners globally*
- Offers partners a wide range of financial and value-added benefits, including excellent sponsorship opportunities
- Levels available to suit any size organization

THOUGHT LEADERSHIP & RESEARCH

- Conducts research and publishes reports and white papers on key subject matters including Horizon Scanning, Emergency Communications and Supply Chain
- Facilitates a number of think tanks globally to gauge the thoughts of regional experts

EVENTS & AWARDS

- Holds a variety of events globally in conjunction with chapters and forums
- Hosts BCI World, one of the largest conference and exhibitions in the industry
- Hosts regional and global awards recognizing the outstanding work of the industry's professionals, teams and organizations

GLOBAL COMMUNITY

- BCI global community is active worldwide through nine chapters and over 50 local forums*
- Allows professionals to meet, network and learn from each other
- Opportunities to hear about the latest developments in the profession
- Contributes to the development of business continuity and resilience globally

*correct at time of printing

TRAINING & EDUCATION

- World-class, award winning education services delivered in partnership with BCI Licensed Training Partners and Approved BCI Instructors
- All instructors are highly experienced business professionals in the continuity and resilience discipline bringing a wealth of real life experience
- Courses to cater for all levels of experience, for both individuals and organizations
- Entry-level awareness training, certification, higher education diploma and in-depth courses for senior professionals
- Classroom based, eLearning, Live interactive distance learning and in-house options available

DO THE MATH
Combine more than 30 expert authors,
with 1,000 years of experience, and countless
problems solved for companies like yours...

{ Your definitive, current, comprehensive Business Continuity textbook and reference – based on international standards and grounded in best practices.

©2014

494 pages + 200 pages of free downloads, illustrations, glossary, index, and Instructional teaching materials.

SBN 978-1-931332-35-4 paperback

ISBN 978-1-931332-76-7 eBook

ISBN 978-1-931332-83-5 ePub

©2014

458 pages, illustrations, glossary, index, and instructional teaching materials.

ISBN 978-1-931332-69-9 paperback

ISBN 978-1-931332-71-2 eBook

ISBN 978-1-931332-87-3 ePub

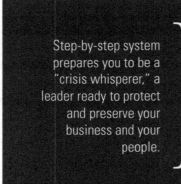

Step-by-step system prepares you to be a "crisis whisperer," a leader ready to protect and preserve your business and your people. }

{ Be prepared! Follow this tested six-phase method to create a plan that you can activate at a moment's notice – to get everyone to safety from any workplace.

©2013

340 pages + 300 pages of free downloads, illustrations, glossary, index, and instructional teaching materials.

ISBN 978-1-931332-56-9 casebound

ISBN 978-1-931332-67-5 eBook

ISBN 978-1-931332-85-9 ePub

...and you have Rothstein Publishing – books
with the *answers* you're looking for.

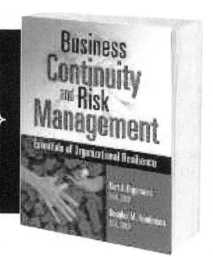

©2012
370 pages,
glossary, index
ISBN 978-1-931332-54-5 paperback

ISBN 978-1-931332-73-6, eBook

ISBN 978-1-931332-89-7 ePub

Ground-breaking
textbook combines
Risk Management and
Business Continuity.
Flexible format adapts to
your needs – today and
tomorrow.

The whole world is
watching! Communicate
effectively when
confronted by a crisis and
the explosive visibility
and reputation risk that
come with it.

©2013
400 pages, glossary, index
ISBN 978-1-931332-57-6
paperback

© 2014
400 pages, glossary, index
ISBN 978-1-931332-66-8
hardcover 6x9

ISBN 978-1-931332-64-4 eBook

ISBN 978-1-931332-81-1 ePub

ROTHSTEIN
PUBLISHING

Since 1989, **Rothstein Publishing** has been your premier source of current,
actionable Organizational Resilience knowledge, solutions, and tools,
authored by industry-leading experts, covering Business Continuity, Risk,
Crisis Management, and more. Rothstein Publishing is a division of Rothstein
Associates Inc., an international management consultancy founded in 1984 by
Philip Jan Rothstein FBCI.

Rothstein publications are distributed worldwide through book retailers and
wholesalers and via eBook databases, including EBSCOHost, ebrary/EBL,
Books24x7, Slicebooks, IngramSpark, MyiLibrary, VItalSource, and iGroup.

www.rothsteinpublishing.com
info@rothstein.com

203.740.7400
4 Arapaho Rd., Brookfield, CT
06804-3104 USA

facebook.com/RothsteinPublishing

linkedin.com/company/rothstein-associates-inc.

How to Get Your FREE DOWNLOAD
of Bonus Resource Materials for This Book

You are entitled to a free download of the **Business Continuity Toolkit** that accompanies your purchase of *Principles and Practice of Business Continuity: Tools and Techniques*, 2nd Edition, by Jim Burtles.

The downloadable **Business Continuity Toolkit** contains dozens of fully editable models, sample plans, templates, forms, PowerPoint presentations, checklists, questionnaires and supplemental content… plus much more!

To access these materials is easy – just login to our website as an existing user or register as a new user, and then register your book by following these simple instructions.

IT'S EASY –
LOGIN OR REGISTER ON OUR WEBSITE

1. FIRST, login as an existing user or register as a new user at **www.rothstein.com/register**. New users will receive an email link to confirm.

THEN REGISTER YOUR BOOK

2. Logging in or registering takes you to our Product Registration page. You'll see a list of books. Simply select your book by clicking the corresponding link to the left and just follow the instructions. You will need to have this book handy to answer the questions.

3. You will receive a confirming email within a few hours with additional information and download instructions.

4. Your registration will also confirm your eligibility for future updates and upgrades if applicable.

If you have any questions or concerns, please email or call us:
Rothstein Associates Inc., Publisher

ROTHSTEIN PUBLISHING
a division of Rothstein Associates Inc.

203.740.7400 or 1-888-ROTHSTEin   fax 203.740.7401
4 Arapaho Road   Brookfield, Connecticut   06804-3104   USA
info@rothstein.com
www.rothsteinpublishing.com
www.rothstein.com